Target Server Settings

Description: vme05

Server Name vmco5

Back End: wdbrpc

IP: 192.168.67.10
↓
15

Console & Redirection : Select All

Computers as Components

Principles of Embedded
Computing System Design

About the Author

Wayne Wolf is a professor of electrical engineering at Princeton University. Before joining Princeton, he was with AT&T Bell Laboratories in Murray Hill, New Jersey. He received his B.S., M.S., and Ph.D. in electrical engineering from Stanford University. He is well known for his research in the areas of hardware/software co-design, embedded computing, VLSI CAD, and multimedia computing systems. He is a fellow of the IEEE and a member of the ACM and SPIE. He was program chair of the First International Workshop on Hardware/Software Co-Design. Wayne was also program chair of the 1996 IEEE International Conference on Computer Design. He is editor-in-chief of *IEEE Transactions on VLSI Systems* (1999–2000) and co-editor of the Kluwer journal *Design Automation for Embedded Systems*. He is also co-series editor of the new Morgan Kaufmann Series in Systems on Silicon.

To Nancy (as always)

Senior Editor Denise E. M. Penrose
Senior Production Editor Cheri Palmer
Editorial Assistant Courtney Garnaas
Cover Design Ross Carron Design
Cover Image © 2000 Estate of Louise Nevelson / Artists Rights Society (ARS), New York
Text Design Rebecca Evans & Associates
Copyeditor Barbara Kohl
Proofreader Jennifer McClain
Composition and Illustration ECOMLINKS
Indexer Ty Koontz
Printer Courier Corporation

ACADEMIC PRESS
A Harcourt Science and Technology Company
525 B Street, Suite 1900, San Diego, CA 92101-4495, USA
http://www.academicpress.com

Academic Press
Harcourt Place, 32 Jamestown Road, London, NW1 7BY, United Kingdom
http://www.academicpress.com

Morgan Kaufmann Publishers
340 Pine Street, Sixth Floor, San Francisco, CA 94104-3205, USA
http://www.mkp.com

Library of Congress Cataloging-in-Publication Data

Wolf, Wayne Hendrix.
 Computers as components: principles of embedded computing system design/
 Wayne Wolf.
 p. cm.
 Includes bibliographical references and index.
 ISBN 1-55860-541-X (case) — ISBN 1-55860-693-9 (paper)
 1. System design. 2. Systems engineering. I. Title.

QA76.9.S88 W64 2001
004.2'1—dc21

00-063323

This book is printed on acid-free paper.

Computers as Components
Principles of Embedded Computing System Design

Wayne Wolf
Princeton University

MORGAN KAUFMANN PUBLISHERS

AN IMPRINT OF ACADEMIC PRESS
A Harcourt Science and Technology Company

SAN FRANCISCO SAN DIEGO NEW YORK BOSTON
LONDON SYDNEY TOKYO

Foreword

by Lynn Conway
Professor Emerita, Electrical Engineering and Computer Science
University of Michigan

Digital system design has entered a new era. At a time when the design of microprocessors has shifted into a classical optimization exercise, the design of embedded computing systems in which microprocessors are merely components has become a wide-open frontier. Wireless systems, wearable systems, networked systems, smart appliances, industrial process systems, advanced automotive systems, and biologically interfaced systems provide a few examples from across this new frontier.

Driven by advances in sensors, transducers, microelectronics, processor performance, operating systems, communications technology, user interfaces, and packaging technology on the one hand, and by a deeper understanding of human needs and market possibilities on the other, a vast new range of systems and applications is opening up. It is now up to the architects and designers of embedded systems to make these possibilities a reality.

However, embedded system design is practiced as a craft at the present time. Although knowledge about the component hardware and software subsystems is clear, there are no system design methodologies in common use for orchestrating the overall design process, and embedded system design is still run in an ad hoc manner in most projects.

Some of the challenges in embedded system design come from changes in underlying technology and the subtleties of how it can all be correctly mingled and integrated. Other challenges come from new and often unfamiliar types of system requirements. Then too, improvements in infrastructure and technology for communication and collaboration have opened up unprecedented

possibilities for fast design response to market needs. However, effective design methodologies and associated design tools haven't been available for rapid follow-up of these opportunities.

At the beginning of the VLSI era, transistors and wires were the fundamental components, and the rapid design of computers on a chip was the dream. Today the CPU and various specialized processors and subsystems are merely basic components, and the rapid, effective design of very complex embedded systems is the dream. Not only are system specifications now much more complex, but they must also meet real-time deadlines, consume little power, effectively support complex real-time user interfaces, be very cost-competitive, and be designed to be upgradable.

Wayne Wolf has created the first textbook to systematically deal with this array of new system design requirements and challenges. He presents formalisms and a methodology for embedded system design that can be employed by the new type of "tall-thin" system architect who really understands the foundations of system design across a very wide range of its component technologies.

Moving from the basics of each technology dimension, Wolf presents formalisms for specifying and modeling system structures and behaviors and then clarifies these ideas through a series of design examples. He explores the complexities involved and how to systematically deal with them. You will emerge with a sense of clarity about the nature of the design challenges ahead and with knowledge of key methods and tools for tackling those challenges.

As the first textbook on embedded system design, this book will prove invaluable as a means for acquiring knowledge in this important and newly emerging field. It will also serve as a reference in actual design practice and will be a trusted companion in the design adventures ahead. I recommend it to you highly.

Contents

Foreword vii

List of Examples xix

Preface xxiii

Chapter 1 **Embedded Computing** 1

1.1 **Introduction** 1

1.2 **Complex Systems and Microprocessors** 2
 1.2.1 Embedding Computers 2
 1.2.2 Characteristics of Embedded Computing Applications 5
 1.2.3 Why Use Microprocessors? 6
 1.2.4 Challenges in Embedded Computing System Design 8

1.3 **The Embedded System Design Process** 10
 1.3.1 Requirements 12
 1.3.2 Specification 17
 1.3.3 Architecture Design 18
 1.3.4 Designing Hardware and Software Components 20
 1.3.5 System Integration 20

1.4 **Formalisms for System Design** 21
 1.4.1 Structural Description 22
 1.4.2 Behavioral Description 29

1.5 Design Example: Model Train Controller **32**

1.5.1 Requirements 34
1.5.2 Conceptual Specification 34
1.5.3 Detailed Specification 39
1.5.4 Lessons Learned 47

1.6 A Guided Tour of This Book **47**

1.6.1 Chapter 2: Instruction Sets 48
1.6.2 Chapter 3: CPUs 48
1.6.3 Chapter 4: The Embedded Computing Platform 49
1.6.4 Chapter 5: Program Design and Analysis 50
1.6.5 Chapter 6: Processes and Operating Systems 51
1.6.6 Chapter 7: CPU Accelerators 52
1.6.7 Chapter 8: Networks 52
1.6.8 Chapter 9: System Design Techniques 53

1.7 Summary **54**

What We Learned **54**

Further Reading **54**

Questions **54**

Lab Exercises **56**

Chapter 2 Instruction Sets **57**

2.1 Introduction **57**

2.2 Preliminaries **58**

2.2.1 Computer Architecture Taxonomy 58
2.2.2 Assembly Language 60

2.3 ARM Processor **62**

2.3.1 Processor and Memory Organization 63
2.3.2 Data Operations 63
2.3.3 Flow of Control 73

2.4 SHARC Processor **82**

2.4.1 Memory Organization 83
2.4.2 Data Operations 83
2.4.3 Flow of Control 93
2.4.4 Parallelism within Instructions 99

2.5 Summary **99**

What We Learned **100**

	Further Reading	**100**
	Questions	**100**
	Lab Exercises	**104**

Chapter 3 **CPUs** **105**

3.1	**Introduction**	**105**
3.2	**Programming Input and Output**	**106**
	3.2.1 Input and Output Devices 106	
	3.2.2 Input and Output Primitives 108	
	3.2.3 Busy-Wait I/O 110	
	3.2.4 Interrupts 112	
3.3	**Supervisor Mode, Exceptions, and Traps**	**128**
	3.3.1 Supervisor Mode 128	
	3.3.2 Exceptions 129	
	3.3.3 Traps 129	
3.4	**Co-Processors**	**130**
3.5	**Memory System Mechanisms**	**131**
	3.5.1 Caches 131	
	3.5.2 Memory Management Units and Address Translation 139	
3.6	**CPU Performance**	**144**
	3.6.1 Pipelining 145	
	3.6.2 Superscalar Execution 149	
	3.6.3 Caching 151	
3.7	**CPU Power Consumption**	**152**
3.8	**Design Example: Data Compressor**	**158**
	3.8.1 Requirements and Algorithm 158	
	3.8.2 Specification 161	
	3.8.3 Program Design 163	
	3.8.4 Testing 170	
3.9	**Summary**	**171**
	What We Learned	**172**
	Further Reading	**172**
	Questions	**173**

Lab Exercises 176

Chapter 4 | **The Embedded Computing Platform** | **177**

4.1 Introduction 177

4.2 The CPU Bus 178

4.2.1 Bus Protocols 178
4.2.2 DMA 186
4.2.3 System Bus Configurations 187
4.2.4 ARM Bus 190
4.2.5 SHARC Bus 191

4.3 Memory Devices 193

4.3.1 Memory Device Organization 194
4.3.2 Random-Access Memories 195
4.3.3 Read-Only Memories 201

4.4 I/O Devices 202

4.4.1 Timers and Counters 202
4.4.2 A/D and D/A Converters 203
4.4.3 Keyboards 204
4.4.4 LEDs 206
4.4.5 Displays 206
4.4.6 Touchscreens 208

4.5 Component Interfacing 209

4.5.1 Memory Interfacing 209
4.5.2 Device Interfacing 211

4.6 Designing with Microprocessors 212

4.6.1 System Architecture 213
4.6.2 Hardware Design 214
4.6.3 The PC as a Platform 216

4.7 Development and Debugging 220

4.7.1 Development Environments 220
4.7.2 Debugging Techniques 221
4.7.3 Debugging Challenges 227

4.8 Manufacturing Testing 228

4.9 Design Example: Alarm Clock 233

4.9.1 Requirements 233

4.9.2 Specification 235
4.9.3 System Architecture 239
4.9.4 Component Design and Testing 240
4.9.5 System Integration and Testing 241

4.10 Summary **241**

What We Learned **241**

Further Reading **242**

Questions **242**

Lab Exercises **244**

| Chapter 5 | **Program Design and Analysis** | **245** |

5.1 Introduction **245**

5.2 Program Design **246**
5.2.1 Design Patterns 246
5.2.2 Design Patterns for Embedded Systems 248

5.3 Models of Programs **252**
5.3.1 Data Flow Graphs 252
5.3.2 Control/Data Flow Graphs 254

5.4 Assembly and Linking **258**
5.4.1 Assemblers 259
5.4.2 Linking 264

5.5 Basic Compilation Techniques **265**
5.5.1 Statement Translation 267
5.5.2 Procedures 273
5.5.3 Data Structures 274
5.5.4 Expression Simplification 275
5.5.5 Dead Code Elimination 277
5.5.6 Procedure Inlining 277
5.5.7 Loop Transformations 278
5.5.8 Register Allocation 280
5.5.9 Scheduling 285
5.5.10 Instruction Selection 287
5.5.11 Understanding and Using Your Compiler 288
5.5.12 Interpreters and JIT Compilers 289

5.6 Analysis and Optimization of Execution Time **290**
5.6.1 Elements of Program Performance 292

5.6.2 Trace-Driven Performance Analysis 296
5.6.3 Optimizing for Execution Speed 304

5.7 Analysis and Optimization of Energy and Power **305**

5.7.1 Program Energy Consumption and Optimization 306

5.8 Analysis and Optimization of Program Size **310**

5.9 Program Validation and Testing **312**

5.9.1 Clear-Box Testing 313
5.9.2 Black-Box Testing 322
5.9.3 Evaluating Function Tests 323
5.9.4 Performance Testing 324

5.10 Design Example: Software Modem **325**

5.10.1 Theory of Operation and Requirements 325
5.10.2 Specification 328
5.10.3 System Architecture 328
5.10.4 Component Design and Testing 329
5.10.5 System Integration and Testing 329

5.11 Summary **330**

What We Learned **330**

Further Reading **331**

Questions **331**

Lab Exercises **339**

Chapter 6 **Processes and Operating Systems** **341**

6.1 Introduction **341**

6.2 Multiple Tasks and Multiple Processes **343**

6.2.1 Multirate Systems 345
6.2.2 Early Multitasking Technology: The Co-Routine 346

6.3 Processes **347**

6.4 Context Switching **351**

6.4.1 Cooperative Multitasking 351
6.4.2 Preemptive Multitasking 356
6.4.3 Processes and Object-Oriented Design 357

6.5 Operating Systems **358**

6.5.1 Process State and Scheduling 358

6.5.2 Operating System Structure 361
6.5.3 Timing Requirements on Processes 362
6.5.4 Interprocess Communication 365
6.5.5 Other Operating System Functions 371

6.6 Scheduling Policies **371**

6.6.1 Rate-Monotonic Scheduling 372
6.6.2 Earliest-Deadline-First Scheduling 377
6.6.3 RMS versus EDF 382
6.6.4 A Closer Look at Our Modeling Assumptions 383
6.6.5 Other POSIX Scheduling Policies 386

6.7 Interprocess Communication Mechanisms **387**

6.7.1 Signals 387
6.7.2 Signals in UML 389
6.7.3 Shared Memory Communication 389
6.7.4 Message-Based Communication 392

6.8 Evaluating Operating System Performance **393**

6.9 Power Optimization Strategies for Processes **396**

6.10 Design Example: Telephone Answering Machine **400**

6.10.1 Theory of Operation and Requirements 400
6.10.2 Specification 404
6.10.3 System Architecture 406
6.10.4 Component Design and Testing 408
6.10.5 System Integration and Testing 409

6.11 Summary **409**

What We Learned **410**

Further Reading **410**

Questions **410**

Lab Exercises **417**

Chapter 7 Hardware Accelerators **419**

7.1 Introduction **419**

7.2 CPUs and Accelerators **420**

7.2.1 Why Accelerators? 421
7.2.2 Accelerator Design 423

7.3 Accelerated System Design **424**

7.3.1 Performance Analysis 424
7.3.2 System Architecture Framework 429
7.3.3 Partitioning 432
7.3.4 Scheduling and Allocation 434
7.3.5 System Integration and Debugging 437

7.4 Design Example: Video Accelerator **437**

7.4.1 Algorithm and Requirements 437
7.4.2 Specification 441
7.4.3 Architecture 441
7.4.4 Component Design 443
7.4.5 System Testing 444

7.5 Summary **445**

What We Learned **446**

Further Reading **446**

Questions **446**

Lab Exercises **447**

Chapter 8 **Networks** **449**

8.1 Introduction **449**

8.2 Distributed Embedded Architectures **450**

8.2.1 Why Distributed? 451
8.2.2 Network Abstractions 452
8.2.3 Hardware and Software Architectures 453
8.2.4 Message Passing Programming 457

8.3 Networks for Embedded Systems **458**

8.3.1 The I^2C Bus 459
8.3.2 The CAN Bus 464
8.3.3 SHARC Link Ports 467
8.3.4 Ethernet 470
8.3.5 Myrinet 472
8.3.6 Internet 473

8.4 Network-Based Design **475**

8.4.1 Communication Analysis 475
8.4.2 System Performance Analysis 481
8.4.3 Hardware Platform Design, Allocation, and Scheduling 482

8.5 Internet-Enabled Systems **484**

8.6 Design Example: Elevator Controller **486**

 8.6.1 Theory of Operation and Requirements 487
 8.6.2 Specification 489
 8.6.3 Architecture 491
 8.6.4 Testing 492

8.7 Summary **493**

What We Learned **493**

Further Reading **493**

Questions **494**

Lab Exercises **496**

Chapter 9 System Design Techniques **497**

9.1 Introduction **497**

9.2 Design Methodologies **498**

 9.2.1 Why Design Methodologies? 498
 9.2.2 Design Flows 500

9.3 Requirements Analysis **507**

9.4 Specifications **509**

 9.4.1 Control-Oriented Specification Languages 509
 9.4.2 Advanced Specifications 512

9.5 System Analysis and Architecture Design **515**

 9.5.1 CRC Cards 516

9.6 Quality Assurance **520**

 9.6.1 Quality Assurance Techniques 523
 9.6.2 Verifying the Specification 525
 9.6.3 Design Reviews 527
 9.6.4 Measurement-Driven Quality Assurance 530

9.7 Design Example: Telephone PBX **534**

 9.7.1 Theory of Operation 535
 9.7.2 System Architecture 537

9.8 Design Example: Ink Jet Printer **539**

 9.8.1 Hardware Design 542
 9.8.2 Software Design 546

9.9 Design Example: Personal Digital Assistants 548

9.10 Design Example: Set-Top Boxes 551

9.11 Systems-on-Silicon 555

9.12 Summary 557

 What We Learned 557

 Further Reading 558

 Questions 558

 Lab Exercises 559

Appendix A **UML Notations** **561**

A.1 Introduction 561

A.2 Primitive Elements 561

A.3 Diagram Types 562

 A.3.1 Class Diagram 563
 A.3.2 State Diagram 564
 A.3.3 Sequence and Collaboration Diagrams 565

Appendix B **Notes on Hardware Design** **567**

B.1 Introduction 567

B.2 Combinational Logic 567

B.3 Sequential Logic 571

 B.3.1 Memory Elements 571
 B.3.2 Synchronous Machines 573
 B.3.3 Asynchronous Machines 576

B.4 Implementation Media 577

 Glossary 579

 References 601

 Index 613

 About the CDs 657

List of Examples

Chapter 1

Application Example 1-1: BMW 850i Brake and Stability Control System 4

Example 1-1: Requirements Analysis of a GPS Moving Map 15

Chapter 2

Example 2-1: Status Bit Computation in the ARM 66

Example 2-2: C Assignments in ARM Instructions 71

Example 2-3: Implementing an if Statement in ARM 74

Example 2-4: Implementing the C Switch Statement in ARM 76

Application Example 2-1: FIR Filters 78

Example 2-5: An FIR Filter for the ARM 78

Example 2-6: Procedure Calls in ARM 81

Example 2-7: Data Operation Status Bits in the SHARC 88

Example 2-8: C Assignments in SHARC Instructions 91

Example 2-9: Implementing an if Statement in SHARC 94

Example 2-10: An FIR Filter for the SHARC 96

Example 2-11: Procedure Calls in SHARC 98

Chapter 3

Application Example 3-1: The 8251 UART 107

Example 3-1: Memory-Mapped I/O on ARM 108

Example 3-2: Memory-Mapped I/O on SHARC 109

Example 3-3: Busy-Wait I/O Programming 110

Example 3-4: Copying Characters from Input to Output Using Busy-Wait I/O 111

Example 3-5: Copying Characters from Input to Output with Basic Interrupts 113

Example 3-6: Copying Characters from Input to Output with
Interrupts and Buffers 114

Example 3-7: Debugging Interrupt Code 119

Example 3-8: I/O with Prioritized Interrupts 122

Example 3-9: Direct-Mapped versus Set-Associative Caches 135

Example 3-10: Code Scheduling for SHARC Data Address Generators 147

Example 3-11: Execution Time of a for Loop on the ARM 148

Application Example 3-2: Energy Efficiency Features in the PowerPC 603 154

Application Example 3-3: Power-Saving Modes of the StrongARM SA-1100 156

Application Example 3-4: Huffman Coding for Text Compression 159

Chapter 4

Example 4-1: A Multichip SRAM Memory System 209

Example 4-2: A Glue Logic Interface 211

Application Example 4-1: System Organization of the Intel
StrongARM SA-1100 and SA-1111 219

Programming Example 4-1: Breakpoints 222

Example 4-3: A Timing Error in Real-Time Code 227

Chapter 5

Programming Example 5-1: A State Machine in C 248

Programming Example 5-2: A Circular Buffer Implementation
of an FIR Filter 251

Example 5-1: Generating a Symbol Table 260

Example 5-2: Compiling an Arithmetic Expression 267

Example 5-3: Generating Code for a Conditional 270

Example 5-4: Loop Unrolling 278

Example 5-5: Register Allocation 280

Example 5-6: Operator Scheduling for Register Allocation 283

Example 5-7: Software Pipelining in SHARC 286

Example 5-8: Data-Dependent Paths in if Statements 293

Example 5-9: Paths in a loop 294

Example 5-10: Data Realignment and Array Padding 302

Application Example 5-1: Code Compression for PowerPC 312

Example 5-11: Controlling and Observing Programs 314

Example 5-12: Choosing the Paths to Test 315

Example 5-13: Condition Testing with the Branch Testing Strategy 318

Chapter 6 Application Example 6-1: Automotive Engine Control 345

Example 6-1: Cooperative Context Switching for the ARM 353

Example 6-2: A Buggy Cooperative Multitasking System 355

Example 6-3: Priority-Driven Scheduling 359

Application Example 6-2: Telephone Calls as Processes 361

Application Example 6-3: A Space Shuttle Software Error 364

Example 6-4: Elastic Buffers as Shared Memory 366

Programming Example 6-1: Test-and-Set Operations 368

Example 6-5: Rate-Monotonic Scheduling 373

Example 6-6: Earliest-Deadline-First Scheduling 378

Example 6-7: Priority Inversion 383

Example 6-8: Data Dependencies and Scheduling 384

Example 6-9: Scheduling and Context Switching Overhead 385

Example 6-10: Effects of Scheduling on the Cache 395

Application Example 6-4: Predictive Shutdown in Pagers 397

Chapter 7 Application Example 7-1: An FPGA-Based Accelerator 429

Application Example 7-2: The ARM Integrator Logic Module 429

Example 7-1: Scheduling and Allocating Processes on a Distributed
Embedded System 434

Chapter 8 Example 8-1: Data-Push Network Architectures 458

Application Example 8-1: A SHARC-Based Multiprocessor 467

Example 8-2: Simple Message Delay for an I^2C Message 476

Example 8-3: Adjusting Messages to Improve Network Delay 477

Application Example 8-2: An Internet Video Camera 485

Chapter 9 Application Example 9-1: Loss of the Mars Climate Observer 499

Example 9-1: Concurrent Engineering Applied to Telephone Systems 505

Application Example 9-2: The TCAS II Specification 512

Example 9-2: CRC Card Analysis 518

Application Example 9-3: The Therac-25 Medical Imaging System 521

Example 9-3: Paperless Code Inspections 529

Application Example 9-4: Software Quality Assurance for Instruments 531

Application Example 9-5: The ROLM PBX 534

Preface

Microprocessors have long been a part of our lives. However, microprocessors have become powerful enough to take on truly sophisticated functions only in the past few years. The result of this explosion in microprocessor power, driven by Moore's Law, is the emergence of embedded computing as a discipline. In the early days of microprocessors, when all the components were relatively small and simple, it was necessary and desirable to concentrate on individual instructions and logic gates. Today, when systems contain tens of millions of transistors and tens of thousands of lines of high-level language code, we must use design techniques that help us deal with complexity.

This book tries to capture some of the basic principles and techniques of this new discipline of embedded computing. Some of the challenges of embedded computing are well known in the desktop computing world. For example, getting the highest performance out of pipelined, cached architectures often requires careful analysis of program traces. Similarly, the techniques developed in software engineering for specifying complex systems have become important with the growing complexity of embedded systems. Another example is the design of systems with multiple processes. The requirements on a desktop general-purpose operating system and a real-time operating system are very different; the real-time techniques developed over the past 30 years for larger real-time systems are now finding common use in microprocessor-based embedded systems.

Other challenges are new to embedded computing. One good example is power consumption. While power consumption has not been a major consideration in traditional computer systems, it is an essential concern for battery-operated embedded computers and is important in many situations in which power supply capacity is limited by weight, cost, or noise. Another challenge is deadline-driven programming. Embedded computers often impose hard

deadlines on completion times for programs; this type of constraint is rare in the desktop world. As embedded processors become faster, caches and other CPU elements also make execution times less predictable. However, by careful analysis and clever programming, we can design embedded programs that have predictable execution times even in the face of unpredictable system components such as caches.

Luckily, there are many tools for dealing with the challenges presented by complex embedded systems: high-level languages, program performance analysis tools, processes and real-time operating systems, and more. But understanding how all these tools work together is itself a complex task. This book takes a bottom-up approach to understanding embedded system design techniques. By first understanding the fundamentals of microprocessor hardware and software, we can build powerful abstractions that help us create complex systems.

A Note to Embedded System Professionals

This book is not a manual for understanding a particular microprocessor. Why should the techniques presented here be of interest to you? There are two reasons. First, techniques such as high-level language programming and real-time operating systems are very important in making large, complex embedded systems that actually work. The industry is littered with failed system designs that didn't work because their designers tried to hack their way out of problems rather than stepping back and taking a wider view of the problem. Second, the components used to build embedded systems are constantly changing, but the principles remain constant. Once you understand the basic principles involved in creating complex embedded systems, you can quickly learn a new microprocessor (or even programming language) and apply the same fundamental principles to your new components.

A Note to Teachers

The traditional microprocessor system design class originated in the 1970s when microprocessors were exotic yet relatively limited. That traditional class emphasizes breadboarding hardware and software to build a complete system. As a result, it concentrates on the characteristics of a particular microprocessor, including its instruction set, bus interface, and so on.

This book takes a more abstract approach to embedded systems. While I have taken every opportunity to discuss real components and applications, this book is fundamentally not a microprocessor data book. As a result, its approach may seem initially unfamiliar. Rather than concentrating on particu-

lars, the book tries to study more generic examples to come up with more generally applicable principles. However, I think that this approach is both fundamentally easier to teach and in the long run more useful to students. It is easier because one can rely less on complex lab setups and spend more time on pencil-and-paper exercises, simulations, and programming exercises. It is more useful to the students because their eventual work in this area will almost certainly use different components and facilities than those used at your school. Once students learn fundamentals, it is much easier for them to learn the details of new components.

Hands-on experience is essential in gaining physical intuition about embedded systems. Some hardware building experience is very valuable; I believe that every student should know the smell of burning plastic integrated circuit packages. But I urge you to avoid the tyranny of hardware building. If you spend too much time building a hardware platform, you will not have enough time to write interesting programs for it. And as a practical matter, most classes don't have the time to let students build sophisticated hardware platforms with high-performance I/O devices and possibly multiple processors. A lot can be learned about hardware by measuring and evaluating an existing hardware platform. The experience of programming complex embedded systems will teach students quite a bit about hardware as well—debugging interrupt-driven code is an experience that few students are likely to forget.

A home page for the book (*www.mkp.com/embed*) includes overheads, instructor's manual, lab materials, links to related Web sites, and a link to a password-protected ftp site that contains solutions to the exercises.

Acknowledgments

I owe a word of thanks to many people who helped me in the preparation of this book. Several people gave me advice about various aspects of the book: Steve Johnson (Indiana University) about specification, Louise Trevillyan and Mark Charney (both IBM Research) on program tracing, Margaret Martonosi (Princeton University) on cache miss equations, Randy Harr (Synopsys) on low power, Phil Koopman (Carnegie Mellon University) on distributed systems, Joerg Henkel (NEC C&C Labs) on low-power computing and accelerators, Lui Sha (University of Illinois) on real-time operating systems, John Rayfield (ARM) on the ARM architecture, David Levine (Analog Devices) on compilers and SHARC, and Con Korikis (Analog Devices) on the SHARC. Many people acted as reviewers at various stages: David Harris (Harvey Mudd College); Jan Rabaey (University of California at Berkeley); David Nagle (Carnegie Mellon University); Randy Harr (Synopsys); Rajesh Gupta, Nikil Dutt, Frederic Doucet, and Vivek Sinha (University of California at Irvine); Ronald D. Williams (University of Virginia); Steve Sapiro (SC Associates); Paul Chow (University of Toronto); Bernd G. Wenzel (Eurostep); Steve Johnson (Indiana University); H. Alan Man-

tooth (University of Arkansas); Margarida Jacome (University of Texas at Austin); John Rayfield (ARM); David Levine (Analog Devices); Ardsher Ahmed (University of Massachusetts/Dartmouth University); and Vijay Madisetti (Georgia Institute of Technology). I also owe a big word of thanks to my editor, Denise Penrose. Denise put in a great deal of effort finding and talking to potential users of this book to help us understand what readers wanted to learn. This book owes a great deal to her insight and persistence. Cheri Palmer and her production team did an excellent job on an impossibly tight schedule. The mistakes and miscues are, of course, all mine.

Chapter

Embedded Computing

- Why we embed microprocessors in systems.

- What is difficult about embedding microprocessors.

- Design methodologies.

- Design description with UML.

- A guided tour of this book.

1.1 Introduction

In this chapter we set the stage for our study of embedded computing system design. In order to understand design processes, we first need to understand how and why microprocessors are used for control, user interface, signal processing, and many other tasks. The **microprocessor** has become so common that it is easy to forget how hard some things are to do without it.

We first review the various uses of microprocessors. We then review the major reasons why microprocessors are used in system design—delivering complex behaviors, fast design turnaround, and so on. Next, in Section 1.3, we walk through the design of an example system to understand the major steps in designing a system. Section 1.4 includes an in-depth look at techniques for specifying embedded systems—we use these specification techniques throughout the book. In Section 1.5, we use a model train controller as an example for applying the specification techniques introduced in Section 1.4 that we use throughout the rest of the book. Section 1.6 provides a chapter-by-chapter tour of the book.

1.2 Complex Systems and Microprocessors

What is an **embedded computer system?** Loosely defined, it is any device that includes a programmable computer but is not itself intended to be a general-purpose computer. Thus, a PC is not itself an embedded computing system, although PCs are often used to build embedded computing systems, as with the PC-based telephone system of Section 9.7. But a fax machine or a clock built from a microprocessor is an embedded computing system.

This means that embedded computing system design is a useful skill for many types of product design. Automobiles, personal digital assistants (PDAs), and even household appliances make extensive use of microprocessors. Designers in many fields must be able to identify where microprocessors can be used, design a hardware platform with I/O devices that can support the required tasks, and implement software that performs the required processing. Computer engineering, like mechanical design or thermodynamics, is a fundamental discipline that can be applied in many different domains. But of course, embedded computing system design does not stand alone. Many of the challenges encountered in the design of an embedded computing system are not computer engineering—for example, they may be mechanical or analog electrical problems. In this book we are primarily interested in the embedded computer itself, so we will concentrate on the hardware and software that enable the desired functions in the final product.

1.2.1 Embedding Computers

Computers have been embedded into applications since the earliest days of computing. One example is the Whirlwind, a computer designed at MIT in the late 1940s and early 1950s. Whirlwind was also the first computer designed to support **real-time** operation and was originally conceived as a mechanism for controlling an aircraft simulator. Even though it was extremely large physically compared to today's computers (it contained over 4,000 vacuum tubes, for example), its complete design from components to system was attuned to the needs of real-time embedded computing. The utility of computers in replacing mechanical or human controllers was evident from the very beginning of the computer era—for example, computers were proposed to control chemical processes in the late 1940s [Sto95].

A microprocessor is a single-chip CPU. **VLSI** (very large scale integration) technology has allowed us to put a complete CPU on a single chip since the 1970s, but those CPUs were very simple. The first microprocessor, the Intel 4004, was designed for an embedded application, namely, a calculator. The calculator was not a general-purpose computer—it merely provided basic arithmetic functions. However, Ted Hoff of Intel realized that a general-purpose

computer programmed properly could implement the required function, and that the computer-on-a-chip could then be reprogrammed for use in other products as well. Since integrated circuit design was (and still is) an expensive and time-consuming process, the ability to reuse the hardware design by changing the software was a key breakthrough. The HP-35 was the first hand-held calculator to perform transcendental functions [Whi72]. It was intro-duced in 1972, so it used several chips to implement the CPU, rather than a single-chip microprocessor. However, the ability to write programs to perform math rather than having to design digital circuits to perform operations like trigonometric functions was critical to the successful design of the calculator.

Automobile designers started making use of the microprocessor soon after single-chip CPUs became available. The most important and sophisticated use of microprocessors in automobiles was to control the engine: determining when spark plugs fire, controlling the fuel/air mixture, and so on. There was a trend toward electronics in automobiles in general—electronic devices could be used to replace the mechanical distributor. But the big push toward microprocessor-based engine control came from two nearly simultaneous developments: The oil shock of the 1970s caused consumers to place much higher value on fuel economy, and fears of pollution resulted in laws restrict-ing automobile engine emissions. The combination of low fuel consumption and low emissions is very difficult to achieve; to meet these goals without compromising engine performance, automobile manufacturers turned to sophisticated control algorithms that could be implemented only with micro-processors.

Microprocessors come in many different levels of sophistication; they are usually classified by their word size. An 8-bit **microcontroller** is designed for low-cost applications and includes on-board memory and I/O devices; a 16-bit microcontroller is often used for more sophisticated applications that may require either longer word lengths or off-chip I/O and memory; and a 32-bit **RISC** microprocessor offers very high performance for computation-intensive applications.

Given the wide variety of microprocessor types available, it should be no surprise that microprocessors are used in many ways. There are many house-hold uses of microprocessors. The typical microwave oven has at least one microprocessor to control oven operation. Many houses have advanced ther-mostat systems, which change the temperature level at various times during the day. The modern camera is a prime example of the powerful features that can be added under microprocessor control. The Canon EOS 3 camera con-tains three microprocessors, including a 32-bit RISC CPU that controls the autofocus and eye control systems [Pho99].

Digital television makes extensive use of embedded processors. In some cases, specialized CPUs are designed to execute important algorithms—an example is the CPU designed for audio processing in the SGS Thomson chip set for DirecTV [Lie98]. This processor is designed to efficiently implement

programs for digital audio decoding. A programmable CPU was used rather than a hardwired unit for two reasons: First, it made the system easier to design and debug; and second, it allowed the possibility of upgrades and using the CPU for other purposes.

A high-end automobile may have 100 microprocessors, but even inexpensive cars today use multiple microprocessors. Some of these microprocessors do very simple things such as detect whether seat belts are in use. Others control critical functions such as the ignition and braking systems. Application Example 1-1 describes some of the microprocessors used in the BMW 850i.

Application Example 1-1

BMW 850i Brake and Stability Control System

The BMW 850i was introduced with a sophisticated system for controlling the wheels of the car. An antilock brake system (ABS) reduces skidding by pumping the brakes. An automatic stability control (ASC+T) system intervenes with the engine during maneuvering to improve the car's stability. These systems actively control critical systems of the car; as control systems, they require inputs from and output to the automobile.

Let's first look at the ABS. The purpose of an ABS is to temporarily release the brake on a wheel when it rotates too slowly—when a wheel stops turning, the car starts skidding and becomes hard to control. It sits between the hydraulic pump, which provides power to the brakes, and the brakes themselves as seen in the following diagram. This hookup allows the ABS system to modulate the brakes in order to keep the wheels from locking. The ABS system uses sensors on each wheel to measure the speed of the wheel. The wheel speeds are used by the ABS system to determine how to vary the hydraulic fluid pressure to prevent the wheels from skidding.

The ASC+T system's job is to control the engine power and the brake to improve the car's stability during maneuvers. The ASC+T controls four different systems: throttle, ignition timing, differential brake, and (on automatic transmission cars) gear shifting. The ASC+T can be turned off by the driver, which can be important when operating with tire snow chains.

The ABS and ASC+T must clearly communicate because the ASC+T interacts with the brake system. Since the ABS was introduced several years earlier than the ASC+T, it was important to be able to interface ASC+T to the existing ABS module, as well as to other existing electronic modules. The engine and control management units include the electronically controlled throttle, digital engine management, and electronic transmission control. The ASC+T control unit has two microprocessors on two printed circuit boards, one of which concentrates on logic-relevant components and the other on performance-specific components.

1.2.2 Characteristics of Embedded Computing Applications

Embedded computing is in many ways much more demanding than the sort of programs that you may have written for PCs or workstations. Functionality is important in both general-purpose computing and embedded computing, but embedded applications must meet many other constraints as well.

On the one hand, embedded computing systems have to provide sophisticated functionality:

- *Complex algorithms:* The operations performed by the microprocessor may be very sophisticated. For example, the microprocessor that controls an automobile engine must perform complicated filtering functions to optimize the performance of the car while minimizing pollution and fuel utilization.

- *User interface:* Microprocessors are frequently used to control complex user interfaces that may include multiple menus and many options. The moving maps in Global Positioning System (GPS) navigation are good examples of sophisticated user interfaces.

To make things more difficult, embedded computing operations must often be performed to meet deadlines:

- *Real time:* Many embedded computing systems have to perform in real time—if the data isn't ready by a certain deadline, the system breaks. In some cases, failure to meet a deadline is unsafe and can even endanger lives. In other cases, missing a deadline doesn't create safety problems but

does create unhappy customers—missed deadlines in printers, for example, can result in scrambled pages.

■ *Multirate:* Not only must operations be completed by deadlines, but many embedded computing systems have several real-time activities going on at the same time. They may simultaneously control some operations that run at slow rates and others that run at high rates. Multimedia applications are prime examples of **multirate** behavior. The audio and video portions of a multimedia stream run at very different rates, but they must remain closely synchronized. Failure to meet a deadline on either the audio or video portions spoils the perception of the entire presentation.

Costs of various sorts are very important:

■ *Manufacturing cost:* The total cost of building the system is very important in many cases. Manufacturing cost is determined by many factors, including the type of microprocessor used, the amount of memory required, and the types of I/O devices.

■ *Power:* Power consumption directly affects the cost of the hardware, since a larger power supply may be necessary. But power consumption also affects battery life, which is important in many applications, as well as heat consumption, which can be important even in desktop applications.

Finally, most embedded computing systems are designed by small teams on tight deadlines. The use of small design teams for microprocessor-based systems is a self-fulfilling prophecy—the fact that systems can be built with microprocessors by only a few people invariably encourages management to assume that all microprocessor-based systems can be built by small teams. Tight deadlines are facts of life in today's internationally competitive environment. However, building a product using embedded software makes a lot of sense: Hardware and software can be debugged somewhat independently and design revisions can be made much more quickly.

1.2.3 Why Use Microprocessors?

There are many ways to design a digital system: custom logic, field-programmable gate arrays (FPGAs), and so on. Why use microprocessors? There are two answers:

■ Microprocessors are a very efficient way to implement digital systems.

■ Microprocessors make it easier to design families of products that can be built to provide various feature sets at different price points and can be extended to provide new features to keep up with rapidly changing markets.

The paradox of digital design is that using a predesigned instruction set processor may in fact result in faster implementation of your application than designing your own custom logic. It is tempting to think that the overhead of fetching, decoding, and executing instructions is so high that it cannot be recouped. But there are two factors that work together to make microprocessor-based designs fast. First, microprocessors execute programs very efficiently. Modern RISC processors can execute one instruction per clock cycle most of the time, and high-performance processors can execute several instructions per cycle. While there is overhead that must be paid for interpreting instructions, it can often be hidden by clever utilization of parallelism within the CPU. Second, microprocessor manufacturers spend a great deal of money to make their CPUs run very fast. They hire large teams of designers to tweak every aspect of the microprocessor to make it run at the highest possible speed. Few products can justify the dozens or hundreds of computer architects and VLSI designers customarily employed in the design of a single microprocessor; chips designed by small design teams are less likely to be as highly optimized for speed (or power) as are microprocessors. They also utilize the latest manufacturing technology. Just the use of the latest generation of VLSI fabrication technology, rather than one-generation-old technology, can make a huge difference in performance. Microprocessors generally dominate new fabrication lines because they can be manufactured in large volume and are guaranteed to command high prices. Customers who wish to fabricate their own logic must often wait to make use of VLSI technology from the latest generation of microprocessors. Thus, even if logic you design avoids all the overhead of executing instructions, the fact that it is built from slower circuits often means that its performance advantage is small and perhaps nonexistent.

It is also surprising but true that microprocessors are very efficient utilizers of logic. The generality of a microprocessor and the need for a separate memory may suggest that microprocessor-based designs are inherently much larger than custom logic designs. However, in many cases the microprocessor is smaller when size is measured in units of logic gates. When special-purpose logic is designed for a particular function, it cannot be used for other functions. A microprocessor, on the other hand, can be used for many different algorithms simply by changing the program it executes. Since so many modern systems make use of complex algorithms and user interfaces, we would generally have to design many different custom logic blocks to implement all the required functionality. Many of those blocks will often sit idle—for example, the processing logic may sit idle when user interface functions are performed. Implementing several functions on a single processor often makes much better use of the available hardware budget.

Given the small or nonexistent gains that can be had by avoiding the use of microprocessors, the fact that microprocessors provide substantial advantages makes them the best choice in a wide variety of systems. The programmability of microprocessors can be a substantial benefit during the design process. It allows program design to be separated (at least to some extent) from design of the hardware on which programs will be run. While one team is designing the board that contains the microprocessor, I/O devices, memory, and so on, others can be writing programs at the same time. Equally important, programmability makes it easier to design families of products. In many cases, high-end products can be created simply by adding code without changing the hardware. This practice substantially reduces manufacturing costs. Even when hardware must be redesigned for next-generation products, it may be possible to reuse software, reducing development time and cost.

1.2.4 Challenges in Embedded Computing System Design

External constraints are one important source of difficulty in embedded system design. Let's consider some important problems that must be taken into account in embedded system design.

How much hardware do we need? We have a great deal of control over the amount of computing power we apply to our problem. Not only can we select the type of microprocessor used, we can select the amount of memory, the peripheral devices, and more. Since we often must meet both performance deadlines and manufacturing cost constraints, the choice of hardware is important—too little hardware and the system fails to meet its deadlines, too much hardware and it becomes too expensive.

How do we meet deadlines? The brute force way of meeting a deadline is to speed up the hardware so that the program runs faster. Of course, that makes the system more expensive. It is also entirely possible that increasing the CPU clock rate may not make enough difference to execution time, since the program's speed may be limited by the memory system.

How do we minimize power consumption? In battery-powered applications, power consumption is extremely important. Even in nonbattery applications, excessive power consumption can increase heat dissipation. One way to make a digital system consume less power is to make it run more slowly, but naively slowing down the system can obviously lead to missed deadlines. Careful design is required to slow down the noncritical parts of the machine for power consumption while still meeting necessary performance goals.

How do we design for upgradeability? The hardware platform may be used over several product generations, or for several different versions of a product in the same generation, with few or no changes. However, we want to be able to add features by changing software. How can we design a machine that will provide the required performance for software that we haven't yet written?

Does it really work? Reliability is always important when selling products—customers rightly expect that products they buy will work. Reliability is especially important in some applications, such as safety-critical systems. If we wait until we have a running system and try to eliminate the bugs, we will be too late—we won't find enough bugs, it will be too expensive to fix them, and it will take too long as well. Another set of challenges comes from the characteristics of the components and systems themselves. If workstation programming is like assembling a machine on a bench, then embedded system design is often more like working on a car—cramped, delicate, and difficult.

Let's consider some ways in which the nature of embedded computing machines makes their design more difficult.

- *Complex testing:* Exercising an embedded system is generally more difficult than typing in some data. We may have to run a real machine in order to generate the proper data. The timing of data is often important, meaning that we cannot separate the testing of an embedded computer from the machine in which it is embedded.

- *Limited observability and controllability:* Embedded computing systems usually do not come with keyboards and screens. This makes it more difficult to see what is going on and to affect the system's operation. We may be forced to watch the values of electrical signals on the microprocessor bus, for example, to know what is going on inside the system. Moreover, in real-time applications we may not be able to easily stop the system to see what is going on inside.

- *Restricted development environments:* The development environments for embedded systems (the tools used to develop software and hardware) are often much more limited than those available for PCs and workstations. We generally compile code on one type of machine, such as a PC, and download it onto the embedded system. To debug the code, we must usually rely on programs that run on the PC or workstation and then look inside the embedded system.

1.3 The Embedded System Design Process

This section provides an overview of the embedded system design process aimed at two objectives. First, it will give us an introduction to the various steps in embedded system design before we delve into them in more detail. Second, it will allow us to consider the design **methodology** itself. A design methodology is important for three reasons. First, it allows us to keep a score-card on a design to ensure that we have done everything we need to do, such as optimizing **performance** or performing functional tests. Second, it allows us to develop computer-aided design tools. Developing a single program that takes in a concept for an embedded system and emits a completed design would be a daunting task, but by first breaking the process into manageable steps, we can work on automating (or at least semiautomating) the steps one at a time. Third, a design methodology makes it much easier for members of a design team to communicate. By defining the overall process, team members can more easily understand what they are supposed to do, what they should receive from other team members at certain times, and what they are to hand off when they complete their assigned steps. Since most embedded systems are designed by teams, coordination is perhaps the most important role of a well-defined design methodology.

Figure 1-1 summarizes the major steps in the embedded system design process. In this top-down view, we start with the system **requirements.** In the next step, **specification,** we create a more detailed description of what we want. But the specification states only how the system behaves, not how it is built. The details of the system's internals begin to take shape when we develop the architecture, which gives the system structure in terms of large components. Once we know the components we need, we can design those components, including both software modules and any specialized hardware we need. Based on those components, we can finally build a complete system.

In this section we will consider design from the **top down**—we will begin with the most abstract description of the system and conclude with concrete details. The alternative is a **bottom-up** view in which we start with components to build a system. Bottom-up design steps are shown in the figure as dashed-line arrows. We need bottom-up design because we do not have perfect insight into how later stages of the design process will turn out. Decisions at one stage of design are based upon estimates of what will happen later: How fast can we make a particular function run? How much memory will we need? How much system bus capacity do we need? If our estimates are inadequate, we may have to backtrack and amend our original decisions to take the new facts into account. In general, the less experience we have with the design of similar systems, the more we will have to rely on bottom-up design information to help us refine the system.

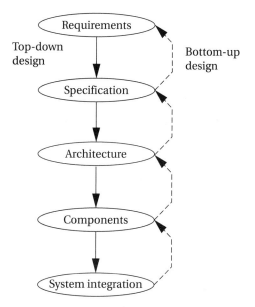

Figure 1-1 *Major levels of abstraction in the design process.*

But the steps in the design process are only one axis along which we can view embedded system design. We also need to consider the major goals of the design:

■ manufacturing cost

■ performance (both overall speed and deadlines)

■ power consumption

■ user interface

We must also consider the tasks we need to perform at every step in the design process. At each step in the design, we add detail:

■ We must *analyze* the design at each step to determine how we can meet the specifications.

■ We must then *refine* the design to add detail.

■ And we must verify the design to ensure that it still meets all system goals, such as cost, speed, and so on.

1.3.1 Requirements

Clearly, before we design a system, we must know what we are designing. The initial stages of the design process capture this information for use in creating the architecture and components. We generally proceed in two phases: First, we gather an informal description from the customers known as requirements, and we refine the requirements into a specification that contains enough information to begin designing the system architecture.

requirements vs. specifications

Separating out requirements analysis and specification is often necessary because of the large gap between what the customers can describe about the system they want and what the architects need to design the system. Consumers of embedded systems are usually not themselves embedded system designers or even product designers. Their understanding of the system is based on how they envision users' interactions with the system. They may have unrealistic expectations as to what can be done within their budgets; and they may also express their desires in a language very different from system architects' jargon. Capturing a consistent set of requirements from the customer and then massaging those requirements into a more formal specification is a structured way to manage the process of translating from the consumer's language to the designer's.

Requirements may be **functional** or **nonfunctional.** We must of course capture the basic functions of the embedded system, but functional description is often not sufficient. Typical nonfunctional requirements include

- *Performance:* The speed of the system is often a major consideration both for the usability of the system and for its ultimate cost. As we have noted, performance may be a combination of soft performance metrics such as approximate time to perform a user-level function and hard deadlines by which a particular operation must be completed.

- *Cost:* The target cost or purchase price for the system is almost always a consideration. Cost typically has two major components: **manufacturing cost** includes the cost of components and assembly; **nonrecurring engineering (NRE)** costs include the personnel and other costs of designing the system.

- *Physical size and weight:* The physical aspects of the final system can vary greatly depending upon the application. An industrial control system for an assembly line may be designed to fit into a standard-size rack with no strict limitations on weight. A handheld device typically has tight requirements on both size and weight that can ripple through the entire system design.

- *Power consumption:* Power, of course, is important in battery-powered systems and is often important in other applications as well. Power can be

specified in the requirements stage in terms of battery life—the customer is unlikely to be able to describe the allowable wattage.

validating requirements

Validating a set of requirements is ultimately a psychological task since it requires understanding both what people want and how they communicate those needs. One good way to refine at least the user interface portion of a system's requirements is to build a **mock-up.** The mock-up may use canned data to simulate functionality in a restricted demonstration, and it may be executed on a PC or a workstation. But it should give the customer a good idea of how the system will be used and how the user can react to it. Physical, nonfunctional models of devices can also give customers a better idea of characteristics such as size and weight.

simple requirements form

Requirements analysis for big systems can be complex and time consuming. However, capturing a relatively small amount of information in a clear, simple format is a good start toward understanding system requirements. To introduce the discipline of requirements analysis as part of system design, we will use a simple requirements methodology.

Figure 1-2 shows a sample **requirements form** that can be filled out at the start of the project. We can use the form as a checklist in considering the basic characteristics of the system. Let's consider the entries in the form:

- *Name:* This is simple but helpful. Giving a name to the project not only simplifies talking about it to other people but can also crystallize the purpose of the machine.

- *Purpose:* This should be a brief one- or two-line description of what the system is supposed to do. If you can't describe the essence of your system in one or two lines, chances are that you don't understand it well enough.

Name

Purpose

Inputs

Outputs

Functions

Performance

Manufacturing cost

Power

Physical size and weight

Figure 1-2 *Sample requirements form.*

- *Inputs and outputs:* These two entries are more complex than they seem. The inputs and outputs to the system encompass a wealth of detail:

 — *Types of data:* Analog electronic signals? Digital data? Mechanical inputs?

 — *Data characteristics:* Periodically arriving data, such as digital audio samples? Occasional user inputs? How many bits per data element?

 — *Types of I/O devices:* Buttons? Analog/digital converters? Video displays?

- *Functions:* This is a more detailed description of what the system does. A good way to approach this is to work from the inputs to the outputs: When the system receives an input, what does it do? How do user interface inputs affect these functions? How do different functions interact?

- *Performance:* Many embedded computing systems spend at least some time controlling physical devices or processing data coming from the physical world. In most of these cases, the computations must be performed within a certain time frame. It is essential that the performance requirements be identified early since they must be carefully measured during implementation to ensure that the system works properly.

- *Manufacturing cost:* This includes primarily the cost of the hardware components. Even if you don't know exactly how much you can afford to spend on system components, you should have some idea of the eventual cost range. Cost has a substantial influence on architecture: A machine that is meant to sell at $10 most likely has a very different internal structure than a $100 system.

- *Power:* Similarly, you may have only a rough idea of how much power the system can consume, but a little information can go a long way. Typically, the most important decision is whether the machine will be battery powered or plugged into the wall. Battery-powered machines must be much more careful about how they spend energy.

- *Physical size and weight:* You should give some indication of the physical size of the system to help guide certain architectural decisions. A desktop machine has much more flexibility in the components used than, for example, a lapel-mounted voice recorder.

A more thorough requirements analysis for a large system might use a form similar to Figure 1-2 as a summary of the longer requirements document. After an introductory section containing this form, a longer requirements document could include details on each of the items mentioned in the introduction. For example, each individual feature described in the introduction in a single sentence may be described in detail in a section of the specification.

internal consistency of requirements After writing the requirements, you should check them for internal consistency: Did you forget to assign a function to an input or output? Did you consider all the modes in which you want the system to operate? Did you place an unrealistic number of features into a battery-powered, low-cost machine?

To practice the capture of system requirements, Example 1-1 creates the requirements for a GPS moving map system.

Example 1-1

Requirements Analysis of a GPS Moving Map

The moving map is a handheld device that displays for the user a map of the terrain around the user's current position; the map display changes as the user and the map device change position. The moving map obtains its position from the GPS, a satellite-based navigation system. The moving map display might look something like the following figure.

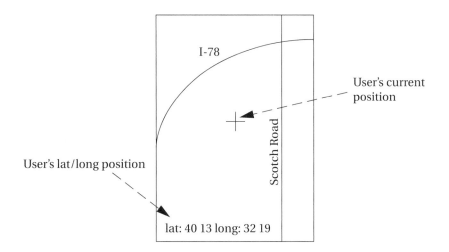

What requirements might we have for our GPS moving map? Here is an initial list:

■ *Functionality:* This system is designed for highway driving and similar uses, not nautical or aviation uses that require more specialized databases and functions. The system should show major roads and other landmarks available in standard topographic databases.

- *User Interface:* The screen should have at least 400 × 600 pixel resolution. The device should be controlled by no more than three buttons. A menu system should pop up on the screen when buttons are pressed to allow the user to make selections to control the system.

- *Performance:* The map should scroll smoothly. Upon power-up, a display should take no more than one second to appear, and the system should be able to verify its position and display the current map within 15 seconds.

- *Cost:* The selling cost (street price) of the unit should be no more than $500.

- *Physical size and weight:* The device should fit comfortably in the palm of the hand.

- *Power consumption:* The device should run for at least eight hours on four AA batteries.

Notice that many of these requirements are not specified in engineering units—for example, physical size is measured relative to a hand, not in centimeters. Although these requirements must ultimately be translated into something that can be used by the designers, keeping a record of what the customer wants can help to resolve questions about the specification that may crop up later during design.

Based on this discussion, let's write a requirements chart for our moving map system:

Name	GPS moving map
Purpose	Consumer-grade moving map for driving use
Inputs	Power button, two control buttons
Outputs	Back-lit LCD display 400 × 600
Functions	Uses 5-receiver GPS system; three user-selectable resolutions; always displays current latitude and longitude
Performance	Updates screen within 0.25 seconds upon movement
Manufacturing cost	$100
Power	100 mW
Physical size and weight	No more than 2" × 6", 12 ounces

This chart adds some requirements in engineering terms that will be of use to the designers. For example, it provides actual dimensions of the device. The manufacturing cost was derived from the selling price by using a simple rule of

thumb: The selling price is four to five times the **cost of goods sold** (the total of all the component costs).

1.3.2 Specification

The specification is more precise—it serves as the contract between the customer and the architects. As such, the specification must be carefully written so that it accurately reflects the customer's requirements and does so in a way that can be clearly followed during design.

Specification is probably the least familiar phase of this methodology for neophyte designers, but it is essential to creating working systems with a minimum of designer effort. Designers who lack a clear idea of what they want to build when they begin typically make faulty assumptions early in the process that aren't obvious until they have a working system. At that point, the only solution is to take the machine apart, throw away some of it, and start again. Not only does this take a lot of extra time, the resulting system is also very likely to be inelegant, kludgy, and bug-ridden.

The specification should be understandable enough so that someone can verify that it meets system requirements and overall expectations of the customer. It should also be unambiguous enough that designers know what they need to build. Designers can run into several different types of problems caused by unclear specifications. If the behavior of some feature in a particular situation is unclear from the specification, the designer may implement the wrong functionality. If global characteristics of the specification are wrong or incomplete, the overall system architecture derived from the specification may be inadequate to meet the needs of implementation.

A specification of the GPS system would include several components:

- data received from the GPS satellite constellation

- map data

- user interface

- operations that must be performed to satisfy customer requests

- background actions required to keep the system running, such as operating the GPS receiver

UML, a language for describing specifications, is introduced in Section 1.4, and we will use it to write a specification in Section 1.5. We will practice writing specifications in each chapter as we work through example system designs. We will also study specification techniques in more detail in Chapter 9.

1.3.3 Architecture Design

The specification does not say how the system does things, only what the system does. Describing how the system implements those functions is the purpose of the architecture. The architecture is a plan for the overall structure of the system that will be used later to design the components that make up the architecture. The creation of the architecture is the first phase of what many designers think of as design.

To understand what an architectural description is, let's look at a sample architecture for the moving map of Example 1-1. Figure 1-3 shows a sample system architecture in the form of a **block diagram** that shows major operations and data flows among them. This block diagram is still quite abstract—we haven't yet specified which operations will be performed by software running on a CPU, what will be done by special-purpose hardware, and so on. The diagram does, however, go a long way toward describing how to implement the functions described in the specification. We clearly see, for example, that we need to search the topographic database and to render (i.e., draw) the results for the display. We have chosen to separate those functions so that we can potentially do them in parallel—performing rendering separately from searching the database may help us update the screen more fluidly.

Only after we have designed an initial architecture that is not biased toward too many implementation details should we refine that system block diagram into two block diagrams: one for hardware and another for software. These two more refined block diagrams are shown in Figure 1-4. The hardware block diagram clearly shows that we have one central CPU surrounded by memory and I/O devices. In particular, we have chosen to use two memories: a frame buffer for the pixels to be displayed and a separate program/data memory for general use by the CPU. The software block diagram fairly closely follows the system block diagram, but we have added a timer to control when we read the buttons on the user interface and render data onto the screen. To have a truly complete architectural description, we require more detail, such as where units in the

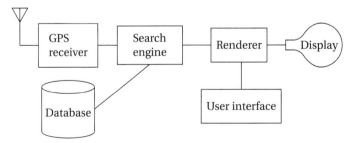

Figure 1-3 *Block diagram for the moving map.*

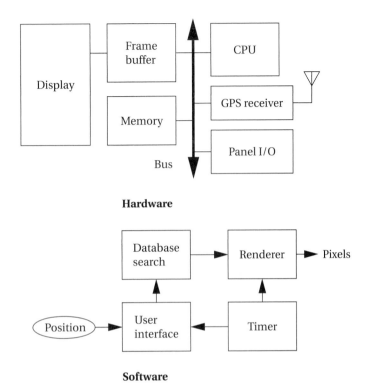

Hardware

Software

Figure 1-4 *Hardware and software architectures for the moving map.*

software block diagram will be executed in the hardware block diagram and when operations will be performed in time.

Architectural descriptions must be designed to satisfy both functional and nonfunctional requirements. Not only must all the required functions be present, but we must meet cost, speed, power, and other nonfunctional constraints. Starting out with a system architecture and refining that to hardware and software architectures is one good way to ensure that we meet all specifications: We can concentrate on the functional elements in the system block diagram, and then consider the nonfunctional constraints when creating the hardware and software architectures.

How do we know that our hardware and software architectures in fact meet constraints on speed, cost, and so on? We must somehow be able to estimate the properties of the components of the block diagrams, such as the search and rendering functions in the moving map system. Accurate estimation derives in part from experience, both general design experience and particular experience with similar systems. However, we can sometimes create simplified models to help us make more accurate estimates. Sound estimates of all

nonfunctional constraints during the architecture phase are crucial, since decisions based on bad data will show up during the final phases of design, indicating that we did not, in fact, meet the specification.

1.3.4 Designing Hardware and Software Components

The architectural description tells us what components we need. The component design effort builds those components in conformance to the architecture and specification. The components will in general include both hardware—field-programmable gate arrays (FPGAs), boards, and so on—and software modules.

Some of the components will be ready-made. The CPU, for example, will be a standard component in almost all cases, as will memory chips and many other components. In the moving map, the GPS receiver is a good example of a specialized component that will nonetheless be a predesigned, standard component. We can also make use of standard software modules. One good example is the topographic database. Standard topographic databases exist, and you probably want to use standard routines to access the database—not only is the data in a predefined format, but it is highly compressed to save storage. Using standard software for these access functions not only saves us design time, but it may give us a faster implementation for specialized functions such as the data decompression phase.

You will have to design some components yourself. Even if you are using only standard integrated circuits, you may have to design the printed circuit board that connects them. You will probably have to do a lot of custom programming as well. When creating these embedded software modules, you must of course make use of your expertise to ensure that the system runs properly in real time and that it doesn't take up more memory space than is allowed. The power consumption of the moving map software example is particularly important. You may need to be very careful about how you read and write memory to minimize power—for example, since memory accesses are a major source of power consumption, memory transactions must be carefully planned to avoid reading the same data several times.

1.3.5 System Integration

Only after the components are built do we have the satisfaction of putting them together and seeing a working system. Of course, this phase usually consists of a lot more than just plugging everything together and standing back. Bugs are typically found during system integration, and good planning can help us find the bugs quickly. By building up the system in phases and running

properly chosen tests, we can often find bugs more easily. If we debug only a few modules at a time, we are more likely to uncover the simple bugs and able to easily recognize them. Only by fixing the simple bugs early will we be able to uncover the more complex or obscure bugs that can be identified only by giving the system a hard workout. We need to ensure during the architectural and component design phases that we make it as easy as possible to assemble the system in phases and test functions relatively independently.

System integration is difficult because it usually uncovers problems. It is often hard to observe the system in sufficient detail to determine exactly what is wrong—the debugging facilities for embedded systems are usually much more limited than what you would find on desktop systems. As a result, determining why things don't work correctly and how they can be fixed is a challenge in itself. Careful attention to inserting appropriate debugging facilities during design can help ease system integration problems, but the nature of embedded computing means that this phase will always be a challenge.

1.4 Formalisms for System Design

As mentioned in the last section, we perform a number of different design tasks at different levels of abstraction throughout this book: creating requirements and specifications, architecting the system, designing code, and designing tests. It is often helpful to conceptualize these tasks in diagrams. Luckily, there is a visual language that can be used to capture all these design tasks: the **Unified Modeling Language (UML)** [Boo99]. UML was designed to be useful at many levels of abstraction in the design process. UML is useful because it encourages design by successive refinement and progressively adding detail to the design, rather than rethinking the design at each new level of abstraction.

UML is an **object-oriented** modeling language. We'll see precisely what we mean by an object in just a moment, but object-oriented design emphasizes two concepts of importance:

- It encourages the design to be described as a number of interacting objects, rather than a few large monolithic blocks of code.

- At least some of those objects will correspond to real pieces of software or hardware in the system. We can also use UML to model the outside world that interacts with our system, in which case the objects may correspond to people or other machines. It is sometimes important to implement something we think of at a high level as a single object using several distinct pieces of code or to otherwise break up the object correspondence in the implementation. However, thinking of the design in terms of actual objects helps us understand the natural structure of the system.

Object-oriented (often abbreviated OO) specification can be seen in two complementary ways:

- Object-oriented specification allows a system to be described in a way that closely models real-world objects and their interactions.

- Object-oriented specification provides a basic set of primitives that can be used to describe systems with particular attributes, irrespective of the relationships of those systems' components to real-world objects.

Both views are useful. At a minimum, object-oriented specification is a set of linguistic mechanisms. In many cases, it is useful to describe a system in terms of real-world analogs. However, performance, cost, and so on may dictate that we change the specification to be different in some ways from the real-world elements we are trying to model and implement. In this case, the object-oriented specification mechanisms are still useful.

object-oriented design vs. programming

What is the relationship between an object-oriented specification and an object-oriented programming language (such as C++)? A specification language may not be executable. But both object-oriented specification and programming languages provide similar basic methods for structuring large systems.

UML is a large language, and covering all of it is beyond the scope of this book. In this section, we introduce only a few basic concepts. In later chapters, as we need a few more UML concepts, we introduce them to the basic modeling elements introduced here. Because UML is so rich, there are many graphical elements in a UML diagram. It is important to be careful to use the correct drawing to describe something—for instance, UML distinguishes between arrows with open and filled-in arrowheads, and solid and broken lines. As you become more familiar with the language, uses of the graphical primitives will become more natural to you.

We also won't take a strict object-oriented approach. We may not always use objects for certain elements of a design—in some cases, such as when taking particular aspects of the implementation into account, it may make sense to use another design style. However, object-oriented design is widely applicable, and no designer can consider himself or herself design literate without understanding it.

1.4.1 Structural Description

By **structural description,** we mean the basic components of the system; we will learn how to describe how these components act in the next section. The principal component of an object-oriented design is, naturally enough, the **object.** An object includes a set of **attributes** that define its internal state.

When implemented in a programming language, these attributes usually become variables or constants held in a data structure. In some cases, we will add the type of the attribute after the attribute name for clarity, but we do not always have to specify a type for an attribute. An object describing a display (such as a CRT screen) is shown in UML notation in Figure 1-5. The text in the folded-corner–page icon is an **annotation;** it does not correspond to an object in the system and only serves as a comment. The attribute is, in this case, an array of pixels that holds the contents of the display. The object is identified in two ways: It has a unique name, and it is a member of a **class.**

classes as types A class is a form of type definition—all objects derived from the same class have the same characteristics, although their attributes may have different values. A class defines the attributes that an object may have. It also defines the **operations** that determine how the object interacts with the rest of the world. In a programming language, the operations would become pieces of code used to manipulate the object. The UML description of the *Display* class is shown in Figure 1-6. The class has the name that we saw used in the *d1* object since *d1* is an instance of class *Display.* The *Display* class defines the *pixels* attribute seen in the object; remember that when we instantiate the class an object, that object will have its own memory so that different objects of the same class have their own values for the attributes. Other classes can examine and modify class

Figure 1-5 *An object in UML notation.*

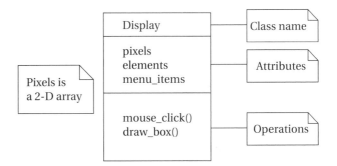

Figure 1-6 *A class in UML notation.*

attributes; if we have to do something more complex than use the attribute directly, we define a behavior to perform that function.

The class definition defines both the **interface** for a particular type of object and that object's **implementation.** When we use an object, we do not directly manipulate its attributes—we can only read or modify the object's state through the operations that define the interface to the object. (The implementation includes both the attributes and whatever code is used to implement the operations.) As long as we do not change the behavior of the object seen at the interface, we can change the implementation as much as we want. This lets us improve the system by, for example, speeding up an operation or reducing the amount of memory required without requiring changes to anything else that uses the object.

choose your interface properly

Clearly, the choice of an interface is a very important decision in object-oriented design. The proper interface must provide ways to access the object's state (since we cannot directly see the attributes) as well as ways to update the state. We need to make the object's interface general enough so that we can make full use of its capabilities. However, excessive generality often makes the object large and slow. Big, complex interfaces also make the class definition difficult for designers to understand and use properly.

There are several types of **relationships** that can exist between objects and classes:

- **Association** occurs between objects that communicate with each other but have no ownership relationship between them.

- **Aggregation** describes a complex object made of smaller objects.

- **Composition** is a type of aggregation in which the owner does not allow access to the component objects.

- **Generalization** allows us to define one class in terms of another.

The elements of a UML class or object do not necessarily directly correspond to statements in a programming language—if the UML is intended to describe something more abstract than a program, there may be a significant gap between the contents of the UML and a program implementing it. The attributes of an object do not necessarily reflect variables in the object. An attribute is some value that reflects the current state of the object. In the program implementation, that value could be computed from some other internal variables. The behaviors of the object would, in a higher-level specification, reflect the basic things that can be done with an object. Implementing all these features may require breaking up a behavior into several smaller behaviors—for example, initialize the object before you start to change its internal state.

Because UML is designed to be used in many stages of design, it is not a programming language. As a result, its concepts may seem abstruse at times. It helps to understand the abstract notions of classes and objects before using them in programming languages. First, let's implement the Display class and the d1 object in the C++ language [Ker88], which directly supports object-oriented techniques. Here is the definition of the Display class:

```
class Display {
        pixels: pixeltype[IMAX,JMAX];
    public:
        Display() { } /* a constructor that creates a class instance */
        pixeltype pixel(int i, int j) {
            return pixels[i,j];
            /* no bounds checking for clarity */
        }
        void set_pixel(pixeltype val, int i, int j) { pixels[i,j] = val; }
    };
```

In C++, the operations are known as **methods.** We have included a list of parameters, a return type, and code for the methods. The C++ code includes more detail than the UML specification; that is natural, since we are using C++ to implement the class, whereas the UML description merely captured the essential characteristics of the system. Here is the instantiation of Display as the object d1:

```
Display d1;
```

The instantiation of d1 creates a data structure in memory that holds the pixel values for d1. For example, the methods defined for the class can be called on d1 to manipulate its pixel values:

```
apixel = d1.pixel(0,0); /* get the value of pixel [0,0] */
```

The notation object.method() says that we are running the method on a particular object. Ensuring that a particular method can be used on a given object is a type checking operation.

Implementing the class and object in a non–object-oriented language like C [Ker88] is a little more challenging but can be done quite well. Here is one way to describe the attributes and operations of the Display class:

```
/* these operations are performed on a two-dimensional array of pixels */
pixel pixelval(pixel *px, int i, int j) { return px[i,j]; }

void set_pixel(pixel *px, pixeltype val, int i, int j) { px[i,j] = val; }
```

Here we have chosen not to define an explicit type for the pixel array since it is a basic two-dimensional array; in other cases, we could use a structure to define the attributes for the object. We have defined two functions to implement the operations. Notice, however, that these functions have an extra argument as compared to the C++ code: The first argument is the array on which we want to apply the operation. In an object-oriented language, some notation such as the object.method() form is used to run an operation on a particular object. When implementing the class in C, we must write the code ourselves that applies the method's operations to a particular set of data that represents an object. This implies that we usually want to keep all the data for an object in a single structure in a C implementation, either an array or a single structure. Requiring the programmer to put the correct data elements in the correct order for each function call on an object would be too time consuming and error-prone.

Here is the instantiation of the d1 object:

```
pixel d1_pixels[IMAX,JMAX];
```

This code simply instantiates the data structure for d1; we have already given the code for the operations. To apply the operations on d1's attributes, we would write code for standard C function calls as follows:

```
apixel = pixelval(d1_pixel,0,0); /* get the [0,0] pixel from the d1_array; */
```

Implementing a class definition and an object in C requires a little more thought and organization than it does in a language like C++ that directly supports object-oriented features. In particular, we want to use comments and code structure to help reflect the structure of the class: We can keep code related to a particular class together and reflect the class definitions in the comments for both the data structures and the functions. However, the time spent defining the classes and objects is not wasted. Not only does designing the class interface help us understand what that element of the system should do, reflecting the class structure in the code will help us maintain the code throughout its lifetime.

derived classes UML, like most object-oriented languages, allows us to define one class in terms of another. An example is shown in Figure 1-7, where we **derive** two particular types of displays. The first, *BW_display*, describes a black-and-white display. This does not require us to add new attributes or operations, but we can specialize both to work on one-bit pixels. The second, *Color_map_display*, uses a graphic device known as a color map to allow the user to select from a large number of available colors even with a small number of bits per pixel. This class defines a *color_map* attribute that determines how pixel values are mapped onto display colors. A **derived class** inherits all the attributes and operations

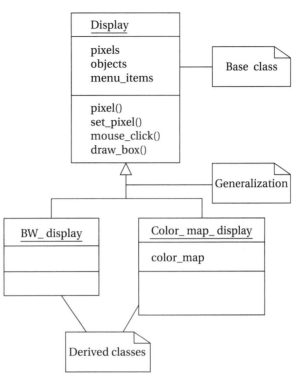

Figure 1-7 *Derived classes as a form of generalization in UML.*

from its **base class.** In this class, *Display* is the base class for the two derived classes. A derived class is defined to include all the attributes of its base class. This relation is transitive—if *Display* were derived from another class, both *BW_display* and *Color_map_display* would inherit all the attributes and operations of *Display's* base class as well. Inheritance has two purposes. It of course allows us to succinctly describe one class that shares some characteristics with another class. Even more important, it captures those relationships between classes and documents them. If we ever need to change any of the classes, knowledge of the class structure helps us determine the reach of changes—for example, should the change affect only *Color_map_display* objects or should it change all *Display* objects?

generalization and inheritance UML considers inheritance to be one form of generalization. A generalization relationship is shown in a UML diagram as an arrow with an open (unfilled) arrowhead. Both *BW_display* and *Color_map_display* are specific versions of *Display,* so *Display* generalizes both of them. UML also allows us to define **multiple inheritance,** in which a class is derived from more than one base class. (Most object-oriented programming languages support multiple

inheritance as well.) An example of multiple inheritance is shown in Figure 1-8; we have omitted the details of the classes' attributes and operations for simplicity. In this case, we have created a *Multimedia_display* class by combining the *Display* class with a *Speaker* class for sound. The derived class inherits all the attributes and operations of both its base classes, *Display* and *Speaker*. Because multiple inheritance causes the sizes of the attribute set and operations to expand so quickly, it should be used with care.

A **link** describes a relationship between objects; association is to link as class is to object. We need links because objects often do not stand alone; associations let us capture type information about these links. Figure 1-9 shows examples of links and an association. When we consider the actual objects in the system, there is a set of messages that keeps track of the current number of active messages (two in this example) and points to the active messages. In this case, the link defines the *contains* relation. When generalized into classes, we define an association between the message set class and the message class. The association is drawn as a line between the two labeled with the name of the association, namely, *contains*. The ball and the number at the message class end indicate that the message set may include zero or more message objects. Sometimes we may want to attach data to the links themselves; we can specify this in the association by attaching a class-like box to the association's edge, which holds the association's data.

Typically, we find that we use a certain combination of elements in an object or class many times. We can give these patterns names, which are called **stereo-**

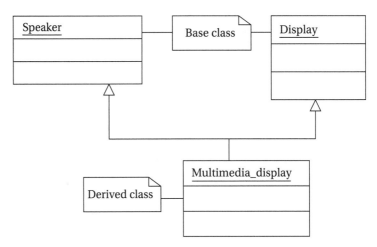

Figure 1-8 *Multiple inheritance in UML.*

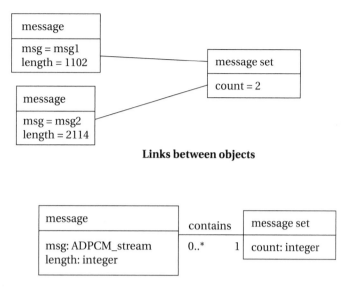

Figure 1-9 *Links and association.*

types in UML. A stereotype name is written in the form <<signal>>. Figure 1-11 shows a stereotype for a signal, which is a communication mechanism.

1.4.2 Behavioral Description

We have to specify the behavior of the system as well as its structure. One way to specify the behavior of an operation is a **state machine.** Figure 1-10 shows UML states; the transition between two states is shown by a skeleton arrow.

These state machines will not rely on the operation of a clock, as in hardware; rather, changes from one state to another are triggered by the occurrence of **events.** An event is some type of action. The event may originate outside the system, such as a user pressing a button. It may also originate inside, such as when one routine finishes its computation and passes the result on to another routine. We will concentrate on the following three types of events defined by UML, as illustrated in Figure 1-11:

■ A **signal** is an asynchronous occurrence. It is defined in UML by an object that is labeled as a *«signal».* The object in the diagram serves as a declaration of the event's existence. Because it is an object, a signal may have parameters that are passed to the signal's receiver.

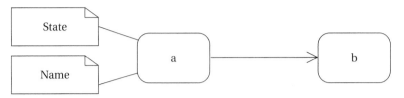

Figure 1-10 *A state and transition in UML.*

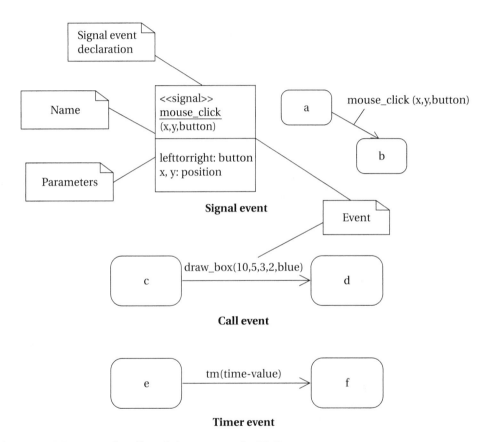

Figure 1-11 *Signal, call, and timer events in UML.*

- A **call event** follows the model of a procedure call in a programming language.

- A **time-out event** causes the machine to leave a state after a certain amount of time. The label *tm(time-value)* on the edge gives the amount of time after which the transition occurs. A time-out is generally implemented with an external timer. This notation simplifies the specification and allows us to defer implementation details about the time-out mechanism.

We show the occurrence of all types of signals in a UML diagram in the same way—as a label on a transition.

Let's consider a simple state machine specification to understand the semantics of UML state machines. A state machine for an operation of the display is shown in Figure 1-12. The start and stop states are special states that help us organize the flow of the state machine. The states in the state machine represent different conceptual operations. In some cases, we take conditional transitions out of states based on inputs or the results of some computation done in the state. In other cases, we make an unconditional transition to the next state. Both the unconditional and conditional transitions make use of the call event. Splitting a complex operation into several states helps document the required steps, much as subroutines can be used to structure code.

It is sometimes useful to show the sequence of operations over time, particularly when several objects are involved. In this case, we can create a sequence diagram, like the one for a mouse click scenario shown in Figure 1-13. A **sequence diagram** is somewhat similar to a hardware timing diagram, although the time flows vertically in a sequence diagram, whereas time typically flows horizontally in a timing diagram. The sequence diagram is designed to show a particular scenario or choice of events—it is not convenient for showing a number of mutually exclusive possibilities. In this case, the sequence shows what happens when a mouse click is on the menu region. Processing includes three objects shown at the top of the diagram. Extending below each object is its *lifeline*, a dashed line that shows how long the object is alive. In this case, all the objects remain alive for the entire sequence, but in other cases objects may be created or destroyed during processing. The boxes along the lifelines show the *focus of control* in the sequence, that is, when the

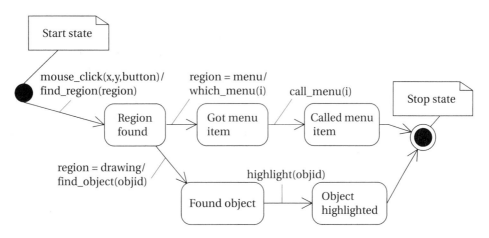

Figure 1-12 *A state machine specification in UML.*

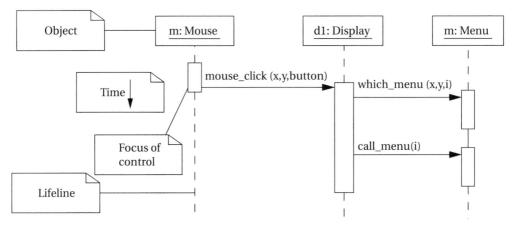

Figure 1-13 *A sequence diagram in UML.*

object is actively processing. In this case, the mouse object is active only long enough to create the *mouse_click* event. The display object remains in play longer; it in turn uses call events to invoke the menu object twice: once to determine which menu item was selected and again to actually execute the menu call. The find_region() call is internal to the display object, so it does not appear as an event in the diagram.

Design Example

1.5 Model Train Controller

In order to learn how to use UML to model systems, we will specify a simple system, a model train controller, which is illustrated in Figure 1-14. The user sends messages to the train with a control box attached to the tracks. The control box may have familiar controls such as a throttle, emergency stop button, and so on. Since the train receives its electrical power from the two rails of the track, the control box can send signals to the train over the tracks by modulating the power supply voltage. As shown in the figure, the control panel sends packets over the tracks to the receiver on the train. The train includes analog electronics to sense the bits being transmitted and a control system to set the train motor's speed and direction based on those commands. Each packet includes an address so that the console can control several trains on the same track; the packet also includes an error correction code (ECC) to guard against

transmission errors. This is a one-way communication system—the model train cannot send commands back to the user.

We start by analyzing the requirements for the train control system. We then develop two specifications: a simple, high-level specification and then a more detailed specification.

Figure 1-14 *A model train control system.*

1.5.1 Requirements

Before we can create a system specification, we have to understand the requirements. Here is a basic set of requirements for the system:

■ The console shall be able to control up to eight trains on a single track.

■ The speed of each train shall be controllable by a throttle to at least 63 different levels in each direction (forward and reverse).

■ There shall be an inertia control that shall allow the user to adjust the responsiveness of the train to commanded changes in speed. Higher inertia means that the train responds more slowly to a change in the throttle, simulating the inertia of a large train. The inertia control will provide at least eight different levels.

■ There shall be an emergency stop button.

■ An error detection scheme will be used to transmit messages.

We can put the requirements into our chart format:

Name	Model train controller
Purpose	Control speed of up to eight model trains
Inputs	Throttle, inertia setting, emergency stop, train number
Outputs	Train control signals
Functions	Set engine speed based upon inertia settings; respond to emergency stop
Performance	Can update train speed at least 10 times per second
Manufacturing cost	$50
Power	10 W (plugs into wall)
Physical size and weight	Console should be comfortable for two hands, approximate size of standard keyboard; weight less than 2 pounds

1.5.2 Conceptual Specification

The conceptual specification allows us to understand the system a little better. We will use the experience gained by writing the conceptual specification to help us write a detailed specification to be given to a system architect.

Because the messages determine what the controller can do, defining the messages will help us understand the functionality of the components. At this point, we are not interested in representing the bits that will be sent down the train track—we only want to capture the information conveyed by the messages. Let's first make a table of commands and then design classes to represent the commands. Here is a set of commands that we can use to implement the requirements placed on the system:

Command name	Parameters
Set-speed	Speed (positive or negative)
Set-inertia	Inertia-value (nonnegative)
Estop	None

Let's first consider how the system console controls the train by sending messages over the tracks. The transmissions are packetized: Each packet includes an address and a message. A typical sequence of train control commands is shown as a UML sequence diagram in Figure 1-15. The focus of the control bars shows that both the console and receiver run continuously. The packets can be sent at any time—there is no global clock controlling when the console sends and the train receives. Since there is only one transmitter, we do

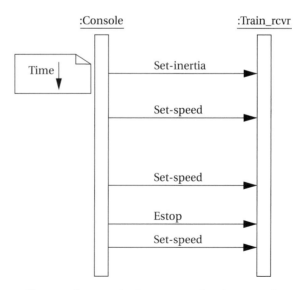

Figure 1-15 *A UML sequence diagram for a typical sequence of train control commands.*

not have to worry about detecting collisions among packets. A *Set-inertia* message will probably be sent infrequently since the train's mass would change only when cars are added or removed. Most of the packets will be speed command messages; when the train receives a speed command, it will speed up or slow down the train smoothly at a rate determined by the current inertia setting. Occasionally, an emergency stop command may be received, which causes the train receiver to immediately shut down the train motor.

commands We can model the commands in UML with a two-level class hierarchy as shown in Figure 1-16. We have created one base class, *Command*, to represent the basic command; there are three subclasses derived from *Command*, one for each specific type of command. This **class diagram** reminds us of the syntax of the messages, showing us what is common among the different messages and what distinguishes them. At this stage of specification, the Command class doesn't have any data fields and seemingly adds little information except to point to the classes for the specific messages. However, we will see in the detailed specification that the command class can be used to describe basic features of all commands, such as error correction, which will be shared by all messages. The *Estop* message class has no parameters because the type of message tells us all we need to know. We have not shown name fields in these classes yet, but we will add this in the detailed specification.

We now need to model the train control system itself. There are clearly two major subsystems: the control-box and the train-board component. Each of these subsystems has its own internal structure. The basic relationship between them is illustrated in Figure 1-17. This figure shows a UML **collaboration diagram;** we could have used another type of figure, such as a class or object diagram, but we wanted to emphasize the transmit/receive relationship between these major subsystems. The console and receiver are each repre-

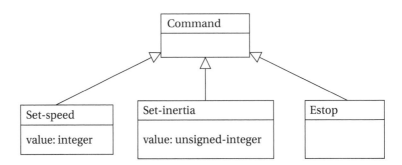

Figure 1-16 *Class diagram for the train controller messages.*

Figure 1-17 *UML collaboration diagram for major subsystems of the train controller system.*

sented by objects; the console sends a sequence of packets to the train's receiver, as illustrated by the arrow. The notation on the arrow provides both the type of message sent and its sequence in a flow of messages; since the console sends all the messages, we have numbered the arrow's messages as 1..n. Those messages are of course carried over the track. Since the track isn't a computer component and is purely passive, it does not appear in the diagram. However, it would be perfectly legitimate to model the track in the collaboration diagram, and in some situations it may be wise to model such nontraditional components in the specification diagrams. For example, if we are worried about what happens when the track breaks, modeling the tracks would help us identify failure modes and possible recovery mechanisms.

Let's break down the console and receiver into their major components. The console needs to perform three functions: read the state of the front panel, format messages, and transmit messages. The train receiver must also perform three major functions: receive the message, interpret the message (taking into account the current speed, inertia setting, etc.), and actually control the motor. In this case, let's use a class diagram to represent the design; we could also use an object diagram if we wished. The UML class diagram is shown in Figure 1-18. It shows the console class using three classes, one for each of its major components. These classes must define some behaviors, but for the moment we will concentrate on the basic characteristics of these classes:

- The *Panel* class describes the console's front panel, which contains the analog knobs and hardware to interface to the digital parts of the system.

- The *Formatter* class includes behaviors that know how to read the panel knobs and creates a bit stream for the required message.

- The *Transmitter* class contains analog electronics to send the message along the track.

There will be one instance of the *Console* class and one instance of each of the component classes, as shown by the numeric values at each end of the relationship links. We've also shown some special classes that represent analog components, ending the name of each with an asterisk:

- *Knobs** describes the actual analog knobs, buttons, and levers on the control panel.

- *Sender** describes the analog electronics that send bits along the track.

Likewise, the *Train* makes use of three other classes that define its components:

- The *Receiver* class knows how to turn the analog signals on the track into digital form.

- The *Controller* class includes behaviors that interpret the commands and figures out how to control the motor.

- The *Motor interface* class defines how to generate the analog signals required to control the motor.

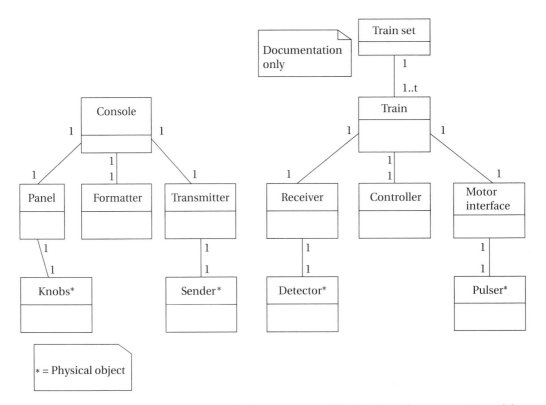

Figure 1-18 *A UML class diagram for the train controller showing the composition of the subsystems.*

We define two classes to represent analog components:

- *Detector** detects analog signals on the track and converts them into digital form.

- *Pulser** turns digital commands into the analog signals required to control the motor speed.

We have also defined a special class, *Train set,* to help us remember that the system can handle multiple trains. The values on the relationship edge show that one train set can have *t* trains. We would not actually implement the train set class, but it does serve as useful documentation of the existence of multiple receivers.

1.5.3 Detailed Specification

Now that we have a conceptual specification that defines the basic classes, let's refine it to create a more detailed specification. We won't make a complete specification, but we will add detail to the classes and look at some of the major decisions in the specification process to get a better handle on how to write good specifications.

At this point, we need to define the analog components in a little more detail because their characteristics will strongly influence the *Formatter* and *Controller.* Figure 1-19 shows a class diagram for these classes; this diagram shows a little more detail than Figure 1-18 since it includes attributes and behaviors of these classes. The *Panel* has three knobs: *train* number (which train is currently being controlled), *speed* (which can be positive or negative), and *inertia.* It also has one button for *emergency-stop.* When we change the train number setting, we also want to reset the other controls to the proper values for that train so that the previous train's control settings are not used to change the current train's settings. To do this, *Knobs** must provide a *set-knobs* behavior that allows the rest of the system to modify the knob settings. (If we wanted or needed to model the user, we would expand on this class definition to provide methods that a user object would call to specify these parameters.) The motor system takes its motor commands in two parts. The *Sender* and *Detector* classes are relatively simple: They simply put out and pick up a bit, respectively.

To understand the *Pulser* class, let's consider how we actually control the train motor's speed. As shown in Figure 1-20, the speed of electric motors is commonly controlled using pulse-width modulation: Power is applied in a pulse for a fraction of some fixed interval, with the fraction of the time that

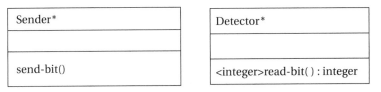

Knobs*
train-knob: integer speed-knob: integer inertia-knob: unsigned-integer emergency-stop: boolean
set-knobs()

Pulser*
pulse-width: unsigned-integer direction: boolean

Sender*
send-bit()

Detector*
<integer>read-bit() : integer

Figure 1-19 *Classes describing analog physical objects in the train control system.*

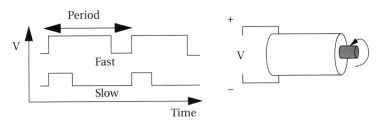

Figure 1-20 *Controlling motor speed by pulse-width modulation.*

power is applied determining the speed. The digital interface to the motor system specifies that pulse width as an integer, with the maximum value being maximum engine speed. A separate binary value controls direction. Note that the motor control takes an unsigned speed with a separate direction, while the panel specifies speed as a signed integer, with negative speeds corresponding to reverse.

Figure 1-21 shows the classes for the panel and motor interfaces. These classes form the software interfaces to their respective physical devices. The *Panel* class defines a behavior for each of the controls on the panel; we have chosen not to define an internal variable for each control since their values can be read directly from the physical device, but a given implementation may choose to use internal variables. The *new-settings* behavior uses the *set-knobs*

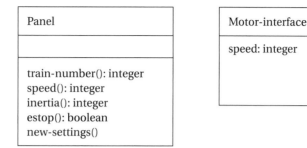

Figure 1-21 *Class diagram for the Panel and Motor interface.*

behavior of the *Knobs** class to change the knobs settings whenever the train number setting is changed. The *Motor-interface* defines an attribute for speed that can be set by other classes. As we will see in a moment, the controller's job is to incrementally adjust the motor's speed to provide smooth acceleration and deceleration.

The *Transmitter* and *Receiver* classes are shown in Figure 1-22. They provide the software interface to the physical devices that send and receive bits along the track. The *Transmitter* provides a distinct behavior for each type of message that can be sent; it internally takes care of formatting the message. The *Receiver* class provides a *read-cmd* behavior to read a message off the tracks. We can assume for now that the receiver object allows this behavior to run continuously to monitor the tracks and intercept the next command. (We consider how to model such continuously running behavior as processes in Chapter 6.) We use an internal variable to hold the current command. Another variable holds a flag showing when the command has been processed. Separate behaviors let us read out the parameters for each type of command; these messages also reset the new flag to show that the command has been processed. We don't need a separate behavior for an *Estop* message since it has no parameters—knowing the type of message is sufficient.

Now that we have specified the subsystems around the formatter and controller, it is easier to see what sorts of interfaces these two subsystems may need.

The *Formatter* class is shown in Figure 1-23. The formatter holds the current control settings for all of the trains. The *send-command* method is a utility function that serves as the interface to the transmitter. The *operate* function performs the basic actions for the object. At this point, we only need a simple specification, which states that the formatter repeatedly reads the panel, determines whether any settings have changed, and sends out the appropriate messages. The *panel-active* behavior returns true whenever the panel's values do not correspond to the current values.

Transmitter	
send-speed(adrs: integer, speed: integer) send-inertia(adrs: integer, val: integer) send-estop(adrs: integer)	

Receiver	
current: command new: boolean	
read-cmd() new-cmd(): boolean rcv-type(msg-type: command) rcv-speed(val: integer) rcv-inertia(val: integer)	

Figure 1-22 *Class diagram for the Transmitter and Receiver.*

Formatter	
current-train: integer current-speed[ntrains]: integer current-inertia[ntrains]: unsigned-integer current-estop[ntrains]: boolean	
send-command() panel-active(): boolean operate()	

Figure 1-23 *Class diagram for the Formatter class.*

The role of the formatter during the panel's operation is illustrated by the sequence diagram of Figure 1-24. The figure shows two changes to the knob settings: first to the throttle, inertia, or emergency stop; then to the train number. The panel is called periodically by the formatter to determine if any control settings have changed. If a setting has changed for the current train, the formatter decides to send a command, issuing a *send-command* behavior to cause the transmitter to send the bits. Because transmission is serial, it takes a noticeable amount of time for the transmitter to finish a command; in the meantime, the formatter continues to check the panel's control settings. If the train number has changed, the formatter must cause the knob settings to be reset to the proper values for the new train.

We have not yet specified the operation of any of the behaviors. We define what a behavior does by writing a state diagram. The state diagram for a very simple version of the *operate* behavior of the *Formatter* class is shown in Figure 1-25. This behavior watches the panel for activity: If the train number changes, it updates the panel display; otherwise, it causes the required message to be sent. Figure 1-26 shows a state diagram for the *panel-active* behavior.

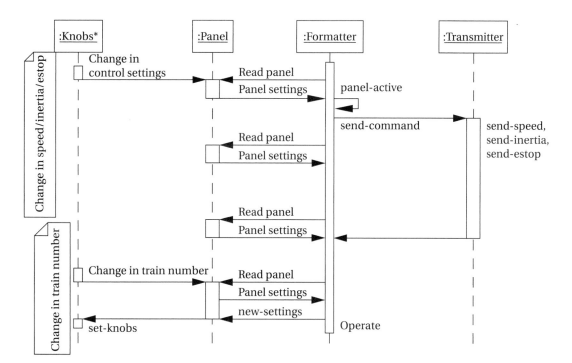

Figure 1-24 *Sequence diagram for transmitting a control input.*

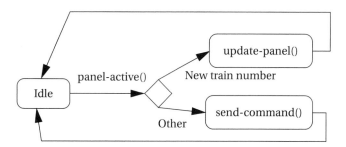

Figure 1-25 *State diagram for the formatter operate behavior.*

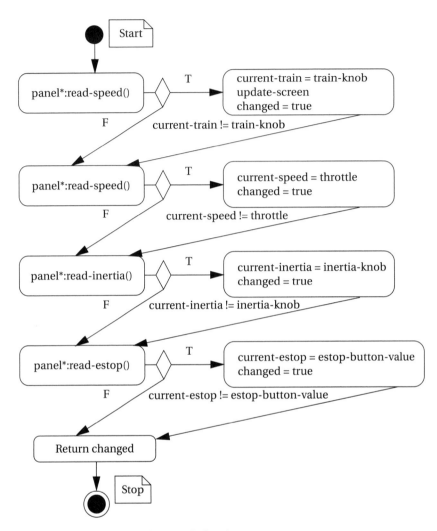

Figure 1-26 *State diagram for the panel-active behavior.*

The definition of the train's *Controller* class is shown in Figure 1-27. The *operate* behavior is called by the receiver when it gets a new command; *operate* looks at the contents of the message and uses the *issue-command* behavior to change the speed, direction, and inertia settings as necessary. A specification for *operate* is shown in Figure 1-28.

The operation of the *Controller* class during the reception of a *set-speed* command is illustrated in Figure 1-29. The *Controller's operate* behavior must execute several behaviors to determine the nature of the message. Once the

```
Controller

current-train: integer
current-speed[ntrains]: unsigned-integer
current-direction[ntrains]: boolean
current-inertia[ntrains]: unsigned-integer

operate()
issue-command()
```

Figure 1-27 *Class diagram for the Controller class.*

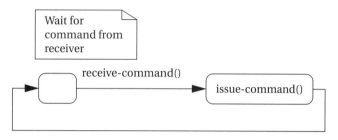

Figure 1-28 *State diagram for the Controller operate behavior.*

speed command has been parsed, it must send a sequence of commands to the motor to smoothly change the train's speed.

refining command classes

It is also a good idea to refine our notion of a command. These changes result from the need to build a potentially upward-compatible system. If the messages were entirely internal, we would have more freedom in specifying messages that we could use during architectural design. But since these messages must work with a variety of trains and we may want to add more commands in a later version of the system, we need to specify the basic features of messages for compatibility. There are three important issues. First, we need to specify the number of bits used to determine the message type. We choose three bits, since that gives us five unused message codes. Second, we need to include information about the length of the data fields, which is determined by the resolution for speeds and inertia set by the requirements. Third, we need to specify the error correction mechanism; we choose to use a single-parity bit. We can update the classes to provide this extra information as shown in Figure 1-30.

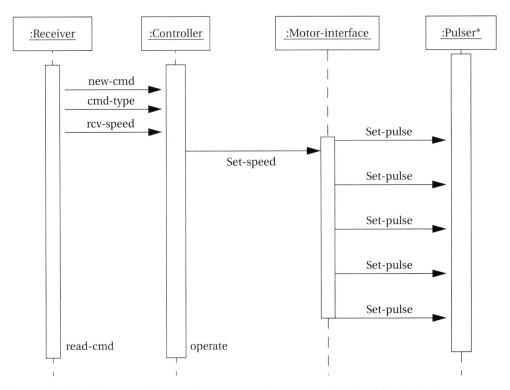

Figure 1-29 *Sequence diagram for a set-speed command received by the train.*

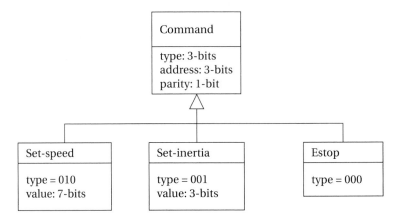

Figure 1-30 *Refined class diagram for the train controller commands.*

1.5.4 Lessons Learned

We've learned a couple of things in this exercise beyond gaining experience with UML notation. First, specification is hard. Even this incomplete specification for a relatively simple system contains a number of subtleties and takes quite a bit of time to complete. You may not be used to thinking at this level of detail before programming. However, such planning is very important. In multiperson projects, the specification is the primary means of communication between programmers. If the specification doesn't provide enough detail, the programmers will have a hard time getting their code modules to work together properly.

The other important lesson is that it is often difficult to completely eliminate architectural decisions from the specification. For instance, we determined that the objects from the formatter and receiver classes had to run continuously to monitor changes in the panel and messages, respectively. Sometimes the cleanest way to write a specification is to make a few basic assumptions about how the system will be designed. As long as those decisions are well understood and well documented, that's okay. However, architectural and other implementation decisions should be kept to a minimum in the specification to avoid creating implementation problems both now and in future versions of the system.

1.6 A Guided Tour of This Book

The most efficient way to learn all the necessary concepts is to move from the bottom up. This book is arranged so that you learn about the properties of components and build toward more complex systems and a more complete view of the system design process. Veteran designers have learned enough bottom-up knowledge from experience to know how to use a top-down approach to designing a system, but when learning things for the first time, the bottom-up approach allows you to build more sophisticated concepts on the basis of lower-level ideas.

We will use several organizational devices throughout the book to help you. Application Examples focus on a particular end-use application and how it relates to embedded system design. We will also make use of Programming Examples to describe software designs. In addition to these examples, each chapter will use a significant system design example to demonstrate the major concepts of the chapter.

Each chapter includes questions that are intended to be answered on paper as homework assignments. The chapters also include lab exercises. These are

more open ended and are intended to suggest activities that can be performed in the lab to help illuminate various concepts in the chapter.

Throughout the book, we will use two CPUs as examples: the ARM RISC processor and the SHARC digital signal processor (DSP). Both are well-known microprocessors used in many embedded applications. Using real microprocessors helps make concepts more concrete. However, our aim is to learn concepts that can be applied to many different microprocessors, not only ARM and SHARC. While microprocessors will evolve over time (Warhol's Law of Computer Architecture [Wol92A] states that every microprocessor architecture will be the price/performance leader for fifteen minutes), the concepts of embedded system design are fundamental and long term.

1.6.1 Chapter 2: Instruction Sets

In Chapter 2, we begin our study of microprocessors by concentrating on **instruction sets.** The chapter covers the instruction sets of the ARM and SHARC microprocessors in separate sections. These two microprocessors are very different. Understanding all details of both is not absolutely necessary to the design of embedded systems. However, comparing the two does provide some interesting lessons in instruction set architectures.

Understanding details of the instruction set is important both for concreteness and for seeing how architectural features can affect performance and other system attributes. But many mechanisms, such as caches and memory management, can be understood in general before we go on to details of how they are implemented in ARM and SHARC.

We do not introduce a design example in this chapter—it is difficult to build even a simple working system without understanding other aspects of the CPU that will be introduced in Chapter 3. However, understanding instruction sets is critical to understanding problems such as execution speed and code size that we study throughout the book.

1.6.2 Chapter 3: CPUs

Chapter 3 rounds out our discussion of microprocessors by focusing on the following important mechanisms that are not part of the instruction set itself:

- The fundamental mechanisms of **input** and **output** are reviewed, including interrupts.

- We also study the **cache** and **memory management unit.**

We also begin to consider how the CPU hardware affects important characteristics of program execution. Program performance and power consumption are very important parameters in embedded system design. An understanding of how architectural aspects such as pipelining and caching affect these system characteristics is a foundation for analyzing and optimizing programs in later chapters.

We use as an example a simple data compression unit, concentrating on the programming of the core compression algorithm.

1.6.3 Chapter 4: The Embedded Computing Platform

Chapter 4 looks at the basic hardware and software platform for embedded computing. The microprocessor is very important, but only part of a system that includes memory, I/O devices, and low-level software. We need to understand the basic characteristics of the platform before we move on to build sophisticated systems.

The basic embedded computing platform includes a microprocessor, I/O hardware, I/O driver software, and memory. Application-specific software and hardware can be added to this platform to turn it into an embedded computing platform. The microprocessor is at the center of both the hardware and software structure of the embedded computing system. The CPU controls the bus that connects to memory and I/O devices; the CPU also runs software that talks to the devices. In particular, I/O is central to embedded computing. Many aspects of I/O are not typically studied in modern computer architecture courses, so we need to master the basic concepts of input and output before we can design embedded systems.

Chapter 4 covers several important aspects of the platform:

- We study in detail how the CPU talks to memory and devices using the microprocessor **bus.**

- Based on our knowledge of bus operation, we study the structure of the **memory system** and types of **memory components.**

- We survey some important types of **I/O devices** to understand how to implement various types of real-world interfaces.

- We look at basic techniques for embedded system **design** and **debugging.**

We use an alarm clock as a design example. The clock does relatively little computation but a lot of I/O: It uses a timer to tell the CPU when to update the time, it reads buttons on the clock to respond to the user, and it continually updates the clock display.

1.6.4 Chapter 5: Program Design and Analysis

Chapter 5 looks inside the CPU to understand how instructions are executed as programs. Given the challenges of embedded programming—meeting strict performance goals, minimizing program size, reducing power consumption—this is an especially important topic. We build upon the fundamentals of computer architecture to understand how to design embedded programs.

- As part of our study of the relationship between programs and instructions, we introduce a model for high-level language programs known as the **control/data flow graph (CDFG).** We use this model extensively to help us analyze and optimize programs.

- Because embedded programs are increasingly written in higher-level languages, we will look at the processes for compiling, assembling, and linking to understand how high-level language programs are translated into instructions and data. Some of the discussion surveys basic techniques for translating high-level language programs, but we also spend time on compilation techniques designed specifically to meet embedded system challenges.

- We develop techniques for the **performance analysis** of programs. It is difficult to determine the speed of a program simply by examining its source code. We learn how to use a combination of the source code, its assembly language implementation, and expected data inputs to analyze program execution time. We also study some basic techniques for optimizing program performance.

- An important topic related to performance analysis is **power analysis.** We build on performance analysis methods to learn how to estimate the power consumption of programs.

- It is critical that the programs that we design function correctly. The control/data flow graph and techniques we have learned for performance analysis are related to techniques for **testing programs.** We develop techniques that can methodically develop a set of tests for a program in order to exercise likely bugs.

Our design example for Chapter 5 is a software modem. A modem translates between the digital world of the microprocessor and the analog transmission scheme of the telephone network. Rather than use analog electronics to build a modem, we can use a microprocessor and special-purpose software. Because the modem has strict real-time deadlines, this example lets us exercise our knowledge of the microprocessor and of program analysis.

1.6.5 Chapter 6: Processes and Operating Systems

Chapter 6 builds on our knowledge of programs to study a special type of software component, the **process,** and operating systems that use processes to create systems. A process is an execution of a program; an embedded system may have several processes running concurrently. A separate **real-time operating system (RTOS)** controls when the processes run on the CPU. Processes are important to embedded system design because they help us juggle multiple events happening at the same time. A real-time embedded system that is designed without processes usually ends up as a mess of spaghetti code that doesn't operate properly.

Throughout the chapter we use the POSIX operating system (a standardized variation of Unix) as an example (Linux is a POSIX-compliant open source operating system). We will study the basic concepts of processes and process-based design in this chapter:

- We begin by introducing the **process abstraction.** A process is defined by a combination of the program being executed and the current state of the program. We will learn how to switch contexts between processes.

- We cover the fundamentals of **interprocess communication,** including the various styles of communication and how they can be implemented.

- In order to make use of processes, we must be able to **schedule** them. We discuss process priorities and how they can be used to guide scheduling.

- The real-time operating system is the software component that implements the process abstraction and scheduling. We study how RTOSs implement schedules, how programs interface to the operating system, and how we can evaluate the performance of systems built from RTOSs.

Chapter 6 uses as a design example a digital telephone answering machine. Not only does an answering machine require real-time operation—telephone data are regularly sampled and stored to memory—but it must juggle several tasks at once. The answering machine must be able to operate the user interface simultaneously with recording voice data. In the most complex version of the answering machine, we must also simultaneously compress voice data during recording and uncompress it during playback. To emphasize the role of processes in structuring real-time computation, we compare the answering machine design with and without processes. It becomes apparent that the implementation that does not use processes will be considerably harder to design and debug.

1.6.6 Chapter 7: CPU Accelerators

We sometimes build embedded systems that include special-purpose function units in addition to the CPU. The CPU calls upon the unit, often called an **accelerator,** to do some of the work. In some cases, we can't do all of the computations we need to do fast enough on a single CPU. In other cases, we can reduce system cost and complexity by putting part of the work on an accelerator and using a smaller CPU for the rest of the operations.

Chapter 7 studies the design of embedded systems with accelerators. Designing an accelerated system requires more than just building the accelerator itself. We have to determine how to connect the accelerator into the hardware and software so that we make best use of its capabilities. For example, the data transfers between the CPU and accelerator can consume all of the time savings created by the accelerator if we are not careful. We can also introduce added parallelism into the system if we have the CPU working on something else while the accelerator does its job.

We use as our example a video accelerator. Digital video requires performing a huge number of operations in real time; video also requires large volumes of data transfers. As such, it provides a good way to study not only the design of the accelerator itself but also how it fits into the overall system.

1.6.7 Chapter 8: Networks

Chapter 8 studies how we can build more complex embedded systems by letting several components communicate on a **network.** The network may include several microprocessors, I/O devices, and special-purpose acceleration units. Embedded systems that are built from multiple microprocessors are called **distributed embedded systems.** The automobile is a prime example of a distributed embedded system: Microprocessors are distributed all over the automobile performing distributed computations and coordinating the operation of the vehicle using networks.

This chapter builds on our knowledge of processes in particular to understand networks and their use in system design as follows:

- We start by discussing the fundamentals of network protocols and how networks differ from buses.

- Based on our knowledge of interprocess communication, we see how to allow processes to communicate over networks. We see how real-time operating systems can be extended to support multiple microprocessors whose processes communicate over a network.

- We study how to break a design into multiple components that communicate over a network. In particular, we need to know how to factor the communication delay of the network into our performance analysis.

Chapter 8 uses as a design example a simple elevator system. An elevator is necessarily a distributed system operating over a network: We must have control in each elevator, but we must also coordinate the elevators to respond to user requests. And because the elevator includes some real-time control requirements—we must be able to stop the elevator at the door to the right floor—it provides a very good example to show how to properly distribute computations over the network to maximize responsiveness.

1.6.8 Chapter 9: System Design Techniques

Chapter 9 is our capstone chapter. This chapter studies the design of large, complex embedded systems. We introduce important concepts that are essential for the successful completion of large embedded system projects, and we use those techniques to help us integrate the knowledge obtained throughout the book.

This chapter delves into several topics related to large-scale embedded system design:

- We revisit the topic of **design methodologies.** Based on our more detailed knowledge of embedded system design, we can better understand the role of methodology and the possible variations in methodologies.

- We study system **specification methods.** Proper specifications become increasingly important as system complexity grows. More formal specification techniques help us capture intent clearly, consistently, and unambiguously.

- We look at **quality assurance** techniques. The program testing techniques covered in Chapter 5 are a good foundation but may not scale easily to complex systems. Additional methods are required to ensure that we exercise complex systems to shake out bugs.

This chapter makes use of several large system examples: a telephone switching system (also known as a PBX), a high-end, ink jet printer, and personal digital assistants. These examples of course help us illustrate specification, methodology, and quality assurance. They also serve to integrate all the lessons of the book, ranging from program performance to process-based design. We also briefly discuss some ideas for more extensive embedded design projects. We then cap off the discussion with a brief survey of systems-on-silicon.

1.7 Summary

Embedded microprocessors are everywhere. Microprocessors allow sophisticated algorithms and user interfaces to be added relatively inexpensively to an amazing variety of products. Microprocessors also help reduce design complexity and time by separating out hardware and software design. Embedded system design is much more complex than programming PCs because we must meet multiple design constraints, including performance, cost, and so on. In the remainder of this book, we will build a set of techniques from the bottom up that will allow us to conceive, design, and implement sophisticated microprocessor-based systems.

What We Learned

■ Embedded computing can be fun. It can also be difficult.

■ Trying to hack together a complex embedded system probably won't work. You need to master a number of skills and understand the design process.

■ Your system must meet certain functional requirements, such as features. It may also have to perform tasks to meet deadlines, limit its power consumption, be of a certain size, or meet other nonfunctional requirements.

■ A hierarchical design process takes the design through several different levels of abstraction. You may need to do both top-down and bottom-up design.

■ We use UML to describe designs at several levels of abstraction.

■ This book takes a bottom-up view of embedded system design.

Further Reading

Spasov [Spa99] describes how 68HC11 microcontrollers are used in Canon EOS cameras. Douglass [Dou98] gives a good introduction to UML for embedded systems. Other foundational books on object-oriented design include Rumbaugh et al. [Rum91], Booch [Boo91], Shlaer and Mellor [Shl92], and Selic et al. [Sel94].

Questions

Q1-1 Briefly describe the distinction between requirements and specification.

Q1-2 Briefly describe the distinction between specification and architecture.

Q1-3 At what stage of the design methodology would we determine what type of CPU to use (8-bit vs. 16-bit vs. 32-bit, which model of a particular type of CPU, etc.)?

Q1-4 At what stage of the design methodology would we choose a programming language?

Q1-5 At what stage of the design methodology would we test our design for functional correctness?

Q1-6 Compare and contrast top-down and bottom-up design.

Q1-7 Provide a concrete example of how bottom-up information from the software programming phase of design may be useful in refining the architectural design.

Q1-8 Give a concrete example of how bottom-up information from I/O device hardware design may be useful in refining the architectural design.

Q1-9 Create a UML state diagram for the *receive-message* behavior of the *Controller* class of Figure 1-27.

Q1-10 Show how a *Set-speed* command flows through the refined class structure described in Figure 1-18, moving from a change on the front panel to the required changes on the train:

 a. Show it in the form of a collaboration diagram.

 b. Show it in the form of a sequence diagram.

Q1-11 Show how a *Set-inertia* command flows through the refined class structure described in Figure 1-18, moving from a change on the front panel to the required changes on the train:

 a. Show it in the form of a collaboration diagram.

 b. Show it in the form of a sequence diagram.

Q1-12 Show how an *Estop* command flows through the refined class structure described in Figure 1-18, moving from a change on the front panel to the required changes on the train:

 a. Show it in the form of a collaboration diagram.

 b. Show it in the form of a sequence diagram.

Q1-13 Draw a state diagram for a behavior that sends the command bits on the track. The machine should generate the address, generate the correct message type, include the parameters, and generate the ECC.

Q1-14 Draw a state diagram for a behavior that parses the received bits. The machine should check the address, determine the message type, read the parameters, and check the ECC.

Q1-15 Draw a class diagram for the classes required in a basic microwave oven. The system should be able to set the microwave power level between 1 and 9 and time a cooking run up to 59 minutes and 59 seconds in one-second increments. Include * classes for the physical interfaces to the telephone line, microphone, speaker, and buttons.

Q1-16 Draw a collaboration diagram for the microwave oven of question Q1-15. The diagram should show the flow of messages when the user first sets the power level to 7, then sets the timer to 2:30, and then runs the oven.

Lab Exercises

L1-1 How would you measure the execution speed of a program running on a microprocessor? You may not always have a system clock available to measure time. To experiment, write a piece of code that performs some function that takes a small but measurable amount of time, such as a matrix algebra function. Compile and load the code onto a microprocessor, and then try to observe the behavior of the code on the microprocessor's pins.

L1-2 Complete the detailed specification of the train controller that was started in Section 1.5.3. Show all the required classes. Specify the behaviors for those classes. Use object diagrams to show the instantiated objects in the complete system. Develop at least one sequence diagram to show system operation.

L1-3 Develop a requirements description for an interesting device. The device may be a household appliance, a computer peripheral, or whatever you wish.

L1-4 Write a specification for an interesting device in UML. Try to use a variety of UML diagrams, including class diagrams, object diagrams, sequence diagrams, and so on.

Instruction Sets

- A brief review of computer architecture taxonomy and assembly language.
- Two very different architectures: ARM and SHARC.

2.1 Introduction

In this chapter, we begin our study of microprocessors by studying **instruction sets**—the programmer's interface to the hardware. Although we hope to do as much programming as possible in high-level languages, the instruction set is the key to analyzing the performance of programs. By understanding the types of instructions that the CPU provides, we gain insight into alternative ways to implement a particular function.

We use two CPUs as examples. The ARM processor [Fur96, Jag95] is widely used in personal digital assistants (PDAs), video games, telephones, and many other systems. (The ARM architecture comes in several versions; we will concentrate on ARM version 7.) The SHARC [ADI97] is a well-known **digital signal processor (DSP).** We do not provide a complete manual on these architectures; instead we survey their features to understand CPU characteristics.

We start with a brief introduction of some terminology about CPUs. Section 2.3 describes the ARM processor, while Section 2.4 describes the SHARC. We do not introduce a design example in this chapter; we postpone the design until the next chapter, when we have a more comprehensive view of the CPU. You may not wish to read about both the ARM and SHARC in detail, particularly if you plan to use only one of them in designs. However, the two instruction sets are very different and comparing them makes for an interesting exercise.

2.2 Preliminaries

2.2.1 Computer Architecture Taxonomy

Before we delve into the details of microprocessor instruction sets, it is helpful to develop some basic terminology. We do so by reviewing a taxonomy of the basic ways we can organize a computer.

von Neumann architectures

A block diagram for one type of computer is shown in Figure 2-1. The computing system consists of a **central processing unit (CPU)** and a **memory.** The memory holds both data and instructions, and can be read or written when given an address. A computer whose memory holds both data and instructions is known as a **von Neumann** machine.

The CPU has several internal **registers** that store values used internally. One of those registers is the **program counter (PC),** which holds the address in memory of an instruction. The CPU fetches the instruction from memory, decodes the instruction, and executes it. The program counter does not directly determine what the machine does next, but only indirectly by pointing to an instruction in memory. By changing only the instructions, we can change what the CPU does. It is this separation of the instruction memory from the CPU that distinguishes a stored-program computer from a general finite-state machine.

Harvard architectures

An alternative to the von Neumann style of organizing computers is the **Harvard architecture,** which is nearly as old as the von Neumann architecture. As shown in Figure 2-2, a Harvard machine has separate memories for data and program. The program counter points to program memory, not data memory. As a result, it is harder to write self-modifying programs (programs

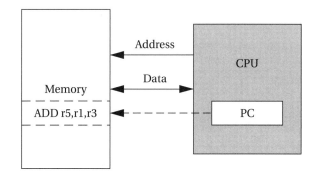

Figure 2-1 *A von Neumann architecture computer.*

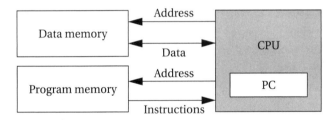

Figure 2-2 *A Harvard architecture.*

that write data values, then use those values as instructions) on Harvard machines.

Harvard architectures are widely used today for one very simple reason—the separation of program and data memories provides higher performance for digital signal processing. Processing signals in real time places great strains on the data access system in two ways: First, large amounts of data flow through the CPU; and second, that data must be processed at precise intervals, not just when the CPU gets around to it. Data sets that arrive continuously and periodically are called **streaming data.** Having two memories with separate ports provides higher memory bandwidth; not making data and memory compete for the same port also makes it easier to move the data at the proper times. DSPs constitute a large fraction of all microprocessors sold today, and most of them are Harvard architectures. A single example shows the importance of DSP: Most of the telephone calls in the world go through at least two DSPs, one at each end of the phone call.

RISC vs. CISC Another axis along which we can organize computer architectures relates to their instructions and how they are executed. Many early computer architectures were what is known today as **complex instruction set computers (CISC).** These machines provided a variety of instructions that may perform very complex tasks, such as string searching; they also generally used a number of different instruction formats of varying lengths. One of the advances in the development of high-performance microprocessors was the concept of **reduced instruction set computers (RISC).** These computers tended to provide somewhat fewer and simpler instructions. The instructions were also chosen so that they could be efficiently executed in **pipelined** processors. Early RISC designs substantially outperformed CISC designs of the period. As it turns out, we can use RISC techniques to efficiently execute at least a common subset of CISC instruction sets, so the performance gap between RISC-like and CISC-like instruction sets has narrowed somewhat.

Beyond the basic RISC/CISC characterization, we can classify computers by several characteristics of their instruction sets. The instruction set of the computer defines the interface between software modules and the underlying

hardware; the instructions define what the hardware will do under certain circumstances. Instructions can have a variety of characteristics, including:

■ fixed versus variable length

■ addressing modes

■ numbers of operands

■ types of operations supported

The set of registers available for use by programs is called the **programming model**, also known as the **programmer model.** (The CPU has many other registers that are used for internal operations and are unavailable to programmers.)

There may be several different implementations of an architecture. In fact, the architecture definition serves to define those characteristics that must be true of all implementations and what may vary from implementation to implementation. Different CPUs may offer different clock speeds, different cache configurations, changes to the bus or interrupt lines, and many other changes that can make one model of CPU more attractive than another for any given application.

2.2.2 Assembly Language

Figure 2-3 shows a fragment of ARM assembly code to remind us of the basic features of assembly languages. Web Aid 2-Assembly provides example ARM and SHARC assembly language files. Assembly languages usually share the same basic features:

■ one instruction appears per line

■ **labels**, which give names to memory locations, start in the first column

■ instructions must start in the second column or after to distinguish them from labels

```
label1    ADR r4,c
          LDR r0,[r4]        ; a comment
          ADR r4,d
          LDR r1,[r4]
          SUB r0,r0,r1       ; another comment
```

Figure 2-3 *An example of ARM assembly language.*

- comments run from some designated comment character (; in the case of ARM) to the end of the line

Assembly language follows this relatively structured form to make it easy for the **assembler** to parse the program and to consider most aspects of the program line by line. (It should be remembered that early assemblers were written in assembly language to fit in a very small amount of memory. Those early restrictions have carried into modern assembly languages by tradition.) Figure 2-4 shows the format of an ARM data processing instruction such as an ADD. For the instruction

ADDGT r0,r3,#5

the *cond* field would be set according to the GT condition (1100), the *opcode* field would be set to the binary code for the ADD instruction (0100), the first *operand* register *Rn* would be set to 3 to represent r3, the destination register *Rd* would be set to 0 for r0, and the *operand 2* field would be set to the immediate value of 5. Figure 2-5 shows the format of one of the SHARC compute-and-move group instructions. The instruction has several fields for specifying registers, read or write, and so on, and a field for a compute operation.

Assemblers must also provide some **pseudo-ops** to help programmers create complete assembly language programs. An example of a pseudo-op is one that allows data values to be loaded into memory locations. These allow

Figure 2-4 *Format of ARM data processing instructions.*

DMD/PMD: read/write

DMDREG, PMDREG: register file locations

Figure 2-5 *Format of the SHARC compute/dreg, DM/dreg, and PM instruction.*

BIGBLOCK % 10

ARM

```
.global BIGBLOCK
.var BIGBLOCK [10] = 0, 0, 0, 0, 0, 0, 0, 0, 0, 0;
```
SHARC

Figure 2-6 *Pseudo-ops for allocating memory.*

constants, for example, to be set into memory. Examples of these pseudo-ops for ARM and SHARC are shown in Figure 2-6. The ARM % pseudo-op allocates a block of memory of the size specified by the operand and initializes those locations to zero. In the SHARC code, you first declare the variable as a global and then initialize it.

2.3 ARM Processor

In this section, we concentrate on the ARM processor. ARM is actually a family of RISC architectures that have been developed over many years. ARM does not manufacture its own VLSI devices; rather, it licenses its architecture to companies who either manufacture the CPU itself or integrate the ARM processor into a larger system.

The textual description of instructions, as opposed to their binary representation, is called an assembly language. ARM instructions are written one per line, starting after the first column. Comments begin with a semicolon and continue to the end of the line. A label, which gives a name to a memory loca-

tion, comes at the beginning of the line, starting in the first column. Here is an example:

```
        LDR r0,[r8] ; a comment
label   ADD r4,r0,r1
```

2.3.1 Processor and Memory Organization

Different versions of the ARM architecture are identified by number. ARM7 is a von Neumann architecture machine, while ARM9 uses a Harvard architecture. However, this difference is invisible to the assembly language programmer, except for possible performance differences.

The ARM architecture supports two basic types of data:

■ the standard ARM word is 32 bits long

■ the word may be divided into four 8-bit bytes

ARM7 allows addresses to be 32 bits long. An address refers to a byte, not a word. Therefore, the word 0 in the ARM address space is at location 0, the word 1 is at 4, the word 2 is at 8, and so on. (As a result, the PC is incremented by 4 in the absence of a branch.) The ARM processor can be configured at power-up to address the bytes in a word in either **little-endian** mode (with the lowest-order byte residing in the low-order bits of the word) or **big-endian** mode (the lowest-order byte stored in the highest bits of the word), as illustrated in Figure 2-7 [Coh81].

General-purpose computers have sophisticated instruction sets. Some of this sophistication is required simply to provide the functionality of a general computer, while other aspects of instruction sets may be provided to increase performance, reduce code size, or otherwise improve program characteristics. In this section, we concentrate on the functionality of the ARM instruction set and will defer performance and other aspects of the CPU to Section 5.6.

2.3.2 Data Operations

Arithmetic and logical operations in C are performed in variables. Variables are implemented as memory locations. Therefore, to be able to write instructions to perform C expressions and assignments, we must consider both the arithmetic and logical instructions as well as instructions for reading and writing memory.

Figure 2-8 shows a sample fragment of C code with data declarations and several assignment statements. The variables a, b, c, x, y, and z all become data locations in memory. In most cases data are kept relatively separate from instructions in the program's memory image.

ARM programming model

In the ARM processor, arithmetic and logical operations cannot be performed directly on memory locations. While some processors allow such operations to directly reference main memory, ARM is a **load-store architecture**—data operands must first be loaded into the CPU and then stored back to main memory to save the results. Figure 2-9 shows the registers in the basic ARM programming model. ARM has 16 general-purpose registers, r0 through r15. Except for r15, they are identical—any operation that can be done on one of them can be done on the others. The r15 register has the same capabilities as the other registers, but it is also used as the program counter. The program counter should of course not be overwritten for use in data operations. However, giving the PC the properties of a general-purpose register allows the program counter value to be used as an operand in computations, which can make certain programming tasks easier.

Figure 2-7 *Byte organizations within an ARM word.*

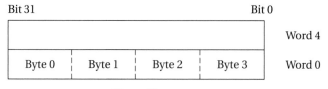

Figure 2-8 *A C fragment with data operations.*

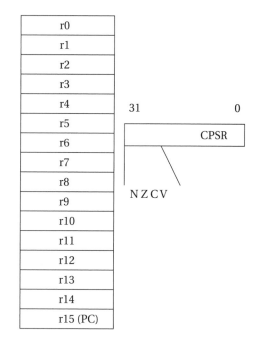

Figure 2-9 *The basic ARM programming model.*

The other important basic register in the programming model is the **current program status register (CPSR).** This register is set automatically during every arithmetic, logical, or shifting operation. The top four bits of the CPSR hold the following useful information about the results of that arithmetic/logical operation:

- The negative (N) bit is set when the result is negative in two's-complement arithmetic.

- The zero (Z) bit is set when every bit of the result is zero.

- The carry (C) bit is set when there is a carry out of the operation.

- The overflow (V) bit is set when an arithmetic operation results in an overflow.

These bits can be used to easily check the results of an arithmetic operation. However, if a chain of arithmetic or logical operations is performed and the intermediate states of the CPSR bits are important, they must be checked at each step since the next operation changes the CPSR values. Example 2-1 illustrates the computation of CPSR bits.

Example 2-1

Status Bit Computation in the ARM

An ARM word is 32 bits. In C notation, a hexadecimal number starts with 0x, such as 0xffffffff, which is a two's-complement representation of −1 in a 32-bit word.

Here are some sample calculations:

- *−1 + 1 = 0:* Written in 32-bit format, this becomes 0xffffffff + 0x1 = 0x0, giving the CPSR value of NZCV = 0110.

- *0 −1 = −1:* 0x0 − 0x1 = 0xffffffff, with NZCV = 1000.

- $2^{31} − 1 + 1 = −2^{31}$*:* 0x7fffffff + 0x1 = 0x80000000, with NZCV = 0101.

The basic form of a data instruction is simple:

ADD r0,r1,r2

This instruction sets register r0 to the sum of the values stored in r1 and r2. In addition to specifying registers as sources for operands, instructions may also provide **immediate operands,** which encode a constant value directly in the instruction. For example,

ADD r0,r1,#2

sets r0 to r1 + 2.

The major data operations are summarized in Figure 2-10. The arithmetic operations perform addition and subtraction; the with-carry versions include the current value of the carry bit in the computation. RSB performs a subtraction with the order of the two operands reversed, so that RSB r0,r1,r2 sets r0 to be r2 − r1. The bit-wise logical operations perform logical AND, OR, and XOR operations (the exclusive or is called EOR). The BIC instruction stands for bit clear: BIC r0,r1,r2 sets r0 to r1 and not r2. This instruction uses the second source operand as a mask: Where a bit in the mask is 1, the corresponding bit in the first source operand is cleared. The MUL instruction multiplies two values, but with some restrictions: No operand may be an immediate, and the two source operands must be different registers. The MLA instruction performs a multiply-accumulate operation, particularly useful in matrix operations and signal processing. The instruction

MLA r0,r1,r2,r3

sets r0 to the value r1 × r2 + r3.

The shift operations are not separate instructions—rather, shifts can be applied to arithmetic and logical instructions. The shift modifier is always applied to the second source operand. A left shift moves bits up toward the

ADD	Add
ADC	Add with carry
SUB	Subtract
SBC	Subtract with carry
RSB	Reverse subtract
RSC	Reverse subtract with carry
MUL	Multiply
MLA	Multiply and accumulate

Arithmetic

AND	Bit-wise and
ORR	Bit-wise or
EOR	Bit-wise exclusive-or
BIC	Bit clear

Logical

LSL	Logical shift left (zero fill)
LSR	Logical shift right (zero fill)
ASL	Arithmetic shift left
ASR	Arithmetic shift right
ROR	Rotate right
RRX	Rotate right extended with C

Shift/rotate

Figure 2-10 *ARM data instructions.*

most-significant bits, while a right shift moves bits down to the least-significant bit in the word. The LSL and LSR modifiers perform left and right logical shifts, filling the least-significant bits of the operand with zeroes. The arithmetic shift left is equivalent to an LSL, but the ASR copies the sign bit—if the sign is 0, a 0 is copied, while if the sign is 1, a 1 is copied. The rotate modifiers always rotate right, moving the bits that fall off the least-significant bit up to the most-significant bit in the word. The RRX modifier performs a 33-bit rotate, with the CPSR's C bit being inserted above the sign bit of the word; this allows the carry bit to be included in the rotation.

The instructions in Figure 2-11 are comparison operands—they do not modify general-purpose registers but only set the values of the NZCV bits of the CPSR register. The compare instruction CMP r0,r1 computes r0 − r1, sets the status bits, and throws away the result of the subtraction. CMN uses an addition to set the status bits. TST performs a bit-wise AND on the operands, while TEQ performs an exclusive-or.

Figure 2-12 summarizes the ARM move instructions. The instruction MOV r0,r1 sets the value of r0 to the current value of r1. The MVN instruction complements the operand bits (one's complement) during the move.

Values are transferred between registers and memory using the load-store instructions summarized in Figure 2-13. LDRB and STRB load and store bytes rather than whole words, while LDRH and SDRH operate on half-words and LDRSH extends the sign bit on loading. An ARM address may be 32 bits long. The ARM load and store instructions do not directly refer to main memory addresses, since a 32-bit address would not fit into an instruction that included

CMP	Compare
CMN	Negated compare
TST	Bit-wise test
TEQ	Bit-wise negated test

Figure 2-11 *ARM comparison instructions.*

MOV	Move
MVN	Move negated

Figure 2-12 *ARM move instructions.*

an opcode and operands. Instead, the ARM uses **register-indirect addressing.** In register-indirect addressing, the value stored in the register is used as the address to be fetched from memory; the result of that fetch is the desired operand value. Thus, as illustrated in Figure 2-14, if we set r1 = 0x100, the instruction

LDR r0,[r1]

sets r0 to the value of memory location 0x100. Similarly, STR r0,[r1] would store the contents of r0 in the memory location whose address is given in r1. There are several possible variations:

LDR r0,[r1, – r2]

LDR	Load
STR	Store
LDRH	Load half-word
STRH	Store half-word
LDRSH	Load half-word signed
LDRB	Load byte
STRB	Store byte
ADR	Set register to address

Figure 2-13 *ARM load-store instructions and pseudo-operations.*

Figure 2-14 *Register-indirect addressing in the ARM.*

loads r0 from the address given by r1 − r2, while

LDR r0,[r1, #4]

loads r0 from the address r1 + 4.

This begs the question of how we get an address into a register—we need to be able to set a register to an arbitrary 32-bit value. In the ARM, the standard way to set a register to an address is by performing arithmetic on the program counter, which is stored in r15. By adding or subtracting to the PC a constant equal to the distance between the current instruction (i.e., the instruction that is computing the address) and the desired location, we can generate the desired address without performing a load. The ARM programming system provides an ADR pseudo-operation to simplify this step. Thus, as shown in Figure 2-15, if we give location 0x100 the name FOO, we can use the pseudo-operation

ADR r1,FOO

to perform the same function of loading r1 with the address 0x100.

Example 2-2 illustrates how to implement C assignments in ARM instruction.

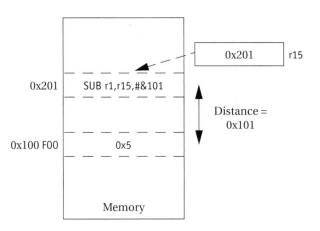

Figure 2-15 *Computing an absolute address using the PC.*

Example 2-2

C Assignments in ARM Instructions

We will use the assignments of Figure 2-8. The semicolon (;) begins a comment after an instruction, which continues to the end of that line. The statement

x = (a + b) – c;

can be implemented by using r0 for a, r1 for b, r2 for c, and r3 for x. We also need registers for indirect addressing. In this case, we will reuse the same indirect addressing register, r4, for each variable load. The code must load the values of a, b, and c into these registers before performing the arithmetic, and it must store the value of x back to memory when it is done. This code performs the following necessary steps:

```
ADR r4,a        ; get address for a
LDR r0,[r4]     ; get value of a
ADR r4,b        ; get address for b, reusing r4
LDR r1,[r4]     ; load value of b
ADD r3,r0,r1    ; set intermediate result for x to a + b
ADR r4,c        ; get address for c
LDR r2,x        ; get value of c
SUB r3,r3,r2    ; complete computation of x
ADR r4,x        ; get address for x
STR r3,[r4]     ; store x at proper location
```

The operation

y = a*(b + c);

can be coded similarly, but in this case we will reuse more registers by using r0 for both a and b, r1 for c, and r2 for y. Once again, we will use r4 to store addresses for indirect addressing. The resulting code is

```
ADR r4,b        ; get address for b
LDR r0,[r4]     ; get value of b
ADR r4,c        ; get address for c
```

```
LDR r1,[r4]        ; get value of c
ADD r2,r0,r1       ; compute partial result of y
ADR r4,a           ; get address for a
LDR r0,[r4]        ; get value of a
MUL r2,r2,r0       ; compute final value of y
ADR r4,y           ; get address for y
STR r2,[r4]        ; store value of y at proper location
```

The C statement

z = (a << 2) | (b & 15);

can be coded using r0 for a and z, r1 for b, and r4 for addresses as follows:

```
ADR r4,a           ; get address for a
LDR r0,[r4]        ; get value of a
MOV r0,r0,LSL 2    ; perform shift
ADR r4,b           ; get address for b
LDR r1,[r4]        ; get value of b
AND r1,r1,#15      ; perform logical AND
ORR r1,r0,r1       ; compute final value of z
ADR r4,z           ; get address for z
STR r1,[r4]        ; store value of z
```

more addressing modes

We have already seen three addressing modes: register, immediate, and indirect. The ARM also supports several forms of **base-plus-offset addressing,** which is related to indirect addressing. But rather than using a register value directly as an address, the register value is added to another value to form the address. For instance,

LDR r0,[r1,#16]

loads r0 with the value stored at location r1 + 16. Here, r1 is referred to as the **base** and the immediate value the **offset.** When the offset is an immediate, it may have any value up to 4096; another register may also be used as the offset. This addressing mode has two other variations: **auto-indexing** and **post-indexing.** Auto-indexing updates the base register, such that

LDR r0,[r1,#16]!

first adds 16 to the value of r1, and then uses that new value as the address. The ! operator causes the base register to be updated with the computed address so that it can be used again later. Our examples of base-plus-offset and auto-indexing instructions will fetch from the same memory location, but auto-indexing will also modify the value of the base register r1. Post-indexing does not perform the offset calculation until after the fetch has been performed. Consequently,

LDR r0,[r1],#16

will load r0 with the value stored at the memory location whose address is given by r1, and then add 16 to r1 and set r1 to the new value. In this case, the post-indexed mode fetches a different value than the other two examples, but ends up with the same final value for r1 as does auto-indexing.

We have used the ADR pseudo-op to load addresses into registers to access variables because this leads to simple, easy-to-read code (at least by assembly language standards). Compilers tend to use other techniques to generate addresses, because they must deal with global variables and automatic variables. Web Aid 2-Addressing provides examples that show how compilers generate code to access variables.

2.3.3 Flow of Control

The B (branch) instruction is the basic mechanism in ARM for changing the flow of control. The address that is the destination of the branch is often called the **branch target**. Branches are **PC-relative**—the branch specifies the offset from the current PC value to the branch target. The offset is in words, but because the ARM is byte-addressable, the offset is multiplied by four (shifted left two bits, actually) to form a byte address. Thus, the instruction

B #100

will add 400 to the current PC value.

We often wish to branch conditionally, based on the result of a given computation. The if statement is a common example. The ARM allows *any* instruction, including branches, to be executed conditionally. This allows branches to be conditional, as well as data operations. Figure 2-16 summarizes the condition codes.

We use Example 2-3 as a way to explore the uses of conditional execution.

EQ	Equals zero	$Z = 1$
NE	Not equal to zero	$Z = 0$
CS	Carry set	$C = 1$
CC	Carry clear	$C = 0$
MI	Minus	$N = 1$
PL	Nonnegative (plus)	$N = 0$
VS	Overflow	$V = 1$
VC	No overflow	$V = 0$
HI	Unsigned higher	$C = 1$ and $Z = 0$
LS	Unsigned lower or same	$C = 0$ or $Z = 1$
GE	Signed greater than or equal	$N = V$
LT	Signed less than	$N \neq V$
GT	Signed greater than	$Z = 0$ and $N = V$
LE	Signed less than or equal	$Z = 1$ or $N \neq V$

Figure 2-16 *Condition codes in ARM.*

Example 2-3

Implementing an if *Statement in ARM*

We will use the following if statement as an example:

```
if (a > b) {
    x = 5;
    y = c + d;
    }
else x = c - d;
```

The first way to implement the above instruction is more traditional and similar to other microprocessors. The following uses conditional branches and unconditional data operations:

```
; compute and test the condition
        ADR r4,a        ; get address for a
        LDR r0,[r4]     ; get value of a
```

```
        ADR r4,b          ; get address for b
        LDR r1,[r4]       ; get value of b
        CMP r0, r1        ; compare a < b
        BGE fblock        ; if a >= b, take branch
; the true block follows
        MOV r0,#5         ; generate value for x
        ADR r4,x          ; get address for x
        STR r0,[r4]       ; store value of x
        ADR r4,c          ; get address for c
        LDR r0,[r4]       ; get value of c
        ADR r4,d          ; get address for d
        LDR r1,[r4]       ; get value of d
        ADD r0,r0,r1      ; compute a + b
        ADR r4,y          ; get address for y
        STR r0,[r4]       ; store value of y
        B after           ; branch around the false block
; the false block follows
fblock  ADR r4,c          ; get address for c
        LDR r0,[r4]       ; get value of c
        ADR r4,d          ; get address for d
        LDR r1,[r4]       ; get value of d
        SUB r0,r0,r1      ; compute a − b
        ADR r4,x          ; get address for x
        STR r0,[r4]       ; store value of x
after   ... ; code after the if statement
```

The second implementation uses conditional execution of instructions. There is no branch; instead, a predicate controls which instructions are executed. The condition codes used to control predicated execution are updated here only by the CMP instructions, not by the arithmetic instructions. Arithmetic instructions may optionally update the condition codes as a side effect, but only if the S bit is set in the arithmetic instruction.

```
; compute and test the condition
        ADR r4,a          ; get address for a
        LDR r0,[r4]       ; get value of a
        ADR r4,b          ; get address for b
        LDR r1,[r4]       ; get value of b
        CMP r0,r1         ; compare a < b
; notice we don't need a branch here
; the true block follows--all instructions conditioned on LT
        MOVLT r0,#5       ; generate value for x
        ADRLT r4,x        ; get address for x
        STRLT r0,[r4]     ; store value of x
```

```
            ADRLT r4,c        ; get address for c
            LDRLT r0,[r4]     ; get value of c
            ADRLT r4,d        ; get address for d
            LDRLT r1,[r4]     ; get value of d
            ADDLT r0,r0,r1    ; compute a + b
            ADRLT r4,y        ; get address for y
            STRLT r0,[r4]     ; store value of y
; we also don't need to branch around the false block
; the false block follows--all instructions conditioned on GE
            ADRGE r4,c        ; get address for c
            LDRGE r0,[r4]     ; get value of c
            ADRGE r4,d        ; get address for d
            LDRGE r1,[r4]     ; get value of d
            SUBGE r0,r0,r1 ; compute a - b
            ADRGE r4,x        ; get address for x
            STRGE r0,[r4]     ; store value of x
```

The ARM is designed to efficiently execute conditioned instructions—there is no penalty for adding the predicate. However, when the condition is false, the instruction still takes the same amount of time, even though it does no useful work. Conditionally executed instructions are best for relatively small conditionals; when too many instructions fail the conditional test, the time required to evaluate those instructions outweighs other gains.

Example 2-4 illustrates an interesting way to implement multiway conditions.

Example 2-4

Implementing the C Switch Statement in ARM

The switch statement in C takes the following form:

```
switch (test) {
case 0: ... break;
case 1: ... break;
...
}
```

The above statement could be coded like an if statement by first testing *test=A*, then *test=B*, and so forth. However, it can be more efficiently implemented by using base-plus-offset addressing and building what is known as a **branch table:**

```
              ADR r2,test        ; get address for test
              LDR r0,[r2]        ; load value for test
              ADR r1,switchtab   ; load address for switch table
              LDR r15,[r1,r0,LSL #2]
switchtab     DCD case0
              DCD case1
              ...
case0         ... ; code for case 0
              ...
case1         ... ; code for case 1
              ...
```

This implementation uses the value of test as an offset into a table, where the table holds the addresses for the blocks of code that implement the various cases. The heart of this code is the LDR instruction, which packs a lot of functionality into a single instruction:

■ It shifts the value of r0 left two bits to turn the offset into a word address.

■ It uses base-plus-offset addressing to add the left-shifted value of test (held in r0) to the address of the base of the table held in r1.

■ It sets the PC (r15) to the new address computed by the instruction.

Each case is implemented by a block of code that is located elsewhere in memory. The branch table begins at the location named switchtab. The DCD statement is a way of loading a 32-bit address into memory at that point, so the branch table holds the addresses of the starting points of the blocks that correspond to the cases.

The loop is a very common C statement. Loops can be naturally implemented using conditional branches. Because loops often operate on values stored in arrays, loops are also a good illustration of another use of the base-plus-offset addressing mode. A simple but common use of a loop is in the FIR filter, which is explained in Application Example 2-1; the loop-based implementation of the FIR filter is described in Example 2-5.

Application Example 2-1

FIR Filters

A **finite impulse response (FIR) filter** is a commonly used method for processing signals; we make use of it in Section 5.10. The FIR filter is a simple sum of products:

$$\sum_{1 \le i \le n} c_i x_i \qquad \text{(EQ 2-1)}$$

In use as a filter, the x_is are assumed to be samples of data taken periodically, while the c_is are coefficients. This computation is usually drawn like this:

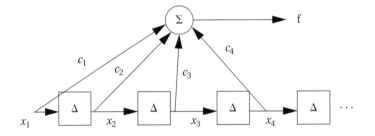

This representation assumes that the samples are coming in periodically and that the FIR filter output is computed once every time a new sample comes in. The Δ boxes represent delay elements that store the recent samples to provide the x_is. The delayed samples are individually multiplied by the c_is and then summed to provide the filter output.

Example 2-5

An FIR Filter for the ARM

The C code for the FIR filter of Application Example 2-1 follows:

```
for (i = 0, f = 0; i < N; i++)
    f = f + c[i] * x[i];
```

We can address the arrays c and x using base-plus-offset addressing: We will load one register with the address of the zeroth element of each array and use the register holding i as the offset.

The C language [Ker88] defines a for loop as equivalent to a while loop with proper initialization and termination. Using that rule, the for loop can be rewritten as

```
i = 0;
f = 0;
while (i < N) {
    f = f + c[i]*x[i];
    i++;
}
```

Here is the code for the loop:

```
        ; loop initiation code
        MOV r0,#0          ; use r0 for i, set to 0
        MOV r8,#0          ; use a separate index for arrays
        ADR r2,N           ; get address for N
        LDR r1,[r2]        ; get value of N for loop termination test
        MOV r2,#0          ; use r2 for f, set to 0
        ADR r3,c           ; load r3 with address of base of c array
        ADR r5,x           ; load r5 with address of base of x array
        ; loop body
loop    LDR r4,[r3,r8]     ; get value of c[i]
        LDR r6,[r5,r8]     ; get value of x[i]
        MUL r4,r4,r6       ; compute c[i]*x[i]
        ADD r2,r2,r4       ; add into running sum f
        ; update loop counter and array index
        ADD r8,r8,#4       ; add one word offset to array index
        ADD r0,r0,#1       ; add 1 to i
        ; test for exit
        CMP r0,r1
        BLT loop           ; if i < N, continue loop
loopend...
```

We have to be careful about numerical accuracy in this type of code, whether it is written in C or assembly language. The result of a 32-bit × 32-bit multiplication is a 64-bit result. The ARM MUL instruction leaves the lower 32 bits of the result in the destination register. So long as the result fits within 32

bits, this is the desired action. If the input values are such that values can sometimes exceed 32 bits, then we must redesign the code to compute higher-resolution values.

Web Aid 2-ARM-Code provides ARM code for the FIR filter.

C functions

The other important class of C statement to consider is the **function.** A C function returns a value (unless its return type is void); **subroutine** or **proce-dure** are the common names for such a construct when it does not return a value. Consider this simple use of a function in C:

```
x = a + b;
foo(x);
y = c − d;
```

A function returns to the code immediately after the function call, in this case the assignment to y. A simple branch is insufficient because we would not know where to return. To properly return, we must save the PC value when the procedure/function is called and, when the procedure is finished, set the PC to the address of the instruction *just after* the call to the procedure. (You don't want to endlessly execute the procedure, after all.)

The branch-and-link instruction is used in the ARM for procedure calls. For instance,

```
BL foo
```

will perform a branch and link to the code starting at location foo (using PC-relative addressing, of course). The branch and link is much like a branch, except that before branching it stores the current PC value in r14. Thus, to return from a procedure, you simply move the value of r14 to r15:

```
MOV r15,r14
```

You should not, of course, overwrite the PC value stored in r14 during the pro-cedure.

But this mechanism only lets us call procedures one level deep. If, for example, we call a C function within another C function, the second function call will overwrite r14, destroying the return address for the first function call. The standard procedure for allowing nested procedure calls (including recur-sive procedure calls) is to build a stack, as illustrated in Figure 2-17. The C code shows a series of functions that call other functions: f1() calls f2(), which in turn calls f3(). The right side of the figure shows the state of the **procedure call**

```
void f1(int a) {
    f2(a);
}

void f2(int r) {
    f3(r,5);
}

void f3(int x, int y) {
    g = x + y;
}

main() {
    f1(xyz);
}
```

C code

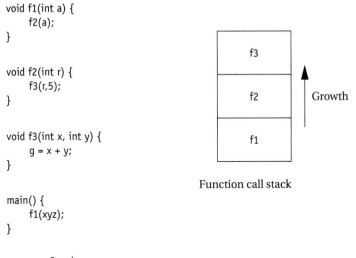

Function call stack

Figure 2-17 *Nested function calls and stacks.*

stack during the execution of f3(). The stack contains one **activation record** for each active procedure. When f3() finishes, it can pop the top of the stack to get its return address, leaving the return address for f2() waiting at the top of the stack for its return.

Most procedures need to pass parameters into the procedure and return values out of the procedure as well as remember their return address.

We can also use the procedure call stack to pass parameters. The conventions used to pass values into and out of procedures is known as **procedure linkage.** To pass parameters into a procedure, the values can be pushed onto the stack just before the procedure call. Once the procedure returns, those values must be popped off the stack by the caller, since they may hide a return address or other useful information on the stack. A procedure may also need to save register values for registers it modifies. The registers can be pushed onto the stack upon entry to the procedure and popped off the stack, restoring the previous values, before returning.

Example 2-6 illustrates the programming of a simple C function.

Example 2-6

Procedure Calls in ARM

We use as an example one of the functions from Figure 2-17:

```
void f1(int a) {
    f2(a);
}
```

The ARM C compiler's convention is to use register r13 to point to the top of the stack. We assume that the argument a has been passed into f1() on the stack and that we must push the argument for f2 (which happens to be the same value) onto the stack before calling f2().

Here is some handwritten code for f1(), which includes a call to f2():

```
f1    LDR r0,[r13]     ; load value of a argument into r0 from stack
      ; call f2()
      STR r13!,[r14]   ; store f1's return address on the stack
      STR r13!,[r0]    ; store argument to f2 onto stack
      BL f2            ; branch and link to f2
      ; return from f1()
      SUB r13,#4       ; pop f2's argument off the stack
      LDR r13!,r15     ; restore registers and return
```

We use base-plus-offset addressing to load the value passed into f1() into a register for use by r1. To call f2(), we first push f1()'s return address, stored in r14 by the branch-and-link instruction executed to get into f1(), onto the stack. We then push f2()'s parameter onto the stack. In both cases, we use autoincrement addressing to both store onto the stack and adjust the stack pointer. To return, we must first adjust the stack to get rid of f2()'s parameter that hides f1()'s return address; we then use autoincrement addressing to pop f1()'s return address off the stack and into the PC (r15).

We will discuss procedure linkage mechanisms for the ARM in more detail in Section 5.5.2.

Web Aid 2-ARM-Code shows compiler-generated code for procedure calls.

2.4 SHARC Processor

In this section, we study the SHARC family of DSPs [ADI97], which uses the Harvard architecture. The SHARC makes a good complement to the ARM CPU because they use fairly different techniques in many aspects of their architectures.

SHARC instructions are written one per line. Because SHARC instructions may use algebraic notation and have several parts, each instruction is terminated with a semicolon (;). A label, which gives a name to an instruction,

comes at the beginning of the line and ends with a colon (:). Comments start with an exclamation point (!) and continue until the end of the line. An example follows:

```
              R1 = DM(M0,I0), R2 = PM(M8,I8); ! a comment
label:        R3 = R1 + R2;
```

2.4.1 Memory Organization

Memory organization is the first area in which the differences between the SHARC and the ARM become apparent. The SHARC uses different word sizes and address space sizes for instructions and data. A SHARC instruction consists of 48 bits; a basic data word, 32 bits; and an address, 32 bits. The SHARC family includes a significant amount of on-chip memory; the smallest member of the family, the 21061, has one megabit of on-chip memory. The internal memory is evenly split between **program memory (PM)** and **data memory (DM),** and more memory can be added off-chip.

The SHARC, in fact, supports the following types of data:

- 32-bit IEEE single-precision floating-point

- 40-bit IEEE extended-precision floating-point

- 32-bit integers

The SHARC is designed to perform floating-point intensive computations, because many signal processing systems are much easier to design and build when arithmetic is performed in the much larger dynamic range provided by floating-point.

The SHARC memory is internally organized as 32-bit words. The SHARC is a modified Harvard architecture that allows the program memory to hold both data and instructions. Not only does this allow extra data to be squeezed into the on-chip memory, but as discussed later, it sometimes allows data to be fetched from both memories in parallel.

2.4.2 Data Operations

SHARC programming model

The programming model for the SHARC is rather large and complex, so for now we will concentrate on that part of the programming model relevant to data operations. The primary data registers, shown in Figure 2-18, have two different names: They are known as R0 through R15 when used for integer operations and as f0 through f15 when used for floating-point operations. All

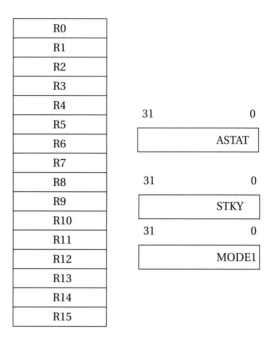

Figure 2-18 *The basic SHARC programming model.*

these data registers are 40 bits long to handle the largest data type, the 40-bit extended-precision floating-point value. When 32-bit data types are stored in the registers, they are put in the most-significant bits of the register.

The CPU has three major data function units: an ALU, a multiplier, and a shifter. These units perform a wide range of operations, as befits a microprocessor designed for numerically intensive programs. The three most-significant mode registers for data operations are *arithmetic status* (ASTAT), *sticky* (STKY), and *mode 1* (MODE1).

SHARC arithmetic

The ALU operations are summarized in Figure 2-19, where *Rn*, *Rx*, and *Ry* are arbitrary data registers R0–R15. All these operations set various status bits in the ASTAT1 and STKY registers as described below. The *COMP* compares two values without modifying any data registers. A dual add-subtract instruction simultaneously computes the sum and difference of two values and can be performed in integer or floating-point. The *CLIP* instruction is used to limit *Rx* within the range given by $[-Ry, Ry]$. If *Rx* is in the range $-Ry \le Rx \le Ry$, then the result is the value of *Rx*. If *Rx* falls beyond the lower end of the range, then the result is $-Ry$; if *Rx* is greater than *Ry*, the result is *Ry*.

All the ALU operations set the AZ (ALU result zero), AN (ALU result negative), AV (ALU result overflow), AC (ALU fixed-point carry), and AI (floating-point invalid) bits in the ASTAT register. The STKY register is a sticky version of some bits in the ASTAT register. The STKY bits are set along with the ASTAT reg-

Rn = Rx + Ry	Add
Rn = Rx – Ry	Subtract
Rn = Rx + Ry + CI	Add with carry
Rn = Rx – Ry + CI – 1	Subtract with borrow
Rn = (Rx + Ry)/2	Average
COMP(Rx,Ry)	Compare
Rn = Rx + CI	Add carry
Rn = Rx + CI – 1	Add borrow
Rn = Rx + 1	Increment
Rn = Rx – 1	Decrement
Rn = – Rx	Negate
Rn = ABS Rx	Absolute value
Rn = PASS Rx	Copy Rx to Rn
Rn = Rx AND Ry	Logical AND
Rn = Rx OR Ry	Logical OR
Rn = Rx XOR Ry	Logical exclusive OR
Rn = NOT Rx	Logical negate
Rn = MIN(Rx,Ry)	Minimum of Rx, Ry
Rn = MAX(Rx,Ry)	Maximum of Rx, Ry
Rn = CLIP Rx by Ry	Clip Rx within range [–Ry,Ry]

Figure 2-19 *Fixed-point ALU operations in the SHARC.*

ister bits, but are not cleared. STKY bits always remain set until cleared by an instruction. This allows programs to evaluate arithmetic problems after a sequence of operations. We will see how these bits are set in more detail in Example 2-7.

The SHARC can perform **saturation arithmetic** on fixed-point values. In saturation arithmetic, an overflow results in the maximum-range value, not the result of wrapping around the numeric range. This style of arithmetic is useful in signal processing applications because it more closely approximates the results of overloading physical systems. Saturation mode is controlled by the ALUSAT bit in the MODE1 register.

The floating-point operations performed by the ALU are summarized in Figure 2-20. A few operations deserve special mention. The *SCALB* operation adds an integer value to the exponent of a floating-point operand. Because the

Fn = Fx + Fy	Add
Fn = Fx – Fy	Subtract
Fn = ABS(Fx + Fy)	Absolute value of sum
Fn = ABS(Fx – Fy)	Absolute value of difference
Fn = (Fx + Fy)/2	Average
COMP(Fx,Fy)	Compare
Fn = –Fx	Negate
Fn = ABS Fx	Absolute value
Fn = PASS Fx	Copy Fx to Fn
Fn = RND Fx	Round
Fn = SCALB Fx by Ry	Scale exponent of Fx by Ry
Rn = MANT Fx	Extract mantissa of Fx
Rn = LOGB Fx	Convert exponent of Fx to integer
Rn = FIX Fx, Rn = TRUNC Fx	Convert floating-point to integer
Fn = FLOAT Rx by Ry, FLOAT Rx	Convert integer to floating-point
Fn = RECIPS Fx	Create seed for reciprocal
Fn = RSQRTS Fx	Create seed for reciprocal square root
Fn = Fx COPYSIGN Fy	Copy sign of Fy to Fx
Fn = MIN(Fx,Fy)	Minimum of Fx, Fy
Fn = MAX(Fx,Fy)	Maximum of Fx, Fy
Fn = CLIP Fx by Fy	Clip Fx within range [–Fy,Fy]

Figure 2-20 *Floating-point ALU operations in the SHARC.*

SHARC doesn't have a divide instruction, programs must compute the reciprocal of a number and then multiply to perform a division. Iterative algorithms are used to compute both reciprocals and square roots. The *RECIPS* and *RSQRTS* operations are used to start these iterative algorithms. Note that some of the results of floating-point operations are integer values, such as extracting the exponent. The rounding modes used for floating-point arithmetic (as specified by the IEEE standard) are controlled by two bits in the MODE1 register. Multiplication sets the MN (multiplier result negative), MV (multiplier overflow), MU (multiplier floating-point underflow), and MI (multiplier floating-point invalid operation) bits in the ASTAT register.

The multiplier performs fixed-point and floating-point multiplication. It can also perform saturation, rounding, and setting the result to 0. Fixed-point multiplication produces an 80-bit result, which can be stored in the MR register and manipulated there. Most of the variations in multiplier operations derive from using various elements of the MR value.

The shifter operations are summarized in Figure 2-21. Logical shifts fill with zeroes, while arithmetic shifts copy sign bits. The distance to shift, supplied by the *Ry* register, may be positive for a left shift or negative for a right shift. Shift operations set the SZ (shifter zero), SV (shifter overflow), and SS (shifter input sign) bits in the ASTAT register.

Rn = LSHIFT Rx by Ry	Logical shift distance Ry
Rn = Rn OR LSHIFT Rx by Ry	Logical shift and logical OR
Rn = ASHIFT Rx by Ry	Arithmetic shift
Rn = Rn OR ASHIFT Rx by Ry	Arithmetic shift and logical OR
Rn = ROT Rx by Ry	Rotate distance Ry
Rn = BCLR Rx by Ry	Clear one bit in Rx
Rn = BSET Rx by Ry	Set one bit in Rx
Rn = BTGL Rx by Ry	Toggle one bit in Rx
BTST Rx by Ry	Test one bit in Rx
Rn = FDEP Rx by Ry	Deposit field from Rx into Rn
Rn = Rn OR FDEP Rx by Ry	Deposit field from Rx using OR
Rn = FDEP Rx by Ry	Deposit and sign extend field from Rx
Rn = Rn OR FDEP Rx by Ry	Deposit and sign extend using OR
Rn = FEXT Rx by Ry	Extract field from Rx
Rn = FEXT Rx by Ry	Extract and sign extend field from Rx
Rn = EXP Rx	Extract exponent field
Rn = EXP Rx (EX)	Extract exponent field from ALU
Rn = LEFTZ Rx	Extract number of leading 0s
Rn = LEFTO Rx	Extract number of leading 1s
Rn = FPACK Fx	Convert 32-bit floating-point to 16-bit floating-point
Fx = FUNPACK Rn	Convert 16-bit floating-point to 32-bit floating-point

Figure 2-21 *Shifter operations in the SHARC.*

Example 2-7 illustrates how status bits are set in the SHARC.

Example 2-7

Data Operation Status Bits in the SHARC

Given the fixed-point ALU calculation $-1 + 1 = 0$, the ASTAT status bits are set as follows: AZ = 1, AU = 0, AN = 0, AV = 0, AC = 1, and AI = 0. The STKY bit AOS (ALU fixed-point underflow) will not be set by this operation, but the bit will retain its value. For the floating-point operation $-1E0 * 1E0 = 0E0$, the bits will be similarly set.

For the fixed-point multiplier operation $-2 * 3$, the ASTAT bits are set as follows: MN = 1, MV = 0, MU = 1, and MI = 0. The multiplier has four STKY bits, none of which will be set by this operation: MOS (multiplier fixed-point overflow), MVS (multiplier floating-point overflow), MUS (multiplier floating-point underflow), and MIS (multiplier floating-point invalid operation).

For the following shifter operation,

```
LSHIFT 0x7fffffff BY 3
```

the ASTAT bits will be set as follows: SZ = 0, SV = 1, and SS = 0. The shifter has no sticky bits.

load and store operations

The SHARC is a load-store architecture—operands must be loaded into registers before operating on them. But unlike many other architectures, SHARC supplies special registers that are used to control loading and storing. The SHARC has two **data address generators (DAGs)** for this purpose—one for the data memory and the other for the program memory. Because there are two DAGs, the SHARC can perform two load-store operations per cycle. Several registers must be set up to perform a load or store; once the setup is complete, the DAG hardware automatically updates their values so that a series of accesses, such as to a series of locations in an array, can be very easily performed. This makes the DAGs quite useful for the sequential accesses found in the array arithmetic common to signal processing programs.

The data address generator registers are illustrated in Figure 2-22. Each data address generator has eight sets of primary registers. Having several sets allows for quicker access of multiple sets of data, such as is required when multiplying two arrays. The registers numbered 0 through 7 belong to DAG1, while registers 8 through 15 belong to DAG2.

DAGs provide the following addressing modes:

■ The simplest addressing mode provides an immediate value that can represent an address. The instruction

R0 = DM(0x2000000);

loads R0 from the location 0x2000000 in data memory. We use the convention that _a is a constant whose value is the address of the variable a, so that

R0 = DM(_a);

loads R0 with the contents of the variable a. A store is written by reversing the arguments:

DM(_a) = R0;

stores R0 into memory location a.

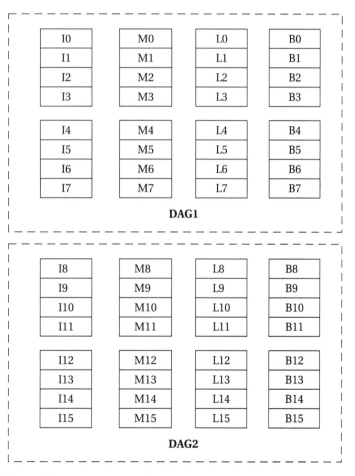

Figure 2-22 *SHARC data address generator registers.*

- An **absolute address** has the entire address in the instruction. This mode is relatively space inefficient because the address bits take up most of the instruction and preclude other operations from being encoded in the instruction.

- A **post-modify with update** mode allows the program to sweep through a range of addresses. This mode uses an I register and a modifier, which may be either an M register or an immediate value. The I register specifies the address and is then updated by the modifier value. An example of a load using this mode is

 `R0 = DM(I3,M1)`

 while an example store is

 `DM(I2,1) = R1`

- The DAGs also support **base-plus-offset** addressing: The address of the location to be fetched is computed as I + M, where I is the base and M is the modifier or offset. Thus, if I0 = 0x2000000 and M1 = 4, the instruction

 `R0 = DM(M1,I0)`

 will load into R0 the contents of location 0x2000004 in the data memory. (Note that we do not have to use I1 with M1—we can mix and match DAG registers, as long as both are in the same DAG.) This form of the instruction does not modify the I register. If the order of M and I are reversed, as in

 `R0 = DM(I0,M1)`

 then I1 is set to the sum of I1 and M0 after performing the load.

- The DAGs also support **circular buffers,** which are commonly used in signal processing (such as the FIR filter of Application Example 2-1). A circular buffer is an array of n elements; when the $n + 1$th element is referenced, the reference goes to buffer location 0, wrapping around from the end to the beginning of the buffer. Circular buffer addresses use the L and B registers: The L register is set with a positive, nonzero value as the starting point in the circular buffer, and the B register of the same number is loaded with the base address of the circular buffer. The I register is loaded with the base address at the same time as the B register. When the I register is used in post-modify mode, the incremented value is compared to the sum of the B and L registers. If the end of the buffer has been reached, the I register is wrapped around.

- The DAGs also support **bit-reversal addressing,** which is useful in the fast Fourier transform (FFT). Bit-reversal addressing can be performed only in I0 and I8, as controlled by the BR0 and BR8 bits in the MODE1 register.

storing data in program memory

The SHARC's modified Harvard architecture allows data to be stored in the program memory. This allows two data fetches per cycle. A DAG is provided for the program memory to support such data fetches. For example,

```
F0 = DM(M0,I0), F1 = PM(M8,I9)
```

will simultaneously load F0 with a value from the data memory and F1 from the program memory. The SHARC C compiler allows the programmer to specify where data are stored. For instance,

```
float dm a[N];
float pm b[N];
```

will place the a[] array in data memory and b[] in program memory. The compiler will then take care of generating the proper instructions to load these values in parallel if the opportunity arises.

When simultaneous memory accesses are performed, those two operations may in fact go to the same memory bank. In these cases, the instruction will require two cycles to execute.

Example 2-8 shows how to implement basic C arithmetic statements on the SHARC.

Example 2-8

C Assignments in SHARC Instructions

In this example, we use the assignments of Figure 2-8. The statement

```
x = (a + b) - c;
```

can be implemented by using r0 for a, r1 for b, r2 for c, and r3 for x. The code must load the values of a, b, and c into these registers before performing the arithmetic, and it must store the value of x back to memory when it is done. We will assume that all variables are in data memory. This code performs the following necessary steps:

```
R0 = DM(_a);        ! get value of a
R1 = DM(_b);        ! load value of b
R3 = R0 + R1;       ! set intermediate result for x to a + b
R2 = DM(_c) ;       ! get value of c
```

```
SUB R3 = R3 – R2 ;    ! complete computation of x
DM(_x) = R3 ;         ! store x at proper location
```

To code the operation

y = a*(b + c);

we will put a and b in data memory and c in program memory to exploit memory parallelism. We will use r0 for a, r1 for b, and r2 for both c and y. The resulting code follows:

```
R1 = DM(_b);              ! load b
R2 = DM(_c);              ! load c
R2 = R1 + R2 ;            ! compute partial result for y
R0 = DM(_a);              ! load a
R2 = R2 * r0 ;            ! compute final value of y
DM(_y) = R2 ;             ! store y
```

The above code can be made shorter by using pointers for the variables as seen below:

```
R2 = DM(I1,M5), R1 = PM(I8,M13);    ! load b and c in parallel
R0 = R2 + R1, R12 = DM(I0,M5);      ! add and load in parallel
R6 = R12*R0 (SSI);                  ! finish y computation
DM(I0,M5) = R8;                     ! store y
```

The C statement

z = (a << 2) | (b & 15);

can be coded using r0 for a and z, r1 for b, and r3 to hold the bit mask to be ANDed as follows:

```
R0 = DM(_a) ;              ! get value of a
R0 = LSHIFT R0 BY #2 ;     ! perform shift
R1 = DM(_b) ;              ! get value of b
R3 = #15 ;                 ! set up the bit mask for ANDing
R1 = R1 AND R3 ;           ! perform logical AND
R0 = R1 OR R0 ;            ! compute final value of z
DM(_z) = R0 ;              ! store value of z
```

2.4.3 Flow of Control

The JUMP instruction is the basic mechanism for changing the flow of control in the SHARC. The instruction

JUMP foo

jumps to the location foo. Jumps in the SHARC can be addressed in any of three ways:

- *Direct:* The instruction specifies a 24-bit address in immediate format. The PC is set to that address.

- *Indirect:* The address is supplied by the DAG2 data address generator.

- *PC-relative:* The instruction specifies an immediate value that is added to the current PC.

Many SHARC instructions, including JUMPs, can be conditionally executed. The condition codes are presented in Figure 2-23. The latter conditions are for elements of the SHARC architecture that we have not yet discussed. Except for LCE and NOT LCE, the conditions have complements, such as LT and GE. The instruction

IF GT JUMP foo;

performs a conditional branch based on the current value of the ASTAT register.
Example 2-9 shows how to implement an if statement in SHARC code.
Loops are the bread and butter of signal processing and numerical code. It should be no surprise that the SHARC provides a specialized loop instruction, DO UNTIL, which allows it to execute loops efficiently. The basic form of the loop instruction is

LCNTR = n, DO label UNTIL LCE;

The loop instruction specifies the following:

- The length of the loop using the loop counter LCNTR

- The label that gives the address for the last instruction in the loop

- The loop termination condition LCE, which stands for "loop counter expired"

True version	Description	Complement version
EQ	ALU = 0	NE
LT	ALU < 0	GE
LE	ALU ≤ 0	GT
AC	ALU carry	NOT AC
AV	ALU overflow	NOT AV
MV	Multiplier overflow	NOT MV
MS	Multiplier sign	NOT MS
SV	Shifter overflow	NOT SV
SZ	Shifter zero	NOT SZ
FLAG0_IN	Flag 0 input	NOT FLAG0_IN
FLAG1_IN	Flag 1 input	NOT FLAG1_IN
FLAG2_IN	Flag 2 input	NOT FLAG2_IN
FLAG3_IN	Flag 3 input	NOT FLAG3_IN
TF	Bit test flag	NOT TF
LCE	Loop counter expired	
NOT LCE	Loop counter not expired	

Figure 2-23 *Condition encoding for SHARC branches.*

Example 2-9

Implementing an if *Statement in SHARC*

As with the ARM, we will use the following if statement as an example:

```
if (a > b) {
    x = 5;
    y = c + d;
```

```
    }
else x = c – d;
```

By placing the true block directly after the test, we can avoid using a branch to get to that block. The condition will jump to the false block if it fails, while the true block will jump past the false block code after it finishes. The code below implements the if statement:

```
! test
            R0 = DM(_a);        ! load a
            R1 = DM(_b);        ! load b
            COMP(R0,R1)         ! compare
            IF GE JUMP fblock;  ! jump if fails test
! true block
tblock:     R0 = 5;             ! get value for x
            DM(_x) = R0;        ! store value for x
            R0 = DM(_c);        ! get c
            R1 = DM(_d);        ! get d
            R1 = R0 + R1;        compute c + d
            DM(_y) = R1;        ! save value for y
            JUMP other;         ! skip false block
! false block
fblock:     R0 = DM(_c);        ! get c
            R1 = DM(_d);        ! get d
            R1 = R0 – R1;       ! compute c – d
            DM(_x) = R1;        ! save value for x
other: ... ! code after if
```

In some cases, we can take advantage of parallelism to reorder the operations in a conditional. Consider this C code fragment:

```
if (a > b)
    y = c – d;
else
    y = c + d;
```

This code computes both the addition and subtraction, and then decides which one to store in y as follows:

```
! load values
            R1 = DM(_a);        ! load a
            R8 = DM(_b);        ! load b
            R2 = DM(_c);        ! load c
```

```
              R4 = DM(_d);          ! load d
! compute both sum and difference
         r12 = r2 + r4, r0 = r2 – r4;
! choose which one to save, copy it into r0 if necessary, then write to y
              comp(r8,r1);          ! now, finally, do the if test
              if ge r0 = r12;       ! if test satisfied, copy sum to r0
              dm(_y) = r0;          ! write to y
```

When control reaches the last instruction in the loop, the machine immediately returns to the head of the loop unless the loop counter has expired. This is known as a zero-overhead loop because the jump back to the top of the loop (and associated delays) are avoided.

The loop instruction makes use of two stacks to handle nested loops (one loop contained inside another). The PC is in fact a stack; a separate stack holds the loop counters for all active loops. These stacks are implemented as part of the programming model outside the memory spaces. The PC stack is 30 deep and holds subroutine return addresses as well as loop addresses, and the loop counter stack is 6 deep. When the DO UNTIL is first encountered, the loop end address is pushed onto the PC stack and the new loop counter value is pushed onto the loop counter stack. When execution reaches the loop end address, the CPU automatically decrements the loop counter and checks its value. (Actually, because the machine is pipelined, it does this *before* reaching the loop end address, as seen in Section 5.6.) If the termination condition (which may be LCE or NOT LCE) is not satisfied, the PC is set to the instruction just after the DO UNTIL for another iteration. If the condition is satisfied, the two stacks are popped and execution continues at the instruction after the loop end address.

Example 2-10 shows how to implement a loop using the SHARC DO instruction.

Example 2-10

An FIR Filter for the SHARC

The C code for the FIR filter of Application Example 2-1 follows:

```
for (i = 0, f = 0; i < N; i++)
    f = f + c[i] * x[i];
```

Here is simple code for the loop that helps us see what is going on:

```
! loop setup
        I0 = _a;              ! I0 points to a[0]
        M0 = 1;               ! set up increment
        I8 = b;               ! I8 points to b[0]
        M8 = 1;               ! set up postincrement mode
! loop body
        LCNTR = N, DO loopend UNTIL LCE;
        ! use postincrement mode
        R1 = DM(I0,M0), R2 = PM(I8,M8);
loopend:R8 = R1*R2, R12 = R12 + R9; ! multiply and accumulate
```

Here is some compiler-generated code that is more highly optimized:

```
! loop setup
        I4 = _a;          ! load a
        I12 = _b;         ! load b
        R4 = R4 xor R4, R1 = DM(I4,M6), R2 = PM(I12,M14);
        MROF = R4, MODIFY(I7,M7);
! start loop
        LCNTR = 20, DO(PC,loop) UNTIL LCE;
loop:   MRF = MRF + R2*R1 (SSI), R1 = DM(I4,M6), R2 = PM(I12,M14);
! loop clean-up
        R0 = MROF;
```

Web Aid 2-SHARC-Code provides code for the FIR filter.

SHARC function calls We discussed the mechanics of C procedures in Section 2.3.3. The SHARC CALL instruction provides procedure calls, as in

CALL foo;

Like JUMPs, CALLs may use absolute, indirect, or PC-relative addressing and may be executed conditionally. For instance,

IF GT CALL (PC,100);

conditionally performs a PC-relative call to a point 100 locations past the current PC value. The CALL instruction pushes the current PC value plus 1 (the location of the return instruction) onto the PC stack before transferring control to the target address.

A return from a procedure call is performed by the RTS (return from subroutine) instruction. This instruction pops the PC stack to return to the instruction after the call.

The SHARC does not include specific instructions for saving and restoring registers for procedure calls. Example 2-11 illustrates the programming of a simple C function.

Example 2-11

Procedure Calls in SHARC

The example here is one of the functions from Figure 2-17:

```
void f1(int a) {
    f2(a);
}
```

Because the SHARC has a PC stack, we do not need to push the return address, only the registers. The SHARC does not have general-purpose stack operators, but we can use the DAGs to implement a stack with a little effort. Pushing onto the stack is relatively easy—we use postincrement mode, and the I register automatically points to the empty location at the top of the stack. Reading values off the stack requires specifying a constant offset in the M field to provide the distance from the end of the stack frame to the variable. Popping the stack means modifying the I register.

Using the above scheme, we use I1 to point to the stack and we assume that M1 has been set to 1, the stack push increment, at the start of the program. Here is handwritten code for f1(), which includes a call to f2():

```
f1:     R0 = DM(I1,−1);       ! load argument a into R0 from stack
        ! call f2()
        DM(I1,M1) = R0;       ! push f2's argument onto the stack
        CALL f2;              ! call f2
        ; return from f1()
        MODIFY(I1,−1);        ! pop one element off stack
        RTS;                  ! return
```

Web Aid 2-SHARC-Code shows compiler-generated code for procedure calls.

2.4.4 Parallelism within Instructions

The SHARC is designed to allow several operations to be performed simultaneously. Although many machines offer parallel execution, the parallelism may be hidden from the programmer. The SHARC's wide instruction word allows the programmer to put together parallel operations in various combinations based upon the need of the application. The machine supports both memory parallelism and operation parallelism. The result is to reduce the number of instructions required for common operations. For example, the basic operation in a dot product loop can be performed in one cycle that performs two fetches, a multiplication, and an addition.

The modified Harvard architecture allows multiple data fetches in a single instruction. The most common instructions allow a memory reference and a computation to be performed at the same time. Memory references can be done two at a time in many instructions, with each reference using a DAG.

The instruction set allows the CPU's function units to be used in various combinations to perform operations. These combinations of operations can be performed in a single instruction, as in

- fixed-point multiply-accumulate and add, subtract, or average;

- floating-point multiplication and ALU operation; and

- multiplication and dual add-subtract.

However, there are restrictions on the sources of the operands when operations are combined. The operands going to the multiplier must come from R0 through R7 (or in the case of floating-point operands, f0 to f7), with one input coming from R0–R3/f0–f3 and the other from R4–R7/f0–f7. The ALU operands must come from R8–R15/f8–f15, with one operand coming from R8–R11/f8–f11 and the other from R12–R15/f12–f15. The results can go to any register. Some other restrictions also apply. An example is the following instruction, which performs three operations:

R6 = R0 * R4, R9 = R8 + R12, R10 = R8 – R12

2.5 Summary

When viewed from high above, all CPUs are similar—they read and write memory, perform data operations, and make decisions. However, there are many ways to design an instruction set, as illustrated by the differences between the ARM and the SHARC. When designing complex systems, we

generally view the programs in high-level language form, which hides many of the details of the instruction set. However, differences in instruction sets can be reflected in nonfunctional characteristics, such as program size and speed.

What We Learned

- Both the von Neumann and Harvard architectures are in common use today.

- The programming model is a description of the architecture relevant to instruction operation.

- ARM is a load-store architecture. It provides a few relatively complex instructions, such as saving and restoring multiple registers.

- SHARC has two on-chip memories for program and data. It allows programmers to encode several operations in a single instruction and provides several optimized mechanisms for loops.

Further Reading

Books by Jaggar [Jag95] and Furber [Fur96] describe the ARM architecture. The ARM Web site, www.arm.com, contains a large number of documents describing various versions of ARM. The *ADSP-2106x SHARC User's Manual* [ADI97] provides a detailed description of the SHARC architecture. Finally, the Analog Devices Web site, www.analog.com, also provides useful information.

Questions

Q2-1 What is the difference between a big-endian and little-endian data representation?

Q2-2 What is the difference between the Harvard and von Neumann architectures?

Q2-3 Answer the following questions about the ARM programming model:
a. How many general-purpose registers are there?
b. What is the purpose of the CPSR?
c. What is the purpose of the Z bit?
d. Where is the program counter kept?

Q2-4 How would the ARM status word be set after these operations?

a. $2 - 3$

b. $-2^{32} + 1 - 1$

c. $-4 + 5$

Q2-5 Write ARM assembly code to implement the following C assignments:

a. x = a + b;

b. y = (c – d) + (e – f);

c. z = a*(b + c) – d*e;

Q2-6 What is the meaning of these ARM condition codes?

a. EQ

b. NE

c. MI

d. VS

e. GE

f. LT

Q2-7 Write ARM assembly code to first read and then write a device memory mapped to location 0x2100.

Q2-8 Write in ARM assembly language an interrupt handler that reads a single character from the device at location 0x2200.

Q2-9 Write ARM assembly code to implement the following C conditional:

```
if (x – y < 3) {
     a = b – c;
     x = 0;
     }
else {
     y = 0;
     d = e + f + g;
     }
```

Q2-10 Write ARM assembly language code for the following loops:

a.

```
for (i = 0; i < 20; i++)
     z[i] = a[i]*b[i];
```

b.
```
for (i = 0; i < 10; i++)
    for (j = 0; j < 10; j++)
        z[i] = a[i,j] * b[i]
```

Q2-11 Explain the operation of the BL instruction, including the state of ARM registers before and after its operation.

Q2-12 How do you return from an ARM procedure?

Q2-13 In the following code, show the contents of the ARM function call stack just after each C function has been entered and just after the function exits. Assume that the function call stack is empty when main() begins.

```
int foo(int x1, int x2) {
    return x1 + x2;
}

int baz(int x1) {
    return x1 + 1;
}

int scum(int r) {
    for (i = 0; i = 2; i++)
        foo(r + i,5);
}

main() {
    scum(3);
    baz(2);
}
```

Q2-14 What data types does the SHARC support?

Q2-15 How many bits long is an IEEE single-precision, floating-point number? An IEEE extended-precision number?

Q2-16 How many general-purpose registers are in the SHARC programming model?

Q2-17 What does the SHARC CLIP instruction do?

Q2-18 How does the SHARC set the ASTAT bits for the following fixed-point operations?

a. $2 - 3$

b. $-2^{32} + 1 - 1$

c. $-4 + 5$

Q2-19 How does SHARC set the ASTAT bits for the following floating-point operations?

a. −0.5 * −2.1

b. 2.5E44 * 4.7E55

c. 1.9E − 17 / 5.5E − 39

Q2-20 Explain how SHARC data address generators are used to perform loads and stores.

Q2-21 Write SHARC assembly code to first read and then write a device memory mapped to location 0x400100.

Q2-22 Write in SHARC assembly language an interrupt handler that reads a single character from the device at location 0x400110.

Q2-23 Write SHARC assembly code to implement the following C conditional:

```
if (x − y < 3) {
    a = b − c;
    x = 0;
    }
else {
    y = 0;
    d = e + f + g;
    }
```

Q2-24 Write SHARC assembly language code for the following loops:

a.

```
for (i = 0; i < 20; i++)
    z[i] = a[i]*b[i];
```

b.

```
for (i = 0; i < 10; i++)
    for (j = 0; j < 10; j++)
        z[i] = a[i,j] * b[i]
```

Q2-25 Explain the operation of the CALL instruction, including the state of SHARC registers before and after its operation.

Q2-26 How do you return from a SHARC procedure?

Q2-27 In the following code, show the contents of the SHARC function call stack just after each C function has been entered and just after the function exits. Assume that the function call stack is empty when main() begins.

```
int foo(int x1, int x2) {
    return x1 + x2;
}

int baz(int x1) {
    return x1 + 1;
}

int scum(int r) {
    for (i = 0; i = 2; i++)
        foo(r + i,5);
}

main() {
    scum(3);
    baz(2);
}
```

Lab Exercises

L2-1 Write a program that uses a circular buffer to perform FIR filtering.

L2-2 Write a simple loop that lets you exercise the cache. By changing the number of statements in the loop body, you can vary the cache hit rate of the loop as it executes. You should be able to observe changes in the speed of execution by observing the microprocessor bus.

Chapter

CPUs

- Input and output mechanisms.
- Supervisor mode, exceptions, and traps.
- Memory management and address translation.
- Caches.
- How architecture affects program performance.
- How architecture affects program power consumption.

3.1 Introduction

This chapter describes aspects of CPUs that do not directly relate to their instruction sets. We consider a number of mechanisms that are important to interfacing to other system elements, such as interrupts and memory management. We also take a first look at aspects of the CPU other than functionality—performance and power consumption are both very important attributes of programs that are only indirectly related to the instructions they use.

In Section 3.2, we study input and output mechanisms such as interrupts. Section 3.3 introduces several mechanisms that are similar to interrupts but are designed to handle internal events. Section 3.4 introduces co-processors that provide optional support for parts of the instruction set. Section 3.5 describes memory systems—both memory management and caches. The next sections look at nonfunctional attributes of execution: Section 3.6 looks at performance, while Section 3.7 considers power consumption. Finally, in Section 3.8 we use a data compressor as an example of a simple yet interesting program.

Programming Input and Output

The basic techniques for I/O programming can be understood relatively independent of the instruction set. In this section, we cover the basics of I/O programming and place them in the contexts of both the ARM and SHARC. We begin by discussing the basic characteristics of I/O devices so that we can understand the requirements they place on programs that communicate with them.

3.2.1 Input and Output Devices

Input and output devices usually have some analog or nonelectronic component—for instance, a disk drive has a rotating disk and analog read/write electronics. But the digital logic in the device that is most closely connected to the CPU very strongly resembles the logic you would expect in any computer system.

Figure 3-1 shows the structure of a typical I/O device and its relationship to the CPU. The interface between the CPU and the device's internals (e.g., the rotating disk and read/write electronics in a disk drive) is a set of registers. The CPU talks to the device by reading and writing the registers. Devices typically have several registers:

■ **Data registers** hold values that are treated as data by the device, such as the data read or written by a disk.

■ **Status registers** provide information about the device's operation, such as whether the current transaction has completed.

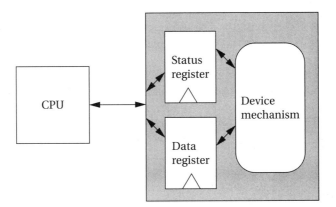

Figure 3-1 *Structure of a typical I/O device.*

Some registers may be read-only, such as a status register that indicates when the device is done, while others may be readable or writable. Application Example 3-1 describes a classic I/O device.

Application Example 3-1

The 8251 UART

The 8251 **UART** (Universal Asynchronous Receiver/Transmitter) [Int82] is the original device used for serial communications, such as the serial port connections on PCs. The 8251 was introduced as a stand-alone integrated circuit for early microprocessors. Today, its functions are typically subsumed by a larger chip, but these more advanced devices still use the basic programming interface defined by the 8251.

The UART is programmable for a variety of transmission and reception parameters. However, the basic format of transmission is simple. Data are transmitted as streams of characters, each of which has the following form:

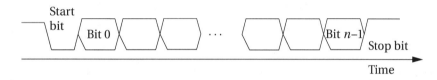

Every character starts with a start bit (a 0) and a stop bit (a 1). The start bit allows the receiver to recognize the start of a new character; the stop bit ensures that there will be a transition at the start of the stop bit. The data bits are sent as high and low voltages at a uniform rate. That rate is known as the **baud rate;** the period of one bit is the inverse of the baud rate.

Before transmitting or receiving data, the CPU must set the UART's mode registers to correspond to the data line's characteristics. The parameters for the serial port are familiar from the parameters for a serial communications program (such as Kermit):

■ the baud rate;

■ the number of bits per character (5 through 8);

■ whether parity is to be included and whether it is even or odd; and

■ the length of a stop bit (1, 1.5, or 2 bits).

The UART includes one 8-bit register that buffers characters between the UART and the CPU bus. The Transmitter Ready output indicates that the

transmitter is ready to accept a data character; the Transmitter Empty signal goes high when the UART has no characters to send. On the receiver side, the Receiver Ready pin goes high when the UART has a character ready to be read by the CPU.

3.2.2 Input and Output Primitives

Microprocessors can provide programming support for input and output in two ways: **I/O instructions** and **memory-mapped I/O.** Some architectures, such as the Intel x86, provide special instructions (in and out in the case of the Intel x86) for input and output. These instructions provide a separate address space for I/O devices.

But the most common way to implement I/O is by memory mapping— even CPUs that provide I/O instructions can also implement memory-mapped I/O. As the name implies, memory-mapped I/O provides addresses for the registers in each I/O device. Programs use the CPU's normal read and write instructions to communicate with the devices. Examples 3-1 and 3-2 illustrate memory-mapped I/O on the ARM and SHARC.

Example 3-1

Memory-Mapped I/O on ARM

We can use the EQU pseudo-op to define a symbolic name for the memory location of our I/O device:

```
DEV1    EQU 0x1000
```

Given that name, we can use the following standard code to read and write the device register:

```
LDR r1,#DEV1    ; set up device address
LDR r0,[r1]     ; read DEV1
LDR r0,#8       ; set up value to write
STR r0,[r1]     ; write 8 to device
```

Example 3-2

Memory-Mapped I/O on SHARC

The lower range of SHARC addresses is assigned to the internal data and program memory banks. A memory-mapped I/O device must be assigned within the external memory space, which starts at 0x400000. But because the data memory can access the entire address space, we can use a DM access to read and write the off-chip device register:

```
I0 = 0x400000
M0 = 0
R1 = DM(i0,M0)
```

How can we directly write I/O devices in a high-level language like C? When we define and use a variable in C, the compiler hides the variable's address from us. But we can use pointers to manipulate addresses of I/O devices. The traditional names for functions that read and write arbitrary memory locations are **peek** and **poke.** The peek function can be written in C as:

```
int peek(char *location) {
    return *location; /* de-reference location pointer */
}
```

The argument to peek is a pointer that is de-referenced by the C * operator to read the location. Thus, to read a device register we can write:

```
#define DEV1 0x1000
...
dev_status = peek(DEV1); /* read device register */
```

The poke function can be implemented as:

```
void poke(char *location, char newval) {
    (*location) = newval; /* write to location */
}
```

To write to the status register, we can use the following code:

```
poke(DEV1,8); /* write 8 to device register */
```

These functions can, of course, be used to read and write arbitrary memory locations, not just devices.

3.2.3 Busy-Wait I/O

The most basic way to use devices in a program is **busy-wait I/O.** Devices are typically slower than the CPU and may require many cycles to complete an operation. If the CPU is performing multiple operations on a single device, such as writing several characters to an output device, then it must wait for one operation to complete before starting the next one. (If we try to start writing the second character before the device has finished with the first one, for example, the device will probably never print the first character.) Asking an I/O device whether it is finished by reading its status register is often called **polling.**

Example 3-3 illustrates busy-wait I/O.

Example 3-3

Busy-Wait I/O Programming

In this example we want to write a sequence of characters to an output device. The device has two registers: one for the character to be written and a status register. The status register's value is 1 when the device is busy writing and 0 when the write transaction has completed.

We will use the peek and poke functions to write the busy-wait routine in C. First, we define symbolic names for the register addresses:

```
#define OUT_CHAR 0x1000 /* output device character register */
#define OUT_STATUS 0x1001 /* output device status register */
```

The sequence of characters is stored in a standard C string, which is terminated by a null (0) character. We can use peek and poke to send the characters and wait for each transaction to complete:

```
char *mystring = "Hello, world." /* string to write */
char *current_char; /* pointer to current position in string */

current_char = mystring; /* point to head of string */
while (*current_char != '\0') { /* until null character */
    poke(OUT_CHAR,*current_char); /* send character to device */
    while (peek(OUT_STATUS) != 0); /* keep checking status */
```

```
    current_char++; /* update character pointer */
}
```

The outer while loop sends the characters one at a time. The inner while loop checks the device status—it implements the busy-wait function by repeatedly checking the device status until the status changes to 0.

Example 3-4 illustrates a combination of input and output.

Example 3-4

Copying Characters from Input to Output Using Busy-Wait I/O

We want to repeatedly read a character from the input device and write it to the output device. First, we need to define the addresses for the device registers:

```
#define IN_DATA 0x1000
#define IN_STATUS 0x1001
#define OUT_DATA 0x1100
#define OUT_STATUS 0x1101
```

The input device sets its status register to 1 when a new character has been read; we must set the status register back to 0 after the character has been read so that the device is ready to read another character. When writing, we must set the output status register to 1 to start writing and wait for it to return to 0. We can use peek and poke to repeatedly perform the read/write operation:

```
while (TRUE) { /* perform operation forever */
    /* read a character into achar */
    while (peek(IN_STATUS) == 0); /* wait until ready */
    achar = (char)peek(IN_DATA); /* read the character */
    /* write achar */
    poke(OUT_DATA,achar);
    poke(OUT_STATUS,1); /* turn on device */
    while (peek(OUT_STATUS) != 0); /* wait until done */
}
```

3.2.4 Interrupts

Basics

Busy-wait I/O is extremely inefficient—the CPU does nothing but test the device status while the I/O transaction is in progress. In many cases, the CPU could do useful work in parallel with the I/O transaction, such as:

- computation, as in determining the next output to send to the device or processing the last input received, and
- control of other I/O devices.

To allow parallelism, we need to introduce new mechanisms into the CPU.

The **interrupt** mechanism allows devices to signal the CPU and to force execution of a particular piece of code. When an interrupt occurs, the program counter's value is changed to point to an **interrupt handler** routine (also commonly known as a **device driver**) that takes care of the device: writing the next data, reading data that have just become ready, and so on. The interrupt mechanism of course saves the value of the PC at the interruption so that the CPU can return to the program that was interrupted. Interrupts therefore allow the flow of control in the CPU to change easily between different **contexts,** such as a foreground computation and multiple I/O devices.

As shown in Figure 3-2, the interface between the CPU and I/O device includes the following signals for interrupting:

- the I/O device asserts the **interrupt request** signal when it wants service from the CPU; and

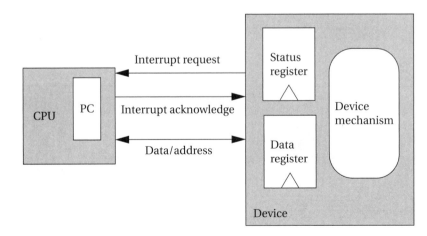

Figure 3-2 *The interrupt mechanism.*

■ the CPU asserts the **interrupt acknowledge** signal when it is ready to handle the I/O device's request.

The I/O device's logic decides when to interrupt; for example, it may generate an interrupt when its status register goes into the ready state. The CPU may not be able to immediately service an interrupt request because it may be doing something else that must be finished first—for example, a program that talks to both a high-speed disk drive and a low-speed keyboard should be designed to finish a disk transaction before handling a keyboard interrupt. Only when the CPU decides to acknowledge the interrupt does the CPU change the program counter to point to the device's handler. The interrupt handler operates much like a subroutine, except that it is not called by the executing program. The program that runs when no interrupt is being handled is often called the **foreground program;** when the interrupt handler finishes, it returns to the foreground program, wherever processing was interrupted.

Before considering the details of how interrupts are implemented, let's look at the interrupt style of processing and compare it to busy-wait I/O. Example 3-5 uses interrupts as a basic replacement for busy-wait I/O; Example 3-6 takes a more sophisticated approach that allows more processing to happen concurrently.

Example 3-5

Copying Characters from Input to Output with Basic Interrupts

As with Example 3-4, we repeatedly read a character from an input device and write it to an output device. We assume that we can write C functions that act as interrupt handlers. Those handlers will work with the devices in much the same way as in busy-wait I/O by reading and writing status and data registers. The main difference is in handling the output—the interrupt signals that the character is done, so the handler doesn't have to do anything.

We will use a global variable achar for the input handler to pass the character to the foreground program. Because the foreground program doesn't know when an interrupt occurs, we also use a global Boolean variable, gotchar, to signal when a new character has been received. The code for the input and output handlers follows:

```
void input_handler() { /* get a character and put in global */
    achar = peek(IN_DATA); /* get character */
    gotchar = TRUE; /* signal to main program */
    poke(IN_STATUS,0); /* reset status to initiate next transfer */
}
```

```
void output_handler() { /* react to character being sent */
    /* don't have to do anything */
}
```

The main program is reminiscent of the busy-wait program. It looks at gotchar to check when a new character has been read and then immediately sends it out to the output device.

```
main() {
    while (TRUE) { /* read then write forever */
        if (gotchar) { /* write a character */
            poke(OUT_DATA,achar); /* put character in device */
            poke(OUT_STATUS,1); /* set status to initiate write */
            gotchar = FALSE; /* reset flag */
        }
    }
}
```

The use of interrupts has made the main program somewhat simpler. But this program design still does not let the foreground program do useful work. Example 3-6 uses a more sophisticated program design to let the foreground program work completely independently of input and output.

Example 3-6

Copying Characters from Input to Output with Interrupts and Buffers

Because we don't need to wait for each character, we can make this I/O program more sophisticated than the one in Example 3-5. Rather than reading a single character and then writing it, the program performs reads and writes independently. The read and write routines communicate through the following global variables:

- A character string io_buf will hold a queue of characters that have been read but not yet written.

- A pair of integers buf_start and buf_end will point to the first and last characters read.

- An integer error will be set to 0 whenever io_buf overflows.

The global variables allow the input and output devices to run at different rates. The queue io_buf acts as a wraparound buffer—we add characters to the tail when an input is received and take characters from the tail when we are ready for output. The head and tail wrap around the end of the buffer array to make most efficient use of the array. Here is the situation at the start of the program's execution, where the tail points to the first available character and the head points to the ready character. As seen below, because the head and tail are equal, we know that the queue is empty.

When the first character is read, the tail is incremented after the character is added to the queue, leaving the buffer and pointers looking like the following:

When the buffer is full, we leave one character in the buffer unused. As the next figure shows, if we added another character and updated the tail buffer (wrapping it around to the head of the buffer), we would be unable to distinguish a full buffer from an empty one.

Here is what happens when the output goes past the end of io_buf:

The following code provides the declarations for the above global variables and some service routines for adding and removing characters from the queue. Because interrupt handlers are regular code, we can use subroutines to structure code just as with any program.

```
#define BUF_SIZE 8
char io_buf[BUF_SIZE]; /* character buffer */
int buf_head = 0, buf_tail = 0; /* current position in buffer */
int error = 0; /* set to 1 if buffer ever overflows */

void empty_buffer() { /* returns TRUE if buffer is empty */
    buf_head == buf_tail;
}

void full_buffer() { /* returns TRUE if buffer is full */
    (buf_tail+1) % BUF_SIZE == buf_head ;
}

int nchars() { /* returns the number of characters in the buffer */
    if (buf_head >= buf_tail) return buf_head - buf_tail;
    else return BUF_SIZE - buf_tail - buf_head;
}

void add_char(char achar) { /* add a character to the buffer head */
    io_buf[buf_tail++] = achar;
    /* check pointer */
    if (buf_tail == BUF_SIZE)
        buf_tail = 0;
}

char remove_char() { /* take a character from the buffer head */
    char achar;
    achar = io_buf[buf_head++];
    /* check pointer */
    if (buf_head == BUF_SIZE)
        buf_head = 0;
}
```

Assume that we have two interrupt handling routines defined in C, input_handler for the input device and output_handler for the output device. These routines work with the device in much the same way as did the busy-wait routines. The only complication is in starting the output device: If io_buf

has characters waiting, the output driver can start a new output transaction by itself. But if there are no characters waiting, an outside agent must start a new output action whenever the new character arrives. Rather than force the foreground program to look at the character buffer, we will have the input handler check to see whether there is only one character in the buffer and start a new transaction.

The code for the input handler follows:

```
#define IN_DATA 0x1000
#define IN_STATUS 0x1001
void input_handler() {
    char achar;
    if (full_buffer()) /* error */
        error = 1;
    else { /* read the character and update pointer */
        achar = peek(IN_DATA); /* read character */
        add_char(achar); /* add to queue */
    }
    poke(IN_STATUS,0); /* set status register back to 0 */
    /* if buffer was empty, start a new output transaction */
    if (nchars() == 1) { /* buffer had been empty until this interrupt */
        poke(OUT_DATA,remove_char()); /* send character */
        poke(OUT_STATUS,1); /* turn device on */
    }
}
```

```
#define OUT_DATA 0x1100
#define OUT_STATUS 0x1101
void output_handler() {
    if (!empty_buffer()) { /* start a new character */
        poke(OUT_DATA,remove_char()); /* send character */
        poke(OUT_STATUS,1); /* turn device on */
    }
}
```

The foreground program does not need to do anything—everything is taken care of by the interrupt handlers. The foreground program is free to do useful work as it is occasionally interrupted by input and output operations. The following sample execution of the program in the form of a UML sequence diagram shows how input and output are interleaved with the foreground program. (We have kept the last input character in the queue until output is complete to make it clearer when input occurs.) The simulation shows that the

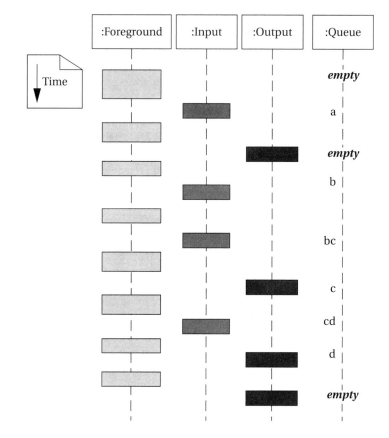

foreground program is not executing continuously, but it continues to run in its regular state independent of the number of characters waiting in the queue.

Interrupts allow a lot of concurrency, which can make very efficient use of the CPU. But when the interrupt handlers are buggy, the errors can be very hard to find. The fact that an interrupt can occur at any time means that the same bug can manifest itself in different ways when the interrupt handler interrupts different segments of the foreground program. Example 3-7 illustrates the problems inherent in debugging interrupt handlers.

Example 3-7

Debugging Interrupt Code

Assume that the foreground code is performing a matrix multiplication operation $y = Ax + b$:

```
for (i = 0; i < M; i++) {
    y[i] = b[i];
    for (j = 0; j < N; j++)
        y[i] = y[i] + A[i,j]*x[j];
}
```

We use the interrupt handlers of Example 3-6 to perform I/O while the matrix computation is performed, but with one small change: read_handler has a bug that causes it to change the value of j. While this may seem far-fetched, remember that when the interrupt handler is written in assembly language such bugs are easy to introduce. Any CPU register that is written by the interrupt handler must be saved before it is modified and restored before the handler exits. Any type of bug—such as forgetting to save the register or to properly restore it—can cause that register to mysteriously change value in the foreground program.

What happens to the foreground program when j changes value during an interrupt depends on when the interrupt handler executes. Because the value of j is reset at each iteration of the outer loop, the bug will affect only one entry of the result y. But clearly the entry that changes will depend on when the interrupt occurs. Furthermore, the change observed in y depends on not only what new value is assigned to j (which may depend on the data handled by the interrupt code), but also when in the inner loop the interrupt occurs. An interrupt at the beginning of the inner loop will give a different result than one that occurs near the end. The number of possible new values for the result vector is much too large to consider manually—the bug can't be found by enumerating the possible wrong values and correlating them with a given root cause. Even recognizing the error can be difficult—for example, an interrupt that occurs at the very end of the inner loop will not cause any change in the foreground program's result. Finding such bugs generally requires a great deal of tedious experimentation and frustration.

The CPU implements interrupts by checking the interrupt request line at the beginning of execution of every instruction. If an interrupt request has

been asserted, the CPU does not fetch the instruction pointed to by the PC. Instead the CPU sets the PC to a predefined location, which is the beginning of the interrupt handling routine. The starting address of the interrupt handler is usually given as a pointer—rather than defining a fixed location for the handler, the CPU defines a location in memory that holds the address of the handler, which can then reside anywhere in memory.

interrupts and subroutines

Because the CPU checks for interrupts at every instruction, it can respond quickly to service requests from devices. However, the interrupt handler must return to the foreground program without disturbing the foreground program's operation. Since subroutines perform a similar function, it is natural to build the CPU's interrupt mechanism to resemble its subroutine function. Most CPUs use the same basic mechanism for remembering the foreground program's PC as is used for subroutines. The subroutine call mechanism in modern microprocessors is typically a stack, so the interrupt mechanism puts the return address on a stack; some CPUs use the same stack as for subroutines while others define a special stack. The use of a procedure-like interface also makes it easier to provide a high-level language interface for interrupt handlers. The details of the C interface to interrupt handling routines vary both with the CPU and the underlying support software.

Web Aid 3-Interrupts provides details of the interrupt handler interface for the ARM and SHARC evaluation boards.

Priorities and Vectors

Providing a practical interrupt system requires having more than a simple interrupt request line. Most systems have more than one I/O device, so there must be some mechanism for allowing multiple devices to interrupt. We also want to have flexibility in the locations of the interrupt handling routines, the addresses for devices, and so on. There are two ways in which interrupts can be generalized to handle multiple devices and to provide more flexible definitions for the associated hardware and software:

- **interrupt priorities** allow the CPU to recognize some interrupts as more important than others, and

- **interrupt vectors** allow the interrupting device to specify its handler.

Prioritized interrupts not only allow multiple devices to be connected to the interrupt line but also allow the CPU to ignore less important interrupt requests while it handles more important requests. As shown in Figure 3-3, the CPU provides several different interrupt request signals, shown here as *L1*, *L2*, up to *Ln*. Typically, the lower-numbered interrupt lines are given higher priority, so in this case, if devices 1, 2, and *n* all requested interrupts simultaneously,

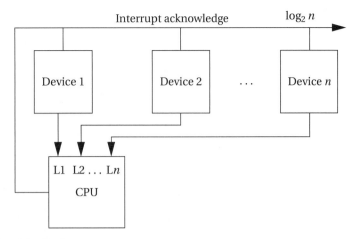

Figure 3-3 *Prioritized device interrupts.*

1's request would be acknowledged because it is connected to the highest-priority interrupt line. Rather than provide a separate interrupt acknowledge line for each device, most CPUs use a set of signals that provide the priority number of the winning interrupt in binary form (so that interrupt level 7 requires 3 bits rather than 7). A device knows that its interrupt request was accepted by seeing its own priority number on the interrupt acknowledge lines.

How do we change the priority of a device? Simply by connecting it to a different interrupt request line. This requires hardware modification, so if priorities need to be changeable, removable cards, programmable switches, or some other mechanism should be provided to make the change easy.

The priority mechanism must ensure that a lower-priority interrupt does not occur when a higher-priority interrupt is being handled. The decision process is known as **masking.** When an interrupt is acknowledged, the CPU stores in an internal register the priority level of that interrupt. When a subsequent interrupt is received, its priority is checked against the priority register; the new request is acknowledged only if it has higher priority than the currently pending interrupt. When the interrupt handler exits, the priority register must be reset. The need to reset the priority register is one reason why most architectures introduce a specialized instruction to return from interrupts rather than using the standard subroutine return instruction.

power-down interrupts The highest-priority interrupt is normally called the **nonmaskable interrupt** or **NMI.** The NMI cannot be turned off and is usually reserved for interrupts caused by power failures—a simple circuit can be used to detect a dangerously low power supply, and the NMI interrupt handler can be used to save critical state in nonvolatile memory, turn off I/O devices to eliminate spurious device operation during power-down, and so on.

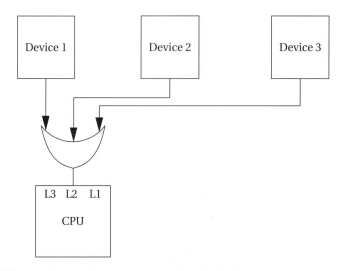

Figure 3-4 *Using polling to share an interrupt over several devices.*

Most CPUs provide a relatively small number of interrupt priority levels, such as eight. While more priority levels can be added with external logic, they may not be necessary in all cases. When several devices naturally assume the same priority (such as when you have several identical keypads attached to a single CPU), you can combine polling with prioritized interrupts to efficiently handle the devices. As shown in Figure 3-4, you can use a small amount of logic external to the CPU to generate an interrupt whenever any of the devices you want to group together request service. The CPU will call the interrupt handler associated with this priority; that handler does not know which of the devices actually requested the interrupt. The handler uses software polling to check the status of each device: In this example, it would read the status registers of *1*, *2*, and *3* to see which of them is ready and requesting service.

Example 3-8 illustrates how priorities affect the order in which I/O requests are handled.

Example 3-8

I/O with Prioritized Interrupts

Assume that we have devices A, B, and C. A has priority 1 (highest priority), B priority 2, and C priority 3. The following UML sequence diagram shows which interrupt handler is executing as a function of time for a sequence of interrupt requests.

In each case, an interrupt handler keeps running until either it is finished or a higher-priority interrupt arrives. The C interrupt, although it arrives early, does not finish for a long time because interrupts from both A and B intervene—system design must take into account the worst-case combinations of interrupts that can occur to ensure that no device goes without service for too long. When both A and B interrupt simultaneously, A's interrupt gets priority; when A's handler is finished, the priority mechanism automatically answers B's pending interrupt.

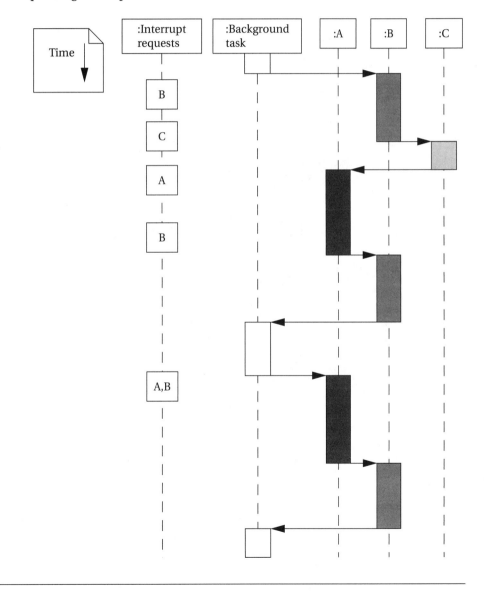

Vectors provide flexibility in a different dimension, namely, the ability to define the interrupt handler that should service a request from a device. Figure 3-5 shows the hardware structure required to support interrupt vectors. In addition to the interrupt request and acknowledge lines, additional interrupt vector lines run from the devices to the CPU. After a device's request is acknowledged, it sends its interrupt vector over those lines to the CPU. The CPU then uses the vector number as an index in a table stored in memory as shown in Figure 3-5. The location referenced in the interrupt vector table by the vector number gives the address of the handler. Figure 3-6 illustrates the sequence of events on the bus: first the request, then the acknowledge, and finally the interrupt vector.

Figure 3-5 *Interrupt vectors.*

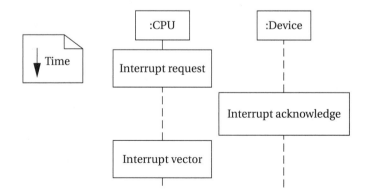

Figure 3-6 *Activity on the bus during a vectored interrupt.*

There are two important things to notice about the interrupt vector mechanism. First, the device, not the CPU, stores its vector number. In this way, a device can be given a new handler simply by changing the vector number it sends, without modifying the system software. For example, vector numbers can be changed by programmable switches. The second thing to notice is that there is no fixed relationship between vector numbers and interrupt handlers. The interrupt vector table allows arbitrary relationships between devices and handlers. The vector mechanism provides great flexibility in the coupling of hardware devices and the software routines that service them.

Most modern CPUs implement both prioritized and vectored interrupts. Priorities determine which device is serviced first, and vectors determine what routine is used to service the interrupt. The combination of the two provides a rich interface between hardware and software.

Interrupt Overhead

Now that we have a basic understanding of the interrupt mechanism, we can consider the complete interrupt handling process. Once a device requests an interrupt, some steps are performed by the CPU, some by the device, and others by software. The basic procedure is described below.

1. *CPU:* The CPU checks for pending interrupts at the beginning of an instruction. It answers the highest-priority interrupt, which has a higher priority than that given in the interrupt priority register.

2. *Device:* The device receives the acknowledgment and sends the CPU its interrupt vector.

3. *CPU:* The CPU looks up the device handler address in the interrupt vector table using the vector as an index. A subroutine-like mechanism is used to save the current value of the PC and possibly other internal CPU state, such as general-purpose registers.

4. *Software:* The device driver may save additional CPU state. It then performs the required operations on the device. It then restores any saved state and executes the interrupt return instruction.

5. *CPU:* The interrupt return instruction restores the PC and other automatically saved states to return execution to the code that was interrupted.

Interrupts do not come without a performance penalty. In addition to the execution time required for the code that talks directly to the devices, there is execution time overhead associated with the interrupt mechanism.

- The interrupt itself has overhead similar to a subroutine call. Because an interrupt causes a change in the program counter, it incurs a branch penalty. In addition, if the interrupt automatically stores CPU registers, that action requires extra cycles, even if the state is not modified by the interrupt handler.

- In addition to the branch delay penalty, the interrupt requires extra cycles to acknowledge the interrupt and obtain the vector from the device.

- The interrupt handler will, in general, save and restore CPU registers that were not automatically saved by the interrupt.

- The interrupt return instruction incurs a branch penalty as well as the time required to restore the automatically saved state.

The time required for the hardware to respond to the interrupt, obtain the vector, and so on cannot be changed by the programmer. In particular, CPUs vary quite a bit in the amount of internal state automatically saved by an interrupt. The programmer does have control over what state is modified by the interrupt handler and therefore it must be saved and restored. Careful programming can sometimes result in a small number of registers used by an interrupt handler, thereby saving time in maintaining the CPU state. However, such tricks usually require coding the interrupt handler in assembly language rather than a high-level language.

Interrupts in ARM

ARM7 supports two types of interrupts: fast interrupt requests (FIQs) and interrupt requests (IRQs). An FIQ takes priority over an IRQ. The interrupt table is always kept in the bottom memory addresses, starting at location 0. The entries in the table typically contain subroutine calls to the appropriate handler.

The ARM7 performs the following steps when responding to an interrupt [ARM99B]:

- saves the appropriate value of the PC to be used to return,

- copies the CPSR into an SPSR (saved program status register),

- forces bits in the CPSR to note the interrupt, and

- forces the PC to the appropriate interrupt vector.

When leaving the interrupt handler, the handler should:

- restore the proper PC value,

- restore the CPSR from the SPSR, and

- clear interrupt disable flags.

The worst-case latency to respond to an interrupt includes the following components:

- two cycles to synchronize the external request,

- up to 20 cycles to complete the current instruction,

- three cycles for data abort, and

- two cycles to enter the interrupt handling state.

This adds up to 27 clock cycles. The best-case latency is 4 clock cycles.

Interrupts in SHARC

SHARC supports three prioritized, vectored, maskable interrupts, each of which calls an interrupt handler subroutine [ADI97]. When processing an interrupt, the SHARC

- outputs the appropriate interrupt vector address;

- pushes the current PC onto the PC stack;

- depending on the type of interrupt, may push the ASTAT and MODE1 registers onto the status stack;

- sets the appropriate bit in the interrupt latch register; and

- changes the interrupt mask pointer to show the current interrupt nesting state.

The RTI instruction is used to return from an interrupt. The RTI instruction

- pops the return address of the PC stack and saves it to the PC,

- pops the status stack if appropriate, and

- clears the appropriate bits in the interrupt latch and mask registers.

The interrupt vector table may be kept either in internal or external memory. The vector table provides interrupt vectors for a number of actions, including reset, the three external interrupts, internal DMA channels, timers, floating-point errors, and user software interrupts.

For most instructions, the latency for an external interrupt is four cycles. Some instructions require multiple cycles to finish and will delay interrupt handling; waiting for external memory may also delay handling.

Supervisor Mode, Exceptions, and Traps

In this section, we consider exceptions and traps. These are mechanisms to handle internal conditions, and they are very similar to interrupts in form. We begin with a discussion of supervisor mode, which some processors use to handle exceptional events and protect executing programs from each other.

3.3.1 Supervisor Mode

As will become clearer in later chapters, complex systems are often implemented as several programs that communicate with each other. These programs may run under the command of an operating system. It may be desirable to provide hardware checks to ensure that the programs do not interfere with each other—for example, by erroneously writing into a segment of memory used by another program. Software debugging is important but can leave some problems in a running system; hardware checks ensure an additional level of safety.

In such cases it is often useful to have a **supervisor mode** provided by the CPU. Normal programs run in **user mode.** The supervisor mode has privileges that user modes do not. For example, we study memory management systems in Section 3.5.2 that allow the addresses of memory locations to be changed dynamically. Control of the memory management unit is typically reserved for supervisor mode to avoid the obvious problems that could occur when program bugs cause inadvertent changes in the memory management registers.

ARM supervisor mode

Not all CPUs have supervisor modes—the SHARC does not, while the ARM does. The ARM instruction that puts the CPU in supervisor mode is called SWI:

```
SWI CODE_1
```

It can, of course, be executed conditionally, as with any ARM instruction. SWI causes the CPU to go into supervisor mode and sets the PC to 0x08. The argument to SWI is a 24-bit immediate value that is passed on to the supervisor mode code; it allows the program to request various services from the supervisor mode.

In supervisor mode, the bottom five bits of the CPSR are all set to 1 to indicate that the CPU is in supervisor mode. The old value of the CPSR just before the SWI is stored in a register called the **saved program status register** (SPSR). There are in fact several SPSRs for different modes; the supervisor mode SPSR is referred to as SPSR_svc.

To return from supervisor mode, the supervisor restores the PC from register r14 and restores the CPSR from the SPSR_svc.

3.3.2 Exceptions

An **exception** is an internally detected error. A simple example is division by zero. One way to handle this problem would be to check every divisor before division to be sure it is not zero, but this would both substantially increase the size of numerical programs and cost a great deal of CPU time evaluating the divisor's value. The CPU can more efficiently check the divisor's value during execution. Since the time at which a zero divisor will be found is not known in advance, this event is similar to an interrupt except that it is generated inside the CPU. The exception mechanism provides a way for the program to react to such unexpected events.

Just as interrupts can be seen as an extension of the subroutine mechanism, exceptions are generally implemented as a variation of an interrupt. Since both deal with changes in the flow of control of a program, it makes sense to use similar mechanisms. However, exceptions are generated internally.

Exceptions in general require both prioritization and vectoring. Exceptions must be prioritized because a single operation may generate more than one exception—for example, an illegal operand and an illegal memory access. The priority of exceptions is usually fixed by the CPU architecture. Vectoring provides a way for the user to specify the handler for the exception condition. The vector number for an exception is usually predefined by the architecture; it is used to index into a table of exception handlers.

3.3.3 Traps

A **trap,** also known as a **software interrupt,** is an instruction that explicitly generates an exception condition. The most common use of a trap is to enter supervisor mode. The entry into supervisor mode must be controlled to maintain security—if the interface between user and supervisor mode is improperly designed, a user program may be able to sneak code into the supervisor mode that could be executed to perform harmful operations.

The ARM provides the SWI interrupt for software interrupts. This instruction causes the CPU to enter supervisor mode. An opcode is embedded in the instruction that can be read by the handler.

SHARC offers three levels of software interrupt, which are activated by setting one of the bits in the IRPTL register. The interrupt vector table establishes vectors for handling the software interrupts.

3.4 Co-Processors

CPU architects often want to provide flexibility in what features are implemented in the CPU. One way to provide such flexibility at the instruction set level is to allow **co-processors,** which are attached to the CPU and implement some of the instructions. For example, floating-point arithmetic was introduced into the Intel architecture by providing separate chips that implemented the floating-point instructions.

To support co-processors, certain opcodes must be reserved in the instruction set for co-processor operations. Because it executes instructions, a co-processor must be tightly coupled to the CPU. When the CPU receives a co-processor instruction, the CPU must activate the co-processor and pass it the relevant instruction. Co-processor instructions can load and store co-processor registers or can perform internal operations. The CPU can suspend execution to wait for the co-processor instruction to finish; it can also take a more superscalar approach and continue executing instructions while waiting for the co-processor to finish.

A CPU may, of course, receive co-processor instructions even when there is no co-processor attached. Most architectures use illegal instruction traps to handle these situations. The trap handler can detect the co-processor instruction and, for example, execute it in software on the main CPU. Emulating co-processor instructions in software is slower but provides compatibility.

co-processors in ARM

The ARM architecture provides support for up to 16 co-processors. Co-processors are able to perform load and store operations on their own registers. They can also move data between the co-processor registers and main ARM registers.

An example ARM co-processor is the floating-point unit. The unit occupies two co-processor units in the ARM architecture, numbered 1 and 2, but it appears as a single unit to the programmer. It provides eight 80-bit floating-point data registers, floating-point status registers, and an optional floating-point status register.

3.5 Memory System Mechanisms

Modern microprocessors do more than just read and write a monolithic memory. Architectural features improve both the speed and capacity of memory systems. Microprocessor clock rates are increasing at a faster rate than memory speeds, such that memories are falling further and further behind microprocessors every day. As a result, computer architects resort to **caches** to increase the average performance of the memory system. Although memory capacity is increasing steadily, program sizes are increasing as well, and designers may not be willing to pay for all the memory demanded by an application. **Memory management units (MMUs)** perform address translations that provide a larger virtual memory space in a small physical memory. In this section, we review both caches and MMUs.

3.5.1 Caches

Caches are widely used to speed up memory system performance. Many microprocessor architectures include caches as part of their definition. The cache speeds up average memory access time when properly used. It increases the variability of memory access times—accesses in the cache will be fast, while access to locations not cached will be slow. This variability in performance makes it especially important to understand how caches work so that we can better understand how to predict cache performance and factor variabilities into system design.

cache controllers A cache is a small, fast memory that holds copies of some of the contents of main memory. Because the cache is fast, it provides higher-speed access for the CPU; but since it is small, not all requests can be satisfied by the cache, forcing the system to wait for the slower main memory. Caching makes sense when the CPU is using only a relatively small set of memory locations at any one time; the set of active locations is often called the **working set.**

Figure 3-7 shows how the cache supports reads in the memory system. A **cache controller** mediates between the CPU and the memory system comprised of the cache and main memory. The cache controller sends a memory request to the cache and main memory. If the requested location is in the cache, the cache controller forwards the location's contents to the CPU and aborts the main memory request; this condition is known as a **cache hit.** If the location is not in the cache, the controller waits for the value from main memory and forwards it to the CPU; this situation is known as a **cache miss.**

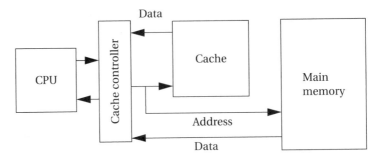

Figure 3-7 *The cache in the memory system.*

We can classify cache misses into several types depending on the situation that generated them:

- a **compulsory miss** (also known as a **cold miss**) occurs the first time a location is used,

- a **capacity miss** is caused by a too-large working set, and

- a **conflict miss** happens when two locations map to the same location in the cache.

memory system performance Even before we consider ways to implement caches, we can write some basic formulas for memory system performance. Let h be the **hit rate,** the probability that a given memory location is in the cache. It follows that $1 - h$ is the **miss rate,** or the probability that the location is not in the cache. Then we can compute the average memory access time as

$$t_{av} = h t_{cache} + (1 - h) t_{main}, \qquad \text{(EQ 3-1)}$$

where t_{cache} is the access time of the cache and t_{main} is the main memory access time. The memory access times are basic parameters available from the memory manufacturer. The hit rate depends on the program being executed and the cache organization, and is typically measured using simulators, as is described in more detail in Section 5.6. The best-case memory access time (ignoring cache controller overhead) is t_{cache}, while the worst-case access time is t_{main}. Given that t_{main} is typically 50 to 60 ns for DRAM, while t_{cache} is at most a few nanoseconds, the spread between worst-case and best-case memory delays is substantial.

Modern CPUs may use multiple levels of cache as shown in Figure 3-8. The **first-level cache** (commonly known as **L1 cache**) is closest to the CPU, the **second-level cache (L2 cache)** feeds the first-level cache, and so on. In today's microprocessors, the first-level cache is often on-chip and the second-level cache is off-chip, although we are starting to see on-chip second-level caches.

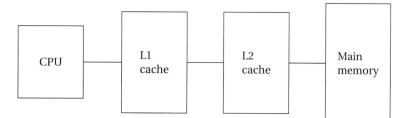

Figure 3-8 *A two-level cache system.*

The second-level cache is much larger but is also slower. If h_1 is the first-level hit rate and h_2 is the rate at which access hit the second-level cache but not the first-level cache, then the average access time for a two-level cache system is

$$t_{av} = h_1 t_{L1} + (h_2 - h_1) t_{L2} + (1 - h_1 - h_2) t_{main}. \qquad \text{(EQ 3-2)}$$

As the program's working set changes, we expect locations to be removed from the cache to make way for new locations. When set-associative caches are used, we have to think about what happens when we throw out a value from the cache to make room for a new value. We do not have this problem in direct-mapped caches because every location maps onto a unique block, but in a set-associative cache we must decide which set will have its block thrown out to make way for the new block. One possible replacement policy is least recently used (LRU), that is, throw out the block that has been used farthest in the past. We can add relatively small amounts of hardware to the cache to keep track of the time since the last access for each block. Another policy is random replacement, which requires even less hardware to implement.

cache organization The simplest way to implement a cache is a **direct-mapped cache,** as shown in Figure 3-9. The cache consists of cache **blocks,** each of which includes a tag to show which memory location is represented by this block, a data field holding the contents of that memory, and a valid tag to show whether the contents of this cache block are valid. An address is divided into three sections. The index is used to select which cache block to check. The tag is compared against the tag value in the block selected by the index. If the address tag matches the tag value in the block, that block includes the desired memory location. If the length of the data field is longer than the minimum addressable unit, then the lowest bits of the address are used as an offset to select the required value from the data field. Given the structure of the cache, there is only one block that must be checked to see whether a location is in the cache—the index uniquely determines that block. If the access is a hit, the data value is read from the cache.

Writes are slightly more complicated than reads because we have to update main memory as well as the cache. There are several ways to do this.

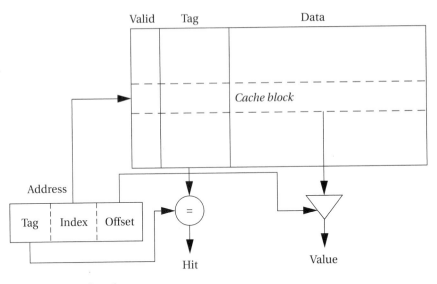

Valid Tag Data

Cache block

Address

Tag Index Offset

=

Hit Value

Figure 3-9 *A direct-mapped cache.*

The simplest scheme is known as **write-through**—every write changes both the cache and the corresponding main memory location (usually through a write buffer). This scheme ensures that the cache and main memory are consistent, but may generate some additional main memory traffic. We can reduce the number of times we write to main memory by using a **write-back** policy: If we write only when we remove a location from the cache, we eliminate the writes when a location is written several times before it is removed from the cache.

The direct-mapped cache is both fast and relatively low cost, but it does have limits in its caching power due to its simple scheme for mapping the cache onto main memory. Consider a direct-mapped cache with four blocks, in which locations 0, 1, 2, and 3 all map to different blocks. But locations 4, 8, 12, ... all map to the same block as location 0; locations 1, 5, 9, 13, ... all map to a single block; and so on. If two popular locations in a program happen to map onto the same block, we will not gain the full benefits of the cache. As seen in Section 5.6, this can create program performance problems.

The limitations of the direct-mapped cache can be reduced by going to the **set-associative** cache structure shown in Figure 3-10. A set-associative cache is characterized by the number of sets it uses, giving an *n*-way set-associative cache. Each set is implemented with a direct-mapped cache. A cache request is broadcast to all sets simultaneously. If any of the sets has the location, the cache reports a hit. Although memory locations map onto blocks in the same way, there are *n* separate blocks for each set of locations. Therefore, we can simultaneously cache several locations that happen to map onto the same

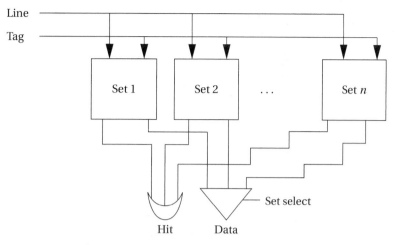

Figure 3-10 *A set-associative cache.*

cache block. The set-associative cache structure incurs a little extra overhead and is somewhat slower than a direct-mapped cache, but the higher hit rates that it can provide often compensate.

The set-associative cache generally provides higher hit rates than the direct-mapped cache because conflicts between a small number of locations can be resolved within the cache. The set-associative cache is somewhat slower, so the CPU designer has to be careful that it doesn't slow down the CPU's cycle time too much. A more important problem with set-associative caches for embedded program design is predictability. Because the time penalty for a cache miss is so severe, we often want to make sure that critical segments of our programs have good behavior in the cache. It is relatively easy to determine when two memory locations will conflict in a direct-mapped cache. Conflicts in a set-associative cache are more subtle, and so the behavior of a set-associative cache is more difficult to analyze for both humans and programs. Example 3-9 compares the behavior of direct-mapped and set-associative caches.

Example 3-9

Direct-Mapped versus Set-Associative Caches

For simplicity, let's consider a very simple caching scheme. We use two bits of the address as the tag. We compare a direct-mapped cache with four blocks

and a two-way set-associative cache with four sets, and we use LRU replacement to make it easy to compare the two caches.

A three-bit address is used for simplicity. The contents of the memory follow:

Address	Data
000	0101
001	1111
010	0000
011	0110
100	1000
101	0001
110	1010
111	0100

We will give each cache the same pattern of addresses (in binary to simplify picking out the index): 001, 010, 011, 100, 101, and 111.

To understand how the direct-mapped cache works, let's see how its state evolves.

After 001 access:

Block	Tag	Data
00	—	—
01	0	1111
10	—	—
11	—	—

After 010 access:

Block	Tag	Data
00	—	—
01	0	1111
10	0	0000
11	—	—

After 011 access:

Block	Tag	Data
00	—	—
01	0	1111
10	0	0000
11	0	0110

After 100 access (notice that the tag bit for this entry is 1):

Block	Tag	Data
00	1	1000
01	0	1111
10	0	0000
11	0	0110

After 101 access (overwrites the 01 block entry):

Block	Tag	Data
00	1	1000
01	1	0001
10	0	0000
11	0	0110

After 111 access (overwrites the 11 block entry):

Block	Tag	Data
00	1	1000
01	1	0001
10	0	0000
11	1	0100

We can use a similar procedure to determine what ends up in the two-way set-associative cache. The only difference is that we have some freedom when we have to replace a block with new data. To make the results easy to understand, we use a least-recently-used replacement policy. The final state of the two-way set-associative cache follows:

Set	Block 0 tag	Block 0 data	Block 1 tag	Block 1 data
00	1	1000	—	—
01	0	1111	1	0001
10	0	0000	—	
11	0	0110	1	0100

Of course, this isn't a fair comparison for performance because the two-way set-associative cache has twice as many entries as the direct-mapped cache. Let's use a two-way, set-associative cache with two sets, giving us four blocks, the same number as in the direct-mapped cache. In this case, the index size is reduced to one bit and the tag grows to two bits.

Set	Block 0 tag	Block 0 data	Block 1 tag	Block 1 data
0	01	0000	10	1000
1	10	0111	11	0100

In this case, the cache contents are significantly different than for either the direct-mapped cache or the four-block, two-way set-associative cache.

The CPU knows when it is fetching an instruction (the PC is used to calculate the address, either directly or indirectly) or data. We can therefore choose whether to cache instructions, data, or both. If cache space is limited, instructions are the highest priority for caching because they will usually provide the highest hit rates. A cache that holds both instructions and data is called a **unified cache.**

ARM and SHARC caches

Various ARM implementations use different cache sizes and organizations [Fur96]. The ARM600 includes a 4-Kbyte, 64-way (wow!) unified instruction/data cache. The StrongARM uses a 16-Kbyte, 32-way instruction cache with a 32-byte block and a 16-Kbyte, 32-way data cache with a 32-byte block; the data cache uses a write-back strategy.

The SHARC includes a 32-instruction, two-way set-associative cache and no data cache.

3.5.2 Memory Management Units and Address Translation

A memory management unit translates addresses between the CPU and physical memory. This translation process is often known as **memory mapping** since addresses are mapped from a logical space into a physical space. Memory management units are not especially common in embedded systems since virtual memory requires a secondary storage device such as a disk. However, that situation is slowly changing with lower component prices in general and the advent of Internet appliances in particular. It is helpful to understand the basics of MMUs for embedded systems complex enough to require them.

Early computers used MMUs to compensate for limited address space in their instruction sets. When memory became cheap enough that physical memory could be larger than the address space defined by the instructions, MMUs allowed software to manage multiple programs in a single physical memory, each with its own address space.

Because modern CPUs typically do not have this limitation, MMUs are used to provide **virtual addressing.** As shown in Figure 3-11, the memory management unit accepts logical addresses from the CPU. Logical addresses refer to the program's abstract address space but do not correspond to actual RAM locations. The MMU translates them from tables to physical addresses that do correspond to RAM. By changing the MMU's tables, you can change the physical location at which the program resides without modifying the program's code or data. (We must, of course, move the program in main memory to correspond to the memory mapping change.)

Furthermore, if we add a secondary storage unit such as a disk, we can eliminate parts of the program from main memory. In a virtual memory system, the MMU keeps track of which logical addresses are actually resident in main memory; those that do not reside in main memory are kept on the secondary storage device. When the CPU requests an address that is not in main

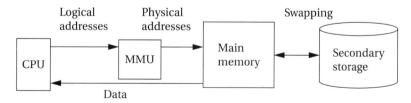

Figure 3-11 *A virtually addressed memory system.*

memory, the MMU generates an exception called a **page fault.** The handler for this exception executes code that reads the requested location from the secondary storage device into main memory. The program that generated the page fault is restarted by the handler only after

- the required memory has been read back into main memory, and

- the MMU's tables have been updated to reflect the changes.

Of course, loading a location into main memory will usually require throwing something out of main memory. The displaced memory is copied into secondary storage before the requested location is read in. As with caches, LRU is a good replacement policy.

There are two styles of address translation: **segmented** and **paged.** Each has advantages and the two can be combined to form a segemented, paged addressing scheme. As illustrated in Figure 3-12, segmenting is designed to support a large, arbitrarily sized region of memory, while pages describe small, equally sized regions. A segment is usually described by its start address and size, allowing different segments to be of different sizes. Pages are of uniform size, which simplifies the hardware required for address translation. A segmented, paged scheme is created by dividing each segment into pages and using two steps for address translation. Paging introduces the possibility of **fragmentation** as program pages are scattered around physical memory.

In a simple segmenting scheme, shown in Figure 3-13, the MMU would maintain a segment register that describes the currently active segment. This register would point to the base of the current segment. The address extracted from an instruction (or from any other source for addresses, such as a register) would be used as the offset for the address. The physical address is formed by adding the segment base to the offset. Most segmentation schemes also check the physical address against the upper limit of the segment by extending the segment register to include the segment size and comparing the offset to the allowed size.

The translation of paged addresses requires more MMU state but a simpler calculation. As shown in Figure 3-14, the logical address is divided into two sections, including a page number and an offset. The page number is used as an index into a page table, which stores the physical address for the start of each page. However, since all pages have the same size and it is easy to ensure that page boundaries fall on the proper boundaries, the MMU simply needs to concatenate the top bits of the page starting address with the bottom bits from the page offset to form the physical address. Pages are small, typically between 512 bytes to 4 Kbytes. As a result, the page table is large for an architecture with a large address space. The page table is normally kept in main memory, which means that an address translation requires memory access.

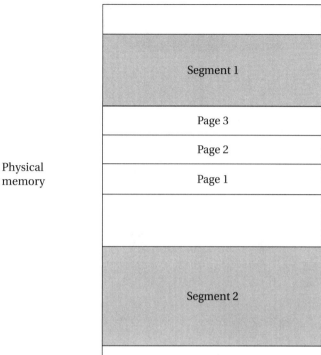

Physical memory

Figure 3-12 *Segments and pages.*

The page table may be organized in several ways, as shown in Figure 3-15. The simplest scheme is a flat table. The table is indexed by the page number and each entry holds the page descriptor. A more sophisticated method is a tree. The root entry of the tree holds pointers to pointer tables at the next level of the tree; each pointer table is indexed by a part of the page number. We eventually (after three levels, in this case) arrive at a descriptor table that includes the page descriptor we are interested in. A tree-structured page table incurs some overhead for the pointers, but it allows us to build a partially populated tree. If some part of the address space is not used, we do not need to build the part of the tree that covers it.

The efficiency of paged address translation may be increased by caching page translation information. A cache for address translation is known as a **translation lookaside buffer (TLB).** The MMU reads the TLB to check whether a page number is currently in the TLB cache and, if so, uses that value rather than reading from memory.

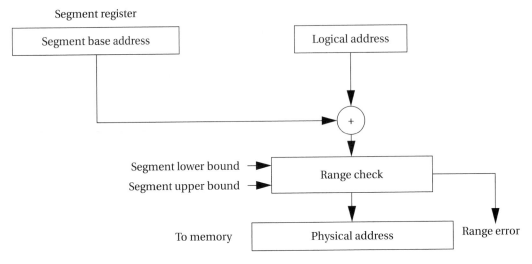

Figure 3-13 *Address translation for a segment.*

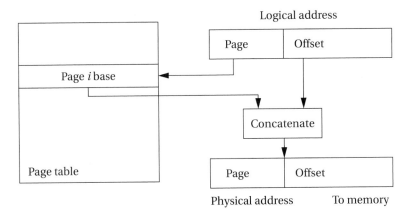

Figure 3-14 *Address translation for a page.*

Virtual memory is typically implemented in a paging or segmented, paged scheme so that only page-sized regions of memory need to be transferred on a page fault. Some extensions to both segmenting and paging are useful for virtual memory:

■ At minimum, a present bit is necessary to show whether the logical segment or page is currently in physical memory.

- A dirty bit shows whether the page/segment has been written to. This bit is maintained by the MMU, since it knows about every write performed by the CPU.

- Permission bits are often used. Some pages/segments may be readable but not writable. If the CPU supports modes, pages/segments may be accessible by the supervisor but not in user mode.

A data or instruction cache may operate either on logical or physical addresses, depending on where it is positioned relative to the MMU.

A memory management unit is an optional part of the ARM architecture. The ARM MMU supports both virtual address translation and memory protection; the architecture requires that the MMU be implemented when cache or write buffers are implemented. The ARM MMU supports the following types of memory regions for address translation:

- a **section** is a 1-Mbyte block of memory,

- a **large page** is 64 Kbytes, and

- a **small page** is 4 Kbytes.

An address is marked as section mapped or page mapped. A two-level scheme is used to translate addresses. The first-level table, which is pointed to by the Translation Table Base register, holds descriptors for section translation and pointers to the second-level tables. The second-level tables describe the

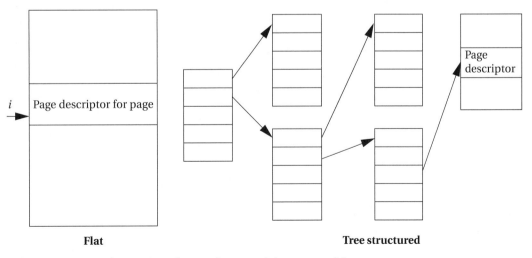

Figure 3-15 *Alternative schemes for organizing page tables.*

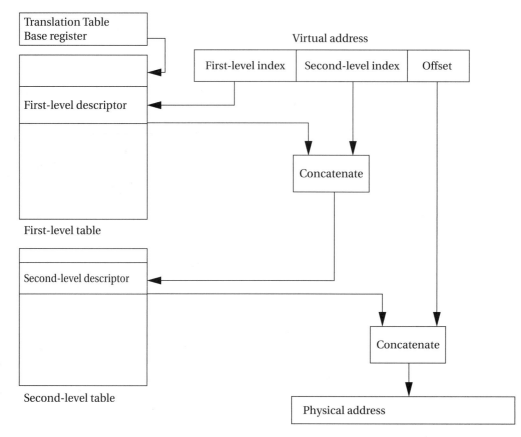

Figure 3-16 *ARM two-stage address translation.*

translation of both large and small pages. The basic two-level process for a large or small page is illustrated in Figure 3-16. The details differ between large and small pages, such as the size of the second-level table index. The first- and second-level pages also contain access control bits for virtual memory and protection.

The SHARC does not have a memory management unit.

3.6 CPU Performance

Now that we have an understanding of the various types of instructions that CPUs can execute, we can move on to a topic particularly important in embedded computing: How fast can the CPU execute instructions? In this section, we

consider three factors that can substantially influence program performance: pipelining, superscalar execution, and caching.

3.6.1 Pipelining

Modern CPUs are designed as **pipelined** machines in which several instructions are executed in parallel. Pipelining greatly increases the efficiency of the CPU. But like any pipeline, a CPU pipeline works best when its contents flow smoothly. Some sequences of instructions can disrupt the flow of information in the pipeline and, temporarily at least, slow down the operation of the CPU.

Both the ARM and the SHARC have a three-stage pipeline:

1. *Fetch:* the instruction is fetched from memory.

2. *Decode:* the instruction's opcode and operands are decoded to determine what function to perform.

3. *Execute:* the decoded instruction is executed.

Each of these operations requires one clock cycle for typical instructions. Thus, a normal instruction requires three clock cycles to completely execute, known as the **latency** of instruction execution. But since the pipeline has three stages, an instruction is completed in every clock cycle. In other words, the pipeline has a **throughput** of one instruction per cycle. Figure 3-17 illustrates the position of instructions in the pipeline during execution using the notation introduced by Hennessy and Patterson [Hen96]. A vertical slice through the timeline shows all instructions in the pipeline at that time. By following an instruction horizontally, we can see the progress of its execution.

RISC machines are designed to keep the pipeline busy. CISC machines may display a wide variation in instruction timing. Pipelined RISC machines typically have more regular timing characteristics—most instructions that do not have pipeline hazards display the same latency.

The one-cycle-per-instruction completion rate does not hold in every case, however. The simplest case for extended execution is when an instruction is too complex to complete the execution phase in a single cycle. A multiple load instruction is an example of an instruction that requires several cycles in the execution phase. Figure 3-18 illustrates a **data stall** in the execution of a sequence of instructions starting with a load multiple (LDMIA) instruction. Since there are two registers to load, the instruction must stay in the execution phase for two cycles. In a multiphase execution, the decode stage is also occupied, since it must continue to remember the decoded instruction. As a result, the SUB instruction is fetched at the normal time but not decoded until the LDMIA is finishing. This delays the fetching of the third instruction, the CMP.

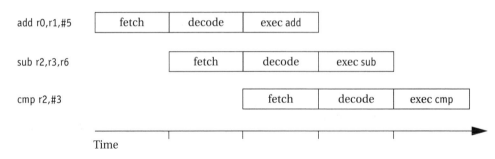

Figure 3-17 *Pipelined execution of ARM instructions.*

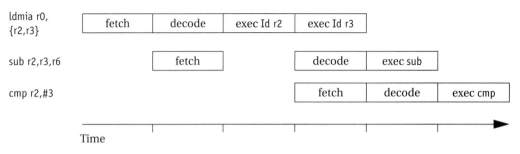

Figure 3-18 *Pipelined execution of multicycle ARM instruction.*

Branches also introduce **control stall** delays into the pipeline, commonly referred to as the **branch penalty,** as shown in Figure 3-19. The decision whether to take the conditional branch BNE is not made until the third clock cycle of that instruction's execution, which computes the branch target address. If the branch is taken, the succeeding instruction at PC+4 has been fetched and started to be decoded. When the branch is taken, the branch target address is used to fetch the branch target instruction. Since we have to wait for the execution cycle to complete before knowing the target, we must throw away two cycles of work on instructions in the path not taken. The CPU uses the two cycles between starting to fetch the branch target and starting to execute that instruction to finish housekeeping tasks related to the execution of the branch.

One way around this problem is to introduce the **delayed branch.** In this style of branch instruction, some number of instructions directly after the branch are always executed, whether or not the branch is taken. This allows the CPU to keep the pipeline full during execution of the branch. However, some of those instructions after the delayed branch may be no-ops. Any instruction in the delayed branch window must be valid for both execution paths, whether

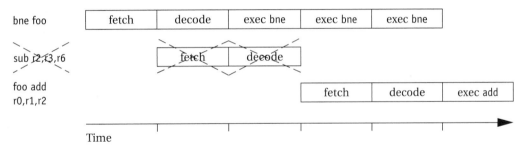

Figure 3-19 *Pipelined execution of a branch in ARM.*

or not the branch is taken. If there are not enough instructions to fill the delayed branch window, it must be filled with no-ops.

SHARC supports both delayed and nondelayed branches. A bit in the branch instruction indicates whether the branch is to be delayed, in which case it will execute two more instructions while fetching and decoding the branch target. In the case of a nondelayed branch, the pipeline will stall for two cycles while waiting for the branch target.

Example 3-10 shows how instructions can be scheduled in the SHARC.

Example 3-10

Code Scheduling for SHARC Data Address Generators

The SHARC contains data address generators (DAGs), illustrated in Figure 2-22, that can be used to efficiently perform memory reads and writes but that also introduce some resource conflicts [ADI97]. A DAG has four types of registers: index(I), modify (M), base (B), and length (L). Each DAG has eight registers of each type. Since a 2106x has two DAGs, the first DAG's registers are I0–I7, and so on, while the second DAG's registers are named I8–I15, and so forth.

Consider this code fragment:

```
L1 = 5;
DM(I0,M1) = R1;
L8 = 8;
DM(i8,M9) = R2;
```

The first two instructions set up a DAG register in DAG unit 1 and then perform a data transfer; the second two instructions do likewise in the second DAG

unit. The CPU cannot load a DAG register and use a register in the same DAG on the next clock cycle because both require the same internal bus. If a DAG register load is immediately followed by a register usage in the same unit, the CPU will insert a NOP to allow the register load to finish. As a result, the CPU will execute two NOPs in this sequence, one after each load of an L register.

We can eliminate the two dead cycles by rescheduling the operations as follows:

```
L1 = 5;
L8 = 8;
DM(I0,M1) = R1;
DM(i8,M9) = R2;
```

The new code is functionally equivalent, but we now interleave operations on the two DAGs. While the load on the first DAG is finishing, we can start the load on the second DAG. While that is finishing, we can initiate the DM operation on the now-idle first DAG unit.

Let's use this knowledge of instruction execution time to evaluate the execution time of some C code, as shown in Example 3-11.

Example 3-11

Execution Time of a for Loop on the ARM

We will use the C code for the FIR filter of Application Example 2-1:

```
for (i = 0, f = 0; i < N; i++)
    f = f + c[i] * x[i];
```

We repeat the ARM code for this loop:

```
; loop initiation code
MOV r0,#0        ; use r0 for i, set to 0
MOV r8,#0        ; use a separate index for arrays
ADR r2,N         ; get address for N
LDR r1,[r2]         ; get value of N for loop termination test
MOV r2,#0        ; use r2 for f, set to 0
ADR r3,c         ; load r3 with address of base of c array
ADR r5,x         ; load r5 with address of base of x array
; loop body
```

```
loop      LDR r4,[r3,r8]        ; get value of c[i]
          LDR r6,[r5,r8]        ; get value of x[i]
          MUL r4,r4,r6          ; compute c[i]*x[i]
          ADD r2,r2,r4          ; add into running sum f
          ; update loop counter and array index
          ADD r8,r8,#4          ; add one word offset to array index
          ADD r0,r0,#1          ; add 1 to i
          ; test for exit
          CMP r0,r1
          BLT loop              ; if i < N, continue loop
loopend...
```

Inspection of the code shows that the only instruction that may take more than one cycle is the conditional branch in the loop test. We can count the number of instructions and associated number of clock cycles in each block as follows:

Block	Variable	# Instructions	# Cycles
Initiation	t_{init}	7	7
Body	t_{body}	4	4
Update	t_{update}	2	2
Test	t_{test}	2	2 best case, 4 worst case

The unconditional branch at the end of the update block always incurs a branch penalty of two cycles. The BLT instruction in the test block incurs a pipeline delay of two cycles when the branch is taken. That happens for all but the last iteration, when the instruction has an execution time of $t_{test,worst}$; the last iteration executes in time $t_{test,best}$. We can write a formula for the total execution time of the loop in cycles as

$$t_{loop} = t_{init} + N(t_{body} + t_{update}) + (N-1)t_{test,worst} + t_{test,best}. \qquad \text{(EQ 3-3)}$$

3.6.2 Superscalar Execution

Another way to improve CPU performance is **superscalar** execution. A superscalar CPU can execute more than one instruction at a time. As illustrated in

Figure 3-20, several instructions are under consideration at once. The programmer cannot tell that the machine is performing several instructions at a time—the results in the programming model are the same. However, the program executes more quickly.

Superscalar is compatible with pipelining. Usually, each of the instruction units in a superscalar machine is pipelined. Controlling a superscalar, pipelined processor is complex, but it can be done. The result is a CPU that can execute several instructions per clock cycle.

It is not always possible to execute arbitrary combinations of instructions simultaneously in a superscalar architecture, because the CPU may not be able to issue as many instructions as it would like. For example, consider the ARM code fragment in Figure 3-21. The first instruction puts the result of an addition in register r2. The second instruction uses that result. We can't perform the second addition until the result of the first addition is available. As a result, the dispatch of the second instruction may be delayed. Many dependencies among instructions may exist. Superscalar processors check on dependencies *dynamically* during execution. (In contrast, a VLIW architecture executes multiple operations, but relies on the compiler to check dependencies and statically select an execution order before execution starts.)

superscalar performance What does superscalar mean for performance? It means that the execution time of a piece of code is even harder to calculate than for a pipelined processor. The CPU must check at execution time whether the combination of instructions presented to it can be executed simultaneously. We cannot consider the execution time of an instruction by itself—we can only determine the execution time when we know the instructions around it. When branches are involved, we must consider the branch-taken and branch-not-taken cases sep-

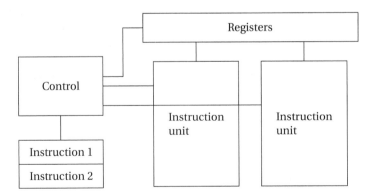

Figure 3-20 *Multiple instruction units in a superscalar processor.*

arately. Hand calculation of execution time is not feasible except for very small code fragments. Even then, the CPU manufacturer may not provide sufficient information to accurately calculate performance. The CPU manufacturer may provide a CPU simulator that calculates performance data.

3.6.3 Caching

We have already discussed caches functionally. Although caches are invisible in the programming model, they have a profound effect on performance. We introduce caches because they substantially reduce memory access time when the requested location is in the cache. However, the desired location is not always in the cache since it is considerably smaller than main memory. As a result, caches cause the time required to access memory to vary considerably. The extra time required to access a memory location not in the cache is often called the **cache miss penalty.** The amount of variation depends on several factors in the system architecture, but a cache miss is often several clock cycles slower than a cache hit.

The time required to access a memory location depends on whether the requested location is in the cache. However, as we have seen, a location may not be in the cache for several reasons.

■ At a compulsory miss, the location has not been referenced before.

```
ADD r2,r0,r1 ; compute a value and store in r2
ADD r3,r2,r5 ; use value just stored in r2
```

ARM instructions

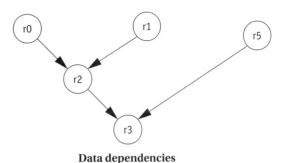

Data dependencies

Figure 3-21 *Problems in superscalar execution.*

- At a conflict miss, two particular memory locations are fighting for the same cache line.

- At a capacity miss, the program's working set is simply too large for the cache.

The contents of the cache can change considerably over the course of execution of a program. When we have several programs running concurrently on the CPU, we can have very dramatic changes in the cache contents. We need to examine the behavior of the programs running on the system to be able to accurately estimate performance when caches are involved. We consider this problem in more detail in Section 5.6.

3.7 CPU Power Consumption

Power consumption is, in some situations, as important as execution time. In this section we study the characteristics of CPUs that influence power consumption and mechanisms provided by CPUs to control how much power they consume.

energy vs. power

First, it is important to distinguish between **energy** and **power.** Power is, of course, energy consumption per unit time. Heat generation depends on power consumption. Battery life, on the other hand, most directly depends on energy consumption. Generally, we will use the term *power* as shorthand for energy and power consumption, distinguishing between them only when necessary.

CMOS power characteristics

The high-level power consumption characteristics of CPUs and other system components are derived from the circuits used to build those components. Today, virtually all digital systems are built with **CMOS** (complementary metal oxide semiconductor) circuitry. The detailed circuit characteristics are best left to a study of VLSI design [Wol98], but the basic sources of CMOS power consumption are easily identified and briefly described below.

- *Voltage drops:* The power consumption of a CMOS circuit is proportional to the square of the power supply voltage (V^2). Therefore, by reducing the power supply voltage to the lowest level that provides the required performance, we can significantly reduce power consumption. We also may be able to add parallel hardware and even further reduce the power supply voltage while maintaining required performance [Cha92].

- *Toggling:* A CMOS circuit uses most of its power when it is changing its output value. This provides two ways to reduce power consumption. By reduc-

ing the speed at which the circuit operates, we can reduce its power consumption (although not the total energy required for the operation, since the result is available later). We can actually reduce energy consumption by eliminating unnecessary changes to the inputs of a CMOS circuit— eliminating unnecessary glitches at the circuit outputs eliminates unnecessary power consumption.

■ *Leakage:* Even when a CMOS circuit is not active, some charge leaks out of the circuit's nodes through the substrate. The only way to eliminate leakage current is to remove the power supply. Completely disconnecting the power supply eliminates power consumption, but it usually takes a significant amount of time to reconnect the system to the power supply and reinitialize its internal state so that it once again performs properly.

As a result, we see the following power-saving strategies used in CMOS CPUs.

■ CPUs can be used at reduced voltage levels. For example, reducing the power supply from 5 V to 3.3 V causes the power consumption to drop by $5^2/3.3^2 = 2.29$.

■ The CPU can be operated at a lower clock frequency to reduce power (but not energy) consumption.

■ The CPU may internally disable certain function units that are not required for the currently executing function. This reduces energy consumption.

■ Some CPUs allow parts of the CPU to be totally disconnected from the power supply to eliminate leakage currents.

static vs. dynamic power management

There are two types of power management features provided by CPUs. A **static power management** mechanism is invoked by the user but does not otherwise depend on CPU activities. An example of a static mechanism is a **power-down mode** intended to save energy. This mode provides a high-level way to reduce unnecessary power consumption. The mode is typically entered with an instruction. If the mode stops the interpretation of instructions, then it clearly cannot be exited by execution of another instruction. Power-down modes typically end upon receipt of an interrupt or other event. A **dynamic power management** mechanism takes actions to control power based upon the dynamic activity in the CPU. For example, the CPU may turn off certain sections of the CPU when the instructions being executed do not need them. Application Example 3-2 describes the static and dynamic energy efficiency features of one of the PowerPC chips.

Application Example 3-2

Energy Efficiency Features in the PowerPC 603

The PowerPC 603 [Gar94] was designed specifically for low-power operation while retaining high performance. It typically dissipates 2.2 W running at 80 MHz. The architecture provides three low-power modes—doze, nap, and sleep—that provide static power management capabilities for use by the programs and operating system.

The 603 also uses a variety of dynamic power management techniques for power minimization that are performed automatically, without program intervention. The CPU is a two-issue, out-of-order superscalar processor. It uses the dynamic techniques summarized below to reduce power consumption.

- An execution unit that is not being used can be shut down.

- The cache, an 8-KB, two-way set-associative cache, was organized into sub-arrays so that at most two out of eight subarrays will be accessed on any given clock cycle. A variety of circuit techniques were also used in the cache to reduce power consumption.

Not all units in the CPU are active all the time; idling them when they are not being used can save power. The table below shows the percentage of time various units in the 603 were idle for the SPEC integer and floating-point benchmarks [Gar94].

Unit	Specint92 (% idle)	Specfp92 (% idle)
Data cache	29	28
Instruction cache	29	17
Load-store	35	17
Fixed-point	38	76
Floating-point	99	30
System register	89	97

Idle units are turned off automatically by switching off their clocks. Various stages of the pipeline are turned on and off, depending on which stages are necessary at the current time. Measurements comparing the chip's power consumption with and without dynamic power management show that dynamic techniques provide significant power savings.

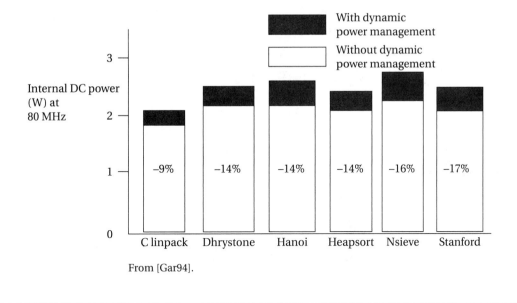

From [Gar94].

A power-down mode provides the opportunity to greatly reduce power consumption because it will typically be entered for a substantial period of time. However, going into and especially out of a power-down mode is not free—it costs both time and energy. The power-down or power-up transition consumes time and energy in order to properly control the CPU's internal logic. Modern pipelined processors require complex control that must be properly initialized to avoid corrupting data in the pipeline. Starting up the processor must also be done carefully to avoid power surges that could cause the chip to malfunction or even damage it.

The modes of a CPU can be modeled by a **power state machine** [Ben00]. An example is shown in Figure 3-22. Each state in the machine represents a different mode of the machine, and every state is labeled with its average power consumption. The example machine has two states: run mode with power consumption P_{run} and sleep mode with power consumption P_{sleep}. Transitions

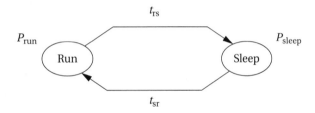

Figure 3-22 *A power state machine for a processor.*

show how the machine can go from state to state; each transition is labeled with the time required to go from the source to the destination state. In a more complex example, it may not be possible to go from a particular state to another particular state—traversing a sequence of states may be necessary. Application Example 3-3 describes the power-down modes of the StrongARM SA-1100.

Application Example 3-3

Power-Saving Modes of the StrongARM SA-1100

The StrongARM SA-1100 [Int99] is designed to provide sophisticated power management capabilities that are controlled by the on-chip power manager. The processor takes two power supplies, as seen in the following figure:

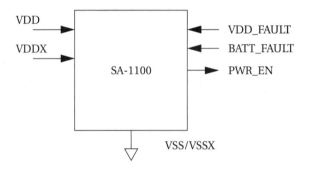

VDD is the main power supply for the core CPU and is nominally 3.3 V. The *VDDX* supply is used for the pins and other logic such as the power manager; it is normally at 1.5 V. (The two supplies share a common ground.) The system can supply two inputs about the status of the power supply. *VDD_FAULT* tells the *CPU* that the main power supply is not being properly regulated, while *BATT_FAULT* indicates that the battery has been removed or is low. Either of these events can cause the CPU to go into a low-power mode. In low-power operation, the *VDD* supply can be turned off (the *VDDX* supply always remains on). When resuming operation, the *PWR_EN* signal is used by the CPU to tell the external power supply to ramp up the *VDD* power supply.

A system power manager can both monitor the CPU and other devices and control their operation to gracefully transition between power modes. It provides several registers that allow programs to control power modes, determine why power modes were entered, determine the current state of power management modes, and so on.

The SA-1100 provides the three power modes described below.

- *Run* mode is normal operation and has the highest power consumption.

- *Idle* mode saves power by stopping the CPU clock. The system unit modules—real-time clock, operating system timer, interrupt control, general-purpose I/O, and power manager—all remain operational. Idle mode is entered by executing a three-instruction sequence. The CPU returns to run mode upon receiving an interrupt from one of the internal system units or from a peripheral or by resetting the CPU. This causes the machine to restart the CPU clock and to resume execution where it left off.

- *Sleep* mode shuts off most of the chip's activity. Entering sleep mode causes the system to shut down on-chip activity, reset the CPU, and negate the PWR_EN pin to tell the external electronics that the chip's power supply should be driven to 0 volts. A separate I/O power supply remains on and supplies power to the power manager so that the CPU can be awakened from sleep mode; the low-speed clock keeps the power manager running at low speeds sufficient to manage sleep mode. The CPU software should set several registers to prepare for sleep mode. Sleep mode is entered by forcing the sleep bit in the power manager control register; it can also be entered by a power supply fault. The sleep shutdown sequence happens in three steps, each of which requires about 30 μs. The machine wakes up from sleep state on a preprogrammed wake-up event. The wake-up sequence has three steps: the PWR_EN pin is asserted to turn on the external power supply and waits for about 10 ms; the 3.686-MHz oscillator is ramped up to speed; and the internal reset is negated and the CPU boot sequence begins.

The power state machine of the SA-1100 [Ben00] is reproduced below.

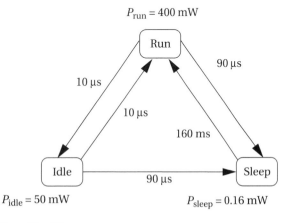

From [Ben00].

The sleep mode saves over three orders of magnitude of power consumption. However, the time required to reenter run mode from sleep is over a tenth of a second.

The SA-1100 has a companion chip, the SA-1111, that provides an integrated set of peripherals. That chip has its own power management modes that complement the SA-1100.

Design Example

3.8 Data Compressor

Our design example for this chapter is a data compressor that takes in data with a constant number of bits per data element and puts out a compressed data stream in which the data is encoded in variable-length symbols. Because this chapter concentrates on CPUs, we focus on the data compression routine itself.

3.8.1 Requirements and Algorithm

We use the **Huffman coding** technique, which is introduced in Application Example 3-4.

We require some understanding of how our compression code fits into a larger system. Figure 3-23 shows a collaboration diagram for the data compression process. The data compressor takes in a sequence of **input symbols** and then produces a stream of **output symbols.** Assume for simplicity that the input symbols are one byte in length. The output symbols are variable length, so we have to choose a format in which to deliver the output data. Delivering each coded symbol separately is tedious, since we would have to supply the length of each symbol and use external code to pack them into words. On the other hand, bit-by-bit delivery is almost certainly too slow. Therefore, we will

Figure 3-23 *UML collaboration diagram for the data compressor.*

rely on the data compressor to pack the coded symbols into an array. There is not a one-to-one relationship between the input and output symbols, and we may have to wait for several input symbols before a packed output word comes out.

Application Example 3-4

Huffman Coding for Text Compression

Text compression algorithms aim at statistical reductions in the volume of data. One commonly used compression algorithm is Huffman coding [Huf52], which makes use of information on the frequency of characters to assign variable-length codes to characters. If shorter bit sequences are used to identify more frequent characters, then the length of the total sequence will be reduced.

In order to be able to decode the incoming bit string, the code characters must have unique prefixes: No code may be a prefix of a longer code for another character. As a simple example of Huffman coding, assume that these characters have the following probabilities P of appearance in a message:

Character	P
a	0.45
b	0.24
c	0.11
d	0.08
e	0.07
f	0.05

We build the code from the bottom up. After sorting the characters by probability, we create a new symbol by adding a bit. We then compute the joint probability of finding either one of those characters and re-sort the table. The result is a tree that we can read top down to find the character codes. The coding tree for our example appears below.

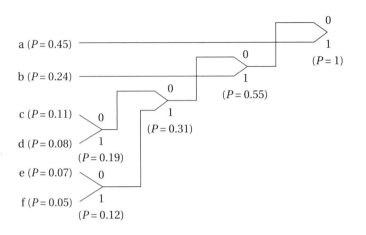

Reading the codes off the tree from the root to the leaves, we obtain the following coding of the characters:

Character	Code
a	1
b	01
c	0000
d	0001
e	0010
f	0011

Once the code has been constructed, which in many applications is done off-line, the codes can be stored in a table for encoding. This makes encoding simple, but clearly the encoded bit rate can vary significantly depending on the input character sequence. On the decoding side, since we do not know a priori the length of a character's bit sequence, the computation time required to decode a character can vary significantly.

The data compressor as discussed above is not a complete system, but we can create at least a partial requirements list for the module as seen below. We used the abbreviation N/A for not applicable to describe some items that don't make sense for a code module.

Name	Data compression module
Purpose	Code module for Huffman data compression
Inputs	Encoding table, uncoded byte-size input symbols
Outputs	Packed compressed output symbols
Functions	Huffman coding
Performance	Requires fast performance
Manufacturing cost	N/A
Power	N/A
Physical size and weight	N/A

3.8.2 Specification

Let's refine the description of Figure 3-23 to come up with a more complete specification for our data compression module. That collaboration diagram concentrates on the steady-state behavior of the system. For a fully functional system, we have to provide the following additional behavior.

■ We have to be able to provide the compressor with a new symbol table.

■ We should be able to flush the symbol buffer to cause the system to release all pending symbols that have been partially packed. We may want to do this when we change the symbol table or in the middle of an encoding session to keep a transmitter busy.

A class description for this refined understanding of the requirements on the module is shown in Figure 3-24. The class's *buffer* and *current-bit* attributes keep track of the state of the encoding, and the *table* attribute provides the current symbol table. The class has three methods as follows:

■ *encode* performs the basic encoding function. It takes in a one-byte input symbol and returns two values: a boolean showing whether it is returning a full buffer and, if the boolean is true, the full buffer itself.

■ *new-symbol-table* installs a new symbol table into the object and throws away the current contents of the internal buffer.

■ *flush* returns the current state of the buffer, including the number of valid bits in the buffer.

We also need to define classes for the data buffer and the symbol table. These classes are shown in Figure 3-25. The *data-buffer* will be used to hold both packed symbols and unpacked ones (such as in the symbol table). It defines the buffer itself and the length of the buffer. We have to define a data type because the longest encoded symbol is longer than an input symbol. The longest Huffman code for an eight-bit input symbol is 256 bits. (Ending up with a symbol this long happens only when the symbol probabilities have the proper values.) The insert function packs a new symbol into the upper bits of the buffer; it also puts the remaining bits in a new buffer if the current buffer is overflowed. The *Symbol-table* class indexes the encoded version of each symbol. The class defines an access behavior for the table; it also defines a *load* behavior to create a new symbol table. The relationships between these classes

Data-compressor

buffer: data-buffer
table: symbol-table
current-bit: integer

encode(): boolean, data-buffer
flush()
new-symbol-table()

Figure 3-24 *Definition of the Data-compressor class.*

Data-buffer

databuf[databuflen]: character
len: integer

insert()
length()

Symbol-table

symbols[nsymbols]: data-buffer

value(): symbol
load()

Figure 3-25 *Additional class definitions for the data compressor.*

are shown in Figure 3-26—a data compressor object includes one buffer and one symbol table.

Figure 3-27 shows a state diagram for the *encode* behavior. It shows that most of the effort goes into filling the buffers with variable-length symbols. Figure 3-28 shows a state diagram for *insert*. It shows that we must consider two cases—the new symbol does not fill the current buffer or it does.

3.8.3 Program Design

OO design in C++

Since we are only building an encoder, the program is fairly simple. We will use this as an opportunity to compare object-oriented and non-OO implementations by coding the design in both C++ and C.

First is the object-oriented design using C++, since this implementation most closely mirrors the specification.

The first step is to design the data buffer. The data buffer needs to be as long as the longest symbol. We also need to implement a function that lets us merge in another data_buffer, shifting the incoming buffer by the proper amount.

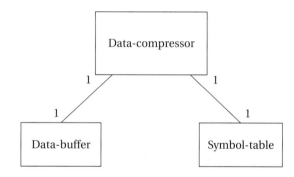

Figure 3-26 *Relationships between classes in the data compressor.*

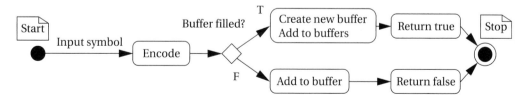

Figure 3-27 *State diagram for encode behavior.*

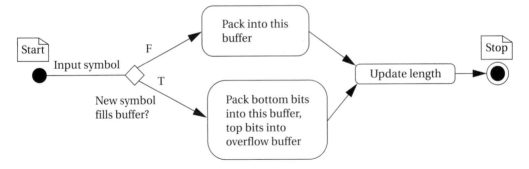

Figure 3-28 *State diagram for insert behavior.*

```
const int databuflen = 8; /* as long in bytes as longest symbol */
const int bitsperbyte = 8; /* definition of byte */
const int bytemask = 0xff; /* use to mask to 8 bits for safety */
const char lowbitsmask[bitsperbyte] = { 0, 1, 3, 7, 15, 31, 63, 127}; /* used to
keep low bits in a byte */
typedef char boolean; /* for clarity */
#define TRUE 1
#define FALSE 0

class data_buffer {
    char databuf[databuflen] ;
    int len;
    int length_in_chars() { return len/bitsperbyte; } /* length in bytes rounded
down--used in implementation */
  public:
    void insert(data_buffer, data_buffer&);
    int length() { return len; } /* returns number of bits in symbol */
    int length_in_bytes() { return (int)ceil(len/8.0); }
    void initialize(); /* initializes the data structure */
    void data_buffer::fill(data_buffer, int); /* puts upper bits
                                        of symbol into buffer */
    data_buffer& operator = (data_buffer&); /* assignment operator */
    data_buffer() { initialize(); } /* C++ constructor */
    ~data_buffer() { } /* C++ destructor */
};

data_buffer empty_buffer; /* use this to initialize other data_buffers */

void data_buffer::insert(data_buffer newval, data_buffer& newbuf) {
    /* This function puts the lower bits of a symbol (newval)
```

into an existing buffer without overflowing the buffer. Puts
spillover, if any, into newbuf. */

```
int i, j, bitstoshift, maxbyte;
/* precalculate number of positions to shift up */
bitstoshift = length() – length_in_bytes()*bitsperbyte;
/* compute how many bytes to transfer--can't run past end
   of this buffer */
maxbyte = newval.length() + length() > databuflen*bitsperbyte ?
                databuflen : newval.length_in_chars();
for (i = 0; i < maxbyte; i++) {
    /* add lower bits of this newval byte */
    databuf[i + length_in_chars()] |= (newval.databuf[i] << bitstoshift) &
bytemask;
    /* add upper bits of this newval byte */
    databuf[i + length_in_chars() + 1] |= (newval.databuf[i] >> (bitsperbyte –
bitstoshift)) & lowbitsmask[bitsperbyte – bitstoshift];
}
/* fill up new buffer if necessary */
if (newval.length() + length() > databuflen*bitsperbyte) {
    /* precalculate number of positions to shift down */
    bitstoshift = length() % bitsperbyte;
    for (i = maxbyte, j = 0; i++, j++; i < = newval.length_in_chars()) {
        newbuf.databuf[j] = (newval.databuf[i] >> bitstoshift) & bytemask;
        newbuf.databuf[j] |= newval.databuf[i + 1] & lowbitsmask
[bitstoshift];
    }
}
/* update length */
len = len + newval.length() > databuflen*bitsperbyte ? databuflen*bitsperbyte
: len + newval.length();
}

data_buffer& data_buffer::operator=(data_buffer& e) {
    /* assignment operator for data buffer */
    int i;
    /* copy the buffer itself */
    for (i = 0; i < databuflen; i++)
        databuf[i] = e.databuf[i];
    /* set length */
    len = e.len;
    /* return */
    return e;
}
```

```
void data_buffer::fill(data_buffer newval, int shiftamt) {
    /* This function puts the upper bits of a symbol (newval) into
    the buffer. */

    int i, bitstoshift, maxbyte;
    /* precalculate number of positions to shift up */
    bitstoshift = length() - length_in_bytes()*bitsperbyte;
    /* compute how many bytes to transfer--can't run past end
      of this buffer */
    maxbyte = newval.length_in_chars() > databuflen ? databuflen :
newval.length_in_chars();
    for (i = 0; i < maxbyte; i++) {
        /* add lower bits of this newval byte */
        databuf[i + length_in_chars()] = newval.databuf[i] << bitstoshift;
        /* add upper bits of this newval byte */
        databuf[i + length_in_chars() + 1] = newval.databuf[i] >> (bitsperbyte -
bitstoshift);
    }
}

void data_buffer::initialize() {
    /* Initialization code for data_buffer. */
    int i;

    /* initialize buffer to all zero bits */
    for (i = 0; i < databuflen; i++)
        databuf[i] = 0;
    /* initialize length to zero */
    len = 0;
}
```

The code for data_buffer is relatively complex, and not all of its complexity was reflected in the state diagram of Figure 3-28. That doesn't mean the specification was bad, but only that it was written at a higher level of abstraction.

The symbol table code can be implemented relatively easily as shown below.

```
const int nsymbols = 256;
class symbol_table {
    data_buffer symbols[nsymbols];
  public:
    data_buffer value(int i) { return symbols[i]; }
    void load(symbol_table&);
```

```
        symbol_table() { } /* C++ constructor */
        ~symbol_table() { } /* C++ destructor */
};

void symbol_table::load(symbol_table& newsyms) {
    int i;
    for (i = 0; i < nsymbols; i++) {
        symbols[i] = newsyms.symbols[i];
    }
}
```

Now let's create the class definition for data_compressor:

```
typedef char boolean; /* for clarity */
class data_compressor {
    data_buffer buffer;
    int current_bit;
    symbol_table table;

    public:
        boolean encode(char, data_buffer&);
        void new_symbol_table(symbol_table newtable)
            { table = newtable; current_bit = 0;
              buffer = empty_buffer; }
        int flush(data_buffer& buf)
            { int temp = current_bit; buf = buffer;
              buffer = empty_buffer; current_bit = 0; return temp; }
        data_compressor() { } /* C++ constructor */
        ~data_compressor() { } /* C++ destructor */
};
```

Now let's implement the encode() method. The main challenge here is managing the buffer.

```
boolean data_compressor::encode(char isymbol, data_buffer& fullbuf) {
    data_buffer temp;
    int overlen;

    /* look up the new symbol */
    temp = table.value(isymbol); /* the symbol itself */
    /* will this symbol overflow the buffer? */
    overlen = temp.length() + current_bit – buffer.length();
            /* amount of overflow */
    if ( overlen > 0 ) { /* we did in fact overflow */
```

```
            data_buffer nextbuf;
            buffer.insert(temp,nextbuf);
            /* return the full buffer and keep the next partial buffer */
            fullbuf = buffer;
            buffer = nextbuf;
            return TRUE;
        } else { /* no overflow */
            data_buffer no_overflow;
            buffer.insert(temp,no_overflow); /* won't use this argument */
            if (current_bit == buffer.length()) { /* return current buffer */
                fullbuf = buffer;
                buffer.initialize(); /* initialize the buffer */
                return TRUE;
                }
            else return FALSE; /* buffer isn't full yet */
        }
    }
}
```

How would we have to modify the implementation for C? We have two choices in implementation, based on whether we want to support multiple simultaneous data compressors. If we want to strictly adhere to the specification, we must be able to run several simultaneous compressors, since in the object-oriented specification we can create as many new *data-compressor* objects as we want.

non–object-oriented implementation We may not have the luxury of coding the algorithm in C++. While C is almost universally supported on embedded processors, support for languages that support object orientation such as C++ or Java is not so universal. How would we have to structure C code to provide multiple instantiations of the data compressor? The fundamental point is that we cannot rely on any global variables—all of the object state must be replicable. We can do this relatively easily, making the code only a little more cumbersome. We create a structure that holds the data part of the object as follows:

```
struct data_compressor_struct {
    data_buffer buffer;
    int current_bit;
    sym_table table;
}
typedef struct data_compressor_struct data_compressor,
    *data_compressor_ptr; /* data type declaration for convenience */
```

We would, of course, have to do something similar for the other classes. Depending on how strict we want to be, we may want to define data access functions to get to fields in the various structures we create. C would permit us

to get to those struct fields without using the access functions, but using the access functions would give us a little extra freedom to modify the structure definitions later.

We then implement the class methods as C functions, passing in a pointer to the data_compressor object we want to operate on. Appearing below is the beginning of the modified encode method showing how we make explicit all references to the data in the object.

```
typedef char boolean; /* for clarity */
#define TRUE 1
#define FALSE 0

boolean data_compressor_encode(data_compressor_ptr mycmprs,
            char isymbol, data_buffer& fullbuf) {
    data_buffer temp;
    int len, overlen;

    /* look up the new symbol */
    temp = mycmprs->table[isymbol].value; /* the symbol itself */
    len = mycmprs->table[isymbol].length; /* its value */
    ...
```

(For C++ afficionados, the above amounts to making explicit the C++ this pointer.)

If, on the other hand, we didn't care about the ability to run multiple compressions simultaneously, we can make the functions a little more readable by using global variables for the class variables:

```
static data_buffer buffer;
static int current_bit;
static sym_table table;
```

We have used the C static declaration to ensure that these globals are not defined outside the file in which they are defined; this gives us a little added modularity. We would, of course, have to update the specification so that it makes clear that only one compressor object can be running at a time. The functions that implement the methods can then operate directly on the globals as seen below.

```
boolean data_compressor_encode(char isymbol,
                                data_buffer& fullbuf) {
    data_buffer temp;
    int len, overlen;
```

```
/* look up the new symbol */
temp = table[isymbol].value; /* the symbol itself */
len = table[isymbol].length; /* its value */
...
```

Notice that this code does not need the structure pointer argument, making it resemble the C++ code a little more closely. However, horrible bugs will ensue if we try to run two different compressions at the same time through this code.

What can we say about the efficiency of this code? Efficiency has many aspects covered in more detail in Chapter 5. For the moment, let's consider instruction selection, that is, how well the compiler does in choosing the right instructions to implement the operations. Bit manipulations such as we do here often raise concerns about efficiency. But if we have a good compiler and we select the right data types, instruction selection is usually not a problem. If we use data types that don't require data type transformations, a good compiler can select the right instructions to efficiently implement the required operations.

3.8.4 Testing

How do we test this program module to be sure it works? We consider testing much more thoroughly in Section 5.9. In the meantime, we can use common sense to come up with some testing techniques.

One way to test the code is to run it and look at the output without considering how the code is written. In this case, we can load up a symbol table, run some symbols through it, and see whether we get the correct result. We can get the symbol table from outside sources (such as the table of Application Example 3-4) or by writing a small program to generate it ourselves. We should test several different symbol tables. We can get an idea of how thoroughly we are covering the possibilities by looking at the encoding trees—if we choose several very different looking encoding trees, we are likely to cover more of the functionality of the module. We also want to test enough symbols for each symbol table. One way to help automate testing is to write a Huffman decoder. As illustrated in Figure 3-29, we can run a set of symbols through the encoder, and then through the decoder, and simply make sure that the input and output are the same. If they are not, we have to check both the encoder and decoder to locate the problem, but since most practical systems will require both in any case, this is a minor concern.

Another way to test the code is to examine the code itself and try to identify potential problem areas. When we read the code, we should look for places where data operations take place to see that they are performed properly. We

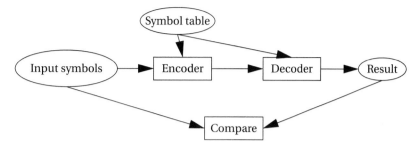

Figure 3-29 *A test of the encoder.*

also want to look at the conditionals to identify different cases that need to be exercised. Some ideas of things to look out for are listed below.

- Is it possible to run past the end of the symbol table?

- What happens when the next symbol does not fill up the buffer?

- What happens when the next symbol exactly fills up the buffer?

- What happens when the next symbol overflows the buffer?

- Do very long encoded symbols work properly? How about very short ones?

- Does flush() work properly?

Testing the internals of code often requires building **scaffolding code.** For example, we may want to test the insert method separately, which would require building a program that calls the method with the proper values. If our programming language comes with an interpreter, building such scaffolding is easier because we don't have to create a complete executable, but we often want to automate such tests even with interpreters because we will usually execute them several times.

3.9 Summary

Numerous mechanisms must be used to implement complete computer systems. For example, interrupts have little direct visibility in the instruction set, but they are very important to input and output operations. Similarly, memory management is invisible to most of the program but is very important to creating a working system.

Although we are not directly concerned with the details of computer architecture, characteristics of the underlying CPU hardware have a major impact

on programs. When designing embedded systems, we are typically concerned about characteristics such as execution speed or power consumption. Having some understanding of the factors that determine performance and power will help you later as you develop techniques for optimizing programs to meet these criteria.

What We Learned

- Two major styles of I/O are polled and interrupt driven.

- Interrupts may be vectorized and prioritized.

- Supervisor mode helps protect the computer from program errors and provides a mechanism for controlling multiple programs.

- An exception is an internal error; a trap or software interrupt is explicitly generated by an instruction. Both are handled similarly to interrupts.

- A cache provides fast storage for a small number of main memory locations. Caches may be direct mapped or set associative.

- A memory management unit translates addresses from logical to physical addresses.

- Co-processors provide a way to optionally implement certain instructions in hardware.

- Program performance can be influenced by pipelining, superscalar execution, and the cache. Of these, the cache introduces the most variability into instruction execution time.

- CPUs may provide static (independent of program behavior) or dynamic (influenced by currently executing instructions) methods for managing power consumption.

Further Reading

As with instruction sets, the ARM and SHARC manuals provide good descriptions of exceptions, memory management, and caches for those processors. Patterson and Hennessy [Pat98] provide a thorough description of computer architecture, including pipelining, caches, and memory management.

Questions

Q3-1 Why do most computer systems use memory-mapped I/O?

Q3-2 Write ARM code that tests a register at location ds1 and continues execution only when the register is nonzero.

Q3-3 Write SHARC code that tests a register at location ds1 and continues execution only when the register is nonzero.

Q3-4 Write ARM code that waits for the low-order bit of device register ds1 to become 1 and then reads a value from register dd1.

Q3-5 Implement peek() and poke() in assembly language for ARM.

Q3-6 Write SHARC code that waits for the low-order bit of device register ds1 to become 1 and then reads a value from register dd1.

Q3-7 Implement peek() and poke() in assembly language for SHARC.

Q3-8 Draw a UML sequence diagram for a busy-wait read of a device. The diagram should include the program running on the CPU and the device.

Q3-9 Draw a UML sequence diagram for a busy-wait write of a device. The diagram should include the program running on the CPU and the device.

Q3-10 Draw a UML sequence diagram for copying characters from an input to an output device using busy-wait I/O. The diagram should include the two devices and the two busy-wait I/O handlers.

Q3-11 When would you prefer to use busy-wait I/O over interrupt-driven I/O?

Q3-12 Draw a UML sequence diagram for an interrupt-driven read of a device. The diagram should include the background program, the handler, and the device.

Q3-13 Draw a UML sequence diagram for an interrupt-driven write of a device. The diagram should include the background program, the handler, and the device.

Q3-14 Draw a UML sequence diagram for a vectored interrupt-driven read of a device. The diagram should include the background program, the interrupt vector table, the handler, and the device.

Q3-15 Draw a UML sequence diagram for copying characters from an input to an output device using interrupt-driven I/O. The diagram should include the two devices and the two I/O handlers.

Q3-16 Draw a UML sequence diagram of a higher-priority interrupt that happens during a lower-priority interrupt handler. The diagram should include the device, the two handlers, and the background program.

Q3-17 Draw a UML sequence diagram of a lower-priority interrupt that happens during a higher-priority interrupt handler. The diagram should include the device, the two handlers, and the background program.

Q3-18 Draw a UML sequence diagram of a nonmaskable interrupt that happens during a low-priority interrupt handler. The diagram should include the device, the two handlers, and the background program.

Q3-19 Three devices are attached to a microprocessor: Device 1 has highest priority and device 3 has lowest priority. Each device's interrupt handler takes 5 time units to execute. Show what interrupt handler (if any) is executing at each time given the sequence of device interrupts displayed below.

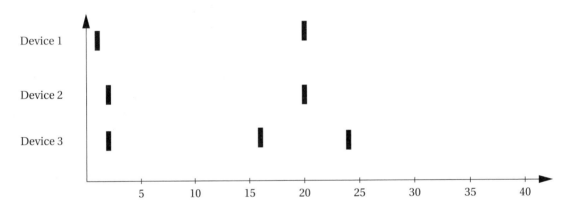

Q3-20 Draw a UML sequence diagram that shows how an ARM processor goes into supervisor mode. The diagram should include the supervisor mode program and the user mode program.

Q3-21 Draw a UML sequence diagram that shows how an ARM processor handles a floating-point exception. The diagram should include the user program, the exception handler, and the exception handler table.

Q3-22 Provide examples of how each of the following can occur in a typical program:

a. compulsory miss

b. capacity miss

c. conflict miss

Q3-23 What is the average memory access time of a machine whose hit rate is 93%, with a cache access time of 5 ns and a main memory access time of 80 ns?

Q3-24 If we want an average memory access time of 6.5 ns, our cache access time is 5 ns, and our main memory access time is 80 ns, what cache hit rate must we achieve?

Q3-25 Assume that a system has a two-level cache: The level 1 cache has a hit rate of 90% and the level 2 cache has a hit rate of 97%. The level 1 cache access time is 4 ns, the level 2 access time is 15 ns, and the level 3 access time is 80 ns. What is the average memory access time?

Q3-26 In the two-way, set-associative cache with four sets of Example 3-9, show the state of the cache after each memory access, as was done for the direct-mapped cache. Use an LRU replacement policy.

Q3-27 The following code is executed by an ARM processor with each instruction executed exactly once:

```
        MOV r0,#0        ; use r0 for i, set to 0
        LDR r1,#10       ; get value of N for loop termination test
        MOV r2,#0        ; use r2 for f, set to 0
        ADR r3,c         ; load r3 with address of base of c array
        ADR r5,x         ; load r5 with address of base of x array
        ; loop test
loop    CMP r0,r1
        BGE loopend      ; if i >= N, exit loop
        ; loop body
        LDR r4,[r3,r0]   ; get value of c[i]
        LDR r6,[r5,r0]   ; get value of x[i]
        MUL r4,r4,r6     ; compute c[i]*x[i]
        ADD r2,r2,r4     ; add into running sum f
        ; update loop counter
        ADD r0,r0,#1     ; add 1 to i
        B loop           ; unconditional branch to top of loop
```

Show the contents of the instruction cache for these configurations, assuming each line holds one ARM instruction:

a. direct-mapped, four lines

b. direct-mapped, eight lines

c. two-way set-associative, four lines per set

Q3-28 Show a UML state diagram for a paged address translation using a flat page table.

Q3-29 Show a UML state diagram for a paged address translation using a three-level, tree-structured page table.

Q3-30 What are the three stages in an ARM pipeline?

Q3-31 What is the difference between latency and throughput?

Q3-32 Draw two pipeline diagrams showing what happens when an ARM BZ instruction is taken and not taken, respectively.

Q3-33 Name three mechanisms by which a CMOS microprocessor consumes power.

Q3-34 Provide a user-level example of

 a. static power management

 b. dynamic power management

Q3-35 Why can't you use the same mechanism to return from a sleep power-saving state as you do from an idle power-saving state?

Lab Exercises

L3-1 Write a simple loop that lets you exercise the cache. By changing the number of statements in the loop body, you can vary the cache hit rate of the loop as it executes. If your microprocessor fetches instructions from off-chip memory, you should be able to observe changes in the speed of execution by observing the microprocessor bus.

L3-2 Try to measure the time required to respond to an interrupt.

Chapter

The Embedded Computing Platform

- CPU buses, I/O devices, and interfacing.

- The CPU system as a framework for understanding design methodology.

- Development environments and debugging.

- An alarm clock design.

4.1 Introduction

In this chapter, we concentrate on **computing platforms** created using microprocessors, I/O devices, and memory components. The microprocessor is an important element of the embedded computing system, but it cannot do its job without memories and I/O devices. We need to understand how to interconnect microprocessors and devices using the CPU bus. Luckily, there are many similarities between the platforms required for different applications, so we can extract some generally useful principles by examining a few basic concepts.

In the next section, we study the CPU bus, which forms the backbone of the hardware system. Because memories are very important components of embedded platforms, Section 4.3 studies types of memory devices. Section 4.4 introduces a variety of types of I/O devices. Section 4.5 introduces basic techniques for interfacing memories and I/O devices to the CPU bus. Section 4.6 focuses on the structure of the complete platform, while Section 4.7 considers development and debugging. In Section 4.8 we will introduce some basic concepts in manufacturing testing, which is important to be sure that the platform

has been properly built. Section 4.9 wraps up with an alarm clock as a design example.

4.2 The CPU Bus

A computer system encompasses much more than the CPU; it also includes memory and I/O devices. The **bus** is the mechanism by which the CPU communicates with memory and devices. A **bus** is, at a minimum, a collection of wires, but the bus also defines a protocol by which the CPU, memory, and devices communicate. One of the major roles of the bus is to provide an interface to memory. (Of course, I/O devices also connect to the bus.) Based on understanding of the bus, we study the characteristics of memory components in this section.

4.2.1 Bus Protocols

The basic building block of most bus protocols is the **four-cycle handshake,** illustrated in Figure 4-1. The handshake ensures that when two devices want to communicate, one is ready to transmit and the other is ready to receive. The handshake uses a pair of wires dedicated to the handshake: **enq** (meaning enquiry) and **ack** (meaning acknowledge). Extra wires are used for the data transmitted during the handshake. The four cycles are described below.

1. *Device 1* raises its output to signal an enquiry, which tells *device 2* that it should get ready to listen for data.

2. When *device 2* is ready to receive, it raises its output to signal an acknowledgment. At this point, *devices 1* and *2* can transmit or receive.

3. Once the data transfer is complete, *device 2* lowers its output, signaling that it has received the data.

4. After seeing that *ack* has been released, *device 1* lowers its output.

At the end of the handshake, both handshaking signals are low, just as they were at the start of the handshake. The system has thus returned to its original state in readiness for another handshake-enabled data transfer.

bus reads and writes Microprocessor buses build on the handshake for communication between the CPU and other system components. The term *bus* is used in two ways. The most basic use is as a set of related wires, such as address wires. However, the term may also mean a protocol for communicating between components. To avoid confusion, we will use the term **bundle** to refer to a set of related signals.

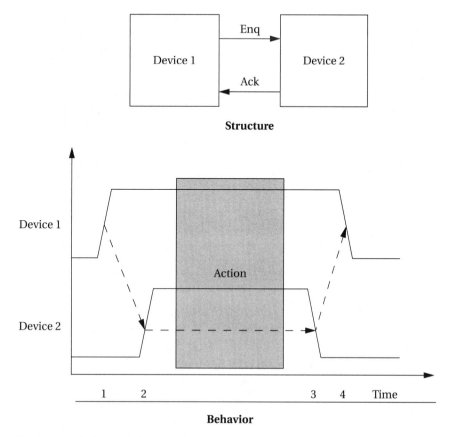

Figure 4-1 *The four-cycle handshake.*

The fundamental bus operations are reading and writing. Figure 4-2 shows the structure of a typical bus that supports reads and writes. The major components follow:

- *Clock* provides synchronization to the bus components,

- *R/W'* is true when the bus is reading and false when the bus is writing,

- *Address* is an *a*-bit bundle of signals that transmits the address for an access,

- *Data* is an *n*-bit bundle of signals that can carry data to or from the CPU, and

- *Data ready'* signals when the values on the data bundle are valid.

All transfers on this basic bus are controlled by the CPU—the CPU can read or write a device or memory, but devices or memory cannot initiate a transfer. This is reflected by the fact that *R/W'* and address are unidirectional signals, since only the CPU can determine the address and direction of the transfer.

The behavior of a bus is most often specified as a **timing diagram.** A timing diagram shows how the signals on a bus vary over time, but since values like the address and data can take on many values, some standard notation is used to describe signals, as shown in Figure 4-3. *A's* value is known at all times, so it

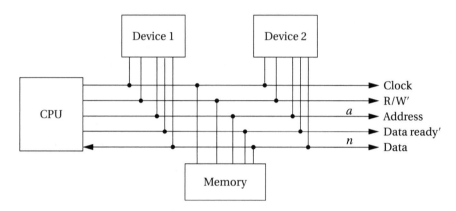

Figure 4-2 *A typical microprocessor bus.*

Figure 4-3 *Timing diagram notation.*

is shown as a standard waveform that changes between zero and one. *B* and *C* alternate between **changing** and **stable** states. A stable signal has, as the name implies, a stable value that could be measured by an oscilloscope, but the exact value of that signal does not matter for purposes of the timing diagram. For example, an address bus may be shown as stable when the address is present, but the bus's timing requirements are independent of the exact address on the bus. A signal can go between a known 0/1 state and a stable/changing state. A changing signal does not have a stable value. Changing signals should not be used for computation. To be sure that signals go to their proper values at the proper times, timing diagrams sometimes show **timing constraints.** We draw timing constraints in two different ways, depending on whether we are concerned with the amount of time between events or only the order of events. The timing constraint from *A* to *B*, for example, shows that *A* must go high before *B* becomes stable. The constraint from *A* to *B* also has a time value of 10 ns, indicating that *A* goes high at least 10 ns before *B* goes stable.

Figure 4-4 shows a timing diagram for the example bus. The diagram shows a read and a write. Timing constraints are shown only for the read operation, but similar constraints apply to the write operation. The bus is normally in the read mode since that does not change the state of any of the devices or memories. The CPU can then ignore the bus data lines until it wants to use the results of a read. Notice also that the direction of data transfer on bidirectional lines is not specified in the timing diagram. During a read, the external device or memory is sending a value on the data lines, while during a write the CPU is controlling the data lines.

With practice, we can see the sequence of operations for a read on the timing diagram as follows:

- A read or write is initiated by setting address enable high after the clock starts to rise. We set $R/W' = 1$ to indicate a read, and the address lines are set to the desired address.

- One clock cycle later, the memory or device is expected to assert the data value at that address on the data lines. Simultaneously, the external device specifies that the data are valid by pulling down the data ready′ line. This line is **active low,** meaning that a logically true value is indicated by a low voltage, in order to provide increased immunity to electrical noise.

- The CPU is free to remove the address at the end of the clock cycle and must do so before the beginning of the next cycle. The external device has a similar requirement for removing the data value from the data lines.

The write operation has a similar timing structure. The read/write sequence does illustrate that timing constraints are required on the transition of the R/W' signal between read and write states. The signal must, of course,

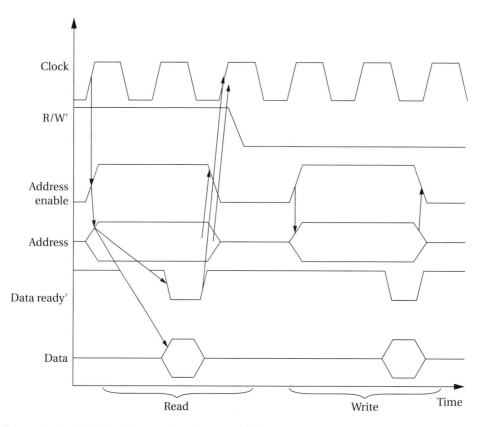

Figure 4-4 *Timing diagram for the example bus.*

remain stable within a read or write. As a result there is a restricted time window in which the CPU can change between read and write modes.

The handshake that tells the CPU and devices when data are to be transferred is formed by data ready' for the acknowledge side, but is implicit for the enquiry side. Since the bus is normally in read mode, enq does not need to be asserted, but the acknowledge must be provided by *data ready'*.

The *data ready'* signal allows the bus to be connected to devices that are slower than the bus. As shown in Figure 4-5, the external device need not immediately assert *data ready'*. The cycles between the minimum time at which data can be asserted and when it is actually asserted are known as **wait states.** Wait states are commonly used to connect slow, inexpensive memories to buses.

We can also use the bus handshaking signals to perform **burst transfers,** as illustrated in Figure 4-6. In this burst read transaction, the CPU sends one address but receives a sequence of data values. We add an extra line to the bus,

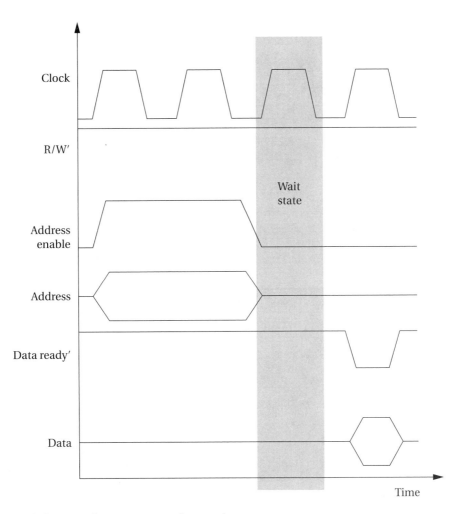

Figure 4-5 *A wait state on a read operation.*

called *burst'* here, which signals when a transaction is actually a burst. Releasing the *burst'* signal tells the device that enough data has been transmitted. To stop receiving data after the end of *data 4*, the CPU releases the *burst'* signal at the end of *data 3* since the device requires some time to recognize the end of the burst. Those values come from successive memory locations starting at the given address.

Some buses provide **disconnected transfers.** In these buses, the request and response are separate. A first operation requests the transfer. The bus can then be used for other operations. The transfer is completed later, when the data are ready.

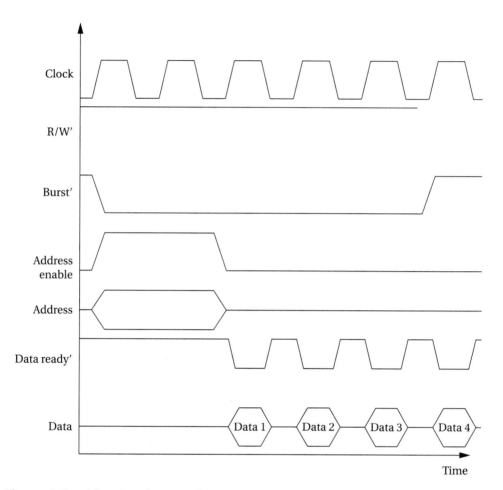

Figure 4-6 *A burst read transaction.*

The state machine view of the bus transaction is also helpful and a useful complement to the timing diagram. Figure 4-7 shows the CPU and device state machines for the read operation. As with a timing diagram, we do not show all the possible values of address and data lines but instead concentrate on the transitions of control signals. When the CPU decides to perform a read transaction, it moves to a new state, sending bus signals that cause the device to behave appropriately. The device's state transition graph captures its side of the protocol.

Some buses have data bundles that are smaller than the natural word size of the CPU. Using fewer data lines reduces the cost of the chip. Such buses are

easiest to design when the CPU is natively addressable. A more complicated protocol hides the smaller data sizes from the instruction execution unit in the CPU. Byte addresses are sequentially sent over the bus, receiving one byte at a time; the bytes are assembled inside the CPU's bus logic before being presented to the CPU proper.

Some buses use multiplexed address and data. As shown in Figure 4-8, additional control lines are provided to tell whether the value on the address/data lines is an address or data. Typically, the address comes first on the combined address/data lines, followed by the data. The address can be held in a register until the data arrive so that both can be presented to the device (such as a RAM) at the same time.

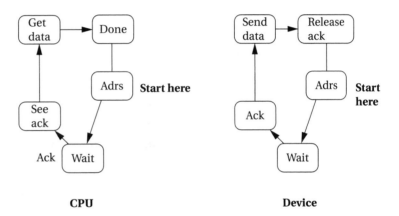

Figure 4-7 *State diagrams for the bus read transaction.*

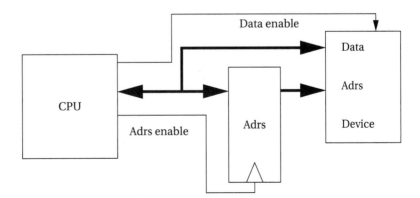

Figure 4-8 *Bus signals for multiplexing address and data.*

4.2.2 DMA

Standard bus transactions require the CPU to be in the middle of every read and write transaction. However, there are certain types of data transfers in which the CPU does not need to be involved. For example, a high-speed I/O device may want to transfer a block of data into memory. While it is possible to write a program that alternately reads the device and writes to memory, it would be faster to eliminate the CPU's involvement and let the device and memory communicate directly. This capability requires that some unit other than the CPU be able to control operations on the bus.

Direct memory access (DMA) is a bus operation that allows reads and writes not controlled by the CPU. A DMA transfer is controlled by a **DMA controller,** which requests control of the bus from the CPU. After gaining control, the DMA controller performs read and write operations directly between devices and memory.

Figure 4-9 shows the configuration of a bus with a DMA controller. The DMA requires the CPU to provide two additional bus signals:

■ The **bus request** is an input to the CPU through which DMA controllers ask for ownership of the bus.

■ The **bus grant** signals that the bus has been granted to the DMA controller.

A device that can initiate its own bus transfer is known as a **bus master.** Devices that do not have the capability to be **bus masters** do not need to connect to a bus request and bus grant. The DMA controller uses these two signals

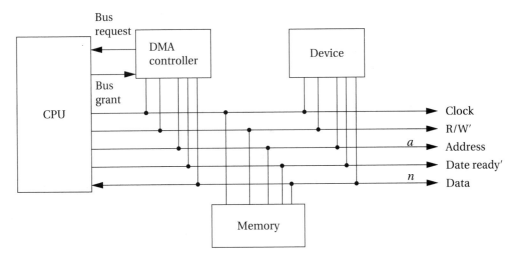

Figure 4-9 *A bus with a DMA controller.*

to gain control of the bus using a classic four-cycle handshake. The bus request is asserted by the DMA controller when it wants to control the bus, and the bus grant is asserted by the CPU when the bus is ready. The CPU will finish all pending bus transactions before granting control of the bus to the DMA controller. When it does grant control, it stops driving the other bus signals: R/W′, address, and so on. Upon becoming bus master, the DMA controller has control of all bus signals (except, of course, for bus request and bus grant).

Once the DMA controller is bus master, it can perform reads and writes using the same bus protocol as with any CPU-driven bus transaction. Memory and devices do not know whether a read or write is performed by the CPU or by a DMA controller. After the transaction is finished, the DMA controller returns the bus to the CPU by deasserting the bus request, causing the CPU to deassert the bus grant.

The CPU controls the DMA operation through registers in the DMA controller. A typical DMA controller includes the following three registers:

- A starting address register specifies where the transfer is to begin.

- A length register specifies the number of words to be transferred.

- A status register allows the DMA controller to be operated by the CPU.

The CPU initiates a DMA transfer by setting the starting address and length registers appropriately and then writing the status register to set its start transfer bit. After the DMA operation is complete, the DMA controller interrupts the CPU to tell it that the transfer is done.

concurrency during DMA

What is the CPU doing during a DMA transfer? It cannot use the bus. As illustrated in Figure 4-10, if the CPU has enough instructions and data in the cache and registers, it may be able to continue doing useful work for quite some time and may not notice the DMA transfer. But once the CPU needs the bus, it stalls until the DMA controller returns bus mastership to the CPU.

To prevent the CPU from idling for too long, most DMA controllers implement modes that occupy the bus for only a few cycles at a time. For example, the transfer may be made 4, 8, or 16 words at a time. As illustrated in Figure 4-11, after each block, the DMA controller returns control of the bus to the CPU and goes to sleep for a preset period, after which it requests the bus again for the next block transfer.

4.2.3 System Bus Configurations

A microprocessor system often has more than one bus. As shown in Figure 4-12, high-speed devices may be connected to a high-performance bus, while lower-speed devices are connected to a different bus. A small block of logic known as a

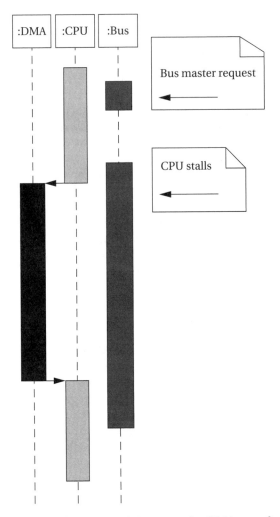

Figure 4-10 *UML sequence diagram of system activity around a DMA transfer.*

bridge allows the buses to connect to each other. Three reasons to do this are summarized below.

- Higher-speed buses may provide wider data connections.

- A high-speed bus usually requires more expensive circuits and connectors. The cost of low-speed devices can be held down by using a lower-speed, lower-cost bus.

■ The bridge may allow the buses to operate independently, thereby providing some parallelism in I/O operations.

In Section 4.6.3, we see that PCs often use this methodology.

bus bridges Let's consider the operation of a bus bridge between what we will call a fast bus and a slow bus as illustrated in Figure 4-13. The bridge is a slave on the fast bus and the master of the slow bus. The bridge takes commands from the fast bus on which it is a slave and issues those commands on the slow bus. It also returns the results from the slow bus to the fast bus—for example, it returns the results of a read on the slow bus to the fast bus.

The upper sequence of states handles a write from the fast bus to the slow bus. These states must read the data from the fast bus and set up the handshake for the slow bus. Operations on the fast and slow sides of the bus bridge should be overlapped as much as possible to reduce the latency of bus-to-bus

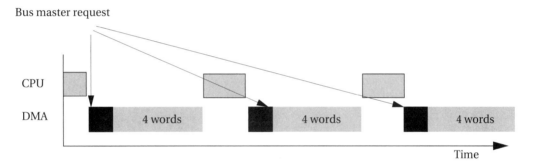

Figure 4-11 *Cyclic scheduling of a DMA request.*

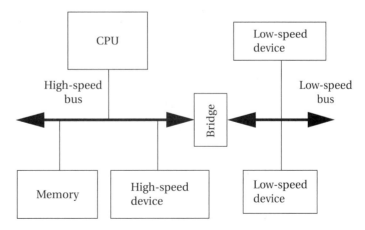

Figure 4-12 *A multibus system.*

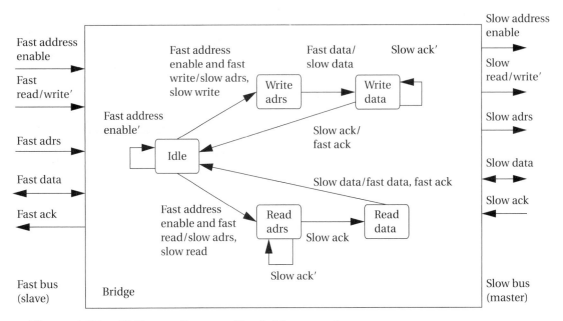

Figure 4-13 *UML state diagram of bus bridge operation.*

transfers. Similarly, the bottom sequence of states reads from the slow bus and writes the data to the fast bus.

The bridge serves as a protocol translator between the two bridges as well. If the bridges are very close in protocol operation and speed, a simple state machine may be enough. If there are larger differences in the protocol and timing between the two buses, the bridge may need to use registers to hold some data values temporarily.

4.2.4 ARM Bus

Since the ARM CPU is manufactured by many different vendors, the bus provided off-chip can vary from chip to chip. ARM has created a separate bus specification for single-chip systems. The AMBA bus [ARM99A] supports CPUs, memories, and peripherals integrated in a system-on-silicon. As shown in Figure 4-14, the AMBA specification includes two buses. The AMBA high-performance bus (AHB) is optimized for high-speed transfers and is directly connected to the CPU. It supports several high-performance features: pipelining, burst transfers, split transactions, and multiple bus masters.

Figure 4-14 *Elements of the ARM AMBA bus system.*

A bridge can be used to connect the AHB to an AMBA peripherals bus (APB). This bus is designed to be simple and easy to implement; it also consumes relatively little power. The AHB assumes that all peripherals act as slaves, simplifying the logic required in both the peripherals and the bus controller. It also does not perform pipelined operations, which simplifies the bus logic.

4.2.5 SHARC Bus

The SHARC uses a different configuration since it contains both program and data memory on-chip. There are two external interfaces of interest: the external memory interface and the host interface. The SHARC's DMA system can be used to transfer data between internal memory and external memory or devices.

external memory interface
The external memory interface allows the SHARC to address up to four gigawords of external memory. External memory can hold either instructions or data. The external data bus can vary in width from 16 to 48 bits, depending on the type of memory accesses (floating-point, instructions, etc.) and whether DMA will be used to mediate the access. Different units in the processor have different amounts of access to the external memory. The DM bus and I/O processor can access the entire external address space, while the PM address bus (which is only 24 bits wide) can access only 12 megawords. The exchanger memory interface is fairly straightforward. Figure 4-15 summarizes the signals in the interface.

External memory is divided into four banks of equal size. Bank 0 starts at 0x00400000, followed by banks 1, 2, and 3. The size is controlled by the internal register MSIZE(3:0); the size can range from 8 K words to 256 M words. The MS'(3:0) outputs signals indicating which bank is being accessed and can be used as chip select signals. Each bank has its own wait state generator. The WAIT register can be used to set up wait states for external memory banks. The memory above the banks is known as **unbanked external memory.**

host interface The host interface is used to connect the SHARC to standard microprocessor buses. Since that CPU will typically be used to set up DSP operations to be performed by the SHARC, it is referred to as the host system. The host interface implements a typical handshake for bus granting. The signals in the host interface are summarized in Figure 4-16. Once the host processor has control of the bus using *HBR'*, *HBG'*, and *REDY*, it can read and write the SHARC's internal memory and the IOP registers.

SHARC DMA The SHARC includes an on-board DMA controller as part of the I/O processor. The DMA controller can perform external port block data transfers and

ADDR(31:0)	External address bus
DATA(47:0)	External data bus
MS'(3:0)	Memory bank select
RD'	Read strobe
WR'	Write strobe
PAGE	DRAM page boundary
SW'	Synchronous write select
ACK	Acknowledge

Figure 4-15 *SHARC external memory interface signals.*

HBR'	Host bus request
HBG'	Host bus grant
CS'	Chip select
REDY	Host bus acknowledge
SBTS'	Suspend bus tristate

Figure 4-16 *SHARC host interface signals.*

data transfers on the link and serial ports. The channels are assigned to various uses, including external memory, link ports, or serial ports. The controller has ten channels that can be directed to any of the external targets. The external and link port DMA channels can be used for bidirectional transfers, while the serial port DMA channels are unidirectional.

A DMA channel operates in a manner similar to the data address generators. An index register (IIx), which holds the base address, and a modify register (IMx), which holds the increment address, configure a data buffer in internal memory. The index register address is actually an offset; that value is offset by 0x00020000 (the address of the first internal RAM location). After each transfer, the DMA controller updates the current address by the IMx value. Each channel also has a count register (Cx) that holds the number of words to be transferred. DMA transfers are mostly fixed priority—serial ports have the highest priority, then link ports, and then external ports. However, external port priorities can be put in a rotating priority mode. A DMA transfer is started by writing parameters to the IIx, IMx, and Cx registers while the DMA enable bit (DEN) is low and then setting DEN to 1 to enable DMA.

Each DMA channel has its own interrupt. When a channel's Cx register goes to zero, an interrupt is generated to signal the end of that transfer. The interrupt priorities of the channels are fixed, but DMA interrupts can be masked and disabled.

The DMA controller supports chained DMA transfers. When used in chain mode, the controller automatically sets up the next DMA operation. A chain pointer register (CP) points to the next set of DMA parameters that are stored in internal memory. Upon completing one transfer, the DMA controller automatically reads the channel parameters from the location pointed to by the CP and uses them to update the registers for the next transfer. The transfer automatically begins without having to set DEN to 0 and back to 1.

4.3 Memory Devices

In this section, we introduce the basic types of memory components that are commonly used in embedded systems. Now that we understand the operation of the bus, we are able to understand the pinouts of these memories and how values are read and written. We also need to understand the varieties of memory cells that are used to build memories. There are several varieties of both read-only and read/write memories, each with its own advantages. After discussing some basic characteristics of memories, we describe RAMs and then ROMs.

4.3.1 Memory Device Organization

The most basic way to characterize a memory is by its capacity, such as 4 Mbits. However, manufacturers usually make several versions of a memory of a given size, each with a different data width. For example, a 4-Mbit memory may be available in the following two versions:

- As a 1 M × 4-bit array, a single memory access obtains a 4-bit data item, with a maximum of 2^{20} different addresses.

- As a 4 M by 1-bit array, a single memory access obtains a 1-bit data item, with a maximum of 2^{22} different addresses.

The height/width ratio of a memory is known as its **aspect ratio.** The best aspect ratio depends on the amount of memory required.

Internally, the data are stored in a two-dimensional array of memory cells as shown in Figure 4-17. Because the array is stored in two dimensions, the *n*-bit address received by the chip is split into a row and a column address (with $n = r + c$). The row and column select a particular memory cell. If the memory's external width is 1 bit, the column address selects a single bit; for wider data widths, the column address can be used to select a subset of the columns. Most memories include an *enable* signal that controls the tri-stating of data onto the

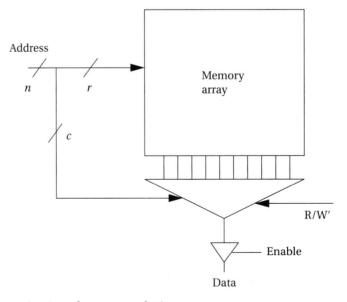

Figure 4-17 *Internal organization of a memory device.*

memory's pins. We will see in Section 4.5.1 how the enable pin can be used to easily build large memories from multiple banks of memory chips. A read/write signal (R/W' in the figure) on read/write memories controls the direction of data transfer; memory chips do not typically have separate read and write data pins.

4.3.2 Random-Access Memories

Random-access memories can be both read and written. They are called random access because, unlike magnetic disks, addresses can be read in any order.

There are two major categories of **random-access memory (RAM): static RAM (SRAM)** and **dynamic RAM (DRAM).** These two types of memory have substantially different characteristics, as summarized below.

- SRAM is faster than DRAM.

- SRAM consumes more power than DRAM.

- More DRAM can be put on a single chip.

- DRAM values must be periodically refreshed.

We don't need to understand the circuit design of static and dynamic memories for our purposes here. Interested readers can find detailed descriptions in numerous sources [Wol98]. Our interest is in the characteristics of memories that influence system design.

static RAM A static RAM and its operation are shown in Figure 4-18. The static RAM has four inputs:

- CE' is the chip enable input. It is active low. When $CE' = 1$, the SRAM's data pins are disabled, and when $CE' = 0$, the data pins are enabled.

- R/W' controls whether the current operation is a read ($R/W' = 1$) or a write ($R/W' = 0$). Read and write are normally specified relative to the CPU, so read means reading from RAM and write means writing to RAM.

- *Adrs* specifies the address for the read or write.

- *Data* is a bidirectional bundle of signals for data transfer. When $R/W' = 1$, the pins are outputs, and when $R/W' = 0$, the data pins are inputs.

Notice that there is no clock signal—SRAMs do have timing constraints on when signals can change, but they do not change relative to a clock.

A read operation on the SRAM occurs as follows:

Interface

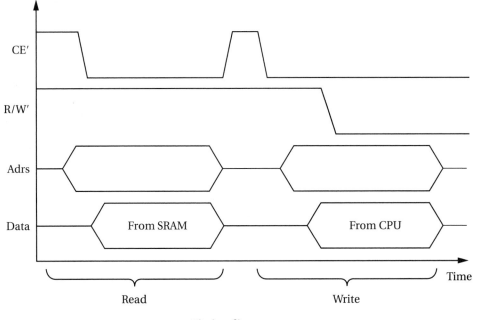

Timing diagram

Figure 4-18 *Static RAM.*

1. *CE'* is set to 0 enabling the chip with $R/W' = 1$.

2. An address is presented on the address lines.

3. After some delay, data appear on the data lines.

A write operation is similar:

1. *CE'* is set to 0.

2. *R/W'* is set to 0 for writing.

3. An address is set on the address lines and data is set on the data lines.

dynamic RAM The interface to a dynamic RAM is more complex because DRAMs are designed to minimize the number of required pins. The interface to a basic dynamic RAM is illustrated in Figure 4-19. In addition to the signals found in an SRAM, the DRAM has **row address select (RAS')** and **column address select (CAS').** These signals are needed because address lines are provided for only half the address. The timing diagram for a read shows that the address is presented in the following two steps:

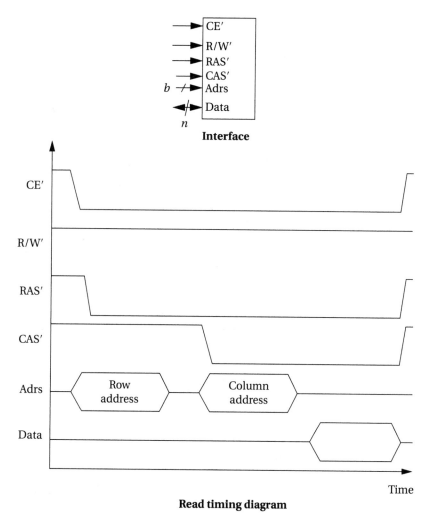

Interface

Read timing diagram

Figure 4-19 *Basic dynamic RAM.*

- First, *RAS'* is set to 0 and the row part of the address (the top bits of the address) is set on the address lines.

- Next, *CAS'* is set to 0 and the column part of the address (the bottom bits of the address) are put on the address lines.

Once again, there is no clock—the control signals are applied asynchronously.

DRAMs must be **refreshed** because of the internal circuitry used to store values. Unlike SRAMs, DRAMs store values on capacitors. Because of parasitic resistances within the chip, the charge stored on the capacitors can leak away. The typical lifetime of data in a dynamic RAM is about a millisecond. The data can be refreshed by performing an internal read operation in which the data value is thrown away. A single refresh request can refresh an entire row of the DRAM. DRAMs provide a special quick refresh mode known as **CAS-before-RAS refresh.** As the name implies, this mode is initiated by setting *CAS'* to 0 before *RAS'* is set to 0. The DRAM keeps an internal counter for the current row to refresh. Asserting *CAS'* before *RAS'* causes the RAM to refresh that row and update the counter. Logic external to the DRAM known as a **memory controller** periodically performs a CAS-before-RAS refresh at a rate that allows the entire memory to be refreshed within the required refresh interval. The interface between the DRAM and the CPU must take refreshes into account—a read or write request cannot be satisfied until a refresh is complete. The memory controller stands between the bus and DRAM and inserts wait states during the intervals in which it is refreshing the memory.

Since programs will often access several locations in the same region of memory, an early feature developed to improve DRAM performance is **page mode.** As shown in Figure 4-20, a page mode access supplies the row address only once but supplies many column addresses. *RAS'* is held down while *CAS'* is strobed to signal the arrival of successive column addresses. Page mode is typically supported for both reads and writes.

An improved version of page mode is known as **EDO** for **extended data out.** A timing diagram for an EDO read is shown in Figure 4-21. An EDO access is similar to page mode in that it allows several column addresses after a single row address. The term *EDO* comes from the fact that the data are held valid until the falling edge of *CAS'*, rather than its rising edge as in page mode.

Another method for improving DRAM performance is to introduce a clock. **Synchronous DRAMs** require events to be referenced to a clock edge; the DRAM's internal circuitry can be made faster because it does not have to derive timing information from asynchronous inputs. As shown in Figure 4-22, a synchronous DRAM has the normal DRAM inputs plus a clock. Changes to the inputs (*RAS'*, *CAS'*, etc.) occur on clock edges, as do DRAM outputs. As a result, the behavior of the part can be described as a finite state machine. The

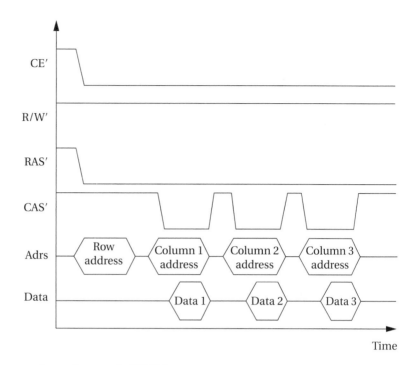

Figure 4-20 *Page mode read access in DRAMs.*

figure shows the basic state transition graph. The default mode for the synchronous DRAM is to be ready to accept a row address; the DRAM can then go into read or write actions, depending on the command it receives from the inputs.

Other types of RAMs with more sophisticated interfaces have been developed for specialized applications:

- A **video RAM** is designed to speed up video operations. It includes a standard parallel interface, as well as a serial interface fed by a shift register. The shift register can provide bit-by-bit access to the data in parallel with other operations performed on the parallel interface. The serial interface is typically connected to a video display while the parallel interface connects to the microprocessor.

- Rambus is designed to be a high-performance but relatively low-cost RAM system. It includes multiple memory banks that can be addressed in parallel. A variety of features, such as separate control and data buses, contribute to a sustained data transfer rate of well over one gigabyte per second.

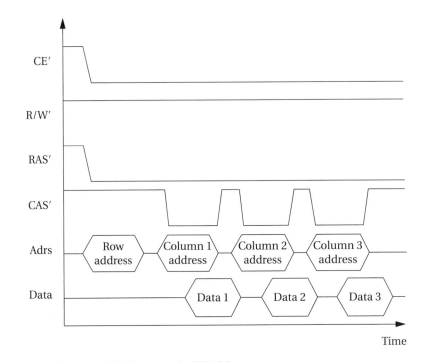

Figure 4-21 *Extended–data-out (EDO) access in DRAMs.*

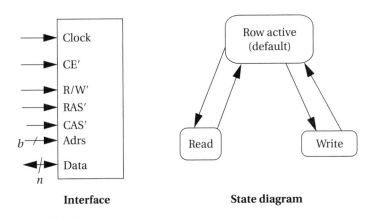

Interface **State diagram**

Figure 4-22 *Synchronous DRAM.*

4.3.3 Read-Only Memories

Read-only memories (ROMs) are preprogrammed with fixed data. They are very useful in embedded systems since a great deal of the code, and perhaps some data, does not change over time. Read-only memories are also less sensitive to radiation-induced errors.

There are several varieties of ROM available. The first-level distinction to be made is between **factory-programmed ROM** (sometimes called **mask-programmed ROM**) and **field-programmable ROM.** Factory-programmed ROMs are ordered from the factory with particular programming. ROMs can typically be ordered in lots of a few thousand, but clearly factory programming is useful only when the ROMs are to be installed in some quantity. Field-programmable ROMs, on the other hand, can be programmed in the lab. Programming units are sometimes known as **ROM burners.** To program the ROM, the user generates a programming file in a standard format, plugs a ROM into the ROM burner, and sends the file to the burner for programming.

There are several different types of field-programmable ROM available, some of which can be programmed only once and others that can be reprogrammed. **Antifuse-programmable ROM** is programmable only once—the programming permanently modifies the chip. This type of ROM is the cheapest but is less flexible than reprogrammable ROM. **UV-erasable PROM (UV-EPROM)** can be erased using ultraviolet light and then reprogrammed. The chip's package includes a window to allow the UV light to penetrate to the chip; the window must be covered when the chip is in use since the UV content of sunlight is sufficient to erase the chip over a period of months. In addition to raw memory, many microcontrollers come with on-board UV-EPROM for program storage.

Flash PROM is the modern form of electrically erasable PROM. Early forms of electrically erasable memory required high voltages for erasure and programming. This meant that the chips had to be removed from the system for reprogramming. Flash memory uses standard system voltage for erasing and programming, allowing it to be reprogrammed inside a typical system. This allows applications such as automatic distribution of upgrades—the flash memory can be reprogrammed while downloading the new memory contents from a telephone line. Early flash memories had to be erased in their entirety; modern devices allow memory to be erased in blocks. Most flash memories today allow certain blocks to be protected. A common application is to keep the boot-up code in a protected block but allow updates to other memory blocks on the device. As a result, this form of flash is commonly known as **boot-block flash.**

4.4 I/O Devices

In this section we survey some input and output devices commonly used in embedded computing systems. Some of these devices are often found as on-chip devices in microcontrollers; others are generally implemented separately but are still commonly used. Looking at a few important devices now will help us understand both the requirements of device interfacing in this chapter and the uses of devices in programming in this and later chapters.

4.4.1 Timers and Counters

Timers and **counters** are distinguished from one another largely by their use, not their logic. Both are built from adder logic with registers to hold the current value, with an increment input that adds one to the current register value. However, a timer has its count connected to a periodic clock signal to measure time intervals, while a counter has its count input connected to an aperiodic signal in order to count the number of occurrences of some external event. Because the same logic can be used for either purpose, the device is often called a **counter/timer.**

Figure 4-23 shows enough of the internals of a counter/timer to illustrate its operation. An *n*-bit counter/timer uses an *n*-bit register to store the current state of the count and an array of *half subtractors* to decrement the count when the count signal is asserted. Combinational logic checks when the count equals zero; the *done* output signals the zero count. It is often useful to be able to control the time-out, rather than require exactly 2^n events to occur. For this purpose, a reset register provides the value with which the count register is to be loaded. The counter/timer provides logic to load the reset register. Most counters provide both cyclic and acyclic modes of operation. In the cyclic mode, once the counter reaches the *done* state, it is automatically reloaded and the counting process continues. In acyclic mode, the counter/timer waits for an explicit signal from the microprocessor to resume counting.

watchdog timer A **watchdog timer** is an I/O device that is used for internal operation of a system. As shown in Figure 4-24, the watchdog timer is connected into the CPU bus and also to the CPU's reset line. The CPU's software is designed to periodically reset the watchdog timer, before the timer ever reaches its time-out limit. If the watchdog timer ever does reach that limit, its time-out action is to reset the processor. In that case, the presumption is that either a software flaw or hardware problem has caused the CPU to misbehave. Rather than diagnose the problem, the system is reset to get it operational as quickly as possible.

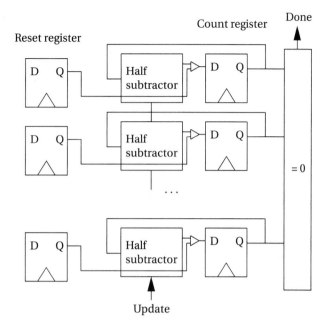

Figure 4-23 *Internals of a counter/timer.*

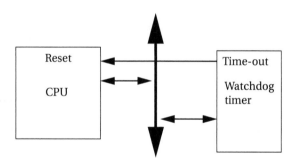

Figure 4-24 *A watchdog timer.*

4.4.2 A/D and D/A Converters

Analog/digital (A/D) and **digital/analog (D/A)** converters (typically known as **ADCs** and **DACs,** respectively) are often used to interface nondigital devices to embedded systems. The design of A/D and D/A converters themselves is beyond the scope of this book; we concentrate instead on the interface to the microprocessor bus. Because A/D conversion requires more complex circuitry, it requires a somewhat more complex interface.

Analog/digital conversion requires sampling the analog input before converting it to digital form. A control signal causes the A/D converter to take a sample and digitize it. There are several different types of A/D converter circuits, some of which take a constant amount of time, while the conversion time of others depends on the sampled value. Variable-time converters provide a done signal so that the microprocessor knows when the value is ready.

A typical A/D interface has, in addition to its analog inputs, two major digital inputs. A data port allows A/D registers to be read and written, and a clock input tells when to start the next conversion.

D/A conversion is relatively simple, so the D/A converter interface generally includes only the data value. The input value is continuously converted to analog form.

4.4.3 Keyboards

A keyboard is basically an array of switches, but it may include some internal logic to help simplify the interface to the microprocessor. In this chapter, we build our understanding from a single switch to a microprocessor-controlled keyboard.

single switch

A switch uses a mechanical contact to make or break an electrical circuit. The major problem with mechanical switches is that they **bounce** as shown in Figure 4-25. When the switch is depressed by pressing on the button attached to the switch's arm, the force of the depression causes the contacts to bounce several times until they settle down. If this is not corrected, it will appear that

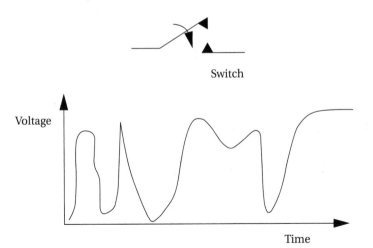

Figure 4-25 *Switch bouncing.*

the switch has been pressed several times, giving false inputs. A hardware **debouncing** circuit can be built using a one-shot timer. Software can also be used to debounce switch inputs. A raw keyboard can be assembled from several switches. Each switch in a raw keyboard has its own pair of terminals, making raw keyboards impractical when a large number of keys is required.

microprocessor controlled

More expensive keyboards, such as those used in PCs, actually contain a microprocessor to preprocess button inputs. PC keyboards typically use a 4-bit microprocessor to provide the interface between the keys and the computer. The microprocessor can provide debouncing, but it also provides other functions as well. An **encoded keyboard** uses some code to represent which switch is currently being depressed. At the heart of the encoded keyboard is the scanned array of switches shown in Figure 4-26. Unlike a raw keyboard, the scanned keyboard array reads only one row of switches at a time. The demultiplexer at the left side of the array selects the row to be read. When the scan input is 1, that value is transmitted to one terminal of each key in the row. If the switch is depressed, the 1 is sensed at that switch's column. Since only one switch in the column is activated, that value uniquely identifies a key. The row address and column output can be used for encoding, or circuitry can be used to give a different encoding.

A consequence of encoding the keyboard is that combinations of keys may not be represented. For example, on a PC keyboard, the encoding must be chosen so that combinations such as control-Q can be recognized and sent to the PC. Another consequence is that **rollover** may not be allowed. For example, if you press 'a', and then press 'b' before releasing 'a', in most applications you want the keyboard to send an 'a' followed by a 'b'. Rollover is very common in typing at even modest rates. A naive implementation of the encoder circuitry will simply throw away any character depressed after the first one until all the

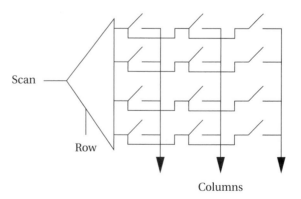

Figure 4-26 *A scanned key array.*

keys are released. The keyboard microcontroller can be programmed to pro-vide **n-key rollover,** so that rollover keys are sensed, put on a stack, and trans-mitted in sequence as keys are released.

4.4.4 LEDs

Light-emitting diodes (LEDs) are often used as simple displays by themselves, and arrays of LEDs may form the basis of more complex displays. Figure 4-27 shows how to connect an LED to a digital output. A resistor is connected between the output pin and the LED to absorb the voltage difference between the digital output voltage and the 0.7 V drop across the on LED. When the digi-tal output goes to 0, the LED voltage is in the device's off region and the LED is not on.

4.4.5 Displays

A display device may be either directly driven or driven from a frame buffer. Typically, displays with a small number of elements are driven directly by logic, while large displays use a RAM frame buffer.

directly driven The *n*-digit array, shown in Figure 4-28, is a simple example of a display that is usually directly driven. A single-digit display typically consists of seven segments; each segment may be either an LED or a **liquid crystal display (LCD)** element. This display relies on the digits being visible for some time after the drive to the digit is removed, which is true for both LEDs and LCDs. The digit input is used to choose which digit is currently being updated, and the selected digit activates its display elements based on the current data

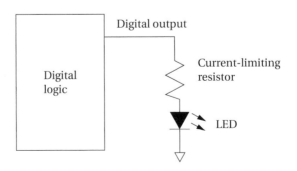

Figure 4-27 *An LED connected to a digital output.*

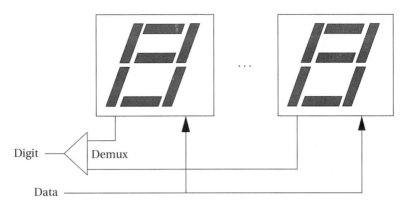

Figure 4-28 *An n-digit display.*

value. The display's driver is responsible for repeatedly scanning through the digits and presenting the current value of each to the display.

A **cathode ray tube (CRT)** can be used as either a directly driven or frame-buffered device. A CRT has horizontal and vertical deflection inputs that position the electron beam over the screen as well as an intensity input that controls the electron beam intensity and therefore the brightness of the pixel at that point. A **calligraphic display** is an example of a directly driven CRT display. For example, if you want to draw a diagonal line, you move the electron beam to the start of the line, turn on the beam, and vary both the horizontal and vertical deflection inputs until you reach the end of the line. CRTs are used in calligraphic mode in aircraft displays because they allow lines to be drawn more brightly.

frame buffer As shown in Figure 4-29, a **frame buffer** is a random-access memory that is attached to the system bus. The microprocessor writes values into the frame buffer in whatever order is desired. When a CRT is connected to a frame buffer, it usually operates in **raster order** by reading pixels sequentially, displaying a row at a time. Because of tradition inherited from broadcast television, displays are scanned from top to bottom and left to right, so the display first draws the topmost line or raster, turns off the beam and moves to the beginning of the second row, and continues to the bottom of the display. At the bottom right corner of the image, the beam is turned off and the vertical and horizontal inputs are returned to the top left corner for the next scan.

LCD panels Large flat panel displays are, at this writing, typically built with LCD. Each pixel in the display is formed by a single liquid crystal. LCD displays present a very different interface to the system because the array of pixel LCDs can be randomly accessed. Early LCD panels were called **passive matrix** because they relied on a two-dimensional grid of wires to address the pixels. Modern LCD panels use an **active matrix** system that puts a transistor at each pixel to

control access to the LCD. Active matrix displays provide higher contrast and a higher-quality display.

4.4.6 Touchscreens

A **touchscreen** is an input device overlaid on an output device. The touchscreen registers the position of a touch to its surface. By overlaying this on a display, the user can react to information shown on the display.

The two most common types of touchscreens are resistive and capacitive. A resistive touchscreen uses a two-dimensional voltmeter to sense position. As shown in Figure 4-30, the touchscreen consists of two conductive sheets separated by spacer balls. The top conductive sheet is flexible so that it can

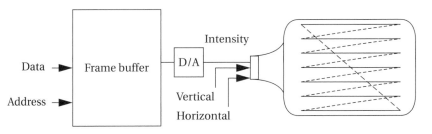

Figure 4-29 *A frame buffer display system.*

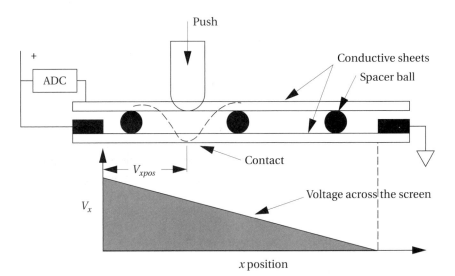

Figure 4-30 *Cross section of a resistive touchscreen.*

be pressed to touch the bottom sheet. A voltage is applied across the sheet; its resistance causes a voltage gradient to appear across the sheet. The top sheet samples the conductive sheet's applied voltage at the contact point. An analog/digital converter is used to measure the voltage and resulting position. The touchscreen alternates between x and y position sensing by alternately applying horizontal and vertical voltage gradients.

4.5 Component Interfacing

Building the logic to interface a device to a bus is not too difficult but does take some attention to detail. We first consider interfacing memory components to the bus, since that is relatively simple, and then use those concepts to interface to other types of devices.

4.5.1 Memory Interfacing

Static RAM is simpler to interface to a bus than is DRAM, due to both the DRAM's RAS'/CAS' multiplexing and the need for refresh. The R/W' on the bus can often be directly connected to the SRAM. The main issue in interfacing SRAM is decoding the address. The chip enable pin is used in RAMs to simplify the interfacing of large memories.

We can easily construct a memory of a given width (8 bits, 16 bits, etc.) by placing RAMs in parallel. After determining the required memory for the application, we can select a particular RAM, such as a 1 M x 8 RAM, depending on availability and cost. If the required number of memory words fits within the height of an available memory, then the interface is simple: The CE' signal is permanently wired to ground so that the chip is always enabled. However, it may not be possible to provide the required memory within a single row of RAMs.

Example 4-1 shows how to design a simple SRAM memory system.

Example 4-1

A Multichip SRAM Memory System

Appearing below is the block diagram for a 2 M $\times$ 16-bit SRAM system built from 1 M $\times$ 8 bit SRAMs. The R/W' signal has been eliminated for clarity.

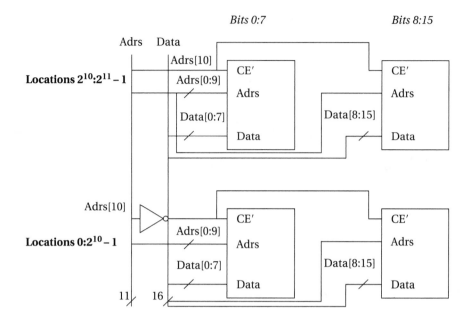

The columns in the figure may be seen as the bytes in the word—the left SRAMs provide the lower eight bits in a word and the right SRAMs give the high-order byte. The 2-megaword memory is built from these 1-megaword rows using the chip enable. A 2-megaword memory requires an 11-bit address, and the 1M SRAMs take 10 bits of memory. The bottom 10 bits of the address can be fed directly from the bus into the address lines. The top bit of the address is used to control *CE'*. The top row of the memory supplies the bottom 1 megaword of memory, so that *adrs[10]* is connected directly to the top row of chips. When addressing the bottom megaword of memory, *adrs[10]* = 0 and the top row of chips is enabled. The inverted form of *adrs[10]* is connected to the chip enables of the bottom row. When addressing the top megaword, *adrs[10]* = 1, so the inverter sets *CE'* = 0 to enable that row of memory.

DRAM interfacing introduces two complications: RAS/CAS addressing and refreshing. The bus address can be split into row and column address with a small amount of logic—a register captures the addresses, a multiplexer selects the row or column portion of the address, and a state machine generates *RAS'* and *CAS'*. The refresh signal can be generated with a counter and a state machine as shown in Figure 4-31. The *counter* times the wait between succes-

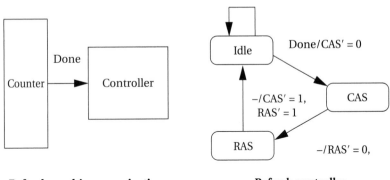

Refresh machine organization **Refresh controller**

Figure 4-31 *A DRAM refresh controller.*

sive refresh actions; the *controller* generates the required signals. In the idle state, the bus signals are passed through to the DRAM to enable reads and writes. When the *counter* rolls over, the *controller* generates *CAS′* and then *RAS′* to induce the next refresh cycle.

4.5.2 Device Interfacing

Some I/O devices are designed to interface directly to a particular bus, forming **glueless interfaces.** But **glue logic** is required when a device is connected to a bus for which it is not designed.

An I/O device typically requires a much smaller range of addresses than a memory, so addresses must be decoded much more finely. Some additional logic is required to cause the bus to read and write the device's registers. Example 4-2 shows one style of interface logic.

Example 4-2

A Glue Logic Interface

Appearing below is an interfacing scheme for a simple I/O device.

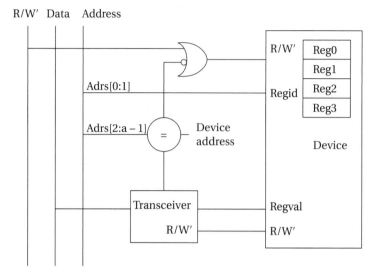

The device has four registers that can be read and written by presenting the register number on the *regid* pins, asserting R/W′ as required, and reading or writing the value on the *regval* pins. To interface to the bus, the bottom two bits of the address are used to refer to registers within the device, and the remaining bits are used to identify the device itself. The top bits of the address are sent to a comparator for testing against the device address. The device's address can be set with switches to allow the address to be easily changed. When the bus address matches the device's, the result is used to enable a *transceiver* for the data pins. When the *transceiver* is disabled, the *regval* pins are disconnected from the data bus. The comparator's output is also used to modify the R/W′ signal: The device's R/W′ pin is given the value (bus R/W′ + not-equal address), so that when the comparator's result is not 1, the device's R/W′ pin always receives a 1 to avoid inadvertently writing the device registers.

4.6 Designing with Microprocessors

In this section we concentrate on how to create an initial working embedded system. The following sections consider how to ensure that the system works properly. Section 4.6.1 considers possible architectures for embedded computing systems. Section 4.6.2 studies techniques for designing the hardware com-

ponents of embedded systems. Section 4.6.3 describes the use of the PC as an embedded computing platform.

4.6.1 System Architecture

We know that an architecture is a set of elements and the relationships between them that together form a single unit. The architecture of an embedded computing system is the blueprint for implementing that system—it tells you what components you need and how you put them together.

The architecture of an embedded computing system includes both hardware and software elements. Let's consider each in turn.

hardware The hardware architecture of an embedded computing system is the more obvious manifestation of the architecture since you can touch it and feel it. It includes several elements, some of which may be less obvious than others.

- *CPU:* An embedded computing system clearly contains a microprocessor. But which one? There are many different architectures, and even within an architecture we can select between models that vary in clock speed, bus data width, integrated peripherals, and so on. The choice of the CPU is one of the most important, but it cannot be made without considering the software that will execute on the machine.

- *Bus:* The choice of a bus is closely tied to that of a CPU, since the bus is an integral part of the microprocessor. But in applications that make intensive use of the bus due to I/O or other data traffic, the bus may be more of a limiting factor than the CPU. Attention must be paid to the required data bandwidths to be sure that the bus can handle the traffic.

- *Memory:* Once again, the question is not whether the system will have memory but the characteristics of that memory. The most obvious characteristic is total size, which depends on both the required data volume and the size of the program instructions. The ratio of ROM to RAM and selection of DRAM versus SRAM can have a significant influence on the cost of the system. The speed of the memory will play a large part in determining system performance.

- *Input and output devices:* The user's view of the input and output mechanisms may not correspond to the devices connected to the microprocessor. For example, a set of switches and knobs on a front panel may all be controlled by a single microcontroller, which is in turn connected to the main CPU. For a given function, there may be several different devices of varying

sophistication and cost that can do the job. The difficulty of using a particular device, such as the amount of glue logic required to interface it, may also play a role in final device selection.

software

You may not think of programs as having architectures, but well-designed programs do have structure that represents an architecture. A fundamental task in software architecture design is **partitioning**—breaking the functionality into pieces in a way that makes it easy to implement, test, and modify.

Most embedded systems will do more than one thing—for example, processing streams of data and handling the user interface. Mixing together different types of functionality into a single code module leads to **spaghetti code,** which has poorly structured control flow, excessive use of global data, and generally unreliable programs.

Breaking the system's functionality into pieces that roughly correspond to the major modes of operation and functions of the device is often a good choice. First, different types of functionality often require different programming styles, so that they will naturally fall into different procedures in the code. Second, the functionality boundaries often correspond to performance requirements. Since at least some of the software components will almost certainly have to finish executing within a given deadline, it is important to be able to identify the code that must satisfy the deadline and to measure the performance of that code.

It is also important to remember that some of the functionality may in fact be implemented in the I/O devices. You may have a choice between using a simple, inexpensive device that requires more software support or a more sophisticated and expensive device that can perform more functions automatically. (An example in the digital audio domain is μ-law scaling, which can be done automatically by some analog/digital converters.) Using DMA to move data rather than a programmed loop is another example of using hardware to substitute for software. Most of the functionality will be in the software, but careful consideration of the hardware architecture can help simplify the software and make it easier for the software to meet its performance requirements.

4.6.2 Hardware Design

The design complexity of the hardware platform can vary greatly, from a totally off-the-shelf solution to a highly customized design.

At the board level, the first step is to consider **evaluation boards** supplied by the microprocessor manufacturer or another company working in collaboration with the manufacturer. Evaluation boards are sold for many microprocessor systems; they typically include the CPU, some memory, a serial link for

downloading programs, and some minimal number of I/O devices. Figure 4-32 shows an ARM evaluation board manufactured by Sharp, and Figure 4-33 shows a SHARC evaluation board from Analog Devices. The evaluation board may be a complete solution or provide what you need with only slight modifications. If the evaluation board is supplied by the microprocessor vendor, its design (netlist, board layout, etc.) may be available from the vendor; companies provide such information to make it easy for customers to use their microprocessors. If the evaluation board comes from a third party, it may be possible to contract them to design a new board with your required modifications, or you can start from scratch on a new board design.

The other major task is the choice of memory and peripheral components. In the case of I/O devices, there are two alternatives for each device: selecting a component from a catalog or designing one yourself. When shopping for devices from a catalog, it is important to read data sheets carefully—it may not be trivial to figure out whether the device does what you need it to do. You

Figure 4-32 *An ARM evaluation board.*

Serial port

Audio input

Audio output

CPU EPROM Reset Power supply

Figure 4-33 *A SHARC evaluation board.*

should also consider the amount of glue logic required to connect the device to your bus. Custom peripherals may be designed as custom **application-specific integrated circuits (ASICs)** or from programmable logic. The design of VLSI ASICs is a discipline in itself [Wol98] and well beyond the scope of this book. Simple peripheral logic can be implemented in **programmable logic devices (PLDs),** while more complex units can be built from **field-programmable gate arrays (FPGAs).**

4.6.3 The PC as a Platform

Personal computers are often used as platforms for embedded computing. A PC offers several important advantages—it is a predesigned hardware platform with a great many features, a wide variety of I/O devices can be purchased for

it, and it provides a rich programming environment. Because a PC-based system does not use custom hardware, it also carries the resulting disadvantages. It is larger, more power-hungry, and more expensive than a custom hardware platform would be. However, for low-volume applications and environments such as factories and offices where size and power are not critical, using a PC to build an embedded system often makes a lot of sense. The term *personal computer* has come to apply to a variety of machines, including IBM-compatibles, Macs, and others. In this section, we describe a generic PC architecture with some discussion of features relevant to different types of PCs. A detailed discussion of any of these platforms is beyond the scope of this book.

As shown in Figure 4-34, a typical PC includes several major hardware components:

- The CPU provides basic computational facilities.

- RAM is used for program storage.

- ROM holds the boot program.

- A DMA controller provides DMA capabilities.

- Timers are used by the operating system for a variety of purposes.

- A high-speed bus, connected to the CPU bus through a bridge, allows fast devices to communicate efficiently with the rest of the system.

- A low-speed bus provides an inexpensive way to connect simpler devices and may be necessary for backward compatibility as well.

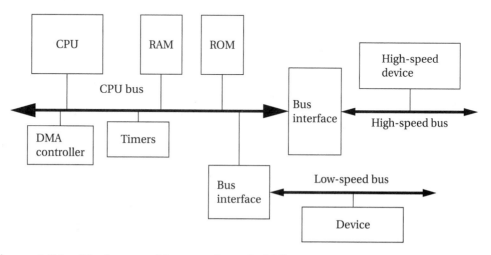

Figure 4-34 *Hardware architecture of a typical PC.*

buses

The typical low-speed bus in IBM-compatible PCs is the **ISA (Industry Standard Architecture)** bus. This bus appeared on the original IBM PC and is closely related to the bus of the Intel 8085 that was used as the IBM PC's CPU. Although relatively high performance for its time, it seems relatively slow by today's standard—the ISA bus runs at 8 MHz. In modern machines it is primarily used for low-speed devices and backward compatibility with older machines.

PCI (peripheral component interconnect) is the dominant high-performance system bus today. PCI uses high-speed data transmission techniques and efficient protocols to achieve high throughput. The original PCI standard allowed operation up to 33 MHz; at that rate, it could achieve a maximum transfer rate of 264 MBytes/sec using 64-bit transfers. The revised PCI standard allows the bus to run up to 66 MHz, giving a maximum transfer rate of 524 MBytes/sec with 64 bit-wide transfers.

ISA and PCI use wide buses with many data and address bits along with multiple control bits. The width of the bus both increases the cost of an interface to the bus and makes the physical connection to the bus more complicated. As a result, PC manufacturers have introduced serial buses to provide high-speed transfers while keeping the cost of connecting to the bus relatively low. **USB** (universal serial bus) and **IEEE 1394** are the two major high-speed serial buses. Both of these buses offer high transfer rates using simple connectors. They also allow devices to be chained together so that users don't have to worry about the order of devices on the bus or other details of connection.

software

A PC also provides a standard software platform that provides interfaces to the underlying hardware as well as more advanced services. At the bottom of the software platform structure in most PCs is a minimal set of software in ROM. This software is designed to load the complete operating system from some other device (disk, network, etc.), and it may also provide low-level hardware interfaces. In the IBM-compatible PC, the low-level software is known as the **BIOS** (basic input/output system). The BIOS provides low-level hardware drivers as well as booting facilities. The operating system provides high-level drivers, control of executing processes, user interfaces, and so on. Because the PC software environment is so rich, developing embedded code for a PC target is much easier than when a host must be connected to a CPU in a development target. However, if the software is delivered directly on a standard version of the operating system, the resulting software package will require significant amounts of RAM as well as occupy a large disk image. Developers often create pared down versions of the operating system for delivering embedded code on PC platforms.

Both the IBM-compatible PC and the Mac provide a combination of hardware and software that allows devices to provide their own configuration information. On the IBM-compatible PC, this is known as the Plug-and-Play standard developed by Microsoft. These standards make it possible to plug in a

single chip

device and have it work directly, without hardware or software intervention from the user.

It is now possible to put all the components (except for memory) for a standard PC on a single chip. A single-chip PC makes the development of certain types of embedded systems much easier, providing the rich software development of a PC with the low cost of a single-chip hardware platform.

The ability to integrate a CPU and devices on a single chip has allowed manufacturers to provide single-chip systems that do not conform to board-level standards. Application Example 4-1 describes one such single-chip system, the Intel StrongARM SA-1100.

Application Example 4-1

System Organization of the Intel StrongARM SA-1100 and SA-1111

The StrongARM SA-1100 provides a number of functions besides the ARM CPU:

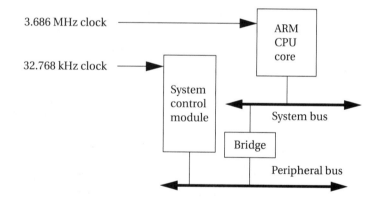

The chip contains two on-chip buses: a high-speed system bus and a lower-speed peripheral bus. The chip also uses two different clocks. A 3.686 MHz clock is used to drive the CPU and high-speed peripherals, and a 32.768 kHz clock is an input to the system control module. The system control module contains the following peripheral devices:

- a real-time clock

- an operating system timer

- 28 general-purpose I/Os (GPIOs)

- an interrupt controller

- a power manager controller

- a reset controller that handles resetting the processor

The 32.768 kHz clock's frequency is chosen to be useful in timing real-time events. The slower clock is also used by the power manager to provide continued operation of the manager at a lower clock rate and therefore lower power consumption.

The SA-1111 is a companion chip that provides a suite of I/O functions. It connects to the SA-1100 through its system bus and provides several functions: a USB host controller; PS/2 ports for keyboards, mice, and so on; a PCMCIA interface; pulse-width modulation outputs; a serial port for digital audio; and an SSP serial port for telecom interfacing.

4.7 Development and Debugging

In this section we take a step back from the platform and consider how it is used during design. We first consider how we can build an effective means for programming and testing an embedded system using hosts. We then see how hosts and other techniques can be used for debugging embedded systems.

4.7.1 Development Environments

A typical embedded computing system has a relatively small amount of everything, including CPU horsepower, memory, I/O devices, and so forth. As a result, it is common to do at least part of the software development on a PC or workstation known as a **host** as illustrated in Figure 4-35. The hardware on which the code will finally run is known as the **target.** The host and target are frequently connected by a serial link, but a higher-speed link such as Ethernet can also be used.

The target must include a small amount of software to talk to the host system. That software will take up some memory, interrupt vectors, and so on, but it should generally leave the smallest possible footprint in the target to avoid interfering with the application software. The host should be able to do the following:

- load programs into the target,

- start and stop program execution on the target, and

- examine memory and CPU registers.

Figure 4-35 *Connecting a host and target system.*

A **cross-compiler** is a compiler that runs on one type of machine but generates code for another. After compilation, the executable code is downloaded to the embedded system by a serial link or perhaps burned in a PROM and plugged in. We also often make use of host-target debuggers, in which the basic hooks for debugging are provided by the target and a more sophisticated user interface is created by the host.

A PC or workstation offers a programming environment that is in many ways much friendlier than the typical embedded computing platform. But one problem with this approach emerges when debugging code talks to I/O devices. Since the host almost certainly will not have the same devices configured in the same way, the embedded code cannot be run as is on the host. In many cases, a **testbench program** can be built to help debug the embedded code. The **testbench** generates inputs to simulate the actions of the input devices; it may also take the output values and compare them against expected values, providing valuable early debugging help. The embedded code may need to be slightly modified to work with the testbench, but careful coding (such as using the #ifdef directive in C) can ensure that the changes can be undone easily and without introducing bugs.

4.7.2 Debugging Techniques

A good deal of software debugging can be done by compiling and executing the code on a PC or workstation. But at some point it inevitably becomes necessary to run code on the embedded hardware platform. Embedded systems are usually

less friendly programming environments than PCs. Nonetheless, the resourceful designer has several options available for debugging the system.

The serial port found on most evaluation boards is one of the most important debugging tools. In fact, it is often a good idea to design a serial port into an embedded system even if it will not be used in the final product; the serial port can be used not only for development debugging but also for diagnosing problems in the field.

Another very important debugging tool is the **breakpoint.** The simplest form of a breakpoint is for the user to specify an address at which the program's execution is to break. When the PC reaches that address, control is returned to the monitor program. From the monitor program, the user can examine and/ or modify CPU registers, after which execution can be continued. Implementing breakpoints does not require using exceptions or external devices. Programming Example 4-1 shows how to use instructions to create breakpoints.

Programming Example 4-1

Breakpoints

A breakpoint is a location in memory at which a program stops executing and returns to the debugging tool or monitor program. Implementing breakpoints is very simple—you simply replace the instruction at the breakpoint location with a subroutine call to the monitor. In the following code, to establish a breakpoint at location 0x40c in some ARM code, we've replaced the branch (B) instruction normally held at that location with a subroutine call (BL) to the breakpoint handling routine:

```
0 × 400  MUL r4,r4,r6          0 × 400  MUL r4,r4,r6
0 × 404  ADD r2,r2,r4          0 × 404  ADD r2,r2,r4
0 × 408  ADD r0,r0,#1    ➤     0 × 408  ADD r0,r0,#1
0 × 40c  B loop               0 × 40c  BL bkpoint
```

When the breakpoint handler is called, it saves all the registers and can then display the CPU state to the user and take commands.

To continue execution, the original instruction must be replaced in the program. If the breakpoint can be erased, the original instruction can simply be replaced and control returned to that instruction. This will normally require fixing the subroutine return address, which will point to the instruction after the breakpoint. If the breakpoint is to remain, then the original instruction can

be replaced and a new temporary breakpoint placed at the next instruction (taking jumps into account, of course). When the temporary breakpoint is reached, the monitor puts back the original breakpoint, removes the temporary one, and resumes execution.

The Unix *dbx* debugger shows the program being debugged in source code form, but that capability is too complex to fit into most embedded systems. Very simple monitors will require you to specify the breakpoint as an absolute address, which requires you to know how the program was linked. A more sophisticated monitor will read the symbol table and allow you to use labels in the assembly code to specify locations.

LEDs as debugging devices

Never underestimate the importance of LEDs (light-emitting diodes) in debugging. As with serial ports, it is often a good idea to design in a few to indicate the system state even if they will not normally be seen in use. LEDs can be used to show error conditions, when the code enters certain routines, or to show idle time activity. LEDs can be entertaining as well—a simple flashing LED can provide a great sense of accomplishment when it first starts to work.

in-circuit emulation

When software tools are insufficient to debug the system, hardware aids can be deployed to give a clearer view of what is happening when the system is running. The **microprocessor in-circuit emulator (ICE)** is a specialized hardware tool that can help debug software in a working embedded system. At the heart of an in-circuit emulator is a special version of the microprocessor that allows its internal registers to be read out when it is stopped. The in-circuit emulator surrounds this specialized microprocessor with additional logic that allows the user to specify breakpoints and examine and modify the CPU state. The CPU provides as much debugging functionality as a debugger within a monitor program, but does not take up any memory. The main drawback to in-circuit emulation is that the machine is specific to a particular microprocessor, even down to the pinout. If you use several microprocessors, maintaining a fleet of in-circuit emulators to match can be very expensive.

logic analyzers

The **logic analyzer** [Ald73] is the other major piece of instrumentation in the embedded system designer's arsenal. Think of a logic analyzer as an array of inexpensive oscilloscopes—the analyzer can sample many different signals simultaneously (tens to hundreds) but can display only 0, 1, or changing values for each. All these logic analysis channels can be connected to the system to record the activity on many signals simultaneously. The logic analyzer records the values on the signals into an internal memory and then displays the results on a display once the memory is full or the run is aborted. The logic analyzer can capture thousands or even millions of samples of data on all of these channels, providing a much larger time window into the operation of the machine than is possible with a conventional oscilloscope.

A typical logic analyzer can acquire data in either of two modes that are typically called **state** and **timing modes.** To understand why two modes are useful and the difference between them, it is important to remember that an oscilloscope trades reduced resolution on the signals for the longer time window. The measurement resolution on each signal is reduced in both voltage and time dimensions. The reduced voltage resolution is accomplished by measuring logic values (0, 1, x) rather than analog voltages. The reduction in timing resolution is accomplished by sampling the signal, rather than capturing a continuous waveform as in an analog oscilloscope.

State and timing mode represent different ways of sampling the values. Timing mode uses an internal clock that is fast enough to take several samples per clock period in a typical system. State mode, on the other hand, uses the system's own clock to control sampling, so it samples each signal only once per clock cycle. As a result, timing mode requires more memory to store a given number of system clock cycles. On the other hand, it provides greater resolution in the signal for detecting glitches. Timing mode is typically used for glitch-oriented debugging, while state mode is used for sequentially oriented problems.

The internal architecture of a logic analyzer is shown in Figure 4-36. The system's data signals are sampled at a latch within the logic analyzer; the latch is controlled by either the system clock or the internal logic analyzer sampling clock, depending on whether the analyzer is being used in state or timing mode. Each sample is copied into a vector memory under the control of a state machine. The latch, timing circuitry, sample memory, and controller must be designed to run at high speed since several samples per system clock cycle

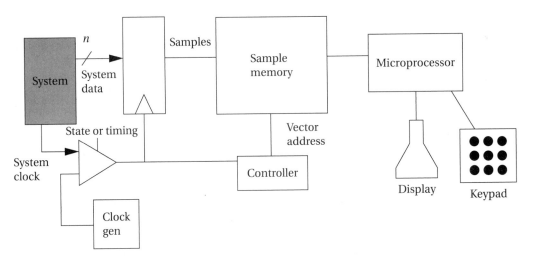

Figure 4-36 *Architecture of a logic analyzer.*

may be required in timing mode. After the sampling is complete, an embedded microprocessor takes over to control the display of the data captured in the sample memory.

Logic analyzers typically provide a number of formats for viewing data. One format is a timing diagram format. Many logic analyzers allow not only customized displays, such as giving names to signals, but also more advanced display options. For example, an inverse assembler can be used to turn vector values into microprocessor instructions. The logic analyzer does not provide access to the internal state of the components, but it does give a very good view of the externally visible signals. That information can be used for both functional and timing debugging.

One common problem is measuring the execution time of a certain piece of code. This can be done in several different ways. If there is a timer available in the system, it can be used to measure the execution time—the program is modified to reset the counter at the start of the code segment and stop it at the end. A logic analyzer can also be used to measure a time interval by having the analyzer watch for starting and stopping addresses on the bus. Logic analyzers are also good at analyzing cache behavior—references to the internal cache will not generate bus activity but cache misses will, so watching the bus gives a good indication of the effectiveness of the cache.

In many circumstances, it is useful to do at least some of the debugging without constructing a development board. (If the system is being built as a single chip, it may not be possible to build a printed circuit board equivalent.) As both the hardware and software in embedded systems have become more complex, designers have been increasingly interested in debugging techniques that don't rely on system integration. This process is often called **hardware/ software co-verification** because it allows hardware and software designs to be validated at the same time, against each other. The types of co-verification techniques available are listed below.

- An **instruction-level simulator** may be used to debug code running on the CPU.

- A **cycle-level simulation tool** may be used for faster simulation of parts of the system.

- A **hardware/software co-simulator** may be used to simulate various parts of the system at different levels of detail.

CPU simulators Rather than run code on a development board, it is often useful to execute it in a simulator. An instruction-level simulator (also known as a CPU simulator) simulates the execution of code to the level of detail provided by the programming model. The instruction-level simulator will not generally tell the number of cycles required to execute an instruction and does not generally simulate the actions of the bus or I/O devices. As a result, it may be possible to

simulate only the computational core of the code. However, the simulator provides a great deal of visibility. For instance, the CPU registers and main memory can easily be examined, traced, and so on. Both the ARM and SHARC processors have instruction-level simulators.

A cycle-based simulator is designed to simulate the hardware operation of a computer to within clock-cycle accuracy. It does not provide detailed timing within a clock cycle, so it cannot be used for low-level debugging of the CPU, but cycle-based simulation runs much faster than lower-level forms of simulation. As a result, enough cycles can usually be simulated to exercise a significant amount of software. A cycle-based simulator may be implemented in software, or it may use a special-purpose computer designed to efficiently execute the basic simulation primitives. Cycle-based simulation is most often used today for the verification of CPU designs themselves, but as single-chip embedded systems become more common, cycle-based simulation tools will probably become more widely used.

co-verification tools

The most common type of co-verification today is **co-simulation.** As illustrated in Figure 4-37, a co-simulator coordinates hardware and software simulations, each of which is responsible for simulating different parts of the design. Software may be executed by simulating compiled code for the target processor or by compiling the code for the simulation host. The challenge in co-simulation is the control of time in simulation. Hardware and software simulation run at different granularities of time—for example, a single step in an instruction-level CPU simulator may require many logic-level simulation steps when simulating an I/O device attached to the CPU.

There are several techniques for implementing co-simulation, including the use of a **simulation bus** to transfer data and timing information between the hardware and software simulators. An alternative technique is to use a *hardware emulator* to run a model of the CPU hardware. A hardware emulator is very different from a microprocessor in-circuit emulator—for instance, the hardware emulator uses FPGAs to implement a logic network. Emulators can often run at several hundred kilohertz and can be plugged into existing systems. If we load a hardware description of a CPU into the emulator, we can then run software on the emulated CPU. Emulators are expensive but are becoming more popular for the co-verification of systems-on-silicon.

Figure 4-37 *Communicating simulations for hardware/software co-simulation.*

4.7.3 Debugging Challenges

Logical errors in software can be hard to track down, but errors in real-time code can create problems that are even harder to diagnose. Real-time programs are required to finish their work within a certain amount of time; if they run too long, they can create very unexpected behavior. Example 4-3 demonstrates one of the problems that can arise.

Example 4-3

A Timing Error in Real-Time Code

Let's consider a simple program that periodically takes an input from an analog/digital converter, does some computations on it, and then outputs the result to a digital/analog converter. To make it easier to compare input to output and see the results of the bug, we assume that the computation produces an output equal to the input, but that a bug causes the computation to run 50% longer than its given time interval. A sample input to the program over several sample periods follows:

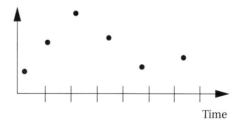

If the program ran fast enough to meet its deadline, the output would simply be a time-shifted copy of the input. But when the program runs over its allotted time, the output will become very different. Exactly what happens depends in part on the behavior of the A/D and D/A converters, so let's make some assumptions. First, the A/D converter holds its current sample in a register until the next sample period, and the D/A converter changes its output whenever it receives a new sample. Next, a reasonable assumption about interrupt systems is that, when an interrupt is not satisfied and the device interrupts again, the device's old value will disappear and be replaced by the new value. The basic situation that develops when the interrupt routine runs too long is summarized below:

1. The A/D converter is prompted by the timer to generate a new value, saves it in the register, and requests an interrupt.

2. The interrupt handler runs too long from the last sample.

3. The A/D converter gets another sample at the next period.

4. The interrupt handler finishes its first request and then immediately responds to the second interrupt. It never sees the first sample and only gets the second one.

Thus, assuming that the interrupt handler takes 1.5 times longer than it should, here is how it would process the sample input:

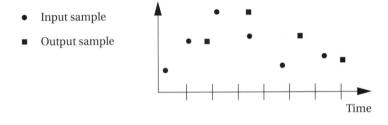

The output waveform is seriously distorted because the interrupt routine grabs the wrong samples and puts the results out at the wrong times.

The exact results of missing real-time deadlines depend on the detailed characteristics of the I/O devices and the nature of the timing violation. This makes debugging real-time problems especially difficult. Unfortunately, the best advice is that if a system exhibits truly unusual behavior, missed deadlines should be suspected. In-circuit emulators, logic analyzers, and even LEDs can be useful tools in checking the execution time of real-time code to determine whether it in fact meets its deadline.

4.8 Manufacturing Testing

Getting the design right is not enough; we must also ensure that the system is manufactured without defects. The goal of the **manufacturing test** is to ensure that errors are not introduced during manufacturing of the system. Even if the design is perfect, there is potential for error in the construction of each copy of the system that rolls off the manufacturing line. One of the tasks of hardware design is to develop manufacturing tests that ensure the desired level of quality

for products coming off the production line. It is generally not a good idea to design the complete system and only then try to figure out how to test it during manufacturing. When building complex systems, it is necessary to take the manufacturing test into account during design. **Design for testability** ensures that the design will not be so difficult to test that we cannot create adequate tests for it.

It is important to remember the distinction between implementation testing and manufacturing testing. Implementation testing's goal is to identify discrepancies between the specification and the way the system works. Manufacturing testing, on the other hand, assumes that the design is correct and looks for variations between the design and copies rolling off the manufacturing line, since the manufacturing process can introduce defects that cause the system to malfunction.

The proportion of working systems produced by a manufacturing process is called the **yield.** Every unit coming off the assembly line must be tested; as a result, it is important to reduce the time required for testing while ensuring that as many faults as possible are discovered before the unit is shipped to the customer. Bad units shipped to customers eventually generate customer returns that cost time, money, and goodwill. Building a system that can be quickly and thoroughly tested usually requires careful up-front design to make sure that the system can be exercised in the ways required to display the effects of manufacturing defects.

fault models At the heart of manufacturing test techniques, and the key difference between manufacturing testing and software testing, is the **fault model.** When we discuss techniques for testing software in Section , you will see that we do not know exactly which potential software faults we are looking for. In the manufacturing test, the fault model describes the types of problems that can occur in the system's components. When we generate tests, we can enumerate what faults might occur in what components. A major challenge in the manufacturing test is to develop a short test that determines whether a particular fault appears. The equipment used to test chips and boards is very expensive. Because the tests must be run on every unit coming off the manufacturing line, testing costs can become a large fraction of total manufacturing costs. As a result, efficient tests are very important.

While there are many types of manufacturing defects possible, a few types of faults often determine the overall yield of the manufacturing process. Once we know the types of faults we wish to target, we can enumerate all possible instances of a fault in a particular design. Given all possible faults we need to test in a unit, we can generate a series of tests that exercises the system to expose the results of those faults. When we test the system, we should be able to distinguish the behaviors of correct and faulty systems. Ideally, we would like to cover all the instantiations of a fault of a particular type. The proportion of faults that we can actually detect with a given series of tests is known as the **fault coverage.**

The classical fault model for digital hardware is the **stuck-at-0/1** model. In this model, a fault in a logic gate causes its output to be constant, independent of its input values. Figure 4-38 shows two examples of stuck-at-0/1 faults: The inverter's output is always 0, even when its input is a 0; and the NAND gate's output is always 1, even when its inputs imply that the output should be 0. When testing a gate, we want to apply an input to the gate that will produce different values when the gate is good or faulty. If, for instance, we applied 10 to the inputs of the NAND gate, we would not be able to tell whether it was good or stuck-at-1. (We would, however, be able to tell if it was stuck-at-0.)

combinational Testing a combinational network is surprisingly challenging. Enumerating all the possible faults in the network is easy: Every gate can be stuck-at-0 and stuck-at-1. Finding tests for these faults is more challenging. Because these gates are embedded within a large logic network, it may not be easy to **control** the inputs to the gate, and it may be difficult to **observe** the value at the outputs. As shown in Figure 4-39, for each test, we need to find a set of values for the network's primary inputs that allows us to justify the required inputs at the gate being tested. We also need to find inputs that allow the test value to propagate to the network's primary outputs.

sequential Testing a sequential network with embedded registers is even more difficult. The registers in the machine supply inputs to the combinational logic and receive outputs from it, but they are not usually directly observable or controllable from the outside. As illustrated in Figure 4-40, the registers propagate val-

Figure 4-38 *Stuck-at 0/1 faults in logic gates.*

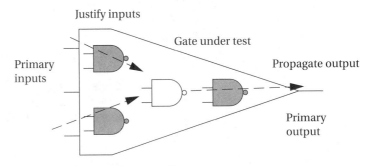

Figure 4-39 *Testing for a fault in a combinational network.*

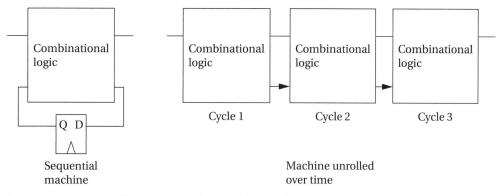

Figure 4-40 *Unrolling a sequential machine in time.*

ues from one clock cycle to the next. This can be envisioned by unrolling the machine in time—each clock cycle gets its own copy of the combinational logic, and the next-state outputs of one cycle are connected to the current-state inputs of the next cycle. Unrolling the sequential machine in time clearly shows the added complexity of testing the sequential machine—the unrolled machine is much larger than the original combinational logic.

scan chain
One way to reduce the complexity of sequential testing is to use **scan chains.** A scan chain is a special type of register that can be operated in two modes. In nonscan mode, it acts as a normal register. In scan mode, it operates as a shift register that allows the current state of the register to be shifted out and the new state to be shifted in. By stopping the machine and using scan mode, we can examine the state of the machine and, if necessary, change the state. Scanning the state out and in takes some time since it is done serially, but this is a small price to pay for the much greater observability and controllability of the system.

Automatic test pattern generation (ATPG) programs generate a series of **test vectors** that exercise the faults in a system. Test pattern generation is an NP-complete problem, so ATPG programs may not be able to find a test for a particular fault even if one exists. But if the logic is *redundant,* there may be no test of any length. It is difficult to distinguish between logic that is redundant and logic that is merely hard to test, so any failure to test a fault should be examined carefully to determine whether the logic is redundant and should be redesigned. If the logic is irredundant and merely difficult to test, it may be possible to redesign the hardware to make it possible to test the fault.

boundary scan
Boundary scan logic helps us solve this problem. Boundary scan is a standard interface for chips. It is also known as JTAG, for Joint Test Action Group, the group that prepared the standard. The JTAG standard prescribes a configuration and control sequence for a scan chain to be added to the pins of the

chip (hence, the term *boundary scan*). As shown in Figure 4-41, the boundary scan registers are organized into a chain on each chip; the boundary scan chains for several chips on a board can be linked together into a larger chain. Boundary scan provides two major advantages in testing a system. First, it allows pins inside the board to be observed and controlled. Second, it allows the chips on the board to be operated somewhat independently. Boundary scan has a surprising number of uses—for example, in-circuit emulators typically use boundary scan to read and update the state of the microprocessor being emulated.

The microprocessor in an embedded system can be used to help test the rest of the system by running test programs that exercise the rest of the machine. However, before the microprocessor can be used for testing, it must itself be tested for correct operation. Boundary scan is very helpful in testing

Figure 4-41 *Organization of boundary scan.*

the microprocessor. Once the minimal microprocessor system has been veri-
fied, diagnostic programs can be run to help test the rest of the system. These
diagnostics can be used not only at the factory but also in the field.

Design Example

4.9 Alarm Clock

Our first system design example will be an alarm clock. We use a microproces-
sor to read the clock's buttons and update the time display. Since we now have
an understanding of I/O, we work through the steps of the methodology to go
from a concept to a completed and tested system.

4.9.1 Requirements

The basic functions of an alarm clock are well understood and easy to enumer-
ate. Figure 4-42 illustrates the front panel design for the alarm clock. The time
is shown as four digits in 12-hour format; we use a light to distinguish between
AM and PM. We use several buttons to set the clock time and alarm time. When
we press the *hour* and *minute* buttons, we advance the hour and minute,
respectively, by one. When setting the time, we must hold down the *set time*
button while we hit the *hour* and *minute* buttons; the *set alarm* button works
in a similar fashion. We turn the alarm on and off with the *alarm on* and *alarm*

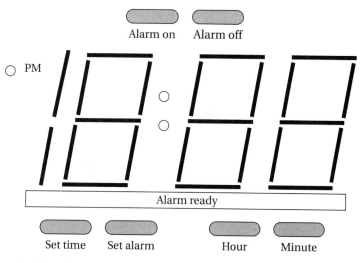

Figure 4-42 *Front panel of the alarm clock.*

off buttons. When the alarm is activated, the *alarm ready* light is on. A separate speaker provides the audible alarm.

We are now ready to create the requirements table:

Name	Alarm clock.
Purpose	A 24-hour digital clock with a single alarm.
Inputs	Six pushbuttons: set time, set alarm, hour, minute, alarm on, alarm off.
Outputs	Four-digit, clock-style output. PM indicator light. Alarm ready light. Buzzer.
Functions	Default mode: the display shows the current time. PM light is on from noon to midnight.
	Hour and minute buttons are used to advance time and alarm, respectively. Pressing one of these buttons increments the hour/minute once.
	Depress set time button: This button is held down while hour/minute buttons are pressed to set time. New time is automatically shown on display.
	Depress set alarm button: While this button is held down, display shifts to current alarm setting; depressing hour/minute buttons sets alarm value in a manner similar to setting time.
	Alarm on: puts clock in alarm-on state, causes clock to turn on buzzer when current time reaches alarm time, turns on alarm ready light.
	Alarm off: turns off buzzer, takes clock out of alarm-on state, turns off alarm ready light.
Performance	Displays hours and minutes but not seconds. Should be accurate within the accuracy of a typical microprocessor clock signal. (Excessive accuracy may unreasonably drive up the cost of generating an accurate clock.)
Manufacturing cost	Consumer product range. Cost will be dominated by the microprocessor system, not the buttons or display.
Power	Powered by AC through a standard power supply.
Physical size and weight	Small enough to fit on a nightstand with expected weight for an alarm clock.

4.9.2 Specification

The basic function of the clock is simple, but we do need to create some classes and associated behaviors to clarify exactly how the user interface works.

Figure 4-43 shows the basic classes for the alarm clock. Borrowing a term from mechanical watches, we call the class that handles the basic clock operation the *Mechanism* class. We have three classes that represent physical elements: *Lights** for all the digits and lights, *Buttons** for all the buttons, and *Speaker** for the sound output. The *Buttons** class can easily be used directly by *Mechanism*. As discussed below, the physical display must be scanned to generate the digits output, so we introduce the *Display* class to abstract the physical lights.

The details of the low-level user interface classes are shown in Figure 4-44. The *Buzzer** class allows the buzzer to be turned on or off; we will use analog electronics to generate the buzz tone for the speaker. The *Buttons** class provides read-only access to the current state of the buttons. The *Lights** class allows us to drive the lights. However, to save pins on the display, *Lights** provides signals for only one digit, along with a set of signals to indicate which digit is currently being addressed. We generate the display by scanning the digits periodically. That function is performed by the *Display* class, which makes the display appear as an unscanned, continuous display to the rest of the system.

The *Mechanism* class is described in Figure 4-45. This class keeps track of the current time, the current alarm time, whether the alarm has been turned on, and whether it is currently buzzing. The clock shows the time only to the minute, but it keeps internal time to the second. The time is kept as discrete digits rather than a single integer to simplify transferring the time to the display. The class provides two behaviors, both of which run continuously. First, *scan-keyboard* is responsible for looking at the inputs and updating the alarm and other functions as requested by the user. Second, *update-time* keeps the current time accurate.

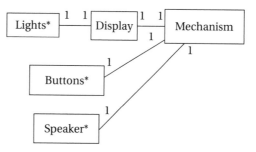

Figure 4-43 *Class diagram for the alarm clock.*

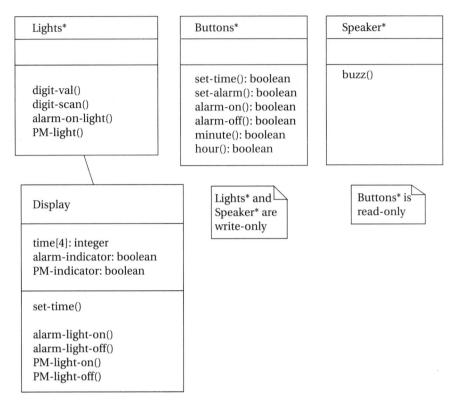

Figure 4-44 *Details of low-level class for the alarm clock.*

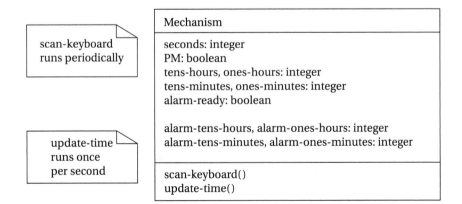

Figure 4-45 *The Mechanism class.*

Figure 4-46 shows the state diagram for *update-time.* This behavior is straightforward, but it must do several things. It is activated once per second and must update the seconds clock. If it has counted 60 seconds, it must then update the displayed time; when it does so, it must roll over between digits and keep track of AM-to-PM and PM-to-AM transitions. It sends the updated time to the display object. It also compares the time with the alarm setting and sets the alarm buzzing under the proper conditions.

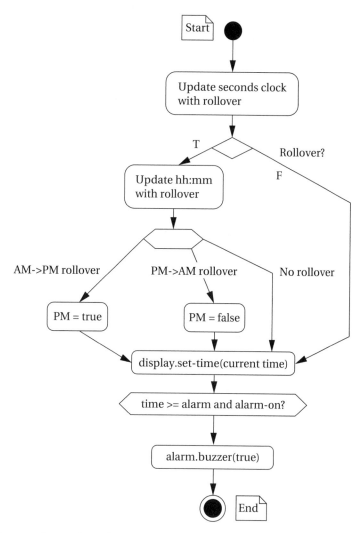

Figure 4-46 *State diagram for update-time.*

The state diagram for *scan-keyboard* is shown in Figure 4-47. This function is called periodically, frequently enough so that all the user's button presses are caught by the system. Because the keyboard will be scanned several times per second, we don't want to register the same button press several times. If, for example, we advanced the minutes count on every keyboard scan when the *set-time* and *minutes* buttons were pressed, the time would be advanced much too fast. To make the buttons respond more reasonably, the function computes button activations—it compares the current state of the button to the button's value on the last scan, and it considers the button activated only when it is on for this scan but was off for the last scan. Once computing the activation values for all the buttons, it looks at the activation combinations and takes the appro-

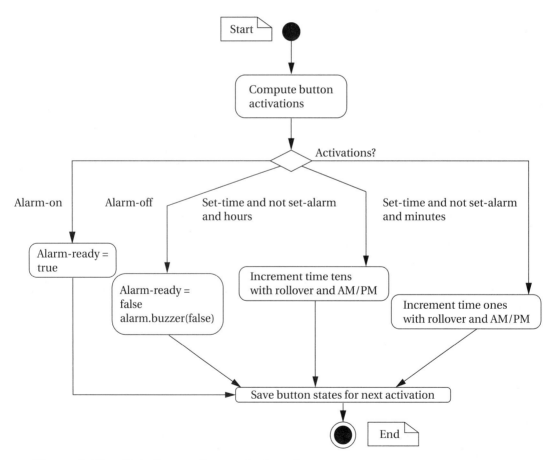

Figure 4-47 *State diagram for scan-keyboard.*

priate actions. Before exiting, it saves the current button values for computing activations the next time this behavior is executed.

4.9.3 System Architecture

The software and hardware architectures of a system are always hard to completely separate, but let's first consider the software architecture and then its implications on the hardware.

The system has both periodic and aperiodic components—the current time must obviously be updated periodically, and the button commands occur occasionally.

It seems reasonable to have the following two major software components:

- An interrupt-driven routine can update the current time. The current time will be kept in a variable in memory. A timer can be used to interrupt periodically and update the time. As seen in the subsequent discussion of the hardware architecture, the display must be sent the new value when the minute value changes. This routine can also maintain the PM indicator.

- A foreground program can poll the buttons and execute their commands. Since buttons are changed at a relatively slow rate, it makes no sense to add the hardware required to connect the buttons to interrupts. Instead, the foreground program will read the button values and then use simple conditional tests to implement the commands, including setting the current time, setting the alarm, and turning off the alarm. Another routine called by the foreground program will turn the buzzer on and off based on the alarm time.

An important question for the interrupt-driven current time handler is how often the timer interrupts occur. A one-minute interval would be very convenient for the software, but a one-minute timer would require a large number of counter bits. It is more realistic to use a one-second timer and to use a program variable to count the seconds in a minute.

The foreground code will be implemented as a while loop:

```
while (TRUE) {
    read_buttons(button_values); /* read inputs */
    process_command(button_values); /* do commands */
    check_alarm(); /* decide whether to turn on the alarm */
}
```

The loop first reads the buttons using read_buttons(). In addition to reading the current button values from the input device, this routine must preprocess

the button values so that the user interface code will respond properly. The buttons will remain depressed for many sample periods since the sample rate is much faster than any person can push and release buttons. We want to make sure that the clock responds to this as a single depression of the button, not one depression per sample interval. As shown in Figure 4-48, this can be done by performing a simple edge detection on the button input—the button event value is 1 for one sample period when the button is depressed and then goes back to 0 and does not return to 1 until the button is depressed and then released. This can be accomplished by a simple two-state machine.

The process_command() function is responsible for responding to button events. The check_alarm() function checks the current time against the alarm time and decides when to turn on the buzzer. This routine is kept separate from the command processing code since the alarm must go on when the proper time is reached, independent of the button inputs.

We have determined from the software architecture that we will need a timer connected to the CPU. We will also need logic to connect the buttons to the CPU bus. In addition to performing edge detection on the button inputs, we must also of course debounce the buttons.

The final step before starting to write code and build hardware is to draw the state transition graph for the clock's commands. That diagram will be used to guide the implementation of the software components.

4.9.4 Component Design and Testing

The two major software components, the interrupt handler and the foreground code, can be implemented relatively straightforwardly. Since most of the functionality of the interrupt handler is in the interruption process itself,

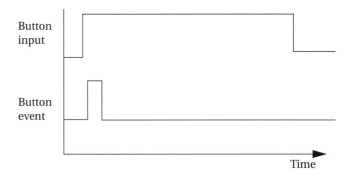

Figure 4-48 *Preprocessing button inputs.*

that code is best tested on the microprocessor platform. The foreground code can be more easily tested on the PC or workstation used for code development. We can create a testbench for this code that generates button depressions to exercise the state machine. We will also need to simulate the advancement of the system clock. Trying to directly execute the interrupt handler to control the clock is probably a bad idea—not only would that require some type of emulation of interrupts, but it would require us to count interrupts second by second. A better testing strategy is to add testing code that updates the clock, perhaps once per four iterations of the foreground while loop.

The timer will probably be a stock component, so we would then focus on implementing logic to interface to the buttons, display, and buzzer. The buttons will require debouncing logic. The display will require a register to hold the current display value in order to drive the display elements.

4.9.5 System Integration and Testing

Because this system has a small number of components, system integration is relatively easy. The software must be checked to ensure that debugging code has been turned off. Three types of tests can be performed. First, the clock's accuracy can be checked against a reference clock. Second, the commands can be exercised from the buttons. Finally, the buzzer's functionality should be verified.

4.10 Summary

The microprocessor is only one component in an embedded computing system—memory and I/O devices are equally important. The microprocessor bus serves as the glue that binds all these components together. Hardware platforms for embedded systems are often built around common platforms with appropriate amounts of memory and I/O devices added on; low-level monitor software also plays an important role in these systems.

What We Learned

- CPU buses are built on handshaking protocols.

- A variety of memory components are available, which vary widely in speed, capacity, and other capabilities.

- An I/O device uses logic to interface to the bus so that the CPU can read and write the device's registers.

- Embedded systems can be debugged using a variety of hardware and software methods.

Further Reading

Shanley and Anderson [Min95] describe the PCI bus in detail. Dahlin [Dah00] describes how to interface to a touchscreen. Collins [Col97] describes the design of microprocessor in-circuit emulators. Earnshaw et al. [Ear97] describe an advanced debugging environment for the ARM architecture. Becker et al. [Bec92] and Coumeri and Thomas [Cou95] describe early hardware/software co-simulation environments.

Questions

Q4-1 Draw a UML sequence diagram that shows a four-cycle handshake between a bus master and a device.

Q4-2 Draw a timing diagram with the following signals (where $[t_1,t_2]$ is the time interval starting at t_1 and ending at t_2):

 a. signal A is stable [0,10], changing [10,15], stable [15,30]

 b. signal B is 1 [0,5], falling [5,7], 0 [7,20], changing [20,30]

 c. signal C is changing [0,10], 0 [10,15], rising [15,18], 1 [18,25], changing [25,30]

Q4-3 Draw a timing diagram for a write operation with no wait states.

Q4-4 Draw a timing diagram for a read operation on a bus in which the read includes two wait states.

Q4-5 Draw a timing diagram for a write operation on a bus in which the write takes two wait states.

Q4-6 Draw a timing diagram for a burst write operation that writes four locations.

Q4-7 Draw a UML state diagram for a burst read operation with wait states. One state diagram is for the bus master and the other is for the device being read.

Q4-8 Draw a UML sequence diagram for a burst read operation with wait states.

Q4-9 Draw timing diagrams for

 a. a device becoming bus master

 b. the device returning control of the bus to the CPU

Q4-10 Draw a timing diagram that shows a complete DMA operation, including handing off the bus to the DMA controller, performing the DMA transfer, and returning bus control back to the CPU.

Q4-11 Draw UML state diagrams for a bus mastership transaction in which one side shows the CPU as the default bus master and the other shows the device that can request bus mastership.

Q4-12 Draw a UML sequence diagram for a bus mastership request, grant, and return.

Q4-13 Draw a UML sequence diagram for a complete DMA transaction, including the DMA controller requesting the bus, the DMA transaction itself, and returning control of the bus to the CPU.

Q4-14 Draw a UML sequence diagram showing a read operation across a bus bridge.

Q4-15 Draw a UML sequence diagram showing a write operation with wait states across a bus bridge.

Q4-16 If you have a choice among several DRAMs of the same capacity but with different data widths, when would you want to use a narrower memory? When would you want to use a taller memory?

Q4-17 Draw a UML sequence diagram for a read transaction that includes a DRAM refresh operation. The sequence diagram should include the CPU, the DRAM interface, and the DRAM internals to show the refresh itself.

Q4-18 Design the logic required to build a 16 M $\times$ 32-bit memory out of 4 M $\times$ 32 memories.

Q4-19 Design the logic required to build a 1 M $\times$ 16 memory out of 1 M $\times$ 4 memories.

Q4-20 Design the logic required to build a 4 M $\times$ 16 memory out of 1 M $\times$ 4 memories.

Q4-21 Draw a UML class diagram that describes a hardware timer/counter. The device can be loaded with a count value. It can decrement the count down to zero based either on a bus signal or by counting some multiple of clock cycles.

Q4-22 Draw a UML class diagram for an analog/digital converter.

Q4-23 Draw a UML class diagram for a digital/analog converter.

Q4-24 Write ARM or SHARC assembly language code that handles a breakpoint. It should save the necessary registers, call a subroutine to communicate with the host, and upon return from the host, cause the breakpointed instruction to be properly executed.

Q4-25 Assume an A/D converter is supplying samples at 44.1 kHz.

a. How much time is available per sample for CPU operations?

b. If the interrupt handler executes 100 instructions obtaining the sample and passing it onto the application routine, how many instructions can be executed on a 20 MHz RISC processor that executes 1 instruction per cycle?

Q4-26 If an interrupt handler executes for too long and the next interrupt occurs before the last call to the handler has finished, what happens?

Q4-27 Consider a system in which an interrupt handler passes on samples to an FIR filter program that runs in the background.

a. If the interrupt handler takes too long, how does the FIR filter's output change?

b. If the FIR filter code takes too long, how does its output change?

Q4-28 Assume that your microprocessor implements an ICE instruction that asserts a bus signal that causes a microprocessor in-circuit emulator to start. Also assume that the microprocessor allows all internal registers to be observed and controlled through a boundary scan chain. Draw a UML sequence diagram of the ICE operation, including execution of the ICE instruction, uploading the microprocessor state to the ICE, and returning control to the microprocessor's program. The sequence diagram should include the microprocessor, the microprocessor in-circuit emulator, and the user.

Lab Exercises

L4-1 Use an instruction-based simulator to simulate a program. How fast was the simulator? Did you have to make any adjustments to your program in order to make it simulate properly?

L4-2 Use a logic analyzer to view system activity on your bus.

L4-3 If your logic analyzer is capable of on-the-fly disassembly, use it to display bus activity in the form of instructions, rather than simply 1s and 0s.

L4-4 Attach LEDs to your system bus so that you can monitor its activity. For example, use an LED to monitor the read/write line on the bus.

L4-5 Design logic to interface an I/O device to your microprocessor.

L4-6 Have someone else deliberately introduce a bug into one of your programs, and then use the appropriate debugging tools to find and correct the bug.

Chapter

Program Design and Analysis

- Program design and design patterns.

- Models of programs, such as data flow and control flow graphs.

- An introduction to compilation methods.

- Optimizing programs for speed, size, and power consumption.

- How to test programs to verify their correctness.

- A software modem.

5.1 Introduction

In this chapter we study in detail the process of programming embedded processors. The creation of embedded programs is at the heart of embedded system design. If you are reading this book, you almost certainly have an understanding of programming, but designing and implementing embedded programs is different and more challenging than writing typical workstation or PC programs. Embedded code must not only provide rich functionality, it must also often run at a required rate to meet system deadlines, fit into the allowed amount of memory, and meet power consumption requirements. Designing code that simultaneously meets multiple design constraints is a considerable challenge, but luckily there are techniques and tools that we can use to help us through the design process. Making sure that the program works is also a challenge, but once again methods and tools come to our aid.

Throughout the discussion we concentrate on high-level programming languages, specifically C. High-level languages were once shunned as too inefficient for embedded microcontrollers, but better compilers, more compiler-friendly architectures, and faster processors and memory have made high-level language programs common. Some sections of a program may still need to be written in assembly language if the compiler doesn't give sufficiently good results, but even when coding in assembly language it is often helpful to think about the program's functionality in high-level form. Many of the analysis and optimization techniques that we study in this chapter are equally applicable to programs written in assembly language.

The next section introduces design patterns as a technique for designing programs. Section 5.3 introduces the control/data flow graph as a model for high-level language programs (which can also be applied to programs written originally in assembly language). Section 5.4 reviews the assembly and linking process and Section 5.5 reviews as background the basic steps in compilation. We talk about optimization techniques specific to embedded computing in the next three sections: performance in Section 5.6, energy consumption in Section 5.7, and size in Section 5.8. In Section 5.9, we discuss techniques for ensuring that the programs you write are correct. We close with a software modem as a design example in Section 5.10.

5.2 Program Design

We begin our study of programs by considering how to design programs. In particular, we examine one popular technique, the use of design patterns. After introducing design patterns, we consider a few useful design patterns for embedded computing.

5.2.1 Design Patterns

A **design pattern** is a generalized description of a way to solve a certain class of problems. As a simple example, we could write C code for one implementation of a linked list, but that code would set in concrete the data items available in the list, actions on errors, and so on. A design pattern describing the list mechanism would capture the essential components and behaviors of the list without adding unnecessary detail. A design pattern can be described in UML; it usually takes the form of a collaboration diagram, which shows how classes work together to perform a given function.

Figure 5-1 shows a simple description of a design pattern as a UML class diagram. The diagram defines two classes: *List* to describe the entire list and

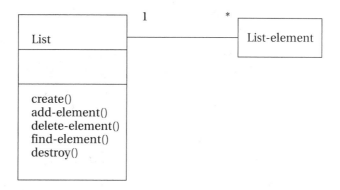

Figure 5-1 *A simple description of a design pattern.*

List-element for one of the items in the list. The *List* class defines the basic operations that you want to do on a list. The details of what goes in the list and so forth can be easily added into this design pattern. A design pattern can be parameterized so that it can be customized to the needs of a particular application. A more complete description of the pattern might include

- state diagrams to describe behavior and

- sequence diagrams to show how classes interact.

Design patterns are primarily intended to help solve midlevel design challenges. A design pattern may include only a single class, but it usually describes a handful of classes. Design patterns rarely include more than a few dozen classes. A design pattern probably will not provide you with the complete architecture of your system, but it can provide you with the architectures for many subsystems in your design: By stitching together and specializing existing design patterns, you may be able to quickly create a large part of your system architecture.

Design patterns are meant to be used in ways similar to how engineers in other disciplines work. A designer can consult catalogs of design patterns to find patterns that seem to fit a particular design problem. The designer can then choose parameters suited to the application and see what that implies for the implementation of the design pattern. The designer can then choose the design pattern that seems to be the best match for the design, parameterize it, and instantiate it.

Design patterns can be of many different types. A few are listed below.

- The digital filter is easily described as a design pattern.

- Data structures and their associated actions can be described as design patterns.

- A reactive system that reacts to external stimuli can be described as a design pattern, leaving the exact state transition diagram as a parameter.

- Douglass [Dou99] describes a policy class that describes a protocol that can be used to implement a variety of policies.

5.2.2 Design Patterns for Embedded Systems

state machine style

In this section, we consider design patterns for two very different styles of programs: the state machine and the circular buffer. State machines are well suited to **reactive systems** such as user interfaces, and circular buffers are useful in digital signal processing.

When inputs appear intermittently rather than as periodic samples, it is often convenient to think of the system as reacting to those inputs. The reaction of most systems can be characterized in terms of the input received and the current state of the system. This leads naturally to a **finite-state machine** style of describing the reactive system's behavior. Moreover, if the behavior is specified in that way, it is natural to write the program implementing that behavior in a state machine style. The state machine style of programming is also an efficient implementation of such computations. Finite-state machines are usually first encountered in the context of hardware design. Programming Example 5-1 shows how to write a finite-state machine in a high-level programming language.

Programming Example 5-1

A State Machine in C

The behavior we want to implement is a simple seat belt controller [Chi94]. The controller's job is to turn on a buzzer if a person sits in a seat and does not fasten the seat belt within a fixed amount of time. This system has three inputs and one output. The inputs are a sensor for the seat to know when a person has sat down, a seat belt sensor that tells when the belt is fastened, and a timer that goes off when the required time interval has elapsed. The output is the buzzer. Appearing below is a state diagram that describes the seat belt controller's behavior.

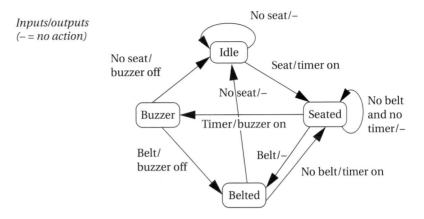

*Inputs/outputs
(– = no action)*

The idle state is in force when there is no person in the seat. When the person sits down, the machine goes into the seated state and turns on the timer. If the timer goes off before the seat belt is fastened, the machine goes into the buzzer state. If the seat belt goes on first, it enters the belted state. When the person leaves the seat, the machine goes back to idle.

To write this behavior in C, we will assume that we have loaded the current values of all three inputs (seat, belt, timer) into variables and will similarly hold the outputs in variables temporarily (timer_on, buzzer_on). We will use a variable named state to hold the current state of the machine and a switch statement to determine what action to take in each state. The code follows:

```
#define IDLE 0
#define SEATED 1
#define BELTED 2
#define BUZZER 3

switch (state) { /* check the current state */
    case IDLE:
        if (seat) { state = SEATED; timer_on = TRUE; }
        /* default case is self-loop */
        break;
    case SEATED:
        if (belt) state = BELTED; /* won't hear the buzzer */
        else if (timer) state = BUZZER; /* didn't put on belt in time */
        /* default is self-loop */
        break;
```

```
        case BELTED:
            if (!seat) state = IDLE; /* person left */
            else if (!belt) state = SEATED; /* person still in seat */
            break;
        case BUZZER:
            if (belt) state = BELTED; /* belt is on--turn off buzzer */
            else if (!seat) state = IDLE; /* no one in seat--turn off buzzer */
            break;
    }
```

This code takes advantage of the fact that the state will remain the same unless explicitly changed; this makes self-loops back to the same state easy to implement. This state machine may be executed forever in a while(TRUE) loop or periodically called by some other code. In either case, the code must be executed regularly so that it can check on the current value of the inputs and, if necessary, go into a new state.

data stream style The data stream style makes sense for data that comes in regularly and must be processed on the fly. The FIR filter of Application Example 2-1 is a classic example of stream-oriented processing. For each sample, the filter must emit one output that depends on the values of the last n inputs. In a typical workstation application, we would process the samples over a given interval by reading them all in from a file and then computing the results all at once in a batch process. In an embedded system we must not only emit outputs in real time, but we must also do so using a minimum amount of memory.

The circular buffer is a data structure that lets us handle streaming data in an efficient way. Figure 5-2 illustrates how a circular buffer stores a subset of the data stream. At each point in time, the algorithm needs a subset of the data stream that forms a window into the stream. The window slides with time as we throw out old values no longer needed and add new values. Since the size of the window does not change, we can use a fixed-size buffer to hold the current data. To avoid constantly copying data within the buffer, we will move the head of the buffer in time. The buffer points to the location at which the next sample will be placed; every time we add a sample, we automatically overwrite the oldest sample, which is the one that needs to be thrown out. When the pointer gets to the end of the buffer, it wraps around to the top. Programming Example 5-2 provides an efficient implementation of a circular buffer.

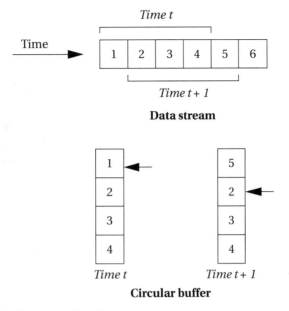

Figure 5-2 *A circular buffer for streaming data.*

Programming Example 5-2

A Circular Buffer Implementation of an FIR Filter

Appearing below are the declarations for the circular buffer and filter coefficients, assuming that N, the number of taps in the filter, has been previously defined.

```
int circ_buffer[N]; /* circular buffer for data */
int circ_buffer_head = 0; /* current head of the buffer */
int c[N]; /* filter coefficients (constants) */
```

To write C code for a circular buffer-based FIR filter, we need to modify the original loop slightly. Because the 0th element of data may not be in the 0th element of the circular buffer, we have to change the way in which we access the data. One of the implications of this is that we need separate loop indices for the circular buffer and coefficients.

```
int ibuf, /* loop index for the circular buffer */
    ic; /* loop index for the coefficient array */
for (f = 0, ibuff = circ_buff_head, ic = 0;
     ic < N;
     ibuff = (ibuff == (N - 1) ? 0 : ibuff++), ic++)
     f = f + c[ic] * circ_buff[ibuf];
```

The above code assumes that some other code, such as an interrupt handler, is replacing the last element of the circular buffer at the appropriate times. The statement ibuff = (ibuff == (N – 1) ? 0 : ibuff++) is a shorthand C way of incrementing ibuff such that it returns to 0 after reaching the end of the circular buffer array.

5.3 Models of Programs

In this section, we develop models for programs that are more general than source code. Why not use the source code directly? First, there are many different types of source code—assembly languages, C code, and so on—but we can use a single model to describe all of them. Once we have such a model, we can perform many useful analyses on the model more easily than we could on the source code.

Our fundamental model for programs is the **control/data flow graph (CDFG).** (We can also model hardware behavior with the CDFG.) As the name implies, the CDFG has constructs that model both data operations (arithmetic and other computations) and control operations (conditionals). Part of the power of the CDFG comes from its combination of control and data constructs. To understand the CDFG, we start with pure data descriptions and then extend the model to control.

5.3.1 Data Flow Graphs

A **data flow graph** is a model of a program with no conditionals. In a high-level programming language, a code segment with no conditionals—more precisely, with only one entry and exit point—is known as a basic block. Figure 5-3 shows a simple basic block. As the C code is executed, we would enter this basic block at the beginning and execute all the statements.

Before we are able to draw the data flow graph for this code we need to modify it slightly. There are two assignments to the variable x—it appears twice on the left side of an assignment. We need to rewrite the code in **single-assignment form,** in which a variable appears only once on the left side. Since our specification is C code, we assume that the statements are executed sequentially, so that any use of a variable refers to its latest assigned value. In this case, x is not reused in this block (presumably it is used elsewhere), so we just have to eliminate the multiple assignment to x. The result is shown in Figure 5-4, where we have used the names x1 and x2 to distinguish the separate uses of x.

The single-assignment form is important because it allows us to identify a unique location in the code where each named location is computed. As an introduction to the data flow graph, we use two types of nodes in the graph— round nodes denote operators and square nodes represent values. The value nodes may be either inputs to the basic block, such as a and b, or variables assigned to within the block, such as w and x1. The data flow graph for our single-assignment code is shown in Figure 5-5. The single-assignment form means that the data flow graph is acyclic—if we assigned to x multiple times, then the second assignment would form a cycle in the graph including x and the operators used to compute x. Keeping the data flow graph acyclic is impor- tant in many types of analyses we want to do on the graph. (Of course, it is important to know whether the source code actually assigns to a variable mul- tiple times, because some of those assignments may be mistakes. We consider the analysis of source code for proper use of assignments in Section 5.9.1.)

The data flow graph is generally drawn in the form shown in Figure 5-6. Here, the variables are not explicitly represented by nodes. Instead, the edges

```
w = a + b;
x = a - c;
y = x + d;
x = a + c;
z = y + e;
```

Figure 5-3 *A basic block in C.*

```
w  = a + b;
x1 = a - c;
y  = x1 + d;
x2 = a + c;
z  = y + e;
```

Figure 5-4 *The basic block in single-assignment form.*

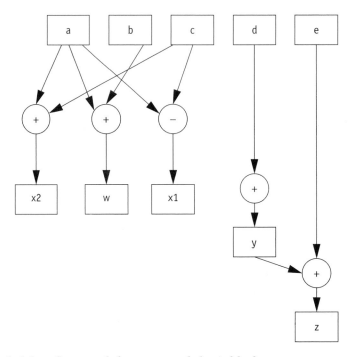

Figure 5-5 *An extended data flow graph for our sample basic block.*

are labeled with the variables they represent. As a result, a variable can be represented by more than one edge. However, the edges are directed and all the edges for a variable must come from a single source. We use this form for its simplicity and compactness.

The data flow graph for the code makes the order in which the operations are performed in the C code much less obvious. This is one of the advantages of the data flow graph. We can use it to determine feasible reorderings of the operations, which may help us to reduce pipeline or cache conflicts. We can also use it when the exact order of operations simply doesn't matter. The data flow graph defines a partial ordering of the operations in the basic block. We must ensure that a value is computed before it is used, but generally there are several possible orderings of evaluating expressions that satisfy this requirement.

5.3.2 Control/Data Flow Graphs

A CDFG uses a data flow graph as an element, adding constructs to describe control. In a basic CDFG, we have two types of nodes: **decision nodes** and **data**

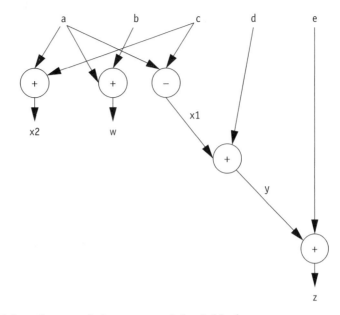

Figure 5-6 *Standard data flow graph for our sample basic block.*

flow nodes. A data flow node encapsulates a complete data flow graph to represent a basic block. We can use one type of decision node to describe all the types of control in a sequential program. (The jump/branch is, after all, the way we implement all those high-level control constructs.)

Figure 5-7 shows a bit of C code with control constructs and the CDFG constructed from it. The rectangular nodes in the graph represent the basic blocks. The basic blocks in the C code have been represented by function calls for simplicity. The diamond-shaped nodes represent the conditionals. The node's condition is given by the label, and the edges are labeled with the possible outcomes of evaluating the condition.

Building a CDFG for a while loop is straightforward, as shown in Figure 5-8. The while loop consists of both a test and a loop body, each of which we know how to represent in a CDFG. We can represent for loops by remembering that, in C, a for loop is defined in terms of a while loop. The following for loop

```
for (i = 0; i < N; i++) {
loop_body();
}
```

is equivalent to

```
if (cond1)
        basic_block_1();
else
        basic_block_2();
basic_block_3();
switch (test1) {
        case c1: basic_block_4(); break;
        case c2: basic_block_5(); break;
        case c3: basic_block_6(): break;
}
```
C code

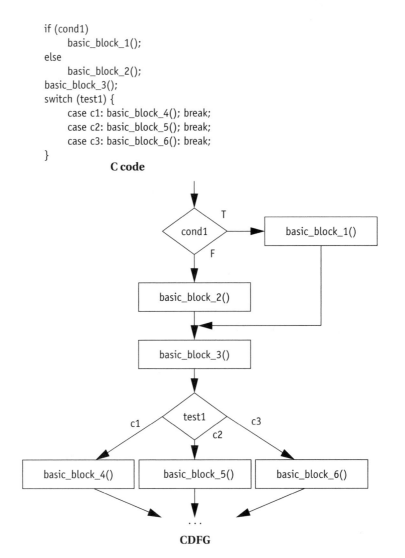

CDFG

Figure 5-7 *C code and its CDFG.*

```
i = 0;
while (i < N) {
loop_body();
i++;
}
```

C code

CDFG

Figure 5-8 *CDFG for a while loop.*

hierarchical representation

For a complete CDFG model, we can use a data flow graph to model each data flow node. Thus, the CDFG is a hierarchical representation—a data flow CDFG can be expanded to reveal a complete data flow graph.

An execution model for a CDFG is very much like the execution of the program it represents. The CDFG does not require explicit declaration of variables, but we assume that the implementation has sufficient memory for all the variables. We can define a state variable that represents a program counter in a CPU. (When studying a drawing of a CDFG, a finger works well for keeping track of the program counter state.) As we execute the program, we either execute the data flow node or compute the decision in the decision node and follow the appropriate edge, depending on the type of node the program counter points on. Even though the data flow nodes may specify only a partial ordering on the data flow computations, the CDFG is a sequential representation of the program. There is only one program counter in our execution model of the CDFG, and operations are not executed in parallel.

The CDFG is not necessarily tied to high-level language control structures. We can also build a CDFG for an assembly language program. A jump instruction corresponds to a nonlocal edge in the CDFG. Some architectures, such as ARM and many VLIW processors, support predicated execution of instructions, which may be represented by special constructs in the CDFG.

5.4 Assembly and Linking

Assembly and linking are the last steps in the compilation process—they turn a list of instructions into an image of the program's bits in memory. In this section, we survey the basic techniques required for assembly linking to help us understand the complete compilation process.

Figure 5-9 highlights the role of assemblers and linkers in the compilation process. This process is often hidden from us by compilation commands that do everything required to generate an executable program. As the figure shows, most compilers do not directly generate machine code, but instead create the instruction-level program in the form of human-readable assembly language. Generating assembly language rather than binary instructions frees the compiler writer from details extraneous to the compilation process, which include the instruction format as well as the exact addresses of instructions and data. The assembler's job is to translate symbolic assembly language statements into bit-level representations of instructions known as **object code.** The assembler takes care of instruction formats and does part of the job of translating labels into addresses. However, since the program may be built from many files, the final steps in determining the addresses of instructions and data are performed by the linker, which produces an **executable binary** file. That file may not necessarily be located in the CPU's memory, however, unless the linker happens to create the executable directly in RAM. The program that brings the program into memory for execution is called a **loader.**

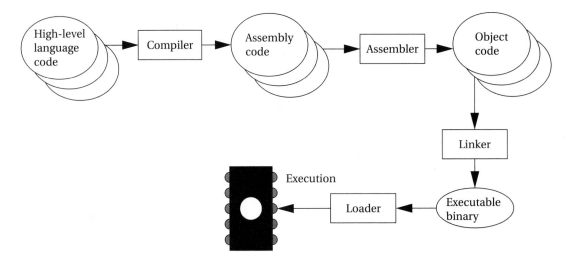

Figure 5-9 *Program generation from compilation through loading.*

The simplest form of the assembler assumes that the starting address of the assembly language program has been specified by the programmer. The addresses in such a program are known as **absolute addresses.** However, in many cases, particularly when we are creating an executable out of several component files, we do not want to specify the starting addresses for all the modules before assembly—if we did, we would have to determine before assembly not only the length of each program in memory but also the order in which they would be linked into the program. Most assemblers therefore allow us to use **relative addresses** by specifying at the start of the file that the origin of the assembly language module is to be computed later. Addresses within the module are then computed relative to the start of the module. The linker is then responsible for translating relative addresses into absolute addresses.

5.4.1 Assemblers

When translating assembly code into object code, the assembler must translate opcodes and format the bits in each instruction, and translate labels into addresses. In this section, we review the translation of assembly language into binary.

Labels make the assembly process more complex, but they are the most important abstraction provided by the assembler. Labels let the programmer (a human programmer or a compiler generating assembly code) avoid worrying about the absolute locations of instructions and data. Label processing requires making two passes through the assembly source code as follows:

1. The first pass scans the code to determine the address of each label.

2. The second pass assembles the instructions using the label values computed in the first pass.

As shown in Figure 5-10, the name of each symbol and its address is stored in a **symbol table** that is built during the first pass. The symbol table is built by

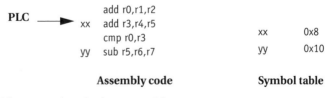

Figure 5-10 *Symbol table processing during assembly.*

scanning from the first instruction to the last. (For the moment, we assume that we know the absolute address of the first instruction in the program; we consider the general case in Section 5.4.2.) During scanning, the current location in memory is kept in a **program location counter (PLC).** Despite the similarity in name to a program counter, the PLC is not used to execute the program, only to assign memory locations to labels. For example, the PLC always makes exactly one pass through the program, whereas the program counter makes many passes over code in a loop. Thus, at the start of the first pass, the PLC is set to the program's starting address and the assembler looks at the first line. After examining the line, the assembler updates the PLC to the next location (since ARM instructions are four bytes long, the PLC would be incremented by four) and looks at the next instruction. If the instruction begins with a label, a new entry is made in the symbol table, which includes the label name and its value. The value of the label is equal to the current value of the PLC. At the end of the first pass, the assembler rewinds to the beginning of the assembly language file to make the second pass. During the second pass, when a label name is found, the label is looked up in the symbol table and its value substituted into the appropriate place in the instruction.

But how do we know the starting value of the PLC? The simplest case is absolute addressing. In this case, one of the first statements in the assembly language program is a pseudo-op that specifies the **origin** of the program, that is, the location of the first address in the program. A common name for this pseudo-op (e.g., the one used for the ARM) is the ORG statement

```
ORG     2000
```

which puts the start of the program at location 2000. This pseudo-op accomplishes this by setting the PLC's value to its argument's value, 2000 in this case. Assemblers generally allow a program to have many ORG statements in case instructions or data must be spread around various spots in memory. Example 5-1 illustrates the use of the PLC in generating the symbol table.

Example 5-1

Generating a Symbol Table

Let's use the following simple example of ARM assembly code:

```
        ORG 100
label1  ADR r4,c
        LDR r0,[r4]
label2  ADR r4,d
        LDR r1,[r4]
label3  SUB r0,r0,r1
```

The initial ORG statement tells us the starting address of the program. To begin, let's initialize the symbol table to an empty state and put the PLC at the initial ORG statement.

PLC = ??

```
        ORG 100
label1  ADR r4,c
        LDR r0,[r4]
label2  ADR r4,d
        LDR r1,[r4]
label3  SUB r0,r0,r1
```

Code **Symbol table**

The PLC value shown is at the beginning of this step, before we have processed the ORG statement. The ORG tells us to set the PLC value to 100.

PLC = 100

```
        ORG 100
label1  ADR r4,c
        LDR r0,[r4]
label2  ADR r4,d
        LDR r1,[r4]
label3  SUB r0,r0,r1
```

Code **Symbol table**

To process the next statement, we move the PLC to point to the next statement. But because the last statement was a pseudo-op that generates no memory values, the PLC value remains at 100.

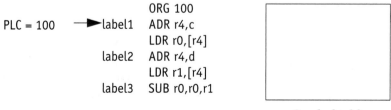

PLC = 100

```
        ORG 100
label1  ADR r4,c
        LDR r0,[r4]
label2  ADR r4,d
        LDR r1,[r4]
label3  SUB r0,r0,r1
```

Code **Symbol table**

Because there is a label in this statement, we add it to the symbol table, taking its value from the current PLC value.

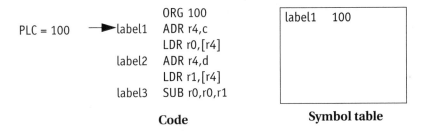

Code **Symbol table**

To process the next statement, we advance the PLC to point to the next line of the program and increment its value by the length in memory of the last line, namely, 4.

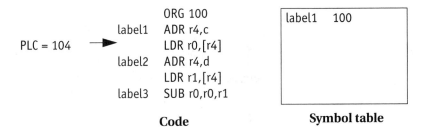

Code **Symbol table**

We continue this process as we scan the program until we reach the end, at which the state of the PLC and symbol table are as shown below.

```
            ORG 100
label1      ADR r4,c
            LDR r0,[r4]
label2      ADR r4,d
            LDR r1,[r4]
PLC = 116 ▶ label3   SUB r0,r0,r1
```

label1	100
label2	108
label3	116

Code **Symbol table**

Assemblers allow labels to be added to the symbol table without occupying space in the program memory. A typical name of this pseudo-op is EQU for equate. For example, in the code

```
          ADD r0,r1,r2
FOO       EQU 5
BAZ       SUB r3,r4,#FOO
```

the EQU pseudo-op adds a label named FOO with the value 5 to the symbol table. The value of the BAZ label is the same as if the EQU pseudo-op were not present, since EQU does not advance the PLC. The new label is used in the subsequent SUB instruction as the name for a constant. EQUs can be used to define symbolic values to help make the assembly code more structured.

The ARM assembler supports one pseudo-op that is particular to the ARM instruction set. In other architectures, an address would be loaded into a register (e.g., for an indirect access) by reading it from a memory location. ARM does not have an instruction that can load an effective address, so the assembler supplies the ADR pseudo-op to create the address in the register. It does so by using ADD or SUB instructions to generate the address. The address to be loaded can be register relative, program relative, or numeric, but it must assemble to a single instruction. More complicated address calculations must be explicitly programmed.

The assembler produces an object file that describes the instructions and data in binary format. A commonly used object file format, originally developed for Unix but now used in other environments as well, is known as COFF (common object file format). The object file must describe the instructions, data, and any addressing information and also usually carries along the symbol table for later use in debugging.

Generating relative code rather than absolute code introduces some new challenges to the assembly language process. Rather than using an ORG statement to provide the starting address, the assembly code uses a pseudo-op to indicate that the code is in fact relocatable. (Relative code is the default for both the ARM and SHARC assemblers.) Similarly, we must mark the output object file as being relative code. We can initialize the PLC to 0 to denote that addresses are relative to the start of the file. However, when we generate code that makes use of those labels, we must be careful, since we do not yet know the actual value that must be put into the bits. We must instead generate relocatable code. We use extra bits in the object file format to mark the relevant fields as relocatable and then insert the label's relative value into the field. The linker must therefore modify the generated code—when it finds a field marked as relative, it uses the absolute addresses that it has generated to replace the relative value with a correct, absolute value for the address. To understand the details of turning relocatable code into absolute executable code, we must understand the linking process described in the next section.

5.4.2 Linking

Many assembly language programs are written as several smaller pieces rather than as a single large file. Breaking a large program into smaller files helps delineate program modularity. If the program uses library routines, those will already be preassembled, and assembly language source code for the libraries may not be available for purchase. A **linker** allows a program to be stitched together out of several smaller pieces. The linker operates on the object files created by the assembler and modifies the assembled code to make the necessary links between files.

Some labels will be both defined and used in the same file. Other labels will be defined in a single file but used elsewhere as illustrated in Figure 5-11. The place in the file where a label is defined is known as an **entry point.** The place in the file where the label is used is called an **external reference.** The main job of the loader is to *resolve* external references based on available entry points. As a result of the need to know how definitions and references connect, the assembler passes to the linker not only the object file but also the symbol table. Even if the entire symbol table is not kept for later debugging purposes, it must at least pass the entry points. External references are identified in the object code by their relative symbol identifiers.

label1	LDR r0,[r1]		label2	ADR var1
	...			...
	ADR a			B label3
	...			...
	B label2		x	% 1
	...		y	% 1
var1	% 1		a	% 10

External references	Entry points
a	label1
label2	var1

External references	Entry points
var1	label2
label3	x
	y
	a

File 1 **File 2**

Figure 5-11 *External references and entry points.*

The linker proceeds in two phases. First, it determines the absolute address of the start of each object file. The order in which object files are to be loaded is given by the user, either by specifying parameters when the loader is run or by creating a **load map** file that gives the order in which files are to be placed in memory. Given the order in which files are to be placed in memory and the length of each object file, it is easy to compute the absolute starting address of each file. At the start of the second phase, the loader merges all symbol tables from the object files into a single, large table. It then edits the object files to change relative addresses into absolute addresses. This is typically performed by having the assembler write extra bits into the object file to identify the instructions and fields that refer to labels. If a label cannot be found in the merged symbol table, it is undefined and an error message is sent to the user.

Controlling where code modules are loaded into memory is important in embedded systems. Some data structures and instructions, such as those used to manage interrupts, must be put at precise memory locations for them to work. In other cases, different types of memory may be installed at different address ranges. For example, if we have EPROM in some locations and DRAM in others, we want to make sure that locations to be written are put in the DRAM locations.

Workstations and PCs provide **dynamically linked libraries,** and certain sophisticated embedded computing environments may provide them as well. Rather than link a separate copy of commonly used routines such as I/O to every executable program on the system, dynamically linked libraries allow them to be linked in at the start of program execution. A brief linking process is run just before execution of the program begins; the dynamic linker uses code libraries to link in the required routines. This not only saves storage space but also allows programs that use those libraries to be easily updated. However, it does introduce a delay before the program starts executing.

5.5 Basic Compilation Techniques

It is useful to understand how a high-level language program is translated into instructions. Since implementing an embedded computing system often requires controlling the instruction sequences used to handle interrupts, placement of data and instructions in memory, and so forth., understanding how the compiler works can help you know when you cannot rely on the compiler. Next, because many applications are also performance sensitive, understanding how code is generated can help you meet your performance goals, either by writing high-level code that gets compiled into the instructions you want or by recognizing when you must write your own assembly code.

compilation =
translation +
optimization

Compilation combines translation and optimization. The high-level language program is translated into the lower-level form of instructions; optimizations try to generate better instruction sequences than would be possible if the brute force technique of independently translating source code statements were used. Optimization techniques focus on more of the program to ensure that compilation decisions that appear to be good for one statement are not unnecessarily problematic for other parts of the program.

The compilation process is summarized in Figure 5-12. Compilation begins with high-level language code such as C and generally produces assembly code. (Directly producing object code simply duplicates the functions of an assembler, which is a very desirable stand-alone program to have.) The high-level language program is parsed to break it into statements and expressions. In addition, a symbol table is generated, which includes all the named objects in the program. Some compilers may then perform higher-level optimizations that can be viewed as modifying the high-level language program input without reference to instructions.

Simplifying arithmetic expressions is one example of a machine-independent optimization. Not all compilers do such optimizations, and compilers can vary widely regarding which combinations of machine-independent optimizations they do perform. Instruction-level optimizations are aimed at generating code. They may work directly on real instructions or on a pseudo-instruction format that is later mapped onto the instructions of the target CPU. This level of optimization also helps modularize the compiler by allowing code

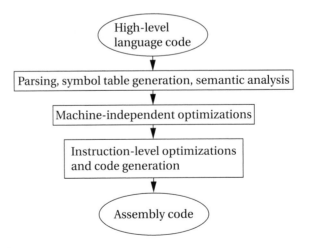

Figure 5-12 *The compilation process.*

generation to create simpler code that is later optimized. For example, consider the following array access code:

x[i] = c*x[i];

A simple code generator would generate the address for x[i] twice, once for each appearance in the statement. The later optimization phases can recognize this as an example of common expressions that need not be duplicated. While in this simple case it would be possible to create a code generator that never generated the redundant expression, taking into account every such optimization at code generation time is very difficult. We get better code and more reliable compilers by generating simple code first and then optimizing it.

5.5.1 Statement Translation

In this section, we consider the basic job of translating the high-level language program with little or no optimization. Let's first consider how to translate an expression. A large amount of the code in a typical application consists of arithmetic and logical expressions. Understanding how to compile a single expression, as described in Example 5-2, is a good first step in understanding the entire compilation process.

Example 5-2

Compiling an Arithmetic Expression

In the following arithmetic expression,

a*b + 5*(c − d)

the variable is written in terms of program variables. In some machines we may be able to perform memory-to-memory arithmetic directly on the locations corresponding to those variables. However, in many machines, such as the ARM, we must first load the variables into registers. This requires choosing which registers receive not only the named variables but also intermediate results such as (c − d).

The code for the expression can be built by walking the data flow graph. The data flow graph for the expression appears below.

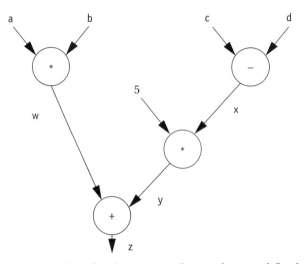

The temporary variables for the intermediate values and final result have been named w, x, y, and z. To generate code, we walk from the tree's root (where z, the final result, is generated) by traversing the nodes in post order. During the walk, we generate instructions to cover the operation at every node. The path is presented below.

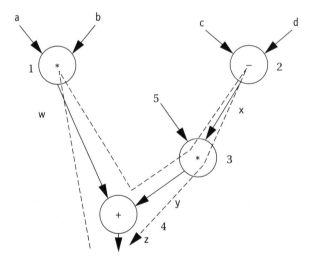

The nodes are numbered in the order in which code is generated. Since every node in the data flow graph corresponds to an operation that is directly supported by the instruction set, we simply generate an instruction at every node. Since we are making an arbitrary register assignment, we can use up the registers in order starting with r1. The resulting ARM code follows:

```
; operator 1 (+)
ADR r4,a          ; get address for a
MOV r1,[r4]       ; load a
ADR r4,b          ; get address for b
MOV r2,[r4]       ; load b
ADD r3,r1,r2      ; put w into r3
; operator 2 (−)
ADR r4,c          ; get address for c
MOV r4,[r4]       ; load c
ADR r4,d          ; get address for d
MOV r5,[r4]       ; load d
SUB r6,r4,r5      ; put x into r6
; operator 3 (*)
MUL r7,r6,#5      ; operator 3, puts y into r7
; operator 4 (+)
ADD r8,r7,r3      ; operator 4, puts z into r8
```

The equivalent SHARC code appears below.

```
! operator 1 (+)
R1 = DM(a);               ! load a
R2 = DM(b);               ! load b
R3 = R1 + R2;             ! compute a + b
! operator 2 (−)
R4 = DM(c);               ! load c
R5 = DM(d);               ! load d
R6 = R4 − R5;             ! compute c − d
! operator 3 (*)
R7 = 5;
R8 = R6 * R7;             ! compute y
! operator 4 (+)
R9 = R3 + R8;             ! compute z
```

One obvious optimization is to reuse a register whose value is no longer needed. In the case of the intermediate values w, x, and y, we know that they cannot be used after the end of the expression (e.g., in another expression) since they have no name in the C program. However, the final result z may in fact be used in a C assignment and the value reused later in the program. In this case we would need to know when the register is no longer needed to determine its best use.

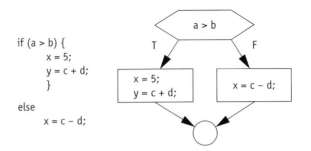

if (a > b) {
 x = 5;
 y = c + d;
 }
else
 x = c – d;

Figure 5-13 *Flow of control in C and control flow diagrams.*

 In the previous example, we made an arbitrary allocation of variables to registers for simplicity. When we have large programs with multiple expressions, we must allocate registers more carefully since CPUs have a limited number of registers. We will consider register allocation in Section 5.5.8.

 We also need to be able to translate control structures. Since conditionals are controlled by expressions, the code generation techniques of the last example can be used for those expressions, leaving us with the task of generating code for the flow of control itself. Figure 5-13 shows a simple example of changing flow of control in C—an if statement, in which the condition controls whether the true or false branch of the if is taken. Figure 5-13 also shows the control flow diagram for the if statement.

 Example 5-3 illustrates how to implement conditionals in assembly language.

Example 5-3

Generating Code for a Conditional

Consider the following C statement:

```
if (a + b > 0)
    x = 5;
else
    x = 7;
```

The CDFG for the statement appears below.

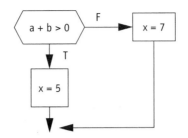

We know how to generate the code for the expressions. We can generate the control flow code by walking the CDFG. One ordered walk through the CDFG follows:

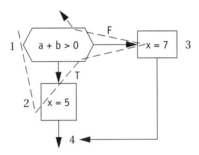

To generate code, we must assign a label to the first instruction at the end of a directed edge and create a branch for each edge that does not go to the immediately following instruction. The exact steps to be taken at the branch points depend on the target architecture. On some machines, evaluating expressions generates condition codes that we can test in subsequent branches, and on other machines we must use test-and-branch instructions. ARM allows us to test condition codes, so we get the following ARM code for the 1-2-3 walk:

```
            ADR r5,a      ; get address for a
            LDR r1,[r5]   ; load a
            ADR r5,b      ; get address for b
            LDR r2,b      ; load b
            ADD r3,r1,r2
            BLE label3    ; true condition falls through branch
; true case
            LDR r3,#5     ; load constant
            ADR r5,x
            STR r3, [r5]  ; store value into x
            B stmtend     ; done with the true case
```

```
; false case
label3       LDR r3,#7    ; load constant
             ADR r5,x     ; get address of x
             STR r3,[r5]  ; store value into x
stmtend      ...
```

The 1-2 and 3-4 edges do not require a branch and label because they are straight-line code. In contrast, the 1-3 and 2-4 edges do require a branch and a label for the target.

Since expressions are generally created as straight-line code, they typically require careful consideration of the order in which the operations are executed. We have much more freedom when generating conditional code because the branches ensure that the flow of control goes to the right block of code. If we walk the CDFG in a different order and lay out the code blocks in a different order in memory, we still get valid code as long as we properly place branches.

Drawing a control flow graph based on the while form of the loop helps us understand how to translate it into instructions.

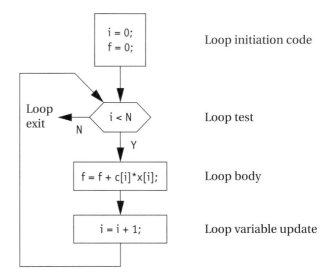

C compilers can generate (using the -s flag) assembler source, which some compilers intersperse with the C code. Such code is a very good way to learn about both assembly language programming and compilation. Web Aid 5-

Assembly has examples of assembly output from C compilers for the ARM and SHARC.

5.5.2 Procedures

Another major code generation problem is the creation of procedures. Generating code for procedures is relatively straightforward once we know the procedure linkage appropriate for the CPU. At the procedure definition, we generate the code to handle the procedure call and return. At each call of the procedure, we set up the procedure parameters and make the call.

The CPU's subroutine call mechanism is usually not sufficient to directly support procedures in modern programming languages. We introduced the procedure stack and procedure linkages in Section 2.3.3. The linkage mechanism provides a way for the program to pass parameters into the program and for the procedure to return a value. It also provides help in restoring the values of registers that the procedure has modified. All procedures in a given programming language use the same linkage mechanism (although different languages may use different linkages). The mechanism can also be used to call handwritten assembly language routines from compiled code.

Procedure stacks are typically built to grow down from high addresses. A **stack pointer** (sp) defines the end of the current frame, while a **frame pointer** (fp) defines the end of the last frame. (The fp is technically necessary only if the stack frame can be grown by the procedure during execution.) The procedure can refer to an element in the frame by addressing relative to sp. When a new procedure is called, the sp and fp are modified to push another frame onto the stack.

The ARM Procedure Call Standard (APCS) is a good illustration of a typical procedure linkage mechanism. Although the stack frames are in main memory, understanding how registers are used is key to understanding the mechanism, as explained below.

- r0–r3 are used to pass parameters into the procedure. r0 is also used to hold the return value. If more than four parameters are required, they are put on the stack frame.

- r4–r7 hold register variables.

- r11 is the frame pointer and r13 is the stack pointer.

- r10 holds the limiting address on stack size, which is used to check for stack overflows.

Other registers have additional uses in the protocol.

Figure 5-14 *Layout of a one-dimensional array in memory.*

5.5.3 Data Structures

The compiler must also translate references to data structures into references to raw memories. In general, this requires address computations. Some of these computations can be done at compile time while others must be done at run time.

arrays

Arrays are interesting because the address of an array element must in general be computed at run time, since the array index may change. Let us first consider one-dimensional arrays:

a[i]

The layout of the array in memory is shown in Figure 5-14: The zeroth element is stored as the first element of the array, the first element directly below, and so on. We can create a pointer for the array that points to the array's head, namely, a[0]. If we call that pointer aptr for convenience, then we can rewrite the reading of a[i] as

*(aptr + i)

Two-dimensional arrays are more challenging. There are multiple possible ways to lay out a two-dimensional array in memory, as shown in Figure 5-15. In this form, which is known as **row major,** the inner variable of the array (j in a[i,j]) varies most quickly. (Fortran uses a different organization known as column major.) Two-dimensional arrays also require more sophisticated addressing—in particular, we must know the size of the array. Let us consider the row-major form. If the a[] array is of size $N \times M$, then we can turn the two-dimensional array access into a one-dimensional array access. Thus,

a[i,j]

Figure 5-15 *Memory layout for two-dimensional arrays.*

becomes

a[i*M + j]

where the maximum value for j is M − 1.

A C struct is easier to address. As shown in Figure 5-16, a structure is implemented as a contiguous block of memory. Fields in the structure can be accessed using constant offsets to the base address of the structure. In this example, if field1 is four bytes long, then field2 can be accessed as

*(aptr + 4)

This addition can usually be done at compile time, requiring only the indirection itself to fetch the memory location during execution.

5.5.4 Expression Simplification

Expression simplification is a useful area for machine-independent transformations. We can use the laws of algebra to simplify expressions. Consider the following expression:

a*b + a*c

We can use the distributive law to rewrite the expression as

a*(b + c)

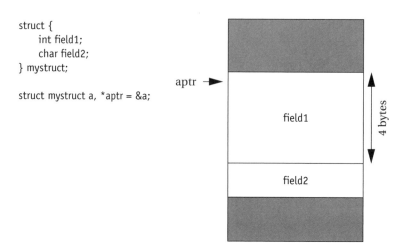

```
struct {
    int field1;
    char field2;
} mystruct;

struct mystruct a, *aptr = &a;
```

Figure 5-16 *C structure layout and access.*

Since the new expression has only two operations rather than three for the original form, it is almost certainly cheaper, because it is both faster and smaller. Such transformations make some broad assumptions about the relative cost of operations. In some cases, simple generalizations about the cost of operations may be misleading. For example, a CPU with a multiply-and-accumulate instruction may be able to do a multiply and addition as cheaply as it can do an addition. However, such situations can often be taken care of in code generation.

We can also use the laws of arithmetic to further simplify expressions on constants. Consider the following C statement:

for (i = 0; i < 8 + 1; i++)

We can simplify 8 + 1 to 9 at compile time—there is no need to perform that arithmetic while the program is executing. Why would a program ever contain expressions that evaluate to constants? Using named constants rather than numbers is good programming practice and often leads to constant expression. The original form of the for statement could have been

for (i = 0; i < NOPS + 1; i++)

where, for example, the added 1 takes care of a trailing null character.

5.5.5 Dead Code Elimination

Code that will never be executed can be safely removed from the program. The general problem of identifying code that will never be executed is difficult, but there are some important special cases where it can be done.

Programmers will intentionally introduce dead code in certain situations. Consider this C code fragment:

```
#define DEBUG 0
...
if (DEBUG) print_debug_stuff();
```

In the above case, the print_debug_stuff() function is never executed, but the code allows the programmer to override the preprocessor variable definition (perhaps with a compile-time flag) to enable the debugging code. This case is easy to analyze because the condition is the constant 0, which C uses for the false condition. Since there is no else clause in the if statement, the compiler can totally eliminate the if statement, rewriting the CDFG to provide a direct edge between the statements before and after the if.

Some dead code may be introduced by the compiler. For example, certain optimizations introduce copy statements that copy one variable to another. If uses of the first variable can be replaced by references to the second one, then the copy statement becomes dead code that can be eliminated.

5.5.6 Procedure Inlining

Another machine-independent transformation that requires a little more evaluation is procedure inlining. An inlined procedure does not have a separate procedure body and procedure linkage; rather, the body of the procedure is substituted in place for the procedure call. Figure 5-17 shows an example of function inlining in C. The C++ programming language provides an inline construct that tells the compiler to generate inline code for a function. In this case, an inlined procedure is generated in expanded form whenever possible. However, inlining is not always the best thing to do. It does eliminate the procedure linkage instructions. However, in a cached system, having multiple copies of the function body may actually slow down the fetches of these instructions. Inlining also increases code size, and memory may be precious.

int foo(a,b,c) { return a + b – c; }

Function definition

z = foo(w,x,y,);

Function call

z = w + x – y;

Inlining result

Figure 5-17 *Function inlining in C.*

5.5.7 Loop Transformations

Loops are important program structures—although they are compactly described in the source code, they often use a large fraction of the computation time. Many techniques have been designed to optimize loops.

A simple but useful transformation is known as **loop unrolling,** which is illustrated in Example 5-4. Loop unrolling is important because it helps expose parallelism that can be used by later stages of the compiler.

Example 5-4

Loop Unrolling

A simple loop in C follows:

```
for (i = 0; i < N; i++) {
    a[i]=b[i]*c[i];
}
```

This loop is executed a fixed number of times, namely, N. A straightforward implementation of the loop would create and initialize the loop variable i, update its value on every iteration, and test it to see whether to exit the loop. However, since the loop is executed a fixed number of times, we can generate more direct code.

If we let $N = 4$, then we can substitute the above C code for the following loop:

```
a[0] = b[0]*c[0];
a[1] = b[1]*c[1];
```

```
a[2] = b[2]*c[2];
a[3] = b[3]*c[3];
```

This unrolled code has no loop overhead code at all, that is, no iteration variable and no tests. But the unrolled loop has the same problems as the inlined procedure—it may interfere with the cache and expands the amount of code required.

We do not, of course, have to fully unroll loops. Rather than unroll the above loop four times, we could unroll it twice. The following code results:

```
for (i = 0; i < 2; i++) {
    a[i*2] = b[i*2]*c[i*2];
    a[i*2 + 1] = b[i*2 + 1]*c[i*2 + 1];
    }
```

In this case, since all operations in the two lines of the loop body are independent, later stages of the compiler may be able to generate code that allows them to be executed efficiently on the CPU's pipeline.

Loop fusion combines two or more loops into a single loop. For this transformation to be legal, two conditions must be satisfied. First, the loops must iterate over the same values. Second, the loop bodies must not have dependencies that would be violated if they are executed together—for example, if the second loop's ith iteration depends on the results of the $i + 1$th iteration of the first loop, the two loops cannot be combined. **Loop distribution** is the opposite of loop fusion, that is, decomposing a single loop into multiple loops.

Loop tiling breaks up a loop into a set of nested loops, with each inner loop performing the operations on a subset of the data. An example is shown in Figure 5-18. Here, each loop is broken up into tiles of size two. Each loop is split into two loops—for example, the inner ii loop iterates within the tile and the outer i loop iterates across the tiles. The result is that the pattern of accesses across the a array is drastically different—rather than walking across one row in its entirety, the code walks through rows and columns following the tile structure. Loop tiling changes the order in which array elements are accessed, thereby allowing us to better control the behavior of the cache during loop execution.

We can also modify the arrays being indexed in loops. **Array padding** adds dummy data elements to a loop in order to change the layout of the array in the cache. Although these array locations will not be used, they do change how the useful array elements fall into cache lines. Judicious padding can in some cases significantly reduce the number of cache conflicts during loop execution.

Code

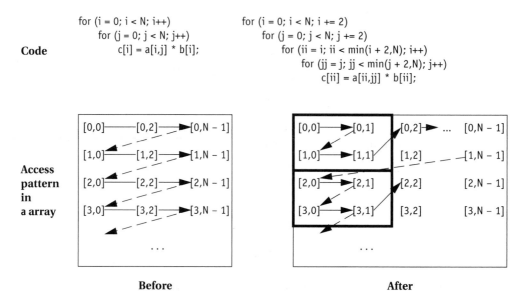

```
for (i = 0; i < N; i++)              for (i = 0; i < N; i += 2)
    for (j = 0; j < N; j++)             for (j = 0; j < N; j += 2)
        c[i] = a[i,j] * b[i];               for (ii = i; ii < min(i + 2,N); i++)
                                                for (jj = j; jj < min(j + 2,N); j++)
                                                    c[ii] = a[ii,jj] * b[ii];
```

**Access
pattern
in
a array**

Before **After**

Figure 5-18 *Loop tiling.*

5.5.8 Register Allocation

Register allocation is a very important compilation phase. Given a block of code, we want to choose assignments of variables (both declared and temporary) to registers to minimize the total number of required registers. Example 5-5 illustrates the importance of proper register allocation.

Example 5-5

Register Allocation

To keep the example small, we assume that we can use only four of the ARM's registers. In fact, such a restriction is not unthinkable—programming conventions can reserve certain registers for special purposes and significantly reduce the number of general-purpose registers available.

Consider the following C code:

```
w = a + b; /* statement 1 */
x = c + w; /* statement 2 */
y = c + d; /* statement 3 */
```

A naive register allocation, assigning each variable to a separate register, would require seven registers for the seven variables in the above code. However, we can do much better by reusing a register once the value stored in the register is no longer needed. To understand how to do this, we can draw a **lifetime graph** that shows the statements on which each statement is used. Appearing below is a lifetime graph in which the *x* axis is the statement number in the C code and the *y* axis shows the variables.

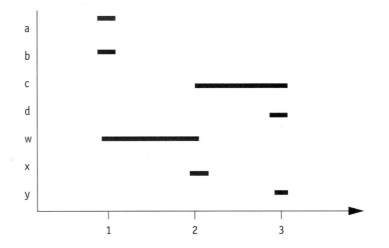

A horizontal line stretches from the first statement where the variable is used to the last use of the variable; a variable is said to be **live** during this interval. At each statement, we can determine every variable currently in use. The maximum number of variables in use at any statement determines the maximum number of registers required. In this case, statement two requires three registers: c, w, and x. This fits within the four registers limitation. By reusing registers once their current values are no longer needed, we can write code that requires no more than four registers. Appearing below is one register assignment.

a	r0
b	r1
c	r2
d	r0
w	r3
x	r0
y	r3

The ARM assembly code that uses the above register assignment follows:

```
LDR r0,[p_a]        ; load a into r0 using pointer to a (p_a)
LDR r1,[p_b]        ; load b into r1
ADD r3,r0,r1        ; compute a + b
STR r3,[p_w]        ; w = a + b
LDR r2,[p_c]        ; load c into r2
ADD r0,r2,r3        ; compute c + w, reusing r0 for x
STR r0,[p_x]        ; x = c + w
LDR r0,[p_d]        ; load d into r0
ADD r3,r2,r0        ; compute c + d, reusing r3 for y
STR r3,[p_y]        ; y = c + d
```

If a section of code requires more registers than are available, we must **spill** some of the values out to memory temporarily. After computing some values, we write the values to temporary memory locations, reuse those registers in other computations, and then reread the old values from the temporary locations to resume work. Spilling registers is problematic in several respects. For example, it requires extra CPU time and uses up both instruction and data memory. Putting effort into register allocation to avoid unnecessary register spills is worth your time.

We can solve register allocation problems by building a **conflict graph** and solving a graph coloring problem. As shown in Figure 5-19, each variable in the high-level language code is represented by a node. An edge is added between two nodes if they are both live at the same time. The graph coloring problem is to use the smallest number of distinct colors to color all the nodes such that no two nodes are directly connected by an edge of the same color. The figure shows a satisfying coloring that uses three colors. Graph coloring is NP-complete, but there are efficient heuristic algorithms that can give good results on typical register allocation problems.

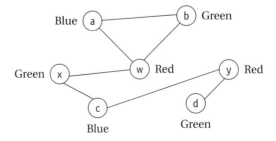

Figure 5-19 *Using graph coloring to solve the problem of Example 5-5.*

Lifetime analysis assumes that we have already determined the order in which we will evaluate operations. In many cases, we have freedom in the order in which we do things. Consider the following expression:

(a + b) * (c - d)

We have to do the multiplication last, but we can do either the addition or the subtraction first. Different orders of loads, stores, and arithmetic operations may also result in different execution times on pipelined machines. If we can keep values in registers without having to reread them from main memory, we can save execution time and reduce code size as well. Example 5-6 illustrates how proper **operator scheduling** can improve register allocation.

Example 5-6

Operator Scheduling for Register Allocation

Here is sample C code fragment:

```
w = a + b; /* statement 1 */
x = c + d; /* statement 2 */
y = x + e; /* statement 3 */
z = a − b; /* statement 4 */
```

If we compile the statements in the order in which they were written, we get the register graph below.

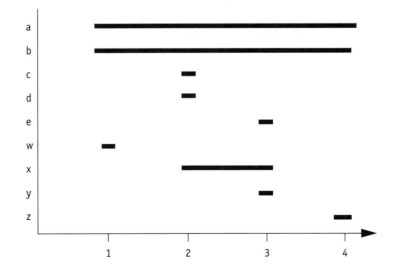

Since w is needed until the last statement, we need five registers at statement 3, even though only three registers are needed for the statement at line 3. If we swap statements 3 and 4 (renumbering them 3′ and 4′), we reduce our requirements to three registers. The modified C code follows:

```
w = a + b; /* statement 1 */
z = a - b; /* statement 2' */
x = c + d; /* statement 3' */
y = x + e; /* statement 4' */
```

The lifetime graph for the new code appears below.

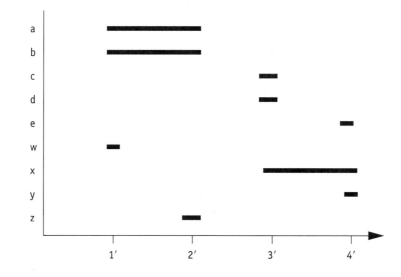

Compare the ARM assembly code for the two code fragments. We have written both assuming that we have only four free registers. In the *before* version, we do not have to write out any values, but we must read a and b twice. The *after* version allows us to retain all values in registers as long as we need them.

Before version

```
LDR r0,a
LDR r1,b
ADD r2,r0,r1
STR r2,w ; w = a + b
LDRr r0,c
LDR r1,d
ADD r2,r0,r1
```

After version

```
LDR r0,a
LDR r1,b
ADD r2,r1,r0
STR r2,w ; w = a + b
SUB r2,r0,r1
STR r2,z ; z = a - b
LDR r0,c
```

```
STR r2,x ; x = c + d          LDR r1,d
LDR r1,e                      ADD r2,r1,r0
ADD r0,r1,r2                  STR r2,x ; x = c + d
STR r0,y ; y = x + e          LDR r1,e
LDR r0,a ; reload a           ADD r0,r1,r2
LDR r1,b ; reload b           STR r0,y ; y = x + e
SUB r2,r1,r0
STR r2,z ; z = a − b
```

5.5.9 Scheduling

We have some freedom to choose the order in which operations will be performed. We can use this to our advantage—for example, we may be able to improve the register allocation by changing the order in which operations are performed, thereby changing the lifetimes of the variables.

We can solve scheduling problems by keeping track of resource utilization over time. We do not have to know the exact microarchitecture of the CPU—all we have to know is that, for example, instruction types 1 and 2 both use resource A while instruction types 3 and 4 use resource B. CPU manufacturers generally disclose enough information about the microarchitecture to allow us to schedule instructions even when they do not provide a detailed description of the CPU's internals.

We can keep track of CPU resources during instruction scheduling using a **reservation table** [Kog81]. As illustrated in Figure 5-20, rows in the table represent instruction execution time slots and columns represent resources that must be scheduled. Before scheduling an instruction to be executed at a particular time, we check the reservation table to determine whether all resources needed by the instruction are available at that time. Upon scheduling the instruction, we update the table to note all resources used by that instruction. Various algorithms can be used for the scheduling itself, depending on the

Time	Resource A	Resource B
t	X	
t + 1	X	X
t + 2	X	
t + 3		X

Figure 5-20 *A reservation table for instruction scheduling.*

types of resources and instructions involved, but the reservation table provides a good summary of the state of an instruction scheduling problem in progress.

We can also schedule instructions to maximize performance. As we know from Section 3.6, when an instruction that takes more cycles than normal to finish is in the pipeline, pipeline bubbles appear that reduce performance. **Software pipelining** is a technique for reordering instructions across several loop iterations to reduce pipeline bubbles. Software pipelining is illustrated in Example 5-7.

Example 5-7

Software Pipelining in SHARC

Software pipelining can be illustrated with a small loop on the SHARC. Consider the following simple loop for a dot product computation:

```
for (i = 0; i < N; i++)
    sum += a[i] * b[i];
```

The SHARC can perform several operations in parallel. However, we can't perform the necessary loads and arithmetic operations on the same cycle.

Assume that we want to rewrite the loop so that we perform two loads, an addition, and a multiplication in one iteration. However, because the result of one operation depends on others, we can't do all these operations for the same iteration at the same time. Instead, the loop body will perform operations from the following three different iterations:

1. The two fetches of the array elements are performed for availability in the next cycle.

2. The multiplication a[i]*b[i] is performed on the operands fetched by the previous loop iteration.

3. The addition into the dot product running sum is performed using the result of the multiplication performed in the previous loop iteration.

When we rewrite the loop, we need to generate special header and trailer code that takes care of the first and last iterations that cannot be pipelined. The C code below is designed to show which operations can be performed in parallel on the SHARC.

```
/* first iteration performed outside loop */
ai = a[0]; bi = b[0]; /* first iteration */
p = ai*bi; ai = a[1]; bi = b[1]; /* second iteration */
/* initiate loads used in second iteration; remaining
    loads will be performed inside the loop */
for (i = 2; i < N – 2; i++) {
    ai = a[i]; bi = b[i]; /* fetch for use in next cycle's multiply */
    p = ai*bi; /* multiply for next iteration's sum */
    sum += p; /* compute sum using p computed in last iteration */
}
/* trailer code */
sum += p; p = ai*bi; /* next-to-last iteration */
sum += p; /* last iteration */
```

In this code, none of the operations in the loop body depend on each other—remember that the p in p = ai*bi is writing a different value than is being used by sum += p, so they can operate in parallel. This allows all the operations to be performed in a single SHARC instruction that performs two data reads, a multiply, and an addition.

5.5.10 Instruction Selection

Selecting the instructions to use to implement each operation is not trivial. There may be several different instructions that can be used to accomplish the same goal, but they may have different execution times. Moreover, using one instruction for one part of the program may affect the instructions that can be used in adjacent code. Although we can't discuss all the problems and methods for code generation here, a little bit of knowledge helps us envision what the compiler is doing.

template matching

One useful technique for generating code is **template matching,** illustrated in Figure 5-21. We have a DAG that represents the expression for which we want to generate code. In order to be able to match up instructions and operations, we represent instructions using the same DAG representation. We shaded the instruction template nodes to distinguish them from code nodes. Each node has a cost, which may be simply the execution time of the instruction or may include factors for size, power consumption, and so on. In this case, we have shown that each instruction takes the same amount of time, and thus all have a cost of 1. Our goal is to cover all nodes in the code DAG with

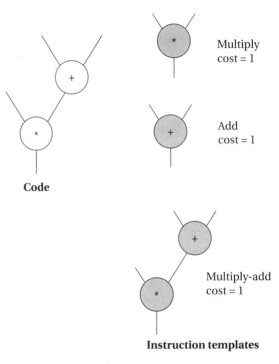

Figure 5-21 *Code generation by template matching.*

instruction DAGs—until we have covered the code DAG we haven't generated code for all the operations in the expression. In this case, the lowest-cost covering uses the multiply-add instruction to cover both nodes. If we first tried to cover the bottom node with the multiply instruction, we would find ourselves blocked from using the multiply-add instruction. Dynamic programming can be used to efficiently find the lowest-cost covering of trees, and heuristics can extend the technique to DAGs.

5.5.11 Understanding and Using Your Compiler

Clearly, the compiler can vastly transform your program during the creation of assembly language. But compilers are also substantially different in terms of the optimizations they perform. Understanding your compiler can help you get the best code out of it.

Studying the assembly language output of the compiler is a good way to learn about what the compiler does. Some compilers will annotate sections of code to help you make the correspondence between the source and assembler output. Starting with small examples that exercise only a few types of state-

ments will help. You can experiment with different optimization levels (the -0 flag on most C compilers). You can also try writing the same algorithm in several ways to see how the compiler's output changes.

If you can't get your compiler to generate the code you want, you may need to write your own assembly language. You can do this by writing it from scratch or modifying the output of the compiler. If you write your own assembly code, you must ensure that it conforms to all compiler conventions, such as procedure call linkage. If you modify the compiler output, you should be sure that you have the algorithm right before you start writing code so that you don't have to repeatedly edit the compiler's assembly language output. You also need to clearly document the fact that the high-level language source is, in fact, not the code used in the system.

5.5.12 Interpreters and JIT Compilers

Programs are not always compiled and then separately executed. In some cases, it may make sense to translate the program into instructions during execution. Two well-known techniques for on-the-fly translation are **interpretation** and **just-in-time (JIT) compilation.** The trade-offs for both techniques are similar. Interpretation or JIT compilation adds overhead—both time and memory—to execution. However, that overhead may be more than made up for in some circumstances. For example, if only parts of the program are executed over some period of time, interpretation or JIT compilation may save memory, even taking overhead into account. Interpretation and JIT compilation also provide added security when programs arrive over the network.

An **interpreter** translates program statements one at a time. The program may be expressed in a high-level language, with Forth being a prime example of an embedded language that is interpreted. An interpreter may also interpret instructions in some abstract machine language. As illustrated in Figure 5-22, the interpreter sits between the program and the machine. It translates one statement of the program at a time. The interpreter may or may not generate an explicit piece of code to represent the statement. Because the interpreter translates only a very small piece of the program at any given time, a small amount of memory is used to hold intermediate representations of the program. In many cases, a Forth program plus the Forth interpreter are smaller than the equivalent native machine code.

JIT compilers have been used for many years, but are best known today for their use in Java environments [Cra97]. A JIT compiler is somewhere between an interpreter and a stand-alone compiler. A JIT compiler produces executable code segments for pieces of the program. However, it compiles a section of the program (such as a function) only when it knows it will be executed. Unlike an interpreter, it saves the compiled version of the code so that the code does not have to be retranslated the next time it is executed. A JIT compiler saves some

Figure 5-22 *Structure of a program interpretation system.*

execution time overhead relative to an interpreter because it does not translate the same piece of code multiple times, but it also uses more memory for the intermediate representation. The JIT compiler usually generates machine code directly rather than building intermediate program representation data structures such as the CDFG. A JIT compiler also usually performs only simple optimizations as compared to a stand-alone compiler.

5.6 Analysis and Optimization of Execution Time

Because embedded systems must perform functions in real time, we often need to know how fast a program runs. The techniques we use to analyze program execution time are also helpful in analyzing properties such as power consumption. In this section, we study how to analyze programs to estimate their run times. We also examine how to optimize programs to improve their execution times; of course, optimization relies on analysis.

Note the word "estimate" in the last paragraph. While we might hope that the execution time of programs could be precisely determined, this is in fact difficult to do in practice. A few of the reasons for such difficulty are summarized below.

- The execution time of a program often varies with the input data values because those values select different execution paths in the program. For example, loops may be executed a varying number of times, and different branches may execute blocks of varying complexity.

- The cache has a major effect on program performance, and once again, the cache's behavior depends in part on the data values input to the program.

- Execution times may vary even at the instruction level. Floating-point operations are the most sensitive to data values, but the normal integer execution pipeline can also introduce data-dependent variations. In general, the execution time of an instruction in a pipeline depends not only on that instruction but on the instructions around it in the pipeline.

measuring
execution speed

We can measure program performance in several ways:

- Some microprocessor manufacturers supply simulators for their CPUs: The simulator runs on a workstation or PC, takes as input an executable for the microprocessor along with input data, and simulates the execution of that program. Some of these simulators go beyond functional simulation to measure the execution time of the program. Simulation is clearly slower than executing the program on the actual microprocessor, but it also provides much greater visibility during execution. Be careful—some microprocessor performance simulators are not 100% accurate, and simulation of I/O-intensive code may be difficult.

- A timer connected to the microprocessor bus can be used to measure performance of executing sections of code. The code to be measured would reset and start the timer at its start and stop the timer at the end of execution. The length of the program that can be measured is limited by the accuracy of the timer.

- A logic analyzer can be connected to the microprocessor bus to measure the start and stop times of a code segment. This technique relies on the code being able to produce identifiable events on the bus to identify the start and stop of execution. The length of code that can be measured is limited by the size of the logic analyzer's buffer.

We are interested in the following three different types of performance measures on programs:

- **average-case execution time:** This is the typical execution time we would expect for typical data. Clearly, the first challenge is defining typical inputs.

- **worst-case execution time:** The longest time that the program can spend on any input sequence is clearly important for systems that must meet deadlines. In some cases, the input set that causes the worst-case execution time is obvious, but in many cases it is not.

- **best-case execution time:** This measure can be important in multirate real-time systems, as seen in Chapter 6.

First, we look at the fundamentals of program performance in more detail. We then consider trace-driven performance based on executing the program and observing its behavior.

5.6.1 Elements of Program Performance

The key to evaluating execution time is breaking the performance problem into parts. Program execution time [Sha89] can be seen as

$$execution\ time = program\ path + instruction\ timing$$

The path is the sequence of instructions executed by the program (or its equivalent in the high-level language representation of the program). The instruction timing is determined based on the sequence of instructions traced by the program path, which takes into account data dependencies, pipeline behavior, and caching. Luckily, these two problems can be solved relatively independently.

Although we can trace the execution path of a program through its high-level language specification, it is hard to get accurate estimates of total execution time from a high-level language program. This is because there is not, as seen in Section 5.5, a direct correspondence between program statements and instructions. The number of memory locations and variables must be estimated, and results may be either saved for reuse or recomputed on the fly, among other effects. These problems become more challenging as the compiler puts more and more effort into optimizing the program. However, some aspects of program performance can be estimated by looking directly at the C program. For example, if a program contains a loop with a large, fixed iteration bound or if one branch of a conditional is much longer than another, we can get at least a rough idea that these are more time-consuming segments of the program.

Of course, a precise estimate of performance also relies on the instructions to be executed, since different instructions take different amounts of time. (In addition, to make life even more difficult, the execution time of one instruction can depend on the instructions executed before and after it.) Example 5-8 illustrates data-dependent program paths.

Example 5-8

Data-Dependent Paths in if *Statements*

Here is a pair of nested if statements:

```
if (a || b) { /* test 1 */
    if (c) /* test 2 */
        { x = r * s + t; /* assignment 1 */ }
    else { y = r + s; /* assignment 2 */ }
    z = r + s + u; /* assignment 3 */
} else {
    if (c) /* test 3 */
        { y = r - t; /* assignment 4 */ }
}
```

The conditional tests and assignments are labeled within each if statement to make it easier to identify paths. What execution paths may be exercised? One way to enumerate all the paths is to create a truth table–like structure. The paths are controlled by the variables in the if conditions, namely, a, b, and c. For any given combination of values of those variables, we can trace through the program to see which branch is taken at each if and which assignments are performed. For example, when a = 1, b = 0, and c = 1, then test 1 is true and test 2 is true. This means we first perform assignment 1 and then assignment 3. Results for all the controlling variable values follow:

a	b	c	Path
0	0	0	test 1 false, test 3 false: no assignments
0	0	1	test 1 false, test 3 true: assignment 4
0	1	0	test 1 true, test 2 false: assignments 2, 3
0	1	1	test 1 true, test 2 true: assignments 1, 3
1	0	0	test 1 true, test 2 false: assignments 2, 3
1	0	1	test 1 true, test 2 true: assignments 1, 3
1	1	0	test 1 true, test 2 false: assignments 2, 3
1	1	1	test 1 true, test 2 true: assignments 1, 3

Notice that there are only four distinct cases: no assignment, assignment 4, assignments 2 and 3, or assignments 1 and 3. These correspond to the possible

paths through the nested ifs; the table adds value by telling us which variable values exercise each of these paths.

Enumerating the paths through a fixed-iteration for loop is seemingly simple. In the code below,

```
for (i = 0; i < N; i++)
    a[i] = b[i]*c[i];
```

the assignment in the loop is performed exactly N times. However, we can't forget the code executed to set up the loop and to test the iteration variable. Example 5-9 illustrates how to determine the path through a loop.

Example 5-9

Paths in a loop

The loop code for the FIR filter of Application Example 2-1 is reproduced below:

```
for (i = 0, f = 0; i < N; i++)
    f = f + c[i] * x[i];
```

By examining the CDFG for the code we can more easily determine how many times various statements are executed. Here is the CDFG once again:

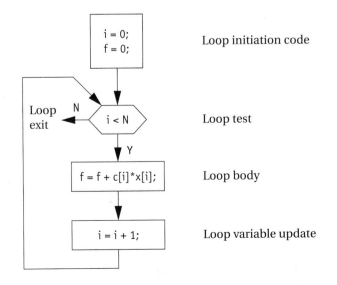

i = 0; f = 0;	Loop initiation code
Loop exit N i < N	Loop test
Y	
f = f + c[i]*x[i];	Loop body
i = i + 1;	Loop variable update

The CDFG makes it clear that the loop initiation block is executed once, the test is executed $N + 1$ times, and the body and loop variable update are each executed N times.

To measure the longest path length, we must find the longest path through the optimized CDFG since the compiler may change the structure of the control and data flow to optimize the program's implementation. It is important to keep in mind that choosing the longest path through a CDFG as measured by the number of nodes or edges touched may not correspond to the longest execution time. Since the execution time of a node in the CDFG will vary greatly depending on the instructions represented by that node, we must keep in mind that the longest path through the CDFG depends on the execution times of the nodes. In general, it is good policy to choose several of what we estimate are the longest paths through the program and measure the lengths of all of them in sufficient detail to be sure that we have in fact captured the longest path.

instruction
timing
Once we know the execution path of the program, we have to measure the execution time of the instructions executed along that path. The simplest estimate is to assume that every instruction takes the same number of clock cycles, which means we need only count the instructions and multiply by the per-instruction execution time to obtain the program's total execution time. However, even ignoring cache effects, this technique is simplistic for the reasons summarized below.

■ *Not all instructions take the same amount of time.* Although RISC architectures tend to provide uniform instruction execution times in order to keep the CPU's pipeline full, even many RISC architectures take different amounts of time to execute certain instructions. Multiple load-store instructions are examples of longer-executing instructions in the ARM architecture. Floating-point instructions show especially wide variations in execution time—while basic multiply and add operations are fast, some transcendental functions can take thousands of cycles to execute.

■ *Execution times of instructions are not independent.* The execution time of one instruction depends on the instructions around it. For example, many CPUs use register bypassing to speed up instruction sequences when the result of one instruction is used in the next instruction. As a result, the execution time of an instruction may depend on whether its destination register is used as a source for the next operation (or vice versa).

■ *The execution time of an instruction may depend on operand values.* This is clearly true of floating-point instructions in which a different number of iterations may be required to calculate the result. Other specialized

instructions can, for example, perform a data-dependent number of integer operations.

We can handle the first two problems more easily than the third. We can look up instruction execution time in a table; the table will be indexed by opcode and possibly by other parameter values such as the registers used. To handle interdependent execution times, we can add columns to the table to consider the effects of nearby instructions. Since these effects are generally limited by the size of the CPU pipeline, we know that we need to consider a relatively small window of instructions to handle such effects. Handling variations due to operand values is difficult to do without actually executing the program using a variety of data values, given the large number of factors that can affect value-dependent instruction timing. Luckily, these effects are often small. Even in floating-point programs, most of the operations are typically additions and multiplications whose execution times have small variances.

caching effects Thus far we have not considered the effect of the cache. Because the access time for main memory can be 10 times larger than the cache access time, caching can have huge effects on instruction execution time by changing both the instruction and data access times. Caching performance inherently depends on the program's execution path since the cache's contents depend on the history of accesses. Because of the complexity of this phenomenon, we consider it in more detail below using both trace-driven and static and dynamic analysis techniques.

5.6.2 Trace-Driven Performance Analysis

A **program trace** (or more succinctly, a **trace**) is a record of the execution path of a program that has been measured during program execution. If we can measure a trace from a running program, we avoid the need to analyze the program's CDFG to determine the execution path. Traces are typically large. Since we usually need to look at the entire execution history of a program, traces can be gigabytes in size. However, because disks to hold the traces are inexpensive and workstations to analyze them are fast and cheap, traces are an appealing way to analyze programs. We have to consider two problems: how to generate a trace and how to use it to determine program performance.

A trace can be captured by using hardware methods. For example, a logic analyzer can be attached to the microprocessor bus to capture memory bus traffic. There are two major limitations to this approach. First, the size of hardware trace buffers is usually limited. The hardware must be able to store instructions at execution speed; if we use high-speed RAM for the buffer, we are limited to perhaps several million instructions. This means that we probably cannot capture a trace of the entire program but only a section of its execution. Second, if the CPU has an on-chip cache, we will not be able to see

internal memory references to the program or the data. Alternatively, a microprocessor emulator can be used to trace the PC over time. Although this technique allows us to see what is going on inside the chip and not just behavior on the memory bus, it is too slow to generate long traces. Since the microprocessor must be stopped for probing and probing is very slow compared to normal execution, capturing long traces would require exorbitant amounts of time.

Some CPUs have hardware facilities for automatically generating trace information. For example, the Pentium family microprocessors generate a special bus cycle, a branch trace message, that shows the source and/or destination address of a branch [Col97]. If we record only traces, we can reconstruct the instructions executed within the basic blocks while greatly reducing the amount of memory required to hold the trace.

There are three major methods for generating a trace by software: **PC sampling, instrumentation instructions,** and **simulation.** The PC sampling technique uses the operating system or some other facility to periodically interrupt the program and save away the current PC value. This method has the same limitations of any sampling method—if the sampling period is too slow, we may miss important behavior; in particular, the wrong sampling interval can be a multiple of some periodic behavior in the program that could be totally missed. Alternatively, instructions can be added to the program that will write out information to the trace buffer. The instructions required depend on the information to be captured. The simplest case is to add code to the start of each basic block that remembers the program execution going through that point. Traces are often used to analyze cache or superscalar behavior, in which case the instrumentation code may need to save additional information about the state of the CPU. Software-based trace generation methods do add execution overhead time to the program, but this usually does not affect the measurement. Simulation methods interpret the instructions to simulate the CPU, and they can generate the required trace information at the same time.

Obtaining a representative trace requires some knowledge of what the program does. Someone needs to supply inputs that properly exercise the program. Program users should have knowledge of the types of data typically presented to the program. However, because they may not know which data inputs will cause worst-case behavior, some collaboration between the program designers and users may be necessary. The techniques of Section 5.9 can be used to measure how thoroughly a set of inputs covers the program's control and data flow, giving you an idea of the representativeness of your traces.

trace analysis Once we have a trace, several things can be done with it. At minimum, the trace tells us the execution path of the program. By assigning the proper execution times to the instructions in the trace (taking into account interactions between instructions, etc.), we can determine the total execution time from the trace. In the case of a trace that does not record the complete execution of a program, we have to infer the trace through the missing pieces. However, if the sampling interval is properly chosen, the missing program fragments can be

easily determined. Traces are often used to analyze cache behavior, allowing us to calculate memory access times throughout the code. This information can be used to select the proper size of the cache to be used with a CPU (either by selecting the proper CPU model with an internal cache or by adding an external cache). It can also be used to optimize the program to improve its cache behavior.

A trace is generated on a particular CPU. We may want to use the trace to analyze the performance of the program on a different CPU. For example, when selecting which microprocessor to use, we may not want to purchase a complete evaluation and compilation system for each potential CPU just to measure the performance of each on our programs. There are limits to what we can do in this case, but the trace can still be useful. We can use the trace to determine the execution path through the program, although we have to be careful that the compilers used for the two CPUs perform similar optimizations. We can approximate the execution time on the new CPU, particularly if the instruction sets of the CPUs are relatively simple. Since many RISC processors have similar basic instructions with similar execution times (and because many compilers use only a small fraction of the CPU's instruction set), we can often obtain reasonable estimates of execution time on the new CPU by examining the trace from another CPU.

Loop Optimizations

Loops are important targets for optimization because programs with loops tend to spend a lot of time executing those loops. There are three important techniques in optimizing loops: **code motion, induction variable elimination, and strength reduction.**

Code motion lets us move unnecessary code out of a loop. If a computation's result does not depend on operations performed in the loop body, then we can safely move it out of the loop. Code motion opportunities can arise because programmers may find some computations clearer and more concise when put in the loop body, even though they are not strictly dependent on the loop iterations. A simple example of code motion is also common. Consider the following loop:

```
for (i = 0; i < N*M; i++) {
    z[i] = a[i] + b[i];
    }
```

The code motion opportunity becomes more obvious when we draw the loop's CDFG as shown in Figure 5-23. The loop bound computation is performed on every iteration during the loop test, even though the result never changes. We can avoid $N \times M - 1$ unnecessary executions of this statement by moving it before the loop, as shown in the figure.

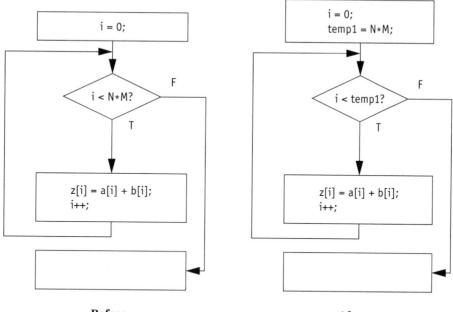

Before **After**

Figure 5-23 *Code motion in a loop.*

An **induction variable** is a variable whose value is derived from the loop iteration variable's value. The compiler often introduces induction variables to help it implement the loop. Properly transformed, we may be able to eliminate some variables and apply strength reduction to others.

A nested loop is a good example of the use of induction variables. A simple nested loop appears below.

```
for (i = 0; i < N; i++)
    for (j = 0; j < M; j++)
        z[i][j] = b[i][j];
```

The compiler uses induction variables to help it address the arrays. Let us rewrite the loop in C using induction variables and pointers. (Later, we use a common induction variable for the two arrays, even though the compiler would probably introduce separate induction variables and then merge them.)

```
for (i = 0; i < N; i++)
    for (j = 0; j < M; j++) {
        zbinduct = i*M + j;
        *(zptr + zbinduct) = *(bptr + zbinduct);
        }
```

In the above code, zptr and bptr are pointers to the heads of the z and b arrays and zbinduct is the shared induction variable. However, we do not need to compute zbinduct afresh each time. Since we are stepping through the arrays sequentially, we can simply add the update value to the induction variable as follows:

```
zbinduct = 0;
for (i = 0; i < N; i++) {
    for (j = 0; j < M; j++) {
        *(zptr + zbinduct) = *(bptr + zbinduct);
        zbinduct++;
        }
    }
```

This is a form of strength reduction since we have eliminated the multiplication from the induction variable computation.

Strength reduction helps us reduce the cost of a loop iteration. Consider the following assignment:

```
y = x * 2;
```

In integer arithmetic, we can use a left shift rather than a multiplication by 2 (as long as we properly keep track of overflows). If the shift is faster than the multiply, we probably want to perform the substitution. This optimization can often be used with induction variables because loops are often indexed with simple expressions. Strength reduction can often be performed with simple substitution rules since there are relatively few interactions between the possible substitutions.

Cache Optimizations

A **loop nest** is a set of loops, one inside the other, as illustrated in Figure 5-24. Loop nests occur when we process arrays. A large body of techniques has been developed for optimizing loop nests. Rewriting a loop nest changes the order in which array elements are accessed. This can expose new parallelism opportunities that can be exploited by later stages of the compiler, and it can also improve cache performance. In this section we concentrate on the analysis of loop nests for cache performance.

Let us first consider the examples of Figure 5-24 in more detail. We can represent the set of array locations indexed by the loop by an **iteration space.** Each point in this space is defined by a vector, each component of which is one of the loop's iteration variables. The points in the space represent the iterations

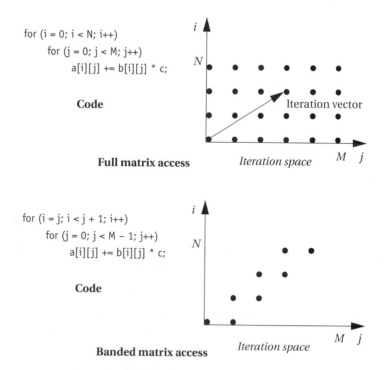

```
for (i = 0; i < N; i++)
    for (j = 0; j < M; j++)
        a[i][j] += b[i][j] * c;
```

Code

Full matrix access

```
for (i = j; i < j + 1; i++)
    for (j = 0; j < M – 1; j++)
        a[i][j] += b[i][j] * c;
```

Code

Banded matrix access

Figure 5-24 *Vector representations of nested loops.*

cache miss equations

executed by the program. The top example in the figure accesses every element of the arrays (the a and b matrices have the same access patterns in this case). The lower example accesses bands in the a and b matrices. We can represent any particular point in the iteration space as an **iteration vector,** such as the vector $i_{3,2} = \langle 3, 2 \rangle$ shown in the figure.

Ghosh et al. [Gho97] developed an analytical technique for describing data cache misses in nested loops. The equations not only describe the set of cache misses but also help us to optimize the program's access patterns. Because numerous equations are necessary to describe a program, the equations are designed to be generated and solved by design tools. Here we concentrate on the basic principles underlying the equations. After understanding these principles, we can apply them by hand in small cases as well as understand what our tools are doing in large cases.

We need to write equations that describe all types of misses, including compulsory, capacity, and conflict. The equations are written in terms of **reuse vectors**—if two iterations i_1 and i_2 use the same array location, the reuse vector that defines that reuse is $r = i_2 - i_1$ (assuming that i_2 comes after i_1). Assume for

the moment that our cache is direct mapped; we need to know the cache's line size so that we can compute which cache line each memory reference falls into. Compulsory misses occur in two cases—in the first access along the reuse vector and when the reuse vector spans more than one cache line. Capacity and conflict misses can be captured in a single form of equation. In the following equation, two references i and j conflict if they access distinct memory lines that map to the same cache line:

$$L(i) = L(j).\qquad\text{(EQ 5-1)}$$

If the cache size is C_s and the line size is L_s, we can rewrite this equation as

$$mem(i) = mem(j) + nC_s + b.\qquad\text{(EQ 5-2)}$$

In Equation 5-2, n is an integer that represents an arbitrary offset and b is an integer in the range $-L_{off} \le b \le Ls - 1 - L_{off}$, where L_{off} is the offset of the memory reference in the cache line.

We can use these equations for a variety of purposes. For instance, if we want to minimize the number of conflicts between array accesses, we can parameterize the equations in terms of the starting addresses of the arrays and the number of elements in each row (by padding the arrays), and then find the values for these parameters that minimize the number of cache conflicts. Example 5-10 illustrates the concepts behind cache miss equations.

Example 5-10

Data Realignment and Array Padding

Assume we want to optimize the cache behavior of the following code:

```
for (j = 0; j < M; j++)
    for (i = 0; i < N; i++)
        a[j][i] = b[j][i] * c;
```

Let us also assume that the a and b arrays are sized with M at 265 and N at 4 and a 256-line, four-way set-associative cache with four words per line. Even though this code does not reuse any data elements, cache conflicts can cause serious performance problems because they interfere with spatial reuse at the cache line level.

Assume that the starting location for a[] is 1024 and the starting location for b[] is 4099. Although a[0][0] and b[0][0] do not map to the same word in the cache, they do map to the same block.

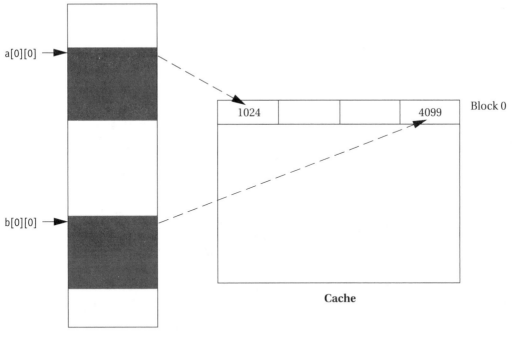

Main memory

Cache

As a result, we see the following scenario in execution:

- The access to a[0][0] brings in the first four words of a[].

- The access to b[0][0] replaces a[0] through a[0][3] with b[0][3] and the contents of the three locations before b[].

- When a[0][1] is accessed, the same cache line is again replaced with the first four elements of a[].

Once the a[0][1] access brings that line into the cache, it remains there for the a[0][2] and a[0][3] accesses since the b[] accesses are now on the next line. However, the scenario repeats itself at a[0][4] and every four iterations of the cache.

One way to eliminate the cache conflicts is to move one of the arrays. We do not have to move it far. If we move b's start to 4100, we eliminate the cache conflicts.

However, that fix won't work in more complex situations. Moving one array may only introduce cache conflicts with another array. In such cases, we can use another technique called padding. If we extend each of the rows of the

arrays to have four elements rather than three, with the padding word placed at the beginning of the row, we eliminate the cache conflicts. In this case, b[0][0] is located at 4100 by the padding. Although padding wastes memory, it substantially improves memory performance. In complex situations with multiple arrays and sophisticated access patterns, we have to use a combination of techniques—relocating arrays and padding them—to be able to minimize cache conflicts.

5.6.3 Optimizing for Execution Speed

If you need to improve the speed of your program, you can attack the problem at several levels of abstraction.

First, make sure that the code really needs to be accelerated. If you are dealing with a large program, the part of the program using the most time may not be obvious. Profiling the program will help you find hot spots. As seen in Chapter 6, many systems are built from multiple programs running as communicating processes; a slow program may not actually limit the overall system performance.

You may be able to redesign your algorithm to improve efficiency. Examining asymptotic performance is often a good guide to efficiency. Doing fewer operations is usually the key to performance. In a few cases, however, brute force may provide a better implementation. A seemingly simple high-level language statement may in fact hide a very long sequence of operations that slows down the algorithm. Using dynamically allocated memory is one example, since managing the heap takes time but is hidden from the programmer. For example, a sophisticated algorithm that uses dynamic storage may be slower in practice than an algorithm that performs more operations on statically allocated memory.

Finally, you can look at the implementation of the program itself. A few hints on program implementation are summarized below.

■ Try to use registers efficiently. Group accesses to a value together so that the value can be brought into a register and kept there.

■ Make use of page mode accesses in the memory system whenever possible. Page mode reads and writes eliminate one step in the memory access. You can increase use of page mode by rearranging your variables so that more can be referenced contiguously.

■ Analyze cache behavior to find major cache conflicts. Restructure the code to eliminate as many of these as you can as follows:

— For instruction conflicts, if the offending code segment is small, try to rewrite the segment to make it as small as possible so that it better fits into the cache. Writing in assembly language may be necessary. For conflicts across larger spans of code, try moving the instructions or padding with NOPs.

— For scalar data conflicts, move the data values to different locations to reduce conflicts.

— For array data conflicts, consider either moving the arrays or changing your array access patterns to reduce conflicts.

5.7 Analysis and Optimization of Energy and Power

Power consumption is a particularly important design metric for battery-powered systems because the battery has a very limited lifetime. However, power consumption is increasingly important in systems that run off the power grid. Fast chips run hot, and controlling power consumption is an important element of increasing reliability and reducing system cost.

How much control do we have over power consumption? Ultimately, we must consume the energy required to perform necessary computations. However, there are opportunities for saving power. Examples appear below.

- We may be able to replace the algorithms with others that do things in clever ways that consume less power.

- Memory accesses are a major component of power consumption in many applications. By optimizing memory accesses we may be able to significantly reduce power.

- We may be able to turn off parts of the system—such as subsystems of the CPU, chips in the system, and so on—when we don't need them in order to save power.

The first step in optimizing a program's energy consumption is knowing how much energy the program consumes. It is possible to measure power consumption for an instruction or a small code fragment [Tiw94]. The technique, illustrated in Figure 5-25, executes the code under test over and over in a loop. By measuring the current flowing into the CPU, we are measuring the power consumption of the complete loop, including both the body and other code. By separately measuring the power consumption of a loop with no body (making sure, of course, that the compiler hasn't optimized away the empty loop), we can calculate the power consumption of the loop body code as the difference between the full loop and the bare loop energy cost of an instruction.

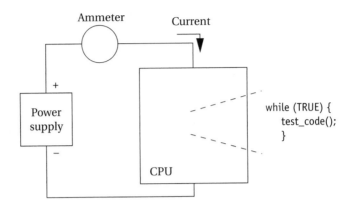

Figure 5-25 *Measuring energy consumption for a piece of code.*

5.7.1 Program Energy Consumption and Optimization

Several factors contribute to the energy consumption of the program.

- Energy consumption varies somewhat from instruction to instruction.
- The sequence of instructions has some influence.
- The opcode and the locations of the operands also matter.

Choosing which instructions to use can make some difference in a program's energy consumption, but concentrating on the instruction opcodes has limited payoffs in most CPUs. The program has to do a certain amount of computation to perform its function. While there may be some clever ways to perform that computation, the energy cost of the basic computation will change only a fairly small amount compared to the total system energy consumption, and usually only after a great deal of effort. We are further hampered in our ability to optimize instruction-level energy consumption because most manufacturers do not provide detailed, instruction-level energy consumption figures for their processors.

memory effects In many applications, the biggest payoff in energy reduction for a given amount of designer effort comes from concentrating on the memory system. As Figure 5-26 shows [Cat98], memory transfers are by far the most expensive type of operation performed by a CPU—a memory transfer takes 33 times more energy than does an addition. As a result, the biggest payoffs in energy optimization come from properly organizing instructions and data in memory. Accesses to registers are the most energy efficient; cache accesses are more energy efficient than main memory accesses.

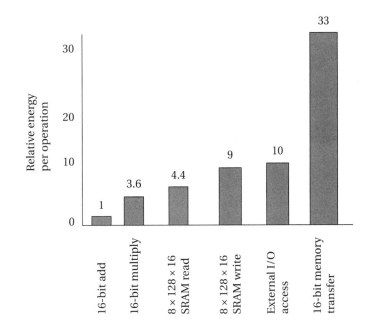

Figure 5-26 *Relative energy consumption of various operations [Cat98].*

Caches are an important factor in energy consumption. On the one hand, a cache hit saves a costly main memory access, and on the other, the cache itself is relatively power hungry because it is built from SRAM, not DRAM. If we can control the size of the cache, we want to choose the smallest cache that provides us with the necessary performance. Li and Henkel [Li98] measured the influence of caches on energy consumption in detail. Figure 5-27 breaks down the energy consumption of a computer running MPEG (a video encoder) into several components: software running on the CPU, main memory, data cache, and instruction cache.

As the instruction cache size increases, the energy cost of the software on the CPU declines, but the instruction cache comes to dominate the energy consumption. Experiments like this on several benchmarks show that many programs have sweet spots in energy consumption. If the cache is too small, the program runs slowly and the system consumes a lot of power due to the high cost of main memory accesses. If the cache is too large, the power consumption is high without a corresponding payoff in performance. At intermediate values, the execution time and power consumption are both good.

energy optimization How can we optimize a program for low power consumption? The best overall advice is that *high performance = low power.* Generally speaking, making the program run faster also reduces energy consumption.

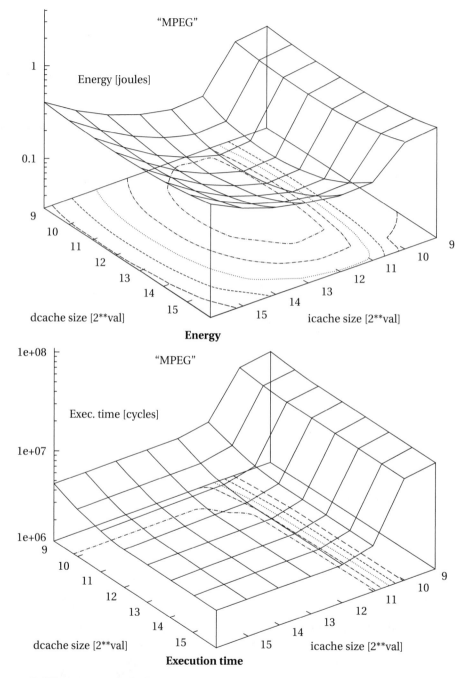

Figure 5-27 *Energy and execution time versus instruction/data cache size for a benchmark program [Li98].*

Clearly, the biggest factor that can be reasonably well controlled by the programmer is the memory access patterns. If the program can be modified to reduce instruction or data cache conflicts, for example, the energy required by the memory system can be significantly reduced. The effectiveness of changes such as reordering instructions or selecting different instructions depends on the processor involved, but they are generally less effective than cache optimizations.

A few optimizations mentioned previously for performance are also often useful for improving energy consumption:

- Try to use registers efficiently. Group accesses to a value together so that the value can be brought into a register and kept there.

- Analyze cache behavior to find major cache conflicts. Restructure the code to eliminate as many of these as you can:

 — For instruction conflicts, if the offending code segment is small, try to rewrite the segment to make it as small as possible so that it better fits into the cache. Writing in assembly language may be necessary. For conflicts across larger spans of code, try moving the instructions or padding with NOPs.

 — For scalar data conflicts, move the data values to different locations to reduce conflicts.

 — For array data conflicts, consider either moving the arrays or changing your array access patterns to reduce conflicts.

- Make use of page mode accesses in the memory system whenever possible. Page mode reads and writes eliminate one step in the memory access, saving a considerable amount of power.

Metha et al. [Met97] present some additional observations about energy optimization as follows:

- Moderate loop unrolling eliminates some loop control overhead. However, when the loop is unrolled too much, power increases due to the lower hit rates of straight-line code.

- Software pipelining reduces pipeline stalls, thereby reducing the average energy per instruction.

- Eliminating recursive procedure calls where possible saves power by getting rid of function call overhead. Tail recursion can often be eliminated; some compilers do this automatically.

5.8 Analysis and Optimization of Program Size

The memory footprint of a program is determined by the size of its data and instructions. Both must be considered to minimize program size.

Data provide an excellent opportunity for minimizing size because the data are most highly dependent on programming style. Because inefficient programs often keep several copies of data, identifying and eliminating duplications can lead to significant memory savings usually with little performance penalty. Buffers should be sized carefully—rather than defining a data array to a large size that the program will never attain, determine the actual maximum amount of data held in the buffer and allocate the array accordingly. Data can sometimes be packed, such as by storing several flags in a single word and extracting them by using bit-level operations.

A very low-level technique for minimizing data is to reuse values. For instance, if several constants happen to have the same value, they can be mapped to the same location. Data buffers can often be reused at several different points in the program. This technique must be used with extreme caution, however, since subsequent versions of the program may not use the same values for the constants. A more generally applicable technique is to generate data on the fly rather than store it. Of course, the code required to generate the data takes up space in the program, but when complex data structures are involved there may be some net space savings from using code to generate data.

Minimizing the size of the instruction text of a program requires a mix of high-level program transformations and careful instruction selection. Encapsulating functions in subroutines can reduce program size when done carefully. Because subroutines have overhead for parameter passing that is not obvious from the high-level language code, there is a minimum-size function body for which a subroutine makes sense. Architectures that have variable-size instruction lengths are particularly good candidates for careful coding to minimize program size, which may require assembly language coding of key program segments. There may also be cases in which one or a sequence of instructions is much smaller than alternative implementations—for example, a multiply-accumulate instruction may be both smaller and faster than separate arithmetic operations.

When reducing the number of instructions in a program, one important technique is the proper use of subroutines. If the program performs identical operations repeatedly, these operations are natural candidates for subroutines. Even if the operations vary somewhat, you may be able to construct a properly parameterized subroutine that saves space. Of course, when considering the code size savings, the subroutine linkage code must be counted

into the equation. There is extra code not only in the subroutine body but in each call to the subroutine that handles parameters. In some cases, proper instruction selection may reduce code size; this is particularly true in CPUs that use variable-length instructions.

Some microprocessor architectures support **dense instruction sets,** specially designed instruction sets that use shorter instruction formats to encode the instructions. The ARM Thumb instruction set and the MIPS-16 instruction set for the MIPS architecture are two examples of this type of instruction set. In many cases, a microprocessor that supports the dense instruction set also supports the normal instruction set, although it is possible to build a microprocessor that executes only the dense instruction set. Special compilation modes produce the program in terms of the dense instruction set. Program size of course varies with the type of program, but programs using the dense instruction set are often 70 to 80% of the size of the standard instruction set equivalents.

Another possibility is to use statistical compression algorithms to compress the program after assembly and then decompress it on the fly. Statistical compression views the data to be compressed as a stream of symbols. It relies on the fact that not all symbols or sequences of symbols are equally probable, so that more probable sections of the data are encoded in a small number of bits while less probable sections are encoded with more bits. File compression programs such as *gzip* can often reduce a file to 50% of its uncompressed size. However, file compression algorithms cannot be directly applied to dynamic code decompression. First, the algorithm must not force us to decompress the entire program before executing—that would defeat the purpose of code compression since the entire program would reside in memory. We must be able to decompress small sections of the program during execution. This creates particular problems for branches, since the address in a branch refers to an uncompressed location, not the location of the branch target in the compressed program. Second, we must be able to decompress the block of code quickly to avoid slowing down the CPU excessively.

There are several techniques for **code compression,** but a common one [Wol92A] is illustrated in Figure 5-28. In this scheme, a block of compressed code is fetched from main memory and decompressed into the cache to satisfy a cache miss. Because decompression occurs only on cache misses, it usually occurs relatively infrequently, and the cache is already organized to handle blocks of code. The code is compressed at the end of compilation after the file has been linked to form an executable; the compression process yields tables that program the decompression unit. Various compression algorithms can be used to generate the compressed code that can also yield fast hardware decompression logic. Application Example 5-1 describes the code compression technique used in PowerPC.

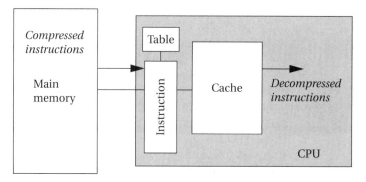

Figure 5-28 *Cache-based instruction decompression.*

Application Example 5-1

Code Compression for PowerPC

IBM has developed a code decompression module for PowerPC processors [Kem98]. Their decompression unit decompresses instructions after they have been fetched from main memory. They found that they could achieve much higher compression ratios by breaking each 32-bit instruction into two 16-bit halves. IBM uses Huffman compression to compress each half, compressing instructions in blocks of 64 bytes. An index table is used to translate uncompressed addresses, such as addresses found in branch instructions, to the new location of the instruction in the compressed code. They also add the K bit to the TLB to indicate whether a page in memory holds compressed instructions. This method compresses benchmark programs to 55 to 65% of their original size.

5.9 Program Validation and Testing

Complex systems need testing to ensure that they work as they are intended. But bugs can be subtle, particularly in embedded systems, where specialized hardware and real-time responsiveness make programming more challenging. Fortunately, there are many available techniques for software testing that can help us generate a comprehensive set of tests to ensure that our system works properly. We examine the role of validation in the overall design methodology

in Section 9.6. In this section, we concentrate on nuts-and-bolts techniques for creating a good set of tests for a given program.

The first question we must ask ourselves is how much testing is enough. Clearly, we cannot test the program for every possible combination of inputs. Because we cannot implement an infinite number of tests, we naturally ask ourselves what a reasonable standard of thoroughness is. One of the major contributions of software testing is to provide us with standards of thoroughness that make sense. Following these standards does not guarantee that we will find all bugs. But by breaking the testing problem into subproblems and analyzing each subproblem, we can identify testing methods that provide reasonable amounts of testing while keeping the testing time within reasonable bounds.

The two major types of testing strategies follow:

- **Black-box** methods generate tests without looking at the internal structure of the program.

- **Clear-box** (also known as **white-box**) methods generate tests based on the program structure.

In this section we cover both types of tests, which complement each other by exercising programs in very different ways.

5.9.1 Clear-Box Testing

The control/data flow graph extracted from a program's source code is an important tool in developing clear-box tests for the program. To adequately test the program, we must exercise both its control and data operations.

In order to execute and evaluate these tests, we must be able to control variables in the program and observe the results of computations, much as in manufacturing testing. In general, we may need to modify the program to make it more testable. By adding new inputs and outputs, we can usually substantially reduce the effort required to find and execute the test. Example 5-11 illustrates the importance of observability and controllability in software testing.

No matter what we are testing, we must accomplish the following three things in a test:

- Provide the program with inputs that exercise the test we are interested in.

- Execute the program to perform the test.

- Examine the outputs to determine whether the test was successful.

Example 5-11

Controlling and Observing Programs

Let's first consider controllability by examining the following FIR filter with a limiter:

```
firout = 0.0; /* initialize filter output */
/* compute buff*c in bottom part of circular buffer */
for (j = curr, k = 0; j < N; j++, k++)
    firout += buff[j] * c[k];
/* compute buff*c in top part of circular buffer */
for (j = 0; j < curr; j++, k++)
    firout += buff[j] * c[k];
/* limit output value */
if (firout > 100.0) firout = 100.0;
if (firout < -100.0) firout = -100.0;
```

The above code computes the output of an FIR filter from a circular buffer of values and then limits the maximum filter output (much as an overloaded speaker will hit a range limit). If we want to test whether the limiting code works, we must be able to generate two out-of-range values for firout: positive and negative. To do that, we must fill the FIR filter's circular buffer with N values in the proper range. Although there are many sets of values that will work, it will still take time for us to properly set up the filter output for each test.

This code also illustrates an observability problem. If we want to test the FIR filter itself, we look at the value of firout before the limiting code executes. We could use a debugger such as dbx to set breakpoints in the code, but this is an awkward way to perform a large number of tests. If we want to test the FIR code independent of the limiting code, we would have to add a mechanism for observing firout independently.

Being able to perform this process for a large number of tests entails some amount of drudgery, but that drudgery can be alleviated with good program design that simplifies controllability and observability.

The next task is to determine the set of tests to be performed. We need to perform many different types of tests to be confident that we have identified a large fraction of the existing bugs. Even if we thoroughly test the program using one criterion, that criterion ignores other aspects of the program. Over the next few pages we will describe several very different criteria for program testing.

execution paths The most fundamental concept in clear-box testing is the path of execution through a program. Previously, we considered paths for performance analysis; we are now concerned with making sure that a path is covered and determining how to ensure that the path is in fact executed. We want to test the program by forcing the program to execute along chosen paths. We force the execution of a path by giving it inputs that cause it to take the appropriate branches. Execution of a path exercises both the control and data aspects of the program. The control is exercised as we take branches; both the computations leading up to the branch decision and other computations performed along the path exercise the data aspects.

Is it possible to execute every complete path in an arbitrary program? The answer is no, since the program may contain a while loop that is not guaranteed to terminate. The same is true for any program that operates on a continuous stream of data, since we cannot arbitrarily define the beginning and end of the data stream. If the program always terminates, then there are indeed a finite number of complete paths that can be enumerated from the path graph. This leads us to the next question: Does it make sense to exercise every path? The answer to this question is no for most programs, since the number of paths, especially for any program with a loop, is extremely large. However, the choice of an appropriate subset of paths to test requires some thought. Example 5-12 illustrates the consequences of two different choices of testing strategies.

Example 5-12

Choosing the Paths to Test

Two reasonable choices for a set of paths to test follow:

- execute every statement at least once
- execute every direction of a branch at least once

These conditions are equivalent for structured programming languages without gotos, but are not the same for unstructured code. Most assembly language is unstructured, and state machines may be coded in high-level languages with gotos.

To understand the difference between statement and branch coverage, consider the CDFG below. We can execute every statement at least once by executing the program along two distinct paths.

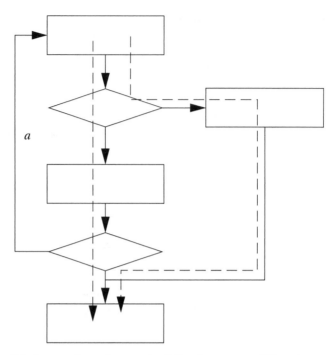

However, this leaves branch *a* out of the lower conditional uncovered. To ensure that we have executed along every edge in the CDFG, we must execute a third path through the program. This path does not test any new statements, but it does cause *a* to be exercised.

How do we choose a set of paths that adequately covers the program's behavior? Intuition tells us that a relatively small number of paths should be able to cover most practical programs. Graph theory helps us get a quantitative handle on the different paths required. In an undirected graph, we can form any path through the graph from combinations of **basis paths.** (Unfortunately, this property does not strictly hold for directed graphs such as CDFGs, but this formulation still helps us understand the nature of selecting a set of covering paths through a program.) The term "basis set" comes from linear algebra. Figure 5-29 shows how to evaluate the basis set of a graph. The graph is represented as an **incidence matrix.** Each row and column represents a node; a 1 is entered for each node pair connected by an edge. We can use standard linear algebra techniques to identify the basis set of the graph. Each vector in the basis set represents a primitive path. We can form new paths by adding the vectors modulo 2. Generally, there is more than one basis set for a graph.

The basis set property provides a metric for test coverage. If we cover all the basis paths, we can consider the control flow adequately covered. Although the

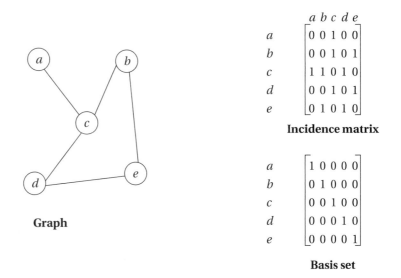

$$
\begin{array}{c}
\quad\quad\quad\quad a\ b\ c\ d\ e \\
\begin{array}{c}
a \\ b \\ c \\ d \\ e
\end{array}
\begin{bmatrix}
0\ 0\ 1\ 0\ 0 \\
0\ 0\ 1\ 0\ 1 \\
1\ 1\ 0\ 1\ 0 \\
0\ 0\ 1\ 0\ 1 \\
0\ 1\ 0\ 1\ 0
\end{bmatrix}
\end{array}
$$

Incidence matrix

$$
\begin{array}{c}
a \\ b \\ c \\ d \\ e
\end{array}
\begin{bmatrix}
1\ 0\ 0\ 0\ 0 \\
0\ 1\ 0\ 0\ 0 \\
0\ 0\ 1\ 0\ 0 \\
0\ 0\ 0\ 1\ 0 \\
0\ 0\ 0\ 0\ 1
\end{bmatrix}
$$

Basis set

Graph

Figure 5-29 *The matrix representation of a graph and its basis set.*

basis set measure is not entirely accurate since the directed edges of the CDFG may make some combinations of paths infeasible, it does provide a reasonable and justifiable measure of test coverage.

There is a simple measure, **cyclomatic complexity** [McC76], which allows us to measure the control complexity of a program. Cyclomatic complexity is an upper bound on the size of the basis set that we found in Section 5.6.1. If e is the number of edges in the flow graph, n the number of nodes, and p the number of components in the graph, then the cyclomatic complexity is given by

$$M = e - n + 2p. \tag{EQ 5-3}$$

For a structured program, M can be computed by counting the number of binary decisions in the flow graph and adding 1. If the CDFG has higher-order branch nodes, add $b - 1$ for each b-way branch. In the example of Figure 5-30, the cyclomatic complexity evaluates to 4. Because there are actually only three distinct paths in the graph, cyclomatic complexity in this case is an overly conservative bound.

Another way of looking at control flow–oriented testing is to analyze the conditions that control the conditional statements. Consider the following if statement:

```
if ((a == b) || (c >= d)) { ... }
```

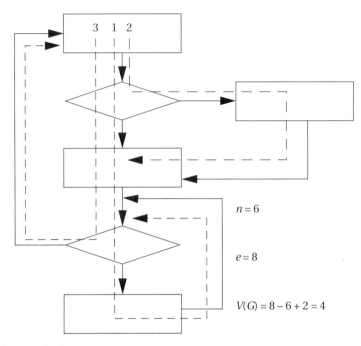

Figure 5-30 *Cyclomatic complexity.*

This complex condition can be exercised in several different ways. If we want to truly exercise the paths through this condition, it is prudent to exercise the conditional's elements in ways related to their own structure, not just the structure of the paths through them. A simple condition testing strategy is known as **branch testing** [Mye79]. This strategy requires the true and false branches of a conditional and every simple condition in the conditional's expression to be tested at least once. Example 5-13 illustrates branch testing.

Example 5-13

Condition Testing with the Branch Testing Strategy

Assume that the code below is what we meant to write.

```
if (a || (b >= c)) { printf("OK\n"); }
```

The code that we mistakenly wrote instead follows:

```
if (a && (b >= c)) { printf("OK\n"); }
```

If we apply branch testing to the code we wrote, one of the tests will use these values: a = 0, b = 3, c = 2 (making a false and b >= c true). In this case, the code should print theOK term [0 || (3 >= 2) is true] but instead doesn't print [0 && (3 >= 2) evaluates to false]. That test picks up the error.

Let's consider another more subtle error that is nonetheless all too common in C. The code we meant to write follows:

```
if ((x == good_pointer) && (x->field1 == 3)) { printf("got the value\n"); }
```

Here is the bad code we actually wrote:

```
if ((x = good_pointer) && (x->field1 == 3)) { printf("got the value\n"); }
```

The problem here is that we typed = rather than ==, creating an assignment rather than a test. The code x = good_pointer first assigns the value good_pointer to x and then, because assignments are also expressions in C, returns good_pointer as the result of evaluating this expression.

If we apply the principles of branch testing, one of the tests we want to use will contain x != good_pointer and x->field1 == 3. Whether this test catches the error depends on the state of the record pointed to by good_pointer. If it is equal to 3 at the time of the test, the message will be printed erroneously. Although this test is not guaranteed to uncover the bug, it has a reasonable chance of success. One of the reasons to use many different types of tests is to maximize the chance that supposedly unrelated elements will cooperate to reveal the error in a particular situation.

Another more sophisticated strategy for testing conditionals is known as **domain testing** [How82], illustrated in Figure 5-31. Domain testing concentrates on linear inequalities. In the figure, the inequality the program should use for the test is j <= i + 1. We test the inequality with three test points—two on the boundary of the valid region and a third outside the region but between the i values of the other two points. When we make some common mistakes in typing the inequality, these three tests are sufficient to uncover them, as shown in the figure.

A potential problem with path coverage is that the paths chosen to cover the CDFG may not have any important relationship to the program's function. Another testing strategy known as **data flow testing** makes use of **def-use analysis** (short for definition-use analysis). It selects paths that have some relationship to the program's function.

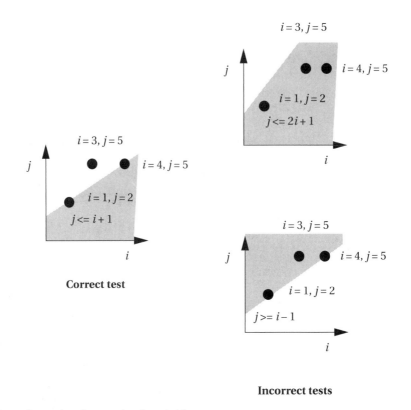

Figure 5-31 *Domain testing for a pair of variables.*

The terms def and use come from compilers, which use def-use analysis for optimization [Aho86]. A variable's value is **defined** when an assignment is made to the variable; it is **used** when it appears on the right side of an assignment (sometimes called a **c-use** for computation use) or in a conditional expression (sometimes called **p-use** for predicate use). A **def-use pair** is a definition of a variable's value and a use of that value. Figure 5-32 shows a code fragment and all the def-use pairs for the first assignment to a. Def-use analysis can be performed on a program using iterative algorithms. Data flow testing chooses tests that exercise chosen def-use pairs. The test first causes a certain value to be assigned at the definition and then observes the result at the use point to be sure that the desired value arrived there. Frankl and Weyuker [Fra88] have defined criteria for choosing which def-use pairs to exercise to satisfy a well-behaved adequacy criterion.

testing loops We can write some specialized tests for loops. Since loops are common and often perform important steps in the program, it is worth developing loop-centric testing methods. If the number of iterations is fixed, then testing is rela-

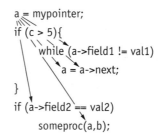

```
a = mypointer;
if (c > 5){
        while (a->field1 != val1)
            a = a->next;
}
if (a->field2 == val2)
        someproc(a,b);
```

Figure 5-32 *Definitions and uses of variables.*

tively simple. However, many loops have bounds that are executed at run time. Consider first the case of a single loop as follows:

```
for (i = 0; i < terminate(); i++)
    proc(i,array);
```

It would be too expensive to evaluate the above loop for all possible termination conditions. However, there are several important cases that we should try at a minimum. These cases are summarized below.

1. Skipping the loop entirely [if possible, such as when terminate() returns 0 on its first call].

2. One loop iteration.

3. Two loop iterations.

4. If there is an upper bound n on the number of loop iterations (which may come from the maximum size of an array), a value that is significantly below that maximum number of iterations.

5. Tests near the upper bound on the number of loop iterations, that is, $n - 1$, n, and $n + 1$.

We can also have nested loops such as the following:

```
for (i = 0; i < terminate1(); i++)
    for (j = 0; j < terminate2(); j++)
        for (k = 0; k < terminate3(); k++)
            proc(i,j,k,array);
```

There are many possible strategies for testing nested loops. One thing to keep in mind is which loops have fixed versus variable numbers of iterations. Beizer [Bei90] suggests an inside-out strategy for testing loops with multiple

variable iteration bounds. First, concentrate on testing the innermost loop as above—the outer loops should be controlled to their minimum numbers of iterations. After the inner loop has been thoroughly tested, the next outer loop can be tested more thoroughly, with the inner loop executing a typical number of iterations. This strategy can be repeated until the entire loop nest has been tested. Clearly, nested loops can require a large number of tests. It may be worthwhile to insert testing code to allow greater control over the loop nest for testing.

5.9.2 Black-Box Testing

Black-box tests are generated without knowledge of the code being tested. When used alone, black-box tests have a low probability of finding all the bugs in a program. But when used in conjunction with clear-box tests they help provide a well-rounded test set, since black-box tests are likely to uncover errors that are unlikely to be found by tests extracted from the code structure. Black-box tests can really work. For instance, when asked to test an instrument whose front panel was run by a microcontroller, one acquaintance of the author used his hand to depress all the buttons simultaneously. The front panel immediately locked up. This situation could occur in practice if the instrument were placed face-down on a table, but discovery of this bug would be very unlikely via clear-box tests.

One important technique is to take tests directly from the specification for the code under design. The specification should state which outputs are expected for certain inputs. Tests should be created that provide specified outputs and evaluate whether the results also satisfy the inputs.

We can't test every possible input combination, but some rules of thumb help us select reasonable sets of inputs. When an input can range across a set of values, it is a very good idea to test at the ends of the range. For example, if an input must be between 1 and 10, 0, 1, 10, and 11 are all important values to test. We should be sure to consider tests both within and outside the range, such as, testing values within the range and outside the range. We may want to consider tests well outside the valid range as well as boundary-condition tests.

Random tests form one category of black-box test. Random values are generated with a given distribution. The expected values are computed independently of the system, and then the test inputs are applied. A large number of tests must be applied for the results to be statistically significant, but the tests are easy to generate.

Another scenario is to test certain types of data values. For example, integer-valued inputs can be generated at interesting values such as 0, 1, and values near the maximum end of the data range. Illegal values can be tested as well.

Regression tests form an extremely important category of tests. When tests are created during earlier stages in the system design or for previous versions of the system, those tests should be saved to apply to the later versions of the system. Clearly, unless the system specification changed, the new system should be able to pass old tests. In some cases old bugs can creep back into systems, such as when an old version of a software module is inadvertently installed. In other cases regression tests simply exercise the code in different ways than would be done for the current version of the code and therefore possibly exercise different bugs.

Some embedded systems, particularly digital signal processing systems, lend themselves to numerical analysis. Signal processing algorithms are frequently implemented with limited-range arithmetic to save hardware costs. Aggressive data sets can be generated to stress the numerical accuracy of the system. These tests can often be generated from the original formulas without reference to the source code.

5.9.3 Evaluating Function Tests

How much testing is enough? Horgan and Mathur [Hor96] evaluated the coverage of two well-known programs, *TeX* and *awk*. They used functional tests for these programs that had been developed over several years of extensive testing. Upon applying those functional tests to the programs, they obtained the code coverage statistics shown in Figure 5-33. The columns refer to various types of test coverage: *block* refers to basic blocks, *decision* to conditionals, *p-use* to a use of a variable in a predicate (decision), and *c-use* to variable use in a nonpredicate computation. These results are at least suggestive that functional testing does not fully exercise the code and that techniques that explicitly generate tests for various pieces of code are necessary to obtain adequate levels of code coverage.

Methodological techniques are important for understanding the quality of your tests. For example, if you keep track of the number of bugs tested each day,

	Block	Decision	P-use	C-use
TeX	85%	72%	53%	48%
awk	70%	59%	48%	55%

Figure 5-33 *Code coverage of functional tests for TeX and awk (after Horgan and Mathur [Hor96]).*

the data you collect over time should show you some trends on the number of errors per page of code to expect on the average, how many bugs are caught by certain kinds of tests, and so on. We address methodological approaches to quality control in more detail in Section 9.6.4.

One interesting method for analyzing the coverage of your tests is **error injection.** First, take your existing code and add bugs to it, keeping track of where the bugs were added. Then run your existing tests on the modified program. By counting the number of added bugs your tests found, you can get an idea of how effective the tests are in uncovering the bugs you haven't yet found. This method assumes that you can deliberately inject bugs that are of similar varieties to those created naturally by programming errors. If the bugs are too easy or too difficult to find or simply require different types of tests, then bug injection's results will not be relevant. Of course, it is essential that you finally use the correct code, not the code with added bugs.

5.9.4 Performance Testing

Because embedded systems often have real-time deadlines, we must concern ourselves with testing for performance, not just functionality. Performance testing determines whether the required result was generated within a certain amount of time. In many cases, we are interested in the worst-case execution time, although in some cases we may want to verify the best-case or average-case execution time.

Performance analysis is very important here. Performance analysis can tell us what path causes the worst-case (or other case) execution time. From there we can determine the inputs required and the expected outputs.

Real-time code with deadlines must always terminate—we know that the code must finish for any possible set of inputs. Functional testing can help us determine whether the program actually terminates.

How do we measure program performance? Functional testing can be performed on any computer in most cases so long as we can compile the code on that platform. Performance testing is not easy. We may be able to use a simulator to measure performance. However, CPU simulators vary widely in the amount of timing information they provide.

Performance can also be measured directly on the hardware. We can use a timer in the system to count execution time. The program resets the timer at the start and checks the timer's value at the end of execution. We can also use logic analyzers as long as the start and end points of the program are visible on the bus.

To obtain truly accurate performance measurements, we must run the program in the environment in which it will operate. For example, the CPU used

must have the same size cache as the target platform will provide. The program should also be run along with other programs that operate concurrently. When several programs (or programs and interrupt drivers) operate concurrently, they can interfere with each other in the cache causing severe performance problems. We consider the analysis of multiple processes in the cache in more detail in Section 6.8.

Design Example

5.10 Software Modem

In this section we design a modem. Low-cost modems generally use specialized chips, but some PCs implement the modem functions in software. Before jumping into the modem design itself, we discuss principles of how to transmit digital data over a telephone line. We will then go through a specification and discuss architecture, module design, and testing.

5.10.1 Theory of Operation and Requirements

The modem will use **frequency-shift keying (FSK),** a technique used in 1200-baud modems. Keying alludes to Morse code–style keying. As shown in Figure 5-34, the FSK scheme transmits sinusoidal tones, with 0 and 1 assigned to different frequencies. Sinusoidal tones are much better suited to transmission over analog phone lines than are the traditional high and low voltages of digital circuits. The 01 bit patterns create the chirping sound characteristic of modems. (Higher-speed modems are backward compatible with the 1200-baud FSK scheme and begin a transmission with a protocol to determine which speed and protocol should be used.)

The scheme used to translate the audio input into a bit stream is illustrated in Figure 5-35. The analog input is sampled and the resulting stream is sent to two digital filters (such as an FIR filter). One filter passes frequencies in the range that represents a 0 and rejects the 1-band frequencies, and the other filter does the converse. The outputs of the filters are sent to detectors, which compute the average value of the signal over the past n samples. When the energy goes above a threshold value, the appropriate bit is detected.

We will send data in units of 8-bit bytes. The transmitting and receiving modems agree in advance on the length of time during which a bit will be transmitted (otherwise known as the baud rate). But the transmitter and receiver are physically separated and therefore are not synchronized in any way. The receiving modem does not know when the transmitter has started to

Figure 5-34 *Frequency-shift keying.*

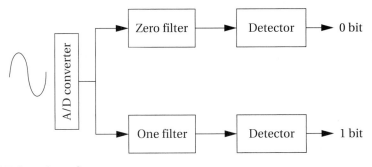

Figure 5-35 *The FSK detection scheme.*

send a byte. Furthermore, even when the receiver does detect a transmission, the clock rates of the transmitter and receiver may vary somewhat, causing them to fall out of sync. In both cases, we can reduce the chances for error by sending the waveforms for a longer time.

The receiving process is illustrated in Figure 5-36. The receiver will detect the start of a byte by looking for a start bit, which is always 0. By measuring the length of the start bit, the receiver knows where to look for the start of the first bit. However, since the receiver may have slightly misjudged the start of the bit, it does not immediately try to detect the bit. Instead, it runs the detection algorithm at the predicted middle of the bit.

Sampling interval

Figure 5-36 *Receiving bits in the modem.*

The modem will not implement a hardware interface to a telephone line or software for dialing a phone number. We will assume that we have analog audio inputs and outputs for sending and receiving. We will also run at a much slower bit rate than 1200 baud to simplify the implementation. Next, we will not implement a serial interface to a host, but rather put the transmitter's message in memory and save the receiver's result in memory as well. Given those understandings, let's fill out the requirements table.

Name	Modem.
Purpose	A fixed baud rate frequency-shift keyed modem.
Inputs	Analog sound input, reset button.
Outputs	Analog sound output, LED bit display.
Functions	Transmitter: Sends data stored in microprocessor memory in 8-bit bytes. Sends start bit for each byte equal in length to one bit. Receiver: Automatically detects bytes and stores results in main memory. Displays currently received bit on LED.
Performance	1200 baud.
Manufacturing cost	Dominated by microprocessor and analog I/O.
Power	Powered by AC through a standard power supply.
Physical size and weight	Small and light enough to fit on a desktop.

5.10.2 Specification

The basic classes for the modem are shown in Figure 5-37.

5.10.3 System Architecture

The modem consists of one small subsystem (the interrupt handlers for the samples) and two major subsystems (transmitter and receiver). Two sample interrupt handlers are required, one for input and another for output, but they are very simple. The transmitter is simpler, so let's consider its software architecture first.

The best way to generate waveforms that retain the proper shape over long intervals is **table lookup.** Software oscillators can be used to generate periodic signals, but numerical problems limit their accuracy. Figure 5-38 shows an

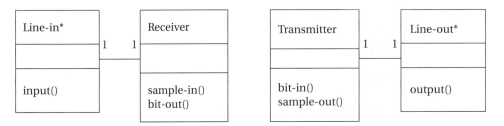

Figure 5-37 *Class diagram for the modem.*

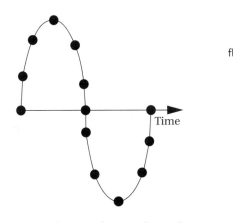

```
float sine_wave[N_SAMP] =
    { 0.0, 0.5, 0.866, 1,
    0.866, 0.5, 0.0, −0.5,
    0.866, −1.0, −0.866, −0.5,
    0};
```

Table

Analog waveform and samples

Figure 5-38 *Waveform generation by table lookup.*

analog waveform with sample points and the C code for these samples. Table lookup can be combined with interpolation to generate high-resolution waveforms without excessive memory costs, which is more accurate than oscillators because no feedback is involved. The required number of samples for the modem can be found by experimentation with the analog/digital converter and the sampling code.

The structure of the receiver is considerably more complex. The filters and detectors of Figure 5-35 can be implemented with circular buffers. But that module must feed a state machine that recognizes the bits. The recognizer state machine must use a timer to determine when to start and stop computing the filter output average based on the starting point of the bit. It must then determine the nature of the bit at the proper interval. It must also detect the start bit and measure it using the counter. The receiver sample interrupt handler is a natural candidate to double as the receiver timer since the receiver's time points are relative to samples.

The hardware architecture is relatively simple. In addition to the analog/digital and digital/analog converters, a timer is required. The amount of memory required to implement the algorithms is relatively small.

5.10.4 Component Design and Testing

The transmitter and receiver can be tested relatively thoroughly on the host platform since the timing-critical code only delivers data samples. The transmitter's output is relatively easy to verify, particularly if the data are plotted. A testbench can be constructed to feed the receiver code sinusoidal inputs and test its bit recognition rate. It is a good idea to test the bit detectors first before testing the complete receiver operation. One potential problem in host-based testing of the receiver is encountered when library code is used for the receiver function. If a DSP library for the target processor is used to implement the filters, then a substitute must be found or built for the host processor testing. The receiver must then be retested when moved to the target system to ensure that it still functions properly with the library code.

Care must be taken to ensure that the receiver does not run too long and miss its deadline. Since the bulk of the computation is in the filters, it is relatively simple to estimate the total computation time early in the implementation process.

5.10.5 System Integration and Testing

There are two ways to test the modem system: by having the modem's transmitter send bits to its receiver, and or by connecting two different modems.

The ultimate test is to connect two different modems, particularly modems designed by different people to be sure that incompatible assumptions or errors were not made. But single-unit testing, called **loop-back** testing in the telecommunications industry, is simpler and a good first step. Loop-back can be performed in two ways. First, a shared variable can be used to directly pass data from the transmitter to the receiver. Second, an audio cable can be used to plug the analog output to the analog input. In this case it is also possible to inject analog noise to test the resiliency of the detection algorithm.

5.11 Summary

The program is a very fundamental unit of embedded system design and it usually contains tightly interacting code. Because we care about more than just functionality, we need to understand how programs are created. Because today's compilers do not take directives such as "compile this to run in less than 1 microsecond," we have to be able to optimize programs ourselves for speed, power, and space. Our earlier understanding of computer architecture is critical to our ability to perform these optimizations. We also need to test programs to make sure they do what we want. Some of our testing techniques can also be useful in exercising the programs for performance optimization.

What We Learned

- We can use data flow graphs to model straight-line code and CDFGs to model complete programs.

- Compilers perform numerous of tasks, such as generating control flow, assigning variables to registers, creating procedure linkages, and so on.

- Remember the performance optimization equation:

 execution time = program path + instruction timing

- Memory and cache optimizations are very important to performance optimization.

- Optimizing for power consumption often goes hand in hand with performance optimization.

- Optimizing programs for size is possible, but don't expect miracles.

- Programs can be tested as black boxes (without knowing the code) or as clear boxes (by examining the code structure).

Further Reading

Aho, Sethi, and Ullman [Aho86] wrote a classic text on compilers, and Muchnick [Muc97] describes advanced compiler techniques in detail. A paper on the ATOM system [Sri94] provides a good description of instrumenting programs for gathering traces. Cramer et al. [Cra97] describe the Java JIT compiler. Li and Malik [Li97D] describe a method for statically analyzing program performance. Banerjee [Ban93, Ban94] describes loop transformations. Two books by Beizer, one on fundamental functional and structural testing techniques [Bei90] and the other on system-level testing [Bei84], provide comprehensive introductions to software testing and, as a bonus, are well written. Lyu [Lyu96] provides a good advanced survey of software reliability. Walsh [Wal97] describes a software modem implemented on an ARM processor.

Questions

Q5-1 Use UML to describe a design pattern for an FIR filter:

 a. class diagram

 b. sequence diagram

Q5-2 Use UML to describe a design pattern for a front panel. The front panel provides displays to output values and two types of inputs: discrete button inputs and continuous knob inputs.

 a. Draw a class diagram.

 b. Draw sequence diagrams for input and output.

Q5-3 For each basic block given below, rewrite it in single-assignment form, and then draw the data flow graph for that form.

 a.

```
x = a + b;
y = c + d;
z = x + e;
```

 b.

```
r = a + b − c;
s = 2 * r;
t = b − d;
r = d + e;
```

c.

```
a = q - r;
b = a + t;
a = r + s;
c = t - u;
```

d.

```
w = a - b + c;
x = w - d;
y = x - 2;
w = a + b - c;
z = y + d;
y = b * c;
```

Q5-4 Draw the CDFG for the following code fragments:

a.

```
if (y == 2) {r = a + b; s = c - d;}
else r = a - c
```

b.

```
x = 1;
if (y == 2) { r = a + b; s = c - d; }
else { r = a - c; }
```

c.

```
x = 2;
while (x < 40) {
    x = foo[x];
}
```

d.

```
for (i = 0; i < N; i++)
    x[i] = a[i]*b[i];
```

e.

```
for (i = 0; i < N; i++) {
    if (a[i] == 0)
        x[i] = 5;
    else
        x[i] = a[i]*b[i];
}
```

Q5-5 Show the contents of the assembler's symbol table at the end of code generation for each line of the following programs:

a.

```
        ORG 200
p1      ADR r4,a
        LDR r0,[r4]
        ADR r4,e
        LDR r1,[r4]
        ADD r0,r0,r1
        CMP  r0,r1
        BNE q1
p2      ADR r4,e
```

b.

```
        ORG 100
p1      CMP r0,r1
        BEQ x1
p2      CMP r0,r2
        BEQ x2
p3      CMP r0,r3
        BEQ x3
```

Q5-6 Your linker uses a single pass through the set of given object files to find and resolve external references. Each object file is processed in the order given, all external references are found, and then the previously loaded files are searched for labels that resolve those references. Will this linker be able to successfully load a program with these external references and entry points?

Object file	Entry points	External references
o1	a, b, c, d	s, t
o2	r, s, t	w, y, d
o3	w, x, y, z	a, c, d

Q5-7 Provide the required order of execution of operations in these data flow graphs. If several operations can be performed in arbitrary order, show them as a set: $\{a + b, c - d\}$.

a.

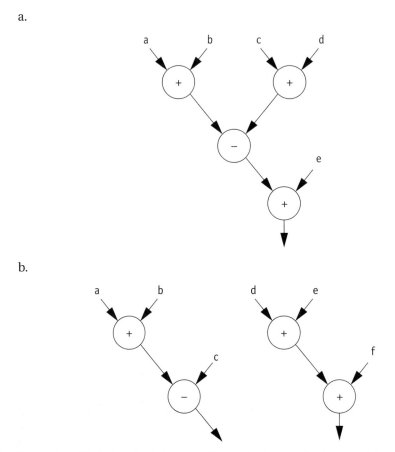

b.

Q5-8 Draw the CDFG for the following C code before and after applying dead code elimination to the if statement:

```
#define DEBUG 0
proc1();
if (DEBUG) debug_stuff();
switch (foo) {
    case A: a_case();
    case B: b_case();
    default: default_case();
    }
```

Q5-9 Unroll the loop below

a. two times

b. three times

```
for (i = 0; i < 32; i++)
    x[i] = a[i] * c[i];
```

Q5-10 Can you apply code motion to the following example? Explain.

```
for (i = 0; i < N; i++)
    for (j = 0; j < M; j++)
        z[i][j] = a[i] * b[i][j];
```

Q5-11 For each of the basic blocks of question Q5-3, determine the minimum number of registers required to perform the operations when they are executed in the order shown in the code. (You can assume that all computed values are used outside the basic blocks, so that no assignments can be eliminated.)

Q5-12 For each of the basic blocks of question Q5-3, determine the order of execution of operations that gives the smallest number of required registers. Next, state the number of registers required in each case. (You can assume that all computed values are used outside the basic blocks, so that no assignments can be eliminated.)

Q5-13 Draw a data flow graph for the code fragment of Example 5-5. Assign an order of execution to the nodes in the graph so that no more than four registers are required. Explain how you arrived at your solution using the structure of the data flow graph.

Q5-14 Determine the longest path through each code fragment, assuming that all statements can be executed in equal time and that all branch directions are equally probable.

a.

```
if (i < CONST1) { x = a + b; }
else { x = c − d; y = e + f; }
```

b.

```
for (i = 0; i < 32; i++)
    if (a[i] < CONST2)
        x[i] = a[i] * c[i];
```

c.

```
if (a < CONST3) {
    if (b < CONST4)
        w = r + s;
    else {
        w = r − s;
        x = s + t;
    }
}
```

```
    } else {
        if (c > CONST5) {
            w = r + t;
            x = r - s;
            y = s + u;
        }
    }
```

Q5-15 For each of the code fragments of question Q5-14, determine the shortest path through each code fragment, assuming that all statements can be executed in equal time and that all branch directions are equally probable.

Q5-16 The loop appearing below is executed on a machine that has a 1K word data cache with four words per cache line.

 a. How must x and a be placed relative to each other in memory to produce a conflict miss every time the inner loop's body is executed?

 b. How must x and a be placed relative to each other in memory to produce a conflict miss one out of every four times the inner loop's body is executed?

 c. How must x and a be placed relative to each other in memory to produce no conflict misses?

```
for (i = 0; i < 50; i++)
    for (j = 0; j < 4; j++)
        x[i][j] = a[i][j] * c[i];
```

Q5-17 Explain why the person generating clear-box program tests should not be the person who wrote the code being tested.

Q5-18 Find the cyclomatic complexity of the CDFGs for each of the code fragments given below.

 a.

```
if (a < b) {
    if (c < d)
        x = 1;
    else
        x = 2;
} else {
    if (e < f)
        x = 3;
    else
        x = 4;
}
```

b.
```
switch (state) {
    case A:
        if (x = 1) { r = a + b; state = B; }
        else { s = a – b; state = C; }
        break;
    case B:
        s = c + d;
        state = A;
        break;
    case C:
        if (x < 5) { r = a – f; state = D; }
        else if (x == 5) { r = b + d; state = A; }
        else { r = c + e; state = D; }
        break;
    case D:
        r = r + 1;
        state = D;
        break;
}
```

c.
```
for (i = 0; i < M; i++)
    for (j = 0; j < N; j++)
        x[i][j] = a[i][j] * c[i];
```

Q5-19 Use the branch condition testing strategy to determine a set of tests for each of the following statements.

a.
```
if (a < b || ptr1 == NULL) proc1();
else proc2();
```

b.
```
switch (x) {
case 0: proc1(); break;
case 1: proc2(); break;
case 2: proc3(); break;
ase 3: proc4(); break;
default; dproc(); break;
}
```

c.
```
if (a < 5 && b > 7) proc1();
else if (a < 5) proc2();
else if (b > 7) proc3();
else proc4();
```

Q5-20 Find all the def-use pairs for each code fragment given below.

a.
```
x = a + b;
if (x < 20) proc1();
else {
    y = c + d;
    while (y < 10)
        y = y + e;
}
```

b.
```
r = 10;
s = a − b;
for (i = 0; i < 10; i++)
    x[i] = a[i] * b[s];
```

c.
```
x = a − b;
y = c − d;
z = e − f;
if (x < 10) {
    q = y + e;
    z = e + f;
}
if (z < y) proc1();
```

Q5-21 For each of the code fragments of question Q5-20, determine values for the variables that will cause each def-use pair to be exercised at least once.

Q5-22 Assume you want to use random tests on an FIR filter program. How would you know when the program under test is executing correctly?

Q5-23 Generate a set of functional tests for a moderate-size program. Evaluate your test coverage in one of two ways: Have someone else independently identify bugs and see how many of those bugs your tests catch (and how many tests they catch that were not found by the human inspector); or inject bugs into the code and see how many of those are caught by your tests.

Lab Exercises

L5-1 Compare the source code and assembly code for a moderate-size program. (Most C compilers will provide an assembly language listing with the -s flag.) Can you trace the high-level language statements in the assembly code? Can you see any optimizations that can be done on the assembly code?

L5-2 Write C code for an FIR filter. Measure the execution time of the filter, either using a simulator or by measuring the time on a running microprocessor. Vary the number of taps in the FIR filter and measure execution time as a function of the filter size.

L5-3 Generate a trace for a program using software techniques. Use the trace to analyze the program's cache behavior.

L5-4 Measure the power consumption of your microprocessor on a simple block of code.

Chapter

6

Processes and Operating Systems

- The process abstraction.

- Switching contexts between programs.

- Real-time operating systems (RTOSs).

- Interprocess communication.

- Performance analysis and power consumption.

- A telephone answering machine design.

6.1 Introduction

Although simple applications can be programmed on a microprocessor by writing a single piece of code, many applications are sophisticated enough that writing one large program does not suffice. When multiple operations must be performed at widely varying times, a single program can easily become too complex and unwieldy. The result is spaghetti code that is too difficult to verify for either performance or functionality.

This chapter studies the two fundamental abstractions that allow us to build complex applications on microprocessors: the **process** and the **operating system (OS).** Together, these two abstractions let us switch the state of the processor between multiple tasks. The process cleanly defines the state of an executing program, while the operating system provides the mechanism for switching execution between the processes.

These two mechanisms together let us build applications with more complex functionality and much greater flexibility to satisfy timing requirements. The need to satisfy complex timing requirements—events happening at very different rates, intermittent events, and so on—causes us to use processes and operating systems to build embedded software. Satisfying complex timing tasks can introduce extremely complex control into programs. Using processes to compartmentalize functions and encapsulating in the operating system the control required to switch between processes make it much easier to satisfy timing requirements with relatively clean control within the processes. We are particularly interested in **real-time operating systems (RTOSs),** which are operating systems that provide facilities for satisfying real-time requirements.

POSIX

Throughout this chapter we use the **POSIX** operating system [Gal95] as our example real-time operating system. POSIX is a version of the Unix operating system created by a standards organization. POSIX-compliant operating systems are source-code compatible—an application can be compiled and run without modification on a new POSIX platform assuming that the application uses only POSIX-standard functions. While Unix was not originally designed as a real-time operating system, POSIX has been extended to support real-time requirements. Many RTOSs are POSIX compliant, and it serves as a good model for basic RTOS techniques. The POSIX standard has many options; particular implementations do not have to support all options. The existence of features is determined by C preprocessor variables—for example, the FOO option would be available if the _POSIX_FOO preprocessor variable were defined. All these options are defined in the system include file, unistd.h.

The **Linux** operating system has become increasingly popular as a platform for embedded computing. Linux is a POSIX-compliant operating system that is available as open source.

More information on POSIX, Linux, and other operating systems for embedded computing can be found at Web Aid 6-OS.

We first use some examples to justify why embedded tasks should often be split into multiple processes. We then introduce the process abstraction. In Section 6.4, we study the **context switch,** which is the mechanism used to share one CPU among several processes. Section 6.5 examines operating systems in more detail. Section 6.6 analyzes several different policies for scheduling processes, and Section 6.7 examines interprocess communication mechanisms. In Section 6.8, we look at some techniques for evaluating performance of operating systems, building on our understanding of program performance analysis. Section 6.9 focuses on operating system–controlled methods for managing system power consumption. Finally, in Section 6.10, we use a telephone answering machine as an example of a system that is much easier to build out of communicating processes.

6.2 **Multiple Tasks and Multiple Processes**

Many (if not most) embedded computing systems do more than one thing—that is, the environment can cause mode changes that in turn cause the embedded system to behave quite differently. For example, when designing a telephone answering machine, we can define recording a phone call and operating the user's control panel as distinct tasks, because they perform logically distinct operations and they must be performed at very different rates. These different **tasks** are part of the system's functionality, but that application-level organization of functionality is often reflected in the structure of the program as well. The need to structure programs to perform multiple tasks is the motivation behind introducing the notion of a process.

To understand why the separation of an application into tasks may be reflected in the program structure, consider how we would build a standalone compression unit based on the compression algorithm we implemented in Section 3.8. As shown in Figure 6-1, this device is connected to serial ports on both ends. The input to the box is an uncompressed stream of

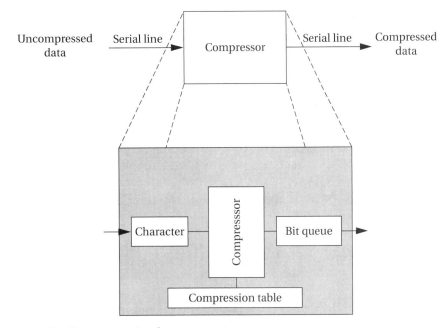

Figure 6-1 *An on-the-fly compression box.*

variable data rates

bytes. The box emits a compressed string of bits on the output serial line, based on a predefined compression table. Such a box may be used, for example, to compress data being sent to a modem.

The need to receive and send data at different rates—for example, the program may emit two bits for the first byte and then seven bits for the second byte—will obviously find itself reflected in the structure of the code. It is easy to create irregular, ungainly code to solve this problem; a more elegant solution is to create a queue of output bits, with those bits being removed from the queue and sent to the serial port in 8-bit sets. But beyond the need to create a clean data structure that simplifies the control structure of the code, we must also ensure that we process the inputs and outputs at the proper rates. For example, if we spend too much time packaging and emitting output characters, we may drop an input character. Solving timing problems is a more challenging problem.

asynchronous input

The text compression box provides a simple example of rate control problems. A control panel on a machine provides an example of a different type of rate control problem, the **asynchronous input.** The control panel of the compression box may, for example, include a compression mode button that disables or enables compression, so that the input text is passed through unchanged when compression is disabled. We certainly don't know when the user will push the compression mode—the button may be depressed asynchronously relative to the arrival of characters for compression.

We do know, however, that the button will be depressed at a much lower rate than characters will be received, since it is not physically possible for a person to repeatedly depress a button at even slow serial line rates. Keeping up with the input and output data while checking on the button can introduce some very complex control code into the program. Sampling the button's state too slowly can cause the machine to miss a button depression entirely, but sampling it too frequently can cause the machine to incorrectly compress data. One solution is to introduce a counter into the main compression loop, so that a subroutine to check the input button is called once every n times the compression loop is executed. But this solution doesn't work when either the compression loop or the button-handling routine has highly variable execution times—if the execution time of either varies significantly, it will cause the other to execute later than expected, possibly causing data to be lost. We need to be able to keep track of these two different tasks separately, applying different timing requirements to each. This is the sort of control that processes allow.

The above two examples illustrate how requirements on timing and execution rate can create major problems in programming. When code is written to satisfy several different timing requirements at once, the control structures necessary to get any sort of solution become very complex very quickly. Worse, such complex control is usually quite difficult to verify for either functional or timing properties.

6.2.1 Multirate Systems

Implementing code that satisfies timing requirements is even more complex when multiple rates of computation must be handled. **Multirate** embedded computing systems are very common, including automobile engines, printers, and telephone PBXs. In all these systems, certain operations must be executed periodically, and each operation is executed at its own rate. Application Example 6-1 describes why automobile engines require multirate control.

Application Example 6-1

Automotive Engine Control

The simplest automotive engine controllers, such as the ignition controller for a basic motorcycle engine, perform only one task—timing the firing of the spark plug, which takes the place of a mechanical distributor. The spark plug must be fired at a certain point in the combustion cycle, but to obtain better performance, the phase relationship between the piston's movement and the spark should change as a function of engine speed. Using a microcontroller that senses the engine crankshaft position allows the spark timing to vary with engine speed. Firing the spark plug is a periodic process (but note that the period depends on the engine's operating speed).

The control algorithm for a modern automobile engine is much more complex, making the need for microprocessors that much greater. Automobile engines must meet strict requirements (mandated by law in the United States) on both emissions and fuel economy. On the other hand, the engines must still satisfy customers not only in terms of performance but also in terms of ease of starting in extreme cold and heat, low maintenance, and so on.

Automobile engine controllers use additional sensors, including the gas pedal position and an oxygen sensor used to control emissions. They also use a multimode control scheme. For example, one mode may be used for engine warm-up, another for cruise, and yet another for climbing steep hills, and so forth. The larger number of sensors and modes increases the number of discrete tasks that must be performed. The highest-rate task is still firing the spark plugs. The throttle setting must be sampled and acted upon regularly, although not as frequently as the crankshaft setting and the spark plugs. The oxygen sensor responds much more slowly than the throttle, so adjustments to the fuel/air mixture suggested by the oxygen sensor can be computed at a much lower rate.

The **period** of a process is the time between successive executions. For example, the period of a digital filter is defined by the time interval between successive input samples. The process's **rate** is the inverse of its period. In a multirate system, each process executes at its own distinct rate.

When a machine's processes have periods that are simply related, designing the code to execute all processes at the proper rates may not be too difficult. For example, if one process operates at half the rate of the other, the faster process's execution loop can use the counter trick to call the inner process on every other loop iteration. However, if the least-common multiple of the periods is large, this solution becomes very unwieldy. The automobile engine poses an interesting problem because some of the computation rates are not constant. Several processes, such as firing the spark plugs, have rates that depend on the engine's rotation speed.

6.2.2 Early Multitasking Technology: The Co-Routine

The **co-routine** was a programming technique commonly used in the early days of embedded computing to handle multiple processes. The co-routine structure is not frequently used today, but it provides a useful example of the problems inherent in trying to devise complex control between multiple processes without using processes.

The basic co-routine structure, which is best understood in assembly language, is illustrated in Figure 6-2. The ARM code in the co-routines is not intended to represent meaningful computations. What is important in this example is the structure of the jumps between the co-routines. Each co-routine has several different entry points; the labels are used here only for convenience. The co-routine generalizes the subroutine register usage so that we can return to either co-routine at the point from which we left it. We use r14 to hold the return address for co-routine 2 and r13 for co-routine 1's return

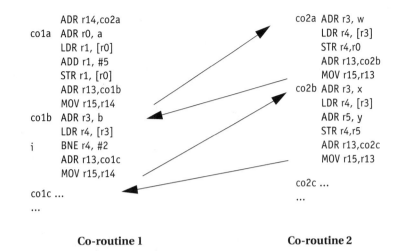

```
          ADR r14,co2a                    co2a ADR r3, w
  co1a ADR r0, a                               LDR r4, [r3]
       LDR r1, [r0]                             STR r4,r0
       ADD r1, #5                               ADR r13,co2b
       STR r1, [r0]                             MOV r15,r13
       ADR r13,co1b                        co2b ADR r3, x
       MOV r15,r14                              LDR r4, [r3]
  co1b ADR r3, b                                ADR r5, y
       LDR r4, [r3]                             STR r4,r5
    i  BNE r4, #2                               ADR r13,co2c
       ADR r13,co1c                             MOV r15,r13
       MOV r15,r14
                                           co2c ...
  co1c ...                                      ...
  ...
```

Co-routine 1 **Co-routine 2**

Figure 6-2 *Flow of control between co-routines.*

address. When one routine wants to transfer control to the other co-routine, it loads up its return address in the proper register and then sets the PC to the other co-routine's return value. The co-routines, of course, must be careful not to destroy values in the registers needed by the other co-routines.

The co-routine structure lets us implement more general kinds of flow of control than is possible with only subroutines; the identification of co-routine entry points provides us with some hooks for nonhierarchical calls and returns within the program. However, the co-routine does not do nearly enough to help us construct complex programs with significant timing properties. The co-routine in general does very little to simplify the design of code that satisfies timing requirements. Furthermore, even without timing constraints, co-routines can be ugly to work with—for example, it is often hard to trace through the flow of control between co-routines, particularly when the system is built from three or more co-routines.

6.3 Processes

The process is the first tool we need to help us tame complex systems—it provides a fundamental abstraction for dealing with multiple simultaneous operations. While the procedure helps us organize source code into manageable units, the process lets us organize executable code into similarly manageable units. Once we have divided the system into processes that interact

cleanly, we can apply operating system techniques to manage the interactions between the processes.

A process is simply a unique execution of a program. That is, a process is defined by both its code and its data. Two copies of a single program executing on their own data constitute two distinct processes. The data set for a process includes not only the CPU registers but also its main memory, since the process's results may be stored in both. (The need to consider all data in a process is strong motivation for avoiding self-modifying code. Processes executing self-modifying code must each have their own copy of the code. If a program does not modify its own instructions, on the other hand, all the processes spawned from it can share a single copy of the instructions.)

We can imply from the above that a process is executed sequentially, since it is written in terms of CPU instructions. Furthermore, a CPU may execute at most one process at a time. However, because we have identified the complete state of the process, we can cause the CPU to stop executing one process and start executing another. By changing the program counter to the new process's code and similarly moving its data into position in the registers and main memory, we cause a context switch to the new process. We study how to implement context switching in detail in Section 6.4.

Figure 6-3 illustrates processes cohabiting on a CPU. The currently executing process (*process 2* in this case) has the program counter pointing within its

Figure 6-3 *Several processes on a single CPU.*

code. The main memory contents for the processes in this example all coexist within main memory. (We could store nonexecuting process code and data on a disk, as is done in most general-purpose systems, but many embedded systems do not require the cost and complexity of a disk.) In addition to the code and data for each process, we need to keep a separate record of the state of each process. The record for a process is often called its **activation record,** since it contains the data used to reactivate the process. The state for *process 2* was copied into the CPU from its activation record at the beginning of the process's current execution. The other, nonexecuting processes have their own activation records that record the CPU internal state when those processes were stopped. That state will be used to reactivate the processes at a later date.

One commonly used form of process in embedded systems is the **lightweight process,** also known as a **thread.** Lightweight processes have their own distinct sets of values for CPU registers, but cohabit the same main memory space. As a result, one lightweight process may inadvertently destroy the data of another lightweight process executing on the machine. Lightweight processes are commonly used in embedded computing to avoid the cost and complexity of memory management units that provide strict separation between memory spaces. General-purpose computing platforms typically run heavyweight processes with full protection of process memory spaces because they may run user code that has not been tested for correctness and safety. A memory management unit can map physical memory into distinct logical memory spaces, ensuring that processes do not interfere with each other. However, since embedded computing platforms generally run only a few programs that can be tested before deployment, it usually makes sense to use a lightweight process model and save the cost of the MMU.

A program is said to be **reentrant** if it can be executed several times without reloading it from some pristine copy. An example of a nonreentrant program is one that first reads some global variable and then writes it—if the program were restarted, it would see a different value for that global variable. Nonreentrant programs are prone to obscure bugs that can be found only when the program is executed many times. A process does not have to be written as a reentrant program, but the system will be easier to debug if all processes are reentrant.

processes in POSIX

Creating a process in POSIX requires somewhat cumbersome code although the underlying principle is elegant. In POSIX, a new process is created by making a copy of an existing process. The copying process creates two different processes that run the same code. The complication enters upon ensuring that one process runs the code intended for the new process while the other process continues the work of the old process.

A process makes a copy of itself by calling the fork() function. That function causes the operating system to create a new process (the child process), which is a nearly exact copy of the process that called fork() (the parent process). Both share the same code and the same data values with one exception, the return value of fork(). The parent process is returned the process ID number of the child process, while the child process gets a return value of 0. We can therefore test the return value of fork() to determine which process is the child as follows:

```
childid = fork();
if (childid == 0) { /* must be the child */
    /* do child process here */
}
```

However, having both processes contain all the code for both the parent and child processes would be clumsy. POSIX provides the exec facility for overloading the code in a process. We can use that mechanism to overlay the child process with the appropriate code. There are several versions of exec; for instance, execv() takes a list of arguments to the process in the form of an array, just as would be accepted by a typical Unix program from the shell. Appearing below is the process call with an overlay of the child's code on the child process.

```
childid = fork();
if (childid == 0) { /* must be the child */
    execv("mychild",childargs);
    perror("execv");
    exit(1);
}
```

The execv() function takes as an argument the name of the file that holds the child's code and the array of arguments. It overlays the process with the new code and starts executing it from the main() function. In the absence of an error, execv() should never return. The code that follows the call to perror() and exit() takes care of the case where execv() fails and returns to the parent process. The exit() function is a C function used to leave a process; it relies on an underlying POSIX function called _exit().

The parent process should use one of the POSIX wait functions before calling exit() for itself. The wait functions not only return the child process's status. In many implementations of POSIX, the functions make sure that the child's resources (namely, memory) are freed. Thus, we can extend our code as follows:

```
childid = fork();
if (childid == 0) { /* must be the child */
```

```
        execv("mychild",childargs);
        perror("execl");
        exit(1);
        }
else { /* is the parent */
        parent_stuff(); /* execute parent functionality */
        wait(&cstatus);
        exit(0);
        }
```

The parent_stuff() function performs the work of the parent function. The wait() function waits for the child process, and sets the integer cstatus variable to the return value of the child process.

POSIX does not implement lightweight processes. Each POSIX process runs in its own address space and cannot directly access the data or code of other processes. As seen in Section 6.7.4, POSIX must supply a mechanism for shared memory to allow processes to communicate in this way.

6.4 Context Switching

The context switch is the mechanism for moving the CPU from one executing process to another. Clearly, the context switch must be bug-free—a process that does not look at a real-time clock should not be able to tell that it was stopped and then restarted. Furthermore, we want context switching to be fast—time spent by the CPU on context switching is time not spent on the computations for which the system is built.

6.4.1 Cooperative Multitasking

Before we study the most general form of context switching, preemptive multitasking, let us consider a more restricted form and its limitations. In a **cooperative multitasking** system, one process gives up the CPU to another voluntarily. This voluntarism can introduce severe bugs.

A context switch in a cooperative multitasking system can be implemented as something that looks like a procedure call, but is not a standard procedure call because it does not immediately return to the caller. As shown in Figure 6-4, each process contains calls to a context switch function (cswitch() in this case). cswitch() does not start a new procedure, but rather copies in the state of another process. When that process makes its own call to cswitch(), the system

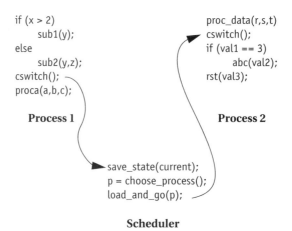

```
if (x > 2)                          proc_data(r,s,t)
     sub1(y);                       cswitch();
else                                if (val1 == 3)
     sub2(y,z);                          abc(val2);
cswitch();                          rst(val3);
proca(a,b,c);

     Process 1                          Process 2

                    save_state(current);
                    p = choose_process();
                    load_and_go(p);

                        Scheduler
```

Figure 6-4 *A set of cooperatively multitasking processes.*

may go back to executing the original process or to executing yet another process. A separate **scheduler** determines the process to be executed next. The scheduler first saves the state of the process that called the scheduler, then determines which process to call next, and finally sets the CPU state to the new process. This structure is similar to the co-routine structure of Section 6.2.2. The main difference is that, rather than directly calling the other process, we use the scheduler to determine which process runs next. This gives us much more flexibility in choosing the order in which processes run, but it still means that a process will continue to execute until it voluntarily turns over control to another process.

The process states are stored in process activation records in main memory. As described below, the CPU's procedure call mechanism is a starting point for the context switch operation.

- The call to cswitch() uses standard procedure call mechanisms to generate a return address.

- cswitch() copies the procedure call state, as well as other registers not saved by the procedure call, to a process state record somewhere in memory.

- After deciding which process will execute next, cswitch() can copy that process's state record into the locations normally used for the procedure call state.

- Executing a standard procedure call will then return control to the selected process.

Example 6-1 describes implementing cswitch() on the ARM in more detail.

Example 6-1

Cooperative Context Switching for the ARM

In this cooperative context switching mechanism for the ARM, we will assume that we have lightweight processes. Our main job, therefore, is to save the user-mode processor registers and restore their values from another process.

The standard way to maintain a process's context [Jag95] is to store a pointer to the current process's context in *r13*. The following illustration shows how the CPU's registers relate to the process context block.

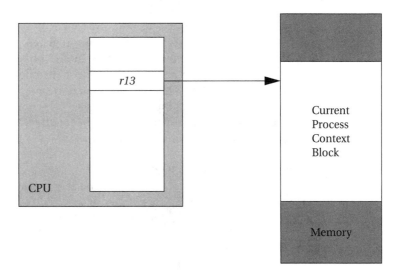

The format we will use to save the registers in a context block appears below. (The reason for this order of appearance of registers will become apparent in a moment.)

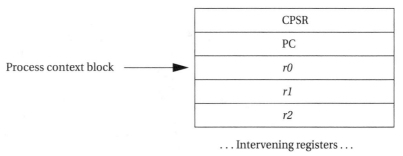

For simplicity, we assume that the next process's context block is pointed to by a variable named NEXTPROC.

To better understand the code, let us separately consider the steps required for saving the old context and restoring the new one. The code for saving the state of the old process follows:

```
STMIA   r13, {r0-r14}^   ; save registers up from [r13]
MRS     r0, SPSR         ; get status register
STMDB   r13, {r0, r15}   ; save status register and PC
```

Remember that *r13* always holds the pointer to the current process's context block. The store multiple instruction (STMIA) stores all user registers in the space pointed to by *r13*. The IA suffix causes the address to be incremented after each register is stored, causing the registers to be stored in ascending order. The ^ directive sets the S bit in the STM instruction, which causes the user-mode registers to be saved. The next instruction (MRS) gets the status register and puts it in r0. The STMDB instruction saves the status register (copied into *r0*) and the PC into the context block.

We can get the new process's state by loading *r13* first and then using it to load all the other registers as seen below.

```
ADR     r0, NEXTPROC     ; get address for pointer
LDR     r13, [r0]        ; get the pointer to the next context block
LDMDB   r13, {r0, r14}   ; get status register and PC
MSR     SPSR, r0         ; set the status register
LDMIA   r13, {r0-r14}^   ; get the registers
MOVS    pc, r14          ; restore the status register
```

If we have a floating-point co-processor, we must save and restore its registers as well.

Cooperative multitasking has been used both in embedded computing and in general-purpose computing systems. However, it is prone to bugs that cause the system to become totally inoperable. The fact that control of the CPU must be voluntarily given up by a process means that simple programming mistakes can cause the system to lock up, failing to respond to input, and to be totally inoperable.

Example 6-2 illustrates a simple case in which program bugs break the cooperative multitasking mechanism. Problems can occur in cooperative multitasking even without logical bugs. If a process executes for too long before passing control back to the scheduler, the system's real-time characteristics are at risk. Cooperative multitasking can work well, but it does not provide a mechanism to overcome bugs introduced by the individual processes that don't properly obey the cooperative multitasking protocol.

Example 6-2

A Buggy Cooperative Multitasking System

As a first example, consider the following program in a cooperative multitasking system:

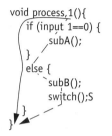

```
void process_1(){
    if (input 1==0) {
        subA();
    }
    else {
        subB();
        switch();S
    }
}
```

The above process is defined as a procedure; when the process is executed once, it will be executed again, since a system will assume that most processes execute repeatedly. The if statement in this process handles different cases for input1, which is presumably set by an input device through another process. If input1 is zero, then a context switch is not executed by this process; switch() is called along one path of execution for process1() (namely, the broken line path), but not for every path (the solid path being an exception). Depending on which other processes are defined and the manner in which the operating system selects processes, failing to allow context switching within process1() may or may not cause the system to lock up.

The previous case is relatively simple and potentially harmless. But other flow-of-control problems can cause the system to completely lock up. Consider the following code:

```
process2() {
    x = global1; /* global1 is an input to the process */
    while (x < 500)
        x = aproc(global2); /* subroutine does its work */
    switch();
}
```

At first glance, it may appear that switch() is called along every execution path of process2(). However, the flow of control depends on the value for x computed by the procedure aproc(). Depending on what the values of global1 and global2 passed into the process and the function performed by aproc(), it is quite possible that x is always less than 500 and that the while loop executes

forever. In this case, unless aproc() calls switch() itself, the operating system will never get a chance to switch contexts because process2() will never exit.

This example illustrates the danger of subroutines in cooperative multitasking systems—the properties of the subroutine, either inherent or in combination with the calling code, can cause the flow of control in the program to be restricted in nonobvious ways that prevent context switches from occurring. The implementation hiding property of the subroutine is, in this case, a distinct disadvantage.

6.4.2 Preemptive Multitasking

The interrupt is an ideal mechanism on which to build context switching for preemptive multitasking. Like the procedure call, the interrupt mechanism is designed to save state and then invisibly return control to an executing program. However, interrupts force the CPU to transfer control to the operating system. Not only does preemption reduce the consequence of programming errors, but we also see in later sections that preemption allows CPU time to be allocated more efficiently between multiple processes with deadlines.

timer-driven preemption Figure 6-5 shows the basic hardware configuration for preemptive multitasking. A timer generates periodic interrupts to the CPU. The interrupt handler for the timer calls the operating system, which saves the previous process's state in an activation record, selects the next process to execute, and switches the context to that process.

As described below, an interrupt-driven, preemptive context switch follows a general flow similar to that of the procedure-driven, cooperative task switch.

- The interrupt causes the flow of control to switch to the interrupt handler, which saves a minimum amount of state.

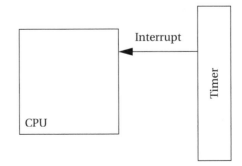

Figure 6-5 *A timer supplying interrupts for preemptive scheduling.*

- The interrupt state is saved in a process state record, along with the remaining registers for the process.

- After choosing the process to run next, the operating system copies its state into the areas used by the interrupt return.

- Returning from the interrupt causes the chosen process to resume execution at the point where it was previously interrupted.

We can implement preemptive context switches using the same basic techniques shown in Example 6-1. The only difference between the two is the triggering event: voluntary release of the CPU in the case of cooperative and timer interrupt in the case of preemptive.

6.4.3 Processes and Object-Oriented Design

We need to design systems with processes as components. In this section, we survey the ways we can describe processes in UML and how to use processes as components in object-oriented design.

UML often refers to processes as **active objects,** that is, objects that have independent threads of control. The class that defines an active object is known as an **active class.** Figure 6-6 shows an example of a UML active class. It has all the normal characteristics of a class, including a name, attributes, and operations. It also provides a set of signals that can be used to communicate with the process. A signal is an object that is passed between processes for asynchronous communication. We describe signals in more detail in Section 6.7.

We can mix active objects and normal objects when describing a system. Figure 6-7 shows a simple collaboration diagram in which an object is used as an interface between two processes: *p1* uses the *w* object to manipulate its data before the data is sent to the *master* process.

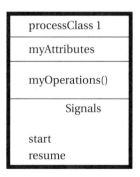

Figure 6-6 *An active class in UML.*

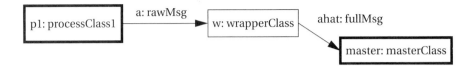

Figure 6-7 *A collaboration diagram with active and normal objects.*

6.5 Operating Systems

The operating system's fundamental job is to allocate resources in the computing system among programs that request them. Naturally, the CPU is the scarcest resource, so scheduling the CPU is the operating system's most important job. In this section, we consider the structure of operating systems, how they schedule processes to meet performance requirements, and how they provide services beyond CPU scheduling.

The operating system is an important abstraction because it vastly simplifies the control code required to coordinate processes. Rather than write spaghetti code to coordinate all the processes, scheduling is centralized in a single algorithm that coordinates computation and the transfer of the CPU state. The simplification of control structure derives from applying a single control strategy for all processes loaded into the CPU. In theory, you can find schedules for a particular application that are more efficient than the general policy of an OS. However, in practice it is difficult to ensure that such special-purpose schedules work when they are crafted by hand. Even when CAD tools are used to create application-specific schedules, the operating system provides a reliable mechanism for switching between processes and implementing the schedule.

6.5.1 Process State and Scheduling

The first job of the operating system is to determine that process runs next. The work of choosing the order of running processes is known as scheduling.

The operating system considers a process to be in one of three basic **scheduling states: waiting, ready,** or **executing.** There is at most one process executing on the CPU at any time. (If there is no useful work to be done, an idling process may be used to perform a null operation.) Any process that could execute is in the ready state; the operating system chooses among the ready processes to select the next executing process. A process may not, however, always be ready to run. For instance, a process may be waiting for data from an I/O device or another process, or it may be set to run from a timer that has not yet expired. Such processes are in the waiting state. Figure 6-8 shows the possible

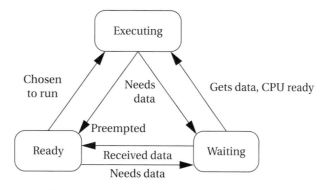

Figure 6-8 *Scheduling states of a process.*

transitions between states available to a process. A process goes into the waiting state when it needs data that it has not yet received or when it has finished all its work for the current period. A process goes into the ready state when it receives its required data and when it enters a new period. A process can go into the executing state only when it has all its data, is ready to run, and the scheduler selects the process as the next process to run.

A common way to choose the next executing process is based on process priorities. Each process is assigned a priority, an integer-valued number. The next process to be chosen to execute is the process in the set of ready processes that has the highest-valued priority. The priority embodies the rules used to select running processes. The seeming simplicity of using a number to determine the next running process hides some important complications, however. Are priorities fixed or can they change during execution? How are priorities determined? We consider these problems in much more detail in Section 6.5.4. In the meantime, Example 6-3 shows how priorities can be used to schedule processes.

Example 6-3

Priority-Driven Scheduling

For this example, we will adopt the following simple rules:

- Each process has a fixed priority that does not vary during the course of execution. (More sophisticated scheduling schemes do, in fact, change the priorities of processes to control what happens next.)

■ The ready process with the highest priority (with 1 as the highest priority of all) is selected for execution.

■ A process continues execution until it completes or it is preempted by a higher-priority process.

Let's define a simple system with three processes as seen below.

Process	Priority	Execution time
P1	1	10
P2	2	30
P3	3	20

In addition to describing the properties of the processes in general, we need to know the environmental setup. We assume that P2 is ready to run when the system is started, P1's data arrive at time 15, and P3's data arrive at time 18.

Once we know the process properties and the environment, we can use the priorities to determine which process is running throughout the complete execution of the system.

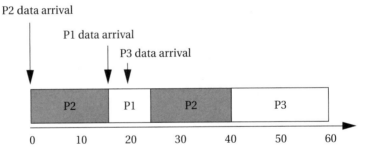

When the system begins execution, P2 is the only ready process, so it is selected for execution. At time 15, P1 becomes ready; it preempts P2 and begins execution since it has a higher priority. Since P1 is the highest-priority process in the system, it is guaranteed to execute until it finishes. P3's data arrive at time 18, but it cannot preempt P1. Even when P1 finishes, P3 is not allowed to run. P2 is still ready and has higher priority than P3. Only after both P1 and P2 finish can P3 execute.

6.5.2 Operating System Structure

The process activation record can be generalized to include all the following data required by the operating system to run the process:

- process priority
- process scheduling state
- starting address of the process

The data structures used to support scheduling depend in part on whether processes can be created during execution. If the system runs a completely fixed set of processes, the process state records can be kept in an array. If processes can be created on the fly during execution, the process state records must be kept in a linked list. While it may initially seem that most embedded computing systems would not create processes on the fly, there are in fact many situations in which it is convenient and efficient to do so. When some events occur aperiodically and infrequently, it may be reasonable to create a process to handle the event when it occurs—see Application Example 6-2 for an example. This is particularly true when all combinations of events are unlikely to occur, since creating processes only when needed will save memory.

Application Example 6-2

Telephone Calls as Processes

A telephone switching system must keep track of some basic information about the call: the two lines connected by the call, billing information such as the length of the call, any special features such as conference calling, and so on. It is therefore convenient to think of each call as a process that is created when the call is initiated and destroyed when the call is complete. Not only does this mean that processes are created and destroyed during the execution of the system, but there may also be a large number of active processes at any one time. A large telephone switch may be capable of handling 10,000 calls. Any implementation that uses processes to represent calls must therefore be able to manipulate processes very efficiently.

Most switching systems use a call process only to keep track of basic information, not to switch the actual call data. Since each call requires high-rate

data transfers (4 kHz for voice), activating even one process at that rate would be impractical, and activating all processes at that rate would be impossible.

The operating system generally executes in protected mode if the microprocessor supports protected mode execution. Even if all the code executing in the system was tested by the designers, running in protected mode gives an extra measure of protection against programming bugs that might cause one process to interfere with another.

The ARM processor uses the SWI (software interrupt) instruction to provide operating system access. This instruction puts the CPU into the supervisor mode; the exception vector table is used to direct execution to the proper place in the operating system. SWI takes one argument that can be used as a parameter to the operating system, which is generally the operating system function being requested (input, output, etc.). If the processes do not share a common address space, the supervisor must save the MMU state as well. The SHARC does not have a supervisor mode and so does not support an equivalent instruction.

6.5.3 Timing Requirements on Processes

Processes can have several different types of timing requirements imposed on them by the application. The timing requirements on a set of processes strongly influence the type of scheduling that is appropriate. A scheduling policy must define the timing requirements that it uses to determine whether a schedule is valid. Before studying scheduling proper, we outline the types of process timing requirements that are useful in embedded system design.

Figure 6-9 illustrates different ways in which we can define two important requirements on processes: **initiation time** and **deadline.** The initiation time is the time at which the process goes from the waiting to the ready state. An aperiodic process is by definition initiated by an event, such as external data arriving or data computed by another process. The initiation time is generally measured from that event, although the system may want to make the process ready at some interval after the event itself. For a periodically executed process, there are two common possibilities. In simpler systems, the process may become ready at the beginning of the period. More sophisticated systems may set the initiation time at the arrival time of certain data, at a time after the start of the period.

A deadline specifies when a computation must be finished. The deadline for an aperiodic process is generally measured from the initiation time, since that is the only reasonable time reference. The deadline for a periodic process may in general occur at some time other than the end of the period. As seen in

Figure 6-9 *Example definitions of initiation times and deadlines.*

Section 6.6.1, some scheduling policies make the simplifying assumption that the deadline occurs at the end of the period.

Rate requirements are also fairly common. A rate requirement specifies how quickly processes must be initiated. The inverse of the rate is the period, which is also called the **initiation interval.** The most common case for periodic processes is for the initiation interval to be equal to the period. However, pipelined execution of processes allows the initiation interval to be less than the period. Figure 6-10 illustrates process execution in a system with four CPUs. The various execution instances of program *P1* have been subscripted to distinguish their initiation times. In this case, the initiation interval is equal to one-fourth of the period. It is possible for a process to have an initiation rate less than the period even in single-CPU systems. If the process execution time is significantly less than the period, it may be possible to initiate multiple copies of a program at slightly offset times.

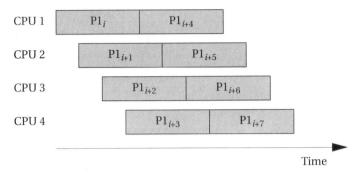

Figure 6-10 *A sequence of processes with a high initiation rate.*

What happens when a process misses a deadline? The practical effects of a timing violation depend on the application—the results can be catastrophic in an automotive control system, whereas a missed deadline in a telephone system may cause a temporary silence on the line. The system can be designed to take a variety of actions when a deadline is missed. Safety-critical systems may try to take compensatory measures such as approximating data or switching into a special safety mode. Systems for which safety is not as important may take simple measures to avoid propagating bad data, such as inserting silence in a phone line, or may completely ignore the failure.

Even if the modules are functionally correct, their timing behavior can introduce major execution errors. Application Example 6-3 describes a timing problem in space shuttle software that caused the delay of the first launch of the shuttle.

Application Example 6-3

A Space Shuttle Software Error

Garman [Gar81] describes a software problem that delayed the first launch of the U.S. space shuttle. No one was hurt and the launch proceeded after the computers were reset. However, this bug was serious and unanticipated.

The shuttle's primary control system was known as the Primary Avionics Software System (PASS). It used four computers to monitor events, with the four machines voting to ensure fault tolerance. Four computers allowed one machine to fail while still leaving three operating machines to vote, such that a majority vote would still be possible to determine operating procedures. If at least two machines failed, control was to be turned over to a fifth computer

called the Backup Flight Control System (BFS). The BFS used the same computer, requirements, programming language, and compiler, but it was developed by a different organization than the one that built the PASS to ensure that methodological errors did not cause simultaneous failure of both systems. The switchover from PASS to BFS was controlled by the astronauts.

During normal operation, the BFS would listen to the operation of the PASS computers so that it could keep track of the state of the shuttle. However, BFS would stop listening when it thought that PASS was compromising data fetching. This would prevent PASS failures from inadvertently destroying the state of the BFS. PASS used an asynchronous, priority-driven software architecture. If high-priority processes take too much time, the operating system can skip or delay lower-priority processing. The BFS, in contrast, used a time-slot system that allocated a fixed amount of time to each process. Since the BFS monitored the PASS, it could get confused by temporary overloads on the primary system. As a result, the PASS was changed late in the design cycle to make its behavior more amenable to the backup system.

On the morning of the launch attempt, the BFS failed to synchronize itself with the primary system. It saw the events on the PASS system as inconsistent and therefore stopped listening to PASS behavior. It turned out that all PASS and BFS processing had been running late relative to telemetry data. This occurred because the system incorrectly calculated its start time.

After much analysis of system traces and software, it was determined that a few minor changes to the software had caused the problem. First, about two years before the incident, a subroutine used to initialize the data bus was modified. Since this routine was run prior to calculating the start time, it introduced an additional, unnoticed delay into that computation. About a year later, a constant was changed in an attempt to fix that problem. As a result of these changes, there was a 1 in 67 probability for a timing problem. When this occurred, almost all computations on the computers would occur a cycle late, leading to the observed failure. The problems were diificult to detect in testing since they required running through all the initialization code; many tests start with a known configuration to save the time required to run the setup code. The changes to the programs were also not obviously related to the final changes in timing.

6.5.4 Interprocess Communication

Processes often need to communicate with each other. **Interprocess communication mechanisms** are provided by the operating system as part of the process abstraction.

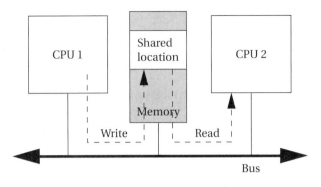

Figure 6-11 *Shared memory communication implemented on a bus.*

In general, a process can send a communication in one of two ways: **blocking** or **nonblocking.** After sending a blocking communication, the process goes into the waiting state until it receives a response. Nonblocking communication allows the process to continue execution after sending the communication. Both types of communication are useful.

There are two major styles of interprocess communication: **shared memory** and **message passing.** The two are logically equivalent—given one, you can build an interface that implements the other. However, some programs may be easier to write using one rather than the other. In addition, the hardware platform may make one easier to implement or more efficient than the other.

Figure 6-11 illustrates how shared memory communication works in a bus-based system. Two components, such as two CPUs, communicate through a shared memory location. The software on CPUs 1 and 2 has been designed to know the address of the shared location. If, as in the figure, CPU 1 wants to send data to CPU 2, it writes to the shared location. CPU 2 then reads the data from that location. The read and write operations are standard and can be encapsulated in a procedural interface. Example 6-4 describes the use of shared memory as a practical communication mechanism.

Example 6-4

Elastic Buffers as Shared Memory

The text compressor of Application Example 3-4 provides a good example of a shared memory. As shown below, the text compressor uses the CPU to compress incoming text, which is then sent on a serial line by a UART.

The input data arrive at a constant rate and are easy to manage. But because the output data are consumed at a variable rate, these data require an elastic buffer. The CPU and output UART share a memory area—the CPU writes compressed characters into the buffer and the UART removes them as necessary to fill the serial line. Because the number of bits in the buffer changes constantly, the compression and transmission processes need additional size information. In this case, coordination is simple—the CPU writes at one end of the buffer and the UART reads at the other end. The only challenge is to make sure that the UART does not overrun the buffer.

As an application of shared memory, let us consider the situation of Figure 6-11 in which programs on two CPUs want to communicate through a shared memory block. There must be a flag that tells one CPU when the data from the other CPU are ready. The flag, an additional shared data location, has a value of 0 when the data are not ready and 1 when the data are ready. CPU 1, for example, would write the data, and then set the flag location to 1. If the flag is used only by CPU 1, then the flag can be implemented using a standard memory write operation. If the same flag is used for bidirectional signaling between CPUs 1 and 2, care must be taken. Consider the following scenario:

1. CPU 1 reads the flag location and sees that it is 0.

2. CPU 2 reads the flag location and sees that it is 0.

3. CPU 1 sets the flag location to 1 and writes data to the shared location.

4. CPU 2 erroneously sets the flag to 1 and overwrites the data left by CPU 1.

race condition The above scenario is caused by a critical timing race between the two programs. To avoid such problems, the microprocessor bus must support an atomic **test-and-set** operation, which is available on a number of microprocessors. The test-and-set operation first reads a location and then sets it to a

specified value. It returns the result of the test. If the location was already set, then the additional set has no effect but the test-and-set instruction returns a false result. If the location was not set, the instruction returns true and the location is in fact set. The bus supports this as an **atomic** operation that cannot be interrupted. Programming Example 6-1 describes a test-and-set operation in more detail.

A test-and-set can be used to implement a **semaphore,** which is a language-level synchronization construct. For the moment, let's assume that the system provides one semaphore that is used to guard access to a block of protected memory. Any process that wants to access the memory must use the semaphore to ensure that no other process is actively using it. As shown below, the semaphore names by tradition are **P()** to gain access to the protected memory and **V()** to release it.

```
/* some nonprotected operations here */
P(); /* wait for semaphore */
/* do protected work here */
V(); /* release semaphore */
```

The P() operation uses a test-and-set to repeatedly test a location that holds a lock on the memory block. The P() operation does not exit until the lock is available; once it is available, the test-and-set automatically sets the lock. Once past the P() operation, the process can work on the protected memory block. The V() operation resets the lock, allowing other processes access to the region by using the P() function.

Programming Example 6-1

Test-and-Set Operations

The following SWP (swap) instruction is used in the ARM to implement atomic test-and-set:

```
SWP        Rd,Rm,Rn
```

The SWP instruction takes three operands—the memory location pointed to by *Rn* is loaded and saved into *Rd,* and the value of *Rm* is then written into the location pointed to by *Rn.* When *Rd* and *Rn* are the same register, the instruction swaps the register's value and the value stored at the address pointed to by *Rd/Rn.* For example, the code sequence

```
        ADR r0, SEMAPHORE          ; get semaphore address
        LDR r1, #1
```

```
GETFLAG     SWP r1,r1,[r0]          ; test-and-set the flag
            BNZ GETFLAG             ; no flag yet, try again
HASFLAG     ...
```

first loads the constant 1 into *r1* and the address of the semaphore FLAG1 into register *r2*, then reads the semaphore into r0 and writes the 1 value into the semaphore. The code then tests whether the semaphore fetched from memory is zero; if it was, the semaphore was not busy and we can enter the critical region that begins with the HASFLAG label. If the flag was nonzero, we loop back to try to get the flag once again.

message passing

Message passing communication complements the shared memory model. As shown in Figure 6-12, each communicating entity has its own message send/receive unit. The message is not stored on the communications link, but rather at the senders/receivers at the endpoints. In contrast, shared memory communication can be seen as a memory block used as a communication device, in which all the data are stored in the communication link/memory.

Applications in which units operate relatively autonomously are natural candidates for message passing communication. For example, a home control system has one microcontroller per household device—lamp, thermostat, faucet, appliance, and so on. The devices must communicate relatively infrequently; furthermore, their physical separation is large enough that we would not naturally think of them as sharing a central pool of memory. Passing communication packets among the devices is a natural way to describe coordination between these devices. Message passing is the natural implementation of communication in many 8-bit microcontrollers that do not normally operate with external memory. We discuss message passing in more detail in Chapter 8.

We almost always need to pass data among processes. There are two distinct cases to consider: communicating processes that execute at the same rate, and those that communicate but operate at different rates.

Figure 6-12 *Message passing communication.*

data dependencies

When communicating processes run at the same rate, we express their relationships using data dependencies. Figure 6-13 shows a set of processes with data dependencies among them. Before a process can become ready, all the processes on which it depends must complete and send their data to it. The data dependencies define a partial ordering on process execution—P1 and P2 can execute in any order (or in interleaved fashion) but must both complete before P3, and P3 must complete before P4. All processes must finish before the end of the period. The data dependencies must form a directed acyclic graph (DAG)—a cycle in the data dependencies is difficult to interpret in a periodically executed system.

A set of processes with data dependencies is known as a **task graph.** Although the terminology for elements of a task graph varies from author to author, we will consider a component of the task graph (a set of nodes connected by data dependencies) as a **task** and the complete graph as the **task set.**

Communication among processes that run at different rates cannot be represented by data dependencies because there is no one-to-one relationship between data coming out of the source process and going into the destination process. Nevertheless, communication among processes of different rates is very common. Figure 6-14 illustrates the communication required among three elements of an MPEG audio/video decoder. Data come into the decoder in the system format, which multiplexes audio and video data. The system

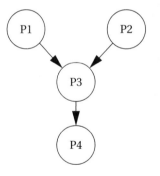

Figure 6-13 *Data dependencies among processes.*

Figure 6-14 *Communication among processes at different rates.*

decoder process demultiplexes the audio and video data and distributes it to the appropriate processes. Multirate communication is necessarily one way—for example, the system process writes data to the video process, but a separate communication mechanism must be provided for communication from the video process back to the system process.

6.5.5 Other Operating System Functions

Beyond scheduling processes, operating systems may provide a wide variety of other services. The role of the operating system may be viewed as managing shared resources. The CPU is clearly shared among the processes, and I/O devices rate a close second as shared resources requiring management. The operating system will generally supply a driver for each device and standard means for communicating with the devices. Network connections are one class of I/O that is becoming increasingly important in embedded computing systems, which may talk either on a local area network or on the Internet.

Advanced embedded operating systems may also provide file system services, with named files accessible for reading and writing. The file system may be kept in RAM and not necessarily on a disk. The file system is a convenient means for organizing large data sets, even if mass storage devices are not built into the hardware platform.

An embedded operating system must also provide powerful debugging facilities that allow system designers to evaluate the state of the system during execution. Debugging facilities are frequently built to take advantage of host PC systems that provide easy-to-use interfaces based on raw data supplied to the host PC by the embedded OS.

6.6 Scheduling Policies

A **scheduling policy** defines how processes are selected for promotion from the ready state to the running state. Every multitasking operating system implements some type of scheduling policy. Choosing the right scheduling policy not only ensures that the system will meet all its timing requirements, but it also has a profound influence on the CPU horsepower required to implement the system's functionality.

As seen in this section, scheduling policies vary widely in the generality of the timing requirements they can handle and the efficiency with which they use the CPU. **Utilization** is one of the key metrics in evaluating a scheduling policy. We will see that some types of timing requirements for a set of processes imply that we cannot utilize 100% of the CPU's execution time on useful work,

even ignoring context switching overhead. However, some scheduling policies can deliver higher CPU utilizations than others, even for the same timing requirements. The best policy depends on the required timing characteristics of the processes being scheduled.

In addition to utilization, we must also consider **scheduling overhead**—the execution time required to choose the next execution process, which is incurred in addition to any context switching overhead. In general, the more sophisticated the scheduling policy, the more CPU time it takes during system operation to implement it. Moreover, we generally achieve higher theoretical CPU utilization by applying more complex scheduling policies with higher overheads. The final decision on a scheduling policy must take into account both theoretical utilization and practical scheduling overhead.

POSIX supports real-time scheduling in the _POSIX_PRIORITY_SCHEDULING resource. Not all processes have to run under the same scheduling policy. The sched_setscheduler() function is used to determine a process's scheduling policy and other parameters. An example appears below.

```
#include <sched.h>
int i, my_process_id;
struct sched_param my_sched_params;

...
i = sched_setscheduler(my_process_id,SCHED_FIFO,&sched_params);
```

This call tells POSIX to use the SCHED_FIFO policy for the process, along with some other scheduling parameters.

The following subsections examine how the scheduling methods supported by POSIX relate to the range of possible scheduling mechanisms.

6.6.1 Rate-Monotonic Scheduling

Rate-monotonic scheduling (RMS), introduced by Liu and Layland [Liu73], was one of the first scheduling policies developed for real-time systems and is still very widely used. We say that RMS is a **static scheduling policy** because it assigns fixed priorities to processes. It turns out that these fixed priorities are sufficient to efficiently schedule the processes in many situations.

The theory underlying RMS is known as **rate-monotonic analysis (RMA).** This theory, as summarized below, uses a relatively simple model of the system.

- All processes run periodically on a single CPU.

- Context switching time is ignored.

- There are no data dependencies between processes.

- The execution time for a process is constant.

- All deadlines are at the ends of their periods.

- The highest-priority ready process is always selected for execution.

The major result of rate-monotonic analysis is that a relatively simple scheduling policy is optimal. Priorities are assigned by rank order of period, with the process with the shortest period being assigned the highest priority. This fixed-priority scheduling policy is the optimum assignment of static priorities to processes, in that it provides the highest CPU utilization while ensuring that all processes meet their deadlines.

Example 6-5 illustrates rate-monotonic scheduling.

Example 6-5

Rate-Monotonic Scheduling

Appearing below is a simple set of processes and their characteristics.

Process	Execution time	Period
P1	1	4
P2	2	6
P3	3	12

Applying the principles of RMA, we give P1 the highest priority, P2 the middle priority, and P3 the lowest priority. To understand all the interactions between the periods, we need to construct a timeline equal in length to the least-common multiple of the process periods, which is 12 in this case. The complete schedule for the least-common multiple of the periods is called the **unrolled schedule.**

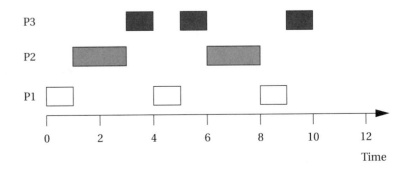

All three periods start at time zero. P1's data arrive first. Since P1 is the highest-priority process, it can start to execute immediately. After one time unit, P1 finishes and goes out of the ready state until the start of its next period. At time 1, P2 starts executing as the highest-priority ready process. At time 3, P2 finishes and P3 starts executing. P1's next iteration starts at time 4, at which point it interrupts P3. P3 gets one more time unit of execution between the second iterations of P1 and P2, but P3 doesn't get to finish until after the third iteration of P1.

Consider the following different set of execution times for these processes, keeping the same deadlines.

Process	Execution time	Period
P1	2	4
P2	3	6
P3	3	12

In this case, we can show that there is no feasible assignment of priorities that guarantees scheduling. Even though each process alone has an execution time significantly less than its period, combinations of processes can require more than 100% of the available CPU cycles. For example, during one 12 time-unit interval, we must execute P1 three times, requiring 6 units of CPU time; P2 twice, costing 6 units of CPU time; and P3 one time, requiring 3 units of CPU time. The total of $6 + 6 + 3 = 15$ units of CPU time is more than the 12 time units available, clearly exceeding the available CPU capacity.

Liu and Layland [Liu73] proved that the RMA priority assignment is optimal using critical-instant analysis. We define the **response time** of a process as the time at which the process finishes. The **critical instant** for a process is defined as the instant during execution at which the task has the largest response time. It is easy to prove that the critical instant for any process P, under the RMA model, occurs when it is ready and all higher-priority processes are also ready—if we change any higher-priority process to waiting, then P's response time can only go down.

We can use critical-instant analysis to determine whether there is any feasible schedule for the system. In the case of the second set of execution times in Example 6-5, there was no feasible schedule. Critical-instant analysis also implies that priorities should be assigned in order of periods. Let the periods and computation times of two processes P1 and P2 be τ_1, τ_2 and T_1, T_2, with $\tau_1 < \tau_2$. We can generalize the result of Example 6-5 to show the total CPU

requirements for the two processes in two cases. In the first case, let P1 have the higher priority. In the worst case we then execute P2 once during its period and as many iterations of P1 as fit in the same interval. Since there are $\lfloor \tau_2 / \tau_1 \rfloor$ iterations of P1 during a single period of P2, the required constraint on CPU time, ignoring context switching overhead, is

$$\left\lfloor \frac{\tau_2}{\tau_1} \right\rfloor T_1 + T_2 \le \tau_2 . \tag{EQ 6-1}$$

If, on the other hand, we give higher priority to P2, then critical-instant analysis tells us that we must execute all of P2 and all of P1 in one of P1's periods in the worst case:

$$T_1 + T_2 \le \tau_1 . \tag{EQ 6-2}$$

CPU utilization

There are cases where the first relationship can be satisfied and the second cannot, but there are no cases where the second relationship can be satisfied and the first cannot. We can inductively show that the process with the shorter period should always be given higher priority for process sets of arbitrary size. It is also possible to prove that RMS always provides a feasible schedule if such a schedule exists.

The bad news is that, although RMS is the optimal static-priority schedule, it does not allow the system to use 100% of the available CPU cycles. The total CPU **utilization** for a set of n tasks is

$$U = \sum_{i = 1}^{n} \frac{T_i}{\tau_i} . \tag{EQ 6-3}$$

It is possible to show that for a set of two tasks under RMS scheduling, the CPU utilization U will be no greater than $2(2^{1/2} - 1) \cong 0.83$. In other words, the CPU will be idle at least 17% of the time. This idle time is due to the fact that priorities are assigned statically; we see in the next section that more aggressive scheduling policies can improve CPU utilization. When there are m tasks, the maximum processor utilization is

$$U = m(2^{1/m} - 1) . \tag{EQ 6-4}$$

As m approaches infinity, the CPU utilization asymptotically approaches ln 2 = 0.69 —the CPU will be idle 31% of the time. We can use processor utilization U as an easy measure of the feasibility of an RMS scheduling problem.

Figure 6-15 shows an example of an RMS schedule for a system in which P1 has a period of 4 and an execution time of 2 and P2 has a period of 12 and an execution time of 1. The execution of P2 is preempted by P1 during P2's first period

and P2's second. The least-common multiple of the periods of the processes is 12, so the CPU utilization of this set of processes is $[(2 \times 3) + (1 \times 12)]/12 = 0.58333$, which is within the feasible utilization of RMS.

implementation The implementation of RMS is very simple. Figure 6-16 shows C code for an RMS scheduler run at the operating system's timer interrupt. The code merely scans through the list of processes in priority order and selects the highest-priority ready process to run. Because the priorities are static, the processes can be sorted by priority in advance before the system starts executing. As a result, this scheduler has an asymptotic complexity of $O(n)$, where n is the

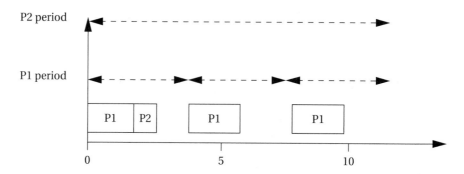

Figure 6-15 *An example of rate-monotonic scheduling.*

```
/* processes[] is an array of process activation records,
   stored in order of priority, with processes[0] being
   the highest-priority process */
Activation_record processes[NPROCESSES];

void RMA(int current) { /* current = currently executing process */
    int i;
    /* turn off current process (may be turned back on) */
    processes[current].state = READY_STATE;
    /* find process to start executing */
    for (i = 0; i < NPROCESSES; i++)
        if (processes[i].state == READY_STATE) {
            /* make this the running process */
            processes[i].state == EXECUTING_STATE;
            break;
        }
}
```

Figure 6-16 *C code for rate-monotonic scheduling.*

number of processes in the system. (This code assumes that processes are not created dynamically. If dynamic process creation is required, the array can be replaced by a linked list of processes, but the asymptotic complexity remains the same.) The RMS scheduler has both low asymptotic complexity and low actual execution time, which helps minimize the discrepancies between the zero-context-switch assumption of rate-monotonic analysis and the actual execution of an RMS system.

POSIX supports rate-monotonic scheduling in the SCHED_FIFO scheduling policy. The name of this policy is unfortunately misleading. It is a strict priority-based scheduling scheme in which a process runs until it is pre-empted or terminates. The term FIFO simply refers to the fact that, within a priority, processes run in first-come, first-served order.

We already saw the sched_setscheduler() function that allows a process to set a scheduling policy. The two useful functions below allow a process to determine the minimum and maximum priority values in the system.

```
minval = sched_get_priority_min(SCHED_RR);
maxval = sched_get_priority_max(SCHED_RR);
```

In the code fragment below, the sched_getparams() function returns the current parameter values for a process and sched_setparams() changes the parameter values.

```
int i, mypid;
struct sched_param my_param;

mypid = getpid();
i = sched_getparam(mypid,&my_params);
my_params.sched_priority = maxval;
i = sched_setparam(mypid,&my_params);
```

Whenever a process changes its priority, it is placed at the back of the queue for that priority level. A process can also explicitly move itself to the end of its priority queue with a call to the sched_yield() function.

6.6.2 Earliest-Deadline-First Scheduling

Earliest deadline first (EDF) is another well-known scheduling policy. It is a dynamic priority scheme—it changes process priorities during execution based on initiation times. As a result, it can achieve higher CPU utilizations than RMS. POSIX does not currently support EDF, but it still serves as a useful comparison to RMS.

The EDF policy is also very simple: It assigns priorities in order of deadline. The highest-priority process is the one whose deadline is nearest in time, and the lowest-priority process is the one whose deadline is farthest away. Clearly, priorities must be recalculated at every completion of a process. However, the final step of the OS during the scheduling procedure is the same as for RMS—the highest-priority ready process is chosen for execution.

Example 6-6 illustrates EDF scheduling in practice.

Example 6-6

Earliest-Deadline-First Scheduling

Consider the following processes:

Process	Execution time	Period
P1	1	3
P2	1	4
P3	2	5

The least-common multiple of the periods is 60, and the utilization is $\frac{1}{3} + \frac{1}{4} + \frac{1}{5} = 0.98333333$. This utilization is too high for RMS, but it can be handled with an earliest-deadline-first schedule. Because the schedule is so long, it is written in table form below.

Time	Running process	Deadlines
0	P1	
1	P2	
2	P3	P1
3	P3	P2
4	P1	P3
5	P2	P1
6	P1	
7	P3	P2

Time	Running process	Deadlines
8	P3	P1
9	P1	P3
10	P2	
11	P3	P1, P2
12	P3	
13	P1	
14	P2	P1, P3
15	P1	P2
16	P2	
17	P3	P1
18	P3	
19	P1	P2, P3
20	P2	P1
21	P1	
22	P3	
23	P3	P1, P2
24	P1	P3
25	P2	
26	P3	P1
27	P3	P2
28	P1	
29	P2	P1, P3
30	P1	
31	P3	P2
32	P3	P1
33	P1	
34	P2	P3
35	P3	P1, P2
36	P1	
37	P2	
38	P3	P1

(continued)

Time	Running process	Deadlines
39	P1	P2, P3
40	P2	
41	P3	P1
42	P1	
43	P3	P2
44	P3	P1, P3
45	P1	
46	P2	
47	P3	P1, P2
48	P3	
49	P1	P3
50	P2	P1
51	P1	P2
52	P3	
53	P3	P1
54	P2	P3
55	P1	P2
56	P2	P1
57	P3	
58	P3	
59	idle	P1, P2, P3

There is one time slot left at the end of this unrolled schedule, which is consistent with our earlier calculation that the CPU utilization is 59/60.

Liu and Layland [Liu73] showed that EDF can achieve 100% utilization. A feasible schedule exists if the CPU utilization (calculated in the same way as for RMA) is less than or equal to 1. They also showed that when an EDF system is overloaded and misses a deadline, it will run at 100% capacity for a time before the deadline is missed. Distinguishing between a system that is running just at

capacity and one that is about to miss a deadline is difficult, making the use of very high deadlines problematic.

The implementation of EDF is more complex than the RMS code. Figure 6-17 outlines one way to implement EDF. The major problem is keeping the processes sorted by time to deadline—since the times to deadlines for the processes change during execution, we cannot presort the processes into an array, as we could for RMS. To avoid re-sorting the entire set of activation records at every change, we can build a binary tree to keep the sorted records

Data structure

```
/* linked list, sorted by deadline */
Activation_record *processes;
/* data structure for sorting processes */
Deadline_tree *deadlines;

void expired_deadline(Activation_record *expired){
    remove(expired); /* remove from the deadline-sorted list */
    add(expired,expired->deadline); /* add at new deadline */
}

Void EDF(int current) { /* current = currently executing process */
    int i;
    /* turn off current process (may be turned back on) */
    processes->state = READY_STATE;
    /* find process to start executing */
    for (alink = processes; alink != NULL; alink = alink->next_deadline)
        if (processes->state == READY_STATE) {
            /* make this the running process */
            processes->state == EXECUTING_STATE;
            break;
        }
}
```

Code

Figure 6-17 *C code for earliest-deadline-first scheduling.*

and incrementally update the sort. At the end of each period, we can move the activation record to its new place in the sorted list by deleting it from the tree and then adding it back to the tree using standard tree manipulation techniques. We must update process priorities by traversing them in sorted order, so the incremental sorting routines must also update the linked list pointers that let us traverse the records in deadline order. (The linked list lets us avoid traversing the tree to go from one node to another, which would require more time.) After putting in the effort to building the sorted list of activation records, selecting the next executing process is done in a manner similar to that of RMS. However, the dynamic sorting adds complexity to the entire scheduling process. Each update of the sorted list requires $O(\log n)$ steps. The EDF code is also significantly more complex than the RMS code.

6.6.3 RMS versus EDF

Which scheduling policy is better: RMS or EDF? That depends on your criteria. EDF can extract higher utilization out of the CPU, but it may be difficult to diagnose the possibility of an imminent overload. Because the scheduler does take some overhead to make scheduling decisions, a factor that is ignored in the schedulability analysis of both EDF and RMS, running a scheduler at very high utilizations is somewhat problematic. RMS achieves lower CPU utilization but is easier to ensure that all deadlines will be satisfied. In some applications, it may be acceptable for some processes to occasionally miss deadlines. For example, a set-top box for video decoding is not a safety-critical application, and the occasional display artifacts caused by missing deadlines may be acceptable in some markets.

What if your set of processes is unschedulable and you need to guarantee that they complete their deadlines? There are several possible ways to solve this problem:

- Get a faster CPU. That will reduce execution times without changing the periods, giving you lower utilization. This will require you to redesign the hardware, but this is often feasible because you are rarely using the fastest CPU available.

- Redesign the processes to take less execution time. This requires knowledge of the code and may or may not be possible.

- Rewrite the specification to change the deadlines. This is unlikely to be feasible, but may be in a few cases where some of the deadlines were initially made tighter than necessary.

6.6.4 A Closer Look at Our Modeling Assumptions

Our analyses of RMS and EDF have made some strong assumptions. These assumptions have made the analyses much more tractable, but the predictions of analysis may not hold up in practice. Since a misprediction may cause a system to miss a critical deadline, it is important to at least understand the consequences of these assumptions.

In all of the above discussions, we have assumed that each process is totally self-contained. However, that is not always the case—for instance, a process may need a system resource, such as an I/O device or the bus, to complete its work. Scheduling the processes without considering the resources those processes require can cause **priority inversion,** in which a low-priority process blocks execution of a higher-priority process by keeping hold of its resource. Example 6-7 illustrates priority inversion.

Example 6-7

Priority Inversion

Consider a system with two processes: the higher-priority P1 and the lower-priority P2. Each uses the microprocessor bus to communicate to peripherals. When P2 executes, it requests the bus from the operating system and receives it. If P1 becomes ready while P2 is using the bus, the operating system will preempt P2 for P1, leaving P2 with control of the bus. When P1 requests the bus, it will be denied the bus, since P2 already owns it. Unless P1 has a way to take the bus from P2, the two processes may deadlock.

The most common method for dealing with priority inversion is to promote the priority of any process when it requests a resource from the operating system. The priority of the process temporarily becomes higher than that of any other process that may use the resource. This ensures that the process will continue executing once it has the resource so that it can finish its work with the resource, return it to the operating system, and allow other processes to use it. Once the process is finished with the resource, its priority is demoted to its normal value.

Rate-monotonic scheduling assumes that there are no data dependencies between processes. Example 6-8 shows that knowledge of data dependencies can help use the CPU more efficiently.

Example 6-8

Data Dependencies and Scheduling

Data dependencies imply that certain combinations of process activations can never occur. Consider the simple example [Mal96] below.

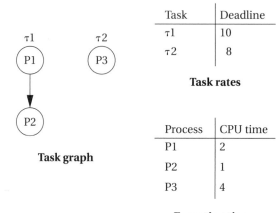

Task	Deadline
$\tau 1$	10
$\tau 2$	8

Task rates

Process	CPU time
P1	2
P2	1
P3	4

Execution times

We know that P1 and P2 cannot execute at the same time, since P1 must finish before P2 can begin. Furthermore, we also know that because P3 has a higher priority, it will not preempt both P1 and P2 in a single iteration. If P3 preempts P1, then P3 will complete before P2 begins; if P3 preempts P2, then it will not interfere with P1 in that iteration. Because we know that some combinations of processes cannot be ready at the same time, we know that our worst-case CPU requirements are less than would be required if all processes could be ready simultaneously.

One important simplification we have made is that contexts can be switched in zero time. On the one hand, this is clearly wrong—we must execute instructions to save and restore context, and we must execute additional instructions to implement the scheduling policy. On the other hand, context switching can be implemented efficiently—context switching need not kill performance. The effects of nonzero context switching time must be carefully analyzed in the context of a particular implementation to be sure that the predictions of an ideal scheduling policy are sufficiently accurate.

Example 6-9 shows that context switching can, in fact, cause a system to miss a deadline.

Example 6-9

Scheduling and Context Switching Overhead

Appearing below is a set of processes and their characteristics.

Process	Execution time	Deadline
P1	3	5
P2	3	10

First, let us try to find a schedule assuming that context switching time is zero. Following is a feasible schedule for a sequence of data arrivals that meets all the deadlines:

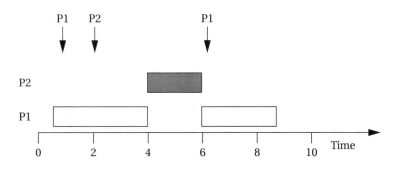

Now let us assume that the total time to initiate a process, including context switching and scheduling policy evaluation, is one time unit. It is easy to see that there is no feasible schedule for the above data arrival sequence, since we require a total of $2T_{P1} + T_{P2} = 2 \times (1 + 3) + (1 + 3) = 11$ time units to execute one period of P2 and two periods of P1.

In Example 6-9, overhead was a large fraction of the process execution time and of the periods. In most real-time operating systems, a context switch requires only a few hundred instructions, with only slightly more overhead for a simple real-time scheduler like RMS. These small overhead times are less likely to cause serious scheduling problems. Problems are most likely to manifest themselves in the highest-rate processes, which are often the most critical in any case. Completely checking that all deadlines will be met with nonzero context switching time requires checking all possible schedules for processes and including the context switch time at each preemption or

process initiation. However, assuming an average number of context switches per process and computing CPU utilization can provide at least an estimate of how close the system is to CPU capacity.

Rhodes and Wolf [Rho97] developed a CAD algorithm for implementing processes that computes exact schedules to accurately predict the effects of context switching. Their algorithm selects between interrupt-driven and polled implementations for processes on a microprocessor. Polled processes introduce less overhead, but they do not respond to events as quickly as interrupt-driven processes. Furthermore, because adding interrupt levels to a microprocessor usually incurs some cost in added logic, we do not want to use interrupt-driven processes when they are not necessary. Their algorithm computes exact schedules for the processes, including the overhead for polling or interrupts as appropriate, and then uses heuristics to select implementations for the processes. The major heuristic starts with all processes implemented as polled mode, and then changes processes that miss deadlines to use interrupts. Some iterative improvement steps try various combinations of interrupt-driven processes to eliminate deadline violations. These heuristics minimize the number of processes implemented with interrupts.

Another important assumption we have made thus far is that process execution time is constant. As seen in Section 5.6, this is definitely not the case—both data-dependent behavior and caching effects can cause large variations in run times. The techniques for bounding the cache-based performance of a single program do not work when multiple programs are in the same cache. The state of the cache depends on the product of the states of all programs executing in the cache, making the state space of the multiple-process system exponentially larger than that for a single program. We discuss this problem in more detail in Section 6.8.

6.6.5 Other POSIX Scheduling Policies

In addition to SCHED_FIFO, POSIX supports two other real-time scheduling policies: SCHED_RR and SCHED_OTHER. SCHED_RR is a combination of real-time and interactive scheduling techniques: Within a priority level, the processes are timesliced. Because interactive systems must ensure that all processes get a chance to run, time is divided into quanta. Processes get the CPU in multiples of quanta. SCHED_RR allows each process to run for a quantum of time and then gives the CPU to the next process to run for its quantum. The length of the quantum can vary with priority level.

The SCHED_OTHER is defined to allow non–real-time processes to intermix with real-time processes. The precise scheduling mechanism used by this policy is not defined. It is used to indicate that the process does not need a real-time scheduling policy.

Remember that different processes in a system can run with different policies. Consequently, some processes may run SCHED_FIFO while others run SCHED_RR.

6.7 Interprocess Communication Mechanisms

In this section, we consider interprocess communication mechanisms in more detail.

6.7.1 Signals

In Section 6.5.4 we stated that the two major forms of interprocess communication are shared memory and message passing. However, Unix supports another, very simple communication mechanism—the **signal.** A signal is simple because it does not pass data beyond the existence of the signal itself. A signal is analogous to an interrupt, but it is entirely a software creation. A signal is generated by a process and transmitted to another process by the operating system.

Figure 6-18 lists basic signal types defined by POSIX. Some of these signals (SIGFPE, SIGILL, SIGSEGV) are used to abstract CPU exceptions to the operating system. Some (SIGALRM, SIGPIPE) relate to operating system services. Several of them (SIGABRT, SIGHUP, SIGINT, SIGKILL, SIGQUIT, SIGTERM) are ways to terminate a process. The SIGUSR1 and SIGUSR2 signals are not used directly by POSIX and are free for application-specific purposes.

The above signals have a fairly limited repertoire of functions—it would be difficult to build a rich set of communicating processes based on error and process termination signals. That point is driven home by the way in which a process generates a signal, namely, the kill() function:

kill(0,SIGABRT);

The previous command sends the SIGABRT signal to all the child processes. Any signal type can be sent by the kill command.

However, a process can control what happens when it receives a signal by declaring a function to handle a signal of a given type. (A control-C in an interactive Unix process usually corresponds to the SIGINT signal. A program that cannot be killed by control-C has told the operating system that it wants to ignore SIGINT signals.) The process declares a handler for a signal using the sigaction() function. The process uses the sigaction data structure to describe

	Name	*Description*
Termination	SIGABRT	Abort process
	SIGTERM	Terminate process
Exceptions	SIGFPE	Floating-point exception
	SIGHUP	Terminal hang-up
	SIGILL	Illegal instruction exception
	ISGINT	Interactive termination
	SIGKILL	Unavoidable process termination
	SIGPIPE	Write to pipe with no readers
	SIGQUIT	Abnormal termination
	SIGSEGV	Memory access exception
	SIGALRM	Real-time clock expired
User-defined	SIGUSR1	User-defined
	SIGUSR2	User-defined

Figure 6-18 *Required POSIX signals.*

which signals it wants the handler to be called for. For example, we can define a handler for the SIGUSR1 function as follows:

```
#include <signal.h>

extern void usr1_handler(int); /* declaration of SIGUSR1 handler */
struct sigaction act, oldact;
int retval;

/* set up the descriptor data structure */
act.sa_flags = 0;
sigemptyset(&act.sa_mask); /* initialize the signal set to empty */
act.sa_handler = usr1_handler; /*add SIGUSR1 handler to the set */
/* tell the operating system about this handler */
retval = sigaction(SIGUSR1,&act,&oldact);
    /* oldact has old action set */
```

These signals have a long history in Unix and POSIX but are not particularly well suited to real-time communication. (The use of the kill() function to send these signals certainly suggests that these signals have one primary use.) Therefore, the POSIX.4 version defines a _POSIX_REALTIME_SIGNALS facility that is much better suited to real-time communication.

The real-time signals are identified by number in the range SIGRTMIN and SIGRTMAX. Although they are named in all capitals, the normal Unix convention for constants, these values can in fact change during execution. Therefore, it is a good idea to refer to signals relative to these bounds—for example, SIGRTMIN + 1.

The sigqueue() function is used to send a signal:

```
if (sigqueue(destpid,SIGRTMAX - 1,sval) < 0) { /* error */ }
```

This code sends the signal SIGRTMAX - 1 to process number destpid. The function returns a negative value if an error occurs sending the signal. As the name of the function implies, signals can be queued—if two processes send a third process containing signals of the same type, the signals are received in the order in which they were sent. However, queueing must be turned on using the SA_SIGINFO bit in the sa_flags field of the sigaction structure.

6.7.2 Signals in UML

A UML signal is actually a generalization of the Unix signal. While a Unix signal carries no parameters other than a condition code, a UML signal is an object. As such, it can carry parameters as object attributes. Figure 6-19 shows the use of a signal in UML. The *sigbehavior()* behavior of the class is responsible for throwing the signal, as indicated by *<<send>>*. The signal object is indicated by the *<<signal>>* stereotype.

6.7.3 Shared Memory Communication

Conceptually, semaphores are the mechanism we use to make shared memory safe. POSIX supports semaphores, but it also supports a direct shared memory mechanism.

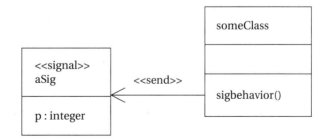

Figure 6-19 *Use of a UML signal.*

POSIX supports counting semaphores in the _POSIX_SEMAPHORES option. A counting semaphore allows more than one process access to a resource at a time. If the semaphore allows up to N resources, then it will not block until N processes have simultaneously passed the semaphore. At that point, the blocked process can resume only after one of the processes has given up its semaphore. The simplest way to think about counting semaphores is that they count down to 0—when the semaphore value is 0, the process must wait until another process gives up the semaphore and increments the count.

Since there may be many semaphores in the system, each one is given a name. Names are similar to file names except that they are not arbitrary paths—they should always start with "/" and should have no other "/". The code fragment below shows how you create a new semaphore called /sem1 and then close it.

```
int i, oflags;
sem_t *my_semaphore; /* descriptor for the semaphore */

my_semaphore = sem_open("/sem1",oflags);
/* do useful work here */
i = sem_close(my_semaphore);
```

The POSIX names for P and V are sem_wait() and sem_post(), respectively. POSIX also provides a sem_trywait() function that tests the semaphore but does not block. Examples of their use follow:

```
int i;
i = sem_wait(my_semaphore); /* P */
/* do useful work */
i = sem_post(my_semaphore); /* V */
/* sem_trywait tests without blocking */
i = sem_trywait(my_semaphore);
```

POSIX shared memory is supported under the _POSIX_SHARED_MEMORY_ OBJECTS option. The shared memory functions create blocks of memory that can be used by several processes. The shm_open() function below opens a shared memory object.

```
objdesc = shm_open("/memobj1",O_RDWR);
```

The above code creates a shared memory object called /memobj1 with read/write access; the O_RDONLY mode allows reading only. It returns an integer that we can use as a descriptor for the shared memory object. The ftruncate() func-

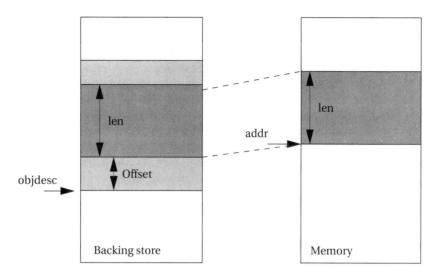

Figure 6-20 *The POSIX* mmap() *function parameters.*

tion allows a process to set the size of the shared memory object as seen in the next example.

```
if (ftruncate(objdesc,1000) < 0) { /* error */ }
```

Before using the shared memory object, we must map it into the process memory space using the mmap() function. POSIX assumes that shared memory objects fundamentally reside in a backing store such as a disk and are then mapped into the address space of the process. Figure 6-20 shows the definitions of the basic mmap() parameters. The value returned by shm_open(), objdesc, is the origin of the shared memory in the backing store. mmap allows the process to map in a subset of that space starting at the offset. The length of the mapped space is len. The start of the block in the process's memory space, addr. mmap(), also requires you to set the protection mode for the mapped memory (O_RDWR, etc.). A sample call to mmap() follows:

```
if (mmap(addr,len,O_RDWR,MAP_SHARED,objdesc,0) == NULL) {
    /* error*/
}
```

The MAP_SHARED parameter tells mmap to propagate all writes to all processes that share this memory block. Use the munmap() function to unmap the memory when the process is done with it as follows:

```
if (munmap(startadrs,len) < 0) { /* error */ }
```

This function unmaps shared memory from startadrs to startadrs+len. Finally, as seen below, the close() function is used to dispose of the shared memory block.

```
close(objdesc);
```

Only one process calls shm_open() to create the shared memory object and close() to destroy it. Every process (including the one that created the object) must use mmap() and mummap() to map the object into its address space.

6.7.4 Message-Based Communication

The shell syntax of the **pipe** is very familiar to Unix users. An example appears below.

```
% foo file1 | baz > file2
```

In this command, the output of foo is sent directly to the baz program's standard input by the operating system. The vertical bar (|) is the shell's notation for a pipe; programs use the pipe() function to create pipes.

A parent process uses the pipe() function to create a pipe to talk to a child. It must do so before the child itself is created or it won't have any way to pass a pointer to the pipe to the child. Each end of a pipe appears to a program as a file—the process at the head of the pipe writes to one file descriptor while the tail process reads from another file descriptor. The pipe() function returns an array of file descriptors, the first for the write end and the second for the read end. An example follows:

```
if (pipe(pipe_ends) < 0) { /* create the pipe, check for errors */
    perror("pipe");
    break;
}
/* create the process */
childid = fork();
if (childid == 0) { /* the child reads from pipe_ends[1]*/
    childargs[0] = pipe_ends[1];
    /* pass the read end descriptor to the new incarnation of child */
    execv("mychild",childargs);
    perror("execv");
    exit(1);
}
```

```
else { /* the parent writes to pipe_ends[0] */
   ...
}
```

POSIX also supports message queues under the _POSIX_MESSAGE_PASSING facility. The advantage of a queue over a pipe is that, since queues have names, we don't have to create the pipe descriptor before creating the other process using it, as with pipes.

The name of a queue follows the same rules as for semaphores and shared memory—it starts with a "/" and contains no other "/" characters. In the code below, the O_CREAT flag to mq_open() causes it to creates the named queue if it doesn't yet exist, and just opens the queue for the process if it does already exist.

```
struct mq_attr mq_attr; /* attributes of the queue */
mqd_t myq; /* the queue descriptor */

mq_attr.mq_maxmsg = 50; /* maximum number of messages */
mq_attr.mq_msgsize = 64; /* maximum size of a message */
mq_attr.mq_flags = 0; /* flags */
myq = mq_open("/q1",O_CREAT | RDWR,S_IRWXU,&mq_attr);
```

We use the following queue descriptor myq to enqueue and dequeue messages:

```
char data[MAXLEN], rcvbuf[MAXLEN];

if (mq_send(myq,data,len,priority) < 0) { /* error */ }
nbytes = mq_receive(myq,rcvbuf,MAXLEN,&prio);
```

Messages can be prioritized, with a priority value between 0 and MQ_PRIO_MAX (there are at least 32 priorities available). Messages are inserted into the queue such that they follow all existing messages of equal or higher priority and precede all lower-priority messages.

When a process is finished with a queue, it calls mq_close() as follows:

```
i = mq_close(myq);
```

6.8 Evaluating Operating System Performance

The scheduling policy does not tell us all that we would like to know about the performance of a real system running processes. Our analysis of scheduling policies makes the following simplifying assumptions:

- We have assumed that context switches require zero time. Although it is often reasonable to neglect context switch time when it is much smaller than the process execution time, context switching can add significant delay in some cases.

- We have assumed that we know the execution time of the processes. In fact, we learned in Section 5.6 that program time is not a single number, but can be bounded by worst-case and best-case execution times.

- We probably determined worst-case or best-case times for the processes in isolation. But, in fact, they interact with each other in the cache. Cache conflicts among processes can drastically degrade process execution time.

Some RTOSs provide simulators or other tools that allow you to view the operation of the processes in the system. These tools will show not only abstract events such as process activations but also context switching time, interrupt response time, and other overheads. This sort of view can be helpful in both functional and performance debugging.

Many real-time systems have been designed based on the assumption that there is no cache present, even though one actually exists. This grossly conservative assumption is made because the system architects lack tools that permit them to analyze the effect of caching. Since they do not know where caching will cause problems, they are forced to retreat to the simplifying assumption that there is no cache. The result is extremely overdesigned hardware, which has much more computational power than is necessary. However, just as experience tells us that a well-designed cache provides significant performance benefits for a single program, a properly sized cache can allow a microprocessor to run a set of processes much more quickly. By analyzing the effects of the cache, we can make much better use of the available hardware.

Li and Wolf [Li99] developed a model for estimating the performance of multiple processes sharing a cache. In the model, some processes can be given reservations in the cache, such that only a particular process can inhabit a reserved section of the cache; other processes are left to share the cache. We generally want to use cache partitions only for performance-critical processes since cache reservations are wasteful of limited cache space. Performance is estimated by constructing a schedule, taking into account not just execution time of the processes but also the state of the cache. Each process in the shared section of the cache is modeled by a binary variable: 1 if present in the cache and 0 if not. Each process is also characterized by three total execution times: assuming no caching, with typical caching, and with all code always resident in the cache. The always-resident time is unrealistically optimistic, but it can be used to find a lower bound on the required schedule time. During construction of the schedule, we can look at the current cache state to see whether the no-

cache or typical-caching execution time should be used at this point in the schedule. We can also update the cache state if the cache is needed for another process. Although this model is simple, it provides much more realistic performance estimates than assuming the cache either is nonexistent or is perfect. Example 6-10 shows how cache management can improve CPU utilization.

Example 6-10

Effects of Scheduling on the Cache

Consider a system containing the following three processes:

Process	Worst-case CPU time	Average-case CPU time
P1	8	6
P2	4	3
P3	4	3

Each process uses half the cache, so only two processes can be in the cache at the same time.

Appearing below is a first schedule that uses a least-recently-used cache replacement policy on a process-by-process basis.

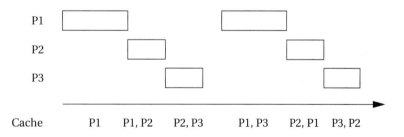

In the first iteration, we must fill up the cache, but even in subsequent iterations, competition among all three processes ensures that a process is never in the cache when it starts to execute. As a result, we must always use the worst-case execution time.

Another schedule in which we have reserved half the cache for P1 is shown below. This leaves P2 and P3 to fight over the other half of the cache.

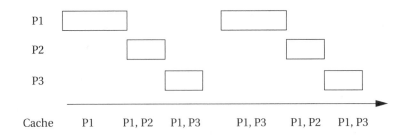

In this case, P2 and P3 still compete, but P1 is always ready. After the first iteration, we can use the average-case execution time for P1, which gives us some spare CPU time that could be used for additional operations.

6.9 Power Optimization Strategies for Processes

We learned in Section 3.7 about the features that CPUs provide to manage power consumption. The RTOS and system architecture can use static and dynamic power management mechanisms to help manage the system's power consumption. A **power management policy** [Ben00] is a strategy for determining when to perform certain power management operations. A power management policy in general examines the state of the system to determine when to take actions. However, the overall strategy embodied in the policy should be designed based on the characteristics of the static and dynamic power management mechanisms.

Going into a low-power mode takes time; generally, the more that is shut off, the longer the delay incurred during reactivation. Because power-down and power-up are not free, modes should be changed carefully. Determining when to switch into and out of a power-up mode requires an analysis of the overall system activity.

- Avoiding a power-down mode can cost unnecessary power.

- Powering down too soon can cause severe performance penalties.

Reentering run mode typically costs a considerable amount of time.

A straightforward method is to power up the system when a request is received. This works as long as the delay in handling the request is acceptable.

A more sophisticated technique is **predictive shutdown.** The goal is to predict when the next request will be made and to start the system just before that time, saving the requestor the start-up time. Clearly, it is possible to exactly

predict request times only in very limited circumstances, but such systems do exist, as described in Application Example 6-4.

Application Example 6-4

Predictive Shutdown in Pagers

A pager can use a predictive shutdown very effectively because the pager network is synchronous. The network assigns a time slot to each pager on the system. The pager uses a timer to determine when the next message should arrive. Between messages, most of the pager remains powered down, while the counter remains on. At the proper time, the timer wakes up the rest of the system, which then listens for its message. Because a typical pager system runs at only 1200 baud, the timer can be built to sufficient accuracy even in a low-power, low-cost system. As a result, the wake-up times are totally predictable.

In general, predictive shutdown techniques are probabilistic—they make guesses about activity patterns based on a probabilistic model of expected behavior. Because they rely on statistics, they may not always correctly guess the time of the next activity. This can cause the following two types of problems:

■ The requestor may have to wait for an activity period. In the worst case, the requestor may not make a deadline due to the delay incurred by system start-up.

■ The system may restart itself when no activity is imminent. As a result, the system will waste power.

Clearly, the choice of a good probabilistic model of service requests is important. The policy mechanism should also not be too complex, since the power it consumes to make decisions is part of the total system power budget.

Several predictive techniques are possible. A very simple technique is to use fixed times. For instance, if the system does not receive inputs during an interval of length T_{on}, it shuts down; a powered-down system waits for a period T_{off} before returning to the power-on mode. The choice of T_{off} and T_{on} must be determined by experimentation. Srivastava and Eustace [Sri94] found one useful rule for graphics terminals. They plotted the observed idle time (T_{off}) of a graphics terminal versus the immediately preceding active time (T_{on}). The result was an L-shaped distribution as illustrated in Figure 6-21. In this distribution, the idle period after a long active period is usually very short, and the

length of the idle period after a short active period is uniformly distributed. Based on this distribution, they proposed a shutdown threshold that depended on the length of the last active period—they shut down when the active period length was below a threshold, putting the system in the vertical portion of the L distribution.

A more advanced technique is based on a more thorough analysis of the system state [Ben99]. As shown in Figure 6-22, we need to consider several elements of the total managed system: The service provider is the machine whose power is being managed; the service requestor is the machine or person making requests of that power-managed system; a queue is used to hold pending requests (e.g., while waiting for the service provider to power up); and the

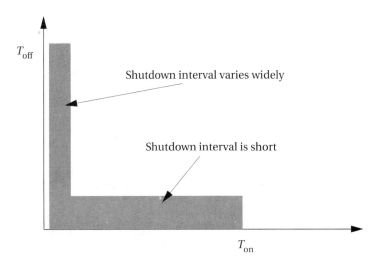

Figure 6-21 *An L-shaped usage distribution.*

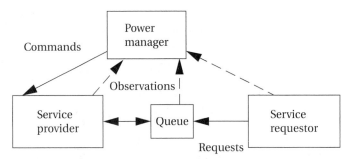

Figure 6-22 *Architecture of a power-managed system.*

power manager is responsible for sending power management commands to the provider. The power manager can observe the behavior of the requestor, provider, and queue. Each of these elements can be modeled by a Markov model, which is a probabilistic state machine. Benini et al. [Ben99] showed that a power management policy that maximizes system performance while meeting a power consumption limitation can be solved in polynomial time.

The **Advanced Configuration and Power Interface (ACPI)** is an open industry standard for power management services. It is designed to be compatible with a wide variety of operating systems. It was targeted initially to PCs. The role of ACPI in the system is illustrated in Figure 6-23. ACPI provides some basic power management facilities and abstracts the hardware layer, the operating system has its own power management module that determines the policy, and the operating system then uses ACPI to send the required controls to the hardware and to observe the hardware's state as input to the power manager.

ACPI supports the following five basic global power states:

■ G3, the mechanical off state, in which the system consumes no power.

■ G2, the soft off state, which requires a full operating system reboot to restore the machine to working condition. This state has four substates:

— S1, a low wake-up latency state with no loss of system context;

Figure 6-23 *The Advanced Configuration and Power Interface and its relationship to a complete system.*

— S2, a low wake-up latency state with a loss of CPU and system cache state;

— S3, a low wake-up latency state in which all system state except for main memory is lost; and

— S4, the lowest-power sleeping state, in which all devices are turned off.

■ G1, the sleeping state, in which the system appears to be off and the time required to return to working condition is inversely proportional to power consumption.

■ G0, the working state, in which the system is fully usable.

■ The legacy state, in which the system does not comply with ACPI.

The power manager typically includes an observer, which receives messages through the ACPI interface that describe the system behavior. It also includes a decision module that determines power management actions based on those observations.

Design Example

6.10 Telephone Answering Machine

In this section we design a digital telephone answering machine. The system will store messages in digital form rather than on an analog tape. To make life more interesting, we use a simple algorithm to compress the voice data so that we can make more efficient use of the limited amount of available memory.

6.10.1 Theory of Operation and Requirements

In addition to studying the compression algorithm, we also need to learn a little about the operation of telephone systems.

The compression scheme we will use is known as **adaptive differential pulse code modulation (ADPCM).** Despite the long name, the technique is relatively simple but can yield 2× compression ratios on voice data.

The ADPCM coding scheme is illustrated in Figure 6-24. Unlike traditional sampling, in which each sample shows the magnitude of the signal at a particular time, ADPCM encodes changes in the signal. The samples are expressed in a **coding alphabet,** whose values are in a relatively small range that spans both negative and positive values. In this case, the value range is {-3,-2,-1,1,2,3}. Each sample is used to predict the value of the signal at the current instant from the previous value. At each point in time, the sample is chosen such that the error between the predicted value and the actual signal value is minimized.

An ADPCM compression system, including an encoder and decoder, is shown in Figure 6-25. The encoder is more complex, but both the encoder and

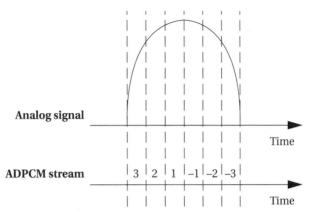

Figure 6-24 *The ADPCM coding scheme.*

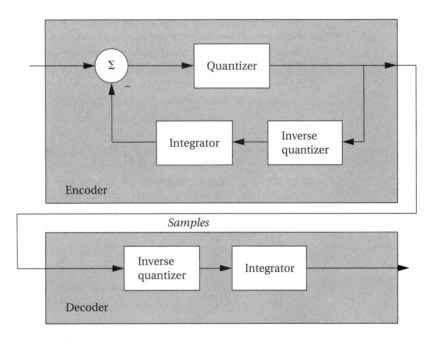

Figure 6-25 *An ADPCM compression system.*

decoder use an integrator to reconstruct the waveform from the samples. The integrator simply computes a running sum of the history of the samples; because the samples are differential, integration reconstructs the original signal. The encoder compares the incoming waveform to the predicted waveform (the waveform that will be generated in the decoder). The quantizer encodes this difference as the best predictor of the next waveform value. The inverse

quantizer allows us to map bit-level symbols onto real numerical values; for example, the eight possible codes in a 3-bit code can be mapped onto floating-point numbers. The decoder simply uses an inverse quantizer and integrator to turn the differential samples into the waveform.

The answering machine will ultimately be connected to a telephone **subscriber line** (although for testing purposes we will construct a simulated line). At the other end of the subscriber line is the **central office.** All information is carried on the phone line in analog form over a pair of wires. In addition to analog/digital and digital/analog converters to send and receive voice data, we need to sense two other characteristics of the line.

- *Ringing:* The central office sends a ringing signal to the telephone when a call is waiting. The ringing signal is in fact a 90 V RMS sinusoid, but we can use analog circuitry to produce 0 for no ringing and 1 for ringing.

- *Off-hook:* The telephone industry term for answering a call is going **off-hook;** the technical term for hanging up is going **on-hook.** (This creates some initial confusion since *off-hook* means the telephone is active and *on-hook* means it is not in use, but the terminology starts to make sense after a few uses.) Our interface will send a digital signal to take the phone line off-hook, which will cause analog circuitry to make the necessary connection so that voice data can be sent and received during the call.

We can now write the requirements for the answering machine. We will assume that the interface is not to the actual phone line but to some circuitry that provides voice samples, off-hook commands, and so on. Such circuitry will let us test our system with a telephone line simulator and then build the analog circuitry necessary to connect to a real phone line. We'll use the term **outgoing message (OGM)** to refer to the message recorded by the owner of the machine and played at the start of every phone call.

Name	Digital telephone answering machine.
Purpose	Telephone answering machine with digital memory, using speech compression.
Inputs	*Telephone:* voice samples, ring indicator. *User interface:* microphone, play messages button, record OGM button.
Outputs	*Telephone:* voice samples, on-hook/off-hook command. *User interface:* speaker, # messages indicator, message light.

Functions	*Default mode:* When machine receives ring indicator, it signals off-hook, plays the OGM, and then records the incoming message. Maximum recording length for incoming message is 30 seconds, at which time the machine hangs up. If the machine runs out of memory, the OGM is played and the machine then hangs up without recording. *Playback mode:* When the play button is depressed, the machine plays all messages. If the play button is depressed again within five seconds, the messages are played again. Messages are erased after playback. *OGM editing mode:* When the user hits the record OGM button, the machine records an outgoing message of up to 10 seconds. When the user holds down the record OGM button and hits the play button, the OGM is played back.
Performance	Should be able to record about 30 minutes of total voice, including incoming and outgoing messages. Voice data are sampled at the standard telephone rate of 8 kHz.
Manufacturing cost	Consumer product range: approximately $50.
Power	Powered by AC through a standard power supply.
Physical size and weight	Comparable in size and weight to a desk telephone.

We have made a few arbitrary decisions about the user interface in these requirements. The amount of voice data that can be saved by the machine should in fact be determined by two factors: the price per unit of DRAM at the time at which the device goes into manufacturing (since the cost will almost certainly drop from the start of design to manufacture) and the projected retail price at which the machine must sell. The protocol when the memory is full is also arbitrary—it would make at least as much sense to throw out old messages and replace them with new ones, and ideally the user could select which protocol to use. Extra features such as an indicator showing the number of messages or a save messages feature would also be nice to have in a real consumer product.

6.10.2 Specification

Figure 6-26 shows the class diagram for the answering machine. In addition to the classes that perform the major functions, we also use classes to describe the incoming and outgoing messages. As seen below, these classes are related.

The definitions of the physical interface classes are shown in Figure 6-27. The buttons and lights simply provide attributes for their input and output values. The phone line, microphone, and speaker are given behaviors that let us sample their current values.

The message classes are defined in Figure 6-28. Since incoming and outgoing message types share many characteristics, we derive both from a more fundamental message type.

The major operational classes—*Controls*, *Record*, and *Playback*—are defined in Figure 6-29. The *Controls* class provides an *operate()* behavior that oversees the user-level operations. The *Record* and *Playback* classes provide behaviors that handle writing and reading sample sequences.

The state diagram for the *Controls activate* behavior is shown in Figure 6-30. Most of the user activities are relatively straightforward. The most complex is answering an incoming call. As with the software modem of Section 5.10, we want to be sure that a single depression of a button causes the required action to be taken exactly once; this requires edge detection on the button signal.

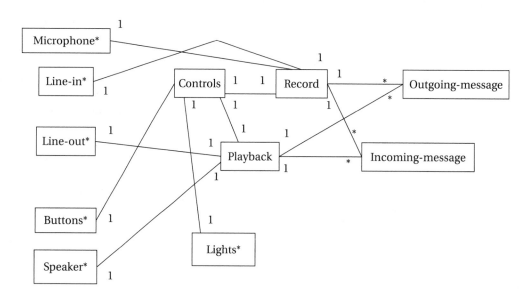

Figure 6-26 *Class diagram for the answering machine.*

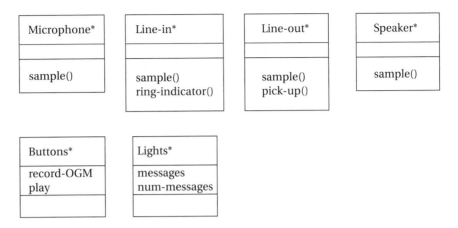

Figure 6-27 *Physical class interfaces for the answering machine.*

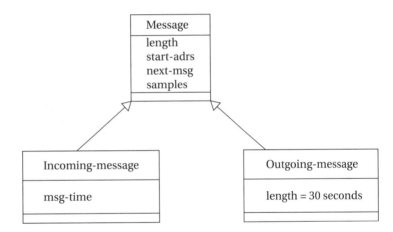

Figure 6-28 *The message classes for the answering machine.*

Figure 6-29 *Operational classes for the answering machine.*

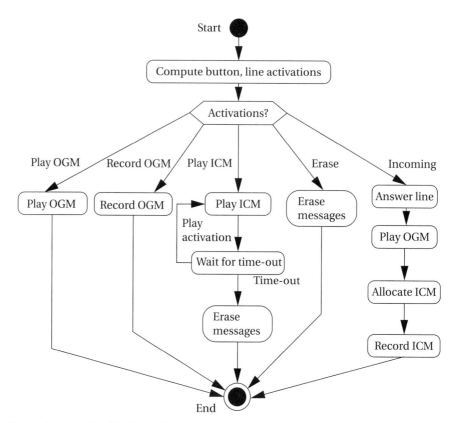

Figure 6-30 *State diagram for the Controls activate behavior.*

State diagrams for *record-msg* and *playback-msg* are shown in Figure 6-31. We have parameterized the specification for *record-msg* so that it can be used either from the phone line or from the microphone. This requires parameterizing the source itself and the termination condition.

6.10.3 System Architecture

The machine consists of two major subsystems from the user's point of view: the user interface and the telephone interface. The user and telephone interfaces both appear internally as I/O devices on the CPU bus with the main memory serving as the storage for the messages.

The software splits into the following seven major pieces:

■ The **front panel module** handles the buttons and lights.

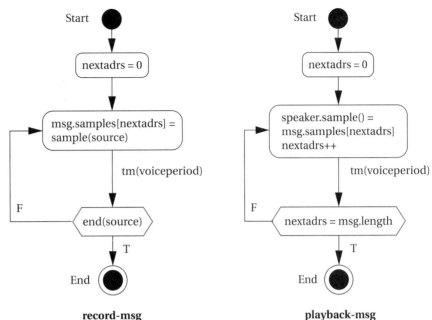

Figure 6-31 *State diagrams for the record-msg and playback-msg behaviors.*

- The **speaker module** handles sending data to the user's speaker.

- The **telephone line module** handles off-hook detection and on-hook commands.

- The **telephone input and output modules** handle receiving samples from and sending samples to the telephone line.

- The **compression module** compresses data and stores it in memory.

- The **decompression module** uncompresses data and sends it to the speaker module.

We can determine the execution model for these modules based on the rates at which they must work and the ways in which they communicate.

- The front panel and telephone line modules must regularly test the buttons and phone line, but this can be done at a fairly low rate. As seen below, they can therefore run as polled processes in the software's main loop.

```
while (TRUE) {
    check_phone_line();
```

```
        run_front_panel();
    }
```

- The speaker and phone input and output modules must run at higher, regular rates and are natural candidates for interrupt processing. These modules don't run all the time and so can be disabled by the front panel and telephone line modules when they are not needed.

- The compression and decompression modules run at the same rate as the speaker and telephone I/O modules, but they are not directly connected to devices. We will therefore call them as subroutines to the interrupt modules.

One subtlety is that we must construct a very simple file system for messages, since we have a variable number of messages of variable lengths. Since messages vary in length, we must record the length of each one. In this simple specification, because we always play back the messages in the order in which they were recorded, we don't have to keep a full-fledged directory. If we allowed users to selectively delete messages and save others, we would have to build some sort of directory structure for the messages.

The hardware architecture is straightforward and illustrated in Figure 6-32. The speaker and telephone I/O devices appear as standard A/D and D/A converters. The telephone line appears as a one-bit input device (ring detect) and a one-bit output device (off-hook/on-hook). The compressed data are kept in main memory.

6.10.4 Component Design and Testing

Performance analysis is important in this case because we want to ensure that we don't spend so much time compressing that we miss voice samples. In a

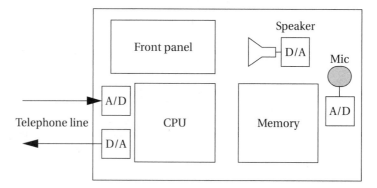

Figure 6-32 *The hardware structure of the answering machine.*

real consumer product, we would carefully design the code so that we could use the slowest, cheapest possible CPU that would still perform the required processing in the available time between samples. In this case, we will choose the microprocessor in advance for simplicity and simply ensure that all the deadlines are met.

An important class of problems that should be adequately tested is memory overflow. The system can run out of memory at any time, not just between messages. The modules should be tested to ensure that they do reasonable things when all the available memory is used up.

6.10.5 System Integration and Testing

We can test partial integrations of the software on our host platform. Final testing with real voice data must wait until the application is moved to the target platform.

Testing your system by connecting it directly to the phone line is not a very good idea. In the United States, the Federal Communications Commission regulates equipment connected to phone lines. Beyond legal problems, a bad circuit can damage the phone line and incur the wrath of your service provider. The required analog circuitry also requires some amount of tuning, and you need a second telephone line to generate phone calls for tests. You can build a telephone line simulator to test the hardware independently of a real telephone line. The phone line simulator consists of A/D and D/A converters plus a speaker and microphone for voice data, an LED for off-hook/on-hook indication, and a button for ring generation. The telephone line interface can easily be adapted to connect to these components, and for purposes of testing the answering machine the simulator behaves identically to the real phone line.

6.11 Summary

The process abstraction is forced on us by the need to satisfy complex timing requirements, particularly for multirate systems. Writing a single program that simultaneously satisfies deadlines at multiple rates is too difficult because the control structure of the program becomes unintelligible. The process encapsulates the state of a computation, allowing us to easily switch among different computations.

The operating system encapsulates the complex control to coordinate the process. The scheme used to determine the transfer of control among processes is known as a scheduling policy. A good scheduling policy is useful

across many different applications while also providing efficient utilization of the available CPU cycles.

It is difficult, however, to achieve 100% utilization of the CPU for complex applications. Because of variations in data arrivals and computation times, reserving some cycles to meet worst-case conditions is necessary. Some scheduling policies achieve higher utilizations than others, but often at the cost of unpredictability—they may not guarantee that all deadlines are met. Knowledge of the characteristics of an application can be used to increase CPU utilization while also complying with deadlines.

What We Learned

- A process is a single thread of execution.

- Preemption is the act of changing the CPU's execution from one process to another.

- A scheduling policy is a set of rules that determines the process to run.

- Rate-monotonic scheduling (RMS) is a simple, but powerful, scheduling policy.

- Several interprocess communication mechanisms exist, including signals, shared memory, and pipes.

- Scheduling analysis often ignores certain real-world effects. Cache interactions between processes are the most important effects to consider when designing a system.

Further Reading

Gallmeister [Gal95] provides a thorough and very readable introduction to POSIX in general and its real-time aspects in particular. Liu and Layland [Liu73] introduce rate-monotonic scheduling; this paper became the foundation for real-time systems analysis and design. Benini et al. [Ben00] provide a good survey of system-level power management techniques. Falik and Intrater [Fal92] describe a custom chip designed to perform answering machine operations.

Questions

Q6-1 Identify activities that operate at different rates in

a. a PDA

b. a laser printer

c. an airplane

Q6-2 Name an embedded system that requires both periodic and aperiodic computation.

Q6-3 An audio system processes samples at a rate of 44.1 kHz. At what rate could we sample the system's front panel to both simplify analysis of the system schedule and provide adequate response to the user's front panel requests?

Q6-4 Which should have lower overhead—a preemptive or cooperative context switch mechanism?

Q6-5 What information is needed in the activation record of a heavyweight process but not a lightweight process?

Q6-6 Which of the following code fragments would be acceptable in a reentrant program?

a.

```
static int xxx = 5;
...
y = xxx * z;
```

b.

```
static int ptr1 = NULL;
...
ptr1 = init_list();
```

c.

```
teststring = "";
...
int i = 0;
while (i < argc && teststring != NULL) {
    teststring = argv[i];
    ...
```

Q6-7 Draw a UML class diagram for a process in an operating system. The process class should include the necessary attributes and behaviors required of a typical process.

Q6-8 Draw a UML sequence diagram showing a cooperative context switch.

Q6-9 Draw a UML sequence diagram showing a preemptive context switch.

Q6-10 What factors provide a lower bound on the period at which the system timer interrupts for preemptive context switching?

Q6-11 What factors provide an upper bound on the period at which the system timer interrupts for preemptive context switching?

Q6-12 What state would be useful to keep in a process that represents a hotel guest?

Q6-13 What is the distinction between the ready and waiting states of process scheduling?

Q6-14 Provide examples of
a. blocking interprocess communication
b. nonblocking interprocess communication

Q6-15 Assuming that you have a routine called swap(int *a,int *b) that atomically swaps the values of the memory locations pointed to a and b, write C code for:
a. P();
b. V()

Q6-16 Draw UML sequence diagrams of two versions of P(): one that incorrectly uses a nonatomic operation to test and set the semaphore location and another that correctly uses an atomic test-and-set.

Q6-17 For the following processes, what is the shortest interval we must examine to see all combinations of deadlines?
a.

Process	Deadline
P1	2
P2	5
P3	10

b.

Process	Deadline
P1	2
P2	4
P3	5
P4	10

c.

Process	Deadline
P1	3
P2	4
P3	5
P4	6
P5	10

Q6-18 Consider the following system of processes executing on a single CPU:

Process	Execution time	Deadline
P1	4	200
P2	1	10
P3	2	40
P4	6	50

Can we add another instance of P1 to the system and still meet all the deadlines using RMS?

Q6-19 Given the following set of processes running on a single CPU, what is the maximum execution time P5 for which all the processes will be schedulable using RMS?

Process	Execution time	Deadline
P1	1	10
P2	18	100
P3	2	20
P4	5	50
P5	x	25

Q6-20 A set of processes is scheduled using RMS. For the process execution times and periods shown below, show the state of the processes at the critical instant for each of these processes.

a. P1

b. P2

c. P3

Process	Time	Deadline
P1	1	4
P2	1	5
P3	1	10

Q6-21 For the given process execution times and periods, show how much CPU time of higher-priority processes will be required during one period of each of the following processes:

a. P1

b. P2

c. P3

d. P4

Process	Time	Deadline
P1	1	5
P2	2	10
P3	2	25
P5	5	50

Q6-22 For the processes shown below:

a. Schedule the processes using an RMS policy.

b. Schedule the processes using an EDF policy.

In each case, compute the schedule for an interval equal to the least-common multiple of the periods of the processes. Time starts at t = 0.

Process	Time	Deadline
P1	1	3
P2	1	4
P3	1	12

Q6-23 For the processes shown below:

 a. Schedule the processes using an RMS policy.

 b. Schedule the processes using an EDF policy.

In each case, compute the schedule for an interval equal to the least-common multiple of the periods of the processes. Time starts at t = 0.

Process	Time	Deadline
P1	1	3
P2	1	4
P3	2	6

Q6-24 For the given set of processes, all of which share the same deadline of 12:

 a. Schedule the processes for the given arrival times using standard rate-monotonic scheduling (no data dependencies).

 b. Schedule the processes taking advantage of the data dependencies. By how much is the CPU utilization reduced?

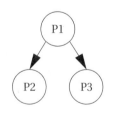

Process	Execution time
P1	2
P2	1
P3	2

Q6-25 For the processes given below, find a valid schedule
a. using standard RMS
b. adding one unit of overhead for each context switch

Process	Time	Deadline
P1	2	30
P2	5	40
P3	7	120
P4	5	60
P5	1	15

Q6-26 For the processes and deadlines given below:
a. Schedule the processes using RMS.
b. Schedule using EDF and compare the number of context switches required for EDF and RMS.

Process	Time	Deadline
P1	1	5
P2	1	10
P3	2	20
P4	10	50
P5	7	100

Q6-27 Draw a UML class diagram for two classes: a front-panel class that reads panel activity and an action class that performs actions based on the front panel requests. The front-panel class uses a Unix signal to communicate with action.

Q6-28 In each circumstance below, would shared memory or message passing communication be better? Explain.
a. A cascaded set of digital filters.
b. A digital video decoder and a process that overlays user menus on the display.
c. A software modem process and a printing process in a fax machine.

Q6-29 If you wanted to reduce the cache conflicts between the most computationally intensive parts of two processes, what are two ways that you could control the locations of the processes' cache footprints?

Q6-30 Draw a state diagram for the predictive shutdown mechanism of a pager. The pager wakes itself up once every five minutes for 0.01 second to listen for its address. It goes back to sleep if it does not hear its address or after it has received its message.

Q6-31 How would you use the ADPCM method to encode an unvarying (DC) signal with the coding alphabet $\{-3,-2,-1,1,2,3\}$?

Lab Exercises

L6-1 Using your favorite operating system, write code to spawn a process that writes "Hello, world" to the screen.

L6-2 Build a small serial port device that lights LEDs based on the last character written to the serial port. Create a process that will light LEDs based on keyboard input.

L6-3 Write a driver for an I/O device.

L6-4 Write context switch code for your favorite CPU.

L6-5 Measure context switching overhead on an operating system.

L6-6 Using a CPU that runs an operating system that uses RMS, try to get the CPU utilization up to 100%. Vary the data arrival times to test the robustness of the system.

L6-7 Using a CPU that runs an operating system that uses EDF, try to get the CPU utilization as close to 100% as possible without failing. Try a variety of data arrival times to determine how sensitive your process set is to environmental variations.

Hardware Accelerators

- Why we design accelerators.

- Performance analysis.

- Architectural templates.

- Architecture design: scheduling and allocation.

- A video accelerator design.

7.1 Introduction

In this chapter, we examine the design of accelerators that are attached to CPU buses to quickly execute certain key functions. Accelerators can provide large performance increases for applications with **computational kernels** that spend a great deal of time in a small section of code. Accelerators can also provide critical speedups for low-latency I/O functions.

The design of accelerated systems is one example of **hardware/software co-design**—the simultaneous design of hardware and software to meet system objectives. Thus far, we have taken the computing platform as a given; by adding accelerators, we can customize the embedded platform to better meet our application's demands.

The next section discusses why designing a custom accelerator makes sense. Section 7.3 develops design techniques for accelerated systems. Section 7.4 designs a video accelerator as an example of an accelerated embedded system.

7.2 CPUs and Accelerators

As illustrated in Figure 7-1, a CPU accelerator is attached to the CPU bus. The CPU is often called the **host.** The CPU talks to the accelerator through data and control registers in the accelerator. These registers allow the CPU to monitor the accelerator's operation and to give the accelerator commands.

The CPU and accelerator may also communicate via shared memory. If the accelerator needs to operate on a large volume of data, it is usually more efficient to leave the data in memory and have the accelerator read and write memory directly rather than to have the CPU shuttle data from memory to accelerator registers and back. The CPU and accelerator use synchronization mechanisms like those described in Section 6.7 to ensure that they do not destroy each other's data.

An accelerator is not a co-processor. A co-processor is connected to the internals of the CPU and processes instructions. An accelerator interacts with the CPU through the programming model interface; it does not execute instructions. Its interface is functionally equivalent to an I/O device, although it usually does not perform input or output.

Accelerators are designed to perform a specific function. We use the generic term **application-specific integrated circuit (ASIC)** for these special-

Figure 7-1 *CPU accelerators in a system.*

function units. We can get an ASIC to suit our needs in one of the following several ways:

- We could, in fact, find a standard component in a catalog that does what we want, though we may have to design interface logic to mate it to our CPU.

- We could design a custom integrated circuit. This requires considerable design and manufacturing time, but may be worth the effort for high-volume designs.

- We could use a programmable logic technology such as a **field-programmable gate array (FPGA),** a programmable logic chip that can quickly be customized to a particular function. FPGAs come in two basic varieties. One-time-programmable devices can be programmed once, while reprogrammable devices can be programmed many times with new logic designs.

Both CPUs and ASICs perform computations required by the specification; at some level we don't care whether the work is done on a programmable CPU or on a custom circuit. We use the term **processing element (PE)** to mean any unit responsible for computation, whether it be a CPU or an ASIC.

7.2.1 Why Accelerators?

Designing an accelerator requires considerable effort and a somewhat different skill set than that required for designing embedded software. To justify the effort, the payoff should be considerable. There are, in fact, several good reasons to add accelerators to embedded systems.

cost/ performance The first reason for building distributed embedded systems is that they offer significantly better cost/performance—that is, performance and functionality per dollar spent on the system—than would be had by spending the same amount of money on a uniprocessor system. The basic reason for this is that processing element purchase price is a *nonlinear* function of performance [Wol98]. The cost of a microprocessor increases greatly as the clock speed increases. We would expect this trend as a normal consequence of VLSI fabrication and market economics. Clock speeds are normally distributed by normal variations in VLSI processes; because the fastest chips are rare, they naturally command a high price in the marketplace.

Because the fastest PEs are very costly, splitting the application so that it can be performed on several smaller PEs is much cheaper. Even with the added costs of assembling those components, the total system comes out to be less expensive. Of course, splitting the application across multiple PEs does entail higher engineering costs and lead times, which must be factored into the project.

In addition to reducing costs, using multiple PEs can also help with real-time performance. We can often meet deadlines and be responsive to interaction much more easily when we put those time-critical processes on separate PEs. Given that scheduling multiple processes on a single CPU incurs overhead in most realistic scheduling models, as discussed in Chapter 6, putting the time-critical processes on PEs that have little or no time-sharing reduces scheduling overhead. Because we pay for that overhead at the nonlinear rate for the PE, as illustrated in Figure 7-2, the savings by segregating time-critical processes can be large—it may take an extremely large and powerful CPU to provide the same responsiveness that can be had from a distributed system.

Of course, there are some real-time problems, such as multidimensional signal processing for video, that are so demanding that they cannot be fit onto a single-chip processor, even one of the most expensive types. When the computations and/or the memory bandwidth required are greater than can be handled by any available processor, designers have no choice but to split the application among multiple PEs.

Appearing below are several types of applications that are well suited to accelerators.

- Some functions require operations that do not map well onto a CPU's data operations. The mismatch may be due to several reasons. For instance, bit-level operations are difficult to perform efficiently on some CPUs; the oper-

Figure 7-2 *Scheduling overhead is paid for at a nonlinear rate.*

ations may require too many registers; or there may be advantages to controlling the precision of the arithmetic.

- Highly responsive input and output operations may be best performed by an accelerator with an attached I/O unit. If data must be read, processed, and written to meet a very tight deadline—for example, in engine control—an accelerator may be more efficient than a CPU.

- Applications with streaming data, such as wireless and multimedia, provide special challenges to CPUs. Streaming data are not well suited to CPU caches since each element of the stream has a limited lifetime. An accelerator with special-purpose data fetch logic may be an efficient way to perform operations on the data stream.

7.2.2 Accelerator Design

The first task in designing an accelerator is determining that our system actually needs one. We have to make sure that the function we want to accelerate will run more quickly on our accelerator than it will executing as software on a CPU. If our system CPU is a small microcontroller, the race may be easily won, but competing against a high-performance CPU is a challenge. We also have to make sure that the accelerated function will speed up the system. If some other operation is in fact the bottleneck, or if moving data into and out of the accelerator is too slow, then adding the accelerator may not be a net gain.

Once we have analyzed the system, we need to design the accelerator itself. In order to have identified our need for an accelerator, we must have a good understanding of the algorithm to be accelerated, which is often in the form of a high-level language program. We must translate the algorithm description into a hardware design, a considerable task in itself. We must also design the interface between the accelerator core and the CPU bus. The interface includes more than bus handshaking logic. For example, we have to determine how the application software on the CPU will communicate with the accelerator and provide the required registers; we may have to implement shared memory synchronization operations; and we may have to add address generation logic to read and write large amounts of data from system memory.

Finally, we will have to design the CPU-side interface to the accelerator. The application software will have to talk to the accelerator, providing it data and telling it what to do. We have to somehow synchronize the operation of the accelerator with the rest of the application so that the accelerator knows when it has the required data and the CPU knows when it has received the desired results.

7.3 Accelerated System Design

In this section we discuss the design of an accelerated system in detail. The design phases most involved are architecture, component design, and system integration. The system specification does not change—the user is unaware of the presence of the accelerator. However, the design of the system architecture is considerably more complicated. An accelerated system is a *custom multi-processor*—the processing elements compute and communicate in parallel. Performance analysis becomes more complicated and we must consider new design tasks as well.

7.3.1 Performance Analysis

In this section, we are most interested in **speedup:** How much faster is the system with the accelerator than the system without it? We may, of course, be concerned with other metrics such as power consumption and manufacturing cost. However, if the accelerator doesn't provide an attractive speedup, questions of cost and power will be moot.

Performance analysis of an accelerated system is a more complex task than what we have done thus far. In Chapter 6, we found that performance analysis of a CPU with multiple processes was more complex than the analysis of a single program. When we have multiple processing elements, the task becomes even more difficult.

The speedup factor depends in part on whether the system is **single threaded** or **multithreaded,** that is, whether the CPU sits idle while the accelerator runs in the single-threaded case or the CPU can do useful work in parallel with the accelerator in the multithreaded case. Another equivalent description is **blocking** versus **nonblocking:** Does the CPU's scheduler block other operations and wait for the accelerator call to complete, or does the CPU allow some other process to run in parallel with the accelerator? The possibilities are shown in Figure 7-3. Data dependencies allow *P2* and *P3* to run independently on the CPU, but *P2* relies on the results of the *A1* process that is implemented by the accelerator. However, in the single-threaded case, the CPU blocks to wait for the accelerator to return the results of its computation. As a result, it doesn't matter whether *P2* or *P3* runs next on the CPU. In the multithreaded case, the CPU continues to do useful work while the accelerator runs, so the CPU can start *P3* just after starting the accelerator and finish the task earlier.

The first task is to analyze the performance of the accelerator. As illustrated in Figure 7-4, the execution time for the accelerator depends on more than just the time required to execute the accelerator's function. It also depends on the time required to get the data into the accelerator and back out of it. Since the

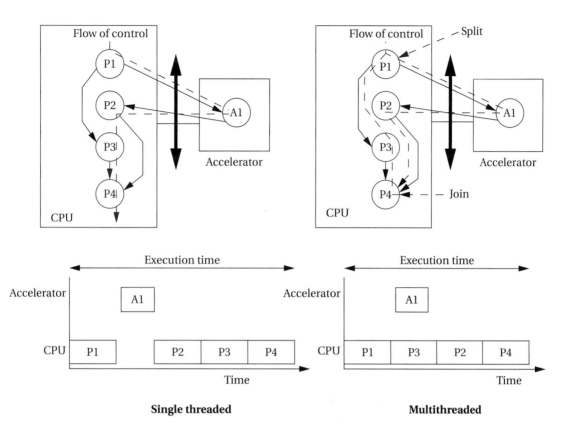

Figure 7-3 *Single-threaded versus multithreaded control of an accelerator.*

CPU's registers are probably not addressable by the accelerator, the data probably reside in main memory.

accelerator
execution time
A simple accelerator will read all its input data, perform the required computation, and then write all its results. In this case, the total execution time may be written as

$$t_{accel} = t_{in} + t_x + t_{out} \qquad\qquad \text{(EQ 7-1)}$$

where t_x is the execution time of the accelerator assuming all data are available, and t_{in} and t_{out} are the times required for reading and writing the required variables, respectively. The values for t_{in} and t_{out} must reflect the time required for the bus transactions, including the following factors:

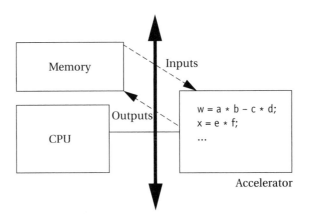

Figure 7-4 *Components of execution time for an accelerator.*

- the time required to flush any register or cache values to main memory, if those values are needed in main memory to communicate with the accelerator; and

- the time required for transfer of control between the CPU and accelerator.

Transferring data into and out of the accelerator may require the accelerator to become a bus master. Since the CPU may delay bus mastership requests, some worst-case value for bus mastership acquisition must be determined based on the CPU characteristics.

A more sophisticated accelerator could try to overlap input and output with computation. For example, it could read a few variables and start computing on those values while reading other values in parallel. In this case, the t_{in} and t_{out} terms would represent the nonoverlapped read/write times rather than the complete input and output times. One important example of overlapped I/O and computation is streaming data applications such as digital filtering. As illustrated in Figure 7-5, an accelerator may take in one or more streams of data and output a stream. Latency requirements generally require that outputs be produced on the fly rather than storing up all the data and then computing; furthermore, it may be impractical to store long streams at all. In this case, the t_{in} and t_{out} terms are determined by the amount of data read in before starting computation and the length of time between the last computation and the last data output.

We are most interested in the speedup obtained by replacing the software implementation with the accelerator. The total speedup S for a kernel can be written as [Hen94]:

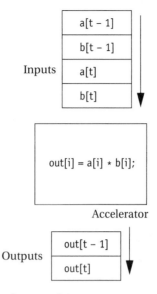

Figure 7-5 *Streaming data in and out of an accelerator.*

$$S = n(t_{CPU} - t_{accel})$$
$$= n[t_{CPU} - (t_{in} + t_x + t_{out})]$$

(EQ 7-2)

where t_{CPU} is the execution time of the equivalent function in software on the CPU and n is the number of times the function will be executed. We can use the techniques of Chapter 5 to determine the value of t_{CPU}. Clearly, the more times the function is evaluated, the more valuable the speedup provided by the accelerator becomes.

system speedup Ultimately, we care not so much about the accelerator's speedup as the speedup for the complete system—that is, how much faster the entire application completes execution. In a single-threaded system, the evaluation of the accelerator's speedup to the total system speedup is simple: The system execution time is reduced by S. The reason is illustrated in Figure 7-6—the single thread of control gives us a single path whose length we can measure to determine the new execution speed.

Evaluating system speedup in a multithreaded environment requires more subtlety. As shown in Figure 7-7, there is now more than one execution path. The total system execution time depends on the **longest path** from the beginning of execution to the end of execution. In this case, the system execution time depends on the relative speeds of *P3* and *P2* plus *A1*. If *P2* and *A1* together take the most time, *P3* will not play a role in determining system execution time. If *P3* takes longer, then *P2* and *A1* will not be a factor. To determine system execution time, we must label each node in the graph with its execution

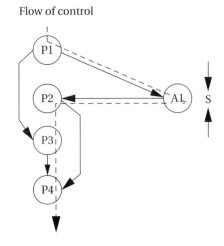

Figure 7-6 *Evaluating system speedup in a single-threaded implementation.*

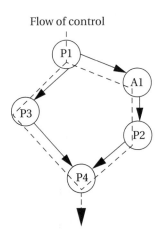

Figure 7-7 *Evaluating system speedup in a multithreaded implementation.*

time. In simple cases we can enumerate the paths, measure the length of each, and select the longest one as the system execution time. Efficient graph algorithms can also be used to compute the longest path.

This analysis shows the importance of selecting the proper functions to be moved to the accelerator. Clearly, if the function selected for speedup isn't a big portion of system execution time, taking the number of times it is executed into account, you won't see much system speedup. We also learned from Equation 7-1 that if too much overhead is incurred getting data into and out of the accelerator, we won't see much speedup.

7.3.2 System Architecture Framework

The complete architectural design of the accelerated system depends on the application being implemented. However, it is helpful to think of an **architectural framework** into which our accelerator fits. Because the same basic techniques for connecting the CPU and accelerator can be applied to many different problems, understanding the framework helps us quickly identify what is unique about our application.

An accelerator can be considered from two angles: its core functionality and its interface to the CPU bus. We often start with the accelerator's basic functionality and work our way out to the bus interface, but in some cases the bus interface and the internal logic are closely intertwined in order to provide high-performance data access. Application Examples 7-1 and 7-2 describe two commercially available accelerators.

Application Example 7-1

An FPGA-Based Accelerator

The Hot II [VCC98] is an accelerator for PCI systems. It uses an FPGA for the accelerator core so that the user can design the accelerator logic using standard synthesis tools. Because it uses a Xilinx SRAM-based FPGA that can be reconfigured many times, it also includes hardware to support run-time reconfiguration. The accelerator can be reconfigured under control of the host processor. A configuration cache manager has access to multiple FPGA configurations and is responsible for loading the proper configuration into the FPGA under host control. The Hot II also includes two data buses and SRAM for local data storage.

Application Example 7-2

The ARM Integrator Logic Module

The ARM Integrator is a series of evaluation boards for the ARM processor. The Integrator Logic Module [ARM00] is an FPGA accelerator board that plugs into the ARM Integrator motherboard. The logic module provides a Xilinx FPGA for reconfigurable logic. The FPGA interfaces to the ARM AMBA bus. The logic

module board does not contain its own SRAM—the FPGA can use the AMBA bus to connect to the SRAM and I/O devices contained on other boards.

accelerator core

The accelerator core typically operates off internal registers. How many registers are required is an important design decision. Main memory accesses will probably take multiple clock cycles, slowing down the accelerator. If the algorithm to be accelerated can predict which data values it will use, the data can be prefetched from main memory and stored in internal registers.

accelerator/CPU interface

The accelerator will almost certainly use registers for basic control. Status registers like those of I/O devices are a good way for the CPU to test the accelerator's state and to perform basic operations such as starting, stopping, and resetting the accelerator.

Large-volume data transfers may be performed by special-purpose read/write logic. Figure 7-8 illustrates an accelerator with read/write units that can supply higher volumes of data without CPU intervention. A register file in the accelerator acts as a buffer between main memory and the accelerator core. The read unit can read ahead of the accelerator's requirements and load the registers with the next required data; similarly, the write unit can send recently completed values to main memory while the core works with other values. In

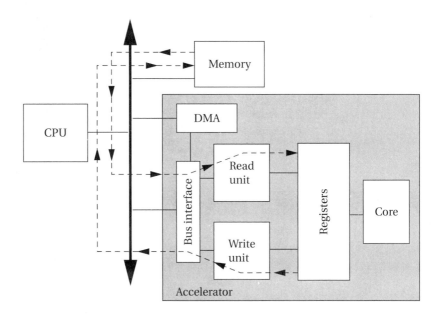

Figure 7-8 *Read/write units in an accelerator.*

order to avoid tying up the CPU, the data transfers can be performed in DMA mode, which means that the accelerator must have the required logic to become a bus master and perform DMA operations.

caching
problems
The CPU cache can cause problems for accelerators. Consider the following sequence of operations, illustrated in Figure 7-9:

1. The *CPU* reads location S.

2. The *accelerator* writes S.

3. The *CPU* again reads S.

If the *CPU* has cached location S, the program will not see the value of S written by the *accelerator*. It will instead get the old value of S stored in the *cache*. To avoid this problem, the CPU's cache must be updated to reflect the fact that this cache entry is invalid. Your CPU may provide cache invalidation instructions; you can also remove the location from the cache by reading another location that is mapped to the same cache line (or, in the case of set-associative caches, enough such locations to replace all the cache sets). Some CPUs are designed to support multiprocessing. The bus interface of such machines provides mechanisms for other processors to tell the CPU of required cache changes. This mechanism can be used by the accelerator to update the cache.

synchronization
If the CPU and accelerator operate concurrently and communicate via shared memory, it is possible that similar problems will occur in main memory, not just in the cache. If one PE reads a value and then updates it, the other PE may change the value, causing the first PE's update to be invalid. In some

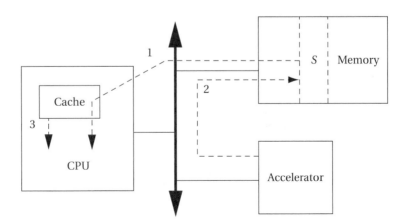

Figure 7-9 *A cache updating problem in an accelerated system.*

cases, it may be possible to use a very simple synchronization scheme for communication: The CPU writes data into a memory buffer, starts the accelerator, waits for the accelerator to finish, and then reads the shared memory area. This amounts to using the accelerator's status registers as a simple semaphore system. If the CPU and accelerator both want access to the same block of memory at the same time, then the accelerator will need to implement a test-and-set operation in order to implement semaphores. Many CPU buses implement test-and-set atomic operations that the accelerator can use for the semaphore operation.

7.3.3 Partitioning

Our specification was written without taking into account the existence of the accelerator. Before we start the architectural design proper, we must **partition** the specification into units that are suitable for architectural design. Some of the partitioned elements will be implemented on the CPU and others on accelerators. We mentioned partitioning in Section 4.6.1; it is especially important in accelerated system design because partitioning can greatly affect system performance as well as our ability to debug it. We want to partition the specification, taking into account the characteristics that make a unit well suited to implementation on the CPU or accelerator.

Partitioning should be driven by performance analysis. We do not want to arbitrarily divide the specified behavior into chunks. Rather, we want to choose a partitioning that will allow us to design a system that meets our performance requirements. Figure 7-10 provides a simple example. The specification at the left provides a single process that performs all the computations. The specifi-

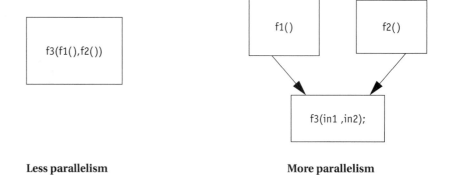

Less parallelism **More parallelism**

Figure 7-10 *Partioning affects available parallelism.*

cation at the right gives three processes with data dependencies among them. We cannot perform the final computation of f3() until we have finished f1() and f2(), but in this case we can perform f1() and f2() in parallel if we so desire.

Partitioning's responsibility is not to choose a single partition for the behavior. Rather, partitioning should identify possible partitions from which the designer can choose. As seen in the last section, both process execution time and communication time affect system performance. We cannot evaluate the quality of a partition without conducting a performance evaluation. Since this is relatively time consuming, we tend to separate the tasks of generating possible partitions and choosing among them.

We can view the partitioning problem as dividing up the CDFGs of the processes so that we can move pieces of a CDFG from one process to another. Figure 7-11 shows one way of partitioning a CDFG [Mad97]. We formed a hierarchical decomposition of the CDFG as follows:

- The basic blocks (blocks 1–3) may be pulled out and made separate processes, giving partitions P1, P2, and P3.

- The conditional containing blocks 1 and 2 may be pulled out as an entire unit to create partition P4.

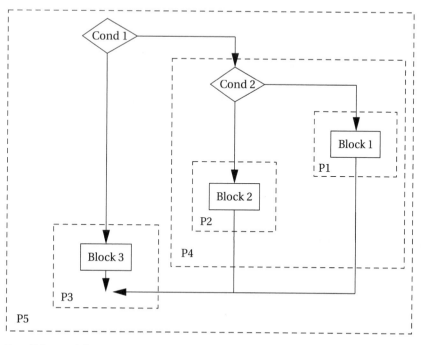

Figure 7-11 *Possible partitions in a CDFG.*

- The outer conditional can be pulled out of the program as a unit to create partition P5.

During design we can evaluate partitions at various levels of granularity as candidates for inclusion in an accelerator. Their suitability depends on global analysis of computation and communication. However, it may be possible to eliminate some partitions as obviously unsuitable using simple back-of-the-envelope calculations.

7.3.4 Scheduling and Allocation

When designing a distributed embedded system, we must deal with the **scheduling** and **allocation** design problems described below.

- We must *schedule* operations in time, including communication on the network and computations on the processing elements. Clearly, the scheduling of operations on the PEs and the communications between the PEs are linked. If one PE finishes its computations too late, it may interfere with another communication on the network as it tries to send its result to the PE that needs it. This is bad for both the PE that needs the result and the other PEs whose communication is interfered with.

- We must *allocate* computations to the processing elements. The allocation of computations to the PEs determines what communications are required—if a value computed on one PE is needed on another PE, it must be transmitted over the network.

Example 7-1 illustrates scheduling and allocation in accelerated embedded systems.

Example 7-1

Scheduling and Allocating Processes on a Distributed Embedded System

We can specify the system as a task graph. However, different processes may end up on different processing elements. Our task graph follows:

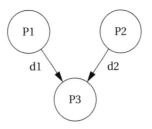

We have labeled the data transmissions on each arc so that we can refer to them later. We want to execute the task on the platform below.

The platform has two processing elements and a single bus connecting both PEs. To make decisions about where to allocate and when to schedule processes, we need to know how fast each process runs on each PE. Process speeds appear below.

	M1	*M2*
P1	5	5
P2	5	6
P3	—	5

The dash (—) entry signifies that the process cannot run on that type of processing element. In practice, a process may be excluded from some PEs for several reasons. If we use an ASIC to implement a special function, it will be able to implement only one process. A small CPU such as a microcontroller may not have enough memory for the process's code or data; it may also simply run too slowly to be useful. A process may run at different speeds on different CPUs for many reasons; even when the CPUs run at the same clock rate, differences in the instruction sets can cause a process to be better suited to a particular CPU.

If two processes are allocated to the same PE, they can communicate using the PE's internal memory and incur no network communication time. Each edge in the task graph corresponds to a data communication that must be carried over the network. Since all PEs communicate at the same rate, the data communication rate is the same for all transmissions between PEs. We need to know how long each communication takes. In this case, *d1* is a short message

requiring 2 time units and *d2* is a longer communication requiring 4 time units.

As an initial design, let us allocate *P1* and *P2* to *M1* and *P3* to *M2*. This allocation would, on the surface, appear to be a good one since *P1* and *P2* are both placed on the processor that runs them the fastest. To evaluate the design, the following schedule shows what happens on all the processing elements and the network:

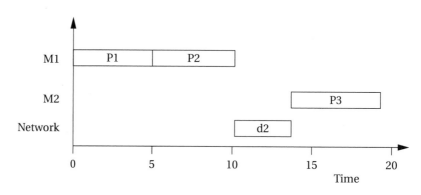

The schedule has length 19. The *d1* message is sent between the processes internal to *P1* and does not appear on the bus.

Let's try a different allocation: *P1* on *M1* and *P2* and *P3* on *M2*. This makes *P2* run more slowly. The schedule follows:

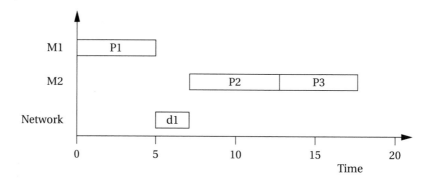

The length of this schedule is 18, or one time unit less than the other schedule. The increased computation time of P2 is more than made up for by being able to transmit a shorter message on the bus. If we had not taken communication into account when analyzing total execution time, we could have made the wrong choice of which processes to put on the same processing element.

7.3.5 System Integration and Debugging

Design of an accelerated system requires both designing your own components and interfacing them to a hardware platform. It is usually good policy to separately debug the basic interface between the accelerator and the rest of the system before integrating the full accelerator into the platform.

Hardware/software co-simulation can be very useful in accelerator design. Because the co-simulator allows you to run software relatively efficiently alongside a hardware simulation, it allows you to exercise the accelerator in a realistic but simulated environment. It is especially difficult to exercise the interface between the accelerator core and the host CPU without running the CPU's accelerator driver. It is much better to do so in a simulator before fabricating the accelerator, rather than to have to modify the hardware prototype of the accelerator.

Design Example

7.4 Video Accelerator

In this section we use a video accelerator as an example of an accelerated embedded system. Digital video is still a computationally intensive task, so it is well suited to acceleration. Motion estimation engines are used in real-time search engines; we may want to have one attached to our personal computer to experiment with video processing techniques.

7.4.1 Algorithm and Requirements

We could build an accelerator for any number of digital video algorithms. We will choose **block motion estimation** as our example here because it is very computation and memory intensive but it is relatively easy to explain.

Block motion estimation is used in digital video compression algorithms so that one frame in the video can be described in terms of the differences between it and another frame. Because objects in the frame often move relatively little, describing one frame in terms of another greatly reduces the number of bits required to describe the video.

motion estimation basics

The concept of block motion estimation is illustrated in Figure 7-12. The goal is to perform a two-dimensional correlation to find the best match between regions in the two frames. We divide the current frame into **macroblocks** (typically, 16×16). For every macroblock in the frame, we want to find the region in the previous frame that most closely matches the macroblock. Searching over the entire previous frame would be too expensive, so we usually limit the search to a given area, centered around the macroblock and larger

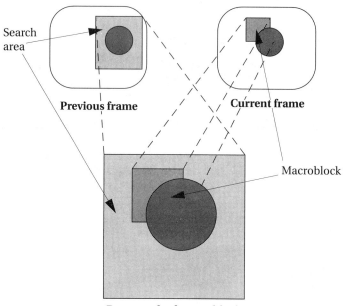

Previous frame Current frame

Search area

Macroblock

Best match of macroblock onto search area

Figure 7-12 *Block motion estimation.*

than the macroblock. We try the macroblock at various offsets in the search area. We measure similarity using the following sum-of-absolute-differences measure:

$$\sum_{1 \le i, j \le n} |M(i, j) - S(i - o_x, j - o_y)| ,$$
(EQ 7-3)

where $M(i,j)$ is the intensity of the macroblock at pixel i,j, $S(i,j)$ is the intensity of the search region, n is the size of the macroblock in one dimension, and $\langle o_x, o_y \rangle$ is the offset between the macroblock and search region. Intensity is measured as an 8-bit luminance that represents a monochrome pixel—color information is not used in motion estimation. We choose the macroblock position relative to the search area that gives us the smallest value for this metric. The offset at this chosen position describes a vector from the search area center to the macroblock's center that is called the **motion vector.**

For simplicity, we will build an engine for a full search, which compares the macroblock and search area at every possible point. Because this is an expensive operation, a number of methods have been proposed for conducting a sparser search of the search area. These methods introduce extra control that would cloud our discussion, but these algorithms may provide good examples.

A good way to describe the algorithm is in C. Some basic parameters of the algorithm are illustrated in Figure 7-13. Appearing below is the C code for a single search, which assumes that the search region does not extend past the boundary of the frame.

```
bestx = 0; besty = 0; /* initialize best location--none yet */
bestsad = MAXSAD; /* best sum-of-absolute-difference thus far */
for (ox = –SEARCHSIZE; ox < SEARCHSIZE; ox++) {
    /* x search ordinate */
    for (oy = –SEARCHSIZE; oy < SEARCHSIZE; oy++) {
        /* y search ordinate */
        int result = 0;
        for (i = 0; i < MBSIZE; i++) {
            for (j = 0; j < MBSIZE; j++) {
                result = result + iabs(mb[i][j] – search[i –
ox + XCENTER][i – oy + YCENTER]);
            }
        }
```

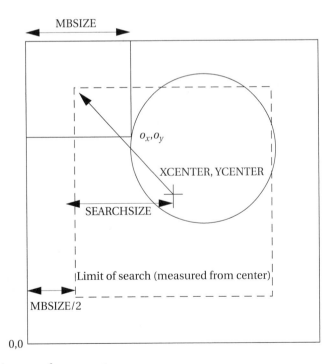

Figure 7-13 *Block motion search parameters.*

```
                if (result <= bestsad) { /* found better match */
                    bestsad = result;
                    bestx = ox; besty = oy;
            }
        }
    }
```

The arithmetic on each pixel is simple, but we have to process a lot of pixels. If MBSIZE is 16 and SEARCHSIZE is 8, and remembering that the search distance in each dimension is 8 + 1 + 8, then we must perform

$$n_{ops} = (16 \times 16) \times (17 \times 17) = 73984 \qquad \text{(EQ 7-4)}$$

absolute difference operations to find the motion vector for a single macroblock, which requires looking at twice as many pixels, one from the search area and one from the macroblock. (We can now see the interest in algorithms that do not require a full search. To process video, we will have to perform this computation on every macroblock of every frame. Adjacent blocks have overlapping search areas, so we will want to try to avoid reloading pixels we already have.

One relatively low-resolution standard video format, common intermediate format (CIF), has a frame size of 352 × 288, which gives an array of 22 × 18 macroblocks. If we want to encode video, we would have to perform motion estimation on every macroblock of most frames (some frames are sent without using motion compensation).

We will build the system using an FPGA connected to the PCI bus of a personal computer. We clearly need a high-bandwidth connection such as the PCI between the accelerator and the CPU. We can use the accelerator to experiment with video processing, among other things. Appearing below are the requirements for the system.

Name	Block motion estimator
Purpose	Perform block motion estimation within a PC system
Inputs	Macroblocks and search areas
Outputs	Motion vectors
Functions	Compute motion vectors using full search algorithms
Performance	As fast as we can get
Manufacturing cost	Hundreds of dollars
Power	Powered by PC power supply
Physical size and weight	Packaged as PCI card for PC

7.4.2 Specification

The specification for the system is relatively straightforward because the algorithm is simple. Figure 7-14 defines some classes that describe basic data types in the system: the motion vector, the macroblock, and the search area. These definitions are straightforward. Because the behavior is simple, we need to define only two classes to describe it: the accelerator itself and the PC. These classes are shown in Figure 7-15. The PC makes its memory accessible to the accelerator. The accelerator provides a behavior compute-mv() that performs the block motion estimation algorithm. Figure 7-16 shows a sequence diagram that describes the operation of compute-mv(). After initiating the behavior, the accelerator reads the search area and macroblock from the PC; after computing the motion vector, it returns it to the PC.

7.4.3 Architecture

The accelerator will be implemented in an FPGA on a card connected to a PC's PCI slot. Such accelerators can be purchased or they can be designed from scratch. If you design such a card from scratch, you have to decide early on

Figure 7-14 *Classes describing basic data types in the video accelerator.*

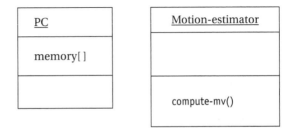

Figure 7-15 *Basic classes for the video accelerator.*

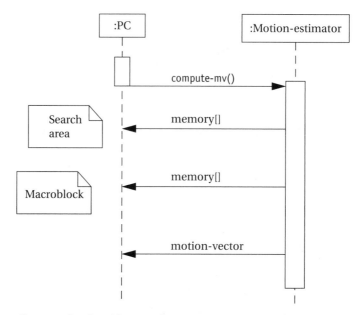

Figure 7-16 *Sequence diagram for the video accelerator.*

whether the card will be used only for this video accelerator or if it should be made general enough to support other applications as well.

The architecture for the accelerator requires some thought because of the large amount of data required by the algorithm. The macroblock has $16 \times 16 = 256$; the search area has $(8 + 8 + 1 + 8 + 8)^2 = 1,089$ pixels. The FPGA probably will not have enough memory to hold 1,089 8-bit values. We have to use a memory external to the FPGA but on the accelerator board to hold the pixels.

There are many possible architectures for the motion estimator. One is shown in Figure 7-17. The machine has two memories, one for the macroblock and another for the search memories. It has 16 processing elements that perform the absolute difference calculation on a pair of pixels; the comparator sums them up and selects the best value to find the motion vector. This architecture can be used to implement algorithms other than a full search by changing the address generation and control. Depending on the number of different motion estimation algorithms that you want to execute on the machine, the networks connecting the memories to the PEs may also be simplified.

Figure 7-18 shows how we can schedule the transfer of pixels from the memories to the PEs in order to efficiently compute a full search on this architecture. The schedule fetches one pixel from the macroblock memory and (in steady state) two pixels from the search area memory per clock cycle. The pixels are distributed to the processing elements in a regular pattern as shown by the schedule. This schedule computes 16 correlations between the macroblock

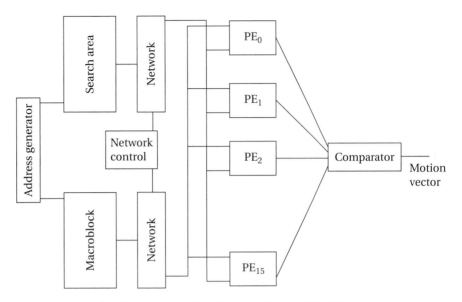

Figure 7-17 *An architecture for the motion estimation accelerator [Dut96].*

and search area simultaneously. The computations for each correlation are distributed among the processing elements; the comparator is responsible for collecting the results, finding the best match value, and remembering the corresponding motion vector.

Based on our understanding of efficient architectures for accelerating motion estimation, we can derive a more detailed definition of the architecture in UML, which is shown in Figure 7-19. The system includes the two memories for pixels, one a single-port memory and the other dual ported. A bus interface module is responsible for communicating with the PCI bus and the rest of the system. The estimation engine reads pixels from the M and S memories, and it takes commands from the bus interface and returns the motion vector to the bus interface.

7.4.4 Component Design

If we want to use a standard FPGA accelerator board to implement the accelerator, we must first make sure that it provides the proper memory required for M and S. Once we have verified that the accelerator board has the required structure, we can concentrate on designing the FPGA logic. Designing an FPGA is, for the most part, a straightforward exercise in logic design. Because the logic for the accelerator is very regular, we can improve the FPGA's clock rate by properly placing the logic in the FPGA to reduce wire lengths.

t	M	S	S′	PE$_0$	PE$_1$	PE$_2$
0	M(0,0)	S(0,0)		\|M(0,0) – S(0,0)\|		
1	M(0,1)	S(0,1)		\|M(0,1) – S(0,1)\|	\|M(0,0) – S(0,1)\|	
2	M(0,2)	S(0,2)		\|M(0,2) – S(0,2)\|	\|M(0,1) – S(0,2)\|	\|M(0,0) – S(0,2)\|
3	M(0,3)	S(0,3)		\|M(0,3) – S(0,3)\|	\|M(0,2) – S(0,3)\|	\|M(0,1) – S(0,3)\|
4	M(0,4)	S(0,4)		\|M(0,4) – S(0,4)\|	\|M(0,3) – S(0,4)\|	\|M(0,2) – S(0,4)\|
5	M(0,5)	S(0,5)		\|M(0,5) – S(0,5)\|	\|M(0,4) – S(0,5)\|	\|M(0,3) – S(0,5)\|
6	M(0,6)	S(0,6)		\|M(0,6) – S(0,6)\|	\|M(0,5) – S(0,6)\|	\|M(0,4) – S(0,6)\|
7	M(0,7)	S(0,7)		\|M(0,7) – S(0,7)\|	\|M(0,6) – S(0,7)\|	\|M(0,5) – S(0,7)\|
8	M(0,8)	S(0,8)		\|M(0,8) – S(0,8)\|	\|M(0,7) – S(0,8)\|	\|M(0,6) – S(0,8)\|
9	M(0,9)	S(0,9)		\|M(0,9) – S(0,9)\|	\|M(0,8) – S(0,9)\|	\|M(0,7) – S(0,9)\|
10	M(0,10)	S(0,10)		\|M(0,10) – S(0,10)\|	\|M(0,9) – S(0,10)\|	\|M(0,8) – S(0,10)\|
11	M(0,11)	S(0,11)		\|M(0,11) – S(0,11)\|	\|M(0,10) – S(0,11)\|	\|M(0,9) – S(0,11)\|
12	M(0,12)	S(0,12)		\|M(0,12) – S(0,12)\|	\|M(0,11) – S(0,12)\|	\|M(0,10) – S(0,12)\|
13	M(0,13)	S(0,13)		\|M(0,13) – S(0,13)\|	\|M(0,12) – S(0,13)\|	\|M(0,11) – S(0,13)\|
14	M(0,14)	S(0,14)		\|M(0,14) – S(0,14)\|	\|M(0,13) – S(0,14)\|	\|M(0,12) – S(0,14)\|
15	M(0,15)	S(0,15)		\|M(0,15) – S(0,15)\|	\|M(0,14) – S(0,15)\|	\|M(0,13) – S(0,15)\|
16	M(1,0)	S(1,0)	S(0,16)	\|M(1,0) – S(1,0)\|	\|M(0,15) – S(0,16)\|	\|M(0,14) – S(0,16)\|
17	M(1,1)	S(1,1)	S(0,17)	\|M(1,1) – S(1,1)\|	\|M(1,0) – S(1,1)\|	\|M(0,15) – S(0,17)\|

Figure 7-18 *A schedule of pixel fetches for a full search [Yan89].*

If we are designing our own accelerator board, we have to design both the video accelerator design proper and the interface to the PCI bus. We can create and exercise the video accelerator architecture in a hardware description language like VHDL or Verilog and simulate its operation. Designing the PCI interface requires somewhat different techniques since we may not have a simulation model for a PCI bus. We may want to verify the operation of the basic PCI interface before we finish implementing the video accelerator logic.

The host PC will probably deal with the accelerator as an I/O device. The accelerator board will have its own driver that is responsible for talking to the board. Since most of the data transfers are performed directly by the board using DMA, the driver can be relatively simple.

7.4.5 System Testing

Testing video algorithms requires a large amount of data. Luckily, the data represents images and video, which are plentiful. Because we are designing only a

Figure 7-19 *Object diagram for the video accelerator.*

motion estimation accelerator and not a complete video compressor, it is probably easiest to use images, not video, for test data. You can use standard video tools to extract a few frames from a digitized video and store them in JPEG format. Open source for JPEG encoders and decoders is available. These programs can be modified to read JPEG images and put out pixels in the format required by your accelerator. With a little more cleverness, the resulting motion vector can be written back onto the image for a visual confirmation of the result. If you want to be adventurous and try motion estimation on video, open source MPEG encoders and decoders are also available.

7.5 Summary

Although the design of an accelerator itself is a hardware design task, the design of an accelerated system requires that we go to a higher level of abstraction. Interactions between the accelerator and the host system, particularly if the host and accelerator execute in parallel, make performance analysis a challenge. Based on the results of performance analysis, we can determine which operations need to go into the accelerator and how to coordinate the actions of the host CPU and the accelerator. Many general-purpose computer systems use accelerators of various types, particularly to support I/O. Adding an accelerator to an embedded system can be an effective way of meeting design requirements.

What We Learned

- An accelerated system is a custom multiprocessor.

- Using an accelerator may increase performance and responsiveness. It can also reduce system cost by allowing you to use a smaller host CPU.

- Performance analysis of an accelerated system is challenging. We must consider the performance of several implementations of an algorithm (CPU, accelerator) as well as communication costs for various configurations.

- We must partition the behavior, schedule operations in time, and allocate operations to processing elements in order to design the system.

Further Reading

Staunstrup and Wolf's edited volume [Sta97] surveys hardware/software co-design, including techniques for accelerated systems like those described in this chapter. Gupta and De Micheli [Gup93] and Ernst et al. [Ern93] describe early techniques for co-synthesis of accelerated systems. Callahan et al. [Cal00] describe an on-chip reconfigurable co-processor connected to a CPU.

Questions

Q7-1 You are designing an embedded system using an Intel 486 as a host. Does it make sense to add an accelerator to implement the function z = ax + by + c? Explain.

Q7-2 You are designing an embedded system using an Intel 486 with no floating-point support as host. Does it make sense to add an accelerator to implement the floating-point function $s = A\sin(2\pi f + \phi)$? Explain.

Q7-3 You are designing an embedded system using an Intel Pentium III as host. Does it make sense to add an accelerator to implement the floating-point function $s = A\sin(2\pi f + \phi)$? Explain.

Q7-4 You are designing an accelerated system that performs the following function as its main task:

```
for (i = 0; i < M; i++)
    for (j = 0; j < N; j++)
        f[i][j] = (pix[i][j – 1] + pix[i – 1][j] + pix[i][j] + pix[i + 1][j] +
        pix[i][j + 1])/(5*MAXVAL);
```

Assume that the accelerator has the entire pix and f arrays in its internal memory during the entire computation—pix is read into the accelerator before the operations begin and f is written out after all computations have been completed.

a. Show a system schedule for the host, accelerator, and bus assuming that the accelerator is inactive during all data transfers. (All data are sent to the accelerator before it starts and data are read from the accelerator after the computations are finished.)

b. Show a system schedule for the host, accelerator, and bus assuming that the accelerator has enough memory for two pix and f arrays and that the host can transfer data for one set of computations while another set is being performed.

Q7-5 Find the longest path through the graph below, using the computation times on the nodes and the communication times on the edges.

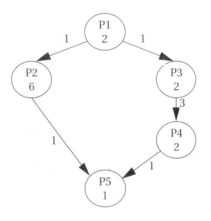

Q7-6 Write pseudocode for an algorithm to determine the longest path through a system execution graph. The longest path is to be measured from one designated entry point to one exit point. Each node in the graph is labeled with a number giving the execution time of the process represented by that node.

Lab Exercises

L7-1 Determine how much logic in an FPGA must be devoted to a PCI bus interface and how much would be left for an accelerator core.

L7-2 Develop a debugging scheme for an accelerator. Determine how you would easily enter data into the accelerator and easily observe its behavior. You will

need to verify the system thoroughly, starting with basic communication and going through algorithmic verification.

L7-3 Develop a generic streaming interface for an accelerator. The interface should allow streaming data to be read by the accelerator from the host's memory. It should also allow streaming data to be written from the accelerator back to memory. The interface should include a host-side mechanism for filling and draining the streaming data buffers.

Chapter

Networks

- Why we build networked embedded systems.

- General network architectures and the ISO network layers.

- Several networks: I^2C, CAN, Ethernet, Myrinet, and SHARC link ports.

- Distributed embedded system design techniques.

- Internet-enabled embedded systems.

- Elevator controller design example.

8.1 Introduction

In this chapter we study **networks** that can be used to build **distributed embedded systems.** In a distributed embedded system, several **processing elements** (either microprocessors or ASICs) are connected by a network that allows them to communicate. The application is distributed over the processing elements, and some of the work is done at each node in the network.

There are several reasons to build network-based embedded systems. When the processing tasks are physically distributed, it may be necessary to put some of the computing power near where the events occur. Consider, for example, an automobile: The short time delays required for tasks such as engine control generally mean that at least parts of the task are done physically close to the engine. Data reduction is another important reason for distributed processing. It may be possible to perform some initial signal processing on captured data to reduce its volume—for example, detecting a certain type of event in a sampled data stream. Reducing the data on a separate processor may significantly reduce the load on the processor that makes use of that data.

Modularity is another motivation for network-based design. For instance, when a large system is assembled out of existing components, those components may use a network port as a clean interface that does not interfere with the internal operation of the component in ways that using the microprocessor bus would. A distributed system can also be easier to debug—the microprocessors in one part of the network can be used to probe components in another part of the network. Finally, in some cases, networks are used to build fault tolerance into systems. Distributed embedded system design is another example of hardware/software co-design, since we must design the network topology as well as the software running on the network nodes.

Of course, the microprocessor bus is a simple type of network. However, we use the term *network* to mean an interconnection scheme that does not provide shared memory communication. In the next section, we develop the basic principles of hardware and software architectures for networks. Section 8.3 examines several different networking systems. Section 8.4 considers techniques for the design of distributed embedded systems. Section 8.5 focuses on how embedded systems can be designed to talk to the Internet. Section 8.6 presents an elevator system as an example of network-based design.

8.2 Distributed Embedded Architectures

A distributed embedded system can be organized in many different ways, but its basic units are the processing element (PE) and the network as illustrated in Figure 8-1. A processing element may be an instruction set processor such as a *DSP, CPU,* or *microcontroller,* as well as a nonprogrammable unit such as the *ASIC*s used to implement *PE 4.* An I/O device such as *PE 1* (which we call here a

Figure 8-1 *An example distributed embedded system.*

sensor or **actuator,** depending on its function) may also be a processing element, as long as it can speak the network protocol to communicate with other processing elements. The network in this case is a bus, but other network topologies are also possible. It is also possible that the system can use more than one network, such as when relatively independent functions require relatively little communication among them. We often refer to the connection between PEs provided by the network as a **communication link.** The system of processing elements and networks forms the **hardware platform** on which the application runs.

However, unlike the system bus of Chapter 4, the distributed embedded system does not have memory on the bus (unless a memory unit is organized as an I/O device that speaks the network protocol). In particular, processing elements do not fetch instructions over the network as they do on the microprocessor bus. We take advantage of this fact when analyzing network performance—the speed at which PEs can communicate over the bus would be difficult if not impossible to predict if we allowed arbitrary instruction and data fetches as we do on microprocessor buses.

8.2.1 Why Distributed?

Building an embedded system with several processing elements talking over a network is definitely more complicated than using a single large microprocessor to perform the same tasks. So why would anyone build a distributed embedded system? All the reasons for designing accelerator systems also apply to distributed embedded systems, and several more reasons are unique to distributed systems.

In some cases, distributed systems are necessary because the devices that the PEs communicate with are physically separated. If the deadlines for processing the data are short, it may be more cost-effective to put the PEs where the data are located rather than build a higher-speed network to carry the data to a distant, fast PE.

An important advantage of a distributed system with several CPUs is that one part of the system can be used to help diagnose problems in another part. Whether you are debugging a prototype or diagnosing a problem in the field, isolating the error to one part of the system can be difficult when everything is done on a single CPU. If you have several CPUs in the system, you can use one to generate inputs for another and to watch its output.

Finally, a system may be required to be distributed if it makes use of component subsystems that have their own embedded microprocessors. A good example is a pen-based computer designed by Rosebrugh and Kwang [Ros92]. This system used a display subsystem purchased from a supplier. The LCD display subsystem included a microcontroller that accepted data to be displayed and controlled the LCD display signals as required. The display inherently

introduced a distributed element into the architecture. Of course, the designers made other uses of the distributed style. Some of the components were connected by a serial bus, which augmented the system bus that connected the high-speed processors with the program/data memory. Notice also that other PEs could not directly talk to the display memory.

8.2.2 Network Abstractions

Networks are complex systems. Ideally, they provide high-level services while hiding many of the details of data transmission from the other components in the system. In order to help understand (and design) networks, the International Standards Organization (ISO) has developed a seven-layer model for networks known as Open Systems Interconnection (OSI) models [Sta97A]. Understanding the OSI layers will help us to understand the details of real networks.

The seven layers of the **OSI model,** shown in Figure 8-2, are intended to cover a broad spectrum of networks and their uses. Some networks may not need the services of one or more layers because the higher layers may be totally missing or an intermediate layer may not be necessary. However, any data network should fit into the OSI model. The OSI layers from lowest to highest level of abstraction are described below.

■ **Physical:** The physical layer defines the basic properties of the interface between systems, including the physical connections (plugs and wires),

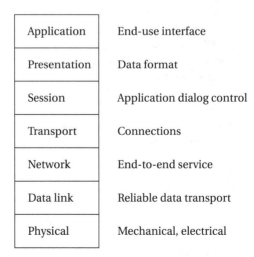

Application	End-use interface
Presentation	Data format
Session	Application dialog control
Transport	Connections
Network	End-to-end service
Data link	Reliable data transport
Physical	Mechanical, electrical

Figure 8-2 *The OSI model layers.*

electrical properties, basic functions of the electrical and physical components, and the basic procedures for exchanging bits.

- **Data link:** The primary purpose of this layer is error detection and control across a single link. However, if the network requires multiple hops over several data links, the data link layer does not define the mechanism for data integrity between hops, but only within a single hop.

- **Network:** This layer defines the basic end-to-end data transmission service. The network layer is particularly important in multihop networks.

- **Transport:** The transport layer defines connection-oriented services that ensure that data are delivered in the proper order and without errors across multiple links. This layer may also try to optimize network resource utilization.

- **Session:** A session provides mechanisms for controlling the interaction of end-user services across a network, such as data grouping and check-pointing.

- **Presentation:** This layer defines data exchange formats and provides transformation utilities to application programs.

- **Application:** The application layer provides the application interface between the network and end-user programs.

Although it may seem that embedded systems would be too simple to require use of the OSI model, the model is in fact quite useful. Even relatively simple embedded networks provide physical, data link, and network services. An increasing number of embedded systems provide Internet service that requires implementing the full range of functions in the OSI model.

8.2.3 Hardware and Software Architectures

Distributed embedded systems can be organized in many different ways depending upon the needs of the application and cost constraints. One good way to understand possible architectures is to consider the different types of interconnection networks that can be used.

point-to-point communication
A **point-to-point** link establishes a connection between exactly two processing elements. Point-to-point links are simple to design precisely because they deal with only two components. We do not have to worry about other processing elements interfering with communication on the link.

Figure 8-3 shows a simple example of a distributed embedded system built from point-to-point links. The input signal is sampled by the input device and

passed to the first digital filter, *F1,* over a point-to-point link. The results of that filter are sent through a second point-to-point link to filter *F2.* The results in turn are sent to the output device over a third point-to-point link. A digital filtering system requires that its outputs arrive at strict intervals, which means that the filters must process their inputs in a timely fashion. Using point-to-point connections allows both *F1* and *F2* to receive a new sample and send a new output at the same time without worrying about collisions on the communications network.

It is possible to build a **full-duplex,** point-to-point connection that can be used for simultaneous communication in both directions between the two PEs. (A **half-duplex** connection allows for only one-way communication.)

buses

A bus is a more general form of network since it allows multiple devices to be connected to it. Like a microprocessor bus, PEs connected to the bus have addresses. Communications on the bus generally take the form of **packets** as illustrated in Figure 8-4. A packet contains an address for the destination and the data to be delivered. It frequently includes error detection/correction information such as parity. It also may include bits that serve to signal to other PEs that the bus is in use, such as the header shown in the figure. The data to be transmitted from one PE to another may not fit exactly into the size of the **data payload** on the packet. It is the responsibility of the transmitting PE to divide its data into packets; the receiving PE must of course reassemble the complete data message from the packets.

Distributed system buses must be arbitrated to control simultaneous access, just as with microprocessor buses. Arbitration scheme types are summarized below.

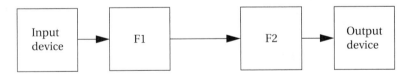

Figure 8-3 *A signal processing system built from point-to-point links.*

Figure 8-4 *Format of a typical message on a bus.*

- **Fixed-priority arbitration** always gives priority to competing devices in the same way. If a high-priority and a low-priority device both have long data transmissions ready at the same time, it is quite possible that the low-priority device will not be able to transmit anything until the high-priority device has sent all its data packets.

- **Fair arbitration** schemes make sure that no device is starved. **Round-robin arbitration** is the most commonly used of the fair arbitration schemes. The PCI bus requires that the arbitration scheme used on the bus must be fair, although it does not specify a particular arbitration scheme. Most implementations of PCI use round-robin arbitration.

general networks A bus has limited available bandwidth. Since all devices connect to the bus, communications can interfere with each other. Other network topologies can be used to reduce communication conflicts. At the opposite end of the generality spectrum from the bus is the **crossbar** network shown in Figure 8-5. A crossbar not only allows any input to be connected to any output, it also allows all combinations of input/output connections to be made. Thus, for example, we can simultaneously connect *in1* to *out4*, *in2* to *out3*, *in3* to *out2*, and *in4* to *out1* or any other combinations of inputs. (Multicast connections can also be made from one input to several outputs.) A **crosspoint** is a switch that connects an input to an output. To connect an input to an output, we activate the crosspoint at the intersection between the corresponding input and output lines in the crossbar. For example, to connect *in2* and *out3* in the figure, we would activate crossbar *A* as shown. The major drawback of the crossbar network is expense: The size of the network grows as the square of the number of inputs (assuming the numbers of inputs and outputs are equal).

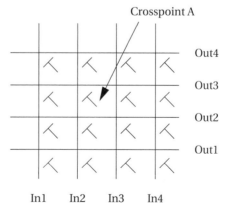

Figure 8-5 *A crossbar network.*

Many other networks have been designed that provide varying amounts of parallel communication at varying hardware costs. Figure 8-6 shows an example **multistage network.** The crossbar of Figure 8-5 is a **direct network** in which messages go from source to destination without going through any memory element. Multistage networks have intermediate routing nodes to guide the data packets.

Most networks are **blocking,** meaning that there are some combinations of sources and destinations for which messages cannot be delivered simultaneously. A bus is a maximally blocking network since any message on the bus blocks messages from any other node.

In general, networks differ from microprocessor buses in how they implement communication protocols. Both need handshaking to ensure that processing elements do not interfere with each other. But in most networks, most of the protocol is performed in software. Microprocessors rely on bus hardware for fast transfers of instructions and data to and from the CPU. Most embedded network ports on microprocessors implement the basic communication functions (such as driving the communications medium) in hardware and implement many other operations in software.

multiple networks An alternative to a nonbus network is to use multiple networks. As with processing elements, it may be cheaper to use two slow, inexpensive networks than a single high-performance, expensive network. If we can segregate critical and noncritical communications onto separate networks, it may be possible to use simpler topologies such as buses. Many systems use serial links for low-speed communication and CPU buses for higher speed and volume data transfers.

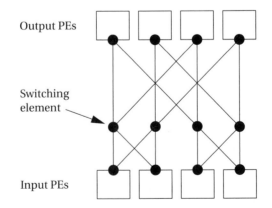

Figure 8-6 *A multistage network.*

8.2.4 Message Passing Programming

Distributed embedded systems do not have shared memory, so they must communicate by passing **messages.** We will refer to a message as the natural communication unit of an algorithm; in general, a message must be broken up into packets to be sent on the network. A procedural interface for sending a packet might look like the following:

```
send_packet(address,data);
```

The routine should return a value to indicate whether the message was sent successfully if the network includes a handshaking protocol. If the message to be sent is longer than a packet, it must be broken up into packet-size data segments as follows:

```
for (i = 0; i < message.length; i = i + PACKET_SIZE)
    send_packet(address,&message.data[i]);
```

The above code uses a loop to break up an arbitrary-length message into packet-size chunks. However, clever system design may be able to recast the message to take advantage of the packet format. For example, clever encoding may reduce the length of the message enough so that it fits into a single packet. On the other hand, if the message is shorter than a packet or not an even multiple of the packet data size, some extra information may be packed into the remaining bits of a packet.

Reception of a packet will probably be implemented with interrupts. The simplest procedural interface will simply check to see whether a received message is waiting in a buffer. In a more complex RTOS-based system, reception of a packet may enable a process for execution.

As seen in Section 6.7, communication may be blocking or nonblocking. Of course, the simplest implementation of message passing is blocking, with the routine not returning until it has transmitted or received. A nonblocking network interface requires a queue of data to be sent, with the network driver sending packets off the head of the queue and placing received packets on the tail of the queue. A nonblocking communication mechanism makes sense only when concurrency is available between computing and data transfer.

Network protocols may encourage a **data-push** design style for the system built around the network. In a single-CPU environment, a program typically initiates a read whenever it wants data. In many networked systems, nodes send values out without any request from the intended user of the system. Data-push programming makes sense for periodic data—if the data will always be used at regular intervals, we can reduce data traffic on the network by automatically sending it when it is needed. Example 8-1 shows an application that can make good use of the data-push architecture.

Example 8-1

Data-Push Network Architectures

Consider the following automobile in which distributed sensors and actuators talk to a central controller:

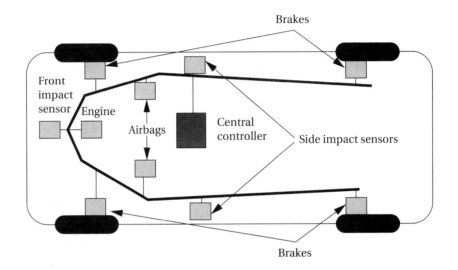

The sensors generally need to be sampled periodically. In such a system, it makes sense for sensors to transmit their data automatically rather than waiting for the controller to request it.

8.3 Networks for Embedded Systems

Many different networks have seen widespread use in distributed embedded systems over the years. Several system buses have been used to build distributed machines as well as for their original purpose of supporting multicard computer systems. Four of these buses are briefly described below.

■ Multibus and VME [DiG90] were developed by Intel and Motorola, respectively, for multicard computer systems and have been widely used in industrial applications.

- The ISA bus [Egg90] has been used to support many I/O cards for PC-based embedded systems.

- The PCI bus [Min95] has replaced ISA for high-speed interfaces in PC-based applications.

Several interconnect networks have been developed especially for distributed embedded computing. Examples are listed below.

- The I^2C bus is used in microcontroller-based systems.

- The controller area network (CAN) bus was developed for automotive electronics. It provides megabit rates and can handle large numbers of devices.

- The Echelon LON network was developed for home and industrial automation.

- Many DSPs supply their own interconnect structures for multiprocessing.

In addition, many networks designed for general-purpose computing have been put to use in embedded applications as well.

In this section, we study several commonly used embedded networks, including the I^2C bus; the CAN system; the SHARC, which supports networks that are representative of the built-in networking elements of many high-performance DSPs; the **Ethernet,** used in local area networking; and **Myrinet,** used in many high-performance signal processing systems. We discuss some basic concepts in the Internet Protocol used in Internet appliances.

8.3.1 The I^2C Bus

The **I^2C bus** [Phi92] is a well-known bus commonly used to link microcontrollers into systems. It has even been used for the command interface in an MPEG-2 video chip [van97]; while a separate bus was used for high-speed video data, setup information was transmitted to the on-chip controller through an I^2C bus interface.

physical layer I^2C is designed to be low cost, easy to implement, and of moderate speed (up to 100 kilobits per second for the standard bus and up to 400 kbits/sec for the extended bus). As a result, it uses only two lines: the **serial data line (SDL)** for data and the **serial clock line (SCL),** which indicates when valid data are on the data line. Figure 8-7 shows the structure of a typical I^2C bus system. Every node in the network is connected to both SCL and SDL. Some nodes may be able to act as bus masters and the bus may have more than one master. Other nodes may act as slaves that only respond to requests from masters.

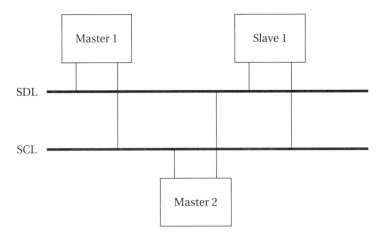

Figure 8-7 *Structure of an I²C bus system.*

electrical interface

The basic electrical interface to the bus is shown in Figure 8-8. The bus does not define particular voltages to be used for high or low so that either bipolar or MOS circuits can be connected to the bus. Both bus signals use open collector/ open drain circuits.[1] A pull-up resistor keeps the default state of the signal high, and transistors are used in each bus device to pull down the signal when a 0 is to be transmitted. Open collector/open drain signaling allows several devices to simultaneously write the bus without causing electrical damage.

The open collector/open drain circuitry allows a slave device to stretch a clock signal during a read from a slave. The master is responsible for generating the SCL clock, but the slave can stretch the low period of the clock (but not the high period) if necessary.

The I²C bus is designed as a multimaster bus—any one of several different devices may act as the master at various times. As a result, there is no global master to generate the clock signal on *SCL*. Instead, a master drives both *SCL* and *SDL* when it is sending data. When the bus is idle, both *SCL* and *SDL* remain high. When two devices try to drive either *SCL* or *SDL* to different values, the open collector/open drain circuitry prevents errors, but each master device must listen to the bus while transmitting to be sure that it is not interfering with another message—if the device receives a different value than it is trying to transmit, then it knows that it is interfering with another message.

data link layer

Every I²C device has an address. The addresses of the devices are determined by the system designer, usually as part of the program for the I²C driver. The addresses must of course be chosen so that no two devices in the system

1. An open collector uses a bipolar transistor, while an open drain circuit uses an MOS transistor.

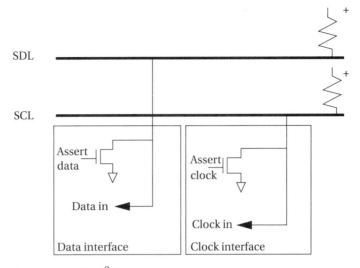

Figure 8-8 *Electrical interface to the I^2C bus.*

have the same address. A device address is 7 bits in the standard I^2C definition (the extended I^2C allows 10-bit addresses). The address 0000000 is used to signal a **general call** or bus broadcast, which can be used to signal all devices simultaneously. The address 11110XX is reserved for the extended 10-bit addressing scheme; there are several other reserved addresses as well.

A **bus transaction** is comprised of a series of one-byte **transmissions** and an address followed by one or more data bytes. I^2C encourages a data-push programming style. When a master wants to write a slave, it transmits the slave's address followed by the data. Since a slave cannot initiate a transfer, the master must send a read request with the slave's address and let the slave transmit the data. Therefore, an address transmission includes the 7-bit address and 1 bit for data direction: 0 for writing from the master to the slave and 1 for reading from the slave to the master. (This explains the 7-bit addresses on the bus.) The format of an address transmission is shown in Figure 8-9.

A bus transaction is initiated by a start signal and completed with an end signal as follows:

■ A start is signaled by leaving the SCL high and sending a 1 to 0 transition on SDL.

■ A stop is signaled by setting the SCL high and sending a 0 to 1 transition on SDL.

However, starts and stops must be paired. A master can write and then read (or read and then write) by sending a start after the data transmission, followed by another address transmission and then more data. The basic state transition graph for the master's actions in a bus transaction is shown in Figure 8-10.

The formats of some typical complete bus transactions are shown in Figure 8-11. In the first example, the master writes two bytes to the addressed slave. In the second, the master requests a read from a slave. In the third, the master writes one byte to the slave, and then sends another start to initiate a read from the slave.

byte format Figure 8-12 shows how a data byte is transmitted on the bus, including start and stop events. The transmission starts when SDL is pulled low while SCL remains high. After this start condition, the clock line is pulled low to initiate the data transfer. At each bit, the clock line goes high while the data line assumes its proper value of 0 or 1. An acknowledgment is sent at the end of every 8-bit transmission, whether it is an address or data. For acknowledgment, the transmitter does not pull down the SDL, allowing the receiver to set the SDL to 0 if it properly received the byte. After acknowledgment, the SDL goes from low to high while the SCL is high, signaling the stop condition.

bus arbitration The bus uses this feature to arbitrate on each message. When sending, devices listen to the bus as well. If a device is trying to send a logic 1 but hears a

Figure 8-9 *Format of an I^2C address transmission.*

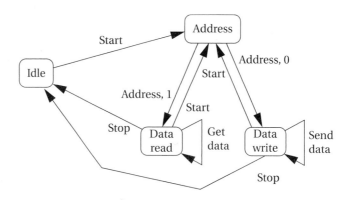

Figure 8-10 *State transition graph for an I^2C bus master.*

Figure 8-11 *Typical bus transactions on the I²C bus.*

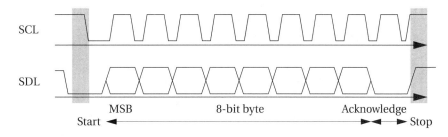

Figure 8-12 *Transmitting a byte on the I²C bus.*

logic 0, it immediately stops transmitting and gives the other sender priority. (The devices should be designed so that they can stop transmitting in time to allow a valid bit to be sent.) In many cases, arbitration will be completed during the address portion of a transmission, but arbitration may continue into the data portion. If two devices are trying to send identical data to the same address, then of course they never interfere and both succeed in sending their message.

application interface

The I²C interface on a microcontroller can be implemented with varying percentages of the functionality in software and hardware [Phi89]. As illustrated in Figure 8-13, a typical system has a 1-bit hardware interface with routines for byte-level functions. The I²C device takes care of generating the clock and data. The application code calls routines to send an address, send a data byte, and so on, which then generates the SCL and SDL, acknowledges, and so forth. One of the microcontroller's timers is typically used to control the length of bits on the bus. Interrupts may be used to recognize bits. However, when used in master mode, polled I/O may be acceptable if no other pending tasks can be performed, since masters initiate their own transfers.

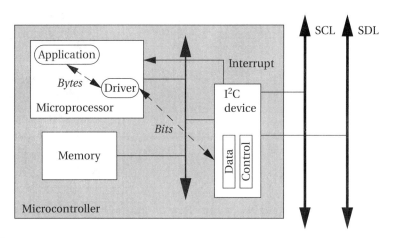

Figure 8-13 *An I²C interface in a microcontroller.*

8.3.2 The CAN Bus

The **CAN bus** was originally designed for automotive electronics. As digital electronics were introduced into automotive components, not only did the individual components get smarter, but the need for them to communicate in order to execute their functions grew. Today, CAN is used in applications other than automotive systems. There are also other network systems used in automotive electronics. However, CAN provides a good example of a distributed network for applications such as automobiles.

The CAN bus uses bit-serial transmission. CAN can run at rates of 1 Mb/second over a twisted pair connection of 40 meters. An optical link can also be used. The bus protocol supports multiple masters on the bus. Many of the details of the CAN and I²C buses are similar, but there are also significant differences.

physical layer As shown in Figure 8-14, each node in the CAN bus has its own electrical drivers and receivers that connect the node to the bus in wired-AND fashion. In CAN terminology, a logical 1 on the bus is called **recessive** and a logical 0 is **dominant.** The driving circuits on the bus cause the bus to be pulled down to 0 if any node on the bus pulls the bus down (making 0 dominant over 1). When all nodes are transmitting 1s, the bus is said to be in the recessive state; when a node transmits a 0, the bus is in the dominant state. Data are sent on the network in packets known as **data frames.**

CAN is a synchronous bus—all transmitters must send at the same time for bus arbitration to work. Nodes synchronize themselves to the bus by listening to the bit transitions on the bus. The first bit of a data frame provides the first synchronization opportunity in a frame. The nodes must also continue to synchronize themselves against later transitions in each frame.

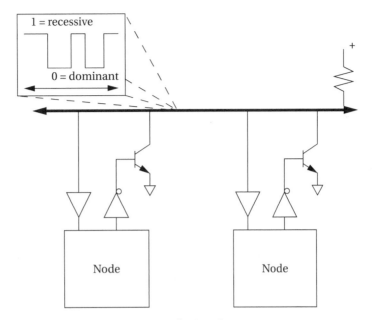

Figure 8-14 *Physical and electrical organization of a CAN bus.*

data frame The format of a CAN data frame is shown in Figure 8-15. A data frame starts with a 1 and ends with a string of seven zeroes. (There are at least three bit fields between data frames.) The first field in the packet contains the packet's destination address and is known as the arbitration field. The destination identifier is 11 bits long. The trailing remote transmission request (RTR) bit is set to 0 if the data frame is used to request data from the device specified by the identifier. When RTR = 1, the packet is used to write data to the destination identifier. The control field provides an identifier extension and a 4-bit length for the data field with a 1 in between. The data field is from 0 to 64 bytes, depending on the value given in the control field. A cyclic redundancy check (CRC) is sent after the data field for error detection. The acknowledge field is used to let the identifier signal whether the frame was correctly received: The sender puts a recessive bit (1) in the ACK slot of the acknowledge field; if the receiver detected an error, it forces the value to a dominant (0) value. If the sender sees a 0 on the bus in the ACK slot, it knows that it must retransmit. The ACK slot is followed by a single bit delimiter followed by the end-of-frame field.

arbitration Control of the CAN bus is arbitrated using a technique known as Carrier Sense Multiple Access with Arbitration on Message Priority (CSMA/AMP). (As seen in Section 8.3.4, Ethernet uses CSMA without AMP.) This method is similar to the I^2C bus's arbitration method; like I^2C, CAN encourages a data-push programming style. Network nodes transmit synchronously, so they all start sending their identifier fields at the same time. When a node hears a

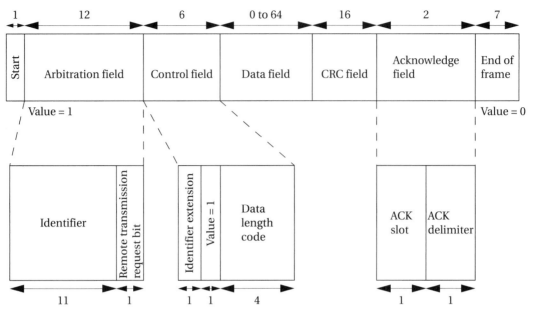

Figure 8-15 *The CAN data frame format.*

dominant bit in the identifier when it tries to send a recessive bit, it stops transmitting. By the end of the arbitration field, only one transmitter will be left. The identifier field acts as a priority identifier, with the all-0 identifier having the highest priority.

remote frames A remote frame is used to request data from another node. The requestor sets the RTR bit to 0 to specify a remote frame; it also specifies zero data bits. The node specified in the identifier field will respond with a data frame that has the requested value. Note that there is no way to send parameters in a remote frame—for example, you cannot use an identifier to specify a device and provide a parameter to say which data value you want from that device. Instead, each possible data request must have its own identifier.

error handling An error frame can be generated by any node that detects an error on the bus. Upon detecting an error, a node interrupts the current transmission with an error frame, which consists of an error flag field followed by an error delimiter field of 8 recessive bits. The error delimiter field allows the bus to return to the quiescent state so that data frame transmission can resume. The bus also supports an overload frame, which is a special error frame sent during the interframe quiescent period. An overload frame signals that a node is overloaded and will not be able to handle the next message. The node can delay the transmission of the next frame with up to two overload frames in a row, hopefully giving it enough time to recover from its overload. The CRC field can be used to check a message's data field for correctness.

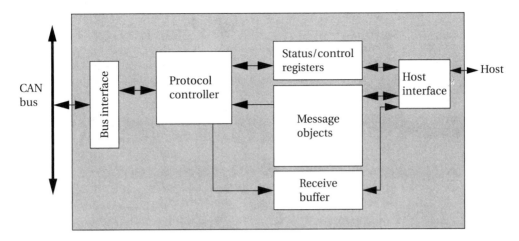

Figure 8-16 *Architecture of a CAN controller.*

If a transmitting node does not receive an acknowledgment for a data frame, it should retransmit the data frame until the data is acknowledged. This action corresponds to the data link layer in the OSI model.

Figure 8-16 shows the basic architecture of a typical CAN controller. The controller implements the physical and data link layers; since CAN is a bus, it does not need network layer services to establish end-to-end connections. The protocol control block is responsible for determining when to send messages, when a message must be resent due to arbitration losses, and when a message should be received.

8.3.3 SHARC Link Ports

The **link ports** of the SHARC [ADI97] are typical of the high-speed links found on many modern DSPs. These ports allow the DSPs to be connected in many different topologies to perform multiprocessing. Application Example 8-1 describes a SHARC multiprocessor that uses the link ports for communication.

Application Example 8-1

A SHARC-Based Multiprocessor

Romano [Rom98] describes a four-CPU multiprocessor built from SHARC DSPs. One interesting characteristic of this multiprocessor is that it contains a

multichip module (MCM), which is a special type of package that can hold several integrated circuits. The MCM provides very small physical size and high-performance interconnections among the DSPs.

The single-MCM multiprocessor was actually produced in two different physical MCM packages, and those packages had different interconnections among the four SHARCs. Appearing below is interconnection topology used in the ceramic quad flat-pack (CQFP) system.

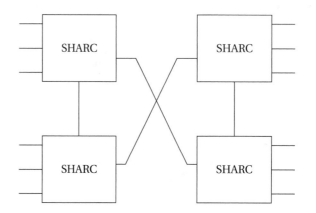

The interconnections are made among the SHARC's serial ports. Since each 21060 SHARC can run at a peak rate of 120 MFlops, the multiprocessor delivers a peak rate of 480 MFlops.

A SHARC with link ports has six such ports. (The ADSP-21061 does not have link ports.) A link port has four data bits that can be clocked twice per clock cycle, providing eight bits of data transfer per clock cycle. Data transfers are packed into 32- or 48-bit words.

Figure 8-17 shows the complete link port connection between two SHARCs. A clock signal is sent with the data, allowing robust transmission of data. Data may be sent to a link port from the DM, PM, or I/O data buses, but not directly. Instead, a link buffer is used to unpack words into four-bit units for transmission or repack after reception. There is no fixed relationship between link buffers and link ports. Instead, a crossbar network allows any link buffer to be connected to any link port. (The link assignment register controls the crossbar configuration.)

Link buffers can be the targets of DMA transfers. Unlike the link port/link buffer relationship, there is a fixed relationship between link buffers and DMA channels. Some of the DMA channels used by link buffers are shared for other uses, such as serial ports. DMA-driven data transfers cause interrupts when

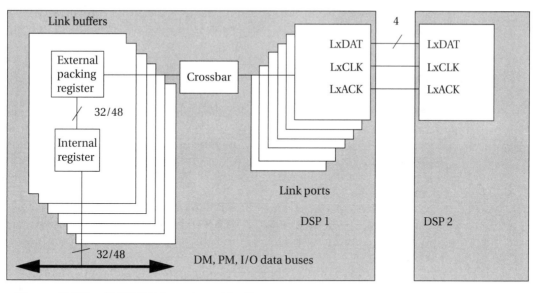

Figure 8-17 *SHARC link ports and buffers.*

the transfer is completed. Link buffer transfers can also be made under direct program control.

In addition to the link access register, two other registers are used to control the link ports. The link buffer control register determines the configuration of the link buffers, including whether transfers are 32 or 48 bits. The link control register enables each link buffer itself, DMA for the link buffer, chaining, and direction of transfer.

half-duplex communication A link port is half-duplex, meaning that data can be sent in only one direction. A link port must be turned around from transmitting to receiving and back under software control. Not only must the link control register be changed for the new transfer direction, but the program must determine that it is safe to do so. Both ends of a link must be turned around: The old transmitter must be switched to receiver mode while the old receiver must be switched to transmit. One way to do this is by passing a token between processors. The token identifies the processor that can write the link port; each processor keeps a memory location to remember whether it currently has the token. At system start-up, one processor is given the token by default. When that processor has completed its transmission, it sends a message to the other processor on the link telling it that it can now transmit. Both processors then change the configuration of their link bits. When using the token method, care must be taken that bugs do not cause the token to be lost (so that no one can transmit) or replicated (causing two link ports to write to the same link). Consideration

should also be given to error conditions to ensure that errors do not cause token loss or replication.

8.3.4 Ethernet

Ethernet is very widely used as a local area network for general-purpose computing. Because of its ubiquity and the low cost of Ethernet interfaces, it has seen significant use as a network for embedded computing. Ethernet is particularly useful when PCs are used as platforms, making it possible to use standard components, and when the network does not have to meet rigorous real-time requirements.

The physical organization of an Ethernet is very simple, as shown in Figure 8-18. The network is a bus with a single signal path; the Ethernet standard allows for several different implementations such as twisted pair and coaxial cable.

Unlike the I^2C or CAN bus, nodes on the Ethernet are not synchronized—they can send their bits at any time. I^2C and CAN rely on the fact that a collision can be detected and quashed within a single bit time thanks to synchronization. But since Ethernet nodes are not synchronized, if two nodes decide to transmit at the same time, the message will be ruined. The Ethernet arbitration scheme is known as **Carrier Sense Multiple Access** with **Collision Detection (CSMA/CD).** The algorithm is outlined in Figure 8-19. A node that has a message waits for the bus to become silent and then starts transmitting. It simultaneously listens, and if it hears another transmission that interferes with its transmission, it stops transmitting and waits to retransmit. The waiting time is random, but weighted by an exponential function of the number of times the message has been aborted. Figure 8-20 shows the exponential backoff function both before and after it is modulated by the random wait time. Since a message may be interfered with several times before it is successfully transmitted, the **exponential backoff** technique helps to ensure that the network does not become overloaded at high demand factors. The random factor in the wait

Figure 8-18 *Ethernet organization.*

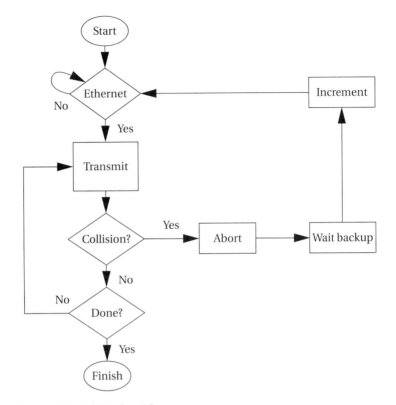

Figure 8-19 *The Ethernet CSMA/CD algorithm.*

time minimizes the chance that two messages will repeatedly interfere with each other.

The maximum length of an Ethernet is determined by the nodes' ability to detect collisions. The worst case occurs when two nodes at opposite ends of the bus are transmitting simultaneously. For the collision to be detected by both nodes, each node's signal must be able to travel to the opposite end of the bus so that it can be heard by the other node. In practice, Ethernets can run up to several hundred meters.

Figure 8-21 shows the basic format of an Ethernet packet. It provides addresses of both the destination and the source. It also provides for a variable-length data payload.

The fact that it may take several attempts to successfully transmit a message and that the waiting time includes a random factor makes Ethernet performance difficult to analyze. It is possible to perform data streaming and other real-time activities on Ethernets, particularly when the total network load is kept to a reasonable level, but care must be taken in designing such systems.

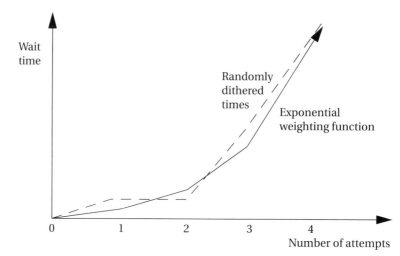

Figure 8-20 *Exponential backoff times.*

Preamble	Start frame	Destination address	Source address	Length	Data	Padding	CRC

Figure 8-21 *Ethernet packet format.*

8.3.5 Myrinet

Myrinet [Bod95] is a very high-performance network that can be used in many environments. It provides a full-duplex connection with 640 Mb/sec, giving a total bandwidth of 1.28 Gb/sec. The technology descended from networks designed for parallel processing systems, which was then redesigned so that it could serve as a local area network. However, its high performance has led it be used in high-performance signal processing systems.

A Myrinet switch is able to route packets between any pair of the links connected to it. A Myrinet network can be constructed in a variety of topologies. A simple network could have a single switch directly connected to processing elements, or switches can be connected to other switches to build multistage networks.

Because the network topology is not predetermined, the format of a Myrinet packet depends in part on the system configuration. A packet starts with a sequence of destinations, which may be switches or ports. Each switch strips off its to-switch field from the packet and passes on the rest. When only a to-host field is left, the packet goes to that node. The data payload may be of variable length and the packet includes error correction codes.

8.3.6 Internet

The **Internet Protocol (IP)** [Los97, Sta97A] is the fundamental protocol on the **Internet.** It provides connectionless, packet-based communication. Industrial automation has long been a good application area for Internet-based embedded systems. Information appliances that use the Internet are rapidly becoming another use of IP in embedded computing.

IP is not defined over a particular physical implementation—it is an **internetworking** standard. Internet packets are assumed to be carried by some other network, such as an Ethernet. In general, an Internet packet will travel over several different networks from source to destination. The IP allows data to flow seamlessly through these networks from one end user to another. The relationship between IP and individual networks is illustrated in Figure 8-22. IP works at the network layer. When node *A* wants to send data to node *B*, the application's data pass through several layers of the protocol stack to get to the Internet Protocol. IP creates packets for routing to the destination, which are then sent to the *data link* and *physical* layers. A node that transmits data among different types of networks is known as a **router.** The router's functionality must go up to the IP layer, but since it is not running applications, it does not need to go to higher levels of the OSI model. In general, a packet may go through several routers to get to its destination. At the destination, the IP layer provides data to the transport layer and ultimately the receiving application. As the data pass through several layers of the protocol stack, the IP packet data are encapsulated in packet formats appropriate to each layer.

The basic format of an IP packet is shown in Figure 8-23. The header and data payload are both of variable length. The maximum total length of the header and data payload is 65,535 bytes.

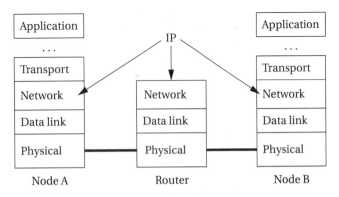

Figure 8-22 *Protocol utilization in Internet communication.*

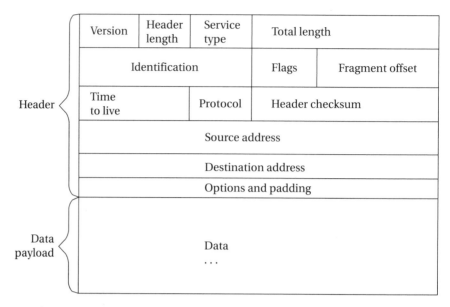

Version	Header length	Service type	Total length	
Identification			Flags	Fragment offset
Time to live		Protocol	Header checksum	
Source address				
Destination address				
Options and padding				
Data . . .				

Figure 8-23 *IP packet structure.*

An Internet address is a number (32 bits in early versions of IP, 128 bits in IPv6). The IP address is typically written in the form xxx.xx.xx.xx. The names by which users and applications typically refer to Internet nodes, such as foo.baz.com, are translated into IP addresses via calls to a **Domain Name Server (DNS),** one of the higher-level services built on top of IP.

The fact that IP works at the network layer tells us that it does not guarantee that a packet is delivered to its destination. Furthermore, packets that do arrive may come out of order. This is referred to as **best-effort routing.** Since routes for data may change quickly with subsequent packets being routed along very different paths with different delays, real-time performance of IP can be hard to predict. When a small network is contained totally within the embedded system, performance can be evaluated through simulation or other methods because the possible inputs are limited. Since the performance of the Internet may depend on worldwide usage patterns, its real-time performance is inherently harder to predict.

The Internet also provides higher-level services built on top of IP. The **Transmission Control Protocol (TCP)** is one such example. It provides a connection-oriented service that ensures that data arrive in the appropriate order, and it uses an acknowledgment protocol to ensure that packets arrive. Because many higher-level services are built on top of TCP, the basic protocol is often referred to as TCP/IP.

Figure 8-24 shows the relationships between IP and higher-level Internet services. Using IP as the foundation, TCP is used to provide **File Transport Pro-**

Figure 8-24 *The Internet service stack.*

tocol (**FTP**) for batch file transfers, **Hypertext Transport Protocol (HTTP)** for World Wide Web service, **Simple Mail Transfer Protocol (SMTP)** for email, and Telnet for virtual terminals. A separate transport protocol, **User Datagram Protocol (UDP),** is used as the basis for the network management services provided by the **Simple Network Management Protocol (SNMP).**

8.4 Network-Based Design

Designing a distributed embedded system around a network involves some of the same design tasks we faced in accelerated systems. We must schedule computations in time and allocate them to processing elements. Scheduling and allocation of communication are important additional design tasks required for many distributed networks. Many embedded networks are designed for low cost and therefore do not provide excessively high communication speed. If we are not careful, the network can become the bottleneck in system design. In this section we concentrate on design tasks unique to network-based distributed embedded systems.

8.4.1 Communication Analysis

We know how to analyze the execution time of programs and systems of processes on single CPUs, but to analyze the performance of networks we must know how to determine the delay incurred by transmitting messages. Let us assume for the moment that messages are sent reliably—we do not have to retransmit a message. The **message delay** for a single message with no contention (as would be the case in a point-to-point connection) can be modeled as

$$t_m = t_x + t_n + t_r \qquad \text{(EQ 8-1)}$$

where t_x is the transmitter-side overhead, t_n is the network transmission time, and t_r is the receiver-side overhead. In I^2C, t_x and t_r are negligible relative to t_n, as illustrated by Example 8-2.

Example 8-2

Simple Message Delay for an I^2C Message

Let's assume that our I^2C bus runs at the rate of 100 kilobits per second and that we need to send one 8-bit byte. Based on the message format shown in Figure 8-9, we can compute the number of bits in the complete packet:

$$n_{packet} = \text{start bit} + \text{address} + \text{data} + \text{stop bit}$$
$$= 1 + 8 + 8 + 1 = 18 \text{ bits}$$

The time required, then, to transmit the packet is

$$t_n = n_{packet} \times t_{bit} = 1.8 \times 10^{-4} \text{sec.}$$

Some of the instructions in the transmitter and receiver drivers—namely, the loops that send bytes to and receive bytes from the network interface—will run concurrently with the message transmission. If we assume that 20 instructions outside of these loops are executed by the transmitter and receiver, overheads on an 8 MHz microcontroller would be as follows:

$$t_x = t_r = 20 \times 0.125 \times 10^{-6} = 2.5 \times 10^{-6}.$$

The total message delay appears below.

$$t_m = 2.5 \times 10^{-6} + 1.8 \times 10^{-4} + 2.5 \times 10^{-6} = 1.85 \times 10^{-4}.$$

Overhead is less than 3% of the total message time in this case.

If messages can interfere with each other in the network, analyzing communication delay becomes difficult. In general, because we must wait for the network to become available and then transmit the message, we can write the **message delay** as

$$t_y = t_d + t_x \qquad \text{(EQ 8-2)}$$

where t_d is the **network availability delay** incurred waiting for the network to become available. The main problem, therefore, is calculating t_d. That value depends on the type of arbitration used in the network.

- If the network uses fixed-priority arbitration, the network availability delay is unbounded for all but the highest-priority device. Since the highest-priority device always gets the network first, unless there is an application-specific limit on how long it will transmit before relinquishing the network, it can keep blocking the other devices indefinitely.

- If the network uses fair arbitration, the network availability delay is bounded. In the case of round-robin arbitration, if there are N devices, then the worst-case network availability delay is $N(t_x + t_{arb})$, where t_{arb} is the delay incurred for arbitration. t_{arb} is usually small compared to transmission time.

Even when round-robin arbitration is used to bound the network availability delay, the waiting time can be very long. It is worthwhile to examine the application to determine whether the message structure can be readjusted to reduce t_d as shown in Example 8-3.

Example 8-3

Adjusting Messages to Improve Network Delay

Assume we want to implement the following task graph:

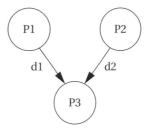

Assume also that we want to implement the task graph on the following network.

We will allocate *P1* to *M1*, *P2* to *M2*, and *P3* to *M3*. *P1* and *P2* run for three time units while *P3* runs for four time units. A complete transmission of either *d1* or *d2* takes four time units. The task graph shows that *P3* cannot start until it receives its data from both *P1* and *P2* over the bus network.

The simplest implementation transmits all the required data in one large message, which is four packets long in this case. Appearing below is a schedule based on that message structure.

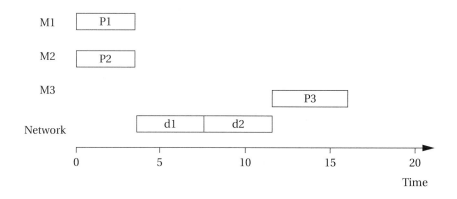

P3 does not start until time 11, when the transmission of the second message has been completed. The total schedule length is 15.

Let's redesign *P3* so that it doesn't require all of both messages to begin. We modify the program so that it reads one packet of data each from *d1* and *d2* and start computing on that. If it finishes what it can do on that data before the next packets from *d1* and *d2* arrive, it waits; otherwise, it picks up the packets and keeps computing. This organization allows us to take advantage of concurrency between the *M3* processing element and the network as shown by the schedule below.

Reorganizing the messages so that they can be sent concurrently with *P3*'s execution reduces the schedule length from 15 to 12, even with *P3* stopping to wait for more data from *P1* and *P2*.

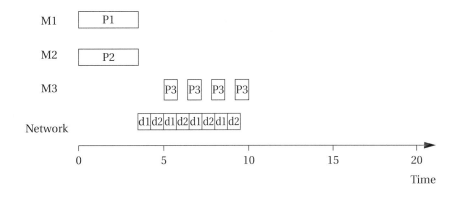

If we add acknowledgment and data corruption into the analysis, figuring network delay is more difficult. Assuming that errors are random, we cannot predict a worst-case delay since every packet may contain an error. We can, however, compute the probability that a packet will be delayed for more than a given amount of time. However, such analysis is beyond the scope of this book.

Arbitration on networks is a form of prioritization. Therefore, we can use the techniques we learned for process scheduling in Chapter 6 to help us schedule communications. In a rate-monotonic communication scheme, the task with the shortest deadline should be assigned the highest priority in the network.

priority inversion in networks

Our process scheduling model assumed that we could interrupt processes at any point. But network communications are organized into packets. In most networks we cannot interrupt a packet transmission to take over the network for a higher-priority packet. As a result, networks exhibit priority inversion like that introduced in Chapter 6. When a low-priority message is on the network, the network is effectively allocated to that low-priority message, allowing it to block higher-priority messages. This cannot cause deadlock since each message has a bounded length, but it can slow down critical communications. The only solution is to analyze network behavior to determine whether priority inversion causes some messages to be delayed for too long.

Of course, a round-robin arbitrated network puts all communications at the same priority. This does not eliminate the priority inversion problem because processes still have priorities.

Thus far we have assumed a **single-hop network:** A message is received at its intended destination directly from the source, without going through any other network node. It is possible to build **multihop networks** in which mes-

sages are routed through network nodes to get to their destinations. (Using a multistage network does not necessarily mean using a multihop network—the stages in a multistage network are generally much smaller than the network processing elements.) Figure 8-25 shows an example of a multihop communication. The hardware platform has two separate networks (perhaps so that communications between subsets of the PEs do not interfere), but there is no direct path from *M1* to *M5*. The message is therefore routed through *M3*, which reads it from one network and sends it on the other one. Analyzing delays through multihop systems is very difficult. For example, the time that the message is held at *M3* depends on both the computational load of *M3* and the other messages that it must handle.

If there is more than one network, we must allocate communications to the networks. We may establish multiple networks so that lower-priority communications can be handled separately without interfering with high-priority communications on the primary network.

Scheduling and allocation of computations and communications are clearly interrelated. If we change the allocation of computations, we change not only the scheduling of processes on those PEs but also potentially the schedules of PEs with which they communicate. For example, if we move a computation to a slower PE, its results will be available later, which may mean rescheduling both the process that uses the value and the communication that sends the value to its destination.

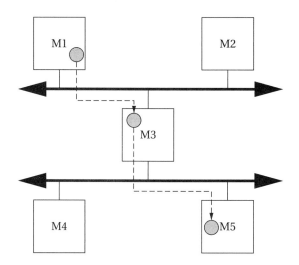

Figure 8-25 *A multihop communication.*

8.4.2 System Performance Analysis

Unfortunately, analyzing the performance of distributed embedded systems is very difficult. We can understand some of the difficulties by starting with simple cases.

Figure 8-26 shows a very simple task graph with two processes and one n-packet data communication. The worst-case execution times of the processes are t_{P1} and t_{P2} and the communication takes nt_x time units. This case is simple because there is no interference from outside elements: We know that the two processes cannot execute simultaneously since there is a data dependency between them and there are no other processes in the system to interfere. Similarly, nothing can interfere with the communication, and everything happens at a single rate. In this case the worst-case execution time is $t_{P1} + nt_x + t_{P2}$.

interference between tasks

When we allow computations and communications to interfere with each other, performance analysis becomes much harder. Consider the example of Figure 8-27, where we have superimposed the task graph on the target architecture. *P2* and *P3* run on the same PE, which helps enable the following chain of events that can affect the whole system:

- The data dependency from *P1* to *P2* translates any uncertainty in the execution time of *P1* into uncertainty about the start time of *P2*.

Figure 8-26 *Delay through a simple task graph.*

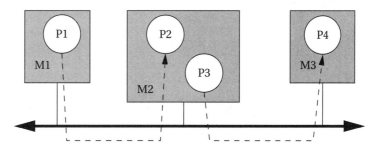

Figure 8-27 *A distributed system with multirate concurrency.*

- The coallocation of *P2* and *P3* to processing element *M3* means that variations in the ready time of *P2* can affect the completion time of *P3*. Of course, variations in the execution time of *P2* also affect *P3*.

- The data dependency from *P3* to *P4* translates variations in the completion time of *P3* to the start time of *P4*.

Therefore, even though *P2* and *P3* are in separate tasks, the fact that they are allocated to the same PE causes them to interact with each other in ways that affect the completion time of every task in the system. Similarly, messages from the two tasks can interfere with each other on the bus, causing yet more variations in completion time.

Complex distributed embedded systems require CAD tools to accurately analyze performance. Algorithms can be used to efficiently determine upper and lower bounds on the start and completion times of processes [Yen98].

If you don't have tools to help you analyze performance, care is essential when hand-designing a system that has to meet hard real-time deadlines. When the system is trying to meet hard deadlines, it is important to make sure that only one task—the critical task—is active. In many cases, user interface activity and other nonessential tasks can be turned off temporarily. When there are several critical tasks that must occur simultaneously, hand design requires allocating them to share nothing—no PEs nor communication links. While this is a conservative design strategy, it makes hand analysis feasible. CAD tools can help loosen some of these restrictions and allow more hardware-efficient designs.

8.4.3 Hardware Platform Design, Allocation, and Scheduling

Now that we know how to compute the delay for messages, we can develop strategies for designing the schedule and allocation of processes and communication. Designing the hardware platform is necessarily closely related to our choices in scheduling and allocating processes. We want to use only as much hardware as is necessary, but we cannot know how much hardware to use until we can construct a system schedule. Creating that schedule requires an allocation of processes to PEs, which in turn requires knowing the available hardware.

When designing the hardware platform, we have the following design choices to make:

- number of PEs required
- types of all PEs
- number of networks required

■ types (and data rates) of the networks

In making these choices, we need to construct allocations and schedules for the processes to evaluate the platform. In turn, allocation and scheduling are driven by system performance analysis.

It helps to start with a basic assessment of the computation and communication needs of the system. A lower bound on the computational needs of the system can be obtained by summing up the worst-case execution times of the processes as follows:

$$t_c = \sum_{process\, i} \frac{T_l}{T_i} t_{Pi}, \qquad \text{(EQ 8-3)}$$

where t_{Pi} is the execution time of process P_i and T_l is the least-common multiple of all the periods T_i. This formula computes the total execution time over the schedule unrolled to the least-common multiple of the periods.

Similarly, we can compute the communication volume over the least-common multiple of the periods as seen below.

$$n_c = \sum_{process\, i} l_i. \qquad \text{(EQ 8-4)}$$

The above formula computes the total number of bytes transmitted in the unrolled schedule by counting the output bytes of all the processes in the system. Of course, these figures do not account for overheads such as operating system scheduling or communication interference. They simply provide lower bounds on our needs.

Depending on the type of system we are designing, the following two strategies may be useful to help us quickly come up with an efficient system:

■ For I/O-intensive systems we will start with the I/O devices and their associated processing.

■ For computation-intensive systems we will start with the processes.

I/O-intensive system design

For systems that do a lot of I/O, we definitely need to support the I/O devices themselves and perhaps do some processing of the data locally before shipping the data over the network.

■ Inventory the required I/O devices.

■ Determine which processing has deadlines short enough that they cannot be met by any network within your price range. I/O devices that do not require local processing may be attached to the network with the simplest available interface.

- Determine which devices can share a processing element or network interface.

- Analyze communication times to determine whether critical communications may interfere with each other. Determine whether a complex network or multiple networks may be required to satisfy communication deadlines.

- Allocate the minimum required PE to go with each I/O device.

- Design the rest of the system using the procedure for computation-intensive systems.

computation-
intensive system
design

For computation-intensive systems, we want to consider the processes and their deadlines and communication as follows:

- Start with the tasks with the shortest deadlines. The shorter the deadline for a task, the more likely it is to require its own processing element or elements. If a high-priority task shares a PE with a low-priority task, not only will a more expensive PE be required, but scheduling overhead will be paid for at the nonlinear rate.

- Analyze communication times to determine whether critical communications may interfere with each other.

- Allocate lower-priority tasks to shared PEs where possible.

After we have designed a basic system that meets our performance goals, we can improve it to satisfy power consumption or other requirements.

Once you have an initial allocation, use the system schedule as a guide for fine tuning. By reallocating processes you may be able to improve one or more attributes, such as hardware cost, slack time in the schedule, power consumption, and so on. In particular, **load balancing** is often a good idea. If you have some PEs that are more heavily loaded than others, it may be possible to move some of those processes to other PEs. Doing so can reduce the chance that the system fails to meet a deadline due to mistaken estimation of run times.

8.5 Internet-Enabled Systems

A very different type of distributed embedded system is rapidly emerging—the **Internet-enabled embedded system** and **Internet appliances.** The Internet is not well suited to the real-time tasks that we have thus far concentrated on in this chapter, but it does provide a rich environment for non–real-time interaction.

The Internet provides a standard way for an embedded system to act in concert with other devices and with users. Examples are listed below.

- One of the earliest Internet-enabled embedded systems was the laser printer. High-end laser printers often use Internet protocols to receive print jobs from host machines.

- A personal digital assistant (PDA) can display Web pages, read email, and synchronize calendar information with remote computers.

- A home control system allows the homeowner to remotely monitor and control home cameras, lights, and so on.

Although there are higher-level services that provide more time-sensitive delivery mechanisms for the Internet, the basic incarnation of the Internet is not well suited to hard real-time operations. However, IP is a very good way to let the embedded system talk to other systems. IP provides a way for both special-purpose and standard programs (such as Web browsers) to talk to the embedded system. This non–real-time interaction can be used to monitor the system, set its configuration, and interact with it.

As seen in Section 8.3.6, the Internet provides a wide range of services built on top of IP. Since code size is an important issue in many embedded systems, one architectural decision that must be made is to determine which Internet services will be needed by the system. This choice depends on the type of data service required, such as connectionless versus connection oriented, streaming versus nonstreaming, and so on. It also depends on the application code and its services: Does the system look to the rest of the Internet like a terminal, a Web server, or something else?

Application Example 8-2 describes an Internet appliance that runs Java to provide useful services.

Application Example 8-2

An Internet Video Camera

Javacam [McD98] is an Internet-accessible video camera that was designed as a demonstration of a Java Nanokernel. The Java Nanokernel is designed to require very little memory. As a result, Javacam can provide an Internet interface with a National Semiconductor NS486SXF microprocessor and 1.5 Mbytes of memory.

Javacam was built from a Connectix QuickCam, a widely available, low-cost video camera for PCs that can send and receive data on a standard PC parallel port.

The illustration below shows how QuickCam operates as a Java applet.

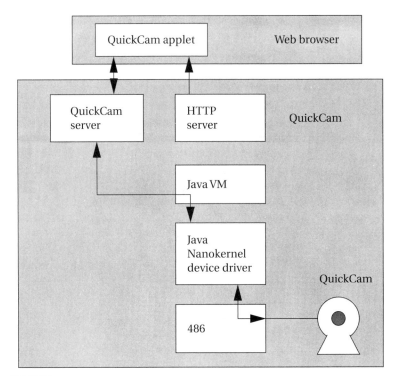

From [McD98].

The HTTP server returns a page containing a piece of Java code that acts as an applet to talk to the device. That Java code running on the Web browser requests an image from the QuickCam server on the QuickCam. The QuickCam server, which executes on top of the Java virtual machine and Java Nanokernel, grabs an image from the QuickCam, performs required transformations, and returns the data to the applet running on the Web browser.

The QuickCam driver communicates with the camera over a parallel port. It provides three basic functions: qc_initialize(); qc_send_command(), which sends commands to the camera; and qc_take_picture(), which returns a picture. Those functions are implemented in C.

Design Example

8.6 Elevator Controller

We will use the principles of distributed system design by designing an elevator controller. The components are physically distributed among the elevators and floors of the building, and the system must meet both hard (making sure the

elevator stops at the right point) and soft (responding to requests for elevators) deadlines.

8.6.1 Theory of Operation and Requirements

We design a multielevator system to increase the challenge. The configuration of a bank of elevators is shown in Figure 8-28. The *elevator car* is the unit that runs up and down the *hoistway* (also known as the shaft) carrying passengers; we will use N to represent the number of hoistways. Each car runs in a hoistway and can stop at any of F floors. (For convenience we will number the floors *1* through *F,* although some of the elevator doors may in fact be in the basement.) Every elevator car has a *car control panel* that allows the passengers to select floors to stop at. Each floor has a single *floor control panel* that calls for an elevator. Each floor also has a set of displays to show the current state of the elevator systems.

The user interface consists of the *elevator control panels,* floor control panels, and *displays.* The car control panels have F buttons to request the floors

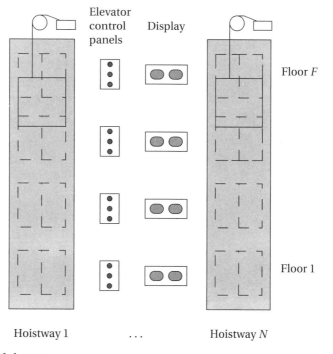

Figure 8-28 *A bank of elevators.*

plus an emergency stop button. Each floor control panel has an up button and a down button that request an elevator going in the chosen direction. There is one display per *hoistway* on each floor. Each *display* has an up light and a down light; if the elevator is idle, neither light is on. The displays for a *hoistway* always show the same state on all floors.

The elevator control system consists of two types of components. First, a single master controller governs the overall behavior of all elevators, and second, on each elevator a car controller runs everything that must be done within the car. The car controller must of course sense button presses on the car control panel, but it must also sense the current position of the elevator. As shown in Figure 8-29, the car controller reads two sets of indicators on the wall of the elevator hoistway to sense position. The *coarse indicators* run the entire length of the hoistway and a *sensor* determines when the elevator passes each one. *Fine indicators* are located only around the stopping point for each floor. There are $2S + 1$ fine indicators on each floor, one at the exact stopping point and S on each side of it. The sensor also reads fine indicators; it puts out separate signals for the coarse and fine indicators. The elevator system can stop at the proper position by counting coarse and fine indicators.

The elevator's movement is controlled by two motor control inputs: one for up and one for down. When both are disabled, the elevator does not move. The system should not enable both up and down on a single hoistway simultaneously.

The master controller has several tasks—it must read inputs from the floor control panels, send signals to the lights on the floor displays, read floor requests from the car controllers, and take inputs from the car sensors. Most importantly, it must tell the elevators when to move and when to stop. It must also schedule the elevators to efficiently answer passenger requests.

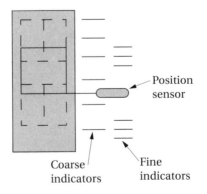

Figure 8-29 *Sensing elevator position.*

The basic requirements for the elevator system follow:

Name	Elevator system
Inputs	F floor control inputs, N position sensors, N car control panels, one master control panel
Outputs	F displays, N motor controllers
Functions	Responds to floor, car, and master control panels; operates cars safely
Performance	Control of elevators is time critical
Manufacturing cost	Cost of electronics is small compared to mechanical systems
Power	Not important
Physical size and weight	Cabling is the major concern

In this design, we are much more aware of the surrounding mechanical elements than we have been in previous examples. The electronics are clearly a small part of the cost and bulk of the elevator system. But because the elevators are controlled by the computers, the proper operation of the embedded hardware and software is very important.

8.6.2 Specification

The basic class diagram for the elevator system is shown in Figure 8-30. This diagram concentrates on the relationships among the classes and the number of objects of each type that the system requires.

The physical interface classes are defined in more detail in Figure 8-31. We have used inheritance to define the sensors, even though these classes represent physical objects. The only difference among the sensors to the elevator controller is whether they indicate coarse or fine positions; other physical distinctions among the sensors do not matter.

The *Car* and *Floor* classes, which describe the control panels on the floors and in the cars, are shown in Figure 8-32. These classes define the basic attributes of the car and floor control panels.

The *Controller* class is defined in Figure 8-33. This class defines attributes that describe the state of the system, including where each car is and whether the system has made an emergency stop. It also defines several behaviors, such as an *operate* behavior and behaviors to check the state of parts of the system.

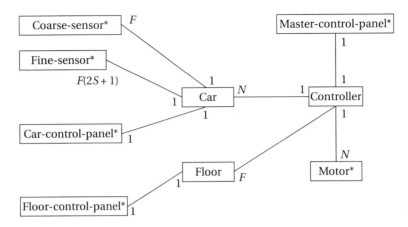

Figure 8-30 *Basic class diagram for the elevator system.*

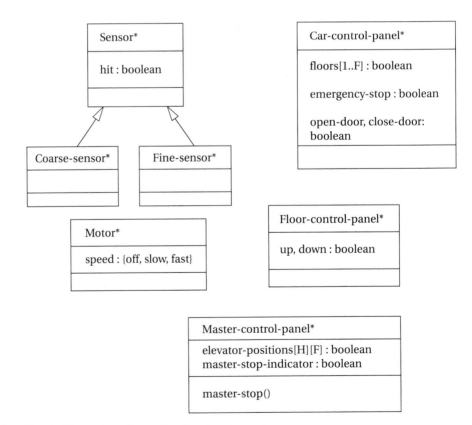

Figure 8-31 *Physical interface classes for the elevator system.*

Car	
request-lights[F] : integer current-floor : integer	

Floor	
up-light, down-light : boolean	

Figure 8-32 *The Car and Floor classes.*

Controller
car-floor[H] : integer
emergency-stop[H] : boolean
scan-cars() scan-floors() scan-master-panel() operate()

Figure 8-33 *The Controller class for the elevator system.*

8.6.3 Architecture

Computation and I/O occur at three major locations in this system: the floor control panels/displays, the elevator cabs, and the system controller. Let's consider the basic operation of each of these subsystems one at a time and then go back and design the network that connects them.

The floor control panels and displays are relatively simple since they have no hard real-time requirements. Each one takes a set of inputs for the up/down indicators and lights the appropriate lights. Each also watches for button events and sends the results to the system controller. We can use a simple microcontroller for all these tasks.

The cab controller must read the cab's buttons and send events to the system controller. It must also read the sensor inputs and send them to the system controller. Reading the sensors is a hard real-time task—proper operation of the elevator requires that the cab controller not miss any of the indicators. We have to decide whether to use one or two PEs in the cab. A conservative design would use separate PEs for the button panel and the sensor. We could also use a single processor to handle both the buttons and the sensor.

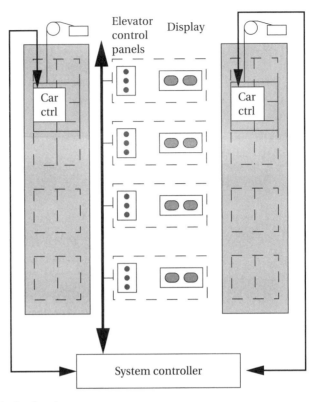

Figure 8-34 *The networks in the elevator system.*

The system controller must take inputs from all these units. Its control of the elevators has both hard and soft real-time aspects: It must constantly monitor all moving elevators to be sure they stop properly, as well as choose which elevator to dispatch to a request.

Figure 8-34 shows the set of networks we will use in the system. The floor control panels/displays are connected along a single bus network. Each elevator car has its own point-to-point link with the system controller.

8.6.4 Testing

The simplest way to test the controllers is to build an elevator simulator using an FPGA. We can easily program an FPGA to simulate several elevators by keeping registers for the current position of each elevator and using counters to control how often the elevators change state. Using an FPGA-based elevator simulator provides good motivation for this example because we can design the FPGA to indicate when an elevator has crashed through the floor or the

ceiling of its shaft. Working with a real-time–oriented elevator simulator helps illustrate the challenges presented by real-time control. We can use a serial link from a PC to provide button inputs, or we can wire up panels of buttons and indicators ourselves.

8.7 Summary

We often need or want to build an embedded system out of a network of connected processors rather than a single CPU with I/O devices. The uses of distributed embedded systems vary greatly, ranging from the real-time networks in an automobile to Internet-enabled information appliances. There are a great many networks that we can choose from to build embedded systems based on constraints of cost, overall throughput, and real-time behavior.

What We Learned

- Distributed embedded systems often make sense for cost, performance, and physical reasons.
- The OSI layer model breaks down the structure of a network into seven layers.
- A large number of networks, many with very different characteristics, are used in embedded systems.
- Performance analysis must take into account network delay.
- Distributed embedded system design requires scheduling of processes and of communication, as well as allocation of processes to processing elements.
- The Internet is not well suited to hard real-time operation, but it can be very useful in building a user interface and in simplifying the integration of systems with multiple nodes.

Further Reading

Kopetz [Kop97] provides a thorough introduction to the design of distributed embedded systems. Stallings [Sta97A] provides a good introduction to data networking. A variety of manufacturers make components for interfacing to popular networks and microprocessors with built-in network interfaces.

Questions

Q8-1 Describe a PC serial interface at the following OSI-compliant levels of detail:

 a. physical

 b. data link

Q8-2 Describe an I^2C bus at the following OSI-compliant levels of detail:

 a. physical

 b. data link

 c. network

 d. transport

Q8-3 Describe a 10Base-T Ethernet at the following OSI-compliant levels of detail:

 a. physical

 b. data link

 c. network

 d. transport

Q8-4 Show the order in which requests would be answered in the timeline below, assuming that each takes one time unit to satisfy, under the following arbitration schemes:

 a. fixed: *a* highest, *b* middle, *c* lowest

 b. round robin

Q8-5 Answer question Q8-4, assuming that each request takes two time units to satisfy.

Q8-6 Answer question Q8-4, using the arrival times below and a request satisfaction time of two time units.

Q8-7 Describe how an IP packet may be sent from a client on one Ethernet to a client on a second Ethernet. The two Ethernets are connected by a router.

Q8-8 What services would the Javacam of Application Example 8-2 require at the following levels of the OSI model:

a. application

b. presentation

c. session

d. transport

Q8-9 Using the methodology of Example 8-2, plot both the transmission time for one byte as a function of the I^2C clock speed and the microcontroller overhead as a function of the number of instructions executed. Determine the values for bus clock speed and the number of instructions at which the transmission delay equals the overhead.

Q8-10 Devise a scenario in which a fixed-priority bus can starve out as many processing elements as possible for an indefinite period.

Q8-11 Devise a scenario in which two processing elements on a fixed-priority bus can starve out all the other processing elements. Do they need to actively cooperate (that is, exchange data during execution to coordinate their starvation effort) to achieve this goal?

Q8-12 What is the longest time that a processing element may have to wait between two successive data transmissions on a round-robin arbitrated bus? Assume that each data transmission requires one time unit.

Q8-13 Derive schedules for the data communication and computation for the data flow graph given below while executing on the network platform shown. Assume that data elements are sent one at a time as they are finished; each data transmission takes one time unit.

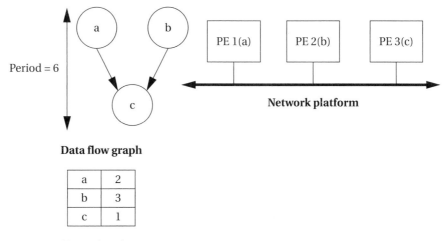

Data flow graph

a	2
b	3
c	1

Execution time

Q8-14 Derive schedules for the data communication and computation for the data flow graph given below while executing on the network platform shown. Assume that data elements are sent one at a time as they are finished; each data transmission requires two time units.

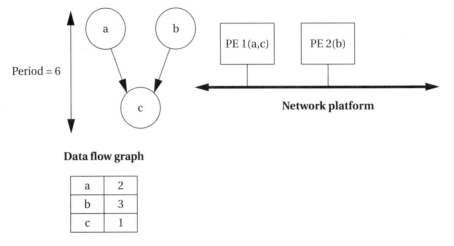

Data flow graph

a	2
b	3
c	1

Execution time

Lab Exercises

L8-1 Build an experimental setup that lets you monitor messages on an embedded network.

L8-2 Measure the effects of collisions on an Ethernet (doing so, of course, on a network where you will not disturb other users). Plot the amount of time required to successfully deliver a message as a function of network load.

Chapter

System Design Techniques

- A deeper look into design methodologies, requirements, specification, and system analysis.

- Quality assurance.

- Several real-world design examples, including a telephone system, an ink jet printer, a PDA, and set-top boxes.

- Systems-on-silicon.

9.1 Introduction

In this chapter we consider the techniques required to create complex embedded systems. Thus far, our design examples have been small so that important concepts can be conveyed relatively simply. However, most real embedded system designs are inherently complex, given that their functional specifications are rich and they must obey multiple other requirements on cost, performance, and so on. Here we examine some real embedded system designs as well as study some techniques that help us get a handle on the design process.

In the next section we look at design methodologies in more detail. Section 9.3 studies requirements analysis, which captures informal descriptions of what a system must do, while Section 9.4 considers techniques for more formally specifying system functionality. Section 9.5 focuses on details of system analysis methodologies. Section 9.6 discusses the topic of quality assurance, which must be considered throughout the design process to ensure a high-quality design. The next three sections describe more complex design examples: Section 9.7 considers a telephone switching system or PBX; Section 9.8 looks at the design of a sophisticated ink jet printer; and Section 9.9 studies the

design of personal digital assistants. Section 9.10 describes the design of television set-top boxes. The next several sections study several real-world design examples. We wrap up with a brief consideration of **systems-on-silicon**—single-chip embedded computing systems.

Design Methodologies

9.2.1 Why Design Methodologies?

This section considers the complete **design methodology**—a **design process**—for embedded computing systems. Process is important because without it, we can't reliably deliver the products we want to create. Thinking about the sequence of steps necessary to build something may seem superfluous. But the fact is that everyone has their own design process, even if they don't articulate it. If you are designing embedded systems in your basement by yourself, having your own work habits is fine. But when several people work together on a project, they need to agree on who will do things and how they will get done. Being explicit about process is important when people work together. Therefore, since many embedded computing systems are too complex to be designed and built by one person, we have to think about design processes.

product metrics The obvious goal of a design process is to create a product that does something useful. Typical specifications for a product will include functionality (e.g., personal digital assistant), manufacturing cost (must have a retail price below $200), performance (must power up within 3 seconds), power consumption (must run for 12 hours on two AA batteries), or other properties. Of course, a design process has several important goals beyond function, performance, and power. Three of these goals are summarized below.

- *Time-to-market.* Customers always want new features. The product that comes out first can win the market, even setting customer preferences for future generations of the product. The profitable market life for some products is three to six months—if you are three months late, you will never make money. In some categories, the competition is against the calendar, not just competitors. Calculators, for example, are disproportionately sold just before school starts in the fall. If you miss your market window, you have to wait a year for another sales season.

- *Design cost.* Many consumer products are very cost sensitive. Industrial buyers are also increasingly concerned about cost. The costs of designing the system are distinct from manufacturing cost—the cost of engineers' salaries, computers used in design, and so on must be spread across the units sold. In some cases, only one or a few copies of an embedded system

may be built, so design costs can dominate manufacturing costs. Design costs can also be important for high-volume consumer devices when time-to-market pressures cause teams to swell in size.

■ *Quality.* Customers not only want their products fast and cheap, they also want them to be right. A design methodology that cranks out shoddy products will soon be forced out of the marketplace. Correctness, reliability, and usability must be explicitly addressed from the beginning of the design job to obtain a high-quality product at the end.

Processes evolve over time. They change due to external and internal forces. Customers may change, requirements change, products change, and available components change. Internally, people learn how to do things better, people move on to other projects and others come in, and companies are bought and sold to merge and shape corporate cultures.

Software engineers have spent a great deal of time thinking about software design processes. Much of this thinking has been motivated by mainframe software such as databases. But embedded applications have also inspired some important thinking about software design processes.

A good methodology is critical to building systems that work properly. Delivering buggy systems to customers always causes dissatisfaction. But in some applications, such as medical and automotive systems, bugs create serious safety problems that can endanger the lives of users. We discuss quality in more detail in Section 9.6. As an introduction, Application Example 9-1 describes problems that led to the loss of an unmanned Martian space probe.

Application Example 9-1

Loss of the Mars Climate Observer

In September 1999, the Mars Climate Observer, an unmanned U.S. spacecraft designed to study Mars, was lost—it most likely exploded as it heated up in the atmosphere of Mars after approaching the planet too closely. The spacecraft came too close to Mars because of a series of problems, according to an analysis by *IEEE Spectrum* and contributing editor James Oberg [Obe99]. From an embedded systems perspective, the first problem is best classified as a requirements problem. The contractors who built the spacecraft at Lockheed Martin calculated values for flight controllers at the Jet Propulsion Laboratory (JPL). JPL did not specify the physical units to be used, but they expected them to be in newtons. The Lockheed Martin engineers returned values in units of pound force. This discrepancy resulted in trajectory adjustments being 4.45 times larger than they should have been. The error was not caught

by a software configuration process nor was it caught by manual inspections. Although there were concerns about the spacecraft's trajectory, errors in the calculation of the spacecraft's position were not caught in time.

9.2.2 Design Flows

A **design flow** is a sequence of steps to be followed during a design. Some of the steps can be performed by tools, such as compilers or CAD systems; other steps can be performed by hand. In this section we look at the basic characteristics of design flows.

waterfall model Figure 9-1 shows the **waterfall model** introduced by Royce [Dav90], the first model proposed for the software development process. The waterfall development model consists of five major phases: *requirements* analysis determines the basic characteristics of the system; *architecture* design decomposes the functionality into major components; *coding* implements the pieces and integrates them; *testing* uncovers bugs; and *maintenance* entails deployment in the field, bug fixes, and upgrades. The waterfall model gets its name from the largely one-way flow of work and information from higher levels of abstraction to more detailed design steps (with a limited amount of feedback to the next-higher level of abstraction). Although top-down design is ideal since it implies good foreknowledge of the implementation during early design phases, most designs are clearly not quite so top down. Most design projects entail experimentation and changes that require bottom-up feedback. As a result, the waterfall model is today cited as an unrealistic design process. However, it is

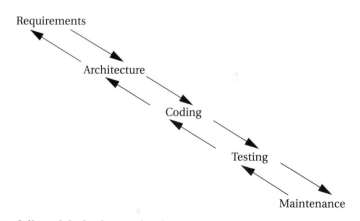

Figure 9-1 *The waterfall model of software development.*

spiral model

important to know what the waterfall model is to be able to understand how others are reacting against it.

Figure 9-2 illustrates an alternative model of software development, called the **spiral model** [Boe87]. While the waterfall model assumes that the system is built once in its entirety, the spiral model assumes that several versions of the system will be built. Early systems will be simple mock-ups constructed to aid designers' intuition and to build experience with the system. As design progresses, more complex systems will be constructed. At each level of design, the designers go through requirements, construction, and testing phases. At later stages when more complete versions of the system are constructed, each phase requires more work, widening the design spiral. This successive refinement approach helps the designers understand the system they are working on through a series of design cycles. The first cycles at the top of the spiral are very small and short, while the final cycles at the spiral's bottom add detail learned from the earlier cycles of the spiral. The spiral model is more realistic than the waterfall model because multiple iterations are often necessary to add enough detail to complete a design. However, a spiral methodology with too many spirals may take too long when design time is a major requirement.

successive refinement

Figure 9-3 shows a **successive refinement** design methodology. In this approach, the system is built several times. A first system is used as a rough

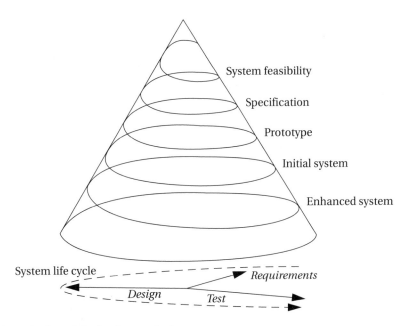

Figure 9-2 *The spiral model of software design.*

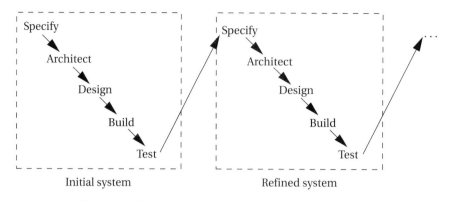

Figure 9-3 *A successive refinement development model.*

prototype, and successive models of the system are further refined. This methodology makes sense when you are relatively unfamiliar with the application domain for which you are building the system. Refining the system by building several increasingly complex systems allows you to test out architecture and design techniques. The various iterations may also be only partially completed; for example, continuing an initial system only through the detailed design phase may teach you enough to help you avoid many mistakes in a second design iteration that is carried through to completion.

Embedded computing systems often involve the design of hardware as well as software. Even if you aren't designing a board, you may be selecting boards and plugging together multiple hardware components as well as writing code. Figure 9-4 shows a design methodology for a combined hardware/software project. Front-end activities such as specification and architecture simultaneously consider hardware and software aspects. Similarly, back-end integration and testing consider the entire system. In the middle, however, development of hardware and software components can go on relatively independently—while testing of one will require stubs of the other, most of the hardware and software work can proceed relatively independently.

hierarchical design flows In fact, many complex embedded systems are themselves built of smaller designs. The complete system may require the design of significant software components, application-specific integrated circuits (ASICs), and so on, and these in turn may be built from smaller components that need to be designed. The design flow follows the levels of abstraction in the system, from complete system design flows at the most abstract to design flows for individual components. The design flow for these complex systems resembles the flow shown in Figure 9-5. The implementation phase of a flow is itself a complete flow from specification through testing. In such a large project, each flow will probably be handled by separate people or teams. The teams must rely on each other's

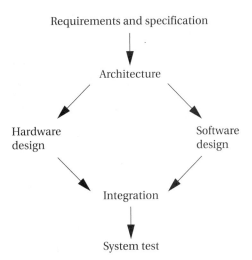

Figure 9-4 *A simple hardware/software design methodology.*

results. The component teams take their requirements from the team handling the next higher level of abstraction, and the higher-level team relies on the quality of design and testing performed by the component team. Good communication is vital in such large projects.

concurrent engineering

When designing a large system along with many people, it is easy to lose track of the complete design flow and have each designer take a narrow view of his or her role in the design flow. **Concurrent engineering** attempts to take a broader approach and optimize the total flow. Reduced design time is an important goal for concurrent engineering, but it can help with any aspect of the design that cuts across the design flow, such as reliability, performance, power consumption, and so on. It tries to eliminate "over-the-wall" design steps, in which one designer performs an isolated task and then throws the result over the wall to the next designer, with little interaction between the two. In particular, reaping the most benefits from concurrent engineering usually requires eliminating the wall between design and manufacturing. Concurrent engineering efforts are comprised of the elements described below.

- *Cross-functional teams* include members from various disciplines involved in the process, including manufacturing, hardware and software design, marketing, and so forth.

- *Concurrent product realization* process activities are at the heart of concurrent engineering. Doing several things at once, such as designing various subsystems simultaneously, is critical to reducing design time.

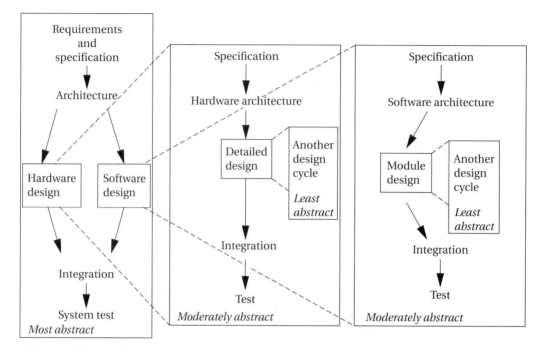

Figure 9-5 *A hierarchical design flow for an embedded system.*

- *Incremental information sharing* and use helps minimize the chance that concurrent product realization will lead to surprises. As soon as new information becomes available, it is shared and integrated into the design. Cross-functional teams are important to the effective sharing of information in a timely fashion.

- *Integrated project management* ensures that someone is responsible for the entire project, and that responsibility is not abdicated once one aspect of the work is done.

- *Early and continual supplier involvement* helps make the best use of suppliers' capabilities.

- *Early and continual customer focus* helps ensure that the product best meets customers' needs.

Example 9-1 describes the experiences of a telephone system design organization with concurrent engineering.

Example 9-1

Concurrent Engineering Applied to Telephone Systems

A group at AT&T applied concurrent engineering to the design of PBXs (telephone switching systems) [Gat94]. The company had a large existing organization and methodology for designing PBXs; their goal was to reengineer their process to reduce design time and make other improvements to the end product. They used the seven-step process described below.

1. *Benchmarking.* They compared themselves to competitors and found that it took them 30% longer to introduce a new product than their best competitors. Based on this study, they decided to shoot for a 40% reduction in design time.

2. *Breakthrough improvement.* Next, they identified the factors that would influence their effort. Three major factors were identified: increased partnership between design and manufacturing; continued existence of the basic organization of design labs and manufacturing; and support of managers at least two levels above the working level. As a result, three groups were established to help manage the effort. A *steering committee* was formed by midlevel managers to provide feedback on the project. A *project office* was formed by an engineering manager and an operations analyst from the AT&T internal consulting organization. Finally, a *core team* of engineers and analysts was formed to make things happen.

3. *Characterization of the current process.* The core team built flowcharts and used other techniques to understand the current product development process. The existing design and manufacturing process resembled the figure below.

 The core team identified several root causes of delays that had to be remedied. First, too many design and manufacturing tasks were performed sequentially. Second, groups tended to focus on intermediate milestones related to their narrow job descriptions, rather than trying to take into account the effects of their decisions on other aspects of the development process. Third, too much time was spent waiting in queues—jobs were handed off from one person to another very frequently. In many cases, the recipient of a set of jobs didn't know how to best prioritize the incoming tasks. Fixing this problem was deemed to be fundamentally a managerial problem, not a technical one. Finally, the team found that too many groups had their own design databases, creating redundant data that had to be maintained and synchronized.

4. *Create the target process.* Based on its studies, the core team created a model for the new development process, which is reproduced below.

From [Gat94].

From [Gat94].

5. *Verify the new process.* The team undertook a pilot product development project to test the new process. The process was found to be basically sound. Some challenges were identified; for example, in the sequential project the design of circuit boards took longer than that of the mechanical enclosures, while in the new process the enclosures ended up taking longer, pointing out the need to start designing them earlier.

6. *Implement across the product line.* After the pilot project, the new methodology was rolled out across the product lines. This activity required training of personnel, documentation of the new standards and procedures, and improvements to information systems.

7. *Measure results and improve.* The performance of the new design flow was measured. The team found that product development time had been reduced from 18–30 months to 11 months.

9.3 Requirements Analysis

Before designing a system, we need to know what we are designing. The terms "requirements" and "specifications" are used in a variety of ways—some people use them as synonyms, while others use them as distinct phases. We use them to mean related but distinct steps in the design process. **Requirements** are informal descriptions of what the customer wants, while **specifications** are more detailed, precise, and consistent descriptions of the system that can be used to create the architecture. Both requirements and specifications are, however, directed to the outward behavior of the system, not its internal structure.

The overall goal of creating a requirements document is effective communication between the customers and the designers. The designers should know what they are expected to design for the customers; the customers, whether they are known in advance or represented by marketing, should understand what they will get.

functional and nonfunctional requirements

We have two types of requirements: **functional** and **nonfunctional.** A functional requirement states what the system must do, such as compute an FFT. A nonfunctional requirement can be any number of other attributes, including physical size, cost, power consumption, design time, reliability, and so on.

A good set of requirements should meet several tests [Dav90]:

- *Correctness:* The requirements should not mistakenly describe what the customer wants. Part of correctness is avoiding overrequiring—the requirements should not add conditions that are not really necessary.

- *Unambiguousness:* The requirements document should be clear and have only one plain language interpretation.

- *Completeness:* All requirements should be included.

- *Verifiability:* There should be a cost-effective way to ensure that each requirement is satisfied in the final product. For example, a requirement that the system package be "attractive" would be hard to verify without some agreed upon definition of attractiveness.

- *Consistency:* One requirement should not contradict another requirement.

- *Modifiability:* The requirements document should be structured so that it can be modified to meet changing requirements without losing consistency, verifiability, and so forth.

- *Traceability:* Each requirement should be traceable in the following ways:

 — We should be able to trace backward from the requirements to know why each requirement exists.

 — We should also be able to trace forward from documents created before the requirements (e.g., marketing memos) to understand how they relate to the final requirements.

 — We should be able to trace forward to understand how each requirement is satisfied in the implementation.

 — We should also be able to trace backward from the implementation to know which requirements they were intended to satisfy.

How do you determine requirements? If the product is a continuation of a series, then many of the requirements are well understood. But even in the most modest upgrade, talking to the customer is valuable. In a large company, marketing or sales departments may do most of the work of asking customers what they want, but a surprising number of companies have designers talk directly with customers. Direct customer contact gives the designer an unfiltered sample of what the customer says. It also helps build empathy with the customer, which often pays off in cleaner, easier-to-use customer interfaces. Talking to the customer may also include conducting surveys, organizing focus groups, or asking selected customers to test a mock-up or prototype.

Specifications

In this section we take a look at some advanced techniques for specification and how they can be used.

9.4.1 Control-Oriented Specification Languages

SDL

We have already seen how to use state machines to specify control in UML. An example of a widely used state machine specification language is the **SDL language** [Roc82], which was developed by the communications industry for specifying communication protocols, telephone systems, and so forth. As illustrated in Figure 9-6, SDL specifications include states, actions, and both conditional and unconditional transitions between states. SDL is an event-oriented state machine model since transitions between states are caused by internal and external events.

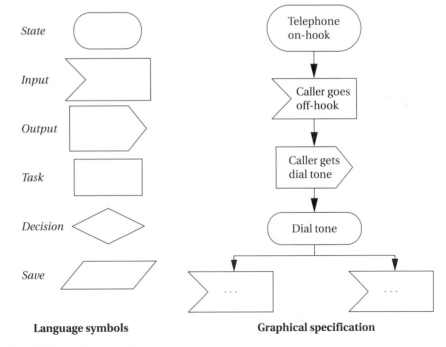

Figure 9-6 *The SDL specification language.*

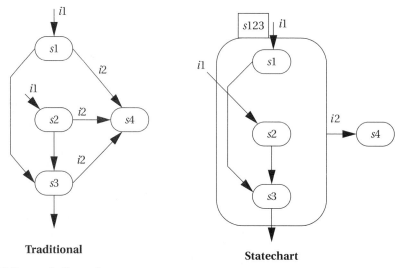

Traditional

Statechart

Figure 9-7 *An OR state in Statecharts.*

Statecharts
Other techniques can be used to eliminate clutter and clarify the important structure of a state-based specification. The **Statechart** [Har87] is one well-known technique for state-based specification that introduced some important concepts. The Statechart notation uses an event-driven model. Statecharts allow states to be grouped together to show common functionality. There are two basic groupings: OR and AND. Figure 9-7 shows an example of an OR state by comparing a traditional state transition diagram with a Statechart described via an OR state. The state machine specifies that the machine goes to state *s4* from any of *s1*, *s2*, or *s3* when they receive the input *i2*. The Statechart denotes this commonality by drawing an OR state around *s1*, *s2*, and *s3* (the name of the OR state is given in the small box at the top of the state). A single transition out of the OR state *s123* specifies that the machine goes into state *s4* when it receives the *i2* input while in any state included in *s123*. The OR state still allows interesting transitions between its member states. There can be multiple ways to get into *s123* (via *s1* or *s2*), and there can be transitions between states within the OR state (such as from *s1* to *s3* or *s2* to *s3*). The OR state is simply a tool for specifying some of the transitions relating to these states.

Figure 9-8 shows an example of an AND state specified in Statechart notation as compared to the equivalent in the traditional state machine model. In the traditional model, there are numerous transitions between the states; there is also one entry point into this cluster of states and one exit transition out of the cluster.

Figure 9-8 *An AND state in Statecharts.*

In the *Statechart*, the AND state *sab* is decomposed into two components, *sa* and *sb*. When the machine enters the AND state, it simultaneously inhabits the state *s1* of component *sa* and the state *s3* of component *sb*. We can think of the system's state as multidimensional. When it enters *sab*, knowing the complete state of the machine requires examining both *sa* and *sb*.

The names of the states in the traditional state machine reveal their relationship to the AND state components. Thus, state *s1-3* corresponds to the Statechart machine having its *sa* component in *s1* and its *sb* component in *s3*, and so forth. We can exit this cluster of states to go to state *s5* only when, in the traditional specification, we are in state *s2-4* and receive input *r*. In the AND state, this corresponds to *sa* in state *s2*, *sb* in state *s4*, and the machine receiving the *r* input while in this composite state. Although the *traditional* and *Statechart* models describe the same behavior, each component has only two states, and the relationships between these states are much simpler to see.

AND/OR tables Leveson et al. [Lev94] used a different format, the **AND/OR table,** to describe similar relationships between states. An example AND/OR table and the Boolean expression it describes are shown in Figure 9-9. The rows in the AND/OR table are labeled with the basic variables in the expresseion. Each column corresponds to an AND term in the expression. For example, the AND term (*cond2* and not *cond3*) is represented in the second column with a *T* for *cond2*, an *F* for *cond3*, and a dash (don't-care) for *cond1*; this corresponds to the fact that *cond2* must be *T* and *cond3* *F* for the AND term to be true. We use the table to evaluate whether a given condition holds in the system. The current states of the variables are compared to the table elements. A column evaluates to true if all the current variable values correspond to the requirements

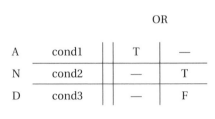

cond1 or (cond2 and !cond3)

Expression

		OR	
A	cond1	T	—
N	cond2	—	T
D	cond3	—	F

AND/OR table

Figure 9-9 *An AND/OR table.*

given in the column. If any one of the columns evaluates to true, then the table's expression evaluates to true, as we would expect for an AND/OR expression. The most important difference between this notation and Statecharts is that don't-cares are explicitly represented in the table, which was found to be of great help in identifying problems in a specification table.

9.4.2 Advanced Specifications

This section is devoted to a single example of a sophisticated system. Application Example 9-2 describes the specification of a real-world, safety-critical system used in aircraft. The specification techniques developed to ensure the correctness and safety of this system can also be used in many applications, particularly in systems where much of the complexity goes into the control structure.

Application Example 9-2

The TCAS II Specification

TCAS II (Traffic Alert and Collision Avoidance System) is a collision avoidance system for aircraft. Based on a variety of information, a TCAS unit in an aircraft keeps track of the position of other nearby aircraft. If TCAS decides that a mid-air collision may be likely, it uses audio commands to suggest evasive action—

for example, a prerecorded voice may warn "DESCEND! DESCEND!" if TCAS believes that an aircraft above poses a threat and that there is room to maneuver below. TCAS makes sophisticated decisions in real time and is clearly safety critical. On the one hand, it must detect as many potential collision events as possible (within the limits of its sensors, etc.). On the other hand, it must generate as few false alarms as possible, since the extreme maneuvers it recommends are themselves potentially dangerous.

Leveson et al. [Lev94] developed a specification for the TCAS II system. We won't cover the entire specification here, but just enough to provide its flavor. The TCAS II specification was written in their RSML language. They use a modified version of Statechart notation for specifying states, in which the inputs to and outputs of the state are made explicit. The notation is illustrated below.

They also use a transition bus to show sets of states in which there are transitions between all (or almost all) states. In the following example, there are transitions from a, b, c, or d to any of the other states:

The top-level description of the collision avoidance system (CAS) appears below.

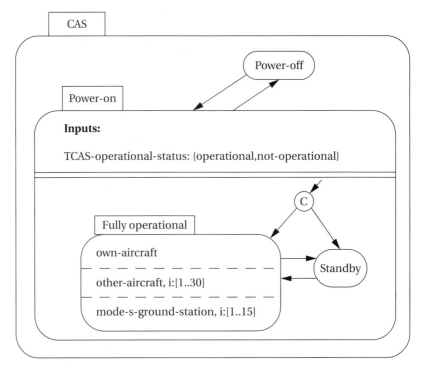

CAS

Power-off

Power-on

Inputs:

TCAS-operational-status: {operational,not-operational}

C

Fully operational

own-aircraft

other-aircraft, i:[1..30]

mode-s-ground-station, i:[1..15]

Standby

From [Lev94].

This diagram specifies that the system has *Power-off* and *Power-on* states. In the power-on state, the system may be in *Standby* or *Fully operational* mode. In the *Fully operational* mode, three components are operating in parallel, as specified by the AND state: the *own-aircraft* subsystem, a subsystem to keep track of up to 30 other aircraft, and a subsystem to keep track of up to 15 Mode S ground stations, which provide radar information.

The next diagram shows a specification of the *Own-Aircraft* AND state. Once again, the behavior of *Own-Aircraft* is an AND composition of several subbehaviors. The *Effective-SL* and *Alt-SL* states are two ways to control the sensitivity level (SL) of the system, with each state representing a different sensitivity level. Differing sensitivities are required depending on distance from the ground and other factors. The *Alt-Layer* state divides the vertical airspace into layers, with this state keeping track of the current layer. *Climb-Inhibit* and *Descent-Inhibit* states are used to selectively inhibit climbs (which may be difficult at high altitudes) or descents (clearly dangerous near the ground), respectively. Similarly, the *Increase-Climb-Inhibit* and *Increase-Descend-Inhibit* states can inhibit high-rate climbs and descents. Because the *Advisory-Status* state is rather complicated, its details are not shown here.

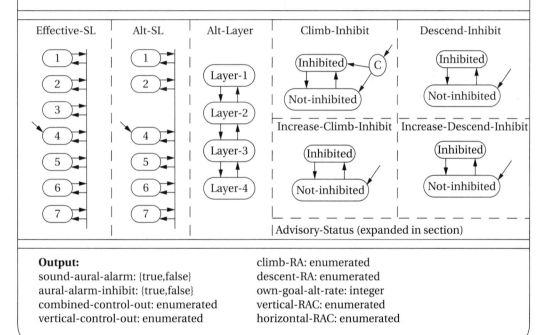

Own-Aircraft

Input:
own-alt-radio: integer
standby-discrete-input: {true,false}
own-alt-barometric: integer
mode-selector: {TA/RA,standby,TA-only,3,4,5,6,7}
radio-altimeter-status: {valid,not-valid}
own-air-status: {airborne,on-ground}
own-mode-s-address: integer
barometric-altimeter-status: {fine-coarse}

traffic-display-permitted: {true,false}
aircraft-altitude-limit: integer
prox-traffic-display: {true,false}
own-alt-rate: integer
config-climb-inhibit: {true,false}
altitude-climb-inhib-active: {true,false}
increase-climb-inhibit-discrete: {true,false}

Effective-SL Alt-SL Alt-Layer Climb-Inhibit Descend-Inhibit

Increase-Climb-Inhibit Increase-Descend-Inhibit

Advisory-Status (expanded in section)

Output:
sound-aural-alarm: {true,false}
aural-alarm-inhibit: {true,false}
combined-control-out: enumerated
vertical-control-out: enumerated

climb-RA: enumerated
descent-RA: enumerated
own-goal-alt-rate: integer
vertical-RAC: enumerated
horizontal-RAC: enumerated

From [Lev94].

9.5 System Analysis and Architecture Design

In this section we consider how to turn a specification into an architecture design. We already have a number of techniques for making specific decisions;

in this section we look at how to get a handle on the overall system architecture. The CRC card methodology for system analysis is one very useful method for understanding the overall structure of a complex system.

9.5.1 CRC Cards

The **CRC card** methodology is a well-known and useful way to help analyze a system's structure. It is particularly well suited to object-oriented design since it encourages the encapsulation of data and functions.

The acronym *CRC* stands for the following three major items that the methodology tries to identify:

- *Classes* define the logical groupings of data and functionality.

- *Responsibilities* describe what the classes do.

- *Collaborators* are the other classes with which a given class works.

The name *CRC card* comes from the fact that the methodology is practiced by having people write on index cards. (In the United States, the standard size for index cards is 3" × 5", so these cards are often called 3 × 5 cards.) An example card is shown in Figure 9-10; it has space to write down the class name, its responsibilities and collaborators, and other information. The essence of the CRC card methodology is to have people write on these cards, talk about them, and update the cards until they are satisfied with the results.

This technique may seem like a primitive way to design computer systems. However, it has several important advantages. First, it is easy to get noncomputer people to create CRC cards. Getting the advice of domain experts (auto-

```
Class name:
Superclasses:
Subclasses:
Responsibilities:        Collaborators:
```

```
Class name:
Class's function:
Attributes:
```

 Front **Back**

Figure 9-10 *Layout of a CRC card.*

mobile designers for automotive electronics or human factors experts for PDA design, for example) is very important in system design. The CRC card methodology is informal enough that it will not intimidate noncomputer specialists and will allow you to capture their input. Second, it aids even computer specialists by encouraging them to work in a group and analyze scenarios. The walkthrough process used with CRC cards is very useful in scoping out a design and determining what parts of a system are poorly understood. This informal technique is valuable to tool-based design and coding. If you still feel a need to use tools to help you practice the CRC methodology, software engineering tools are available that automate the creation of CRC cards.

Before going through the methodology, let's review the CRC concepts in a little more detail. We are familiar with classes—they encapsulate functionality. A class may represent a real-world object or it may describe an object that has been created solely to help architect the system. A class has both an internal state and a functional interface; the functional interface describes the class's capabilities. The responsibility set is an informal way of describing that functional interface. The responsibilities provide the class's interface, not its internal implementation. Unlike describing a class in a programming language, however, the responsibilities may be described informally in English (or your favorite language). The collaborators of a class are simply the classes that it talks to, that is, classes that use its capabilities or that it calls upon to help it do its work.

The class terminology is a little misleading when an object-oriented programmer looks at CRC cards. In the methodology, a class is actually used more like an object in an OO programming language—the CRC card class is used to represent a real actor in the system. However, the CRC card class is easily transformable into a class definition in an object-oriented design.

CRC card analysis is performed by a team of people. It is possible to use it by yourself, but a lot of the benefit of the method comes from talking about the developing classes with others. Before becoming the process, you should create a large number of CRC cards using the basic format shown in Figure 9-10. As you are working in your group, you will be writing on these cards; you will probably discard many of them and rewrite them as the system evolves. The CRC card methodology is informal, but you should go through the following steps when using it to analyze a system:

1. *Develop an initial list of classes.* Write down the class name and perhaps a few words on what it does. A class may represent a real-world object or an architectural object. Identifying which category the class falls into (perhaps by putting a star next to the name of a real-world object) is helpful. Each person can be responsible for handling a part of the system, but team members should talk during this process to be sure that no classes are missed and that duplicate classes are not created.

2. *Write an initial list of responsibilities and collaborators.* The responsibilities list helps describe in a little more detail what the class does. The collaborators list should be built from obvious relationships between classes. Both the responsibilities and collaborators will be refined in the later stages.

3. *Create some usage scenarios.* These scenarios describe what the system does. Scenarios probably begin with some type of outside stimulus, which is one important reason for identifying the relevant real-world objects.

4. *Walk through the scenarios.* This is the heart of the methodology. During the walkthrough, each person on the team represents one or more classes. The scenario should be simulated by acting: people can call out what their class is doing, ask other classes to perform operations, and so on. Moving around, for example, to show the transfer of data, may help you visualize the system's operation. During the walkthrough, all of the information created so far is targeted for updating and refinement, including the classes, their responsibilities and collaborators, and the usage scenarios. Classes may be created, destroyed, or modified during this process. You will also probably find many holes in the scenario itself.

5. *Refine the classes, responsibilities, and collaborators.* Some of this will be done during the course of the walkthrough, but making a second pass after the scenarios is a good idea. The longer perspective will help you make more global changes to the CRC cards.

6. *Add class relationships.* Once the CRC cards have been refined, subclass and superclass relationships should become clearer and can be added to the cards.

Once you have the CRC cards, you need to somehow use them to help drive the implementation. In some cases, it may work best to use the CRC cards as direct source material for the implementors; this is particularly true if you can get the designers involved in the CRC card process. In other cases, you may want to write a more formal description, in UML or another language, of the information that was captured during the CRC card analysis, and then use that formal description as the design document for the system implementors.

Example 9-2 illustrates the use of the CRC card methodology.

Example 9-2

CRC Card Analysis

Let's perform a CRC card analysis of the elevator system of Section 8.6. First, we need the following basic set of classes:

- *Real-world classes:* elevator car, passenger, floor control, car control, and car sensor.

- *Architectural classes:* car state, floor control reader, car control reader, car control sender, and scheduler.

For each class, we need the following initial set of responsibilities and collaborators. (An asterisk is used to remind ourselves which classes represent real-world objects.)

Class	Responsibilities	Collaborators
Elevator car*	Moves up and down	Car control, car sensor, car control sender
Passenger*	Pushes floor control and car control buttons	Floor control, car control
Floor control*	Transmits floor requests	Passenger, floor control reader
Car control*	Transmits car requests	Passenger, car control reader
Car sensor*	Senses car position	Scheduler
Car state	Records current position of car	Scheduler, car sensor
Floor control reader	Interface between floor control and rest of system	Floor control, scheduler
Car control reader	Interface between car control and rest of system	Car control, scheduler
Car control sender	Interface between scheduler and car	Scheduler, elevator car
Scheduler	Sends commands to cars based upon requests	Floor control reader, car control reader, car control sender, car state

Several usage scenarios define the basic operation of the elevator system as well as some unusual scenarios:

1. One passenger requests a car on a floor, gets in the car when it arrives, requests another floor, and gets out when the car reaches that floor.

2. One passenger requests a car on a floor, gets in the car when it arrives, and requests the floor that the car is currently on.

3. A second passenger requests a car while another passenger is riding in the elevator.

4. Two people push floor buttons on different floors at the same time.

5. Two people push car control buttons in different cars at the same time.

At this point, we need to walk through the scenarios and make sure they are reasonable. Find a set of people and walk through these scenarios. Do the classes, responsibilities, collaborators, and scenarios make sense? How would you modify them to improve the system specification?

9.6 Quality Assurance

The quality of a product or service can be judged by how well it satisfies its intended function. A product can be of low quality for several reasons, such as it was shoddily manufactured, its components were improperly designed, its architecture was poorly conceived, and the product's requirements were poorly understood. Quality must be designed in. You can't test out enough bugs to deliver a high-quality product. The **quality assurance (QA)** process is vital for the delivery of a satisfactory system. In this section we will concentrate on portions of the methodology particularly aimed at improving the quality of the resulting system.

The software testing techniques described earlier in the book constitute one component of quality assurance, but the pursuit of quality extends throughout the design flow. For example, settling on the proper requirements and specification cannot be overlooked as an important determinant of quality. If the system is too difficult to design, it will probably be difficult to keep it working properly. Customers may desire features that sound nice but in fact don't add much to the overall usefulness of the system. In many cases, having too many features only makes the design more complicated and the final device more prone to breakage.

In this section, we review the quality assurance process in more detail. Section 9.6.1 introduces the quality assurance process, Section 9.6.2 focuses on verifying requirements and specifications, Section 9.6.3 discusses design reviews, and Section 9.6.4 examines measurement-driven quality assurance.

To help us understand the importance of quality assurance, Application Example 9-3 describes serious safety problems in one computer-controlled medical system. Medical equipment, like aviation electronics, is a safety-critical application; unfortunately, this medical equipment caused deaths before its design errors were properly understood. This example also allows us

to use specification techniques to understand software design problems. In the rest of the section, we look at several ways of improving quality: design reviews, measurement-based quality assurance, and techniques for debugging large systems.

Application Example 9-3

The Therac-25 Medical Imaging System

The Therac-25 medical imaging system caused what Leveson and Turner called "the most serious computer-related accidents to date (at least nonmilitary and admitted)" [Lev93]. In the course of six known accidents, these machines delivered massive radiation overdoses, causing deaths and serious injuries. Leveson and Turner analyzed the Therac-25 system and the causes for these accidents.

The Therac-25 was controlled by a PDP-11 minicomputer. The computer was responsible for controlling a radiation gun that delivered a dose of radiation to the patient. It also runs a terminal that presents the main user interface. The machine's software was developed by a single programmer in PDP-11 assembly language over several years. The software includes four major components: stored data, a scheduler, a set of tasks, and interrupt services. The three major critical tasks in the system follow:

- A treatment monitor controls and monitors the setup and delivery of the treatment in eight phases.

- A servo task controls the radiation gun, machine motions, and so on.

- A housekeeper task takes care of system status interlocks and limit checks. (A limit check determines whether some system parameter has gone beyond preset limits.)

The code was relatively crude—the software allowed several processes access to shared memory, there was no synchronization mechanism aside from shared variables, and test-and-set for shared variables were not indivisible operations.

Let us examine the software problems responsible for one series of accidents. Leveson and Turner reverse-engineered a specification for the relevant software as follows:

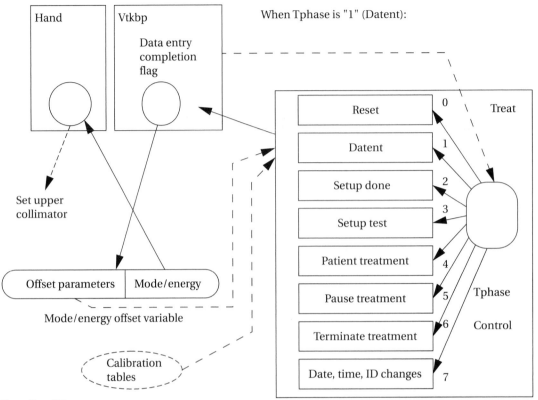

When Tphase is "1" (Datent):

From [Lev 93].

Treat is the treatment monitor task, divided into eight subroutines (*Reset, Datent,* and so on). *Tphase* is a variable that controls which of these subroutines is currently executing. *Treat* reschedules itself after the execution of each subroutine. The *Datent* subroutine communicates with the keyboard entry task via the data entry completion flag, which is a shared variable. *Datent* looks at this flag to determine when it should leave the data entry mode and go to the *Setup test* mode. The *Mode/energy offset* variable is a shared variable: The top byte holds offset parameters used by the *Datent* subroutine, and the low-order byte holds mode and energy offset used by the *Hand* task.

When the machine is run, the operator is forced to enter the mode and energy (there is one mode in which the energy is set to a default), but the operator can later edit the mode and energy separately. The software's behavior is timing dependent. If the keyboard handler sets the completion variable before the operator changes the *Mode/energy* data, the *Datent* task will not detect the change—once *Treat* leaves *Datent*, it will not enter that subroutine again during the treatment. However, the *Hand* task, which runs concurrently, will see

the new *Mode/energy* information. Apparently, the software included no checks to detect the incompatible data.

After the *Mode/energy* data are set, the software sends parameters to a digital/analog converter and then calls a Magnet subroutine to set the bending magnets. Setting the magnets takes about 8 seconds and a subroutine called Ptime is used to introduce a time delay. Due to the way that *Datent*, Magnet, and Ptime are written, it is possible that changes to the parameters made by the user can be shown on the screen but will not be sensed by *Datent*. One accident occurred when the operator initially entered *Mode/energy*, went to the command line, changed Mode/energy, and returned to the command line within 8 seconds. The error therefore depended on the typing speed of the operator. Since operators become faster and more skillful with the machine over time, this error is more likely to occur with experienced operators.

Leveson and Turner emphasize that the following poor design methodologies and flawed architectures were at the root of the particular bugs that led to the accidents:

- The designers performed a very limited safety analysis. For example, low probabilities were assigend to certain errors with no apparent justification.

- Mechanical backups were not used to check the operation of the machine (such as testing beam energy), even though such backups were employed in earlier models of the machine.

- Programmers created overly complex programs based on unreliable coding styles.

In summary, the designers of the Therac-25 relied on system testing with insufficient module testing or formal analysis.

9.6.1 Quality Assurance Techniques

The International Standards Organization (ISO) has created a set of quality standards known as **ISO 9000.** ISO 9000 was created to apply to a broad range of industries, including but not limited to embedded hardware and software. A standard developed for a particular product, such as wooden construction beams, could specify criteria particular to that product, such as the load that a beam must be able to carry. However, a wide-ranging standard such as ISO 9000 cannot specify the detailed standards for every industry. Consequently, ISO 9000 concentrates on processes used to create the product or service. The processes used to satisfy ISO 9000 affect the entire organization as well as the individual steps taken during design and manufacturing.

A detailed description of ISO 9000 is beyond the scope of this book; several books [Sch94, Jen95] describe ISO 9000's applicability to software development. We can, however, make the following observations about quality management based on ISO 9000:

- *Process is crucial.* Haphazard development leads to haphazard products and low quality. Knowing what steps are to be followed to create a high-quality product is essential to ensuring that all the necessary steps are in fact followed.

- *Documentation is important.* Documentation has several roles: The creation of the documents describing processes helps those involved understand the processes; documentation helps internal quality monitoring groups to ensure that the required processes are actually being followed; and documentation also helps outside groups (customers, auditors, etc.) understand the processes and how they are being implemented.

- *Communication is important.* Quality ultimately relies on people. Good documentation is an aid for helping people understand the total quality process. The people in the organization should understand not only their specific tasks but also how their jobs can affect overall system quality.

Many types of techniques can be used to verify system designs and ensure quality. Techniques can be either *manual* or *tool based*. Manual techniques are surprisingly effective in practice. In Section 9.6.3 we discuss design reviews, which are simply meetings at which the design is discussed and which are very successful in identifying bugs. Many of the software testing techniques described in Section 5.9 can be applied manually by tracing through the program to determine the required tests. Tool-based verification helps considerably in managing large quantities of information that may be generated in a complex design. Test generation programs can automate much of the drudgery of creating test sets for programs. Tracking tools can help ensure that various steps have been performed. Design flow tools automate the process of running design data through other tools.

Metrics are important to the quality control process. To know whether we have achieved high levels of quality, we must be able to measure aspects of the system and our design process. We can measure certain aspects of the system itself, such as the execution speed of programs or the coverage of test patterns. We can also measure aspects of the design process, such as the rate at which bugs are found. Section 9.6.4 describes ways in which measurements can be used in the quality assurance process.

Tool and manual techniques must fit into an overall process. The details of that process will be determined by several factors, including the type of product being designed (e.g., video game, laser printer, air traffic control system), the number of units to be manufactured and the time allowed for design, the

existing practices in the company into which any new processes must be integrated, and many other factors. An important role of ISO 9000 is to help organizations study their total process, not just particular segments that may appear to be important at a particular time.

One well-known way of measuring the quality of an organization's software development process is the **Capability Maturity Model (CMM)** developed by Carnegie Mellon University's Software Engineering Institute [SEI99]. The CMM provides a model for judging an organization. It defines the following five levels of maturity:

1. *Initial.* A poorly organized process, with very few well-defined processes. Success of a project depends on the efforts of individuals, not the organization itself.

2. *Repeatable.* This level provides basic tracking mechanisms that allow management to understand cost, scheduling, and how well the systems under development meet their goals.

3. *Defined.* The management and engineering processes are documented and standardized. All projects make use of documented and approved standard methods.

4. *Managed.* This phase makes detailed measurements of the development process and product quality.

5. *Optimizing.* At the highest level, feedback from detailed measurements is used to continually improve the organization's processes.

The Software Engineering Institute has found very few organizations anywhere in the world that meet the highest level of continuous improvement and quite a few organizations that operate under the chaotic processes of the initial level. However, the Capability Maturity Model provides a benchmark by which organizations can judge themselves and use that information for improvement.

9.6.2 Verifying the Specification

The requirements and specification are generated very early in the design process. Verifying the requirements and specification is very important for the simple reason that bugs in the requirements or specification can be extremely expensive to fix later on. Figure 9-11 shows how the cost of fixing bugs grows over the course of the design process (we use the waterfall model as a simple example, but the same holds for any design flow). The longer a bug survives in the system, the more expensive it will be to fix. A coding bug, if not found until after system deployment, will cost money to recall and reprogram existing

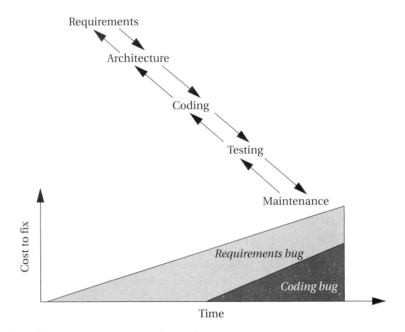

Figure 9-11 *Long-lived bugs are more expensive to fix.*

systems, among other things. But a bug introduced earlier in the flow and not discovered until the same point will accrue all those costs and more costs as well. A bug introduced in the requirements or specification and left until maintenance could force an entire redesign of the product, not just the replacement of a ROM. Discovering bugs early is crucial because it prevents bugs from being released to customers, minimizes design costs, and reduces design time. While some requirements and specification bugs will become apparent in the detailed design stages—for example, as the consequences of certain requirements are better understood—it is possible and desirable to weed out many bugs during the generation of the requirements and spec.

The goal of validating the requirements and specification is to ensure that they satisfy the criteria we originally applied in Section 9.3 to creating the specification, including correctness, completeness, consistency, and so on. Validation is in fact part of the effort of generating the requirements and specification. Some techniques can be applied while they are being created to help you understand the requirements and specifications, while others are applied on a draft, with results used to modify the specs.

requirements validation Since requirements come from the customer and are inherently somewhat informal, it may seem like a challenge to validate them. However, there are many things that can be done to ensure that the customer and the person actually writing the requirements are communicating. **Prototypes** are a very

existing practices in the company into which any new processes must be integrated, and many other factors. An important role of ISO 9000 is to help organizations study their total process, not just particular segments that may appear to be important at a particular time.

One well-known way of measuring the quality of an organization's software development process is the **Capability Maturity Model (CMM)** developed by Carnegie Mellon University's Software Engineering Institute [SEI99]. The CMM provides a model for judging an organization. It defines the following five levels of maturity:

1. *Initial.* A poorly organized process, with very few well-defined processes. Success of a project depends on the efforts of individuals, not the organization itself.

2. *Repeatable.* This level provides basic tracking mechanisms that allow management to understand cost, scheduling, and how well the systems under development meet their goals.

3. *Defined.* The management and engineering processes are documented and standardized. All projects make use of documented and approved standard methods.

4. *Managed.* This phase makes detailed measurements of the development process and product quality.

5. *Optimizing.* At the highest level, feedback from detailed measurements is used to continually improve the organization's processes.

The Software Engineering Institute has found very few organizations anywhere in the world that meet the highest level of continuous improvement and quite a few organizations that operate under the chaotic processes of the initial level. However, the Capability Maturity Model provides a benchmark by which organizations can judge themselves and use that information for improvement.

9.6.2 Verifying the Specification

The requirements and specification are generated very early in the design process. Verifying the requirements and specification is very important for the simple reason that bugs in the requirements or specification can be extremely expensive to fix later on. Figure 9-11 shows how the cost of fixing bugs grows over the course of the design process (we use the waterfall model as a simple example, but the same holds for any design flow). The longer a bug survives in the system, the more expensive it will be to fix. A coding bug, if not found until after system deployment, will cost money to recall and reprogram existing

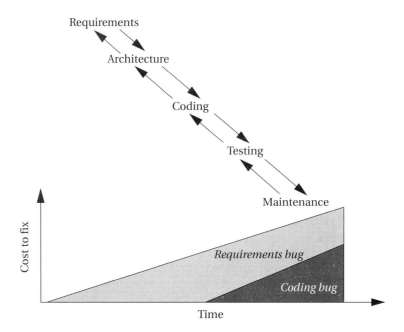

Figure 9-11 *Long-lived bugs are more expensive to fix.*

systems, among other things. But a bug introduced earlier in the flow and not discovered until the same point will accrue all those costs and more costs as well. A bug introduced in the requirements or specification and left until maintenance could force an entire redesign of the product, not just the replacement of a ROM. Discovering bugs early is crucial because it prevents bugs from being released to customers, minimizes design costs, and reduces design time. While some requirements and specification bugs will become apparent in the detailed design stages—for example, as the consequences of certain requirements are better understood—it is possible and desirable to weed out many bugs during the generation of the requirements and spec.

The goal of validating the requirements and specification is to ensure that they satisfy the criteria we originally applied in Section 9.3 to creating the specification, including correctness, completeness, consistency, and so on. Validation is in fact part of the effort of generating the requirements and specification. Some techniques can be applied while they are being created to help you understand the requirements and specifications, while others are applied on a draft, with results used to modify the specs.

requirements validation

Since requirements come from the customer and are inherently somewhat informal, it may seem like a challenge to validate them. However, there are many things that can be done to ensure that the customer and the person actually writing the requirements are communicating. **Prototypes** are a very

useful tool when dealing with end users—rather than simply describe the system to them in broad, technical terms, a prototype can let them see, hear, and touch at least some of the important aspects of the system. Of course, the prototype will not be fully functional since the design work has not yet been done. However, user interfaces in particular are well suited to prototyping and user testing. Canned or randomly generated data can be used to simulate the internal operation of the system. A prototype can help the end user critique numerous functional and nonfunctional requirements, such as data displays, speed of operation, size, weight, and so forth. Certain programming languages, sometimes called **prototyping languages** or **specification languages,** are especially well suited to prototyping. Very high-level languages (such as Matlab in the signal processing domain) may be able to perform functional attributes, such as the mathematical function to be performed, but not nonfunctional attributes such as the speed of execution. **Preexisting systems** can also be used to help the end user articulate his or her needs. Specifying what someone does or doesn't like about an existing machine is much easier than having them talk about the new system in the abstract. In some cases, it may be possible to construct a prototype of the new system from the preexisting system.

specification validation

The techniques used to validate requirements are also useful in verifying that the specifications are correct. Building prototypes, specification languages, and comparisons to preexisting systems are as useful to system analysis and designers as they are to end users. Auditing tools may be useful in verifying consistency, completeness, and so forth. Working through **usage scenarios** often helps designers fill out the details of a specification and ensure its completeness and correctness. In some cases, **formal techniques** (that is, design techniques that make use of mathematical proofs) may be useful. Proofs may be done either manually or automatically. In some cases, proving that a particular condition can or cannot occur according to the specification is important. Automated proofs are particularly useful in certain types of complex systems that can be specified succinctly but whose behavior over time is complex. For example, complex protocols have been successfully formally verified.

9.6.3 Design Reviews

The **design review** [Fag76] is a critical component of any quality assurance process. The design review is a simple, low-cost way to catch bugs early in the design process. A design review is simply a meeting in which team members discuss a design, reviewing how a component of the system works. Some bugs are caught simply by preparing for the meeting, as the designer is forced to think through the design in detail. Other bugs are caught by people attending the meeting, who will notice problems that may not be caught by the unit's designer. By catching bugs early and not allowing them to propagate into the

implementation, we reduce the time required to get a working system. We can also use the design review to improve the quality of the implementation and make future changes easier to implement.

*design review
format*

A design review is held to review a particular component of the system. A design review team has the following members:

- The *designers* of the component being reviewed are, of course, central to the design process. They present their design to the rest of the team for review and analysis.

- The *review leader* coordinates the premeeting activities, the design review itself, and the postmeeting follow-up.

- The *review scribe* records the minutes of the meeting so that designers and others know which problems need to be fixed.

- The *review audience* studies the component. Audience members will naturally include other members of the project for which this component is being designed. Audience members from other projects often add valuable perspective and may notice problems that team members have missed.

The design review process begins before the meeting itself. The design team prepares a set of documents (code listings, flowcharts, specifications, etc.) that will be used to describe the component. These documents are distributed to other members of the review team in advance of the meeting, so that everyone has time to become familiar with the material. The review leader coordinates the meeting time, distribution of handouts, and so forth.

During the meeting, the leader is responsible for ensuring that the meeting runs smoothly, while the scribe takes notes about what happens. The designers are responsible for presenting the component design. A top-down presentation often works well, beginning with the requirements and interface description, followed by the overall structure of the component, the details, and then the testing strategy. The audience should look for all types of problems at every level of detail, including the problems listed below.

- Is the design team's view of the component's specification consistent with the overall system specification, or has the team misinterpreted something?

- Is the interface specification correct?

- Does the component's internal architecture work well?

- Are there coding errors in the component?

- Is the testing strategy adequate?

The notes taken by the scribe are used in meeting follow-up. The design team should correct bugs and address concerns raised at the meeting. While

doing so, the team should keep notes describing what they did. The design review leader coordinates with the design team, both to make sure that the changes are made and to distribute the change results to the audience. If the changes are straightforward, a written report of them is probably adequate. If the errors found during the review caused a major reworking of the component, a new design review meeting for the new implementation, using as many of the original team members as possible, may be useful.

Example 9-3 describes the use of modern software tools for paperless software design reviews.

Example 9-3

Paperless Code Inspections

A paperless code inspection methodology was set up within AT&T Bell Laboratories for large software projects [Hsu94]. The inspection process used the following off-the-shelf tools:

- The Procase SMARTsystem provided facilities for analysis, reverse engineering, and management of C code.

- FrameMaker was used for document preparation.

- nmake, an updated version of the traditional Unix make facility, was used for controlling software builds.

- Sablime was used to control versions of source code.

- The cimgr program was used to annotate documents.

Participants in the code reviews used tools at all points during the process. The moderator could use an on-line calendar to schedule the meeting. The designer used cimgr and the SMARTsystem to store the code, using nmake to ensure that the proper versions were saved. cimgr also allowed the designer to link the source code to Frame documents to provide background documentation. Reviewers used cimgr to find the appropriate set of code and documents for the review and used the other tools to help them review the code; they could also use the annotation tools to provide notes before the meeting. During the meeting, all the participants used cimgr to manage documents and provide annotations, with the moderator eliminating redundant annotations. After the meeting, the designer used the tools to make the changes. cimgr can be used to collect statistics on the meeting, such as the amount of code reviewed, preparation time per inspector, and so forth.

9.6.4 Measurement-Driven Quality Assurance

The design review is an inspection-based system—it cannot be fully automated because we don't have formal criteria for finding all types of bugs. The inspection process is important because there will always be creative ways to introduce bugs that require human analysis. However, we can make measurements of bug rates in our system and use those statistics to help us. Not only do bug statistics help us determine the proper amount of testing for a system, we can also use the knowledge gained in one project to predict where bugs are likely to occur in later projects.

Measurements of the design process are important for the same reason that measurements help us in all sorts of other activities—they provide accurate information that leads to insight. Early studies of software development provide important insight into the software development process, and those basic lessons are still relevant today. One study of software projects at IBM [End75] found that 46% of the errors found in its sample set of software were rooted in misunderstanding of the problem, poor communication, inadequate knowledge of problem-solving techniques, and so forth, while only 38% were amenable to better tools and other technological fixes. Some of the results of another study at IBM [Jon78] are shown in Figure 9-12. These tables show both the original source of the errors and the steps in the development process where they were found (*defect removal efficiency* is simply the ratio of defects found before release to defects found before and after release). These results show that many errors were due to high-level problems such as poor functional design and bad documentation. They also show that defect removal procedures added a small number of new bugs by incorrectly fixing the problems found. On the positive side, the results also show that design reviews caught many errors and that multiple levels of review caught new bugs.

The Hitachi Software Quality Evaluation (SQE) system [Cus91] is one early example of a successful measurement-driven quality assurance program. The SQE methodology kept track of customer-identified defects and, together with information on bugs found during in-house data reviews, predicted the number of bugs to be expected in similar products and identified tests to find these bugs. The Hitachi effort measured relatively simple properties of programs, including program size and structure, amount of code written in high-level languages, number of design and test work hours, as well as other relevant parameters.

The purpose of measuring your design process is not to entirely eliminate bugs—as Figure 9-12 illustrates, even bug removal processes can introduce new bugs. Rather, measurement-driven quality assurance is essential to continuous process improvement. While we cannot expect perfection, we can always improve on what we are doing; measuring design processes and using those results to improve processes allow us to continuously improve how we work and what we do.

Functional design and misunderstandings	15%
Logic design and misunderstandings	20%
Coding problems	30%
Documentation and others (not shown)	35%

Percentage defects by source

	Efficiency % against defects in			% incorrect repairs
	Function	Logic	Coding	
Functional specification review	50	—	—	+1
Logic specification review	40	50	—	+2
Module specification review	60	70	—	+2
Module code inspection	65	75	70	+3
Unit test	10	10	25	+4
Function test	20	25	55	+5
Component test	15	20	65	+5
Subsystem test	15	15	55	+7
System test	10	10	40	+10
Cumulative efficiency	98	98	99	
Net cumulative efficiency	98			

Defect removal efficiency by source

Figure 9-12 *Early statistics on software development [Jon 78].*

Application Example 9-4 describes the quality assurance process for microprocessor-controlled instruments.

Application Example 9-4

Software Quality Assurance for Instruments

Asada and Yan [Asa98] describe improvements they made to the software quality assurance process used at the Hewlett-Packard Kobe Instrument Division. The process they used through the early 1990s separated unit and integration test from system test. The R&D group was responsible for unit

and integration testing; R&D handed over the complete product to a software quality assurance group for system testing. The system test phase occurred just before product shipment.

But as time-to-market pressures reduced the amount of development time available while simultaneously requiring products to be extended with new features, they noticed that more single-function defects made it past unit and integration testing into the system testing phase. Consequently, system testing failed to result in stable defect reporting rates. As illustrated below, defects as a function of time should stabilize for a well-tested product but will continue to climb when testing is incomplete.

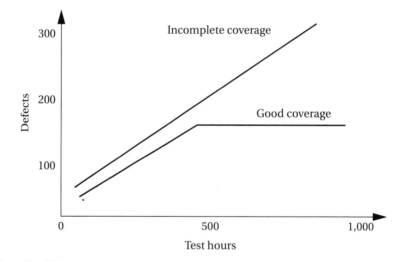

From [Asa98].

They found that, for a product designed in 1990, 17.8% of the defects found in system test were single-function defects, but that number climbed to 48.0% for a product designed in 1996. Because so many single-function defects were making it into system testing, it became more difficult to uncover multiple-function defects. As a result, the cost per function of an enhancement rose from 61.3 hours in 1991 to 132 hours in 1995.

To find bugs earlier and reduce total testing costs, they changed the development process. First, they brought software Q&A into the unit and integration process, rather than waiting until system testing. Bringing in Q&A early helped them integrate design and testing to catch problems earlier. The definition of instrument functions was captured early in tables such as the one below.

Command	Range	Initial value	Description
POIN <val>	2 to 801 (int)	201 (NA,ZA), 801 (SA)	In SWPT != List, set MEAS point of sweep.
SPAN <val> (Hz)	0 to 510 M(Hz)	500 MHz	In SWPT != LIST, set SPAN value of sweep parameter.
STAR <val> (Hz)	0 to max (Hz)	0 Hz	In SWPT != LIST, set START value of sweep parameter. Min and max value of START, STOP, CENTER depend on RBW.
Stop <val> (Hz)	min to 510 M(Hz)	500 MHz	In SWPT != LIST, set STOP value of sweep parameter. Min and max value of START, STOP, CENTER depend on RBW.

From [Asa98].

The function descriptions faciliate the design phase by allowing incomplete function definitions, conflicts between functions, and other problems to be caught early, before code is written. The descriptions are useful in the process by driving an automatic test generation process. Engineers manually write scripts, based on the function descriptions, to automatically generate unit and integration tests. They use equivalence partitioning and boundary value analysis to design test scripts for single-function defects. The function definitions guide the design of tests for multiple-function defects. The test scripts allow tests to be run immediately after new code for a function is written.

The new methodology helped reduce product design costs. The authors compared a Project Y to a Project X product of which Y was an extension. Project X's original design required 1,049 testing hours to find 309 defects. Project Y's tests naturally covered Project X code as well as changes made for Project Y; 88 defects were found in Project X code in 200 hours of testing for Project Y. These 88 defects had remained in Project X even though they had spent over 1,000 hours testing the original product. Engineer-months per defect went from 0.0402 for Project X to 0.0273 in Project Y. As illustrated in the figure below, testing costs declined significantly for Project Y, even though they spent more time on test pattern generation.

From [Asa98].

Design Example

 9.7 **Telephone PBX**

A telephone **private branch exchange (PBX)** presents an interesting array of problems to the embedded system designer, including high data rates, sophisticated functionality, low cost, and high reliability. We will use TigerSwitch, a PC-based PBX designed at Princeton University [Wol96] as the basis for our discussion. The basic principles of TigerSwitch apply to non–PC-based PBXs, such as the ROLM PBX of Application Example 9-5, and some commercial PBXs are in fact built on standard PCs. After describing the basic principles of operation of a PBX, we describe the system architecture.

Application Example 9-5

The ROLM PBX

The ROLM PBX was based on a general-purpose computer. As seen in the figure below, it uses two buses:

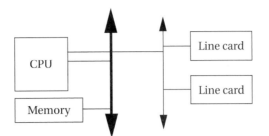

The CPU has one bus for data and instruction fetching. The telephone interfaces (called line cards) were attached to a separate bus. Using two buses kept the CPU operations from interfering with telephone data transfers.

The PBX used data transfers between line cards to make phone calls. At each sampling interval, the CPU would transfer voice data between the phone lines involved in the call. A table in memory told the CPU which phone lines were connected by calls.

9.7.1 Theory of Operation

The first problem is to understand the procedure for completing calls. Each distinct telephone connection is called a *line,* so a call is completed by connecting two lines. We briefly described telephone calls when we designed the answering machine of Section 6.10—remember that a telephone can be on-hook or off-hook and that telephone voice data are sampled at an 8 kHz rate.

When making a call, actions are required on each of the two lines to be connected—one must initiate the call by dialing a number, while the other side must pick up the phone. We can describe the operations on each of the lines using a single state transition graph that covers placing and receiving calls. The state transition graph for a single phone line, showing both placing and receiving calls, is shown in Figure 9-13. To understand the state transition diagram, assume that the phone line starts *on-hook.* When a call is placed to this line, the phone starts to ring. If the phone is *taken off-hook* while the line is ringing, the call is completed. Once the phone is put back *on-hook,* the call is terminated and the line goes back to its initial state. To place a call, the user takes the phone *off-hook.* At this point, the user must wait until a dialing decoder is ready before a *dial tone* is sent over the line. We will see that the dialing decoder consumes significant resources and not all telephones can be dialed simultaneously. Once the *dial tone* is received, the *dialing* procedure can

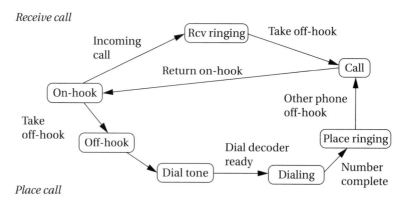

Figure 9-13 *States of a telephone line for making and receiving calls.*

begin. When the PBX recognizes that it has received a complete call, it goes into its own ringing state and waits for an answer. The *rcv ringing* and *place ringing* states are distinct even though they both denote a line ringing: in the *place ringing* state, another line is ringing, while in the *rcv* ringing state this line is ringing.

The behavior of the entire PBX can be understood as a set of loosely coupled state machines, one for each line, as illustrated in Figure 9-14. Each line is represented by a state machine. An additional state machine takes care of the coordination and interaction between lines—for example, when a receiving line goes off-hook, the placing line must be put in the call state. This specification style naturally captures the parallelism in a phone system—calls are independent and do not interact.

One of the important steps in placing a call is routing the call based on the telephone number. If the telephone call is to another line within the PBX, the call is sent there directly. If the call is outside the PBX, then it must be routed through an external line (called a *trunk line*) to another telephone switching system, which requires that the PBX set up a connection with the external switch.

We use *dual-tone multifrequency (DTMF)* dialing rather than pulse dialing. As illustrated in Figure 9-15, each key on a DTMF dialing pad generates two tones when depressed, one to designate its row and another for its column. The PBX senses digits dialed by looking for pairs of frequencies. The two tones must be simultaneously present for at least 0.1 second for a digit to be registered.

The PBX must also collect billing information for all calls. This function requires keeping track of the destination number and duration of each call. The length of a call must be determined accurately to create accurate billing statements. Some telephone companies use their finer time measurement

Figure 9-14 *The PBX as a set of coordinated lines.*

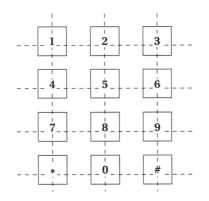

Figure 9-15 *Frequencies assigned to DTMF digits.*

granularity in their marketing, but that finer-grained measurement of call times adds to the CPU load on the PBX.

Finally, the PBX must support standard maintenance operations, such as adding new telephone lines and corresponding phone numbers, updating call routing information, and testing the PBX.

9.7.2 System Architecture

The basic hardware architecture of a PBX is shown in Figure 9-16. Each telephone line is an I/O device. The interface logic between the telephone and the PBX is known as a **line card;** it contains A/D and D/A converters, circuitry for the ringing signal, and so on. The CPU copies data between the line cards to make telephone calls—at each sampling interval, the CPU reads the A/D converter from one line and sends it to the other line's D/A converter, then

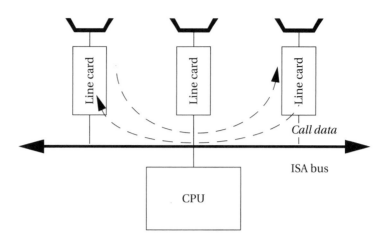

Figure 9-16 *Basic hardware architecture of TigerSwitch.*

performs the copy in the opposite direction. (The standard PC timer cannot generate interrupts at an 8 kHz rate, so we built a special 8 kHz interrupt timer as an I/O card for TigerSwitch.)

Before considering other operations such as dialing, let's determine the architecture of the basic call mechanism. For each call placed, we must perform two reads (from each line's A/D) and two writes (to each line's D/A) at the 8 kHz sampling rate. The specification of Figure 9-14 would suggest that we implement each line as a separate process. However, that would lead to disastrous performance consequences during calls: Each of the two lines involved in a call would have to be activated at the 8 kHz sampling rate. Even a small number of calls would introduce so much context switching overhead as to overload a typical PC.

An alternative is to implement one call handling process that performs the data transfers for all active calls. We build a table that shows the connections between lines. At each sampling interval, we loop through the active calls and perform the necessary transfers as follows:

```
for (i = 0; i < n_calls; i++) {
    /* transfer data from line 1 to line 2 */
    data = read_line(call[i].line1);
    write_line(call[i].line2,data);
    /* transfer data from line 2 to line 1 */
    data = read_line(call[i].line2);
    write_line(call[i].line1,data);
}
```

This code is much more efficient than using separate processes for the lines. The loop structure can be understood as a very simple implementation of the processes. An operating system would keep a table of the current state of all processes; the call[] table in the loop corresponds to that process state table. However, since the loop deals with only a small amount of data, it need not save and restore the complete system state between iterations.

Call initiation and completion can be handled by a lower-priority process that runs much slower than the sampling rate. For instance, when a line goes off-hook, this process can sense the off-hook state by polling the line cards, and then initiate the next action based on the current state of the line.

Sensing the DTMF signals during dialing can be expensive. Since dialing takes a relatively small fraction of the total time a phone line is in use, most switching systems provide only a few DTMF detectors. Thus, when a line goes off-hook, it will not get a dial tone until one of the detectors is available. The tones can be sensed using a bank of filters, one for each frequency. We could use an analog filter bank on each line card, but that would be expensive. (Although our PBX has a relatively small number of line cards, large PBXs have 10,000 line cards, which account for the largest single cost component of the machine.) We can also use digital filters, which can be implemented either on the CPU or on a separate card with a DSP attached to the bus. While it may seem expensive to build a separate card with a DSP solely for DTMF detection, it must be remembered that the digital filters will compete with the call activity when placed on the main CPU. The call handling process is being activated at the 8 kHz rate, and the DTMF detection process would be activated at that rate as well. Since DTMF detection requires more CPU time than call handling, it can cause significant CPU loads. Our experiments indicated that putting DTMF detection on the main CPU would require us to use a Pentium processor, while off-loading DTMF detection to a separate low-end DSP would allow us to use an 80386 for the main CPU. At the time of our project, the difference in cost between the x386 and the Pentium was over $500, while the DSP cost only a few dollars.

Call routing and maintenance can both be implemented as low-priority processes. Call routing has a soft deadline, since we do not want to excessively delay the call setup. Maintenance for the most part does not require deadlines, although certain shutdown operations may require timely execution.

Design Example

9.8 Ink Jet Printer

The HP DesignJet drafting plotter [Boe92, Meb92] is a large ink jet plotter designed for creating engineering drawings. It can plot on paper up to 36 inches wide at a resolution of 300 dots per inch (dpi).

At a very high level, the plotting process is comprised of the steps shown in Figure 9-17. The plot is given to the plotter in a *page description language (PDL).* The original DesignJet used *HP-GL/2,* an HP graphics language, and later versions also used *PostScript,* a well-known page description language. The page description is interpreted and then converted into *raster format,* which describes the picture as a two-dimensional array of dots, very similar to a television picture. At each point in the raster, a quadruplet of intensities for red, green, blue, and black are stored to describe the picture. A plotter controller reads the rasterized image and sends commands to the *plotter carriage* to put ink on paper in accordance with the raster. The plotter carriage and related units are called the *print engine.*

Appearing below are several important considerations in the design of this system.

■ *Memory space is important.* A complete 36-inch plot described at 300 dpi would require a large amount of memory. Memory is always a significant cost factor and at the time this system was designed, using a brute force solution and requiring enough memory to rasterize a complete D-size plot

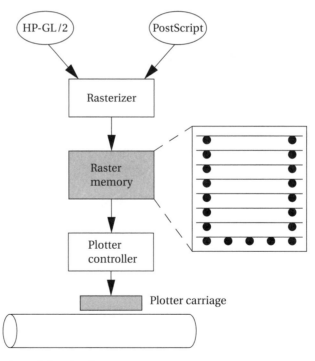

Figure 9-17 *A high-level view of the plotting process.*

would make the system too expensive for most of the target customers. A variety of techniques had to be developed to reduce the amount of raster memory.

- *Real-time control is required.* The ink jet requires some very high-speed control in order to transfer the ink from the cartridge to the paper. The intensity of each ink jet must be carefully controlled based on the rasterized information. In addition, the ink jet head must be scanned across the page and the paper must be moved up and down with servos.

- *Multiple events are happening at once.* While the ink jets are spitting ink, the head is moving across the paper. The paper may move at the same time as the carriage is being positioned for the next pass.

The design team considered several different architectures early in the project. They first considered specialized graphics processors, but found that they were much too slow for parsing the page description language. They then considered using a general-purpose processor for parsing and other tasks while using a graphics chip for raster conversion. This architecture was deemed too expensive since in general parsing and raster conversion would not be running simultaneously.

The design team finally chose a single RISC microprocessor, the Intel 80960KA, to perform parsing, rasterization, and print engine control. One reason to choose the 960 was that its bus multiplexes address and data, which reduces the pin count for the application-specific ICs (ASICs) that would be used to speed up certain functions. Another reason was that another version, the 960KB, had a floating-point unit and was pin compatible with the KA. If they determined in midproject that faster floating-point arithmetic was required, the design could easily be upgraded.

Other decisions made early in the design process are summarized below.

- The design team decided to add a modular I/O (MIO) port to allow I/O ports to be added to the machine by the user. The RS-232/422 and parallel interfaces were retained as basic interfaces. MIO modules for both HP-IB (an instrumentation bus) and Ethernet were provided.

- They decided against using a disk to hold intermediate data during plotting. A disk would have added too much to the cost of the plotter. However, since some users with more complex plots might need more memory, they chose to add sockets for single inline memory modules (SIMMs).

To understand the plotter, let's first look at the hardware architecture and then the software that runs on that hardware platform.

9.8.1 Hardware Design

The hardware architecture is shown in Figure 9-18. This system is rather complex, including a RISC microprocessor, two microcontrollers, and three application-specific ICs (ASICs). This architecture is complex because the system performs several different types of processing—parsing the page description language, rasterizing, and controlling the print engine—and must do so at reasonable cost. Both ASICs and microcontrollers were added as separate processing elements to enhance performance over the basic main processor system.

Notice that the hardware architecture doesn't strictly fit the typical accelerated system architecture of accelerators attached to a single CPU bus. The

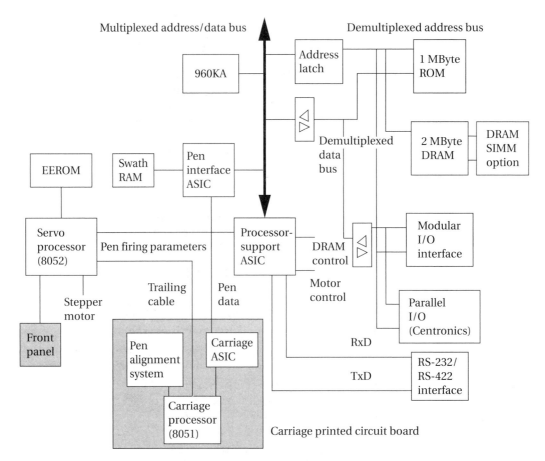

Figure 9-18 *Block diagram of the electronics of the HP DesignJet plotter [Meb92].*

servo processor is only loosely coupled to the i960. This makes sense since the servo commands are relatively simple on the i960 side, but control of the servo itself requires fast responses.

The system includes 2 MBytes of DRAM (with SIMM sockets to hold more) and 1 MByte of ROM. In addition to the main CPU (the i960KA), there are three ASICs: the pen interface ASIC, the processor support ASIC, and the carriage ASIC (which is part of the pen alignment system). There are also two microcontrollers. The servo processor controls a servo motor on the print carriage, controls the front panel display and scans its keyboard, and runs a service station for the ink jet pens.

We can make better sense of Figure 9-18 by identifying the major operations and the flow of data through the system. Figure 9-19 shows how the data flow during three major operations. First, the page description comes through an I/O port (the parallel port in this instance) to the main processor and its main memory. Here, the page description is parsed and pixels are generated. Second, the generated pixels are stored in a *swath*—a section of the rasterized plot. The swath memory is kept separate from the main processor memory because it is more than a buffer for the generated pixels. The pixels are generated by the main processor in row order, but they must be fed to the ink jet pens in column order. The swath memory is used by the pen interface ASIC to accomplish this task. To actually plot, the pixels are read from the swath memory and transferred to the carriage control system in the appropriate order.

The servo processor, which is an 8052, operates as a slave to the main processor. The processor-support ASIC implements a bidirectional port that can be used either to send commands or as a mailbox through which the servo processor can send data back to the main processor or generate several different types of interrupts on the 960. Using an external processing element was found to significantly off-load the main processor. The microcontroller was both faster to design and cheaper to manufacture than an ASIC.

The ink jet pens each have 50 nozzles and the pens may not be closely aligned with each other—tight alignment would make the pens difficult for the user to install and would be hard to maintain in any case. As a result, the hardware includes units to measure the current alignment of the pens and to compensate for misalignments during printing. To align itself, the printer first prints a test pattern on a piece of paper and then scans the result to determine misalignment of the pens. The carriage processor microcontroller, an 8051, controls the optical alignment system. The carriage processor also provides the serial communication link from the 960 to the servo processor.

The processor-support ASIC, whose block diagram is shown in Figure 9-20, performs several different functions in the printer, all of which were collected in a single chip. It connects to both the 960 and the servo processor, and provides both interrupt-driven unidirectional transfers and polled, bidirectional mailboxes. The *main processor interface* allows it to talk to the 960 and to generate interrupts. The *servo processor interface* talks to the 8052. The *interprocessor*

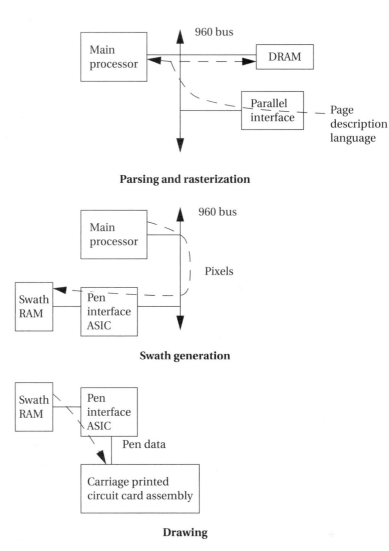

Figure 9-19 *Major operations in the DesignJet plotter.*

communication block intermediates the communication between the two processors.

The *motion controller* block decodes the position of the print carriage and paper axes, based on encoded signals provided to it. It also senses the servo motor current and uses a watchdog timer to determine if the servo has run out of control; if the servo runs for too long, the controller shuts it off. The carriage axis and paper axis outputs are pulse-width modulated (as with the model

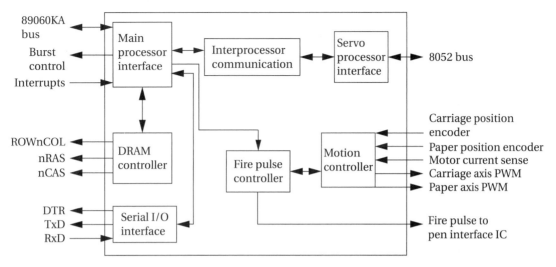

Figure 9-20 *The processor-support ASIC for the DesignJet printer [Meb92].*

train controller). The *fire pulse controller* block generates a synchronizing output for each column of pen data.

The remaining blocks provide basic service functions. The *DRAM controller* block generates refresh signals for the DRAM. The *serial I/O interface* provides the basic RS-232/422 interface.

The pen interface ASIC architecture is shown in Figure 9-21. The pen interface is a key component of the shuffler subsystem, which maps the pixels generated by the main processor in a row orientation to a column orientation to feed the pens. This chip includes interfaces to the main processor bus, the swath memory, and the serial link to the carriage ASIC. The pen interface reads pixels from the swath in a predetermined order according to a predetermined pattern. Keeping the swath memory on a separate bus greatly reduces traffic on the main processor bus and also makes it easier to support different pen nozzle configurations. When data are copied from the main processor to memory, data flow from the main processor interface to the swath RAM; when printing, the data flow from the swath RAM to the serial interface. The pixel address generator includes an SRAM array for a programmable sequencer, a column counter, and an adder. The sequencer memory is loaded with pixel address offsets for each pen. Since the printer head prints in both directions, it must be able to run through sequences in both directions. A pixel counter counts the number of pixels to be printed, and this value can be used to calculate ink use.

The carriage ASIC block diagram is shown in Figure 9-22. This ASIC interfaces to the carriage processor bus, the pen interface ASIC, and the servo processor. The carriage ASIC reads timing control registers using the processor

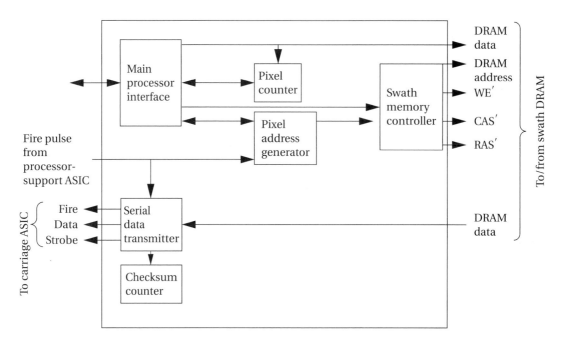

Figure 9-21 *The pen interface ASIC for the DesignJet plotter [Meb92].*

bus. The pen interface data come in serial form and are converted into parallel form on-chip and used to drive four different pen channels. The delayed pipeline registers are programmed with delay values in order to control the pen alignment.

Since the shuffling algorithm implemented in the pen interface and carriage ASICs had not been previously built, the algorithms were developed using a behavioral model written in C. Graphical stubs were written for both input and output to help visualize the results of processing. This allowed the shuffling algorithm to be debugged before designing the ASICs.

In order to be able to develop the printer software in parallel with the hardware, the design team built emulators for the ASICs. The processor-support and pen-notify ASICs were built with a combination of fast PLDs, standard parts, and UARTs, and the high-speed PLDs were required to meet the fast clock speeds for these subsystems. The carriage ASIC emulator was built from an FPGA since it did not have to run as fast.

9.8.2 Software Design

The design team identified three major challenges for developing the plotter software. First, the hardware platform would not be available until several

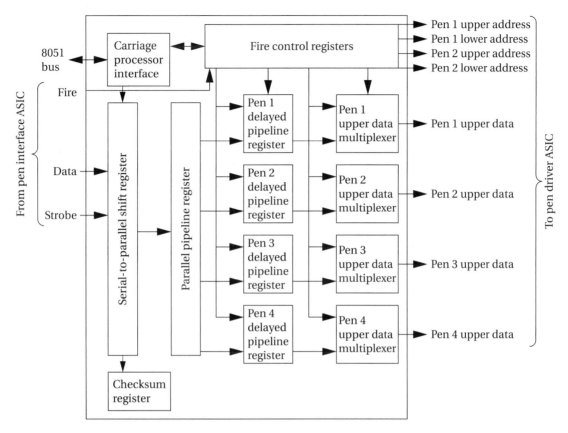

Figure 9-22 *The carriage ASIC for the DesignJet plotter [Meb92].*

months after programming had begun. Second, the team was unfamiliar with the 960. Third, the design team was small. To solve all three problems, they created a software development environment that did not require the hardware platform and maximized programmer productivity.

The software development environment created for the plotter design allowed software to be run either on a Unix workstation or on the target platform. The main differences between the two lay in the I/O and print engine subsystems. The I/O subsystem code was easily modified to accommodate file I/O when running on the host workstation. The print engine was emulated on the host using an X Windows interface that showed the current state of the swath.

The main processor software was developed around a real-time operating system developed in-house. An RTOS was chosen for two reasons: First, it provided standard mechanisms for interprocess communication, and second, it

eliminated many common timing problems by providing preemptive scheduling. The team reported very few timing problems in the design of the printer.

The software running on the main processor included both a parser for the page description language and a rasterizer. The DesignJet team used an HP-GL/2 language subsystem that had been used on several other printers. This reduced both development and debugging time. They rewrote an existing vector-to-raster converter from assembly language into C. This was clearly necessary since they were using a new processor.

To debug 960 code when running on the target platform, they used a remote debugger. The GNU debugger for the 960, gdb960, runs as a monitor program on the main processor and communicates with the workstation using a serial interface. The debugger provided C source-level debugging while running on the target.

The front panel interface was developed using a simulator running on a PC. Marketing and user interface experts were able to use the simulator to design their own front panels.

The process of loading paper into the printer evolved substantially over the course of the design. The basic algorithms were developed by mechanical engineers working on a breadboard. The mechanical engineers provided graphical descriptions of their work to software engineers who wrote programs to implement the necessary actions.

Design Example

9.9 Personal Digital Assistants

Personal digital assistants (PDAs) have become an important example of the information appliance—a device that can be used to receive, display, and transcribe information. Although this product category is evolving rapidly, we can identify several important characteristics of these machines' architectures [Man99].

An ideal PDA has several important characteristics. It is cheap, physically small, lightweight, has a long battery life, and provides many features to the user. Some of these characteristics depend on mechanical design and the properties of important components, such as the display. However, many of the characteristics also greatly influence the design of the digital hardware platform and the software running on that platform.

The Apple Newton MessagePad is considered to be the first modern PDA. The hardware organization of the Newton is shown in Figure 9-23 [Fur96]. The first-generation Newton used the ARM 610 processor (a later version used the StrongARM). The following support operations were bundled into a single ASIC known as the Runt: DMA control, real-time clock, timers, bus interface and CPU control, digitizer and LCD interface, audio generation, and PCMCIA and infrared support. The bulk of the software was written in the NewtonScript

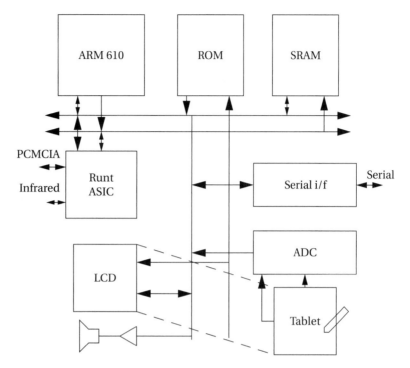

Figure 9-23 *Hardware architecture of the Newton MessagePad [Fur96].*

language, which was an interpreted byte-code language supporting an object-oriented model. The software was organized around a real-time operating system that preemptively scheduled processes on the platform. All processes used a single address space, but the ARM MMU was used to provide memory protection via its subpage mechanism.

The Motorola Envoy PDA appeared in 1994; its hardware architecture is shown in Figure 9-24. The hardware architecture is in many ways similar to the Newton. In addition to a CPU (a Motorola 68349 in this case), an ASIC is used to encapsulate many system functions; other chips supply I/O functions for the touchscreen, and so on. The Envoy used the Magic Cap operating system, which made use of object-oriented software design.

One major design challenge in PDAs is *feature creep*—the tendency for the final system to contain more features than the architecture can adequately support. Features can be added in the form of additional interfaces for new types of devices. New interfaces not only increase power consumption but also make the mechanical design of the system more difficult and may contribute to electromagnetic interference. Features can also enter in the form of software modules. Such features may tax the available RAM and ROM in the system. If the added software causes memory thrashing, the penalty is felt not only in

Figure 9-24 *Hardware architecture of the Motorola Envoy PDA [Man99].*

slower execution time but also in decreased battery life due to the increased memory activity.

The design of the power supply is another important aspect of PDA design. A large amount of data is kept in RAM during execution; if the machine loses power suddenly, the PDA could be rendered useless. Many batteries have hard-to-predict lifetimes—voltage may go from an acceptable value to near zero very quickly. To combat this problem, Intel and Duracell developed the Smart Battery System. In this system, the battery is packaged with a microcontroller and a small amount of memory, and the PDA or other device can talk to the battery's microcontroller over a simple serial bus. The battery's internal electronics can read the battery's charge status more accurately, allowing the system to read battery lifetime more accurately and provide for a safe shutdown before power fails.

An influential system for even more advanced handheld functions was the InfoPad [Tru98]. The InfoPad provided not only a portable computer with a screen but also a wireless link and the ability to handle audio and video data. Because it had a wireless link, InfoPad was designed to act as a remote I/O interface. It used remote computers, accessed over the wireless network, to provide many computational functions. This feature helped with power, size, and weight. However, it did contain a significant amount of computational power itself in the form of an ARM60 running at 10 MHz, 512 MB of RAM, and 128 KB of ROM. As illustrated in Figure 9-25, the CPU was viewed as one element of the overall system. Some operations were implemented in special-

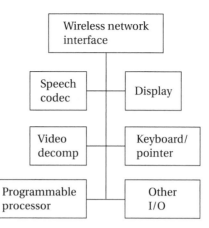

Figure 9-25 *Organization of the InfoPad [Tru98].*

purpose hardware in order to save power, and others were implemented in the ARM60 in order to provide more flexibility. For this reason, the ARM60 was referred to as a peripheral processing unit, being viewed as a controller rather than as the central unit in the system.

Design Example

9.10 Set-Top Boxes

In this section we study two related hardware and software designs [Aki96, Rat96] of **set-top boxes**—devices used to interface a video delivery service, such as cable or satellite, with a consumer television. Set-top boxes for cable TV were traditionally based on analog circuitry for the television signal with a small amount of user interface functionality provided by a microcontroller. We concentrate here on set-top boxes for digital television, which typically provide more advanced user interfaces as well. Figure 9-26 shows the relationship of the set-top box to the complete television delivery system. The box decodes the digital TV signal and converts it into a form suitable for the consumer TV. It also provides user interface features, both by generating on-TV displays and by listening to a remote control through an infrared (IR) interface. Some boxes also transmit information to the content provider through a **back channel,** often using a telephone line, for purchase of special programs or other options.

Set-top boxes are very cost sensitive. These designs were targeted to a selling price of $250 to $350 per box, or about equal to the cost of a midrange television, when produced in volumes of tens of millions of units.

Figure 9-27 shows the hardware architecture of a set-top box designed for a telephone company for a fiber-to-the-curb video delivery system. The network

interface module receives and transmits data over the fiber optic network. The video is delivered in the form of MPEG, an international standard for compressed video and audio. A collection of units turns the compressed bit stream into analog signals for the television set. The MPEG transport demultiplexer separates (demultiplexes) the MPEG data stream into audio and video components, which are then decoded by the MPEG audio and video decoders. A radio frequency (RF) modulator, an NTSC encoder, and analog D/A converters convert the digital signal into analog form for the television. The host microprocessor is a Motorola MC68341, which includes a 68020 CPU, two channels of DMA control, two serial channels, a timer, and a serial peripheral interface. A CD-I graphics processor can be used to generate graphics on the screen. An I/O microprocessor talks to the box's keyboard, the IR link that receives commands from the remote, and a card reader. A PCMCIA slot provides the ability to expand memory. Note that the MPEG system, the host microprocessor, and the I/O microprocessor each have their own bus. Separating the MPEG system and the host processor is particularly important to ensure that video decoding receives enough bus capacity. Note also that many subsystems have their own memory—memory bandwidth would probably be too high if all memory were shared on a single bus.

The software architecture of the box is shown in Figure 9-28. The host processor runs the OS-9 operating system, whose application programming interface (API) is known as DAVID. Note that the MPEG2 decoder operates under the operating system. Because these functions are implemented in special-

Figure 9-26 *Role of a set-top box in digital TV system.*

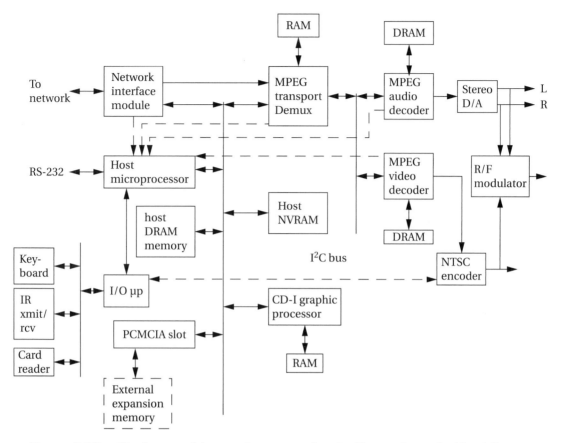

Figure 9-27 *Hardware architecture for a set-top box for fiber-to-the-curb video delivery [Aki96].*

purpose hardware, they appear as very low-level operations that do not directly affect the scheduling of the application on the host processor.

Figure 9-29 shows the software architecture of a different set-top box [Rat96] in more detail than that shown in Figure 9-28. The hardware architecture of this box is slightly different but has the same flavor as that of Figure 9-27. As with the other system, this box is built on top of the OS-9 operating system. The system level includes a number of basic processes. The software is structured so that all operations are performed on objects structured as files; for example, the MPEG stream appears as a file. RTNFM is the real-time network file manager that handles all the file objects. SPF is the sequential packet file manager that handles the network interface. MPEG decoding is controlled by MPFM, the MPEG file manager. The CD-I graphics

Figure 9-28 *Software architecture of a set-top box [Aki96].*

processor is managed by UCM, the user communication manager task. PCFM is the PDI-CIA port manager.

At the application level, the navigator is the primary user interface. The navigator is in fact a distributed application that processes some commands locally and dispatches others to network elements. The *Level 1* and *Level 2* gateways provide means to get services from the network. The *Level 1* gateway is used to download new applications to the terminal; this could be used, for example, to supply video games. The *Level 2* gateway is used for the video stream of a video-on-demand service. The configuration application sets up the network address and other utilities. The display process provides a virtual terminal display on the TV set for messages from other applications. The *Emergency Broadcast Services* process provides notice of warnings about natural disasters and other emergencies that are transmitted over the network. The IAT application allows the user to send messages upstream to the provider, such as for interacting with game shows.

Figure 9-29 *Software architecture of another set-top box [Rat96].*

9.11 Systems-on-Silicon

While embedded systems have traditionally been built as multiple chips connected on a printed circuit board, an increasing number of embedded systems are single-chip systems known as **systems-on-silicon** or **systems-on-a-chip.** A system-on-silicon presents all the challenges of traditional embedded system design as well as many more.

An example embedded processor for systems-on-silicon is shown in Figure 9-30. The IBM PowerPC 405GP includes a CPU core, 16 K instruction and 8 K data caches, an SDRAM controller, peripheral controllers, and PCI and Ethernet interfaces. The design is available as a component that can be placed on a system-on-silicon, along with whatever other logic and memory is desired.

While a system-on-silicon does not inherently require an embedded CPU, most do for several reasons. Programming an embedded CPU provides a much more productive design technique than hardwired controllers. The embedded

Figure 9-30 *An embedded processor for systems-on-silicon (courtesy of IBM Microelectronics).*

CPU also takes advantage of embedded RAM technology—since large amounts of RAM are available on-chip, it makes sense to choose a design methodology that takes advantage of it. Embedded software is also more easily upgradeable to new releases and versions of the product.

design challenges However, systems-on-silicon pose several unique challenges. Integrated circuit fabrication technology makes traditional embedded system debugging impractical. Fabricating the chip takes weeks or months and costs tens or hundreds of thousands of dollars. Although a printed circuit board design can be modified by fixing the printed circuit board (cutting traces, adding wires) or by replacing chips (e.g., reprogramming the PROM), none of these techniques work on an integrated circuit. If the system can be tested only by changing the

hardware, that change will incur the same costs in time and money of fabricating the original version. Furthermore, observing signals on the chip is much more difficult than attaching a logic analyzer to a printed circuit board.

As a result, systems-on-silicon must be designed under methodologies that aim for **first-time correctness.** Systems-on-silicon design makes more extensive use of computer-aided design in the following ways:

- Analysis tools help determine the characteristics of a proposed architecture.

- Synthesis tools help configure the hardware and software architectures.

- Co-simulation tools allow the system design to be exercised before building the complete system.

The cost of architectural mistakes in embedded systems has always been high, but it is extremely high in systems-on-silicon due to the time and expense of a design iteration.

An important advantage of systems-on-silicon is that we can customize components—we do not have to use stock microprocessors or other components. We can easily, for example, select the cache size and even cache organization to suit the needs of our application. It is even possible to modify the instruction set of the processor to suit our needs. An **application-specific instruction processor (ASIP)** is a CPU whose instruction set has been optimized for a particular set of applications.

9.12 Summary

System design takes a comprehensive view of the application and the system under design. To ensure that we design an acceptable system, we must understand the application and its requirements. Numerous techniques, such as object-oriented design, can be used to create useful architectures from the system's original requirements. Along the way, by measuring our design processes, we can gain a clearer understanding of where bugs are introduced, how to fix them, and how to avoid introducing them in the future.

What We Learned

- Design methodologies and design flows can be organized in many different ways.

- Building a system mock-up is one good way to help understand system requirements.

- Statecharts are valuable in the specification of control and are part of UML.

- CRC cards help us understand the system architecture in the initial phases of architecture design.

- Systems-on-silicon provide new opportunities and challenges for embedded computing.

Further Reading

Pressman [Pre97] provides a thorough introduction to software engineering. Davis [Dav90] gives a good survey of software requirements. Beizer [Bei84] surveys system-level testing techniques. Leveson [Lev86] provides a good introduction to software safety. Schmauch [Sch94] and Jenner [Jen95] both describe ISO 9000 for software development. A tutorial edited by Chow [Cho85] includes a number of important early papers on software quality assurance. Cusumano [Cus91] provides a fascinating account of software factories in both the United States and Japan. Newman [New94] describes a small PBX design based on a microcontroller, and a later article [New96] describes phone line interfaces.

Questions

Q9-1 Briefly describe the differences between the waterfall and spiral development models.

Q9-2 What skills might be useful in a cross-functional team that is responsible for designing a set-top box?

Q9-3 Describe how you might use a spiral development model to design a PBX like the one described in Section 9.7.

Q9-4 Describe how you might use successive refinement to design a printer like the one described in Section 9.8.

Q9-5 Describe how concurrent engineering practices might be applied to the design of a PDA like those described in Section 9.9.

Q9-6 Provide realistic examples of how a requirements document may be:

a. ambiguous

b. incorrect

c. incomplete

d. unverifiable

Q9-7 Develop a state diagram that defines the basic actions of a telephone call, including going off-hook, dialing, connecting, talking, hanging up, and tearing down the call. Use AND and OR states whenever possible.

Q9-8 Develop a state diagram that describes how a user of a set-top box can select a channel from an on-screen display using up and down buttons to select the desired channel. Use AND and OR states whenever possible.

Q9-9 Develop a set of CRC card descriptions for the PBX of Section 9.7.

Q9-10 Develop a set of CRC card descriptions for a PDA like the ones described in Section 9.9.

Q9-11 Develop a set of UML diagrams that describe a design pattern for an on-screen user interface; the design pattern should be applicable to both PDAs and set-top boxes.

Lab Exercises

L9-1 Develop UML diagrams to describe some of the systems in this chapter, either as specifications or as architectural diagrams.

L9-2 Draw a diagram showing the developmental steps of one of the projects you recently designed. Which development model did you follow (waterfall, spiral, etc.)?

L9-3 Find a detailed description of a system of interest to you. Write your own description of what it does and how it works.

Appendix

UML Notations

A.1 Introduction

In this appendix we review the basics of UML notation for easy reference. We do not cover all the aspects of UML. For a more thorough treatment of UML, see references such as Booch et al. [Boo99]. This appendix includes only a basic summary of UML diagrams; for a more detailed introduction to what these symbols mean, see Section 1.4.

A.2 Primitive Elements

The most fundamental primitives of UML are the object and the class; an object is an instance of a class. In addition, various types of relations between objects and classes are possible. Other types of elements have also been defined. Primitives are summarized in Figure A-1. A *class* has attributes and behaviors. An *object* may have its attributes assigned particular values. An anonymous object belongs to a class but has no name, probably because it does not play a major role in the system. A *package* is an organizational unit of the system that may contain class definitions, objects, and so on. A *state* is used in state diagrams to describe *behavior*. A physical processor is a hardware element. A component is a physical part of a system that implements a set of interfaces.

561

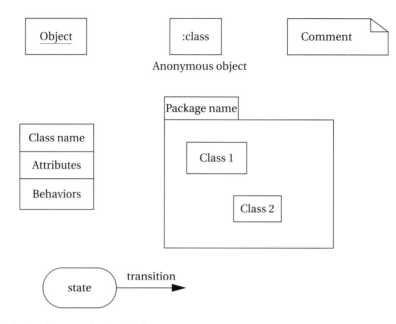

Figure A-1 *Primitive elements for UML diagrams.*

Figure A-2 *A UML stereotype.*

We often find that we use a certain combination of elements in an object or class many times. We can give these combinations names; such a definition is called a **stereotype** in UML. The *<<signal>>* shown in Figure A-2 is an example of a stereotype.

An active class is a class that will implement a separate thread of control. As shown in Figure A-3, an active class is identified by its heavy border.

A.3 Diagram Types

The UML primitives can be put together in a number of ways. This section provides examples of several of the basic UML diagram types that we use in this book.

A.3.1 Class Diagram

The class diagram defines classes and describes the relationships between them. One type of relationship between classes is subtype/supertype, which is shown in Figure A-4; note that the derivation arrows go from derived to base. In the upper part of the figure, *Class 2* is derived from *Class 1*. In the lower part of the figure, *Class b* is derived from both *Class a1* and *Class a2*, an example of multiple inheritance.

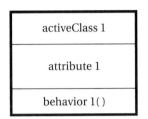

Figure A-3 *An active class.*

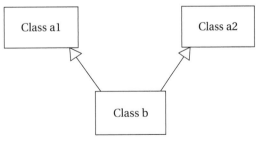

Figure A-4 *Class derivation in a UML class diagram.*

Many relationships other than inheritance can be represented in UML. A class diagram with associations and their multiplicities is shown in Figure A-5. This diagram shows how many objects of one class interact with a given number of objects of another class.

A.3.2 State Diagram

The state diagram shows the structure of states and transitions for a behavior. A basic state diagram is shown in Figure A-6. A transition may be labeled with the event that causes entry onto that transition and the actions taken on the transition.

UML allows you to describe Statechart-style substates. Examples of sequential and concurrent substates are shown in Figure A-7. The sequential substates (similar to the Statechart OR state) describe detailed behavior within an overall system state; the concurrent substates (similar to the Statechart AND state) describe two distinct activities going on concurrently within the same system state.

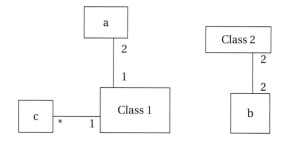

Figure A-5 *A UML class diagram showing associations.*

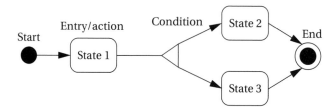

Figure A-6 *A state diagram in UML.*

A.3.3 Sequence and Collaboration Diagrams

Sequence and collaboration diagrams both illustrate scenarios, but in different ways. Figure A-8 shows a UML sequence diagram that includes a timeline. The bars show when different objects are active. Figure A-9 shows a UML collaboration diagram for the same sequence of events. In this diagram, messages are given sequence numbers to indicate time.

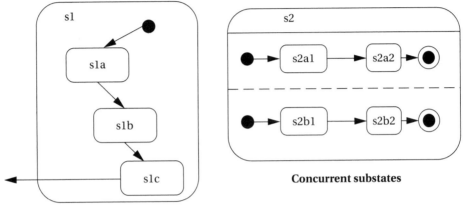

Sequential substates

Concurrent substates

Figure A-7 *Substates in UML.*

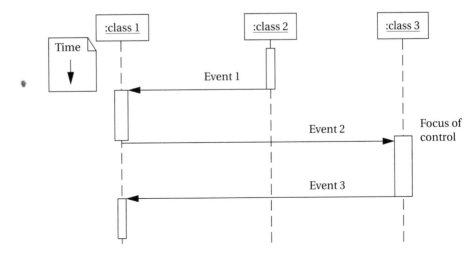

Figure A-8 *A sequence diagram in UML.*

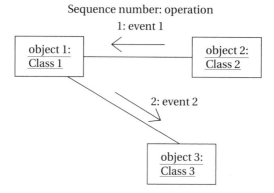

Figure A-9 *A UML collaboration diagram.*

Notes on Hardware Design

B.1 Introduction

This appendix overviews some basic concepts in hardware design. It is not intended to be a complete introduction to hardware design. Rather, it is intended to refresh some basic concepts in the mind of the reader and to outline our terminology. Many excellent textbooks describe logic design in detail. We describe combinational logic and sequential machines and then describe the various devices that can be used to implement logic.

B.2 Combinational Logic

Combinational logic is so named because the output of the combinational logic block is a combination of its inputs. Unlike a sequential machine, the output of combinational logic does not depend on the state of the machine or previous inputs.

Boolean algebra Combinational logic can be specified using Boolean algebra. The Boolean primitives AND ($\cdot$), OR ($+$), and NOT ($-$) are functions in Boolean algebra. A set of operators is said to be **complete** if we can generate any possible formula using the operators. Generally, a set of operators must include inversion to be complete. Because of the nature of digital circuits, we often work with NANDs and NORs. NAND is, by itself, a complete set of Boolean operators. Similarly,

NOR is a complete set. However, {AND, OR} is not a complete set. We often interchangeably refer to the TRUE logic value as a logic 1 and FALSE as logic 0; if we use the arithmetic multiplication, addition, and negation operations on 0 and 1 values, we find the results are consistent with the TRUE and FALSE model.

A **logic gate** is a digital circuit used to compute a logic function. The dominant circuit technology today is **CMOS (complementary metal oxide semiconductor).** CMOS uses voltages to represent logic levels, as shown in Figure B-1. The power supply terminals are known as V_{DD} (high voltage) and V_{SS} (low voltage); we use V_{DD} to represent a logic 1 and V_{SS} to represent a logic 0. Because of a variety of physical effects, we allow a logic level to be represented by a range of voltages. A range of voltages between the logic 0 and 1 ranges represents no logic value, referred to as X or unknown. A logic gate's output normally goes through the X region only temporarily during transitions between logic 0 and 1.

CMOS transistors

The basic characteristics of a CMOS transistor relevant to basic digital operation are illustrated in Figure B-2. The device has three relevant terminals: *source, drain,* and *gate.* The current between *drain* and *source,* I_{ds}, is considered the device's output. It is controlled by the *gate* voltage V_{gs}. In the case of the **n-type transistor** shown, when V_{gs} is large, the *drain* current is large; when the *gate* voltage is small, the *drain* current is cut off. CMOS also supplies another complementary type of transistor known as the **p-type.** That device has opposite characteristics: When V_{gs} is small, the *drain* current is large.

inverter operation

The logic gate that performs negation is known as an **inverter.** The operation of a CMOS inverter is shown in Figure B-3. We can use the CMOS transistors as switches controlled by their gate inputs. Consider, for example, the steady state case in which a low voltage is applied to the inverter's input. In this case, the *n-type transistor* will be off and the *p-type transistor* will be on. This

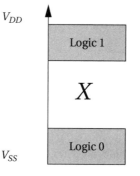

Figure B-1 *Logic levels and voltages in CMOS.*

Figure B-2 *Operation of a CMOS n-type transistor.*

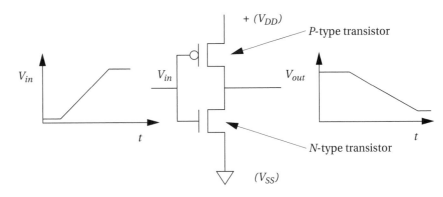

Figure B-3 *Operation of a CMOS inverter.*

will cause current to flow through the *p-type transistor* that, by charging the capacitance that naturally occurs at the input of the next logic gate, produces a logic 1 at the output. When the inverter's input is a high voltage, only the *n-type transistor* is on and the resulting output is a logic 0. When the inverter's inputs transition between 0 to 1, as shown in the figure, the output naturally transitions as well.

power consumption of CMOS gates

The operation of the CMOS inverter helps explain the power consumption characteristics of CMOS logic. During steady state, both the *p-type* and *n-type transistors* are not on. As a result, there is no current-carrying path from V_{DD} to V_{SS}. There is a very small leakage current through the devices that is several orders of magnitude smaller than the current consumed during transitions. However, the power consumption of a CMOS gate is very small while it is not transitioning. When the gate inputs and outputs change, the *p-type* and *n-type transistors* may both be on at the same time; during this interval, there is significant current from V_{DD} to V_{SS}. As a result, the gate's power consumption goes up when its outputs are changing.

Figure B-4 shows the standard schematic symbols used for logic gates. The bubble shown at the outputs of these gates represents logical inversion. We can draw an AND gate, for example, by removing the inversion bubble from the output of the NAND symbol.

We connect logic gates together to form **combinational logic networks** that compute logical functions. Logic gates correspond to operations in the Boolean formula that defines the function. In general, there are many equivalent forms of a Boolean function, so there are also many different logic networks that implement the desired function. Figure B-5 shows two different logic networks that implement the same logical function. On the left side, we have built a logic network for $(a' + b)''$ using a NOR gate and inverters. However, we can use De Morgan's Law to rewrite that formula to $(ab')'$. This gives us the logic network on the right side of the figure.

evaluating logic networks Although many logic networks are equivalent in their Boolean function, they may be very different in other characteristics. **Combinational logic delay** is the time required for a change at one of the inputs to propagate to the network's output. We are usually interested in the worst-case delay caused by any input change. The physical *size* of the network is roughly proportional to the total number of logic gate inputs in the network. The *power consumption* of the logic network depends on the network's structure as well as the transition characteristics of the expected inputs. All these characteristics can be used to judge the appropriateness of a logic network to an application.

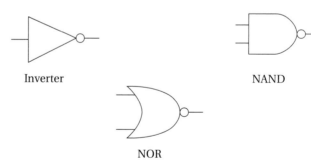

Inverter NAND

NOR

Figure B-4 *Schematic symbols for logic gates.*

Figure B-5 *Two equivalent combinational logic networks.*

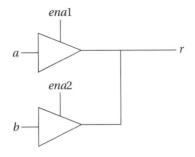

Figure B-6 *Three-state logic.*

typical logic blocks

Numerous logic functions that provide commonly used functions have been given names. One of the most important and thoroughly studied logic networks is the **adder.** An adder computes a sum and a carry from a pair of binary numbers (and possibly a carry-in). The design of fast adders is an art in itself. The **multiplexer,** another common logic function, has n data inputs and a control input; the output is one of the n data inputs, as determined by the current value of the control input.

three-state logic

One useful form of combinational logic gate is the **three-state** gate. A three-state gate has an additional enable input. When the enable input is active, the gate behaves normally; when disabled, the gate's output is disconnected from its internal circuitry so that neither a logic 0 nor a logic 1 can appear on the gate's output. When output is disabled, the output is said to be in a **high-impedance** state. Figure B-6 shows two noninverting three-state buffers attached to a common output r. These gates pass their inputs to their outputs when enabled and present a high-impedance output when disabled. When *ena*1 is enabled and *ena*2 is disabled, the value of r is determined by the a input; when *ena*1 = 0 and *ena*2 = 1, r is determined by b. When neither is enabled, r is in an unknown state. When both are enabled, problems occur when a and b have different values—the two three-state gates fight each other. Not only does this cause an indeterminate value on r, but the high currents flowing through the output stages of the two states can cause burnout.

B.3 Sequential Logic

B.3.1 Memory Elements

A **memory element** stores a logic value. The presence of memory elements distinguishes the sequential logic network from combinational logic. The schematic symbol and operation of a memory element are shown in Figure B-7.

Access to the internal memory is controlled by the *clock* signal. At the proper event on the *clock* input, the memory element samples the *D* input. It stores the value internally and presents it to the *Q* output. The output remains at the same value until the *clock* causes the memory element to store a new value.

The two major types of memory elements are described below.

■ The **flip-flop** samples the input at a clock transition. Its output makes a nearly instantaneous change from one value to another.

■ The **latch** is transparent—its output is connected to its input as long as the clock signal is active. The output stabilizes only when the clock signal becomes inactive.

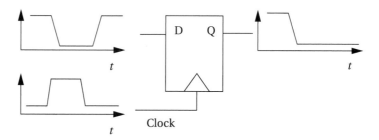

Figure B-7 *A memory element.*

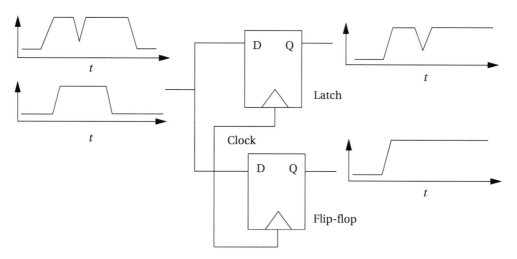

Figure B-8 *Latch and flip-flop behavior compared.*

Figure B-8 compares the behavior of a *latch* and a *flip-flop* to the same data and *clock* input.

The D-type memory element we have used thus far copies its input to its output. There are other types of memory elements, such as the T, which toggles its output.

timing
requirements
Both latches and flip-flops share the following major timing requirements:

- **Setup time** is the minimum time required for the data input to be stable before the clock edge that controls the memory element.

- **Hold time** is the minimum time that the data input must remain stable after the end of the controlling clock edge.

Setup and hold times for a positive edge-triggered D flip-flop are shown in Figure B-9.

B.3.2 Synchronous Machines

synchronous
machines run off
a central clock
We can use combinational logic and memory elements to build *synchronous* sequential machines. A synchronous machine uses a clock to synchronize the transitions between states of the machine. We design synchronous machines because they provide simple timing characteristics. Our goal is to design a machine that has a single timing constraint—we slow down the clock until the machine starts to work, and the machine will continue to work at any slower clock rate.

flip-flop–based
machines
Let's first consider how to build a sequential machine out of flip-flops. Figure B-10 shows the structure of such a machine. The machine's combina-

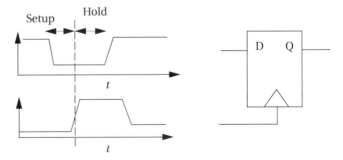

Figure B-9 *Setup and hold times.*

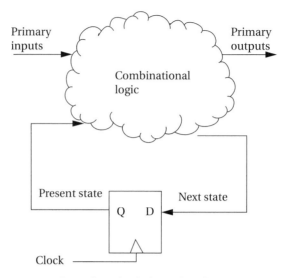

Figure B-10 *A synchronous sequential machine built from flip-flops.*

tional logic takes two sets of inputs: **primary inputs** that come from the out-side world and **present state inputs** that derive from the memory elements. It computes two sets of outputs: the **primary outputs** that are sent to the external world and the **next state** outputs that go to the flip-flops. At the command of the clock, the next state is transferred to the flip-flops and becomes the present state for the next cycle.

The timing requirement on this machine is simple to analyze. If the delay through the combinational logic to the next state outputs is longer than the clock period, then the next state will not be ready when the next clock edge causes the next state to be loaded into the flip-flop. Therefore, at high clock speeds, the machine doesn't work. When we slow down the clock so that the combinational logic has time to compute the next state, the machine starts to work, and it continues to work at any lower clock speed.

latch-based machines Using a latch to build a synchronous machine requires a little more effort. The structure is shown in Figure B-11. This machine divides the combinational logic into two portions and puts latches between the portions. The latches are organized such that a signal must go through two latches on every clock cycle. The clock itself actually consists of two phases as shown in Figure B-12—one phase controls one rank of latches and the other phase controls the other rank. The two ranks of latches are necessary because latches are transparent. If we used the structure of Figure B-10 with latches, then the machine would have a lower bound on the clock period as well as an upper bound. Thus, if the clock

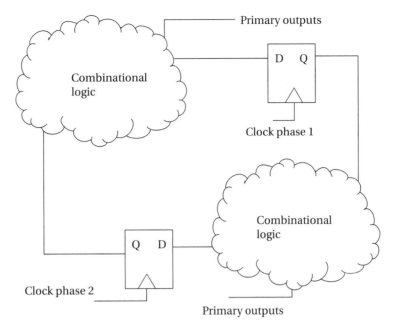

Figure B-11 *A synchronous sequential machine built from latches.*

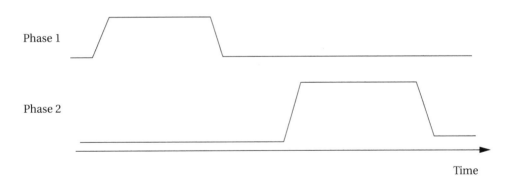

Figure B-12 *A two-phase clock.*

ran too slowly, then a signal would have time to go from the present state output of the latch through the combinational logic and back into the latch. Because the latch is transparent, we cannot allow its input to change while the clock is active. Using two ranks of latches along with a pair of clock phases that are not both active at once ensures that this will not happen.

B.3.3 Asynchronous Machines

An *asynchronous* sequential machine is not under the control of a master clock. We use asynchronous machines, for example, at the interface between blocks of logic that operate under separate clocks. Many microprocessor buses are at least partially asynchronous because the CPU and the other devices on the bus may not be under the control of the same clock.

timing diagrams In order to understand sequential machines, it is helpful to first understand the **timing diagram,** a common way to specify the behavior of sequential machines. A sample timing diagram is shown in Figure B-13. The timing diagram shows the behavior of signals over time. Some signals may take known values such as logic 0 or 1. However, we often specify a signal as **stable** (the signal holds some value, but we don't know whether it is 0 or 1) or **changing** (the signal has not reached its desired value).

min, max Beyond signal values themselves, we also use timing diagrams to describe
constraints constraints between the times at which signal events can occur. Figure B-13 shows a **minimum** (also known as **min**) **timing constraint.** This constraint gives the minimum elapsed time that is required between two signal events— in this case, the minimum time from when *b* becomes stable to the time at which *c* can change from 0 to 1. We may also need to specify **maximum** (or **max**) **timing constraints** that give the maximum allowable time between events.

Figure B-14 illustrates why minimum timing constraints occur. Some of the signals in the timing diagram are used as clock inputs for latches or flip-flops

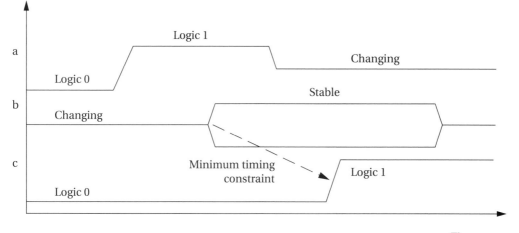

Figure B-13 *A timing diagram.*

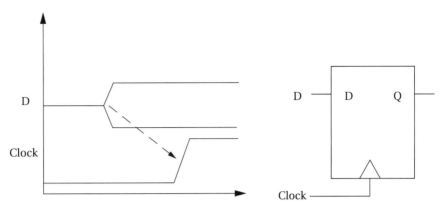

Figure B-14 *Why minimum timing contraints are needed.*

in the asynchronous machine. The memory elements have setup and hold requirements that are translated into minimum timing requirements in the timing diagram. We can see that the data signal *D* must become stable before the *clock* signal is asserted, creating a minimum timing requirement. However, the signals used as clocks may not be explicitly identified as such in the component specification; we can only infer the uses of the signals by examining the timing diagrams and the constraints they describe.

B.4 Implementation Media

We can implement combinational logic and sequential machines in a variety of forms. Each form has its own advantages and disadvantages, and each is useful in different situations.

custom chips

We could design a **custom chip** for the logic. A custom chip requires a great deal of work, as well as significant lead time to design and manufacture the circuit. However, the custom chip is often the fastest chip. In large volumes, the custom chip may be the low-cost solution as well.

programmable logic

There are many types of **programmable logic** devices as well. These chips have some standard structure that can be programmed to customize the device's behavior. We can classify programmable logic in the following ways:

■ *Factory-programmed versus field-programmed:* Some devices are programmed at the factory. For example, when ordering a factory-programmed ROM, you supply the factory with the desired contents of the memory. The factory returns to you chips that have the desired contents. You can program

other chips in the field, generally by using some sort of programming device.

■ *One-time-programmable versus reprogrammable:* Some devices can be programmed only once; an antifuse is commonly used as the programmable structure in these devices. The programming in other devices can be erased so that they can be reprogrammed.

■ *Erasure technique:* Some devices may be erased with ultraviolet light. Other devices are electrically erasable. Still others make use of SRAM to store their programming, so that they lose their programming when power is removed.

■ *Logic structure:* Some devices are structured as fully addressable memories, while others are used to describe logic functions. Some random logic devices support only two levels of logic; others allow you to implement multiple levels of logic.

PLDs vs. FPGAs When designing random logic and state machines, the most commonly used devices are **programmable logic devices (PLDs)** and **field-programmable gate arrays (FPGAs).** The most basic distinction between them is that PLDs implement two-level logic while FPGAs can be used to implement multilevel logic.

hardware description languages We can occasionally use a very low-level description of logic such as a netlist or a ROM table. However, we usually use a **hardware description language (HDL)** to describe the logic we want to build. The two most common hardware description languages are **VHDL** and **Verilog.** Both these languages are designed to support simulation. They can also be used as the input to synthesize systems that generate a final hardware description.

A hardware description language can be used to describe hardware at the following levels of abstraction:

■ *Gate level:* The primitives in the hardware description are the actual gates, latches, and flip-flops used in the hardware.

■ *Register-transfer level:* The combinational functions for next state and outputs are defined, but not necessarily in the form that will be used for the logic gate implementation.

■ *Behavioral level:* A behavioral model does not specify the exact cycle-by-cycle behavior of the machine. Synthesis would determine what operations happen on what clock cycles.

Web Aid C-HDL provides some example VHDL and Verilog descriptions.

Glossary

absolute address An address of an exact location in memory (Section 2.4.2, Section 5.4).

ack Short for *acknowledge*, a signal used in handshaking protocols (Section 4.2.1).

ACPI Advanced Configuration and Power Interface, an industry standard for power management interfaces (Section 6.9).

activation record A data structure that describes the information required by a currently active procedure call (Section 2.3.3). A data structure used to describe the state of a process (Section 6.3).

active class A UML class that can create its own thread of control (Section 6.4.3).

active low A logic 0 that denotes activity for a device, as compared to the normal logic 1 (Section 4.2.1).

actuator A physical output device (Section 8.2).

A/D converter See *analog/digital converter.*

ADPCM Adaptive differential pulse code modulation (Section 6.10.1).

allocation The assignment of responsibility for a computation to a processing element (Section 7.3.4).

analog/digital converter A device that converts an analog signal into digital form (Section 4.4.2).

AND/OR table A technique for specifying control-oriented functionality (Section 9.4).

antifuse-programmable ROM A type of ROM that can be programmed once (Section 4.3.3).

application layer In the OSI model, the end-user interface (Section 8.2.2).

ASIC Application-specific integrated circuit (Section 4.6.2, Section 7.2).

aspect ratio In a memory, the ratio of the number of addressable units to the number of bits read per request (Section 4.3.1).

assembler A program that creates object code from a symbolic description of instructions (Section 5.4).

asynchronous An event not coordinated with a clock (Section 4.3.2).

atomic operation An operation that cannot be interrupted (Section 6.5.4).

ATPG See *automatic test pattern generation.*

auto-indexing Automatically incrementing or decrementing a value before or after using it (Section 2.3.2).

automatic test pattern generation Automatically creating a set of manufacturing tests for a digital system (Section 4.8).

average-case execution time A typical execution time for typical inputs (Section 5.6).

base-plus-offset addressing Calculating the address by adding a base address to an offset (usually contained in a register) (Section 2.3.2).

basis paths A set of execution paths that cover the possible execution paths (Section 5.9.1).

best-case execution time The shortest execution time for any possible set of inputs (Section 5.6).

best-effort routing The Internet routing methodology, which does not guarantee completion (Section 8.3.6).

big-endian A data format in which the low-order byte is stored in the highest bits of the word (Section 2.3.1).

BIOS Basic Input/Output System. Originally, low-level IBM PC software; today, low-level operating software in any computer system (Section 4.6.3).

black-box testing Testing a program without knowledge of its implementation (Section 5.9.2).

blocking communication Communication that requires a process to wait after sending a message (Section 6.5.4).

boot-block flash A type of flash memory that protects some of its contents (Section 4.3.3).

bottom-up design Using information from lower levels of abstraction to modify the design at higher levels of abstraction (Section 1.3).

bounce Repeated make-break contacts upon activation of a switch (Section 4.4.3).

boundary scan A technique for allowing access to the internal state of chips on boards (Section 4.8).

branch table A multiway branching mechanism that uses a value to index into a table of branch targets (Example 2-5).

branch target The destination address of a branch (Section 2.3.3).

branch testing A technique to generate a set of tests for conditionals (Section 5.9.1).

breakpoint A stopping point for system execution (Section 4.7.2).

bridge A logic unit that acts as an interface between two buses (Section 4.2.3).

bundle A collection of logically related signals (Section 4.2.1).

burst transfer A bus transfer that transfers several contiguous locations without separate addresses for each (Section 4.2.1).

bus Generally, a shared connection. CPUs use buses to connect themselves to external devices and memory (Section 4.2).

bus grant The granting of ownership of the bus to a device (Section 4.2.2).

bus master The current owner of the bus (Section 4.2.2).

bus request A request to obtain ownership of the bus (Section 4.2.2).

busy-wait I/O Servicing an I/O device by executing instructions that test the device's state (Section 3.2.3).

cache A small memory that holds copies of certain main memory locations for fast access (Section 3.5.1).

cache hit A memory reference to a location currently held in the cache (Section 3.5.1).

cache miss A memory reference to a location not currently in the cache (Section 3.5.1).

cache miss penalty The extra time incurred for a memory reference that is a cache miss (Section 3.6.3).

calligraphic display A display that writes arbitrary vectors (Section 4.4.5).

CAN bus A serial bus for networked embedded systems (Section 8.3.2).

Capability Maturity Model A method developed at the Software Engineering Institute of Carnegie Mellon University for assessing the quality of software development processes (Section 9.6.1).

capacity miss A cache miss that occurs because the program's working set is too large for the cache (Section 3.5.1).

CAS See *column address select.*

CAS-before-RAS refresh A scheme for signaling refresh requests to a DRAM (Section 4.3.2).

CDFG See *control/data flow graph.*

central processing unit The part of the computer system responsible for executing instructions fetched from memory (Section 2.2).

changing In logic timing analysis, a signal whose value is changing at a particular moment in time (Section 4.2.1).

circular buffer An array used to hold a window of a stream of data (Section 2.4.2).

CISC Complex instruction set computer. Typically uses a number of instruction formats of varying length and provides complex operations in some instructions (Section 2.2).

class A type description in an object-oriented language (Section 1.4).

class diagram A UML diagram that defines classes and shows derivation relationships among them (Section 1.5.2).

clear-box testing Generating tests for a program with knowledge of its structure (Section 5.9.1).

CMM See *Capability Maturity Model.*

CMOS Complementary metal oxide semiconductor, the dominant VLSI technology today (Section 3.7).

code compression Compressing instructions so that they can be dynamically decompressed during execution (Section 5.8).

code motion A technique for moving operations in a program without affecting its behavior (Section 5.6.2).

cold miss See *compulsory miss.*

collaboration diagram A UML diagram that shows communication among classes without the use of a timeline (Section 1.5.2, Section A.3.3). See also *sequence diagram.*

column address select A DRAM signal that indicates the column part of the address is being presented to the memory (Section 4.3.2).

communication link A connection between processing elements (Section 8.2).

compulsory miss A cache miss that occurs the first time a location is used (Section 3.5.1).

computational kernel A small portion of an algorithm that performs a long function (Section 7.1).

computing platform A hardware system used for embedded computing (Section 4.1).

concurrent engineering Simultaneous design of several different system components (Section 9.2.2).

conflict graph A graph that represents incompatibilities between entities; used in register allocation (Section 5.5.8).

conflict miss A cache miss caused by two locations in use mapping to the same cache location (Section 3.5.1).

control In testing, the ability to set an input to a desired value (Section 4.8).

control/data flow graph A graph that models both the data and control operations in a program (Section 5.3).

cooperative multitasking A scheme for sharing the CPU among multiple processors in which the processes voluntarily give up control of the CPU (Section 6.4.1).

co-processor An optional unit added to a CPU that is responsible for executing some of the CPU's instructions (Section 3.4).

co-routine A manual method of programming concurrency (Section 6.2.2).

co-simulation See *hardware/software co-simulation.*

counter A device that counts asynchronous external events (Section 4.4.1).

CPSR Current program status register in the ARM processor (Section 2.3.2).

CPU See *central processing unit.*

CRC card A technique for capturing design information (Section 9.5.1).

critical instant In RMA, the worst-case combination of process activations (Section 6.6.1).

CRT Cathode ray tube (Section 4.4.5).

cycle-level simulator A CPU simulation that is accurate to the clock-cycle level (Section 4.7.2).

cyclomatic complexity A measure of the control complexity of a program (Section 5.9.1).

D/A converter See *digital/analog converter.*

DAG Data address generator in SHARC (Section 2.4.2).

data address generator Registers in SHARC used for addressing data and program memory (Section 2.4.2).

data flow graph A graph that models data operations without conditionals (Section 5.3.1).

data flow testing A technique for generating tests by examining the data flow representation of a program (Section 5.9.1).

data link layer In the OSI model, the layer responsible for reliable data transport (Section 8.2.2).

data memory Memory bank in the SHARC reserved for data (Section 2.4.1).

dead code elimination Eliminating code that can never be executed (Section 5.5.5).

deadline The time at which a process must finish (Section 6.5.3).

debouncing Eliminating the bouncing of a switch (Section 4.4.3).

decision node A node in a CDFG that models a conditional (Section 5.3.2).

def-use analysis Analyzing the relationships between reads and writes of variables in a program (Section 5.9.1).

delayed branch A branch instruction that always executes one or more instructions after the branch, independent of whether the branch is taken (Section 3.6.1).

dense instruction set An instruction set designed to provide compact code (Section 5.8).

design flow A series of steps used to implement a system (Section 9.2.2).

design for testability Designing a system so that it is easy to test (Section 4.8).

design methodology A method of proceeding through levels of abstraction to complete a design (Section 9.2).

design pattern A generic design for a software component that can be adapted to a variety of circumstances (Section 5.2.1).

design process See *design methodology.*

digital/analog converter A device that converts a sequence of digital values into an analog waveform (Section 4.4.2).

digital signal processor A microprocessor whose architecture is optimized for digital signal processing applications (Section 2.1).

direct-mapped cache A cache with a single set (Section 3.5.1).

direct memory access A bus transfer performed by a device without executing instructions on the CPU (Section 4.2.2).

distributed embedded system An embedded system built around a network (Section 8.1).

DM Data memory in SHARC (Section 2.4.1).

DMA See *direct memory access.*

DMA controller A logic unit designed to execute DMA transfers (Section 4.2.2).

DNS See *domain name server.*

Domain Name Service An Internet service that translates names to Internet addresses (Section 8.3.6).

DRAM See *dynamic random access memory.*

DSP See *digital signal processor.*

dynamic power management A power management technique that looks at the CPU activity (Section 3.7).

dynamic random access memory A memory that relies on stored charge (Section 4.3.2).

dynamically linked library A code library that is linked into the program at the start of execution (Section 5.4.2).

earliest deadline first A variable priority scheduling scheme (Section 6.6.2).

EDF See *earliest deadline first.*

EDO RAM Extended–data-out RAM, a memory that provides looser constraints on data timing (Section 4.3.2).

embedded computer system A computer used to implement some of the functionality of something other than a general-purpose computer (Section 1.2).

encoded keyboard A keyboard that produces codes for key depressions (Section 4.4.3).

energy The ability to do work (Section 3.7).

enq Short for *enquiry*, a signal used in handshaking protocols (Section 4.2.1).

entry point A label in an assembly language module that can be referred to by other program modules (Section 5.4.2).

EPROM See *erasable PROM*.

erasable PROM A programmable read-only memory that can be erased and reprogrammed (Section 4.3.3).

error injection Evaluating test coverage by inserting errors into a program and using your tests to try to find those errors (Section 5.9.3).

Ethernet A local area network (Section 8.3.4).

evaluation board A printed circuit board designed to provide a typical platform (Section 4.6.2).

executable binary An object program that is ready for execution (Section 5.4).

exception Any unusual condition in the CPU that is recognized during execution (Section 3.3.2).

expression simplification Rewriting an arithmetic expression (Section 5.5.4).

external reference A reference in an assembly language program to another module's entry point (Section 5.4.2).

factory-programmed ROM A ROM that is programmed during manufacture (Section 4.3.3).

fault coverage The proportion of faults covered by a set of tests (Section 4.8).

fault model A model of possible faults (Section 4.8).

field-programmable gate array An integrated circuit that can be programmed by the user and that provides multilevel logic (Section 4.6.2, Section 7.2).

field-programmable ROM A ROM that can be programmed by the user after manufacture (Section 4.3.3).

first-level cache The cache closest to the CPU (Section 3.5.1).

flash PROM A programmable read-only memory that can be electrically erased and reprogrammed with standard voltages (Section 4.3.3).

four-cycle handshake A handshaking protocol that goes through four states (Section 4.2.1).

FPGA See *field-programmable gate array.*

frame pointer Points to the end of a procedure stack frame (Section 5.5.2).

function In a programming language, a procedure that can return a value to the caller (Section 2.3.3).

functional requirements Requirements that describe the logical behavior of the system (Section 9.3).

glue logic Interface logic (Section 4.5.2).

glueless interface An interface between components that requires no glue logic (Section 4.5.2).

handshake A protocol designed to confirm the arrival of data (Section 4.2.1).

hardware/software co-design The simultaneous design of hardware and software components to meet system requirements (Section 7.1).

hardware/software co-simulation Simultaneous simulation of hardware and software at different time granularities (Section 4.7.2).

hardware/software co-verification Any technique for simultaneously verifying hardware and software components (Section 4.7.2).

Harvard architecture A computer architecture that provides separate memories for instructions and data (Section 2.2.1).

hit rate The probability of a memory access being a cache hit (Section 3.5.1).

host system Any system that is used as an interface to another system (Section 4.7.1, Section 7.2).

Huffman coding A method of data compression (Section 3.8.1).

I^2C bus A serial bus for distributed embedded systems (Section 8.3.1).

IEEE 1394 A high-speed serial network for peripherals (Section 4.6.3).

immediate operand An operand embedded in an instruction rather than fetched from another location (Section 2.3.2).

induction variable elimination A loop optimization technique that eliminates references to variables derived from the loop control variable (Section 5.6.2).

initiation time The time at which a process becomes ready to execute (Section 6.5.3).

instruction-level simulator A CPU simulator that is accurate to the level of the programming model but not to timing (Section 4.7.2).

instruction set The definition of the operations performed by a CPU (Section 2.1).

Internet A worldwide network based on the Internet Protocol (Section 8.3.6).

Internet appliance An information system that makes use of the Internet (Section 8.5).

Internet-enabled embedded system Any embedded system that includes an Internet interface (Section 8.5).

Internet Protocol A packet-based protocol (Section 8.3.6).

interpreter A program that executes a given program by analyzing a high-level description of the program at execution time (Section 5.5.12).

interprocess communication A mechanism for communication between processes (Section 6.5.4).

interrupt A mechanism that allows a device to request service from the CPU (Section 3.2.4).

interrupt handler A routine called upon an interrupt to service the interrupting device (Section 3.2.4).

interrupt priority Priorities used to determine which of several interrupts gets attention first (Section 3.2.4).

interrupt vector Information used to select which segment of the program should be used to handle the interrupt request (Section 3.2.4).

I/O Input/output (Section 3.2).

IP See *Internet Protocol.*

ISA bus Industry Standard Architecture bus, an early bus for PCs (Section 4.6.3).

ISO 9000 A series of international standards for quality process management (Section 9.6.1).

iteration vector A specification of the loop iteration variable values that describe a particular iteration of a set of nested loops (Section 5.6.2).

JIT compiler A just-in-time compiler; compiles program sections on demand during execution (Section 5.5.12).

L1 cache See *first-level cache.*

L2 cache See *second-level cache.*

label In assembly language, a symbolic name for a memory location (Section 2.2.2).

LCD Liquid-crystal display (Section 4.4.5).

LED Light emitting diode (Section 4.4.4).

lightweight process A process that shares its memory spaces with other processes (Section 6.3).

link port A CPU-to-CPU networking system for SHARC (Section 8.3.3).

linker A program that combines multiple object program units, resolving references between them (Section 5.4.2).

Linux A well-known, open-source version of Unix (Section 6.1).

little-endian A data format in which the low-order byte is stored in the lowest bits of the word (Section 2.3.1).

load balancing Adjusting scheduling and allocation to even out system load in a network (Section 8.4.3).

loader A program that loads a given program into memory for execution (Section 5.4).

load map A description of where object modules should be placed in memory (Section 5.4.2).

load-store architecture An architecture in which only load and store operations can be used to access data and ALU, and other instructions cannot directly access memory (Section 2.3.2).

logic analyzer A machine that captures multiple channels of digital signals to produce a timing diagram view of execution (Section 4.7.2).

longest path The path through a weighted graph that gives the largest total sum of weights (Section 7.3.1).

loop nest A set of loops, one inside the other (Section 5.6.2).

loop unrolling Rewriting a loop so that several instances of the loop body are included in a single iteration of the modified loop (Section 5.5.7).

manufacturing test Testing for errors introduced during manufacturing (Section 4.8).

masking In interrupts, causing lower-priority interrupts to be held in order to service higher-priority interrupts (Section 3.2.4).

memory controller A logic unit designed as an interface between DRAM and other logic (Section 4.3.2).

memory management unit A unit responsible for translating logical addresses into physical addresses (Section 3.5.2).

memory-mapped I/O Performing I/O by reading and writing memory locations that correspond to device registers (Section 3.2.2).

memory mapping Translating addresses from logical to physical form (Section 3.5.2).

message delay The delay required to send a message on a network with no interference (Section 8.4.1).

message passing A style of interprocess communication (Section 6.5.4, Section 8.2.4).

methodology Used to describe an overall design process (Section 1.3).

microcontroller A microprocessor that includes memory and I/O devices, often including timers, on a single chip (Section 1.2).

miss rate The probability that a memory access will be a cache miss (Section 3.5.1).

MMU See *memory management unit.*

motion vector A vector describing the displacement between two units of an image (Section 7.4.1).

multihop network A network in which messages may go through an intermediate PE when traveling from source to destination (Section 8.4.1).

multirate Operations that have different deadlines, causing the operations to be performed at different rates (Section 1.2, Section 6.2.1).

Myrinet A high-performance network (Section 8.3.5).

network A system for communicating between components (Section 8.1).

network availability delay The delay incurred waiting for the network to become available (Section 8.4.1).

network layer In the OSI model, the layer that provides end-to-end service (Section 8.2.2).

n-key rollover Reading the correct sequence of key depressions when keys are depressed simultaneously (Section 4.4.3).

NMI See *nonmaskable interrupt.*

nonblocking communication Interprocess communication that allows the sender to continue execution after sending a message (Section 6.5.4).

nonfunctional requirements Requirements that do not describe the logical behavior of the system; examples include size, weight, and power consumption (Section 1.3.1, Section 9.3).

nonmaskable interrupt An interrupt that must always be handled, independent of other system activity (Section 3.2.4).

object A program unit that includes both internal data and methods that provide an interface to the data (Section 1.4).

object code A program in binary form (Section 5.4).

object oriented Any use of objects and classes in design; can be applied at many different levels of abstraction (Section 1.4).

observe In testing, the ability to see an output (Section 4.8).

operating system A program responsible for scheduling the CPU and controlling access to devices (Section 6.1).

origin The starting address of an assembly language module (Section 5.4.1).

OSI model A model for levels of abstraction in networks (Section 8.2.2).

overhead In operating systems, the CPU time required for the operating system to switch contexts (Section 6.6).

P() Traditional name for the procedure that takes a semaphore (Section 6.5.4).

page fault A reference to a memory page not currently in physical memory (Section 3.5.2).

page mode An addressing mechanism for RAMs (Section 4.3.2).

paged addressing Division of memory into equal-sized pages (Section 3.5.2).

partitioning Dividing a functional description into processes that can execute in parallel or modules that can be separately implemented (Section 4.6.1, Section 7.3.3).

PBX Private branch exchange, a telephone switching system (Section 9.7).

PC 1. In computer architecture, see *program counter*. 2. Personal computer (Section 4.6.3).

PC sampling Generating a program trace by periodically sampling the PC during execution (Section 5.6.2).

PCI A high-performance bus for PCs and other applications (Section 4.6.3).

PC-relative addressing An addressing mode that adds a value to the current PC (Section 2.3.3, Section 2.4.3).

PDA Personal digital assistant (Section 9.9).

PE See *processing element*.

peek A high-level language routine that reads an arbitrary memory location (Section 3.2.2).

performance The speed at which operations occur (Section 1.3).

period In real-time scheduling, a periodic interval of execution (Section 6.2.1).

physical layer In the OSI model, the layer that defines electrical and mechanical properties (Section 8.2.2).

pipe A Unix interprocess communication mechanism (Section 6.7.2).

pipeline A logic structure that allows several operations of the same type to be performed simultaneously on multiple values, with each value having a different part of the operation performed at any one time (Section 3.6.1).

PLC See *program location counter*.

PLD Programmable logic device (Section B.4).

PM Program memory in SHARC (Section 2.4.1).

poke A high-level language routine that writes an arbitrary location (Section 3.2.2).

polling Testing one or more devices to determine whether they are ready (Section 3.2.3).

POSIX A standardized version of Unix (Section 6.1).

post-indexing An addressing mode in which an index is added to the base address after the fetch (Section 2.3.2).

power Energy per unit time (Section 3.7).

power-down mode A mode invoked in a CPU that causes the CPU to reduce its power consumption (Section 3.7).

power management policy A scheme for making power management decisions (Section 6.9).

power state machine A finite-state machine model for the behavior of a component under power management (Section 3.7).

predictive shutdown A power management technique that predicts appropriate times for system shutdown (Section 6.9).

preemptive multitasking A scheme for sharing the CPU in which the operating system can interrupt the execution of processes (Section 6.4.2).

presentation layer In the OSI model, the layer responsible for data formats (Section 8.2.2).

priority-driven scheduling Any scheduling technique that uses priorities of processes to determine the running process (Section 6.5).

priority inversion A situation in which a lower-priority process prevents a higher-priority process from executing (Section 6.6.4).

procedure A programming language construct that allows a single piece of code to be called at multiple points in the program (Section 2.3.3). Generally, a synonym for *subroutine;* see also *function.*

procedure call stack A stack of activation records for currently active processes (Section 2.3.3).

procedure linkage A convention for passing parameters and other actions required to call a procedure (Section 2.3.3).

process A unique execution of a program (Section 6.1).

processing element A component that performs a computation under the coordination of the system (Section 7.2, Section 8.1).

program counter A common name for the register that holds the address of the currently executing instruction (Section 2.2.1).

program location counter A variable used by an assembler to assign memory addresses to instructions and data in the assembled program (Section 5.4.1).

program memory Memory bank on the SHARC normally used for instructions, but that also can be used for data (Section 2.4.1).

programming model The CPU registers visible to the programmer (Section 2.2.1).

pseudo-op An assembly language statement that does not generate code or data (Section 2.2.2, Section 5.4.1).

quality assurance A process for ensuring that systems are designed and built to high quality standards (Section 9.6).

RAM See *random-access memory.*

random-access memory A memory that can be addressed in arbitrary order (Section 4.3.2).

random testing Testing a program using randomly generated inputs (Section 5.9.2).

RAS See *row address select.*

raster scan (or order) display A display that writes pixels by rows and columns (Section 4.4.5).

rate Inverse of period (Section 6.2.1).

rate-monotonic scheduling A fixed-priority scheduling scheme (Section 6.6.1).

reactive system A system designed to react to external events (Section 5.5.2).

read-only memory A memory with fixed contents (Section 4.3.3).

real time A system that must perform operations by a certain time (Section 1.2).

real-time operating system An operating system designed to be able to satisfy real-time constraints (Section 6.1).

reentrancy The ability of a program to be executed multiple times, using the same memory image without error (Section 6.3).

refresh Restoring the values kept in a DRAM (Section 4.3.2).

register Generally, an electronic component that holds state. In the context of computer programming, storage internal to the CPU that is part of the programming model (Section 2.2.1).

register allocation Assigning variables to registers (Section 5.5.8).

register-indirect addressing Fetching from a first memory location to find the address of the memory location that contains the operand (Section 2.3.2).

regression testing Testing hardware or software by applying previously used tests (Section 5.9.2).

relative address An address measured relative to some other location, such as the start of an object module (Section 5.4).

requirements An informal description of what a system should do (Section 1.3). A precursor to a specification.

reservation table A hardware technique for scheduling instructions (Section 5.5.9).

response time The time span between the initial request for a process and its completion (Section 6.6.1).

RISC Reduced instruction set computer (Section 2.2).

RMA Rate-monotonic analysis, another term for *rate-monotonic scheduling*.

rollover Reading multiple keys when two keys are pressed at once (Section 4.4.3).

ROM See *read-only memory*.

row address select A DRAM signal that indicates the row part of the address is being presented (Section 4.3.2).

RTOS See *real-time operating system*.

saturation arithmetic An arithmetic system that provides a result at the maximum/minimum value on overflow/underflow (Section 2.4.2).

scan chain A set of registers that can be configured as a shift register to allow access to a machine's internal state (Section 4.8).

scheduling Determining the time at which an operation will occur (Section 7.3.4).

scheduling overhead The execution time required to make a scheduling decision (Section 6.6.4).

scheduling policy A methodology for making scheduling decisions (Section 6.6).

SDL A software specification language (Section 9.4.1).

second-level cache A cache after the first-level cache but before main memory (Section 3.5.1).

segmented addressing Dividing memory into large, unequal-sized segments (Section 3.5.2).

semaphore A mechanism for coordinating communicating processes (Section 6.5.4).

sensor An input device that reads a physical value (Section 8.2).

sequence diagram A UML diagram type that shows how objects communicate over time using a timeline (Section 1.4.2). See also *collaboration diagram.*

session layer In the OSI model, the layer responsible for application dialog control (Section 8.2.2).

set-associative cache A cache with multiple sets (Section 3.5.1).

set-top box A system used for cable or satellite television reception (Section 9.10).

shared memory A communication style that allows multiple processes to access the same memory locations (Section 6.5.4).

signal 1. A Unix interprocess communication method (Section 6.7.1). 2. A UML stereotype for communication (Section 6.7.2).

single-assignment form A program that writes to each variable once at most (Section 5.3.1).

single-hop network A network in which messages can travel from one PE to any other PE without going through a third PE (Section 8.4.1).

software interrupt See *trap.*

software pipelining A technique for scheduling instructions in loops (Section 5.5.9).

specification A formal description of what a system should do (Section 1.3). More precise than a requirements document.

speedup The ratio of system performance before and after a design modification (Section 7.3.1).

spill Writing a register value to main memory so that the register can be used for another purpose (Section 5.5.8).

spiral model A design methodology in which the design iterates through specification, design, and test at increasingly detailed levels of abstraction (Section 9.2.2).

SRAM See *static random-access memory.*

stable In logic timing analysis, a signal whose value is not changing at a particular moment in time (Section 4.2.1).

stack pointer Points to the top of a procedure call stack (Section 5.5.2).

Statecharts A specification technique that uses compound states (Section 9.4.1).

state machine Generally, a machine that goes through a sequence of states over time. May be implemented in software (Section 1.4.2, Section 5.2.2).

state mode A logic analyzer mode that provides reduced timing resolution in return for longer time spans (Section 4.7.2).

static power management A power management technique that does not consider the current CPU behavior (Section 3.7).

static random-access memory A RAM that consumes power to continuously maintain its stored values (Section 4.3.2).

static scheduling A scheduling policy in which process priorities are fixed (Section 6.6.1).

streaming data A sequence of data values that is received periodically, such as in digital signal processing (Section 2.2.1).

strength reduction Replacing an operation with another equivalent operation that is less expensive (Section 5.6.2).

stuck-at-0/1 A type of fault model in which faults cause an output to be always 0 or always 1 (Section 4.8).

subroutine A synonym for *procedure* (Section 2.3.3).

successive refinement A design methodology in which the design goes through the levels of abstraction several times, adding detail in each refinement phase (Section 9.2.2).

superscalar An execution method that can perform several different instructions simultaneously (Section 3.6.2).

supervisor mode A CPU execution mode with unlimited privileges (Section 3.3.1). See also *user mode*.

symbol table Generally, a table relating symbols in a program to their meaning; in an assembler, a table giving the locations specified by labels (Section 5.4.1).

synchronous DRAM A memory that uses a clock (Section 4.3.2).

system-on-silicon A single-chip system that includes computation, memory, and I/O (Section 9.11).

target system A system being debugged with the aid of a host (Section 4.7.1).

task graph A graph that shows processes and data dependencies among them (Section 6.5.4).

TCP See *Transmission Control Protocol.*

testbench A setup used to test a design; may be implemented in software to test other software (Section 4.7.1).

testbench program A program running on a host used to interface to a debugger that runs on an embedded processor (Section 4.7.1).

test vector A test input (Section 4.8).

thread See *lightweight process.*

timer A device that measures time from a clock input (Section 4.4.1).

timing constraint A relationship among two or more events on signals in a logic network (Section 4.2.1).

timing diagram A diagram that shows the relationships between signal transitions, possibly with arrows showing timing constraints (Section 4.2.1).

timing mode A logic analyzer mode that provides increased timing resolution (Section 4.7.2).

TLB See *translation lookaside buffer.*

top-down design Designing from higher levels of abstraction to lower levels of abstraction (Section 1.3).

touchscreen A combination display and input device that allows pointing (Section 4.4.6).

trace A record of the execution path of a program (Section 5.6.2).

trace-driven analysis Analyzing a trace of a program's execution (Section 5.6.2).

translation lookaside buffer A cache used to speed up virtual-to-physical address translation (Section 3.5.2).

Transmission Control Protocol A connection-oriented protocol built upon the IP (Section 8.3.6).

transport layer In the OSI model, the layer responsible for connections (Section 8.2.2).

trap An instruction that causes the CPU to execute a predetermined handler (Section 3.3.3).

UART Universal Asynchronous Receiver/Transmitter, a serial I/O device (Section 3.2.1).

UML See Unified Modeling Language.

unified cache A cache that holds both instructions and data (Section 3.5.1).

Unified Modeling Language A widely used graphical language that can be used to describe designs at many levels of abstraction (Section 1.4).

usage scenario A description of how a system will be used (Section 9.6.2).

USB Universal serial bus, a high-performance serial bus for PCs and other systems (Section 4.6.3).

user mode A CPU execution mode with limited privileges (Section 3.3.1). See also *supervisor mode.*

UV-EPROM An EPROM that can be erased with ultraviolet light (Section 4.3.3).

V() Traditional name for the procedure that releases a semaphore (Section 6.5.4).

video RAM A two-port RAM with one parallel and one serial port, designed for video memories (Section 4.3.2).

virtual addressing Translating an address from a logical to a physical location (Section 3.5.2).

VLSI Acronym for *very large scale integration;* generally means any modern integrated circuit fabrication process (Section 1.2).

von Neumann architecture A computer architecture that stores instructions and data in the same memory (Section 2.2).

wait state A state in a bus transaction that waits for the response of a memory or device (Section 4.2.1).

watchdog timer A timer that resets the system when the system fails to periodically reset the timer (Section 4.4.1).

waterfall model A design methodology in which the design proceeds from higher to lower levels of abstraction (Section 9.2.2).

white-box testing See *clear-box testing.*

word The basic unit of memory access in a computer (Section 2.3.1).

working set The set of memory locations used during a chosen interval of a program's execution (Section 3.5.1).

worst-case execution time The longest execution time for any possible set of inputs (Section 5.6).

write-back Writing to main memory only when a line is removed from the cache (Section 3.5.1).

write-through Writing to main memory for every write into the cache (Section 3.5.1).

yield The proportion of working devices obtained from manufacturing (Section 4.8).

References

[ADI97] Analog Devices, Inc., *ADSP-2106x SHARC User's Manual,* second edition, Analog Devices, 1997.

[Aho86] Alfred V. Aho, Ravi Sethi, and Jeffrey D. Ullman, *Compilers: Principles, Techniques, and Tools,* Reading MA: Addison-Wesley, 1986.

[Aki96] Olu Akiwumu-Assani and Marnix Vlot, "Multi-media terminal architecture," *Philips Journal of Research,* 50(1/2), 1996, pp. 169–184.

[Ald73] Robin Alder, Mark Baker, and Howard D. Marshall, "The logic analyzer: A new instrument for observing logic signals," *Hewlett-Packard Journal,* 25(2), October 1973, pp. 2–16.

[ARM99A] ARM Limited, *AMBA(TM) Specification (Rev 2.0),* 1999. Available at www.arm.com.

[ARM99B] ARM Limited, *ARM7TDMI-S Technical Reference Manual,* 1999. Available at www.arm.com.

[ARM00] ARM Limited, *Integrator/LM-XCV400+ Logic Module,* ARM DUI 0130A, February 2000. Available at www.arm.com.

[Asa98] Mutsuhiko Asada and Pong Mang Yan, "Strengthening Software Quality Assurance," *Hewlett-Packard Journal,* 49(2), May, 1998, pp. 89–97.

[Ban93] Uptal Banerjee, *Loop Transformations for Restructuring Compilers: The Foundations,* Boston: Kluwer Academic Publishers, 1993.

[Ban94] Uptal Banerjee, *Loop Parallelization,* Boston: Kluwer Academic Publishers, 1994.

[Bec92] David Becker, Raj K. Singh, and Stephen G. Tell, "An engineering environment for hardware/software co-simulation," in *Proceedings, 29th ACM/ IEEE Design Automation Conference*, Los Alamitos CA: IEEE Computer Society Press, 1992, pp. 129–134.

[Bei84] Boris Beizer, *Software System Testing and Quality Assurance*, New York: Van Nostrand Reinhold, 1984.

[Bei90] Boris Beizer, *Software Testing Techniques*, second edition, New York: Van Nostrand Reinhold, 1990.

[Ben99] L. Benini, A. Bogliolo, G. A. Paleologo, and G. DeMicheli, "Policy optimization for dynamic power management," *IEEE Transactions on Computer-Aided Design,* 18(6), June 1999, pp. 742–760.

[Ben00] L. Benini, A. Bogliolo, and G. De Micheli, "A survey of design techniques for system-level dynamic power management," *IEEE Transactions on VLSI Systems*, 8(3), June 2000, pp. 299–316.

[Bod95] Nanette J. Boden, Danny Cohen, Robert E. Felderman, Alan E. Kulawik, Charles L. Seitz, Jakov N. Seizovic, and Wen-King Su, "Myrinet—a gigabit-per-second local-area network," *IEEE Micro*, February 1995, pp. 29–36.

[Boe84] Barry W. Boehm, "Verifying and validating software requirements and design specifications," *IEEE Software*, 1(1), January 1984, pp. 75–88.

[Boe87] Barry W. Boehm, "A spiral model of software development and enhancement," in *Software Engineering Project Management*, 1987, pp. 128–142. Reprinted in Richard H. Thayer and Merlin Dorfman, eds., *System and Software Requirements Engineering*, Los Alamitos CA: IEEE Computer Society Press, 1990.

[Boe92] Robert A. Boeller, Samuel A. Stodder, John F. Meyer, and Victor T. Escobedo, "A large-format thermal inkjet drafting plotter," *Hewlett-Packard Journal*, 43(6), December, 1992, pp. 6–15.

[Boo91] Grady Booch, *Object-Oriented Design*, Redwood City CA: Benjamin/ Cummings, 1991.

[Boo99] Grady Booch, James Rumbaugh, and Ivar Jacobson, *The Unified Modeling Language User Guide*, Reading MA: Addison-Wesley, 1999.

[Cal00] Timothy J. Callahan, John R. Hauser, and John Wawrzynek, "The Garp architecture and C compiler," *IEEE Computer*, 33(4), April 2000, pp. 62–69.

[Cat98] Francky Catthoor, Sven Wuytack, Eddy De Greef, Florin Balasa, Lode Nachtergaele, and Arnout Vandecappelle, *Custom Memory Management Methodology: Exploration of Memory Organization for Embedded Multimedia System Design*, Norwell MA: Kluwer Academic Publishers, 1998.

[Cha92] Anantha P. Chandrakasan, Samuel Sheng, and Robert W. Brodersen, "Low-power CMOS digital design," *IEEE Journal of Solid-State Circuits*, 27(4), April 1992, pp. 473–484.

[Chi94] M. Chiodo, P. Giusto, H. Hsieh, A. Jurecska, L. Lavagno, and A. Sangiovanni-Vincentelli, "Hardware/software co-design of embedded systems," *IEEE Micro*, 14(4), August 1994, pp. 26–36.

[Cho85] Tsun S. Chow, *Tutorial: Software Quality Assurance: A Practical Approach*, Silver Spring MD: IEEE Computer Society Press, 1985.

[Coh81] Danny Cohen, "On holy wars and a plea for peace," *Computer*, 14(10), October 1981, pp. 48–54.

[Col97] Robert R. Collins, "In-circuit emulation," *Dr. Dobb's Journal*, September 1997, pp. 111–113.

[Cou95] Sari L. Coumeri and Donald E. Thomas, "A simulation environment for hardware-software codesign," in *Proceedings, ICCD '95*, Los Alamitos CA: IEEE Computer Society Press, 1995, pp. 58–63.

[Cra97] Timothy Cramer, Richard Friedman, Terrence Miller, David Seberger, Robert Wilson, and Mario Wolczko, "Compiling Java just in time," *IEEE Micro*, May/June 1997, pp. 36–43.

[Cus91] Michael A. Cusumano, *Japan's Software Factories*, New York: Oxford University Press, 1991.

[Dah00] Tom Dahlin, "Reach out and touch: Designing a resistive touch screen," *Circuit Cellar*, 114, January 2000, pp. 20–25.

[Dav90] Alan M. Davis, *Software Requirements: Analysis and Specification*, Englewood Cliffs NJ: Prentice Hall, 1990.

[DiG90] Joseph Di Giacomo, *Digital Bus Handbook*, New York: McGraw-Hill, 1990.

[Dou98] Bruce Powel Douglass, *Real-Time UML: Developing Efficient Objects for Embedded Systems*, Reading MA: Addison-Wesley Longman, 1998.

[Dou99] Bruce Powel Douglass, *Doing Hard Time: Developing Real-Time Systems with UML, Objects, Frameworks, and Patterns*, Reading MA: Addison-Wesley Longman, 1999.

[Dut96] Santanu Dutta and Wayne Wolf, "A flexible parallel architecture adapted to block-matching motion-estimation algorithms," *IEEE Transactions on Circuits and Systems for Video Technology*, 6(1), February 1996, pp. 74–86.

[Ear97] Richard W. Earnshaw, Lee D. Smith, and Kevin Welton, "Challenges in cross-development," *IEEE Micro*, July/August 1997, pp. 28–36.

[Egg90] Lewis C. Eggebrecht, *Interfacing to the IBM Personal Computer*, second edition, Carmel IN: Howard W. Sams and Co., 1990.

[End75] Albert Endres, "An analysis of errors and their causes in system programs," *IEEE Transactions on Software Engineering*, June 1975, pp. 140–149.

[Ern93] Rolf Ernst, Joerg Henkel, and Thomas Benner, "Hardware-software cosynthesis for microcontrollers," *IEEE Design and Test of Computers,* 10(4), December 1993, pp. 64–75.

[FAA98] Federal Aviation Administration, *Aeronautical Information Manual*, Washington DC: Government Printing Office, 1998.

[Fag76] M. E. Fagan, "Design and code inspections to reduce errors in program development," *IBM Systems Journal*, 15(3), 1976, pp. 219–248.

[Fal92] Ohad Falik and Gideon Intrater, "NSC's Digital Answering Machine Solution," in *Proceedings, ICCD '92*, Los Alamitos CA: IEEE Computer Society Press, 1992.

[Fra88] Phyllis G. Frankl and Elaine J. Weyuker, "An applicable family of data flow testing criteria," *IEEE Transactions on Software Engineering,* 14(10), October 1988, pp. 1483–1498.

[Fur96] Steve Furber, *ARM System Architecture*, Harlow, England: Addison-Wesley, 1996.

[Gal95] Bill O. Gallmeister, *Posix.4: Programming for the Real World*, Sebastopol CA: O'Reilly and Associates, 1995.

[Gar81] John R. Garman, "The 'bug' heard 'round the world," *Software Engineering Notes*, 6(5), October 1981, pp. 3–10.

[Gar94] Sonya Gary, Pete Ippolito, Gianfranco Gerosa, Carl Dietz, Jim Eno, and Hector Sanchez, "PowerPC 603, a microprocessor for portable computers," *IEEE Design and Test of Computers*, 11(4), Winter 1994, pp. 14–23.

[Gat94] David A. Gatenby, Paul M. Lee, Randall E. Howard, Kaveh Hushyar, Rich Layendecker, and John Wesner, "Concurrent engineering: An enabler for fast, high-quality product realization," *AT&T Technical Journal*, January/February 1994, pp. 34–47.

[Gho97] Somnath Ghosh, Margaret Martonosi, and Sharad Malik, "Cache miss equations: An analytical representation of cache misses," in *Proceedings of the 11th ACM International Conference in Supercomputing*, ACM Press, 1997.

[Gup93] Rajesh K. Gupta and Giovanni De Micheli, "Hardware-software cosynthesis for digital systems," *IEEE Design and Test of Computers*, 10(3), September 1993, pp. 29–40.

[Har87] D. Harel, "Statecharts: A visual formalism for complex systems," *Science of Computer Programming*, 8, 1987, pp. 231–274.

[Hat88] Derek J. Hatley and Imtiaz A. Pirbhai, *Strategies for Real-Time System Specification*, New York: Dorset House, 1988.

[Hen94] J. Henkel, R. Ernst, U. Holtmann, and T. Benner, "Adaptation of partitioning and high-level synthesis in hardware/software co-synthesis," in *Proceedings, ICCAD-94*, Los Alamitos CA: IEEE Computer Society Press, 1994, pp. 96–100.

[Hen96] John L. Hennessy and David A. Patterson, *Computer Architecture: A Quantitative Approach,* second edition, San Francisco: Morgan Kaufmann, 1996.

[Hor96] Joseph R. Horgan and Aditya P. Mathur, "Software testing and reliability," Chapter 13 in Michael R. Lyu, ed., *Handbook of Software Reliability Engineering*, Los Alamitos CA: IEEE Computer Society Press/McGraw-Hill, 1996, pp. 531–566.

[How82] W. E. Howden, "Weak mutation testing and the completeness of test cases," *IEEE Transactions on Software Engineering*, SE-8(4), July 1982, pp. 371–379.

[Hsu94] T. Richard Hsueh, Thomas F. Houghton, Joseph F. Maranzano, and Gerald P. Pasternack, "Software production: From art/craft to engineering," *AT&T Technical Journal*, January/February 1994, pp. 59–68.

[Huf52] David A. Huffman, "A method for the construction of minimum-redundancy codes," *Proceedings of the IRE*, September 1952, pp. 1098–1101.

[Int82] Intel, *Microprocessor and Peripheral Handbook*, 1982.

[Int89] Intel, *80960KB Hardware Designer's Reference Manual*, 1989. ISBN 1-55512-100-4.

[Int91] Intel, *i960 KA/KB Microprocessor Programmer's Reference Manual*, 1991. ISBN 1-55512-137-3.

[Int96] Intel, Microsoft, and Toshiba, *Advanced Configuration and Power Interface Specification*, 1996. Available at http://www.teleport.com/~acpi.

[Int99] Intel, *Intel StrongARM SA-1100 Microprocessor Technical Reference Manual*, March 1999. Available at http://www.intel.com.

[Jag95] Dave Jaggar, ed., *Advanced RISC Machines Architectural Reference Manual,* London: Prentice Hall, 1995.

[Jen95] Michael G. Jenner, *Software Quality Management and ISO 9001: How to Make Them Work for You,* New York: John Wiley and Sons, 1995.

[Jon78] T. C. Jones, "Measuring programming quality and productivity," *IBM Systems Journal,* 17(1), 1978, pp. 39–63.

[Kas79] J. M. Kasson, "The ROLM Computerized Branch Exchange: An advanced digital PBX," *IEEE Computer,* June 1979, pp. 24–31.

[Kem98] T. M. Kemp, R. K. Montoye, J. D. Harper, J. D. Palmer, and D. J. Auerbach, "A decompression core for PowerPC," *IBM Journal of Research and Development,* 42(6), November 1998, pp. 807–812.

[Ker88] Brian W. Kernighan and Dennis M. Ritchie, *The C Programming Language,* second edition, New York: Prentice Hall, 1988.

[Kog81] Peter M. Kogge, *The Architecture of Pipelined Computers,* New York: McGraw-Hill, 1981.

[Kop97] Hermann Kopetz, *Real-Time Systems: Design Principles for Distributed Embedded Applications,* Boston: Kluwer Academic Publishers, 1997.

[Lev86] Nancy G. Leveson, "Software safety: Why, what, and how," *Computing Surveys,* 18(2), June 1986, pp. 125–163.

[Lev93] Nancy G. Leveson and Clark S. Turner, "An investigation of the Therac-25 accidents," *IEEE Computer,* July 1993, pp. 18–41.

[Lev94] Nancy G. Leveson, Mats Per Erik Heimdahl, Holly Hildreth, and Jon Damon Reese, "Requirements specification for process-control systems," *IEEE Transactions on Software Engineering,* 20(9), September 1994, pp. 684–707.

[Li97A] Yanbing Li and Wayne Wolf, "Scheduling and allocation of multirate real-time embedded systems," in *Proceedings, ED&TC '97,* Los Alamitos CA: IEEE Computer Society Press, 1997, pp. 134–139.

[Li97B] Yanbing Li and Wayne Wolf, "A task-level hierarchical memory model for system synthesis of multiprocessors," in *Proceedings, 34th Design Automation Conference,* ACM Press, 1997, pp. 153–156.

[Li97C] Yanbing Li, Miodrag Potkonjak, and Wayne Wolf, "Real-time operating systems for embedded computing," in *Proceedings, ICCD '97,* Los Alamitos CA: IEEE Computer Society Press, 1997.

[Li97D] Yau-Tsun Steven Li and Sharad Malik, "Performance analysis of embedded software using implicit path enumeration," *IEEE Transactions on CAD/ICAS*, 16(12), December 1997, pp. 1477–1487.

[Li98] Yanbing Li and Joerg Henkel, "A framework for estimating and minimizing energy dissipation of embedded HW/SW systems," in *Proceedings, DAC '98*, New York: ACM Press, 1998, pp. 188–193.

[Li99] Yanbing Li and Wayne Wolf, "A task-level hierarchical memory model for system synthesis of multiprocessors," *IEEE Transactions on CAD*, 18(10), October 1999, pp. 1405–1417.

[Lie98] Clifford Liem and Pierre Paulin, "Compilation Techniques and Tools for Embedded Processor Architectures," Chapter 5 in J. Staunstrup and W. Wolf, eds., *Hardware/Software Co-Design: Principles and Practice*, Boston: Kluwer Academic Publishers, 1998.

[Liu73] C. L. Liu and James W. Layland, "Scheduling algorithms for multiprogramming in a hard–real-time environment," *Journal of the ACM*, 20(1), January 1973, pp. 46–61.

[Los97] Pete Loshin, *TCP/IP Clearly Explained*, second edition, New York: Academic Press, 1997.

[Lyu96] Michael R. Lyu, ed., *Handbook of Software Reliability Engineering*, Los Alamitos, CA: IEEE Computer Society Press/McGraw-Hill, 1996.

[Mad97] J. Madsen, J. Grode, P. V. Knudsen, M. E. Peterson, and A. Haxthausen, "LYCOS: The Lungby Co-Synthesis System," *Design Automation for Embedded Systems*, 2(2), March 1997, pp. 165–195.

[Mal96] Sharad Malik, Wayne Wolf, Andrew Wolfe, Yao-Tsun Steven Li, and Ti-Yen Yen, "Performance analysis of embedded systems," in G. De Micheli and M. Sami, eds., *Hardware-Software Co-Design*, Boston: Kluwer Academic Publishers, 1996.

[Man99] William H. Mangione-Smith, "Technical challenges for designing personal digital assistants," *Design Automation for Embedded Systems*, 4(1), January 1999, pp. 23–40.

[McC76] T. J. McCabe, "A complexity measure," *IEEE Transactions on Software Engineering*, 2, 1976, pp. 308–320.

[McD98] Charles E. McDowell, Bruce R. Montague, Michael R. Allen, Elizabeth A. Baldwin, and Marcelo E. Montoreano, "Javacam: Trimming Java down to size," *IEEE Internet Computing*, May/June 1998, pp. 53–59.

[Meb92] Alfred Holt Mebane IV, James R. Schmedake, Iue-Shuenn Chen, and Anne P. Kadonaga, "Electronic and firmware design of the HP DesignJet Drafting Plotter," *Hewlett-Packard Journal*, 43(6), December 1992, pp. 16–23.

[Met97] Hufeza Metha, Robert Michael Owens, Mary Jane Irwin, Rita Chen, and Debashree Ghosh, "Techniques for low energy software," in *Proceedings, 1997 International Symposium on Low Power Electronics and Design*, New York: ACM Press, 1997, pp. 72–75.

[Min95] Mindshare, Inc., Tom Shanley and Don Anderson, *PCI System Architecture*, third edition, Reading MA: Addison-Wesley, 1995.

[Muc97] Steven S. Muchnick, *Advanced Compiler Design and Implementation*, San Francisco: Morgan Kaufmann, 1997.

[Mye79] G. Myers, *The Art of Software Testing*, New York: John Wiley and Sons, 1979.

[New94] Richard Newman, "The Personal PBX," *Circuit Cellar INK*, 48, July 1994, pp. 14–22.

[New96] Richard Newman, "Connect the Personal PBX to the real world," *Circuit Cellar INK*, 67, February 1996, pp. 18–24.

[Obe99] James Oberg, "Why the Mars probe went off course," *IEEE Spectrum*, December 1999, pp. 34–39.

[Pan99] Preeti Ranjan Panda, Nikil Dutt, and Alexandru Nicolau, *Memory Issues in Embedded Systems-on-Chip: Optimizations and Exploration*, Norwell MA: Kluwer Academic Publishers, 1999.

[Pat98] David A. Patterson and John L. Hennessy, *Computer Organization and Design: The Hardware/Software Interface*, second edition, San Francisco: Morgan Kaufmann, 1998.

[Phi89] "Using the 8XC751 microcontroller as an I^2C bus master," Philips Application Note AN422, September 1989, revised June 1993, in *Application Notes and Development Tools for 80C51 Microcontrollers*, Philips Semiconductors, 1995.

[Phi92] "The I^2C bus and how to use it (including specification)," January 1992, in *Application Notes and Development Tools for 80C51 Microcontrollers*, Philips Semiconductors, 1995.

[Pho99] "User Report: Canon EOS-3," *Photographic* 27(12), April 1999, pp. 76–80.

[Pre97] Roger S. Pressman, *Software Engineering: A Practitioner's Approach,* New York: McGraw-Hill, 1997.

[Rat96] Kamlesh Rath and James W. Wendorf, "Set-top box control software: A key component in digital video," *Philips Journal of Research,* 50(1/2), 1996, pp. 185–199.

[Rho97] David L. Rhodes and Wayne Wolf, "Allocation and data arrival design of hard real-time systems," in *Proceedings, ICCD '97,* Los Alamitos CA: IEEE Computer Society Press, 1997.

[Roc82] Anders Rockström and Roberto Saracco, "SDL—CCITT specification and description language," *IEEE Transactions on Communication,* 30(6), June 1982, pp. 1310–1318.

[Rom98] Glenn M. Romano, "Design and test of a multi-processor DSP multi-chip module," 1998. Available at http://www.analog.com.

[Ros92] Christopher Rosebrugh and Eng-Kee Kwang, "Multiple microcontrollers in an embedded system," *Dr. Dobb's Journal,* January 1992, pp. 48–57.

[Rum91] James Rumbaugh, Michael Blaha, William Premerlani, Frederick Eddy, and William Lorensen, *Object-Oriented Modeling and Design,* Englewood Cliffs NJ: Prentice Hall, 1991.

[Sch94] Charles H. Schmauch, *ISO 9000 for Software Developers,* Milwaukee: ASQC Quality Press, 1994.

[SEI99] Software Engineering Institute, "Capability Maturity Model (SW-CMM) for Software," 1999. Available at www.sei.cmu.edu/cmm/cmm.html.

[Seg97] Simon Segars, "ARM7TDMI power consumption," *IEEE Micro,* July/August 1997, pp. 12–19.

[Sel94] Bran Selic, Garth Gullekson, and Paul T. Ward, *Real-Time Object-Oriented Modeling,* New York: John Wiley and Sons, 1994.

[Sha89] Alan C. Shaw, "Reasoning about time in higher-level language software," *IEEE Transactions on Software Engineering,* 15, July 1989, pp. 875–889.

[Shl92] Sally Shlaer and Stephen J. Mellor, *Object Lifecycles: Modeling the World in States,* New York: Yourdon Press Computing Series, 1992.

[Spa99] Peter Spasov, *Microcontroller Technology: The 68HC11,* third edition, Upper Saddle River NJ: Prentice Hall, 1999.

[Sri94] Amitabh Srivastava and Alan Eustace, "ATOM: A system for building customized program analysis tools," Digital Equipment Corp., WRL Research Report 94/2, March 1994. Available at www.research.digital.com.

[Sta97A] William Stallings, *Data and Computer Communication,* fifth edition, Upper Saddle River NJ: Prentice Hall, 1997.

[Sta97B] J. Staunstrup and W. Wolf, eds., *Hardware/Software Co-Design: Principles and Practice,* Boston: Kluwer Academic Publishers, 1997.

[Sto95] Thomas M. Stout and Theodore J. Williams, "Pioneering work in the field of computer process control," *IEEE Annals of the History of Computing,* 17(1), 1995, pp. 6–18.

[Tha90] Richard H. Thayer and Merlin Dorfman, eds., *System and Software Requirements Engineering,* Los Alamitos CA: IEEE Computer Society Press, 1990.

[Tiw94] Vivek Tiwari, Sharad Malik, and Andrew Wolfe, "Power analysis of embedded software: A first step toward software power minimization," *IEEE Transactions on VLSI Systems,* 2(4), December 1994, pp. 437–445.

[Tru98] T. E. Truman, T. Pering, R. Doering, and R. W. Brodersen, "The Info-Pad multimedia terminal: A portable device for wireless information access," *IEEE Transactions on Computers,* 47(10), October 1998, pp. 1073–1087.

[van97] Albert van der Werf, Font Brüls, Richard Kleinhorst, Erwin Waterlander, Matt Verstraeler, and Thomas Friedrich, "I.McIC: A single-chip MPEG2 video encoder for storage," in *ISSCC '97 Digest of Technical Papers,* Castine ME: John W. Wuorinen, 1997, pp. 254–255.

[VCC98] Virtual Computer Corporation, "Hot II Architecture," Technical Bulletin, October 1998. Available at //www.annapmicro.com.

[Vos89] L. D. Vos and M. Stegherr, "Parameterizable VLSI architectures for the full-search block-matching algorithm," *IEEE Transactions on Circuits and Systems,* 36(10), October 1989, pp. 1309–1316.

[Wal97] Dave Walsh, "Reducing system cost with software modems," *IEEE Micro,* July/August 1997, pp. 37–55.

[Whi72] Thomas M. Whitney, France Rode, and Chung C. Tung, "The 'powerful pocketful': An electronic calculator challenges the slide rule," *Hewlett-Packard Journal,* 1972, pp. 2–9.

[Whi80] L. J. White and E. I. Cohen, "A domain strategy for program testing," *IEEE Transactions on Software Engineering,* 14(6), June 1980, pp. 868–874.

[Wol92A] Wayne Wolf, "Expert opinion: In search of simpler software integration," *IEEE Spectrum,* January 1992, p. 31.

[Wol92B] Andrew Wolfe and Alex Chanin, "Executing compressed programs on an embedded RISC architecture," in *Proceedings, 25th Annual International Symposium on Microarchitecture*, 1992, pp. 81–91.

[Wol96] Wayne Wolf, Andrew Wolfe, Steve Chinatti, Ravi Koshy, Gary Slater, and Spencer Sun, "Lessons from the design of a PC-based private branch exchange," *Design Automation for Embedded System*s, 1(4), 1996, pp. 297–314.

[Wol97] Wayne Wolf, "Hardware/software co-design for multimedia," in *Advanced Signal Processing: Algorithms, Architectures, and Implementations VII*, Society of Photo-Optical Instrumentation Engineers, 1997.

[Wol98] Wayne Wolf, *Modern VLSI Design: Systems on Silicon*, Upper Saddle River NJ: Prentice Hall, 1998.

[Yan89] Kun-Min Yang, Ming-Ting Sun, and Lancelot Wu, "A family of VLSI designs for the motion compensation block-matching algorithm," *IEEE Transactions on Circuits and Systems,* 36(10), October 1989, pp. 1317–1325.

[Yen98] Ti-Yen Yen and Wayne Wolf, "Performance analysis of distributed embedded systems," *IEEE Transactions on Parallel and Distributed Systems*, 9(11), November 1998, pp. 1125–1136.

Index

* (asterisk) in special class names, 37
: (colon) for SHARC label termination, 82–83
! (exclamation point) for SHARC comments, 83
; (semicolon)
 for ARM comments, 62
 for SHARC instruction termination, 82
8-bit microprocessors, 3
16-bit microprocessors, 3
4004 microprocessor (Intel), 2
8251 UART example, 107–108
80960KA RISC microprocessor, 541

ABS (antilock brake system) example, 4–5
absolute address
 ARM computation using PC, 70
 defined, 259
 in SHARC, 90
accelerators, 419–448
 accelerated system design, 424–437
 as hardware/software co-design, 419
 partitioning, 432–434
 performance analysis, 423, 424–428
 scheduling and allocation, 434–436
 system architecture framework, 429–432
 accelerator design, 423
 advantages of, 419, 421–422
 applications suited to, 422–423
 ARM Integrator example, 429–430
 caching problems, 431

co-processors vs., 420
CPUs and, 420–423
 blocking vs. nonblocking schedulers, 424
 caching problems, 431
 co-processors vs. accelerators, 420
 cost and performance issues, 421–423
 interface, 420, 421, 430–431
 partitioning, 432
 single-threaded vs. multithreaded systems, 424, 425, 427–428
 synchronization, 431–432
FPGA-based example, 429
performance, 423, 424–428
 cost/performance, 421
 partitioning and, 432–433
 real-time performance, 422
video accelerator example, 437–445
ack wire in four-cycle handshake, 178, 179
ACPI (Advanced Configuration and Power Interface), 399–400
activate behavior (telephone answering machine example), 404
activation record, 81, 349, 361
active classes, 357, 563
active matrix LCD panels, 207–208
active objects, 357–358
actuator, 451
A/D (analog/digital) converters, 203–204, 227–228
adaptive differential pulse code modulation (ADPCM), 400–401

ADCs (analog/digital converters), 203–204, 227–228

adders, 571

addressing
absolute address, 70, 90, 259
ARM processor
absolute address computation using PC, 70
auto-indexing, 72–73
base-plus-offset, 72, 73
computing absolute address using PC, 70
immediate, 66
PC-relative, 73
post-indexing, 72, 73
register-indirect, 69–70
word length, 63
MMUs and address translation, 139–144
in ARM, 143–144
paged address translation, 140–142
segmented address translation, 140, 142
virtual memory, 142–143
relative addresses, 259
SHARC processor
absolute address, 90
base-plus-offset, 90
bit-reversal, 90
for CALLs, 97
circular buffers, 90
data address generators (DAGs), 88–90
for jumps, 93
PC-relative, 93, 97
post-modify with update mode, 90
virtual addressing, 139–140

ADPCM (adaptive differential pulse code modulation), 400–401

ADR pseudo-operation in ARM, 70

Advanced Configuration and Power Interface (ACPI), 399–400

aggregation, 24

alarm clock example, 233–241

algorithms
complexity of embedded computing applications, 5
Huffman compression, 158–160, 312
program execution time optimization and, 304
statistical compression of programs, 311
video accelerator, 437–440

allocation
of communication, process scheduling and, 480
of computations in accelerated systems, 434–436
of memory, 61–62
of registers during compilation, 280–285

ALU operations in SHARC, 84–86

AMBA bus system in ARM, 190–191

analog waveform with sample points, 328–329

analog/digital (A/D) converters, 203–204, 227–228

analysis. See also requirements; testing
CRC card analysis, 516–520
elevator system example, 518–520
methodology, 516–518
critical-instant analysis, 374–375
def-use analysis, 319–320, 321
distributed embedded system design
communication analysis, 475–480
system performance analysis, 481–482
in embedded computing system design, 11
of energy and power, 305–306
of network communication, 475–480
of program execution time, 290–305
of program performance, 324–325
of program size, 310–311
of program test coverage, 323–324
rate-monotonic analysis (RMA), 372–373
requirements analysis, 507–508
system analysis and architecture design, 515–520

AND
AND/OR tables, 511–512
in Boolean logic, 567–568
Own-Aircraft AND state, 514–515
in Statecharts, 510–511

AND/OR tables, 511–512

annotations in UML, 23

answering machine example. See telephone answering machine example

antifuse-programmable ROM, 210

antilock brake system (ABS) example, 4–5

APCS (ARM Procedure Call Standard), 273

Apple Newton MessagePad, 548–549

application interface of I^2C bus, 463–464

application layer of OSI model, 453

application-specific instruction processors (ASIPs), 557

application-specific integrated circuits (ASICs). See also accelerators
for custom peripherals, 216

defined, 420–421
ink jet printer example, 543–544,
545–546, 547
sources of, 421
applications suited to accelerators,
422–423
arbitration of buses
CAN bus, 465–466
Carrier Sense Multiple Access with Arbi-
tration on Message Priority (CSMA/
AMP), 465–466
Ethernet, 470–471, 472
fair arbitration, 455, 477
fixed-priority arbitration, 455, 477
I^2C bus, 462–463
need for, 454
network availability delay and, 477–479
round-robin arbitration, 455, 477
architectural classes (elevator controller
example), 519
architecture
accelerator framework, 429–432
alarm clock example, 239–240
distributed embedded systems, 450–451,
453–456
elevator controller example, 491–492,
518–520
Harvard architecture
in ARM9 processor, 63
overview, 58–59
in SHARC processor, 82, 91, 99
implementations of, 60
ink jet printer example, 542–546
load-store, 64
of logic analyzers, 224–225
of networks, 453–456
blocking, 456
buses, 454–455
crossbar, 455
data-push, 457–458
direct, 456
multiple networks, 456
multistage, 456
OSI model, 452–453
point-to-point communication,
453–454
set-top boxes example
hardware architecture, 551–552
software architecture, 552–554, 555
software modem example, 328–329
system analysis and architecture design,
515–520
CRC card methodology, 516–518

elevator system example, 518–520
taxonomy of computer architecture,
58–59
telephone answering machine example,
406–408
telephone PBX example, 537–539
video accelerator example, 441–443
von Neumann, 58, 63
in waterfall model of software develop-
ment, 500
architecture design
alarm clock example, 239–240
block diagrams, 18–19
elevator controller example, 491–492,
518–520
estimating component properties, 19–20
hardware architecture, 213–214
Harvard architecture, 58–59
implementations, 60
ink jet printer example, 542–546
overview, 18–20
RISC vs. CISC, 59
set-top boxes example
hardware architecture, 551–552
software architecture, 552–554, 555
software architecture, 214
software modem example, 328–329
taxonomy of computer architecture,
58–59
telephone answering machine example,
406–408
telephone PBX example, 537–539
video accelerator example, 441–443
von Neumann architecture, 58
arithmetic expression compilation,
267–269
arithmetic instructions
ARM processor, 66, 67
SHARC processor, 84–88
ALU operations, 84–86
C statements, 91–92
multiplier operations, 87
saturation arithmetic, 85
shifter operations, 87–88
ARM processor, 62–82
ARM7 vs. ARM9, 63
ARM Integrator boards, 429–430
ARM Procedure Call Standard (APCS),
273
assembly language defined, 62
caches in, 138
co-processors in, 130
co-routine structure, 346–347

ARM processor (*continued*)
 comments, 62
 compilation
 of arithmetic expression, 268–269
 conditional code generation, 271–272
 cooperative context switching, 353–354
 CPU bus (AMBA), 190–191
 data operations, 63–73
 absolute address computation using
 PC, 70
 arithmetic instructions, 66, 67
 ARM programming model, 64–65
 auto-indexing addressing, 72–73
 base-plus-offset addressing, 72, 73
 C assignments in instructions, 70–72
 comparison instructions, 68
 current program status register
 (CPSR), 65–66
 data instructions, 66–68
 immediate operands, 66
 load-store architecture, 64
 load-store instructions, 68–69
 logical instructions, 66, 67
 move instructions, 68
 post-indexing addressing, 72, 73
 programming model, 64–66
 pseudo-operations, 62, 69, 70
 register-indirect addressing, 69–70
 shift/rotate instructions, 67–68
 data types supported, 63
 flow of control, 73–82
 branch target, 73
 C switch statement implementation,
 76–77
 condition codes, 73, 74
 condition execution, 73–76
 finite impulse response (FIR) filter,
 78–80
 functions, 80–82
 if statement implementation,
 74–76
 loops, 77–80
 multiway conditions, 76–77
 PC-relative branches, 73
 predicates for condition execution,
 75–76
 procedure calls, 81–82
 interrupts in, 126–127
 labels, 62–63
 memory management units (MMUs),
 143–144
 memory-mapped I/O, 108
 in PDAs, 548, 550–551
 pipelining, 145, 146–147, 148–149

 processor and memory organization, 63
 pseudo-ops, 62, 69, 70, 263
 register allocation, 280–282
 software interrupts (traps), 130
 StrongARM
 SA-1100 power-saving modes,
 156–158
 system organization, 219–220
 supervisor mode, 128–129, 362
 symbol table generation, 260–261
 test-and-set operations, 368–369
 Thumb instruction set, 311
 uses for, 57
 version used in this book, 57
 VLSI devices for, 62
arrays
 array padding, 279
 compiling, 274–275
 iteration space, 300–301
 padding and data realignment, 302–304
Asada, Mutsuhiko, 531
ASC+T (automatic stability control) system
 example, 4–5
ASICs (application-specific integrated cir-
 cuits). *See also* accelerators
 for custom peripherals, 216
 defined, 420–421
 ink jet printer example, 543–544,
 545–546, 547
 sources of, 421
ASIPs (application-specific instruction
 processors), 557
aspect ratio of memory, 194
ASR modifier in ARM, 68
assemblers, 258–263
 addressing by, 259
 COFF file format, 263
 label processing by, 259, 262–263
 object code generation, 263
 parsing by, 61
 program location counter (PLC), 260
 pseudo-ops, 61–62
 role of, 258
 symbol table processing by, 259–262
assembly language
 basic features, 60–61
 CDFGs for, 257
 notation, 60–61
 overview, 60–62
 parsing by assemblers, 61
 pseudo-ops, 61–62
 writing assembly code, 289
association
 described, 24

links and, 28, 29
ASTAT register in SHARC, 84, 86, 87, 88
asterisk (*) in special class names, 37
asynchronous input, 344
asynchronous machines, 576–577
atomic test-and-set operations, 367–369
ATPG (automatic test pattern generation),
 231
attributes
 operations manipulating, 24
 overview, 22–23
 variables vs., 24
auditing tools for specification validation,
 527
auto-indexing addressing in ARM proces-
 sor, 72–73
automatic stability control (ASC+T) system
 example, 4–5
automatic test pattern generation (ATPG),
 231
automobiles
 automotive engine control example,
 345–346
 BMW 850i brake and stability control
 system, 4–5
 data-push network architectures, 458
 distributed embedded systems in, 449
 microprocessor use in, 3, 4
availability delay in networks, 477–479
average-case execution time, 291

Backup Flight Control System (BFS), 365
base class, 27
base-plus-offset addressing
 ARM processor
 auto-indexing variation, 72–73
 overview, 72
 post-indexing variation, 72, 73
 SHARC processor, 90
basic input/output system (BIOS), 218
basis paths, 316–317
baud rate, 107
behavioral description, 29–32
 events, 29–31
 sequence diagrams, 31–32
 state machines, 29, 30, 31
behavioral level in hardware description
 languages, 578
behaviors in UML, 561
Beizer, Boris, 321
Benini, L., 399
best-case execution time, 292

best-effort routing in IP, 474
BFS (Backup Flight Control System), 365
BIC instruction in ARM, 66
big-endian mode, 63, 64
BIOS (basic input/output system), 218
bit-reversal addressing in SHARC, 90
black-box testing, 322–323
block diagrams for architecture design,
 18–19
block motion estimation algorithm,
 437–440
blocking CPU schedulers, 424
blocking networks, 456
blocks, cache, 133
BMW 850i brake and stability control sys-
 tem, 4–5
Boolean algebra, 567–568
boot-block flash PROM, 201
bottom-up design, 10, 11
bounce in single-switch keyboards,
 204–205
boundary scan logic, 231–233
branch penalty in pipelining, 146–147
branch table, 77
branch target, 73
branches. *See also* condition execution
 in ARM, 73, 77
 SHARC condition encoding, 93, 94
breakpoints, 222–223
bridge (CPU bus)
 ARM bus, 191
 bridge logic, 187–189
 bridges, 189–190
buffers
 circular buffer addresses in SHARC, 90
 circular buffer implementation of FIR fil-
 ter, 251–252
 copying characters from input to output
 using, 114–118
 elastic buffers as shared memory,
 366–367
 frame buffers, 207
 reusing data buffers, 310
 SHARC link buffers, 368–369
buggy cooperative multitasking system
 example, 354–356
bugs. *See* debugging
bundle, 178
burst transfers (CPU bus), 182–183, 184
bus grant signals, 186
bus master devices, 186–187
bus networks, 454–455

bus request signal, 186
bus transactions in I^2C, 461–462, 463
buses. *See also* CPU bus
 accelerator bus mastership, 426
 arbitration
 CAN bus, 465–466
 Carrier Sense Multiple Access with
 Arbitration on Message Priority
 (CSMA/AMP), 465–466
 Ethernet, 470–471, 472
 fair, 455, 477
 fixed-priority, 455, 477
 I^2C bus, 462–463
 need for, 454
 network availability delay and,
 477–479
 round-robin, 455, 477
 bus networks, 454–455
 CPU bus, 178–193
 ARM processor, 190–191
 bus master devices, 186–187
 components, 179
 defined, 178
 DMA, 186–187, 189
 hardware architecture design and, 213
 protocols, 178–185
 SHARC processor, 191–193
 system bus configurations, 187–190
 typical bus structure, 180
 IEEE 1394 bus, 218
 ISA (Industry Standard Architecture)
 bus, 218
 network system buses
 CAN (controller area network) bus,
 464–467
 I^2C bus, 459–464
 overview, 458–459
 PC platform, 218
 PCI (peripheral component intercon-
 nect) bus, 218
 shared memory interprocess communi-
 cation, 366, 367
 simulation bus, 226
 USB (universal serial bus), 218
busy-wait I/O, 110–111
 copying characters from input to output,
 111
 described, 110
 inefficiency of, 112
 polling, 110
 programming example, 110–111
Buttons* class
 alarm clock example, 235, 236

telephone answering machine example,
 405
bytes
 format in I^2C bus, 462, 463
 word organization in ARM, 63, 64

C
 arithmetic and logical operations in, 63
 assignments
 in ARM instructions, 70–72
 in SHARC instructions, 91–92
 CDFG code, 255, 256
 class and object implementation in,
 25–26
 earliest-deadline-first scheduling code,
 381
 finite impulse response (FIR) filter
 in ARM, 78–79
 in SHARC, 96
 function inlining, 277–278
 functions in ARM, 80–82
 I/O devices, writing directly, 109–110
 loop unrolling, 278–279
 procedure calls
 in ARM, 81–82
 in SHARC, 98
 rate-montonic scheduling code, 376
 state machine implementation, 248–250
 switch statement implementation in
 ARM, 76–77
C++
 class and object implementation in, 25
 data compressor program design,
 163–168
 inline construct, 277
C (carry) bit of ARM CPSR, 65
c-use, 320
caches, 131–139
 accelerators and, 431
 in ARM, 138
 cache controllers, 131–132
 cache miss equations, 301–302
 cache miss penalty, 151–152
 cache-based instruction compression,
 311–312
 CPU performance and, 151–152
 described, 131
 direct-mapped, 133–134
 direct-mapped vs. set-associative,
 135–138
 energy efficiency and, 306–307, 308
 optimizations, 300–304
 cache miss equations, 301–302

conflict elimination, 304–305, 309
data realignment and array padding,
 302–304
for energy efficiency, 307, 308, 309
nested loops and, 300–301
performance
 CPU, 151–152
 instruction execution time, 296
 memory system, 132–133
 process scheduling and, 394–396
PowerPC 603 energy efficiency features,
 154
process scheduling and, 394–396
program execution time optimization
 and, 304–305
set-associative, 134–135
in SHARC, 139
trace capturing and, 297
unified, 138
call events, 30
CALL instruction in SHARC, 97
calligraphic displays, 207
cameras, microprocessor use in, 3
CAN (controller area network) bus,
 464–467
 arbitration, 465–466
 data frame, 465
 error handling, 466–467
 physical layer, 464–465
 remote frames, 466
 as synchronous bus, 464
 uses, 459
Canon EOS 3 camera, 3
Capability Maturity Model (CMM), 525
capacitive touchscreens, 208
capturing a trace, 296–297
Car class (elevator controller example),
 489, 491
Car control* class (elevator controller
 example), 519
Car control reader class (elevator controller
 example), 519
Car control sender class (elevator control-
 ler example), 519
Car sensor* class (elevator controller exam-
 ple), 519
Car state class (elevator controller exam-
 ple), 519
Car-control-panel* class (elevator control-
 ler example), 490
Carnegie Mellon University, 525
carriage ASIC (ink jet printer example),
 545–546, 547

Carrier Sense Multiple Access with Arbitra-
 tion on Message Priority (CSMA/
 AMP), 465–466
carry (C) bit of ARM CPSR, 65
cathode ray tube (CRT) displays, 207
CDFGs. See control/data flow graphs
 (CDFGs)
central office, 402
central processing units. See CPUs; micro-
 processors
changing states (CPU bus), 181
check_alarm() function (alarm clock exam-
 ple), 239, 240
CIF (common intermediate format) for
 video, 440
cimgr program, 529
circular buffer
 addresses in SHARC, 90
 FIR filter implementation, 251–252
 streaming data and, 250–251
CISC microprocessors
 pipelining, 145
 RISC vs., 59
class diagrams
 active class, 357
 alarm clock example, 235, 236
 data compressor example, 162
 of design pattern, 246–247
 elevator controller example, 489,
 490–491
 model train controller example, 36, 37,
 38, 40, 41, 42, 45, 46
 overview, 36, 563–564
 software modem example, 328
 telephone answering machine example,
 404–405
classes
 active, 357, 563
 alarm clock example, 235–239
 data compressor example, 161–163
 derived, 26–27, 563
 elevator controller example, 489–491,
 519
 model train controller example, 37–46
 operations, 23
 overview, 23–24
 relationship types, 24
 software implementation of, 25–26
 software modem example, 328
 telephone answering machine example,
 404–406
 in UML notation, 561
 video accelerator example, 441

clear-box testing, 313–322
 condition testing, 317–320
 execution paths for, 315–317
 loop testing, 320–322
 observability and controllability issues, 313–314
 tasks, 313–314
CLIP instruction in SHARC, 84
close() function in POSIX, 392
CMM (Capability Maturity Model), 525
CMN instruction in ARM, 68
CMOS (complementary metal oxide semiconductor)
 leakage, 153
 as logic gate technology, 568
 power characteristics, 152–153
 power consumption of gates, 569–570
 power-saving strategies, 153
 toggling, 152–153
 transistors, 568
 voltage and power consumption, 152, 153
CMP instruction in ARM, 68
co-design, hardware/software, 419, 450
co-processors, 130, 420
co-routine structure, 346–347
co-simulation, 226, 437
co-verification techniques
 co-simulation, 226, 437
 co-verification tools, 226
 CPU simulators, 225–226
 cycle-based simulators, 226
 simulation bus, 226
Coarse-sensor* class (elevator controller example), 490
code compression, 311–312
code inspections, paperless, 529
code motion loop optimization, 298–299
coding alphabet (ADPCM), 400, 401
coding in waterfall model of software development, 500
COFF (common object file format), 263
collaboration diagrams
 active and normal objects, 358
 model train controller example, 36–37
 overview, 565–566
 relationships emphasized by, 36
colon (:) for SHARC label termination, 82–83
combinational logic, 567–571
 adders, 571
 Boolean algebra, 567–568

CMOS transistors, 568
 described, 567
 inverter operation, 568–569
 logic network evaluation, 570
 multiplexers, 571
 power consumption of CMOS gates, 569–570
 three-state logic, 571
combinational logic networks, 570
combinational network, manufacturing testing and, 230
comments
 in ARM, 62
 in assembly language, 61
 in SHARC, 83
common intermediate format (CIF) for video, 440
common object file format (COFF), 263
communication links for PEs, 451
COMP instruction in SHARC, 84
comparison instructions in ARM, 68
compilation, 258–290
 arithmetic expression example, 267–269
 arrays, 274–275
 assembly, 258–263
 conditional code generation example, 270–272
 data structures, 274–275
 dead code elimination, 277
 expression simplification, 275–276
 instruction selection, 287–288
 interpreters, 289
 JIT (just-in-time) compilers, 289–290
 linking, 258, 264–265
 loop transformations, 278–280
 procedure creation, 273
 procedure inlining, 277–278
 register allocation, 280–285
 scheduling, 285–287
 reservation table, 285–286
 software pipelining, 286–287
 statement translation, 267–273
 summary of process, 266
 template matching, 287–288
 as translation plus optimization, 266–267
 understanding and using compilers, 288–289
compilers
 cross-compilers, 221
 interpreters, 289
 JIT (just-in-time), 289–290

understanding and using, 288–289
complementary metal oxide semiconduc-
 tor. *See* CMOS (complementary
 metal oxide semiconductor)
completeness test for requirements, 508
complex instruction set computers. *See*
 CISC microprocessors
complexity, cyclomatic, 317, 318
component design
 alarm clock example, 240–241
 overview, 20
 software modem example, 329
 standard and ready-made components,
 20
 telephone answering machine example,
 408–409
 video accelerator example, 443–444
component interfacing, 209–212
 device interfacing, 211–212
 glue logic interface, 211–212
 memory interfacing, 209–211
 multichip SRAM memory system,
 209–210
composition, 24
compression. *See also* data compressor
 example
 ADPCM system, 400–402
 code compression, 311–312
 data compressor example, 158–171,
 366–367
 file compression, 311
 program compression, 311
 stand-alone compression unit, 343–344
 telephone answering machine example,
 407, 408
compression module (telephone answer-
 ing machine example), 407, 408
computational kernels, 419
computation-intensive system design, 484
computing platform. *See* platform
concurrency during DMA, 187
concurrent engineering, 503–507
 elements of, 503–504
 goals, 503
 telephone systems example, 505–507
cond field in assembly language, 61
condition codes in ARM, 73, 74
condition execution. *See also* loops
 ARM processor, 73–77
 C switch statement implementation,
 76–77
 condition codes, 73, 74

execution time evaluation, 148–149
 if statement implementation, 74–76
 loops, 77–80
 multiway conditions, 76–77
 predicate used for, 75–76
 clear-box testing, 317–320
 compilation example, 270–272
 control flow graph for while loop, 272
 SHARC processor
 encoding for branches, 93, 94
 if statement implementation, 94–96
 JUMP instruction, 93
 loops, 93, 96–97
condition testing, 317–321
 analyzing conditions, 317–318
 with branch testing strategy, 318–319
 data flow testing, 319–320
 def-use analysis, 319–320, 321
 domain testing, 319, 320
conflict graph, 282
Connectix QuickCam, 485–486
consistency of requirements, 15, 508
Console class (model train controller
 example), 37
constants, reusing values for, 310
context switching, 351–358
 cooperative multitasking, 351–356
 ARM processor, 353–354
 as bug-prone, 354
 buggy system example, 354–356
 cswitch() function, 351–352
 defined, 351
 procedure call mechanism and, 352
 defined, 342
 object-oriented design and processes,
 357–358
 overhead, 384–386
 preemptive multitasking, 356–357
 interrupt mechanism for, 356–357
 timer-driven preemption, 356–357
control flow-oriented testing. *See* clear-box
 testing
control stall delays in pipelining, 146–147
control-oriented specifications languages,
 509–512
 AND/OR tables, 511–512
 SDL, 509
 Statecharts, 510–511
control/data flow graphs (CDFGs), 254–257
 for assembly language programs, 257
 C code for, 255, 256
 data flow nodes, 254–255

control/data flow graphs (CDFGs)
(*continued*)
 decision nodes, 254–255
 for determining statement execution
 repetitions, 294–295
 execution model, 257
 as fundamental model for programs, 252
 hierarchical representation, 257
 for partitioning, 433–434
 for while loops, 255–257, 272
controllability as design challenge, 9
controller area network bus. *See* CAN (con-
 troller area network) bus
Controller class
 elevator controller example, 489, 491
 model train controller example, 38, 39,
 44–45
Controls class (telephone answering
 machine example), 404–406
cooperative multitasking, 351–356
 ARM processor, 353–354
 as bug-prone, 354
 buggy system example, 354–356
 context switching in, 351–352
 cswitch() function, 351–352
 defined, 351
 procedure call mechanism and, 352
copying characters from input to output
 with basic interrupts, 113–114
 with interrupts and buffers, 114–118
 using busy-wait I/O, 111
correctness test for requirements, 508
costs. *See also* manufacturing cost
 accelerators and, 421
 as design goals, 11, 498–499
 of fixing bugs, 525–526
 as nonfunctional requirements, 12
 nonrecurring engineering (NRE), 12
 power consumption, 6
counter/timers
 internals, 203
 overview, 202
CPSR. *See* current program status register
 (CPSR) in ARM
CPU bus, 178–193
 bus master devices, 186–187
 components, 179
 DMA, 186–187, 189
 four-cycle handshake, 178, 179
 hardware architecture design and, 213
 protocols, 178–185
 bus reads and writes, 178–185
 four-cycle handshake, 178, 179

reads and writes, 178–185
 SHARC processor, 191–193
 system bus configurations, 187–190
 typical bus structure, 180
CPU simulators, 225–226
CPUs. *See also* accelerators; ARM proces-
 sor; instruction sets; microproces-
 sors; SHARC processor
 accelerators and, 420–423
 blocking vs. nonblocking schedulers,
 424
 caching problems, 431
 co-processors vs. accelerators, 420
 cost and performance issues, 421–423
 interface, 420, 421, 430–431
 partitioning, 432
 single-threaded vs. multithreaded sys-
 tems, 424, 425, 427–428
 synchronization, 431–432
 application-specific instruction proces-
 sors (ASIPs), 557
 bus, 178–193
 ARM processor, 190–191
 bus master devices, 186–187
 components, 179
 defined, 178
 DMA, 186–187, 189
 four-cycle handshake, 178, 179
 hardware architecture design and,
 213
 protocols, 178–185
 reads and writes, 178–185
 SHARC processor, 191–193
 system bus configurations, 187–190
 typical bus structure, 180
 co-processors, 130, 420
 cost/performance issues, 421
 data compressor example, 158–171
 data function units in SHARC, 84
 exceptions, 129
 hardware architecture design and, 213
 in Harvard architecture, 59
 implementations of an architecture,
 60
 for instruction set examples, 57
 interrupt handling, 119–120, 125
 I/O programming, 106–128
 busy-wait I/O, 110–111
 input and output devices, 106–108
 input and output primitives, 108–110
 interrupts, 112–128
 memory system mechanisms, 131–144
 caches, 131–139

MMUs and address translation, 139–144
multiple, in distributed systems, 451
performance, 144–152
 caching, 132–133, 151–152
 pipelining, 145–149
 superscalar execution, 149–151
power consumption, 152–158
 CMOS power characteristics, 152–153
 energy vs. power, 152
 power state machine, 155–156
 power-down modes, 153, 155–156
 PowerPC 603 energy efficiency features, 154–155
 static vs. dynamic power management, 153, 155–156
 StrongARM SA-1100 power-saving modes, 156–158
process cohabitation on, 348–349
ROLM PBX, 535
simulators, 225–226
supervisor mode, 128–129, 362
systems-on-silicon, 555–557
trace generation by, 297
traps, 129–130
utilization and scheduling policies
 earliest-deadline-first scheduling, 380–381
 overview, 371–372
 rate-montonic scheduling, 375–376
 RMS vs. EDF, 382
in von Neumann architecture, 58
CRC card analysis
 elevator system example, 518–520
 methodology, 516–518
critical instant of processes, 374
critical-instant analysis, 374–375
crossbar networks, 455
cross-compilers, 221
cross-functional teams in concurrent engineering, 503
crosspoints, 455
CRT (cathode ray tube) displays, 207
CSMA/AMP (Carrier Sense Multiple Access with Arbitration on Message Priority), 465–466
cswitch() function, 351–352
current program status register (CPSR) in ARM
 automatic setting of, 65
 checking arithmetic operations, 65, 66
 interrupts and, 126

supervisor mode and, 129
top four bits, 65
custom chips, 577
custom logic designs
 for ASICs, 421
 microprocessors vs., 6–8
customer focus in concurrent engineering, 504
cycle-based simulators, 226
cyclomatic complexity, 317, 318

DACs (digital/analog converters), 203–204, 227
DAGs. *See* data address generators (DAGs) in SHARC
data
 for accelerators, 424–425
 distributed processing for reducing, 449
 program size and, 310
 streaming, 59, 250–251, 423
data address generators (DAGs) in SHARC, 88–90
 absolute address mode, 90
 base-plus-offset addressing, 90
 bit-reversal addressing, 90
 circular buffers, 90
 code scheduling for, 147–148
 post-modify with update mode, 90
data bits for SHARC link ports, 468
data compressor example, 158–171
data dependencies
 message-based interprocess communication and, 370–371
 scheduling processes and, 383–384
 task graph, 370
 task set, 370
data flow graphs, 252–254
 control/data flow graphs (CDFGs), 254–257
 defined, 252
 extended, 253–254
 single-assignment form, 253
 uses of, 254
data flow nodes in CDFGs, 254–255
data flow testing, 319–320
data frame of CAN bus, 465
data instructions in ARM processor, 66–68
data link layer
 I^2C bus, 460–462
 IP routing and, 473
 OSI model, 453
data memory (DM) in SHARC, 83

data operations
 ARM processor, 63–73
 absolute address computation using PC, 70
 arithmetic instructions, 66, 67
 ARM programming model, 64–65
 auto-indexing addressing, 72–73
 base-plus-offset addressing, 72, 73
 C assignments in ARM instructions, 70–72
 comparison instructions, 68
 current program status register (CPSR), 65–66
 data instructions, 66–68
 immediate operands, 66
 load-store architecture, 64
 load-store instructions, 68–69
 logical instructions, 66, 67
 move instructions, 68
 post-indexing addressing, 72, 73
 pseudo-operations, 69
 register-indirect addressing, 69–70
 shift/rotate instructions, 67–68
 SHARC processor, 83–92
 ALU operations, 84–86
 arithmetic operations, 84–88
 C assignments in instructions, 91–92
 CPU data function units, 84
 floating-point operations, 83, 85–87
 load-and-store operations, 88–90
 multiplier operations, 87
 programming model, 83–84
 saturation arithmetic, 85
 shifter operations, 87–88
 status bits, 88
 storing data in program memory, 91–92
data rates, variable, 344
data realignment and array padding, 302–304
data registers. *See* registers
data stall in pipelining, 145
data stream style program design patterns, 250–252
data structures, compiling, 274–275
data types in SHARC, 83
data value tests, 322
data words. *See* words (data)
data-buffer class (data compressor example), 162
Data-compressor class, 161–163

data-dependent program paths, 293–294
data-push network architectures, 457–458
DAVID API, 552
dead code elimination, 277
deadline of processes
 computation-intensive system design and, 484
 earliest-deadline-first scheduling (EDF), 377–382
 I/O-intensive system design and, 483
 overview, 362–363, 364
deadlines
 for microprocessor design, 6, 8
 real-time operations and, 5–6
debouncing circuits for single-switch keyboards, 205
debugging, 221–228. *See also* quality assurance (QA); testing
 accelerated systems, 437
 black-box testing, 322–323
 breakpoints, 222–223
 clear-box testing, 313–322
 condition testing, 317–320
 execution paths for, 315–317
 loop testing, 320–322
 observability and controllability issues, 313–314
 tasks, 313–314
 co-verification techniques
 co-verification tools, 226
 CPU simulators, 225–226
 cycle-based simulators, 226
 costs of fixing bugs, 525–526
 data value tests, 322
 distributed embedded systems, 450
 during system integration, 20–21
 facilities for embedded systems, 21
 in-circuit emulation, 223
 ink jet printer example, 548
 interrupts, 118–119
 LEDs as debugging devices, 223
 logic analyzers, 223–225
 operating system facilities, 371
 on platform, 221–228
 challenges, 227–228
 techniques, 221–226
 program validation and testing, 312–324
 black-box testing, 322–323
 clear-box testing, 313–322
 evaluating function tests, 323–324

major strategies, 313
observability and controllability
issues, 313–314
tasks, 313–314
random tests, 322
real-time code, 227–228
regression tests, 323
serial ports and, 222
decision nodes in CDFGs, 254–255
decompression module (telephone
answering machine example), 407,
408
defect removal efficiency, 530, 531
Defined level of maturity, 525
def-use analysis, 319–320, 321
def-use pair, 320
delayed branch in pipelining, 146–147
dense instruction sets, 311
dependency checking, dynamic, 150
derived classes, 26–27, 563
design. *See* architecture design; distributed
embedded system design; embed-
ded computing system design;
hardware design; program design
design flows, 500–504
concurrent engineering, 503–507
defined, 500
hierarchical, 502–503, 504
spiral model, 502
successive refinement development
model, 501–502, 503
waterfall model, 500–501
design for testability, 229
design reviews, 527–529
described, 527–528
format for, 528–529
paperless code inspections, 529
review team, 528
DesignJet plotter. *See* ink jet printer
example
Detector* class (model train controller
example), 39, 40
development environments, 9, 220–221
device drivers, 112
device interfacing. *See also* interfaces
glue logic, 211–212
glueless, 211
devices. *See* hardware; I/O devices
dialing procedure (telephone PBX exam-
ple), 535–536
digital signal processors. *See* DSPs (digital
signal processors)

digital/analog (D/A) converters, 203–204,
227
direct addressing for jumps in SHARC, 93
direct memory access. *See* DMA (direct
memory access)
direct networks, 456
direct-mapped caches
blocks, 133
limitations, 134
overview, 133–134
reads, 133
set-associative caches vs., 135–138
writes, 133–134
directly-driven displays, 206–207
DirecTV, 3–4
disconnected transfers (CPU bus), 183
Display class (alarm clock example), 235,
236
displays, 206–208
directly driven, 206–207
frame buffer, 207, 208
LCD panels, 207–208
distributed embedded system design,
475–484
accelerated systems, scheduling and
allocation problems, 434–436
communication analysis, 475–480
for computation-intensive systems, 484
elevator controller example, 486–493
hardware platform, 451, 482–484
as hardware/software co-design, 450
for I/O-intensive systems, 483–484
networks for, 458–475
CAN (controller area network) bus,
464–467
Ethernet, 470–472
I^2C bus, 459–464
Internet, 473–475
Myrinet, 472
SHARC link ports, 467–470
system buses, 458–459
performance analysis, 481–482
system performance analysis, 481–482
distributed embedded systems. *See also*
distributed embedded system
design; networks
architectures, 450–451, 453–456
blocking, 456
buses, 454–455
crossbar, 455
data-push, 457–458
direct, 456

distributed embedded systems, architec-
tures (*continued*)
multiple networks, 456
multistage, 456
point-to-point communication,
453–454
computation-intensive, 484
debugging, 450
described, 449
interference between tasks, 481–482
Internet-enabled embedded systems,
484–486
I/O-intensive, 483–484
message passing programming, 457–458
modularity, 450
need for, 451–452
OSI model, 452–453
performance analysis, 481–482
processing element (PE), 449, 450–451
reasons for, 449–450, 451
DLLs (dynamically linked libraries), 265
DM (data memory) in SHARC, 83
DMA (direct memory access), 186–187
cyclic scheduling of DMA request, 189
SHARC processor, 192–193
DO UNTIL instruction in SHARC, 93, 96–97
Domain Name Server (DNS), 474
domain testing, 319, 320
done output of counter/timers, 202
DRAM. *See* dynamic RAM (DRAM); memory
DSPs (digital signal processors)
link ports, 467
telephone PBX example, 539
dual-tone multifrequency (DTMF) dialing,
536, 539
dynamic dependency checking, 150
dynamic power management
in PowerPC 603, 154–155
static vs., 153, 155–156
dynamic RAM (DRAM), 197–200
EDO (extended data out), 198, 200
hardware architecture design and, 213
ink jet printer example, 543
inputs (control signals), 197–198
interface, 197, 210–211
memory controller, 198
page mode access, 198, 199
refreshing, 198, 211
SRAM vs., 195
synchronous DRAM, 198–199, 200
timing diagram, 197
dynamically linked libraries, 265

earliest-deadline-first scheduling (EDF),
377–382
CPU utilization, 380–381, 382
as dynamic priority scheme, 377
example, 378–380
high deadlines and, 380–381
implementation, 381–382
RMS vs., 382
Echelon LON network, 459
EDF. *See* earliest-deadline-first scheduling
(EDF)
EDO (extended data out) DRAM, 198, 200
efficiency. *See also* optimization; perfor-
mance; power consumption
busy-wait I/O and, 112
energy efficiency
caches and, 306–307, 308
microprocessor features, 154–158
of microprocessors, 6, 7
elastic buffers as shared memory, 366–367
electrical interface
CAN bus, 464, 465
I^2C bus, 460, 461
Elevator car* class (elevator controller
example), 519
elevator controller example, 486–493
architecture, 491–492
CRC card analysis, 518–520
requirements, 489
specification, 489–491
testing, 492–493
theory of operation, 487–488
embedded computer systems. *See also* dis-
tributed embedded systems
application characteristics, 5–6
defined, 2
multirate systems, 345–346
PCs vs., 2
embedded computing platform. *See*
platform
embedded computing system design. *See
also* distributed embedded system
design; platform; processes; pro-
gramming embedded processors;
requirements; specification
accelerated system design, 424–437
video accelerator example, 437–445
alarm clock example, 233–241
architecture design, 18–20
challenges, 8–9
component design, 20
concerns of this book, 2

custom logic designs vs. microproces-
 sors, 6–8
data compressor example, 158–171
deadlines, 6, 8
design for testability, 229
development environments, 9, 220–221
distributed embedded system design,
 475–484
formalisms, 21–32
 behavioral description, 29–32
 structural description, 22–29
 Unified Modeling Language (UML),
 21–22
goals, 11, 498–499
hardware/software co-design, 419, 450
ink jet printer example, 539–548
 ASICs, 543–544, 545–546, 547
 design considerations, 540–541
 early design decisions, 541
 hardware design, 542–546
 HP DesignJet plotter described,
 539–540
 software design, 546–548
methodologies
 defined, 498
 design flows, 500–504
 Mars Climate Observer example,
 499–500
 need for, 10, 498–499
 product metrics, 498–499
 telephone systems example, 505–507
with microprocessors, 212–220
 hardware architecture, 213–214
 hardware design, 214–216
 PCs as platforms, 216–219
 programmability benefits, 8
 software architecture, 214
 StrongARM system organization,
 219–220
model train controller example, 32–47
 conceptual specification, 34–39
 detailed specification, 39–46
 overview, 32–33
 requirements, 34
object-oriented design, 21
object-oriented design and processes,
 357–358
personal digital assistants (PDAs) exam-
 ple, 548–551
 Apple Newton MessagePad, 548–549
 characteristics, 548
 feature creep issues, 549–550
 InfoPad, 550–551

Motorola Envoy PDA, 549, 550
 power supply design, 550
process overview, 10–11
program design patterns, 248–252
programmability benefits for, 8
quality assurance (QA), 520–534
 as design goal, 499
requirements, 12–17, 507–508
set-top boxes example, 551–555
 cost sensitivity, 551
 hardware architecture, 551–552
 role of set-top boxes, 551, 552
 software architecture, 552–554, 555
 user interface, 554
small teams for, 6
software modem example, 325–330
specifications, 509–515
 overview, 17
system analysis and architecture design,
 515–520
 CRC card methodology, 516–518
 elevator system example, 518–520
system integration, 20–21
systems-on-silicon, 555–557
tasks in steps of, 11
telephone answering machine example,
 400–409
telephone PBX examples
 concurrent engineering at AT&T,
 505–507
 ROLM PBX, 534–539
top-down vs. bottom-up, 10
video accelerator example, 437–445
encode method (Data-compressor class),
 161
encoded keyboards, 205
energy. *See also* power consumption
 optimization, 307–309
 power vs., 152
energy efficiency features. *See also* power
 consumption; power management
 of PowerPC 603, 154–155
 of StrongARM SA-1100, 156–158
enq wire in four-cycle handshake, 178, 179
Envoy PDA, 549, 550
error handling
 CAN bus, 466–467
 exceptions, 129, 387, 388
 traps, 129–130
error injection, 324
Ethernet, 470–472
 arbitration, 470–471, 472
 maximum length, 471

Ethernet (*continued*)
 packet format, 471, 472
 performance, 471
 physical organization, 470
 uses, 459, 470
Eustace, Alan, 397
events
 call events, 30
 overview, 29–31
 signals, 29, 30
 time-out events, 30
exceptions
 overview, 129
 POSIX signals, 387, 388
exclamation point (!) for SHARC com-
 ments, 83
executable binary file, 258
executing state of processes, 358, 359
execution model for CDFGs, 257
execution time of accelerators, 425–427
execution time of programs, 290–305
 average-case, 291
 best-case, 292
 caching effects, 296
 data-dependent program paths, 293–294
 difficulties estimating, 290–291
 formula for, 292
 instruction timing, 295–296
 measuring execution speed, 291
 optimization for execution speed,
 304–305
 paths in loops, 294–295
 scheduling overhead, 372, 422
 trace-driven performance analysis,
 296–304
 types of performance measures,
 291–292
 worst-case, 291
execv() function (POSIX), 350
exit() function (POSIX), 350
expression simplification, 275–276
extended data out (EDO) DRAM, 198, 200
external memory interface of SHARC CPU
 bus, 191–192

factory-programmed ROM, 201
fair arbitration, 455, 477
FALSE value in Boolean logic, 568
fast interrupt requests (FIQs), 126
fault coverage, 229
fault models, 229–230
 fault coverage, 229
 overview, 229

stuck-at-0/1 model, 230
feature creep, 549–550
field-programmable gate arrays (FPGAs)
 for accelerators, 421, 429, 440, 443–444
 for ASICs, 216
 elevator simulator using, 492–493
 programmable logic devices (PLDs) vs.,
 578
field-programmable ROM, 201
file compression, 311
file system services of operating systems,
 371
File Transport Protocol (FTP), 474–475
Fine-sensor* class (elevator controller
 example), 490
finite impulse response (FIR) filter
 in ARM, 78–80
 circular buffer implementation, 251–252
 observability problem for testing, 314
 overview, 78
 paths in loop, 294–295
 in SHARC, 96–97
 stream-oriented processing, 250
finite-state machines. *See also* state
 machines
 C implementation, 248–250
 reactive systems and, 248
FIQs (fast interrupt requests), 126
FIR filter. *See* finite impulse response (FIR)
 filter
first-time correctness, 557
fixed-priority arbitration, 455, 477
flash PROM, 201
flip-flop memory elements, 572, 573
flip-flop-based synchronous machines,
 573–574
floating-point operations
 ARM co-processor, 130
 SHARC processor, 83, 85–87
Floor class (elevator controller example),
 489, 491
Floor control* class (elevator controller
 example), 519
Floor control reader class (elevator control-
 ler example), 519
Floor-control-panel* class (elevator con-
 troller example), 490
flow of control
 ARM processor, 73–82
 branch table, 77
 branch target, 73
 C switch statement implementation,
 76–77

condition codes, 73, 74
condition execution, 73–77
finite impulse response (FIR) filter, 78–80
functions, 80–82
if statement implementation, 74–76
loops, 77–80
multiway conditions, 76–77
PC-relative branches, 73
predicates for condition execution, 75–76
procedure calls, 81–82
co-routine structure, 346–347
interrupts and, 112
SHARC processor, 93–98
C procedure calls, 98
CALL instruction, 97
conditional encoding for branches, 93, 94
DO UNTIL instruction, 93, 96–97
FIR filter, 96–97
function calls, 97–98
if statement implementation, 94–96
JUMP instruction, 93
loops, 93, 96–97
flush method (Data-compressor class), 161
focus of control in sequence diagrams, 31–32
foreground programs, 113
fork() function (POSIX), 350
formal techniques for specification validation, 527
formalisms for system design, 21–32. *See also* behavioral description; structural description
behavioral description, 29–32
object-oriented design, 21–22
structural description, 22–29
Unified Modeling Language (UML), 21–22
Formatter class (model train controller example), 37, 39, 41–43
Forth language, 289
four-cycle handshake, 178, 179
FPGAs (field-programmable gate arrays). *See* field-programmable gate arrays (FPGAs)
fragmentation of program pages in memory, 140
frame pointer, 273
FrameMaker, 529
frequency-shift keying (FSK), 325–326

front panel module (telephone answering machine example), 406, 407–408
FTP (File Transport Protocol), 474–475
full-duplex point-to-point connections, 454
functionality requirements
alarm clock example, 234
data compressor example, 161
elevator controller example, 489
GPS requirements example, 15, 16
model train controller example, 34
requirements form, 14
software modem example, 327
telephone answering machine example, 403
video accelerator example, 440
functions. *See also* procedures
in ARM, 80–82
procedure calls
in ARM, 81–82
cooperative multitasking and, 352
energy optimization and recursive calls, 309
in SHARC, 98
for processes in POSIX, 350–351
in SHARC, 97–98
subroutines or procedures, 80

Garman, John R., 364
gate level in hardware description languages, 578
general call of I^2C bus, 461
generalization, 24, 27
Ghosh, Somnath, 301
Global Positioning System (GPS)
architecture design example, 18–19
requirements analysis example, 15–17
specification example, 17
user interface, 5
glue logic interface, 211–212
goals. *See also* purpose
of concurrent engineering, 503
of embedded computing system design, 11, 498–499
of manufacturing testing, 238–239
of requirements and specification validation, 526
GPS. *See* Global Positioning System (GPS)
gzip program, 311

half subtractors in counter/timers, 202, 203

half-duplex communication
 point-to-point connections, 454
 SHARC link ports, 469–470
handshake, four-cycle, 178, 179
hardware. *See also* microprocessors; plat-
 form
 accelerators, 419–448
 architecture design, 18–19, 213–214
 changing device priorities, 121
 component design, 20
 component interfacing, 209–212
 CPU bus, 178–193
 ARM processor, 190–191
 bus master devices, 186–187
 components, 179
 defined, 178
 DMA, 186–187, 189
 hardware architecture design and, 213
 protocols, 178–185
 SHARC processor, 191–193
 system bus configurations, 187–190
 typical bus structure, 180
 as design challenge, 8
 designing, 214–216, 567–578
 accelerators, 423
 combinational logic, 567–571
 custom peripherals, 216
 evaluation boards, 214–215
 implementation media, 577–578
 ink jet printer example, 542–546
 I/O device choices, 215–216
 sequential logic, 571–577
 set-top boxes example, 551–552
 hardware description languages (HDLs),
 578
 hardware/software co-design, 419, 450
 interrupt handling and, 125
 I/O devices, 106–108, 202–209
 A/D and D/A converters, 203–204,
 227–228
 architecture design and, 213–214
 counter/timers, 202–203
 displays, 206–208
 8251 UART example, 107–108
 hardware architecture design and,
 213–214
 hardware design and, 215–216
 I/O programming and, 106–108
 keyboards, 204–206
 LEDs, 206
 polling, 110
 registers, 106–107
 timers, 202–203

 touchscreens, 208–209
 typical device structure, 106
 writing directly in C, 109–110
 memory devices, 193–201
 organization, 194–195
 random-access memories,
 195–200
 read-only memories (ROMs), 201
 trace capturing methods, 296–297
hardware accelerators. *See* accelerators
hardware description languages (HDLs),
 578
hardware design, 214–216, 567–578
 accelerators, 423
 combinational logic, 567–571
 adders, 571
 Boolean algebra, 567–568
 CMOS transistors, 568
 described, 567
 inverter operation, 568–569
 logic network evaluation, 570
 multiplexers, 571
 power consumption of CMOS gates,
 569–570
 three-state logic, 571
 custom peripherals, 216
 evaluation boards, 214–215
 implementation media, 577–578
 ink jet printer example, 542–546
 I/O device choices, 215–216
 sequential logic, 571–577
 asynchronous machines, 576–577
 memory elements, 571–573
 synchronous machines, 573–575
 set-top boxes example, 551–552
hardware platform. *See* platform
hardware/software co-design, 419, 450
hardware/software co-verification
 co-simulation, 226, 437
 co-verification tools, 226
 CPU simulators, 225–226
 cycle-based simulators, 226
 simulation bus, 226
Harvard architecture
 in ARM9 processor, 63
 overview, 58–59
 in SHARC processor, 82, 91, 99
HDLs (hardware description languages),
 578
Hewlett-Packard Kobe Instrument Divi-
 sion, 531
hierarchical design flows, 502–503, 504
high-impedance state, 571

Hitachi Software Quality Evaluation (SQE) system, 530
Hoff, Ted, 2
hold time for sequential logic memory elements, 573
Horgan, Joseph R., 323
host (development environment), 220, 221
host interface of SHARC CPU bus, 192
Hot II accelerator, 429
household uses of microprocessors, 3
HP DesignJet plotter. *See* ink jet printer example
HP-35, 3
HTTP (Hypertext Transport Protocol), 475
Huffman coding, 158–160, 312
Hypertext Transport Protocol (HTTP), 475

IBM PowerPC 405GP, 555, 556
I^2C bus, 459–464
 application interface, 463–464
 arbitration, 462–463
 bus transactions, 461–462
 byte format, 462, 463
 data link layer, 460–462
 electrical interface, 460, 461
 message delay, 476
 as multimaster bus, 460
 physical layer, 459–460
 serial clock line (SCL), 459–460, 461, 462, 463
 serial data line (SDL), 459–460, 461, 462, 463
 uses, 459
ICE (in-circuit emulator), 223
idle mode, 157
IEEE 1394 bus, 218
if statement
 ARM implementation, 74–76
 data-dependent paths, 293–294
 SHARC implementation, 94–96
immediate operands in ARM, 66
implementation media, 577–578
implementation of objects in class definitions, 24
implementations of an architecture, 60
incidence matrix, 217, 316
in-circuit emulator (ICE), 223
Incoming-message class (telephone answering machine example), 405
incremental information sharing in concurrent engineering, 504
indirect addressing for jumps in SHARC, 93

induction variable elimination for loop optimization, 299–300
Industry Standard Architecture (ISA) bus, 218, 459
InfoPad, 550–551
inheritance
 generalization and, 27
 multiple, 27–28
Initial level of maturity, 525
initiation interval of processes, 363, 364
initiation time of processes, 362, 363
ink jet printer example, 539–548
 ASICs, 543–544, 545–546, 547
 design considerations, 540–541
 early design decisions, 541
 hardware design, 542–546
 HP DesignJet plotter described, 539–540
 software design, 546–548
input devices. *See* I/O devices
inputs. *See also* I/O devices; I/O programming
 asynchronous, 344
 copying characters to output
 using basic interrupts, 113–114
 using busy-wait I/O, 111
 using interrupts and buffers, 114–118
 dynamic RAM (DRAM) control signals, 197–198
 flip-flop-based synchronous machines, 574
 primitives, 108–110
 stand-alone compression unit, 343–344
 static RAM (SRAM) control signals, 195
 variable data rates, 344
instruction sets, 57–104. *See also* ARM processor; SHARC processor
 architecture taxonomy, 58–59
 ARM processor, 62–82
 data operations, 63–73
 flow of control, 73–82
 notation, 62–63
 processor and memory organization, 63
 assembly language overview, 60–62
 characteristics of, 59–60
 CPUs for examples, 57
 custom logic vs., 7
 defined, 57
 dense, 311
 for general-purpose computers, 63
 RISC vs. CISC, 59
 SHARC processor, 82–99

instruction timing, 295–296
instruction-level optimization, 266–267
instruction-level simulators, 225–226
instructions. *See also* ARM processor;
 SHARC processor
 in assembly language, 60
 energy consumption and, 306
 execution times, 295–296
 instrumentation instructions for trace
 generation, 297
 program size optimization, 310–311
 scheduling in compilation, 285–287
 selection in compilation, 287–288
 software pipelining, 286–287
 template matching, 287–288
instrumentation instructions for trace gen-
 eration, 297
integrated project management in concur-
 rent engineering, 504
Intel
 4004 microprocessor, 2
 80960KA RISC microprocessor, 541
 Multibus, 458
interfaces
 of ADCs, 204
 component interfacing, 209–212
 device interfacing, 211–212
 glue logic interface, 211–212
 memory interfacing, 209–211
 multichip SRAM memory system,
 209–210
 of DACs, 204
 of dynamic RAM (DRAM), 197
 of hardware accelerators, 423
 I^2C application interface, 463–464
 of objects
 choosing properly, 24
 in class definitions, 24
 set-top box user interface, 554
 of static RAM (SRAM), 196
internal consistency of requirements, 15
International Standards Organization. *See*
 ISO (International Standards Orga-
 nization)
Internet
 higher-level services, 474–475
 Internet appliances, 484, 485–486
 Internet Protocol (IP), 473–475
 Internet-enabled embedded systems,
 484–485
 protocol utilization, 473
 Transmission Control Protocol (TCP),
 474

 video camera example, 485–486
Internet Protocol (IP)
 as internetworking standard, 473
 IP addresses, 474
 packet format, 473–474
 relationship with higher-level services,
 474–475
 routing, 473, 474
interpreters, 289
interprocess communication mecha-
 nisms, 365–371, 387–393
 blocking vs. nonblocking, 366
 message-based communication,
 369–371, 392–393
 autonomously operating units and,
 369
 data dependencies, 370–371
 in POSIX, 393
 for processes running at different
 rates, 370–371
 for processes running at the same
 rate, 370
 shared memory communication vs.,
 366, 369
 in Unix, 392–393
 shared memory communication,
 366–369, 389–392
 in bus-based systems, 366, 367
 elastic buffers as shared memory,
 366–367
 message passing communication vs.,
 366
 in POSIX, 390–392
 race condition, 367–369
 test-and-set operations, 367–369
 text compressor example, 366–367
 UML signals, 389
 Unix signals, 387–389
interrupt requests (IRQs), 126
interrupts, 112–128
 alarm clock example, 239
 in ARM, 126–127
 basics, 112–120
 contexts, 112
 copying characters from input to output,
 113–118
 CPU checking for, 119–120, 125
 debugging, 118–119
 interrupt acknowledge signal, 113
 interrupt handler, 112, 122–123, 124, 125
 interrupt mechanism, 112
 interrupt request signal, 112
 latency, 127, 128

overhead, 125–126
performance issues, 125–126
preemptive multitasking and,
 356–357
priorities, 120–123, 125
in SHARC, 127–128
software (traps), 129–130
vectors, 120, 124–125
inverter operation, 568–569
I/O devices, 106–108, 202–209
 A/D and D/A converters, 203–204,
 227–228
 accelerators, 423
 counter/timers, 202–203
 displays, 206–208
 directly driven, 206–207
 frame buffer, 207, 208
 LCD panels, 207–208
 8251 UART example, 107–108
 hardware architecture design and,
 213–214
 hardware design and, 215–216
 interfacing, 211–212
 I/O programming and, 106–108
 keyboards, 204–206
 microprocessor controlled, 205–206
 single switch, 204–205
 LEDs, 206
 operating system services, 371
 polling, 110
 as processing elements (PEs), 450–451
 registers, 106–107, 211–212
 timers, 202–203
 touchscreens, 208–209
 typical device structure, 106
 writing directly in C, 109–110
I/O instructions, 108
I/O programming, 106–128. *See also* inter-
 rupts
 busy-wait I/O, 110–111
 input and output devices, 106–108
 8251 UART example, 107–108
 polling, 110
 registers, 106–107
 typical device structure, 106
 writing directly in C, 109–110
 input and output primitives, 108–110
 I/O instructions, 108
 memory-mapped I/O, 108–110
 interrupts, 112–128
 in ARM, 126–127
 basics, 112–120
 overhead, 125–126

priorities, 120–123, 125
 in SHARC, 127–128
 vectors, 120, 124–125
parallelism, 112
polling, 110
I/O-intensive system design, 483–484
IP. *See* Internet Protocol (IP)
IRPTL register in SHARC, 130
IRQs (interrupt requests), 126
ISA (Industry Standard Architecture) bus,
 218, 459
ISO (International Standards Organization)
 9000 standard, 523–524
 OSI model, 452–453
iteration space, 300–301

Java Nanokernel, 485
Javacam, 485–486
JIT (just-in-time) compilers, 289–290
Joint Test Action Group (JTAG), 231
JUMP instruction in SHARC, 93
just-in-time (JIT) compilers, 289–290

keyboards, 204–206
 bounce, 204–205
 encoded, 205
 microprocessor controlled, 205–206
 rollover, 205–206
 single switch, 204–205
Knobs* class (model train controller exam-
 ple), 38, 39, 40, 41
Kwang, Eng-Kee, 451

labels
 in ARM, 62–63
 assembler processing of, 259
 in assembly language, 60
 in SHARC, 82, 83
 symbol table processing and, 262–263
latch memory elements, 572–573
latch-based synchronous machines,
 574–575
latency. *See also* performance
 of bus-to-bus transfers, 189–190
 interrupts, 127, 128
 pipelining, 145
layers in OSI model, 452–453
Layland, James W., 374, 380
LCDs. *See* liquid crystal displays (LCDs)
LDMA instruction in ARM, 145
LDRB instruction in ARM, 68
LDRH instruction in ARM, 68
LDRSH instruction in ARM, 68

leakage, CMOS power consumption and, 153
LEDs (light-emitting diodes)
as debugging devices, 223
in directly-driven displays, 206
overview, 206
Leveson, Nancy G., 511, 513, 521, 523
Li, Yanbing, 394
lifelines in sequence diagrams, 31
lifetime graphs, 281, 283, 284
light-emitting diodes. *See* LEDs (light-emitting diodes)
Lights* class
alarm clock example, 235, 236
telephone answering machine example, 405
lightweight processes, 349
line card for PBX, 537–538
Line-in* class (telephone answering machine example), 405
Line-out* class (telephone answering machine example), 405
lines (telephone)
PBX, 535
trunk lines, 546
link ports in SHARC, 467–470
data bits, 468
half-duplex communication, 469–470
link buffers, 368–369
registers, 469
SHARC-based multiprocessor example, 467–468
words, 468
linkers, 264, 265
linking, 264–265
dynamically linked libraries, 265
loading code modules into memory, 165
role of, 258, 264
subroutine linkage and program size, 310–311
symbol table processing, 264, 265
two-phase process, 265
links between objects, 28, 29
Linux, as POSIX-compliant, 342
liquid crystal displays (LCDs)
directly driven, 206–207
flat panels, 207–208
little-endian mode, 63, 64
Liu, C. L., 374, 380
live variables, 281
load balancing, 484
loader, 258

load-store architecture, 64
load-store instructions
ARM co-processors, 130
ARM processor, 68–69
SHARC processor, 88–90
logic analyzers, 223–225
logic gates. *See also* CMOS (complementary metal oxide semiconductor); combinational logic
combinational logic networks, 570
overview, 568
power consumption of CMOS gates, 569–570
testing for faults in, 230
logic network evaluation, 570
logical instructions, ARM processor, 66, 67
LON network, 459
loop transformations
array padding, 279
loop distribution, 279
loop fusion, 279
loop tiling, 279, 280
loop unrolling, 278–279
loops
alarm clock example, 239–240
in ARM
execution time evaluation, 148–149
FIR filter, 78–80
overview, 77–80
CDFGs for while loops, 255–257
clear-box testing, 320–322
energy optimization and, 309
finite impulse response (FIR) filter
in ARM, 78–80
overview, 78
in SHARC, 96–97
iteration space, 300–301
nested, 300, 321–322
optimizations, 298–300
code motion, 298–299
induction variable elimination, 299–300
strength reduction, 300
paths in, 294–295
in SHARC
DO UNTIL instruction, 93, 96
FIR filter, 96–97
software pipelining, 286–287
transformations, 278–280
LSL modifier in ARM, 68
LSR modifier in ARM, 68

machine-independent optimization, 266
Macroblock class (video accelerator example), 441
maintenance in waterfall model of software development, 500
Managed level of maturity, 525
manual vs. tool-based QA techniques, 524
manufacturing cost
 as design goal, 11
 overview, 6
manufacturing testing, 228–233
 automatic test pattern generation (ATPG), 231
 boundary scan logic, 231–233
 combinational network, 230
 design for testability, 229
 fault models, 229–230
 goal, 238–239
 scan chains, 231
 sequential network, 230–231
 using the microprocessor, 232–233
 yield, 229
Mars Climate Observer example, 499–500
mask-programmed ROM, 201
masking, 121
Master-control-panel* class (elevator controller example), 490
Mathur, Aditya P., 323
maximum timing constraints on asynchronous machines, 576–577
Mbit capacity of memory, 194
measurement-driven quality assurance
 overview, 530–531
 software quality example, 531–534
Mechanism class (alarm clock example), 235–239
memory. *See also* caches
 ARM processor organization, 63
 array layouts, 274–275
 aspect ratio, 194
 assembly language restrictions, 61
 C struct layout, 275, 276
 described, 58
 device organization, 194–195
 energy reduction, 306–307, 308, 309
 external memory interface (SHARC CPU bus), 191–192
 hardware architecture design and, 213
 in Harvard architecture, 58–59
 ink jet printer requirements, 540–541
 interfacing, 209–211
 dynamic RAM (DRAM), 210–211

multichip SRAM memory system, 209–210
 static RAM (SRAM), 209–210
Mbit capacity, 194
memory-mapped I/O, 108–110
 ARM processor, 108
 described, 108
 SHARC processor, 109
 writing directly in C, 109–110
multichip SRAM memory system, 209–210
power consumption and memory transactions, 20
pseudo-op for allocating, 61–62
random-access memories, 195–200
 described, 195
 dynamic RAM (DRAM), 197–200, 210–211
 Rambus, 199
 static RAM (SRAM), 195–196, 209–210
 video RAM, 199
read-only memories (ROMs), 201
sequential logic memory elements, 571–573
 flip-flop, 572, 573
 latch, 572–573
 timing requirements, 573
SHARC processor organization, 83
storing data in program memory in SHARC, 91–92
system mechanisms, 131–144
 caches, 131–139
 MMUs and address translation, 139–144
virtual memory extensions, 142–143
in von Neumann architecture, 58
memory controller for DRAM, 198
memory devices, 193–201
 hardware architecture design and, 213
 organization, 194–195
 random-access memories, 195–200
 described, 195
 dynamic RAM (DRAM), 197–200, 210–211, 213, 543
 frame buffers, 207
 Rambus, 199
 static RAM (SRAM), 195–196, 209–210, 213
 video RAM, 199
 read-only memories (ROMs), 201
memory elements in sequential logic, 571–573
 flip-flop, 572, 573

memory elements in sequential logic
(*continued*)
latch, 572–573
timing requirements, 573
memory management units (MMUs),
139–144
in ARM, 143–144
described, 131
fragmentation, 140
page faults, 140
paged address translation, 140–142
segmented address translation, 140, 142
SHARC and, 144
virtual addressing, 139–140
virtual memory extensions, 142–143
message classes (telephone answering
machine example), 404, 405
message delay, 475–477
for I²C message, 476
network availability delay and, 476–477
for single message with no contention,
475–476
message passing interprocess communica-
tion. *See* message-based interpro-
cess communication
message passing programming for net-
works, 457–458
message-based interprocess communica-
tion, 369–371, 392–393
autonomously operating units and, 369
data dependencies, 370–371
in POSIX, 393
for processes running at different rates,
370–371
for processes running at the same rate,
370
shared memory communication vs., 366,
369
in Unix, 392–393
methodologies for design
CRC card analysis, 516–520
defined, 498
design flows, 500–504
concurrent engineering, 503–507
defined, 500
hierarchical, 502–503, 504
spiral model, 502
successive refinement development
model, 501–502, 503
waterfall model, 500–501
first-time correctness, 557
Mars Climate Observer example,
499–500
need for, 10, 498–499

paperless code inspections, 529
product metrics, 498–499
telephone systems example, 505–507
methods
Data-compressor class, 161
defined, 25
microcontrollers. *See* microprocessors
Microphone* class (telephone answering
machine example), 405
microprocessors. *See also* ARM processor;
CPUs; instruction sets; SHARC pro-
cessor
CISC, 59, 145
classification of, 3
co-processors, 130, 420
CPU bus, 178–193, 213
CPU performance, 144–152
caching, 151–152
pipelining, 145–149
superscalar execution, 149–151
CPU power consumption, 152–158
CMOS power characteristics,
152–153
energy vs. power, 152
power state machine, 155–156
power-down modes, 153, 155–156
PowerPC 603 energy efficiency fea-
tures, 154–155
static vs. dynamic power manage-
ment, 153–158
StrongARM SA-1100 power-saving
modes, 156–158
custom logic designs vs., 6–8
data compressor example, 158–171
defined, 2
designing with, 212–220
hardware architecture, 213–214
hardware design, 214–216
PCs as platforms, 216–219
programmability benefits, 8
software architecture, 214
StrongARM system organization,
219–220
efficiency of, 6, 7
evolution of, 2–3
exceptions, 129
in-circuit emulator (ICE), 223
instruction sets, 57–104
ARM processor, 62–82
assembly language overview, 60–62
defined, 57
SHARC processor, 82–99
taxonomy of computer architecture,
58–59

interrupt checking, 119–120
I/O programming, 106–128
 busy-wait I/O, 110–111
 input and output devices, 106–108
 input and output primitives, 108–110
 interrupts, 112–128
keyboards controlled by, 205–206
manufacturing testing using, 232–233
memory system mechanisms, 131–144
 caches, 131–139
 MMUs and address translation,
 139–144
RISC, 3, 59, 145, 541
supervisor mode, 128–129, 362
systems-on-silicon, 555–557
traps, 129–130
uses of, 2, 3–4
minimum timing constraints on asynchro-
 nous machines, 576–577
MIPS-16 instruction set, 311
MLA instruction in ARM, 66
mmap() function in POSIX, 391–392
MMUs. *See* memory management units
 (MMUs)
mock-ups for validating requirements, 13
MODE1 register in SHARC, 85, 86
model train controller example, 32–47
 conceptual specification, 34–39
 class diagrams, 36, 37
 classes, 37–39
 collaboration diagram, 36–37
 commands, 35–36
 transmission packets, 35–36
 detailed specification, 39–46
 class diagrams, 40, 41, 42, 45, 46
 Controller class, 39, 44–45
 Detector* class, 39, 40
 Formatter class, 39, 41–43
 Knobs* class, 39, 40, 41
 Motor interface class, 41
 Panel class, 39, 40–41
 Pulser* class, 39–40
 Receiver class, 41, 42
 refining command classes, 45–46
 Sender* class, 39, 40
 sequence diagrams, 43, 46
 state diagrams, 43, 44, 45
 Transmitter class, 41, 42
 lessons learned, 47
 overview, 32–33
 requirements, 34
modeling assumptions for scheduling poli-
 cies, 383–386

context switching overhead, 384–386
data dependencies, 383–384
priority inversion, 383
models of programs, 252–257. *See also* pro-
 gramming model
 control/data flow graphs (CDFGs), 252,
 254–257
 data flow graphs, 252–254
modems
 frequency-shift keying (FSK), 325–326
 software modem example, 325–330
 theory of operation, 325–326
modifiability test for requirements, 508
modularity, 450
Motion-estimator class (video accelerator
 example), 441
Motion-vector class (video accelerator
 example), 441
Motor* class (elevator controller example),
 490
Motor interface class (model train control-
 ler example), 38, 41
Motorola
 Envoy PDA, 549, 550
 VME, 458
move instructions in ARM, 68
MPEG, set-top boxes and, 552, 553
MUL instruction in ARM, 66
Multibus, 458
multichip SRAM memory system, 209–210
multidimensional signal processing for
 video, 422
multihop networks, 479–480
multimaster buses, 460. *See also* I^2C bus
multiple inheritance, 27–28
multiple networks, 456
multiplexed address and data (CPU bus),
 185
multiplexers, 571
multiplier operations in SHARC, 87
multiprocessors, SHARC-based, 467–468
multirate behaviors, 6
multirate communication, 371
multirate systems, 345–346
multistage networks, 456
multitasking
 co-routine structure, 346–347
 cooperative, 351–356
 ARM processor, 353–354
 as bug-prone, 354
 buggy system example, 354–356
 context switching in, 351–352
 cswitch() function, 351–352

multitasking, cooperative (*continued*)
 defined, 351
 procedure call mechanism and, 352
 preemptive, 356–357
 interrupt mechanism for, 356–357
 timer-driven preemption, 356–357
multithreaded accelerator control, 424,
 425, 427–428
multiway conditions in ARM, 76–77
munmap() function in POSIX, 391–392
Myrinet, 459, 472

N (negative) bit of ARM CPSR, 65
n-key rollover in keyboards, 206
NANDs in Boolean logic, 567–568
negative (N) bit of ARM CPSR, 65
nested loops, 300, 321–322
network delay
 adjusting messages to improve, 477–479
 arbitration and, 477–479
 message delay and, 476–477
network layer of OSI model, 453
network-based design. *See* distributed
 embedded system design
networks, 449–496. *See also* distributed
 embedded system design; distrib-
 uted embedded systems
 architectures, 453–456
 availability delay, 477–479
 CAN (controller area network) bus,
 464–467
 communication analysis, 475–480
 communication links for PEs, 451
 defined, 450
 elevator controller example, 486–493
 Ethernet, 470–472
 I²C bus, 459–464
 Internet, 473–475
 Internet-enabled embedded systems,
 484–486
 manufacturing testing
 combinational network, 230
 sequential network, 230–231
 message delay, 475–477
 modularity, 450
 multihop, 479–480
 Myrinet, 459, 472
 operating system I/O services, 371
 OSI model, 452–453
 predictive shutdown in pagers, 397
 priority inversion, 479
 SHARC link ports, 467–470
 single-hop, 479

system buses, 458–459
new-symbol-table method (Data-
 compressor class), 161
Newton MessagePad, 548–549
next state outputs for flip-flop-based syn-
 chronous machines, 574
nmake Unix facility, 529
NMIs (nonmaskable interrupts), 121
nonfunctional requirements
 architecture design and, 19
 overview, 12–13, 507
nonmaskable interrupts (NMIs), 121
nonrecurring engineering (NRE) costs, 12
NORs in Boolean logic, 567–568
NOT in Boolean logic, 567
notations
 ARM, 62–63
 assembly language, 60–61
 SHARC, 82–83
 UML, 561–566
 diagram types, 562–566
 primitive elements, 561–562
NRE (nonrecurring engineering) costs, 12

Oberg, James, 499
object code, 258
object diagram for video accelerator, 445
object-oriented design
 overview, 21
 processes and, 357–358
object-oriented programming, 22, 24–25
object-oriented specification, 22, 24–25
objects
 active, 357–358
 attributes, 22–23
 described, 22–23
 implementation, 24
 interface, 24
 links, 28, 29
 relationship types, 24
 software implementation of, 25–26
 in UML notation, 23, 561
observability, as design challenge, 9
off-hook (telephone), 402, 535, 536
offset
 base-plus-offset addressing
 in ARM, 72–73
 in SHARC, 90
 PC-relative branches in ARM, 73
on-hook (telephone), 402, 535, 536
opcode field
 in assembly language, 61
 coprocessors and, 130

open collector/open drain signaling, 460
Open Systems Interconnect (OSI) model,
 452–453
operand values and instruction execution
 time, 295–296
operating systems, 358–371. *See also*
 POSIX; real-time operating systems
 (RTOSs)
 complex programs and, 341–342
 context switching, 351–358
 data structures to support scheduling,
 361
 debugging facilities, 371
 described, 341
 file system services, 371
 interprocess communication mecha-
 nisms, 365–371, 387–393
 blocking vs. nonblocking, 366
 message-based communication,
 369–371, 392–393
 shared memory communication,
 366–369, 389–392
 UML signals, 389
 Unix signals, 387–389
 I/O services, 371
 multitasking
 co-routine structure, 346–347
 cooperative, 351–356
 preemptive, 356–357
 in PCs, 218
 performance evaluation, 393–396
 process scheduling
 allocation of communication and,
 480
 caching and, 394–396
 priority-driven scheduling, 359–360
 process states and, 358–360
 protected mode, 362
 tasks, 343
 timing requirements on processes,
 362–365
 deadline, 362–363, 364
 initiation interval, 363, 364
 initiation time, 362, 363
 rate requirements, 363
 space shuttle software error example,
 364–365
operations. *See also* data operations
 in class definitions, 23
 methods as, 25
 software implementation of classes and
 objects, 25–26

operator scheduling for register allocation,
 283–285
optimization
 cache optimizations, 300–304
 cache miss equations, 301–302
 conflict elimination, 304–305, 309
 data realignment and array padding,
 302–304
 for energy efficiency, 307, 308, 309
 nested loops and, 300–301
 compilation as translation plus optimi-
 zation, 266–267
 dead code elimination, 277
 of energy and power, 306–309
 energy optimization, 307–309
 instruction choices, 306
 memory effects, 306–307
 opportunities for saving power, 305
 for processes, 396–397
 expression simplification, 275–276
 instruction-level, 266–267
 loop optimizations, 298–300
 code motion, 298–299
 induction variable elimination,
 299–300
 strength reduction, 300
 loop transformations, 278–280
 machine-independent, 266
 procedure inlining, 277–278
 of program execution speed, 304–305
 of program size, 310–312
Optimizing level of maturity, 525
OR
 AND/OR tables, 511–512
 in Boolean logic, 567–568
 in Statecharts, 510
OSI (Open Systems Interconnect) model,
 452–453
Outgoing-message class (telephone
 answering machine example), 405
output devices. *See* I/O devices
outputs. *See also* I/O devices; I/O program-
 ming
 CMOS power consumption and, 152–153
 copying characters from input
 with basic interrupts, 113–114
 with interrupts and buffers, 114–118
 using busy-wait I/O, 111
 counter/timer done output, 202
 flip-flop-based synchronous machines,
 574
 primitives, 108–110

outputs, primitives (*continued*(
 variable data rates, 344
overflow (V) bit, of ARM CPSR, 65
Own-Aircraft AND state, 514–515

P() semaphore name, 368, 390. *See also*
 semaphores
p-use, 320
packages in UML, 561
packets
 data payload, 454
 described, 454
 Ethernet packet format, 471, 472
 IP packet format, 473–474
 message passing programming, 457–458
 Myrinet, 472
page faults, 140
page mode
 DRAM access, 198, 199
 program execution time optimization
 and, 304
paged address translation, 140–142
pagers, predictive shutdown in, 397
Panel class (model train controller exam-
 ple), 37, 39, 40–41
paperless code inspections, 529
parallelism
 concurrency during DMA, 187
 I/O programming and, 112
 partitioning and, 432–433
 within instructions in SHARC, 99
parent_stuff() function (POSIX), 351
parity, UART setting, 107
parsing by assemblers, 61
partitioning
 accelerated system design and, 432–434
 software architecture design and, 214
PASS (Primary Avionics Software System),
 364–365
Passenger* class (elevator controller exam-
 ple), 519
passing messages in interprocess commu-
 nication. *See* message-based inter-
 process communication
passing values into and out of procedures
 in ARM, 81
passive matrix LCD panels, 207
paths of execution
 basis paths, 316–317
 for clear-box testing, 315–317
 cyclomatic complexity, 317, 318
 data-dependent, 293–294

in loops, 294–295
overview, 292
PBX examples. *See* telephone PBX exam-
 ples
PC class (video accelerator example), 441
PC (program counter). *See* program
 counter (PC)
PCI (peripheral component interconnect)
 bus, 218, 459
PCs
 embedded computer systems vs., 2
 Hot II accelerator for, 429
 as platforms, 216–219
 advantages, 216–217
 buses, 218
 hardware components, 217
 single-chip PCs, 219–220
 software, 218–219
 StrongARM SA-1100 and 1111,
 219–220
PDAs. *See* personal digital assistants
 (PDAs) example
PE (processing element), 421, 449, 450–451
pen interface ASIC (ink jet printer exam-
 ple), 545, 546
pen-based computer system, 451–452
performance
 accelerators and
 accelerator execution time, 425–427
 blocking vs. nonblocking CPU sched-
 ulers, 424
 cost/performance, 421
 partitioning, 432–433
 performance analysis, 423, 424–428
 real-time performance, 422
 single-threaded vs. multithreaded sys-
 tems, 424, 425, 427–428
 system speedup, 424, 426–428
 caches and
 CPU performance, 151–152
 instruction execution time, 296
 memory system performance,
 132–133
 process scheduling, 394–396
 context switching overhead, 384–386
 of CPUs, 144–152
 caching, 132–133, 151–152
 pipelining, 145–149
 superscalar execution, 149–151
 as design goal, 11
 design methodology and, 10
 distributed embedded systems, 481–482

Ethernet, 471
execution time measurement, 225
interrupts and, 125–126
model train controller example, 34
nonlinear functions, 421, 422
operating systems, 393–396
optimization
 of energy and power, 305–309,
 396–400
 of program execution speed, 304–305
 of program size, 310–312
power consumption and, 307
process scheduling and, 393–396
program execution time, 290–305
 caching effects, 296
 data-dependent program paths,
 293–294
 difficulties estimating, 290–291
 execution time formula, 292
 instruction timing, 295–296
 measuring execution speed, 291
 optimization for execution speed,
 304–305
 paths in loops, 294–295
 scheduling overhead, 372, 422
 trace-driven performance analysis,
 296–304
 types of performance measures,
 291–292
program testing, 324–325
scheduling overhead, 372
scheduling policy CPU utilization
 earliest-deadline-first scheduling,
 380–381
 overview, 371–372
 rate-monotonic scheduling, 375–376
 RMS vs. EDF, 382
SRAM vs. DRAM, 195
telephone answering machine example,
 408–409
trace-driven performance analysis,
 296–304
 cache optimizations, 300–304
 capturing a trace, 296–297
 CPU generation of traces, 297
 loop optimizations, 298–300
 software generation of traces, 297
 trace analysis, 297–298
 trace defined, 296
period of a process, 346
peripheral component interconnect (PCI)
 bus, 218, 459
perror() function (POSIX), 350

personal computers. *See* PCs
personal digital assistants (PDAs) example,
 548–551
 Apple Newton MessagePad, 548–549
 characteristics, 548
 feature creep issues, 549–550
 InfoPad, 550–551
 Motorola Envoy PDA, 549, 550
 power supply design, 550
phone input module (telephone answering
 machine example), 407, 408
phone output module (telephone answer-
 ing machine example), 407, 408
physical interface classes
 elevator controller example, 489, 490
 telephone answering machine example,
 404, 405
physical layer
 CAN bus, 464–465
 Ethernet, 470
 I^2C bus, 459–460
 IP routing and, 473
 OSI model, 452–453
pipe() function in Unix, 392–393
pipelining, 145–149
 in ARM, 145, 148–149
 branch penalty, 146–147
 in CISC machines, 145
 code scheduling for SHARC DAGs,
 147–148
 control stall delays, 146–147
 data stall, 145
 delayed branch, 146–147
 energy optimization and, 309
 evaluation time for loop in ARM,
 148–149
 latency, 145
 RISC architecture and, 59
 in RISC machines, 59, 145
 in SHARC, 145, 147–148, 286–287
 software pipelining, 286–287
 superscalar execution and, 150
 three-stage pipeline, 145
 throughput, 145
place ringing state (telephone PBX exam-
 ple), 536
platform, 177–244
 alarm clock example, 233–241
 component design and testing,
 240–241
 requirements, 233–234
 specification, 235–239
 system architecture, 239–240

platform, alarm clock example (*continued*)
system integration and testing, 241
component interfacing, 209–212
device interfacing, 211–212
glue logic interface, 211–212
memory interfacing, 209–211
multichip SRAM memory system,
209–210
CPU bus, 178–193
ARM processor, 190–191
bus master devices, 186–187
components, 179
defined, 178
DMA, 186–187, 189
hardware architecture design and, 213
protocols, 178–185
SHARC processor, 191–193
system bus configurations, 187–190
typical bus structure, 180
debugging, 221–228
breakpoints, 222–223
challenges, 227–228
co-verification tools, 226
CPU simulators for, 225–226
cycle-based simulators for, 226
hardware/software co-verification
techniques, 225–226
in-circuit emulation, 223
LEDs as debugging devices, 223
logic analyzers for, 223–225
real-time code, 227–228
techniques, 221–226
designing with microprocessors,
212–220
hardware architecture, 213–214
hardware design, 214–216
PCs as platforms, 216–219
programmability benefits, 8
software architecture, 214
StrongARM system organization,
219–220
development environments, 9, 220–221
distributed embedded system design,
482–484
computation-intensive systems, 484
I/O-intensive systems, 483–484
platform defined, 451
I/O devices, 202–209
A/D and D/A converters, 203–204,
227–228
counter/timers, 202–203
displays, 206–208

hardware architecture design and,
213–214
hardware design and, 215–216
keyboards, 204–206
LEDs, 206
timers, 202–203
touchscreens, 208–209
manufacturing testing, 228–233
automatic test pattern generation
(ATPG), 231
boundary scan logic, 231–233
combinational network, 230
design for testability, 229
fault models, 229–230
goal, 238–239
scan chains, 231
sequential network, 230–231
using the microprocessor, 232–233
yield, 229
memory devices, 193–201
organization, 194–195
random-access memories, 195–200
read-only memories (ROMs), 201
PCs as platforms, 216–219
advantages, 216–217
buses, 218
hardware components, 217
single-chip PCs, 219–220
software, 218–219
StrongARM SA-1100 and 1111,
219–220
Playback class (telephone answering
machine example), 404–406, 407
playback-msg behavior (telephone
answering machine example), 406,
407
PLC (program location counter), 260
PLDs (programmable logic devices), 216,
577–578
Plug-and-Play standard, 218–219
PM (program memory) in SHARC, 83
point-to-point links, 453–454
polling
defined, 110
with prioritized interrupts, 122
POSIX
compliance with, 342
described, 342
interprocess communication
message-based, 393
shared memory, 389–392
signals, 387–389

processes in, 349–351
scheduling policies for processes
earliest-deadline-first scheduling
(EDF), 377–382
modeling assumptions, 383–386
_POSIX_PRIORITY_SCHEDULING resource,
372
rate-monotonic scheduling (RMS),
372–377
RMS vs. EDF, 382
SCHED_FIFO policy, 377
SCHED_OTHER policy, 386–387
SCHED_RR policy, 386–387
signals, 387–389
exceptions, 387, 388
for interprocess communication,
387–389
real-time, 388–389
sigqueue() function, 389
termination, 387, 388
user-defined, 387, 388
_POSIX_MESSAGE_PASSING facility, 393
_POSIX_PRIORITY_SCHEDULING resource, 372
_POSIX_REALTIME_SIGNALS facility, 378–379
_POSIX_SEMAPHORES option, 390
_POSIX_SHARED_MEMORY_OBJECTS option,
390–392
post-indexing addressing in ARM, 72, 73
post-modify addressing in SHARC, 90
power consumption. *See also* power man-
agement
analysis, 305–306
of CMOS gates, 569–570
costs affected by, 6
CPU power consumption, 152–158
CMOS power characteristics, 152–153
energy vs. power, 152
power state machine, 155–156
power-down modes, 153, 155–156
PowerPC 603 energy efficiency fea-
tures, 154–155
static vs. dynamic power manage-
ment, 153, 155–156
StrongARM SA-1100 power-saving
modes, 156–158
as design challenge, 8
as design goal, 11
energy vs. power, 152
measuring for code fragments, 305–306
memory accesses and, 20
optimization, 306–309
energy optimization, 307–309
instruction choices, 306

memory effects, 306–307
opportunities for saving power, 305
for processes, 396–400
SRAM vs. DRAM, 195
power management
Advanced Configuration and Power
Interface (ACPI), 399–400
optimization strategies, 396–400
power management policy, 396
power state machine, 155–156
power-down modes, 153, 155–156
PowerPC 603 energy efficiency features,
154–155
predictive shutdown, 396–399
for processes, 396–400
static vs. dynamic, 153, 155–156
StrongARM SA-1100 power-saving
modes, 156–158
power state machine, 155–156
power-down modes
Advanced Configuration and Power
Interface (ACPI), 399–400
idle mode, 157
overview, 153, 155–156
power state machine, 155–156
in PowerPC 603, 154
predictive shutdown, 396–399
sleep mode, 155–156, 157–158
in StrongARM SA-1100, 157–158
PowerPC
code compression for, 312
energy efficiency features, 154–155
for systems-on-silicon, 555, 556
power-saving modes of StrongARM SA-
1100, 156–158
predicates for condition execution in ARM,
75–76
predictive shutdown, 396–399
goal of, 396–397
in pagers, 397
predictive techniques, 397–399
preemptive multitasking, 356–357
interrupt mechanism for, 356–357
timer-driven preemption, 356–357
present state inputs for flip-flop-based
synchronous machines, 574
presentation layer of OSI model, 453
Primary Avionics Software System (PASS),
364–365
primary inputs for flip-flop-based synchro-
nous machines, 574
primary outputs for flip-flop-based syn-
chronous machines, 574

primitives
 input and output, 108–110
 object-oriented specification, 22
 UML elements, 561–562
prioritization. *See also* arbitration of
 buses
 of exceptions, 129
 of messages in POSIX, 393
prioritized interrupts, 120–123, 125
 advantages of, 120–121
 changing device priorities, 121
 described, 120
 I/O example, 122–123
 masking, 121
 nonmaskable interrupts (NMIs), 121
 polling with, 122
priority inversion
 among processes, 383
 in networks, 479
priority-driven process scheduling,
 359–360
private branch exchange (PBX) examples.
 See telephone PBX examples
Procase SMARTsystem, 529
procedure call stack in arm, 80–81
procedure calls
 in ARM, 81–82, 273
 cooperative multitasking and, 352
 energy optimization and recursive calls,
 309
 in SHARC, 98
procedure linkage, 81
procedures. *See also* functions
 in ARM, 80–82, 273
 creating in compilation, 273
 defined, 80
 frame pointer, 273
 inlining, 277–278
 in SHARC, 97–98
 stack pointer, 273
process_command() function (alarm clock
 example), 239, 240
processes
 activation record, 349, 361
 complex programs and, 341–342
 computation-intensive system design,
 484
 context switching, 351–358
 cooperative multitasking, 351–356
 defined, 342
 object-oriented design and pro-
 cesses, 357–358
 overhead, 384–386
 preemptive multitasking, 356–357

CPU cohabitation by, 348–349
 critical instance, 374
 data dependencies, 370–371, 383–384
 defined, 348
 described, 341
 executing state, 358, 359
 interprocess communication mecha-
 nisms, 365–371, 387–393
 blocking vs. nonblocking, 366
 message-based communication,
 369–371, 392–393
 shared memory communication,
 366–369, 389–392
 UML signals, 389
 Unix signals, 387–389
 I/O-intensive system design, 483–484
 lightweight processes, 349
 multiple tasks and, 343–347
 object-oriented design and, 357–358
 operating system data structures to sup-
 port scheduling, 361
 overview, 347–349
 performance evaluation, 393–396
 period of a process, 346
 platform design and, 482–484
 in POSIX, 349–351
 power optimization strategies, 396–400
 Advanced Configuration and Power
 Interface (ACPI), 399–400
 power management policy, 396
 predictive shutdown, 396–399
 priority inversion, 383
 rate, 346
 ready state, 358, 359
 reentrant programs, 349
 response time, 374
 scheduling by operating systems,
 358–360
 accelerated systems and, 434–436
 allocation of communication and,
 480
 caching and, 394–396
 priority-driven scheduling, 359–360
 process states and, 358–359
 scheduling policies, 371–387
 CPU utilization, 371–372, 375–376,
 380–381, 382
 defined, 371
 earliest-deadline-first scheduling
 (EDF), 377–382
 modeling assumptions, 383–386
 performance evaluation, 393–396
 POSIX SCHED_OTHER policy, 386–387
 POSIX SCHED_RR policy, 386–387

rate-monotonic scheduling (RMS),
372–377
RMS vs. EDF, 382
scheduling overhead, 372, 422
telephone answering machine example,
400–409
component design and testing,
408–409
requirements, 402–403
specification, 404–406
system architecture, 406–408
system integration and testing, 409
theory of operation, 400–402
telephone calls as, 361–362
threads, 349
timing requirements, 362–365
deadline, 362–363, 364
initiation interval, 363, 364
initiation time, 362, 363
rate requirements, 363
space shuttle software error example,
364–365
waiting state, 358–359
processing element (PE), 421, 449, 450–451
processor-support ASIC (ink jet printer
example), 543–544, 545
product metrics, 498–499
product realization, concurrent, 503
program counter (PC)
computing absolute address using
(ARM), 70
in Harvard architecture, 58–59
PC-relative addressing
in ARM, 73
in SHARC, 93, 97
PC-relative branches in ARM, 73
trace generation by sampling, 297
in von Neumann architecture, 58
program design, 246–252
data compressor example, 163–170
non–object-oriented implementation,
168–170
object-oriented implementation,
163–168
shared memory in, 366–367
design patterns
circular buffer implementation of FIR
filter, 251–252
data stream style, 250–252
for embedded systems, 248–252
overview, 246–247
state machine style, 248–250
software modem example, 325–330

component design and testing,
329
requirements, 327
specification, 328
system architecture, 328–329
system integration and testing,
329–330
theory of operation, 325–326
program location counter (PLC), 260
program memory (PM) in SHARC, 83
program trace, 296. *See also* trace-driven
performance analysis
programmability, design benefits of, 8
programmable logic devices (PLDs), 216,
577–578
programmer model. *See* programming
model
programming embedded processors
assembly, 258–263
compilation techniques, 258–263
arithmetic expression example,
267–269
arrays, 274–275
conditional code generation example,
270–272
data structures, 274–275
dead code elimination, 277
expression simplification, 275–276
instruction selection, 287–288
interpreters, 289
JIT (just-in-time) compilers, 289–290
loop transformations, 278–280
procedure creation, 273
procedure inlining, 277–278
register allocation, 280–285
scheduling, 285–287
statement translation, 267–273
template matching, 287–288
as translation plus optimization,
266–267
understanding and using compilers,
288–289
energy and power analysis and optimi-
zation, 305–309
measuring power consumption for
code fragments, 305–306
opportunities for saving power, 305
optimization, 306–309
execution time analysis and optimiza-
tion, 290–305
caching effects, 296
data-dependent program paths,
293–294

programming embedded processors, execution time analysis and optimization (*continued*)
 difficulties for estimating run times, 290–291
 execution time formula, 292
 instruction timing, 295–296
 measuring execution speed, 291
 optimization for execution speed, 304–305
 paths in loops, 294–295
 trace-driven performance analysis, 296–304
 types of performance measures, 291–292
linking, 258, 264–265
models of programs, 252–257
 control/data flow graphs (CDFGs), 252, 254–257
 data flow graphs, 252–254
program design patterns
 circular buffer implementation of FIR filter, 251–252
 class diagram, 246–247
 data stream style, 250–252
 for embedded systems, 248–252
 state machine style, 248–250
 types of, 247–248
 uses for, 247
program size analysis and optimization, 310–312
program validation and testing, 312–325
 black-box testing, 322–323
 clear-box testing, 313–322
 evaluating function tests, 323–324
 major strategies, 313
 observability and controllability issues, 313–314
 performance testing, 324–325
 software modem example, 329–330
 tasks, 313–314
 thoroughness required, 313
software modem example, 325–330
 component design and testing, 329
 requirements, 327
 specification, 328
 system architecture, 328–329
 system integration and testing, 329–330
 theory of operation, 325–326
programming model. *See also* models of programs
 ARM processor, 64–66

defined, 60
SHARC processor, 83–84
programs. *See* software
PROM
 flash, 201
 UV-erasable (UV-EPROM), 201
protected mode, 362
protocols
 CPU bus, 178–185
 bus reads and writes, 178–185
 four-cycle handshake, 178, 179
 Internet, 473–475
prototypes, 527
prototyping languages, 527
pseudo-operations
 ARM processor, 62, 69, 70, 263
 for memory allocation, 61–62
 overview, 61–62
 SHARC processor, 62
Pulser* class (model train controller example), 39–40
purpose. *See also* goals
 alarm clock example, 234
 data compressor example, 161
 model train controller example, 34
 on requirements form, 13
 software modem example, 327
 telephone answering machine example, 402
 video accelerator example, 440

quality assurance (QA), 520–534. *See also* debugging; testing
 defect removal efficiency, 530, 531
 as design goal, 499
 design reviews, 527–529
 described, 527–528
 format for, 528–529
 paperless code inspections, 529
 review team, 528
 measurement-driven, 530–531
 overview, 520
 software QA example, 531–534
 techniques, 523–525
 Capability Maturity Model (CMM), 525
 ISO 9000 standard, 523–524
 manual vs. tool based, 524
 overall process, 524–525
 Therac-25 medical imaging system example, 521–523
 verifying the specification, 525–527
QuickCam, 485–486

race condition in shared memory communication, 367–369
RAM. *See* random-access memories
random tests, 322
random-access memories, 195–200
 described, 195
 dynamic RAM (DRAM), 197–200
 EDO (extended data out), 198, 200
 inputs (control signals), 197–198
 interface, 197, 199, 210–211
 memory controller, 198
 page mode access, 198, 199
 refreshing, 198, 211
 SRAM vs., 195
 synchronous DRAM, 198–199, 200
 timing diagram, 197
 frame buffers, 207
 hardware architecture design and, 213
 Rambus, 199
 static RAM (SRAM), 195–196
 DRAM vs., 195
 inputs (control signals), 195
 interface, 196, 209–210
 multichip SRAM memory system, 209–210
 read operation, 195–196
 timing diagram, 196
 video RAM, 199
raster order for CRT displays, 207
rate control problems, 344
rate of a process, 346
rate requirements for processes, 363
rate-monotonic analysis (RMA), 372–373, 374
rate-monotonic scheduling (RMS), 372–377
 CPU utilization, 375–376, 382
 critical-instant analysis, 374–375
 EDF vs., 382
 example, 373–374
 implementation, 376–377
 rate-monotonic analysis (RMA), 372–373, 374
rcv ringing state (telephone PBX example), 536
reactive systems, state machines and, 248
read operations for static RAM (SRAM), 195–196
read_buttons() function (alarm clock example), 239–240
read-only memories (ROMs)
 hardware architecture design and, 213
 overview, 201

reads and writes (CPU bus), 178–185
 burst transfers, 182–183, 184
 changing and stable states, 181
 data bundles smaller than word size, 184–185
 disconnected transfers, 183
 multiplexed address and data, 185
 read sequence of operations, 181
 state machine view, 184, 185
 timing constraints, 181
 timing diagram, 180–181
 wait states, 182
 write sequence of operations, 181–182
ready state of processes, 358, 359
real-time code
 debugging, 227–228
 termination of, 324
real-time network file manager (RTNFM), 553
real-time operating systems (RTOSs). *See also* POSIX
 defined, 342
 ink jet printer example, 541, 547–548
 process evaluation tools, 394
real-time operations
 overview, 5–6
 of Whirlwind, 2
real-time performance and accelerators, 422
real-time signals in POSIX, 388–389
real-world classes (elevator controller example), 519
real-world modeling in object-oriented specification, 22
Receiver class (model train controller example), 38, 41, 42
RECIPS operation in SHARC, 86
Record class (telephone answering machine example), 404–406, 407
record-msg behavior (telephone answering machine example), 406, 407
recursive procedure calls, 309
reduced instruction set computers. *See* RISC microprocessors
reentrant programs, 349
refinement in design, 11
refreshing DRAM, 198, 211
register-transfer level in hardware description languages, 578
registers
 accelerators and, 425
 allocation during compiling, 280–285
 ARM example, 280–282

registers, allocation during compiling
(*continued*)
conflict graph, 282
lifetime graphs, 281, 283, 284
live variables, 281
operator scheduling, 283–285
spilling registers, 282
ARM processor
allocation, 280–282
co-processors and, 130
current program status register
(CPSR), 65–66, 126, 129
general purpose registers, 64
interrupt handling and, 126
register-indirect addressing, 69–70
saved program status register (SPSR),
126, 129
supervisor mode and, 129
in assembly language, 61
energy efficiency and, 306, 309
in I/O devices, 106–107, 211–212
program execution time optimization
and, 304
programming model, 60
register-transfer level in hardware
description languages, 578
SHARC processor
ASTAT register, 84, 86, 87, 88
interrupt handling and, 127
IRPTL register, 130
link port registers, 469
MODE1 register, 85, 86
primary data registers, 83–84
Ry register, 87
STKY register, 84–85, 88
UART, 107–108
in von Neumann architecture, 58
regression tests, 323
relationships
aggregation, 24
association, 24, 28, 29
composition, 24
generalization, 24
links, 28, 29
relative addresses, 259
reliability, as design challenge, 9
remote frames in CAN bus, 466
Repeatable level of maturity, 525
requirements
alarm clock example, 233–234
analysis, 507–508
data compressor example, 160–161
defined, 507

determining, 508
elevator controller example, 489
functional vs. nonfunctional, 12, 507
GPS system example, 15–17
internal consistency of, 15
mock-ups, 13
model train controller example, 34
nonfunctional, 12–13, 19, 507
overview, 12–17
sample form for, 13–14
specifications vs., 12, 507
in spiral model of software design,
502
telephone answering machine example,
402–403
tests for good requirements, 507–508
validation, 13, 526–527
video accelerator example, 440
in waterfall model of software develop-
ment, 500
requirements form, 13–14
reservation table, 285–286
resistive touchscreens, 208–209
response time of processes, 374
reusing values, 310
Rhodes, David L., 386
ringing, sensing for telephone, 402
RISC microprocessors. *See also* PowerPC
CISC vs., 59
in ink jet printer example, 541
pipelining, 59, 145
uses of, 3
RMA (rate-monotonic analysis), 372–373,
374
RMS. *See* rate-monotonic scheduling
(RMS)
rollover in keyboards, 205–206
ROLM PBX example, 534–535
ROM burners, 201
Romano, Glenn M., 467
ROMs. *See* read-only memories (ROMs)
Rosebrugh, Christopher, 451
rotate instructions. *See* shift/rotate instruc-
tions
round-robin arbitration, 455, 477
routers
best-effort routing, 474
defined, 473
row major array form, 274
RRX modifier in ARM, 68
RSB instructions in ARM, 66
RSQRTS operation in SHARC, 86
RTI instruction in SHARC, 127

RTNFM (real-time network file manager), 553

RTOSs. *See* real-time operating systems (RTOSs)

run times. *See* execution time of programs

Ry register in SHARC, 87

Sablime, 529

saturation arithmetic in SHARC, 85

saved program status register (SPSR) in ARM, 126, 129

SCALB operation in SHARC, 85–86

scan chains, 231

scan-keyboard behavior (alarm clock example), 235, 236, 238–239

SCHED_FIFO policy in POSIX, 377

SCHED_OTHER policy in POSIX, 386–387

SCHED_RR policy in POSIX, 386–387

sched_setscheduler() function in POSIX, 372

Scheduler class (elevator controller example), 519

scheduling operations during compilation, 285–287

scheduling processes
 for accelerated systems, 434–436
 allocation of communication and, 480
 caching and, 394–396
 context switching overhead and, 384–386
 CPU utilization, 371–372, 375–376, 380–381, 382
 data dependencies and, 383–384
 overhead, 372, 422
 priority inversion, 383
 priority-driven scheduling, 359–360
 process states and, 358–359
 scheduling policies, 371–387

SCL (serial clock line) of I^2C bus, 459–460, 461, 462, 463

SDL (serial data line) of I^2C bus, 459–460, 461, 462, 463

SDL specification language, 509

SDRAM (synchronous DRAM), 198–199, 200

SDRB instruction in ARM, 68

SDRH instruction in ARM, 68

Search-area class (video accelerator example), 441

segmented address translation, 140, 142

self-modifying programs, 58–59

semaphores
 defined, 368

in POSIX, 389–390
 test-and-set operation, 368–369

semicolon (;)
 for ARM comments, 62
 for SHARC instruction termination, 82

sem_post() function in POSIX, 390

sem_trywait() function in POSIX, 390

sem_wait() function in POSIX, 390

Sender* class (model train controller example), 38, 39, 40

sensor, 451

Sensor* class (elevator controller example), 490

sequence diagrams
 focus of control in, 31–32
 lifelines, 31
 model train controller example, 43, 46
 overview, 31–32, 565
 video accelerator example, 441, 442

sequential logic, 571–577
 asynchronous machines, 576–577
 memory elements, 571–573
 synchronous machines, 573–575

sequential networks, manufacturing testing and, 230–231

serial clock line (SCL) of I^2C bus, 459–460, 461, 462, 463

serial data line (SDL) of I^2C bus, 459–460, 461, 462, 463

serial port as debugging tool, 222

session layer of OSI model, 453

set-associative caches
 direct-mapped caches vs., 135–138
 hit rates, 135
 limitations, 135
 overhead, 134–135
 overview, 134–135

set-top boxes example, 551–555
 cost sensitivity, 551
 hardware architecture, 551–552
 role of set-top boxes, 551, 552
 software architecture, 552–554, 555
 user interface, 554

setup time for sequential logic memory elements, 573

SGS Thomson chip set, 3–4

SHARC processor, 82–99
 caches in, 139
 comments, 83
 compilation of arithmetic expression, 269
 compute-and-move instructions, 61, 62

SHARC processor, (*continued*)
CPU bus, 191–193
DMA, 192–193
external memory interface, 191–192
host interface, 192
data operations, 83–92
ALU operations, 84–86
arithmetic operations, 84–88
C assignments in instructions, 91–92
CPU data function units, 84
floating-point operations, 83, 85–87
load-and-store operations, 88–90
multiplier operations, 87
programming model, 83–84
saturation arithmetic, 85
shifter operations, 87–88
status bits, 88
storing data in program memory, 91–92
flow of control, 93–98
C procedure calls, 98
CALL instruction, 97
conditional encoding for branches, 93, 94
DO UNTIL instruction, 93, 96–97
FIR filter, 96–97
function calls, 97–98
if statement implementation, 94–96
JUMP instruction, 93
loops, 93, 96–97
instruction termination, 82
interrupts in, 127–128
labels, 82, 83
link ports, 467–470
data bits, 468
half-duplex communication, 469–470
link buffers, 368–369
registers, 469
SHARC-based multiprocessor example, 467–468
words, 468
memory management units (MMUs) and, 144
memory organization, 83
memory-mapped I/O, 109
notation, 82–83
parallelism within instructions, 99
pipelining, 145, 147–148, 286–287
pseudo-ops for allocating memory, 62
software interrupts (traps), 130
software pipelining, 286–287
supervisor mode and, 128

shared memory interprocess communication, 366–369, 389–392
in bus-based systems, 366, 367
elastic buffers as shared memory, 366–367
message passing communication vs., 366
in POSIX, 389–392
race condition, 367–369
test-and-set operations, 367–369
text compressor example, 366–367
shell syntax of pipe in Unix, 392–393
shift/rotate instructions
ARM processor, 67–68
SHARC processor, 87–88
shm_open() function in POSIX, 390, 392
signals
CPU bus components, 179
dynamic RAM (DRAM) control signals, 197–198
interprocess communication
POSIX signals, 387–389
UML signals, 389
multidimensional signal processing for video, 422
open collector/open drain signaling, 460
overview, 29, 30
static RAM (SRAM) control signals, 195
sigqueue() function in POSIX, 389
Simple Mail Transfer Protocol (SMTP), 475
Simple Network Management Protocol (SNMP), 475
simulation
hardware/software co-verification
co-simulation, 226, 437
co-verification tools, 226
CPU simulators, 225–226
cycle-based simulators, 226
simulation bus, 226
trace generation, 297
simulation bus, 226
single switch keyboards, 204–205
single-assignment form, 253
single-chip PCs, 219–220
single-hop networks, 479
single-threaded accelerator control, 424, 425, 427, 428
size
custom logic designs vs. microprocessors, 7
program size analysis and optimization, 310–312
sleep mode, 155–156, 157–158

Smart Battery System, 550
SMARTsystem, 529
SMTP (Simple Mail Transfer Protocol), 475
SNMP (Simple Network Management Protocol), 475
software. *See also* debugging; processes; programming embedded processors
 alarm clock example, 239–240
 architecture, 214
 architecture design, 18–19
 breakpoints, 222–223
 complex programs, 341–342
 component design, 20
 design benefits of programmability, 8
 development environments, 9, 220–221
 hardware/software co-design, 419, 450
 implementation of classes and objects, 25–26
 ink jet printer example, 546–548
 interrupt handling and, 125
 interrupts (traps), 129–130
 modem example, 325–330
 partitioning, 214
 PC platform software, 218–219
 pipelining, 286–287, 309
 program size analysis and optimization, 310–312
 programming embedded processors
 assembly, 258–263
 compilation techniques, 258–290
 energy and power analysis and optimization, 305–309
 execution time analysis and optimization, 290–305
 linking, 258, 264–265
 models of programs, 252–257
 program design patterns, 246–252
 program size analysis and optimization, 310–312
 program validation and testing, 312–325
 software modem example, 325–330
 quality assurance example, 531–534
 reentrant programs, 349
 set-top boxes example, 552–554, 555
 spaghetti code, 214, 341
 trace generation, 297
Software Engineering Institute, 525
software pipelining, 286–287, 309
Software Quality Evaluation (SQE) system, 530

space shuttle software error example, 364–365
spaghetti code, 214, 341
Speaker* class
 alarm clock example, 235, 236
 telephone answering machine example, 405
speaker module (telephone answering machine example), 407, 408
specifications, 509–515
 alarm clock example, 235–239
 class diagram, 36, 37
 collaboration diagram, 36–37
 control-oriented languages, 509–512
 AND/OR tables, 511–512
 SDL, 509
 Statecharts, 510–511
 data compressor example, 161–163
 elevator controller example, 489–491
 GPS system example, 17
 model train controller example
 conceptual specification, 34–39
 detailed specification, 39–46
 object-oriented, 22
 overview, 17, 509–515
 requirements vs., 12, 507
 software modem example, 328
 specification languages, 527
 of state machine in UML, 31
 TCAS II (Traffic Alert and Collision Avoidance System) example, 512–515
 telephone answering machine example, 404–406
 validation, 526, 527
 verifying, 525–527
 video accelerator example, 441
speed. *See* performance
spilling registers, 282
spiral model of software design, 502
SPSR (saved program status register) in ARM, 126, 129
SQE (Software Quality Evaluation) system, 530
SRAM. *See* memory; static RAM (SRAM)
Srivasta, Amitabh, 397
stable states (CPU bus), 181
stack pointer, 273
stand-alone compression unit, 343–344
start bits, 107
state diagrams
 alarm clock example, 237, 238
 bus bridge operation, 189, 190

state diagrams (*continued*)
 data compressor example, 163, 164
 model train controller example, 43, 44, 45
 overview, 564
 telephone answering machine example, 406, 407
state machines
 C implementation, 248–250
 CPU bus, 184, 185
 events, 29–30
 finite-state, 248
 reactive systems and, 248
 specification in UML, 31
 states and transitions in UML, 29, 30
state mode of logic analyzers, 224
state transition graph for I^2C bus master, 462
Statecharts specification language, 510–511
statement translation, 267–273
 arithmetic expression compilation, 267–269
 compilation as translation plus optimization, 266–267
states in UML, 561
static power management
 dynamic vs., 153, 155–156
 in PowerPC 603, 154–155
static RAM (SRAM)
 DRAM vs., 195
 hardware architecture design and, 213
 inputs (control signals), 195
 interface, 196, 209–210
 multichip SRAM memory system, 209–210
 overview, 195–196
 read operation, 195–196
 timing diagram, 196
statistical compression of programs, 311
status registers. *See* registers
stereotypes, 28–29, 562
STKY register in SHARC, 84–85, 88
stop bits, 107
storing data in program memory in SHARC, 91–92
STR instruction in ARM, 69–70
streaming data
 accelerators and, 423
 circular buffer for, 250–251
 in Harvard architecture, 59
strength reduction for loop optimization, 300

StrongARM
 SA-1100 power-saving modes, 156–158
 system organization, 219–220
structural description, 22–29
 class notation, 23–24
 defined, 22
 derived classes, 26–27
 generalization and inheritance, 27–28
 interface choice, 24
 links, 28, 29
 object notation, 23
 relationships, 24
 software implementation of classes and objects, 25–26
 stereotypes, 28–29
stuck-at-0/1 fault model, 230
subroutines. *See also* functions; procedures
 defined, 80
 program size reduction and, 310–311
subscriber line, 402
successive refinement development model, 501–502, 503
superscalar execution, 149–151
 dynamic dependency checking, 150
 overview, 149–150
 performance, 150–151
 pipelining and, 150
supervisor mode
 overview, 128–129
 SWI instruction in ARM, 128–129, 130, 362
 traps and, 129–130
supplier involvement in concurrent engineering, 504
SWI instruction in ARM, 128–129, 130, 362
SWP instruction in ARM, 368–369
symbol table processing
 in ARM, 260–262
 by assemblers, 259–260
 labels and, 262–263
 by linkers, 264, 265
Symbol-table class (data compressor example), 162
synchronous bus, 464. *See also* CAN (controller area network) bus
synchronous DRAM, 198–199, 200
synchronous machines, 573–575
 central clock for, 573
 flip-flop-based, 573–574
 latch-based, 574–575
system architecture. *See also* architecture
 accelerator framework, 429–432
 alarm clock example, 239–240

software modem example, 328–329
system analysis and architecture design,
515–520
CRC card methodology, 516–518
elevator system example, 518–520
telephone answering machine example,
406–408
telephone PBX example, 537–539
system design. *See* embedded computing
system design
system integration
accelerated systems, 437
alarm clock example, 241
debugging during, 20–21
overview, 20–21
software modem example, 329–330
telephone answering machine example,
409
systems-on-a-chip, 555–557
systems-on-silicon, 555–557

table lookup, 328–329
target in development environment, 220,
221
task graph, 370
task set, 370
tasks, 343
taxonomy of computer architecture, 58–59
TCAS II (Traffic Alert and Collision Avoid-
ance System) specification,
512–515
CAS system, 513–515
Own-Aircraft AND state, 514–515
TCP (Transmission Control Protocol),
474–475
telephone answering machine example,
400–409
component design and testing, 408–409
requirements, 402–403
specification, 404–406
system architecture, 406–408
system integration and testing, 409
theory of operation, 400–402
telephone calls as processes, 361–362
telephone line module (telephone answer-
ing machine example), 406,
407–408
telephone PBX examples
concurrent engineering at AT&T,
505–507
ROLM PBX, 534–539
telephone systems concurrent engineering
example, 505–507

television, microprocessor use in, 3–4
template matching, 287–288
TEQ instruction in ARM, 68
termination signals in POSIX, 387, 388
test-and-set operations, 367–369
testbench programs, 221
testing. *See also* debugging; quality assur-
ance (QA)
alarm clock example, 140–141
black-box testing, 322–323
clear-box testing, 313–322
condition testing, 317–320
execution paths for, 315–317
loop testing, 320–322
observability and controllability
issues, 313–314
tasks, 313–314
complexity as design challenge, 9
data compressor example, 170–171
data value tests, 322
design for testability, 229
elevator controller example, 492–493
manufacturing testing, 228–233
automatic test pattern generation
(ATPG), 231
boundary scan logic, 231–233
combinational network, 230
design for testability, 229
fault models, 229–230
goal, 238–239
scan chains, 231
sequential network, 230–231
using the microprocessor, 232–233
yield, 229
program validation and testing,
312–325
black-box testing, 322–323
clear-box testing, 313–322
evaluating function tests, 323–324
major strategies, 313
observability and controllability
issues, 313–314
performance testing, 324–325
software modem example, 329–330
tasks, 313–314
thoroughness required, 313
random tests, 322
regression tests, 323
software modem example, 329–330
in spiral model of software design, 502
telephone answering machine example,
408–409
testbench programs, 221

testing (*continued*)
 video accelerator example, 444–445
 in waterfall model of software development, 500
text compression example. *See* data compressor example
theory of operation
 elevator controller example, 487–488
 software modem example, 325–326
 telephone PBX example, 535–537
Therac-25 medical imaging system example, 521–523
threads. *See also* processes
 defined, 349
 single-threaded vs. multithreaded accelerator control, 424, 425, 427–428
three-state logic, 571
throughput, pipelining, 145
Thumb instruction set in ARM, 311
time for program execution. *See* execution time of programs
time-out events, 30
time-to-market, 498
timer-driven preemption, 356–357
timers, 202–203
 counter/timers, 202, 203
 overview, 202
 watchdog timer, 202–203
timing constraints on asynchronous machines, 576–577
timing diagrams
 asynchronous machines, 576
 CPU bus, 180–181
 dynamic RAM (DRAM), 197
 static RAM (SRAM), 196
timing error in real-time code, debugging, 227–228
timing instructions, 295–296
timing mode of logic analyzers, 224
timing requirements
 for flip-flop-based synchronous machines, 574
 on processes, 362–365
 deadline, 362–363, 364
 initiation interval, 363, 364
 initiation time, 362, 363
 rate requirements, 363
 space shuttle software error example, 364–365
 for sequential logic memory elements, 573
toggling and CMOS power consumption, 152–153

tool-based vs. manual QA techniques, 524
top-down design, 10, 11
touchscreens, 208–209
trace, 296
trace-driven performance analysis, 296–304
 cache optimizations, 300–304
 cache miss equations, 301–302
 data realignment and array padding, 302–304
 nested loops and, 300–301
 capturing a trace, 296–297
 CPU generation of traces, 297
 loop optimizations, 298–300
 code motion, 298–299
 induction variable elimination, 299–300
 strength reduction, 300
 software generation of traces, 297
 trace analysis, 297–298
 trace defined, 296
traceability test for requirements, 508
Traffic Alert and Collision Avoidance System. *See* TCAS II (Traffic Alert and Collision Avoidance System) specification
Train class (model train controller example), 38
Train set class (model train controller example), 39
transitions in state machines, 29, 30, 31
Transmission Control Protocol (TCP), 474–475
Transmitter class (model train controller example), 37, 41, 42
Transmitter Empty signal of UART, 108
Transmitter Ready output of UART, 107–108
transport layer of OSI model, 453
traps, 129–130
TRUE value in Boolean logic, 568
trunk lines, telephone, 536
TST instruction in ARM, 68
Turner, Clark S., 511, 513, 521, 523

UART (Universal Asynchronous Receiver/Transmitter) example, 107–108
UDP (User Datagram Protocol), 475
UML. *See* Unified Modeling Language (UML)
unambiguousness test for requirements, 508

unified caches, 138
Unified Modeling Language (UML),
 561–566
 active class, 357
 annotations, 23
 class diagrams, 563–564
 class notation, 23–24
 collaboration diagrams, 565–566
 derived classes, 26–27
 inheritance, 27–28
 interprocess communication signals,
 389
 links, 28, 29
 notations, 561–566
 diagram types, 562–566
 primitive elements, 561–562
 object notation, 23
 object-oriented programming languages
 vs., 22, 24–25
 overview, 21–22
 relationships, 24
 scope of this book and, 22
 sequence diagrams, 31–32, 565
 signals, 389
 software implementation of classes and
 objects, 25–26
 state diagrams, 564
 stereotypes, 28–29, 562
Universal Asynchronous Receiver/
 Transmitter (UART) example,
 107–108
universal serial bus (USB), 218
Unix. *See also* POSIX
 interprocess communication
 message-based, 392–393
 signals, 387–389
 POSIX standard, 342
 shell syntax of pipe, 392–393
 signals, 387
update-time behavior (alarm clock exam-
 ple), 235, 236, 237
upgradeability as design challenge, 9
usage scenarios, 527
USB (universal serial bus), 218
User Datagram Protocol (UDP), 475
user interface
 as design goal, 11
 GPS requirements example, 16
 overview, 5
user mode, 128
user-defined signals in POSIX, 387, 388

utilization of CPUs, scheduling policies
 and
 earliest-deadline-first scheduling,
 380–381
 overview, 371–372
 rate-monotonic scheduling, 375–376
 RMS vs. EDF, 382
UV-erasable PROM (UV-EPROM), 201

V (overflow) bit of ARM CPSR, 65
V() semaphore name, 368, 390. *See also*
 semaphores
validation. *See also* testing
 program validation and testing, 312–325
 black-box testing, 322–323
 clear-box testing, 313–322
 evaluating function tests, 323–324
 major strategies, 313
 observability and controllability
 issues, 313–314
 performance testing, 324–325
 software modem example, 329–330
 tasks, 313–314
 thoroughness required, 313
 of requirements, 13, 526–527
 of specifications, 527
variable data rates, 344
variables
 for arithmetic and logical operations in
 C, 63
 attributes vs., 24
 def-use analysis, 319–320, 321
 induction variable elimination, 299–300
 live, 281
 used, 320
 value defined for, 320
vectored interrupts, 124–125
 described, 120
 hardware structure for, 124
 interrupt handlers and, 124, 125
 in SHARC, 127
 vector number, 124, 125
 vector table, 124, 127
vectoring of exceptions, 129
verifiability test for requirements, 508
verification
 co-verification techniques, 225–226
 in embedded computing system design,
 11
 of the specification, 525–527
Verilog, 578

very large scale integration. *See* VLSI (very large scale integration) technology

VHDL language, 578

video accelerator example, 437–445

 algorithm, 437–440

 architecture, 441–443

 component design, 443–444

 requirements, 440

 specification, 441

 testing, 444–445

video camera, Internet, 485–486

video RAM, 199

virtual addressing, 139–140

virtual memory, MMU extensions, 142–143

VLSI (very large scale integration) technology

 for ARM processors, 62

 custom logic designs vs. microprocessors, 7

 single-chip CPUs and, 2

VME, 458

voltage and CMOS power consumption, 152, 153

von Neumann architecture

 in ARM7 processor, 63

 overview, 58

VRAM (video RAM), 199

wait states (CPU bus), 182

waiting state of processes, 358–359

watchdog timer, 202–203

waterfall model of software development, 500–501

Whirlwind computer, 2

white-box testing. *See* clear-box testing

Wolf, Wayne, 386, 394

words (data)

 ARM processor, 63, 64

 big-endian mode, 63, 64

 CPU bus data bundles smaller than word size, 184–185

 little-endian mode, 63, 64

 SHARC link ports, 468

 SHARC processor, 83

worst-case execution time, 291

write-back scheme for direct-mapped caches, 134

write-through scheme for direct-mapped caches, 134

writes (CPU bus). *See* reads and writes (CPU bus)

Yan, Pong Mang, 531

yield, 229

Z (zero) bit, of ARM CPSR, 65

zero (Z) bit, of ARM CPSR, 65

About the CD

Two CDs accompany this hardcover book: the ARM Developer Suite™ v1.0 and the Analog Devices Inc.'s VisualDSP test drive. The following pages detail the materials on each CD, the system requirements for each CD, and how to get started. The license agreement for the VisualDSP CD follows, while the license agreement for the ARM Developer Suite is on the CD. The software is provided to you on an "AS IS" basis. Morgan Kaufmann Publishers will replace defective CDs at no charge. In the case that a CD is defective, please call 1.800.321.5068 or fax your request to 1.800.874.6418. Proof of purchase must be submitted along with your request. To replace the VisualDSP CD, refer to ISBN 1-55860-725-0. To replace the ARM Developer Suite v1.0 CD, refer to ISBN 1-55860-726-9. The CDs do not accompany the softcover (ISE) version of the text.

ARM DEVELOPER SUITE v1.0

Description of the CD-ROM Materials

This evaluation CD contains the ARM Developer Suite (ADS). ADS includes all of the tools necessary for developing applications for the ARM architecture. This evaluation version includes C and C++ compilers, assembler and linker, an integrated development environment, powerful GUI debugger, instruction set simulators, and ROM-based debug tools. It also provides support for new cores (including the ARM9E™ and ARM10™ cores), an interactive demonstration of features and benefits of ADS, and documentation in PDF format.

The ARM Developer Suite replaces the existing ARM Software Development Toolkit (SDT) v2.50. It enhances some existing SDT components and replaces others with new elements. The tools included in this evaluation version have the same functionality as those provided for the full product. Once installed, the software will operate for 45 days.

System Requirements

This CD is intended for use on a Pentium or faster IBM-compatible PC. This CD will run on Windows 95, 98, or NT 4.0. Hardware requirements include a minimum of 32MB RAM; hard disk space of 85MB, 120MB with manuals, or 130MB with manuals plus Adobe Acrobat Reader install option; and a CD-ROM Drive. To install the Evaluation Toolkit, you should remove any previous versions of ADS or the ARM Software Development Toolkit.

Getting Started

Insert the CD into the CD-ROM. Execute the setup.exe program from the CD-ROM, and follow the on-screen instructions.

Copyright Notice

shall not be liable for any loss or damage arising from the use of any information in this document or any error or omission in such information.

VisualDSP® Test Drive

Description of the CD-ROM Materials

Analog Devices, Inc.'s VisualDSP is a Windows®-based evaluation software development environment for Analog Devices Digital Signal Processors (DSP). It is a project management environment, comprised of an integrated development environment and debugger. The project development and debug environments are integrated, allowing movement between editing, building, and debugging activities.

The software provides an integrated development environment with support for editing programs, managing projects, and controlling build tools. The integrated development environment will define all project and tool configurations through property page dialog boxes, set project-wide or individual file settings for debug or release mode project builds, and create source files using an integrated, full-featured editor with syntax highlighting, OLE drag and drop, and bookmarks.

The CD also provides a source level, object-oriented debugger with support for DSP simulation and emulation. With the debugger, the user will be able to view source files in C, assembly, or mixed C and assembly; profile and trace instruction execution of C and assembly programs; set watch points on processor registers and stacks, as well as program and data memory; create custom register windows; and simulate standard I/O, interrupts, and streams.

Analog Devices provides online access to all documentation for this product via PDF files.

This test drive supports the SHARC® DSP family. VisualDSP not only supports the SHARC DSP family, but also supports the TigerSHARC® DSP family, and the ADSP-218x and ADSP-219x DSP.

System Requirements

This CD is intended for use on a Pentium 166 MHz or faster (Pentium II recommended). To install this CD, you must have Windows 95 OSR B, Windows 98, Windows NT 4.0 (service pack 3 or later), Windows 2000, or Solaris 2.5.1. Hardware requirements include a minimum of 32MB RAM, hard disk space of 100MB, and a VGA display adapter and monitor. A two-button pointing device (mouse) is highly recommended.

Getting Started

To evaluate the test drive you must register at www.analog.com/industry/dsp/tools/test_drive.html. When registration is complete you will be given a serial number that will activate the software. Once installed, the software will operate fully for 30 days.

Copyright Notice

Analog Devices, Inc. reserves the right to make changes to or to discontinue any product or service identified in this publication without notice. Analog Devices assumes no liability for Analog Devices applications assistance, customer product design, customer software performance, or infringement of patents or services described herein. In addition, Analog Devices shall not be held liable for special, collateral, incidental or consequential damages in connection with or arising out of the furnishing, performance, or use of this product. Analog Devices products are not intended for use in life-support applications, devices, or systems. Use of an Analog Devices product in such applications without the written consent of the Analog Devices officer is prohibited. Users are restricted from copying, modifying, distributing, reverse engineering, and reverse assembling or reverse compiling the operational software (one copy may be made for back-up purposes only). No part of this document may be reproduced in any form without permission. Trademarks are property of their respective holders.

ANALOG DEVICES SOFTWARE LICENSE AGREEMENT

This is a legal document between you (either an individual or entity) and Analog Devices, Inc. (ADI). **Read the following terms and conditions carefully before opening the accompanying software packets.** They define your rights and obligations with respect to the enclosed ADI software and documentation (SOFTWARE). If you do not agree to the terms of this agreement, promptly return the sealed software packet(s) and accompanying documentation to the place you obtained them or to Analog Devices Inc. If the return is postmarked, or is received, within thirty (30) days of shipment, charges for the software will be removed from your bill. **OPENING THE SEALED SOFTWARE PACKET INDICATES YOUR AGREEMENT WITH AND ACCEPTANCE OF THE FOLLOWING TERMS AND CONDITIONS. AN INDIVIDUAL WHO DOES NOT HAVE AUTHORITY TO BIND THE ENTITY USING THE SOFTWARE SHOULD NOT**

OPEN THE SOFTWARE PACKET WITHOUT OBTAINING APPROVAL OF THIS AGREEMENT FROM A PERSON HAVING SUCH AUTHORITY.

1. SOFTWARE LICENSE GRANT

 A. You are granted a non-exclusive license to use this serialized copy of copyrighted SOFTWARE, only in accordance with this license agreement.

2. YOUR RESTRICTIONS, OBLIGATIONS AND DUTIES

 A. Use of this SOFTWARE is restricted to the execution of the SOFTWARE on one workstation at a time. You may not have more than one user concurrently access the SOFTWARE unless a separate license has been purchased for additional concurrent users.

 B. You may make up to two (2) copies to be used only for backup or archival purposes. All copyright notices and legends shall be reproduced on the backup copies.

 C. You may not disclose or transfer any portion of the SOFTWARE to any other party for any reason. Upon discontinuation of use of the SOFTWARE or termination of this license, you agree to destroy all copies, including partial copies, of the SOFTWARE.

 D. You may not disassemble, decompile, reverse engineer or alter the SOFTWARE.

3. TERMS, TERMINATION/CANCELLATION

 A. ADI may terminate this license upon your failure to comply with any of the terms and conditions of this agreement.

4. LIMITED WARRANTY AND LIMITATIONS OF LIABILITY AND REMEDY

 A. ADI warrants the SOFTWARE media against manufacturing defects for a period of ninety (90) days from the date of receipt. ADI will replace defective media at no charge to you through the Publisher. Contact the Publisher directly for a replacement CD. The SOFTWARE itself is otherwise provided to you on an "AS IS" basis. ADI does not provide any warranty or make any representation, either express or implied, that the SOFTWARE meets your needs or expectations, that it will function as anticipated, or that its use will not infringe on the intellectual property rights of any third party, although, to the best of its knowledge ADI is not aware of any such IP rights. You assume the full responsibility for

the selection, use and performance of the SOFTWARE. **WITH RESPECT TO THIS SOFTWARE, THE ABOVE LIMITED MEDIA WARRANTY IS IN LIEU OF ALL OTHER WARRANTIES. ADI MAKES NO OTHER WARRANTY, EITHER EXPRESS OR IMPLIED, INCLUDING THE IMPLIED WARRANTIES OF MERCHANTABILITY AND FITNESS FOR A PARTICULAR PURPOSE, AND SUCH WARRANTIES ARE EXPRESSLY DISCLAIMED.**

B. Replacement of defective media is your sole and exclusive remedy to any SOFTWARE claims. ADI is not liable nor responsible for any special, incidental, direct or consequential damage, including but not limited to lost profits, downtime, or damages to property, resulting from any cause whatsoever.

5. GENERAL

A. This agreement is the complete and exclusive statement of the SOFTWARE Agreement between you and ADI and supersedes all prior oral and written communications, agreements, representations, statements and undertakings with respect to the SOFTWARE, including any terms and conditions on your purchase order. No modification, termination, extension, renewal or waiver of, nor addition to the terms and conditions of this agreement shall be binding upon ADI unless specifically set forth in writing, and signed by an authorized official of ADI.

B. Title to the SOFTWARE and all copies and portions thereof shall remain in the copyright holder, and you only purchase the limited license set forth in this agreement.

C. You may neither assign any right or license granted under this agreement nor delegate any obligation under this agreement.

D. This agreement shall be governed by the substantive laws of the Commonwealth of Massachusetts, and you consent to the jurisdiction of the Courts of the Commonwealth of Massachusetts for resolution of any dispute involving this agreement.

You acknowledge that you have read this agreement, that you understand it, that you agree to be bound by its terms and conditions.